S0-CKX-531

Seriously Dangerous Religion

SERIOUSLY DANGEROUS RELIGION

WHAT THE OLD TESTAMENT REALLY SAYS AND WHY IT MATTERS

IAIN PROVAN

BAYLOR UNIVERSITY PRESS

© 2014 by Baylor University Press, Waco, Texas 76798

All Rights Reserved. No part of this publication may be reproduced, stored in a retrieval system, or transmitted, in any form or by any means, electronic, mechanical, photocopying, recording or otherwise, without the prior permission in writing of Baylor University Press.

Cover Design by *the*BookDesigners

Cover Image: "The Death of Samson (Judges XVI)," from *The Bible Gallery*, illustrated by Gustave Doré and descriptive letterpress by Talbot W. Chambers (New York: Cassell and Company, 1880). Image provided by Shutterstock/Nicku.

The Library of Congress has catalogued the hardcover edition as follows:

Library of Congress Cataloging-in-Publication Data

Provan, Iain W. (Iain William), 1957–

  Seriously dangerous religion : what the Old Testament really says and why it matters / Iain Provan.

  512 pages cm

  Includes bibliographical references and index.

  ISBN 978-1-4813-0022-3 (hardback : alk. paper)

1. Bible. Genesis—Theology. 2. Bible. Genesis—Criticism, interpretation, etc. 3. Bible. Old Testament—Criticism, interpretation, etc. I. Title.

  BS1235.52.P76 2014

  221.6—dc23

2013020060

The paperback ISBN for this title is 978-1-4813-0023-0.

Printed in the United States of America on acid-free paper.

For Loren and Mary Ruth

CONTENTS

ACKNOWLEDGMENTS

This book—and another closely related one, *Convenient Myths: The Axial Age, Dark Green Religion, and the World That Never Was* (Baylor University Press, 2013)—has been a long time in the making, and I have many people and institutions to thank for help and support along the way.

On the institutional side, first of all, I want to thank my employers at Regent College for their support for the project in terms of two periods of sabbatical leave in the winter semesters of 2009 and 2012. Thanks are also due, with respect to the second of these sabbaticals, to the University of Erfurt in Germany, and in particular to my host there, Christoph Bultmann, and his wife, Ursula, both of whom went out of their way to make my wife and me welcome. I must also thank most warmly the Alexander von Humboldt-Stiftung in Germany, which funded my stay in Erfurt, and the Lilly Foundation, whose Theological Research Grants Program covered our travel and other expenses.

On the personal side of things I want to thank five research assistants at Regent College who completed an enormous amount of work on this project. Merely to name each one does not seem sufficient, but this is what one does, apparently: Jen Gilbertson, Alex Breitkopf, Rachel Toombs, Benjamin Petroelje, and Stacey Van Dyk. I also want to thank various colleagues, friends, and students who read the book proposal or sections of the manuscript and made helpful comments. In alphabetical order except for the first, these are: my wife, Lynette, then Travis Black, Scott and Monica Cousens, Don Curry, Dennis Danielson, Craig Gay, Edwin Hui, Mariam Kamell, Preston Manning, Bethany Sollereder, John Stackhouse, and Paul Teel. Almost finally, I am most grateful to both Walter Brueggemann and Tremper Longman, who took the time to write supportive letters with respect to my application for the Lilly Foundation grant. And finally, thank you to all my students and colleagues at Regent College over the last sixteen years, without whose stimulation, insight, criticism, and sometimes annoying denseness the thinking behind this book could not have developed as it needed to do, and the book would almost certainly not have been written. I feel rather as John Steinbeck is reported to have felt about his book, *East of Eden*: "It has everything in it I have been able to learn about my craft or profession in all these years . . . I think everything else I have written has been, in a sense, practice for this." At least, that is what Wikipedia says he felt.

This book is dedicated to Loren and Mary Ruth Wilkinson: inspirational friends and colleagues who have not only helped me to think well about the relationship between biblical and other thinking but also lived the integration that they preach. Their impact for good on the Regent College community in the course of their membership in it, and on the wider world, will never be adequately measured on this side of eternity. Only a small part of this book was actually written where they live, on Galiano Island in British Columbia, Canada. It was written over a three-day period in May 2011, in a cottage adjacent to their home, at a desk that looks out over one of the most beautiful bays I know. Yet the book owes a lot to them, as I hope they recognize. I even dare to hope that they like it.

Iain Provan
Vancouver, Canada, 2013

1

Of Mice, and Men, and Hobbits

Stories, Art, and Life

The biggest challenge humanity faces in carving out a
better future is to reimagine how we perceive the world, our place
within it, and our highest priorities. By creating a vision of what
must be, we then determine the way we act.

David Suzuki[1]

It's all a question of story. We are in trouble just now because
we do not have a good story. We are in between stories. The old
story, the account of how the world came to be and how we fit
into it—is no longer effective. Yet we have not learned the new
story. . . . We need something that will supply in our times what
was supplied formerly by our traditional religious story. . . .
We need a story that will educate us, a story that will heal,
guide, and discipline us.

Thomas Berry[2]

This is a book about seriously dangerous religion. But for reasons that
will become clear in a moment, it begins with a comparison of two not
so seriously dangerous novels.

The first is *The Hitchhiker's Guide to the Galaxy*.[3] In this novel,
Douglas Adams imagines the world as a huge, complex computer. The

backstory concerns a group of pan-dimensional beings who have been seeking the answer to the ultimate question of life, the universe, and everything. They have found the answer, which is 42, but they still do not know the question. In pursuit of the question, they construct the Earth—a computer that incorporates within it living beings (including its pan-dimensional creators, who assume the form of mice). In the end their quest fails, since the Earth is destroyed a mere five minutes before completion of the program. It turns out, as the series of Hitchhiker novels proceeds, that both the ultimate question and the ultimate answer can, in fact, never be known in the same universe. If they are, that universe will disappear and be replaced by something even more bizarre.

This is a world, then, of which its inhabitants can make no ultimate sense—neither the mice nor the men. Absurdity rules. This means (among other things) that there exists in this "world" no coherent basis for moral action—no foundation upon which to build a moral vision. The novel's characters are lost in space.

Contrast the situation as we find it in the scene in J. R. R. Tolkien's *The Lord of the Rings*, where the two hobbits, Frodo and Sam, are preparing to enter the evil realm of Mordor.[4] There they hope to be able to destroy the ring of power that will otherwise assure the victory of evil over good and the dominion of the dark lord Sauron. They sit down to eat together, and they talk about their journey—the story in which they find themselves—and about other famous journeys and stories of the past. "I wonder," muses Sam, "what sort of tale we've fallen into?" Frodo confesses that he does not know, but "that's the way of a real tale. Take any one that you're fond of. You may know, or guess, what kind of a tale it is, happy-ending or sad-ending, but the people in it don't know. And you don't want them to." This prompts in Sam a revelation, as he considers the old story of Beren, Luthien, and the Silmarils, a long tale that "goes on past . . . happiness and into grief and beyond it." Considering this, he realizes that some of the light of a Silmaril lies close by them in the star glass gifted to Frodo by the Lady Galadriel: "Why, to think of it, we're in the same tale still! It's going on. Don't the great tales never end?"[5]

The old tale that the hobbits recall here is not itself told in *The Lord of the Rings*; it lies far behind it. But, through Lothlorien and Galadriel, they realize, they are connected to this tale, and this realization gives them hope. They discover that they are part of a larger, coherent story that clarifies what it is that they are doing, and what they *must* now do. The larger story helps them to make sense of things—to locate themselves in the present and to move on resolutely into the future. This story in which they find themselves, it might be said, provides their ground for moral action—the foundation upon which they can build a moral vision.

ON ART AND LIFE

Why begin here, with such contrasting novels? I do so because, in one way or another, we too each find ourselves in the midst of a story. It could not be otherwise—it is the way that human beings are. Regardless of whether one believes in *larger* stories, each individual indisputably inhabits *the story of his or her own life.* Our telling of this story is an integral part of the way in which we not only relate to others but also understand and shape who we are. Yet, almost inevitably, this personal story, as important as it is, feels "partial," for at least two reasons. First, there is usually a great deal of mystery surrounding the beginning of each of our personal stories—a beginning dimly and only partially remembered. Second, there is an even greater degree of mystery about the *end* of our own story. Much of the story is still to be written, and we do not yet know where it will end. Lacking a comprehensive account of the beginning and any account of the end, we have great difficulty in giving an account of *ourselves*—of knowing who we really are, and what we should be doing with our lives. The past and the future being so incompletely known, we find ourselves "inextricably middled" in our own story and therefore often comprehensively *muddled* about the present in which we find ourselves.[6] Sometimes "muddle" appears to be all there *is.* Our stories lose all coherence.

Others have found themselves in this muddled place in the past. Among them is the thirteenth-century Florentine nobleman Dante Alighieri, the author of the *Divine Comedy*—the medieval (but also very contemporary) story of one man's journey down into the pit of hell, up the great mountain of purgatory, and out through all the circles of heaven, until he is given a vision of God. It is a physical journey, but it is also a journey that Dante takes into himself. His story begins: *Nel mezzo del camin di nostra vita, Mi ritrovai per una selva oscura, Che la diritta via era smarrita* (Midway this way of life we're bound upon, I woke to find myself in a dark wood, where the right road was wholly lost and gone).[7] This is the original midlife crisis. The speaker finds himself lost in the middle of a story whose end is a mystery to him. He is middled—in the middle of a story, in the middle of a journey. And he is also muddled—muddled about where to go and muddled about what to do.

The solution in Dante's case is similar to the one discovered by Frodo and Sam. He joins his own story to a much larger story—a story in which the beginning and the ending are already known. The direction for his present moment is therefore also clarified; the "right road . . . wholly lost and gone" is once again found. In precisely the same way, each of us needs the clarity that a larger, coherent story can provide. As Alasdair MacIntyre puts it in *After Virtue*,

> I can only answer the question "What am I to do?" if I can answer the prior question "Of what story or stories do I find myself a part?" We enter human society, that is, with one or more imputed characters—roles into which we have been drafted—and we have to learn what they are in order to be able to understand how others respond to us and how our responses to them are apt to be construed. It is through hearing stories about wicked stepmothers, lost children, good but misguided kings, wolves that suckle twin boys, youngest sons who receive no inheritance but must make their own way in the world . . . that children learn or mis-learn both what a child and what a parent is, what the cast of characters may be in the drama in which they have been born and what the ways of the world are. Deprive children of stories and you leave them unscripted, anxious stutterers in their actions as in their words.[8]

I can only answer the question "What am I to do?" if I can answer the prior question "Of what story or stories do I find myself a part?" It is a profound point. Without an understanding of the story in which we find ourselves, we lack direction and purpose. We do not know what to do next. We do not even understand what we are doing *now*.

Tom Stoppard explores this theme in his amusing but tragic play *Rosencrantz and Guildenstern Are Dead*. In this play the action of Shakespeare's *Hamlet* is seen through the eyes of two of its minor characters, Rosencrantz and Guildenstern, who are portrayed as inhabiting a world completely beyond their comprehension. They fail to understand their world because they have no access to the overarching story of which they are a part. They have not read *Hamlet*. Unsure of their direction (and unsure even who they are and where they have come from), they depend upon their brief interactions with other characters to give their lives meaning. The rest is waiting—for what, they do not know. And while they wait, they play games. That is their life. Absurdity rules.

Our great human need, claims MacIntyre, is to find out which story we are in and to locate our place in it. I find myself in the middle of a story—but which story? Is it only my own personal story? Or is there some larger tale of which I am a part? And is that larger tale coherent? On the answers to these questions hangs everything else—my sense of who I am, where I should be heading, and what I should do next. Among the realities impacted by such answers will be my art. Both Dante and Tolkien, for example, wrote fiction that reflects their deep *Christian* convictions about the ultimate coherence of the larger story in which we are all bound up—a story that is being told, in the end, by God. Adams, however, wrote fiction that reflects not the Christian convictions of his youth but the atheism of his adult life. As in art, so (often) in life; as in life, so (often) in art.

LIFE, THE UNIVERSE, AND EVERYTHING

As we open ourselves up to such questions, we find that there are many larger stories ("metanarratives") that compete for our attention. There are ancient ones, like the stories told in Hinduism or Buddhism; there are not so ancient but still very old ones, like the story told in Islam; and then there are fairly modern ones, like the story told in Marxism. Each of these important metanarratives claims to offer a coherent account of "life, the universe, and everything" and a foundation for the moral and spiritual life. Many of them will be discussed in this book at some point and to some degree, but here I am interested in only four stories—three modern and one ancient. I shall explain my particular interest in these four stories shortly.

The Story of the Axial Age

At the heart of the first of the three modern stories lies the "big idea" of an "axial age." This idea was first introduced to the world by the German existentialist philosopher Karl Jaspers in the period right after the Second World War.[9] Jaspers had just lived through a period marked by barbarism, nationalism, and fanaticism—a period of total war. He was concerned, in the aftermath of the war, to identify something that modern human beings hold in common—a story that might unify humanity and help us all to live peaceably together. He believed that he had discovered what was needed not in any single religious or philosophical perspective but in a specific historical experience: the axial age. Modern human beings stand, he proposed, on the far side of this crucial turning point in history (the period 800–200 B.C.). This is the period that produced the basic categories for modern thought—the period that saw the emergence of "world religions." For Jaspers, the cultures that experienced this new beginning, in China, India, and the West, constantly return to it for renewal. As they do so, they recognize what they hold in common, beyond all particular differences of faith. It is to this common past that we ourselves must *now* return, as we strive to make the unity of humankind concrete in the present. We must return to this axial age—the wellspring from which all faith once emerged, behind and beneath all specific religious and philosophical worldviews and their secularized political forms. And having gone back, we must move forward to build a new world order. We must birth a new axial age—an age of world peace.

Few readers of this book will have heard of Karl Jaspers. It is more likely that they will be familiar with authors who have made "axial age thinking" more accessible to the general public—authors like the religious studies expert John Hick or the popular religious historian Karen Armstrong.[10] They may not have encountered axial age thinking at a sophisticated level, therefore, but they will certainly have encountered it in the kind of unsophisticated statements that often appear in such books (e.g., about the ways in which all religions "are in essence really just the same" or about the present necessity of moving beyond absolutist ideologies to a more pluralist approach to truth). An increasing number of readers will also have encountered this story in educational curricula or privately by way of books emerging from the discipline of religious studies.

The Story of the Dark Green Golden Age

The second modern story also has at its heart a "big idea." It is the idea of what I shall refer to as "the dark green golden age." This story is in some respects older than the story of the axial age. Some of its roots lie in previous notions of a past golden age that go back at least as far as the Renaissance. In its present form, the story is specifically connected with what Bron Taylor has called "dark green religion."[11] It is dark green both because it is very serious and because it is somewhat sinister. The storytellers in this case also believe in something like an axial age, but they do not look back to it for inspiration. In this story, the axial age is an age not of enlightenment but of repression. Axial age civilizations destroyed prior societies based around natural and cosmological cycles. They broke the human connection with the earth. They also broke down human *community*, as *individual* religious identity developed. Axial age ("world") religions, since they were not connected with particular places, inevitably reduced the importance of place, unless that "place" was in a spiritual afterlife. Much of what is wrong with human life now results from this embrace of "civilization." To recover ourselves we must now *reject* civilization. We must get back behind the axial age, in order to recover a more authentic way of being. We must get back to the Paleolithic Age and reconnect with our hunter-gatherer ancestors in the state of nature. Central to our recovery will be the renewed embrace of preaxial spirituality. If the story of the axial age is about achieving world peace, the story of the dark green golden age looks to achieve something still greater—the salvation of the planet.

Many readers of this book will have encountered the "dark green" story in some form or another. They may well have read accessible books that promote it, written by such notables as the best-selling author Thomas Berry, the ecologist David Suzuki, or the anarcho-primitivist Derrick Jensen.[12] Further, they may be familiar with some of its leading ideas, such as the notion that people in ancient hunter-gatherer societies lived much happier lives than we modern people do or that they did a much better job of looking after the environment. It is a story that, in its popular forms, has a wide reach.

The Story of the Scientific New Age

At the heart of the third modern story in which I am interested lies the "big idea" of what I shall refer to as "the scientific new age." This is the story told in very recent times by the writers whom others have called "the new atheists"—writers like Richard Dawkins, Daniel Dennett, Sam Harris, and Christopher Hitchens.[13] It has been extensively discussed in the public domain over the last several years, and it is likely to be the one of my three modern stories that is, at present, most familiar to my readers. A useful starting point in describing it is provided by the following sentences from a relevant website:

> Tolerance of pervasive myth and superstition in modern society is not a virtue. Religious fundamentalism has gone main stream [sic] and its toll on education, science, and social progress is disheartening. Wake up people!! We are smart enough now to kill our invisible gods and oppressive beliefs. It is the responsibility of the educated to educate the uneducated, lest we fall prey to the tyranny of ignorance.[14]

This third story is different in character from the other two. Those who tell the other stories are looking to the *past* for paradigms or models that might help us in moving ahead into the future, and for this purpose they are particularly interested in recovering *religious* perspectives from the past. The new atheists, however, look fundamentally to the *present* for their inspiration, and they are profoundly *hostile* to religion (both past and present). The world (they claim) would be a much better place if we could get over our childish infatuation with God (or the gods) and if we could embrace modern, empirical science as the only (or at least the best) basis for true knowledge of the world—including knowledge about our moral obligations. Indeed (they contend), science will one day comprehensively demonstrate (or has already done so) that religious belief is entirely explicable as a product of biological evolution.

Convinced of their case, the new atheists have set out in a conscious, dedicated, and public manner to convince as many people as possible that to believe in God (the gods) is to be deluded, that religion is bad for both individuals and societies, and that abandoning religious perspectives will lead to greater human fulfillment and happiness. This (they believe) is a story worth telling, and they tell it not only through books, television, and the Internet but also through speaking engagements and "atheist bus campaigns," in which buses travel around different countries or regions carrying slogans like, "There's probably no God. Now stop worrying and enjoy your life."[5]

A Common Thread

Each of these three modern stories claims to offer a coherent account of life, the universe, and everything" and therefore a foundation for the moral and spiritual life. Each has been told and retold in recent times by well-intentioned people who want to make the world a better place—to usher in world peace or to save the planet or to increase individual (and communal) happiness and well-being. All the stories have proved to be remarkably influential. Many people are drawn to them, and, in recognition of the demand, their proponents' books are well represented in bookstores. These are stories that *sell*, and one could spend a considerable amount of time discussing the many interesting things that are said in each one. One could also spend time reflecting on how far one or the other of them is likely to be true and how far their vision of the world is good—for since they are so very different from each other, they cannot all be entirely true, and their visions of the world cannot all be entirely good.

For the moment, however, my interest does not lie in what differentiates the modern storytellers from each other or in evaluating their various claims about truth and goodness, and indeed beauty.[16] Rather, I am interested in one thing they share in common *as they offer* their differing evaluations of truth, goodness, and beauty: they all agree that the Old Story (as I shall now refer to it, taking my lead from Thomas Berry in the second epigraph to this chapter) into which the likes of Dante and Tolkien once read their lives—the biblical story—is neither true nor good nor beautiful. Each of the new stories is, indeed, consciously told in an attempt to displace, above all other old stories, this dominant Old Story of Western culture.

For example, it is to a version of this Old Story that Berry himself refers when he says, "Our traditional story of the universe sustained us [in the West, mainly] for a long period of time. It shaped our emotional attitudes, provided us with life purposes, and energized action. It consecrated suffering and integrated knowledge. We awoke in the morning and knew where we were."[7] However, it is this story that Berry also has in mind when he tells us that "the old story, the account of how the world came to be and how we fit into it—is no longer effective." It once oriented us and gave us a sense of who we are, but now it no longer "works."

Berry offers us here only a mild form of what is a common contemporary criticism in the West of the biblical story: it is typically more aggressively argued. For, nowadays, this Old Story is routinely regarded by thoughtful people concerned about our world and its future, not just as "ineffective" but as dangerous. Such critics of the Bible are often particularly antagonistic to what Christians call the Old Testament and

Jews call the Tanakh. The best thing one can say about the Old Testament is that it is a poor rendition of the timeless truths of authentic spirituality, the common beliefs at the core of the world's major religions and philosophies. The worst thing one can say about the Old Testament is that it is not only quite untrue but also bad for us—and bad *even* for its original recipients. It alienated them from each other, from other peoples, and especially from their fellow creatures and our common home, the earth. The telling of its story has continued to do damage down through the ages, precipitating violence, war, and ecological disaster. Religion in itself may not be dangerous—our various modern storytellers disagree on that point—but monotheistic religion is certainly dangerous, and *biblical* monotheism is *seriously* dangerous.

Therefore we can be sure that when someone like David Suzuki (in the first epigraph to this chapter) writes about creating a "story" that might serve us well in the future—about our need to "reimagine how we perceive the world, our place within it, and our highest priorities"—he is not thinking about going back to the Old Story for his inspiration. For our modern storytellers and their followers, this is self-evidently *not* where we should be going any longer for our account of life, the universe, and everything. This is simply not the story into which I should be reading myself in order to gain (in MacIntyre's words) "my sense of who I am, where I should be heading, and what I should do next."

AN INVITATION TO RECONSIDER

It is in the light of this thoroughgoing modern assault on the Old Story from all sides that I have written this book. To put my agenda simply, in one of its aspects, I do not think that many of its critics understand this Story very well, and I hope to persuade them of this fact. Whether accidently or deliberately, they have misrepresented the Story in pursuit of their own agendas. It has suffered *such* a level of violence, in fact, that it is no longer recognizable to people like myself, a lifelong Bible reader and now a professional biblical scholar, in many of their presentations of it. It has been seriously distorted.

I have also written this book, however, for the *readers* of the critics. We live in a time, at least in the post-Christian West, when popular knowledge of the Bible is at a very low ebb. A 2010 survey conducted by the Pew Forum on Religion and Public Life in the U.S.A., for example, evidenced a startling inability among residents of that country to answer even the most basic questions about the Bible and Christianity.[18] Among committed white evangelical Protestant Christians, for example, the average rate of correct response was only 7.3 out of 12. The *overall* Protestant average fell to 6.5; the Roman Catholic average was 5.4; and the "unaffiliated" average was 5.3.[19] The biblical story is not well understood at present, even in its basic shape and among people we might expect to be familiar with it. Average readers of the modern storytellers described above, then, do not have much to fall back upon when trying to make an assessment of the latter's assault on the Old Story, even assuming that such readers are already reading the Bible for themselves in the first place. All too often what people *think* they know about the biblical story appears, in fact, to have been gleaned from authors like Armstrong or Dawkins. It is not surprising, then, that many who have never read the Bible nor made it their business to study the history of its reading (or the actions of its readers) just "know" that the biblical story is bad news—that it is a dangerous lie. It is my hope that my book will help those who would like to gain a degree of independent judgment on what the modern storytellers have to say— who would like to enter into a discussion both about the biblical story and about other stories that have sought to displace it, rather than just being a "groupie" of one heroic author or another. This book is, essentially, an invitation to reconsider the Bible and to reconsider the Old Testament more particularly. What does it really have to say? Is it really as obviously untrue as many modern people appear to think? And is it dangerous?

The Questions to Be Asked

My invitation to reconsider is embodied in what follows, first of all, in the answers I shall try to give to a number of important questions I pose to the Old Testament literature:

What is the world?

Who is God?

Who are man and woman?

Why do evil and suffering mark the world?

What am I to do about evil and suffering?

How am I to relate to God?

How am I to relate to my neighbor?

How am I to relate to the rest of creation?

Which society should I be helping to build?

What am I to hope for?

I have chosen these questions because they are precisely the kind that religions and philosophies have always tried to answer and about which we would expect any serious religious or philosophical literature to have something to say, either explicitly or implicitly. It is reasonable to ask them also of the Old Testament literature, which was coming into its final form precisely during that period of significant intellectual and religious flourishing in the world that others have called the "axial age." Here I agree with University of Chicago professor Leon Kass in what he says specifically about the book of Genesis in his large and insightful book, *The Beginning of Wisdom*.[20] Defining philosophy as the single-minded and wholehearted (yet thoughtful and self-critical) pursuit of "the truth about the world and our place within it" and hoping thereby to find "guidance for how we are to live," Kass tells us, "This book results from my efforts to read the book of Genesis in this spirit, the same spirit in which I read Plato's *Republic* or Aristotle's *Nicomachean Ethics*—indeed, any great book—seeking wisdom regarding human life lived well in relation to the whole."[21] I share Kass' conviction that Genesis (and indeed the whole Old Testament) seeks to provide wisdom. I therefore agree that it makes sense to read this literature in pursuit of its authors' conception of this wisdom. We should not read it *in exactly the same way* as we read Plato or Aristotle (not least because our various biblical texts *are* embedded in one overarching story, whereas our various Platonic and Aristotelian texts are not), but we should certainly read the biblical literature in the same *spirit*.

Indeed, I shall be referring in what follows to some of the answers offered to my ten questions in nonbiblical religious or philosophical traditions, comparing and contrasting them to what the biblical story implies or states as its own answers. My aim is obviously not to be exhaustive with respect to these other traditions, although I shall mention important aspects of many of them.[22] It is simply to sharpen our understanding of what the biblical material has to say by placing it in relation to various alternatives offered in the so-called preaxial and axial ages, as well as in later periods. In this way, I hope that we shall arrive at a reliable understanding of the biblical tradition as it sits within the course of human intellectual and religious history from the axial age down to the present. In the process, I hope that it will become clear just how often and how notably what the Old Testament *really* says—about how the cosmos came to be, what our place in it is, and how we should live here—diverges from what our modern story-tellers *claim* that it says. To be blunt, the rhetoric of the advocates of the three "ages" described earlier is simply that—rhetoric—and their claims about the Old Story are false.

A Constraint to Be Observed

Each of the questions listed earlier is considered at chapter-length in chapters 2–11. In answering each one, I shall restrict myself to the literature that forms the older part of the Old Story (i.e., the Tanakh or Old Testament). This is not *only* because modern critics of the Bible are usually particularly antagonistic toward this part of the story. There is another good reason I have accepted this self-limitation, even though I am personally convinced that we need the New Testament to fill out and complete the biblical answers to the questions I have posed. It lies in the fact that this older part of the Old Story has been not only much misunderstood by *outsiders* to the story but also somewhat misunderstood by *insiders*. Sadly, even those who have held it to be *the* Story that defines what is good and true and beautiful have not always read it well. There are many reasons for this, but one of them has been the unfortunate tendency to read the Old Testament only through the lens of the New Testament, rather than for its own sake. The *real* Story becomes, as it were, the New Testament story, making what lies beforehand only a kind of shadowy background.

This may strike readers unfamiliar with the history of Bible-reading as a somewhat bizarre way to approach *any* body of literature, much less one that possesses (for Christians) an overarching narrative structure (from Genesis to Revelation), in which comprehension of the later texts appears to *require* prior comprehension of the earlier ones. I can only agree; it is bizarre. I am reporting the reality, not endorsing the approach. Certainly such an approach to the Old Testament has led, among other things, to a degree of imposition on the Old Testament texts—a narrowing of scope and vision and a distortion (in places) of what is actually there. In turn, these "insider" mistakes have influenced the views of outsiders themselves as to what Old Testament texts are about. The later "outsider" mistakes are often only the earlier "insider" ones writ large—as when the post-Christian "person on the street" somehow just "knows" (if he any longer does) that the God of the Old Testament is a very angry God, whereas the God of the New Testament is only sweetness and light. We "insiders," to this extent, have only ourselves to blame.

I think it best, then, to set aside the newer part of the Old Story in the first instance, so that we can see with renewed clarity what the older part is really about. Once we have gained this clarity, I do consider it important to return to the New Testament to see how that part of the Story claims to continue, develop, and bring to completion what the earlier part has to say. It is at that point, in chapter 12, that my "invitation to reconsider" will involve the whole (Christian) biblical tradition.

A Strategy to Be Followed

We are, of course, dealing in the case of the Old Testament with a relatively large body of literature. This has forced me to decide upon a workable strategy for opening up access to its various perspectives for the reader who may know little of these in advance. I have settled, then, upon this approach: I shall ground in the book of Genesis, specifically, my answer to each of the questions I am asking. I shall then branch out from Genesis to connect each theme with other Old Testament texts. This is, I think, a sound strategy, not least because the book of Genesis is where the biblical story begins and no story can be read well if the beginning is not properly understood. If we misconstrue the beginning, mistakes and misunderstandings in what follows are (nearly) inevitable. I have just made the same point with respect to reading the Old Testament before we read the New.

Some modern authors, of course, have deliberately exploited this basic rule of reading ("begin at the beginning") in pursuit of their own literary goals. In Agatha Christie's novel *The Murder of Roger Ackroyd*, for example, the impact of the story depends on the reader's misapprehension, at the very beginning of the book, that the first-person voice telling the story is reliable and truthful.[23] In actual fact, however, the narrator turns out to be the murderer, and the reader is forced at the end of the book to revisit the "reading" with which she began. In sum: our understanding of the beginning of any story deeply influences our reading of the entire story.

It has certainly been this way, historically, with the biblical story. The ways in which the first three chapters of Genesis have been read—or not read—have profoundly shaped the reader's understanding of what follows. My reference to "not reading" may once again puzzle readers unfamiliar with the history of Bible reading. Why would any reader of the Old Testament *not* begin with Genesis 1–3? The answer is, once again (remembering what I just said about the New Testament), that many readers have been driven by convictions about where the "real" biblical story begins. In the modern period, these convictions have often been connected to assessments about where real *history* begins in the Bible—with Abraham, perhaps, or with Moses or with David. They have also often been connected with assessments about when different parts of the Old Testament were first written down: is the story about creation, for example, "later" than the story about the Exodus from Egypt? If so (some have assumed), the creation story should not be given the role of "framing" what follows.

The effects of "not reading" the first three chapters of Genesis in their opening position have often been striking—again, imposition on the Old Testament texts, the narrowing of scope and vision, and the distortion of what is actually there. In turn (again), these "insider" mistakes have influenced the views of *outsiders* on what Old Testament texts are about—as when Richard Dawkins reads particular Old Testament texts about God without any regard for their larger narrative context and particularly without any regard for the opening sections of the biblical story in Genesis 1–3. We shall come back to this matter later (chap. 3). Here, let me simply emphasize that it is precisely because of the importance of the beginning of *any* story that I shall give particular attention in what follows to Genesis 1–3.

The Questions to Be Ignored

I want to be explicit at this point not only about the questions I *shall* be asking in chapters 2–11 but also about the questions I shall *ignore*—particularly with respect to the book of Genesis. This is necessary precisely because of the various ways in which Genesis has been read in the last 150 years and the expectations that this reading tradition may have lodged in the reader's mind.

In the scholarly world, first, analysis of Genesis has lain at the center of many of the most significant developments in modern critical reading of the Bible, including source, form, and redaction-critical reading and, more recently, narrative-critical reading.[24] Our understanding of Genesis as ancient literature has no doubt increased as a result of such analysis, although it has raised challenging and unresolved questions about the process by which the book came into existence. In the Christian church and in society at large, second, the emphasis in the reading of the book of Genesis has more often lain not upon the history *of* the text (how it might have been composed) but upon the text's relationship to history itself. There has been a particular fascination with what Genesis might have to say about the origins of the cosmos and about the origins and early development of humanity. The discussion that has followed from this emphasis has tended to become quickly polarized. Genesis is regarded, on the one hand, negatively in terms of its historical and scientific accuracy, and, on the other, positively as the very font of knowledge when it comes to such matters.[25] Whether at the scholarly or popular level, then, we find in much of the reading of Genesis in recent times a pronounced historical and scientific interest.

I want to underline that these are not the emphases that mark my own reading of Genesis in this book. I am of course interested, personally, in how we are to understand what Genesis says about the world in the light of what modern science tells us. But it is, in my view, premature even to pursue this question before we know what it is, in fact, that Genesis itself is trying to *say*. So I shall not be asking questions about Genesis and science in what follows in chapters 2–11. I *shall*, however, return to this question to some extent in chapter 13.

I am equally interested in the ways in which it is best to understand biblical perspectives on the ancient Near Eastern past in the light of modern historical research. I have coauthored a large book that explores this question.[26] Yet it must be said that the biblical story is told not simply for its own sake but to communicate what its authors hold to be true—and not *just* historically true. The primary purpose of recounting the past in this biblical story is, instead, to tell us important things about God, the world, and how we should live. These are the things in which I am primarily interested in *this* particular book; I shall therefore not be asking questions in it about the historicity of the Genesis narratives (or of any others).

Finally, I am also interested in all the many questions that biblical scholars have asked about how our biblical texts came to be in their present form—which sources of information might have been used, who might have written the texts, and when (and why). For the purposes of this book, however, it does not matter *how*, precisely, the book of Genesis and the remainder of the Old Testament literature came into being, for I am interested in what this body of literature as a whole has to say, whenever its various parts came to be embraced as aspects of the tradition and wherever they came from. It is the worldview implicit and explicit in the biblical literature as we have it—reading that literature as making up a story that unfolds from Genesis onward—that is the focus of my concern. Further, it is not the statement that this or that biblical author uttered at this or that particular time that is of ultimate importance to me in this book—whenever that time might be; rather, it is the answers that our biblical texts taken together may reasonably be held to provide to my ten questions. So I shall not be asking about the precise date, authorship, and provenance of this or that biblical text. There are many other books that offer insight on such matters—as indeed there are many that discuss the other matters mentioned in the last three paragraphs.

To be completely clear, then, my interest in Genesis (and the remainder of the Old Testament), in this particular book that you are now reading, lies not in its potential for answering historical and scientific questions but in its potential for answering religious and philosophical questions.

Conclusions to Be Drawn

In the end, of course, we need to get back to the questions of truth and danger with which we began. Many thoughtful modern people consider the biblical metanarrative to be both untrue and dangerous. I am inviting them to reconsider. *Is* the Old Story, as it is restated in chapters 2–12, *really* as obviously untrue as people think? This is the question I address in chapter 13. *Does* it present us with seriously dangerous religion? That is the question for chapter 14. I shall argue that, contrary to popular belief, the biblical story does deserve to be taken seriously as a series of truth claims about the world and our place and destiny within it. I shall also argue that biblical religion *is* seriously dangerous—but not in the way that most people think. Overall, the Old Story can still be regarded as a true and helpful account of "life, the universe, and everything." In fact, when properly understood, it provides a solid point of departure for precisely the path out of trouble and into a better future for which its detractors are often looking.

THE BOOK IN THE LIFE OF THE READER

Earlier I said *something* about the readership I have in mind for this book. I want to close this opening chapter by saying something *more*.

Nonideal Readers

First of all, for whom have I *not* written this book? I have not written this book, first, for the ideologically committed—those who are already so convinced of their own story that they are incapable of hearing a critique of it. This is not a book that will be much enjoyed by, or be of much use to, people who believe that they already know precisely what the Old Story is all about—whether they are well disposed or antagonistic toward it. It is certainly a book that will exasperate those who are so devoted to one of the "modern stories" I have described that they are not open to revising their opinions about the "old" one. I recognize that I have as much chance of persuading such ideologically committed readers that there is reality outside their "box" as the lion Aslan had in *The Last Battle* of persuading the dwarves that there was a reality outside their stable.[27] "Never, never think outside the box," the home-owner is reputed to have instructed his cat. In the case of the ideologically committed, no such instruction is even necessary; they will, in *fact*, never think outside the box. For my book to "work," however, there needs to be some genuine interest on the reader's part in questioning received opinion and in learning something new. In sum, I have not written this book either for the closed-minded Christian or for the closed-minded critic of Christian faith—or indeed for closed-minded people of any persuasion.

Nor have I written it, second, even for the open-minded reader who thinks that truth can be easily and quickly identified and grasped. If you are a reader who is dismissive of books that give careful attention to texts, ideas, and arguments—of *long* books, which try to operate at the length that their subject matter properly requires—then this book is not for you. This is a book that requires commitment—to reading texts well and to the hard, critical thinking without which wrong ideas cannot be differentiated from right ones.

However (and third), I have also not written this book for those readers—colleagues of mine in the academic community, for example—whose normal business is careful attention to texts, ideas, and arguments in pursuit of expertise in fairly small, isolated areas of ancient and modern life. I value such expertise, and I possess some small amount of my own in the area of biblical studies. This book will bear scrutiny by such colleagues, but it has not been written to increase the sum of such narrow expert knowledge. It is a work of synthesis—a book that ranges broadly over multiple areas of expertise. About some of these areas I know a great deal; about some I know less. But I range broadly, nonetheless, in the hope of helping the general reader to make discriminating judgments about the new and the old stories that are my central concern.

Ideal Readers

For which kind of reader, then, *have* I written this book? I have in mind, first, the reader who has been influenced even at a distance (and perhaps without knowing it) by the three modern stories described earlier. I am thinking of the reader who has harbored doubts about these stories, and has long wanted to explore the matter, but has lacked resources to do so. I include among these readers open-minded *tellers* of the modern stories who have come to realize that they are not well educated about the Bible, and would like to understand this literature better.

I am thinking, second, of students or ex-students who have often heard in the course of their education, at high school or at university, about the problematic or dangerous character of the biblical tradition, yet have read enough of the Bible, or have met enough people who read it differently, that they have come to question what they have been taught.

I have in mind, third, teachers who have come to doubt the veracity of what they have been teaching in religious studies or history (or indeed English literature), especially as it concerns the Old Testament, but who lack the resources that might expand their own horizons and to which they might send puzzled students.

I am thinking, fourth, of readers who know very little about biblical faith to begin with and would value a reliable guide to the Old Story that I am retelling here.

Finally, I am hopeful that this book will be read by many Christian readers who have long known the contents of the biblical story and have felt it to be very important but have become dissatisfied with the way they have been taught to read it (especially the Old Testament). I am hoping for readers who have found it difficult to bring their reading of the Old Testament into any kind of meaningful connection with everyday life—who feel that they are missing something in this ancient story and are open to finding out what it is.

These are the readers I consciously had in mind in writing the book. But the list is not meant to exclude. You are very welcome as a reader, whoever you might be!

2

THE UP QUARK, THE DOWN QUARK, AND OTHER COOL STUFF

What Is the World?

The most incomprehensible thing about the world is that
it is comprehensible.

Albert Einstein[1]

When I was born I was so surprised I couldn't talk
for a year and a half.

Gracie Allen[2]

We can all empathize with Gracie Allen. We are each thrown uncer-
emoniously (so it seems) into a world that we had no reason to suspect
existed and whose nature we have no initial way of comprehending.
Gradually most of us begin to make some sense of it, in the most basic
ways. We learn to discriminate between living and nonliving things and
between strangers, on the one hand, and our parents and other familiar people, on the other. We learn to count and to organize. We learn
that objects have names, and we learn to speak these names. However,
such comprehension does not belong strictly to ourselves; we "learn"
the world in community with others, who give us the language that
helps us to make sense of it. These "others" do this quite specifically,
in terms of our mother tongue: we learn French, Cantonese, Swahili,

or whatever the language of our family or tribe might be. But they also do it more generally, gradually imparting to us their views about the very nature of our world. As young children, we are each introduced into a *story* about the reality that we are now encountering outside our mother's womb—a story that we simply accept, at first, as a true story, because it cannot and does not occur to us that it could be otherwise. In other words, we do not simply *enter* a world at birth; we are, in fact, progressively *given* a world in which to live. In this world meaning and significance are already attached to things, and we are guided by other people in "making" what we "make" of them.

For example, how are we to understand the sun? Is it a god, as many ancient peoples believed, or is it not, as many modern people believe? Are storms simply storms, or are we to see in them the activity of nature deities? Is the earth a disk, or is it a sphere? Our first beliefs about such things will be determined by what we are told by our family and tribal members. As we grow up we may discover, through education or travel perhaps, that the story we have been told is not true—or, at least, that it is not large enough to account for all reality as we now understand it (including up quarks and down quarks and electrons).[3] We may well discover this *without* much education of a formal kind, or much travel, because life itself may teach us that the world we have been given is not big enough and to some extent is based on falsehood or illusion. There are many ways, then, in which our world can be shattered, in whole or in part. For some, it is the pain and heartbreak of loss, which afflicts educated travelers no more and no less than the uneducated. For others, merely the awareness that, contrary to what we have been told, there are people who "live in a different world," may be enough to shake our confidence in our own "world." Still others simply become tired of the conflict and violence that can arise when different "stories" about the world collide, and they look for some larger story that can reconcile people. Whatever the reason may be, many of us come at some point in our lives to ask the question: what *is* it all about, then? What *is* the world, really, behind all these stories that are told about it and behind all the opinions that are voiced about it?

The biblical book of Genesis provides a particular set of answers to this question, grounded in its opening line: "in the beginning God created the heavens and the earth" (Genesis 1:1).[4] Here "heavens and earth" simply *mean* "world"—everything that makes up the reality of our cosmos, including not only the earth upon which we walk but also the sky in which we see the stars and planets move.[5] And Genesis claims that this world—heavens and earth—is a *creation*. In the beginning someone created the world.[6] There are at least two initial aspects to this claim that require immediate clarification, so that, even at this early stage in our inquiry, the Genesis way of looking at reality can be clearly differentiated from some alternatives.

THE WORLD IS NOT ETERNAL

First of all, in the book of Genesis the world is not eternal. It has a beginning, and although Genesis does not itself say this, other biblical texts tell us that it also has an end. The book of Isaiah imagines "a new heavens and a new earth" after the world of our present experience passes away (65:17). We live in a world that once came into being and one day will come to its end. This became one of the fundamental beliefs for each of the three major religions that either take the biblical literature as their Scripture or have been heavily influenced by it—the so-called Abrahamic religions of Judaism, Christianity, and Islam.[7]

Theirs is a very different view of the cosmos than the one found, for example, in Hinduism, in which what is ultimately real is the eternal and all-embracing "Brahman." What is Brahman? It is "oneness in contrast to multiplicity . . . the one source of all . . . prior to all forms and divisions."[8] It is the unchanging ground of being, understood in much Hindu tradition as being entirely impersonal. Everything else in the cosmos evolves from this "One" by a mechanistic process. This includes human beings, whose "real" self (atman) is eternal and formless and, in essence, *nothing other than* Brahman. In the end, then, it is an illusion that we creatures living in the cosmos are Many. We are, in fact, all the same thing. We are all the eternal One. This way of looking at the world is typically referred to as "monism." The world, in this sense, is eternal:

> We fail to realize our true divine nature, mistaking our lower selves for our higher selves. Our lower selves, because they are transitory and inconstant, are ultimately not real. Until we fully recognize the truth about Brahman and *atman*, we continue to suffer on the wheel of samsara [an endless series of birth, death, and rebirth] because we continue to generate karma [action and consequence], which binds us to the phenomenal world.[9]

Buddhism and Jainism (another Indian religion), although different from Hinduism in various ways, embrace this same idea of the eternal cosmos: "In Jainism, as well as Hinduism and Buddhism, one encounters a universe without beginning or end."[10]

As in the East, so also in the West, in the thinking of the Greek philosopher Aristotle. Since matter, motion, and time are eternal, he believed, the world must be eternal too. "Aristotle's main contention [in *On the Heavens*] is that the physical universe is spatially finite but temporally infinite: it is a vast but bounded sphere which has existed without beginning and will exist without end."[11]

Over against these various opinions, the book of Genesis proposes that the world has a beginning. Other books of the Bible, recognizing the implication of such a "beginning," assert that it has an end as well.

THE WORLD WAS CREATED BY A PERSON

The beginning, second, was initiated in *personal* terms, according to Genesis. "*God* created the heavens and the earth," and as we read further in Genesis 1–2 we discover that this God speaks, makes things out of clay—including human persons who are said to be made "in his own image" (Genesis 1:27)—and displays such things as love and anger. We shall discuss these matters much more extensively in chapters 3 and 4. God is a person, in biblical thinking. Like the idea of the time-bounded nature of creation, this notion of a personal Creator has also been embraced in Judaism, Christianity, and Islam, but it is also very different from what we find in much of the philosophy of ancient Greece.[12] From early on, this philosophy set out to identify a single impersonal substance out of which everything else in the world was derived. Among the pre-Socratic philosophers, Thales and Anaximenes thought that this "One" was a substance visible to us (water and air, respectively), and Anaximander believed that it was an unlimited primordial mass existing prior to all things visible. Later, Plato in his *Republic* posited a "Form of the Good" that is "the final cause of everything that we do . . . [and] 'the cause' of the knowability and even of the very being of his favourite entities, the Forms."[13] It is ultimate reality—the highest idea of the good, the beautiful and the true—but it is impersonal. The same can be said of Aristotle's "unmoved mover," existing outside the universe, as well as the heavenly bodies within it to which he often refers as divine. As Jonathan Barnes puts it,

Aristotle's gods are too abstract, remote, and impersonal to be regarded as the objects of religious worship. Rather, we might connect Aristotle's remarks about the divinity of the universe with the sense of wonderment which nature and its works produced in him.[14]

The biblical notion of a personal Creator is also different from what we find in much of the religion of the East.[15] Buddhism's founder, Siddhartha Gautama, taught his followers that the "ultimate" they should seek is not a god, but simply "truth" (dharma). This "truth" is a transcendental entity operating in the world itself. It is not a person, but "the universal ordering principle that penetrates everywhere and is operative in everything. . . . There is no god who causes everything."[16] Jainism, likewise, does not envision a supreme personal being who creates the world. Jains regard the world as operating "according to its own innate laws, in world cycles of evolution and degeneration without beginning and without end."[17] They "do not affirm the idea of a God, at least as this idea is understood in the Abrahamic religions—a creator and moral arbiter of the universe."[18]

The major religions or philosophies of China, likewise, teach that there is one unified world, outside of which there is no transcendent God. Neo-Confucianism knows of an ultimate principle in the cosmos that holds all things together—"the sum total of the principles of all things and also the highest principle in each."[19] This principle is eternal and unchanging, but it is not personal: "in their view of ultimate reality, Neo-Confucianist teachers have effectively excluded the idea of a personal God who rules over all."[20] Classical Daoists attempt to be in harmony with the movement of dao, the eternal source of all reality that exists prior to the multiplicity of phenomena that make up our existence. Dao is once again impersonal: "infinite and boundless, it cannot be named; it belongs to where there are no beings."[21]

The term "classical Daoist" implies a distinction that needs to be unpacked and permits an important general clarification with respect to what follows in this book. The clarification pertains to the questions of unity/diversity and personal/impersonal. One of the difficulties in writing about the Eastern religions just mentioned, and also about Hinduism, is that if one simply refers to Hinduism or Daoism on these questions, one will inevitably mislead by oversimplifying. It is quite true that much Hindu tradition holds Brahman to be impersonal, but in Hinduism the ultimate can also have personal qualities, and (moreover) the many personal gods of the Hindu pantheon *can* be regarded simply as different manifestations of this ultimate reality.[22] Gautama did teach that the "ultimate" is not a personal god, but many Buddhists are nevertheless devoted to gods.[23] The dao is impersonal, but Daoists often regard the founder of Daoism, Laozi, as having been deified—as a personification of the dao and "an active, conscious creator who is set apart from the world and gives it shape."[24]

To a great extent, the coexistence of the personal with the impersonal—the one with the many—in these religions and philosophies is the result of developments in each tradition that postdate their originators. In these developments, originally distinctive and considerably antipolytheistic ideas were reintegrated back into the polytheistic cultures that the originators were attempting to transcend.[25] It is to reflect this reality, and to avoid the need for countless (no doubt irritating) qualifications, that I have adopted the term "classical." It may not be an ideal term, but I cannot think of a less problematic one. In what follows, then, when "classical" appears before one of the traditions mentioned earlier, I mean by it the version of that religion that holds ultimate reality to be one and impersonal. I do not mean to refer to its polytheistic (and personal) expressions. Polytheism, as an approach to life, the universe, and everything, shall be considered separately throughout the book.

Taking our first two points in this chapter together, then, we may rightly say that the book of Genesis proposes something quite different from what is proposed by many thinkers in both East and West about the nature of the world. It proposes that a *personal* God *created* the heavens and the earth. This is only the first of many ways in which, to echo Blaise Pascal's words in his *Mémorial*, the God of Abraham, Isaac, and Jacob of whom Genesis speaks is not the god of the philosophers (insofar as the term "god" is even an appropriate term for the "One" that these philosophers envisage).[26] It is also only the first of many ways in which the axial age thesis about the deep commonality of the great religions and philosophies is revealed to be deeply flawed.

CREATION IS ORDERED

The story in which we find ourselves, the book of Genesis claims, is the story of a creation. That is why there is an *order* to the world that enables life to flourish upon the planet Earth. Planets need not possess this kind of order, of course—that is obvious. There is certainly no other planet in our own solar system, and possibly none anywhere in the universe, that possesses it. Our own planet is the only one known to us that is ordered in this way; it is the only planet where life is known to exist. How are we to explain this? The book of Genesis explains it in terms of a personal creation; the Creator has produced order. Interestingly, this same connection is hinted at in a passage from Aristotle's *Metaphysics*, quoted by Jonathan Barnes to illustrate Aristotle's reverence for the excellence of the universe:

> The excellence of an army resides both in its orderliness and in its general, and especially in the latter . . . And all things—fish and birds and plants—are ordered in a way, yet not in the same way; and it is not the case that there is no connection between one thing and another—there is a connection.[27]

Aristotle's analogy implies a "general" who brings order to creation. That is, indeed, the kind of person that Genesis envisages, but Aristotle in the end (and in spite of his analogy) does not.

This ordered environment, according to Genesis, has not always existed. Genesis 1:2 describes, in fact, precisely its opposite: "The earth was formless and empty, darkness was over the surface of the deep, and the Spirit of God was hovering over the waters." Pictured here is an environment that could not support life as we know it. The earth was "formless"—a word used elsewhere in the Old Testament for landscape that is inhospitable and dangerous, as in Deuteronomy 32:10 ("In a desert land he found him, in a barren and howling *waste*") and Job 6:18 ("Caravans turn aside from their routes; they go up into the *wasteland* and perish"). The earth was also "empty" of life—no doubt what we would expect from a formless place.[28] There was a vast ocean, over which "darkness" brooded—problematic for many creatures, who need light to see by and firm ground to walk upon. Darkness evokes not only night rather than day but also death rather than life ("The people walking in darkness have seen a great light; on those living in the land of the shadow of death a light has dawned"; Isaiah 9:1). The raw materials out of which the beginnings of the heavens and the earth will be made are certainly present in Genesis 1:2, but they have not yet been ordered, and then supplemented, so as *actually* to bring a habitable world into being. The Spirit of God does hover like a bird over the primeval ocean, surveying the scene and preparing for action, but no action has yet occurred.

Creation itself takes place in the six days described in Genesis 1:3-31: the creation of light on day one; of the heavens on day two; of earth and seas, vegetation, plants, and trees on day three; of sun, moon, and stars on day four; of sea creatures and birds on day five; and, finally, of land creatures on day six. Days one through three deal with the problem of the world's "formlessness." Here the world is given a particular structure and shape, in which light is separated from darkness, the heavens are separated from the earth, and the earth is separated from the seas. Darkness is in this way contained and made useful, as night corresponding to day; the primeval deep is tamed and made useful, as seas separate from land and as rain that falls upon the land. In other words, the world is made habitable. Days four through six deal with the world's "emptiness." God fills the newly ordered cosmos with inhabitants created for each of its newly created habitations—planets and stars for the heavens; birds and sea creatures for the air and the seas; and land creatures for the earth.

There is a lyrical feel to all of this, as the language used to describe God speaking the world into being itself *evokes* order in its repetition of key phrases: "and God said"; "let there be"; "God saw that it was good"; "and there was evening, and there was morning." These words of God are, however, marked not only by repetition (and thus by orderliness) but also by progression. They increase in number as we move through each group of three days, suggesting the increasing complexity and (perhaps) importance of the creation as we approach the final day. More weight is thus given to the earth than to the heavens, and more interest is shown in the creation of human beings than in anything else. This is not surprising. Both those who wrote these words and those for whom they were first written were themselves human beings. Among their questions, then, about the world in which they found themselves would be the following: what does it *mean* to be a human being? This is a question we ourselves shall explore further in chapter 4. For the moment, let us simply notice that the order in the world whose complexity and wondrousness we begin to comprehend as we encounter it first as a child and then as an adult—this order is attributed by Genesis to a personal Creator. It does not arise as a result of chance or impersonal forces. The Creator makes things the way they are, providing both the habitations and the inhabitants that make up our world.

CREATION IS SEPARATE FROM GOD,
AND IS NOT DIVINE

This creation is not only ordered *by* God; it is also separate *from* God. I do not mean by this that God is not present in the creation and cannot be encountered in the creation. On the contrary, Genesis 3:8 envisages God as "walking in the garden in the cool of the day" and conversing with the human creatures he meets there.[29] God is not "separate from creation" in that sense. But in the book of Genesis God and creation *are* separate "beings." The word "being" is not an ideal word to use here, because creation in the Genesis story is not so much *a* being as a *collection* of beings and "things" (inanimate objects such as mountains). Yet "being" is certainly a better word than, for example, "entity," or some such term. "Entity" is an entirely inappropriate word to use in reference to God, who is a person, and it is also inappropriate in reference to creation, insofar as creation embraces a rich tapestry of living beings bound together into one organic, interdependent whole. My main point here, though, is not to argue for this or that term in describing the reality in which I am interested; it is to ensure a proper description of the reality itself. According to Genesis, God is not creation nor an aspect of creation nor a superior being within creation; neither is creation God, nor is any part of it God. In chapter 3 we shall return to this matter (in reference to who *God* is in biblical faith), and we shall think about it more deeply. For the moment, it is important only to notice that in the book of Genesis, *creation* is not to be *identified* with God in any way. Genesis 1 communicates this reality implicitly in the metaphor of God's *speaking* creation into being. God speaks, and "over there," as it were, creation begins to take shape. There is no "natural" point of contact between the transcendent God and the creation. The word of God goes *out*, which is to say that creation is distinct from this God-who-speaks.[30]

By way of contrast, consider the very different view of the world that was widely shared in its broad contours in "complex" societies across the ancient Near East, from Egypt to Mesopotamia.[31] These societies provide the broader milieu in which the ancient Israelites lived and against the background of which biblical literature must largely be understood. As in the later philosophies and religions of both East and West I mentioned earlier, in ancient Near Eastern thinking the world as we know it emerges from a process through which the One becomes the Many. Separation occurs *within the One*, and singularity gives way to multiplicity in the emerging world. The gods of the various pantheons are themselves products of this process of separation and are thus part *of* the world, not separate *from* it. In this way they are closely connected with what modern Western people might call the "natural" phenomena of the world. Indeed, all sorts of aspects of what modern Western people call the natural world were, in the ancient Near East, directly associated with deities, such that for these ancients there was no "natural world" at all. Everything was imbued with the supernatural. Sun gods were active in and through the sun, storms gods in and through storms, and so on. Yet, importantly, these gods were not "creators" in the way that Genesis imagines a Creator. At most they were *managers* of the cosmos of which they formed a part, caretakers of the very "stuff" from which they had emerged. They could "create" new things only within the parameters already set forth in the cosmos as it developed out of the One. In this way they were just like human beings, whose other characteristics (e.g., the ability to procreate) they are often pictured as sharing. Essentially, these ancient peoples worshipped the cosmos itself as divine—as the collective manifestation of the gods. The significant continuity between the One and the Many, which included the gods, invited such worship.[32]

In Genesis, however, there is no such continuity, and nowhere in the Old Testament is such continuity suggested. In biblical thinking, the Creator God has no origin, and the world, which *does* have an origin, certainly does not originate from "within" God. Creation is essentially separate from God, who sustains and interacts with it from "outside." The cosmic phenomena of the heavens and the earth are therefore not manifestations of divine attributes, although they *are* understood to be instruments of God's sovereignty. With respect to *earthly* phenomena, this is perhaps best seen not in Genesis but in the story of Elijah (1 Kings 19:11-12), where the Hebrew prophet encounters God—not in the heavens but on the earth. While this encounter does occur in the midst of an upheaval in the natural world marked by wind, earthquake, and lightning ("fire"), the narrator makes it clear that "the LORD was not in the wind . . . not in the earthquake . . . [and] not in the fire." Instead, if God is to be found anywhere in the midst of this upheaval, it is only in the "gentle whisper" that follows the fire.[33] Natural elements are not divine, although God does speak in the midst of them. Neither are *heavenly* phenomena (sun, moon, stars) manifestations of the divine. The sun and the moon were two of the most important gods in the ancient Near Eastern pantheons, often named Shamash and Yar-ich, respectively. The stars were widely held to control human destiny. In Genesis 1, the creation of these heavenly bodies is described at far greater length than anything else, except for the creation of human beings (Genesis 1:14-18). The authors do have something important to say about them. *What* they say, however, is that these heavenly bodies are not divine managers of the cosmos, but only creatures of God—and impersonal ones at that. The sun and moon, specifically, are merely "lights" designed to be helpful to the creatures of the earth—and par-ticularly to human beings, for whom they mark "seasons and days and years" (Genesis 1:14). They are not, like the Hittite sun god, gods "from eternity." Probably to underline this fact, Genesis 1 avoids altogether the standard Hebrew terms used elsewhere in the Old Testament (*shemesh* and *yareakh*) for sun and moon—terms that would have been unhelp-fully reminiscent, for ancient readers, of Shamash and Yarich.

In sum: according to the biblical perspective and to the Abrahamic religions that embraced it or were influenced by it, creation is not to be worshipped, for it is not divine. There is separation between God and the world, and God, not the world, is to be worshipped. In gen-eral, for the peoples of the ancient Near East, "nature" was entirely *per-sonal*—the very place where the gods were to be found. That which they perceived to be *beyond* the world was resolutely impersonal and ultimately irrelevant to their lives. Biblical faith, conversely, sees nature as *impersonal*, divesting it of the many gods who might be worshipped there. What lies *beyond* the world, however, is profoundly personal and profoundly relevant to life.

CREATION IS NOT DIVINE, BUT IT IS SACRED

At first it might seem that the nondivinity of the world should lead to a devaluation of the world in Hebrew thinking, relative to the valuation of the world that is found in ancient Near Eastern religion more gener-ally. This is typically the argument advanced by dark green religionists concerning axial age religions, including the religion of the Old Testa-ment. These religions have secularized the world, they claim, thereby making it into a collection of mere objects that exist for the purpose of human exploitation. The world has become "disenchanted," and human beings no longer feel any constraint in "using" it. An essay that has exerted great influence on contemporary thinking in this regard is Lynn White's "The Historical Roots of Our Ecologic Crisis" (1967). White says this about the Christian worldview specifically:

> By gradual stages a loving and all-powerful God had created light and darkness, the heavenly bodies, the earth and all its plants, animals, birds and fishes. Finally, God had created Adam and, as an afterthought, Eve to keep man from being lonely. Man named all the animals, thus establishing his dominance over them. God planned all of this explicitly for man's benefit and rule: no item in the physical creation had any purpose save to serve man's purposes. And, although man's body is made of clay, he is not simply part of nature: he is made in God's image. Especially in its Western form, Christianity is the most anthropocentric religion the world has seen.[34]

This is, however, a quite wrong-headed critique of biblical faith. Even though the world is not divine in Hebrew thinking, it is nevertheless a *sacred* place in which God has chosen to make himself known to his creatures. It is, therefore, a place that is to be revered and protected out of love and respect not only for the Creator but also for the creation itself.[35]

The Cosmos as Temple

The sacred nature of the world is first intimated in Genesis 1 through the metaphor of the temple. Temples in the ancient Near East were designed primarily as residences for the gods, rather than as places of worship.[36] They were built on previously identified sacred space, and their ordered arrangement and decoration mirrored the order and fertility of the cosmos as a whole. More than a mirror, however, a temple was considered to be *the very center* of the cosmos, from which emanated all the good of society. It was often viewed as incorporating within it (or as having been built upon) a spring, which represented the primeval waters out of which the world ultimately evolved. These waters of life were imagined to flow out of the temple and into the whole world, watering the four corners of the earth.[37] Given this close connection between temple and cosmos in the ancient mind, it is unsurprising that ancient Near Eastern texts concerning the creation of the world should show a marked similarity to ancient Near Eastern texts concerning the construction of temples. Both kinds of text tell the story of how a stable and ordered environment was brought about in which divinity could find "rest," enjoying (along with his worshippers) the peace and security of the cosmos.[38]

It is this close connection between cosmos construction and temple construction that we see also in Genesis 1:1–2:4, where the cosmos is presented *as* God's temple. First, temple-dedication ceremonies in the ancient Near East often lasted seven days; in Genesis 1 (along with the opening verses of Genesis 2) we are told that the creative process lasts six days, but the six are completed by a seventh in which God comes to "rest." Near the beginning of the creative process, second, we are told of God's gathering of the waters into one place so that they could serve a useful purpose as seas (Genesis 1:9). This reflects the reality of the later temple in Israel's capital city of Jerusalem, within whose precincts was to be found an impressive "sea of cast metal, circular in shape" (1 Kings 7:23-26). Third, we also read in Genesis about the creation of the sun and the moon (Genesis 1:14-16), and I noted earlier the curiosity that they are not named but are simply "lights." I suggested that the authors wished to avoid evoking the picture of well-known ancient gods, but in addition we should note that the Hebrew word used here for "light" (*ma'or*) is most frequently used elsewhere in the Old Testament for the sanctuary light in the tabernacle (the Israelites' portable temple prior to Solomon's time).[39] Fourth, the *end* of the creation account in Genesis 1:1–2:4 *also* reminds us of the construction of the tabernacle. In Exodus 40:33, Moses "finished the work" on that sanctuary, just as God "finished his work" on creation in Genesis 2:2.[40] Finally, before God finishes this creative work, we read in Genesis that he places an "image" in creation (1:26-28). In the ancient Near East more generally, a deity's presence in his temple was also marked by an image, in which the reality of the deity was thought to be embodied.[41] We shall return later (in chapter 4) to the precise significance of this Genesis reference to the divine image for the biblical understanding of humanity.

In Genesis 1:1–2:4, then, we read about the construction of a temple-cosmos. This cosmos is neither *merely* utilitarian nor *solely* functional. It is *sacred space*.[42]

The Impossible Garden

The sacred nature of the world is also strongly suggested by the metaphor of the garden that is used for it in Genesis 2. This is often missed, however, because of a long reading tradition that understands this garden ("in the east, in Eden"; 2:8) as a place *within* the world rather than as a picture *of* the world. Indeed, there stands behind the modern reader a long series of speculations about its particular *location* within the world. Before returning to the metaphor in itself, then, I must first digress briefly into a discussion of the "geography" of Eden.

The authors of Genesis almost certainly did not have a particular location in mind when writing about this garden. Three features of their description strongly suggest this. First, the region to the "east" of ancient Israel was Mesopotamia, so if we *were* looking for a particular location, we might well assume that this is where we should look. However, as we read the first eleven chapters of the Genesis story, we discover that human beings only *end up* in Mesopotamia as the result of an eastward migration from their starting point in the garden. They first leave the garden via the entrance/exit on its east side (this is where the cherubim guards are placed to prevent reentry; Genesis 3:24). Once out of the garden, Cain's failures lead him further eastward into the land of Nod (4:16); further eastward migration ultimately leads to Babylon (11:2). Eden, it seems, must actually be in the *west*—and indeed, one ancient tradition identifies the garden with the oasis city of Damascus in Syria. It seems impossible to hold these two very different ideas together. Is Eden in the east, or is it in the west? This suggests that there is, at the very least, something wrong with the translation "in the east" for the Hebrew word *miqqedem* in Genesis 2:8, and we shall return to this question in a moment.

Second, we must remember that Genesis 2 follows Genesis 1, which has just outlined a human vocation that involves ruling over the whole earth. It has already described the creation of trees in that global context (1:11-12, 29), as well as the creation of beasts, birds, and humans (female as well as male; Genesis 1:20-27). Chapter 2 repeats all of this in the context of the garden. The natural implication is that the garden is not located somewhere *on* the earth, but represents the *whole* earth. It is the very place in which we find all the plants and trees, all the beasts and birds (they are all there to be named in Genesis 2:19-20), and all the images of God (human beings) who are placed in God's temple-cosmos. Put succinctly, the creation narrative of Genesis 1 is retold in Genesis 2, this time through the metaphor of the garden rather than the temple. Indeed, if the garden is *not* the whole earth, it is unclear how the whole earth is supposed to be populated and governed by human beings in line with Genesis 1:28, for there is no hint in Genesis 1–3 that human beings were ever *supposed* to leave the garden. They leave it in Genesis 3 only because they become implicated in moral evil (Genesis 3:23).

Third, there is the puzzling matter of the geography of Genesis 2:10-14:

> A river watering the garden flowed from Eden; from there it was separated into four headwaters. The name of the first is the Pishon; it winds through the entire land of Havilah, where there is gold. (The gold of that land is good; aromatic resin and onyx are also there.) The name of the second river is the Gihon; it winds through the entire land of Cush. The name of the third river is the Tigris; it runs along the east side of Asshur. And the fourth river is the Euphrates.

The presence of two known rivers of the ancient Near East (the Tigris and the Euphrates) among the four mentioned here has prompted speculation about the identity of the other two (the Pishon and the Gihon) amid attempts to identify the location of "the garden." The Pishon has been identified, for example, with the Indus or the Ganges, in which case the "land of Havilah, where there is gold" would be India. The Gihon has frequently been identified with the Nile because of its stated connection with the land of Cush, which is an ancient name for the southern part of Egypt.[43] A reading of the Old Testament itself, however, would suggest that we associate Havilah with Arabia (Genesis 10:29; 25:18). It would further suggest that we associate Gihon with Palestine; Gihon elsewhere in the Old Testament is the name of an important spring in the Kidron Valley beneath Jerusalem (e.g., in 1 Kings 1:33, 38), access to which was important enough to the inhabitants of the city to prompt the early construction of a complex water system. Those who are looking for a specific geographical location for the garden thus need to reckon with a river flowing from one starting point in Eden and dividing, then, into four, resulting in two rivers in Mesopotamia (the Tigris and the Euphrates), one in Arabia (the Pishon), and one that apparently flowed through Egypt but also Palestine (the Gihon). It is difficult to conceive of such a river, especially when it is considered that the Tigris and Euphrates both flow from north to south, and the Nile from south to north—facts as obvious to ancient as to modern observers.[44] These various rivers evidently do not come from the same "place."

Where, then, is Eden? I submit that this is the wrong question. We are not dealing in Genesis 2 with a garden that inhabits a space within the world in terms of normal physical geography. We are dealing, I believe, with something else.

Garden and Temple

We can gain some clarity about this "something else" if we invest our time, not in speculating about "where Eden was" but in becoming better informed about how gardens functioned and what they stood for in the ancient Near East. In ancient Mesopotamia, the palace complexes of kings commonly featured gardens. Given the supposed divinity of kings in that world, we can see right away an association between gardens and divinity. The major temple complexes in Mesopotamia also featured, along with the temple, both a ziggurat and a garden. The ziggurat was a pyramid-like structure with a staircase running down it by which the gods were thought to enter the earthly realm, descending to the temple at the ziggurat's foot to receive the gifts and worship of the people.[45] The garden had a twofold function: it symbolized the fertility that flowed *from* the deity, and it provided some of the food for the offerings made *to* the deity. These temple gardens were viewed as being watered by the primeval streams flowing out from the temple that I described a moment ago, and they featured pools, trees and plants, and animals. Finally, the gods themselves are sometimes said in ancient Near Eastern literature to live in a garden paradise. The Mesopotamian *Epic of Gilgamesh* speaks of such a place—a mountain sanctuary characterized by luxuriant trees, into which no mortal being may enter. The myth of *Enki and Ninhursag* further describes the land of Dilmun, watered by streams emerging from the earth to bring life to it. It is in this land that Enki and Ninhursag have sexual intercourse.[46]

What we are *likely* dealing with in Genesis 2, then, is exactly what we are *certainly* dealing with in Genesis 1. It is the idea that the whole world is sacred space. In Genesis 2, however, this idea is developed using garden imagery. Like other temples in the ancient world, this (cosmic) garden-temple incorporates within it a spring, from which the primeval waters flow out to water the four corners of the earth (2:6)—the world known to ancient Israel as bounded by Egypt and Arabia to the south, Mesopotamia to the north and east, and by the Mediterranean Sea to the west.[47] The Jerusalem temple itself could be envisaged as a garden-sanctuary of this kind. We see this in 1 Kings 6, where its interior is said to be "carved with gourds and open flowers . . . palm trees and open flowers" (1 Kings 6:18, 29). We see it also in Ezekiel 47:1-12, where the prophet, in a vision, observes water flowing out "from under the threshold of the Temple toward the east (for the Temple faced east)," giving life to the world around it (cf. Psalm 46:14; Zechariah 14:8). Like the Jerusalem temple, we note, the entrance to the garden in Eden is on its east side (Genesis 3:24) and is guarded by "cherubim"—mysterious winged beings who appear elsewhere in the Old Testament only in connection with the Jerusalem temple and the tabernacle (e.g., Exodus 25:18-22; 26:1, 31; 1 Kings 6:23-28). Ezekiel's vision then goes on to describe the many fruit trees that flank the river of life that emerges from the temple, reminding us of the trees in the garden in Eden that were "pleasing to the eye and good for food" (Genesis 2:9). God's abundant provision for his creatures, described in both Genesis 1 and 2, is itself represented in the Jerusalem temple by the "bread of the presence" that is displayed there (1 Kings 7:48; cf. Exodus 25:30). The particular "tree" that is the tree of life in the garden (Genesis 2:9) is represented in the Tabernacle by the branched lampstand with its floral motifs (Exodus 25:31-40; 37:17-24). Such "trees of life," symbolizing the fertility of nature, are commonly found in ancient Near Eastern artistic representation.

In Genesis 2, then, the whole world is sacred garden space. It is into this space that human beings are placed by God, just as they are placed in the temple-cosmos in Genesis 1. They are located there for a particular purpose: "to work it and take care of it" (Genesis 2:15)—or more literally, "to serve it [Heb. 'avad] and keep/guard it [Heb. shamar]." This language is also significant for our understanding of the nature of the garden, for it is the same language that is used in Numbers 3:7-8 about the tasks of the priests in the tabernacle. These priests "are to perform (shamar) duties . . . by doing the work ('avad) of the Tabernacle. They are to take care of (shamar) all the furnishings of the Tent of Meeting, fulfilling the obligations of the Israelites by doing the work ('avad) of the Tabernacle." From the biblical perspective, then, the work of human beings in God's world is religious work. We are to look after sacred space—the dwelling place of God—on behalf of the one who created it. This connection between garden and tabernacle is made clear in a different way in Leviticus 26:11-12, where God promises, "I will put my dwelling place (tabernacle) among you, and I will not abhor you. I will walk among you and be your God, and you will be my people." God walks among his people in the tabernacle, just as he once walked among them in the garden. The same form of the Hebrew verb (to walk) is used of God's presence in Genesis 3:8, where he is found "walking in the garden in the cool of the day" and looking for communion with his human creatures.

In sum to this point: when the Genesis creation account is read against the background of ancient Near Eastern thinking and practice more generally, as well as other biblical texts, it becomes clear that through its use of the metaphor of the garden, just as through its use of the metaphor of the temple, it accords to creation a sacred character.

In saying this, I do not mean to suggest that our biblical authors are using metaphor and imagery in just the same way that ancient Mesopotamians (in particular) did. For example, while it is true that the motif of the primeval waters flowing out of the temple is common both to the Old Testament and to other ancient literature, in biblical faith these primeval waters are not the source out of which everything else in the world ultimately evolved. It is likewise true that the biblical garden in Eden is somewhat like the garden of the gods described in ancient Near Eastern literature. However, in the garden of the gods the many trees provide food *for the gods*; in Genesis, they provide food for human beings. In the *Epic of Gilgamesh*, the sacred garden space is barred to human beings; in Genesis it is the very place in which human beings should be living, along with God and their fellow creatures. Human beings—the image bearers of God—are, in fact, the only "gods" to be found in the biblical garden. It is only they who have the capacity to engage in sexual intercourse (Genesis 2:24)—to "be fruitful and increase in number" (Genesis 1:28)—for the biblical God is not like Enki or Ninhursag, and he does not engage in sex. So Genesis does clearly *use* the ancient imagery of the garden, and readers must reckon with the great extent to which this is so if they are to understand what the book means to say. However, our biblical authors always use this imagery consistently with their overall (and distinctive) view of God and creation. They make it their own.

Living in the Garden

The garden in Eden, then (or the "garden of God," as other biblical texts call it; e.g., Isaiah 51:3; Ezekiel 28:13), is best thought of as a picture of the whole world. It is the same temple-cosmos in which God is to be found "at rest" in Genesis 1:1–2:4. It is not a specific *location* in the world. It is, rather, a *state of being* in the world, in which God exists in harmony with his creatures and in which his creatures exist in harmony with each other. In Genesis 3, this state of being is envisaged as having been lost by the first human beings, but it was once a global reality. This brings us back around to the Hebrew word *miqqedem* in Genesis 2:8, which has so often been translated as "in the east." It is in fact much better understood as referring to this ancient state of harmony. It is not so much an expression of physical direction as it is an allusion to the way things once were for all of humanity and then ceased to be. *Miqqedem* runs in two directions. It alludes, first, to God's complete communion with his creatures in the world. The sun rises in the east (*miqqedem*), and light is a common Old Testament metaphor for the divine presence.[48] It alludes, secondly, to the *loss* of this communion—for *miqqedem* is frequently used in the Old Testament in another sense, referring to that which is "from of old" (e.g., Isaiah 45:21; 46:10).[49] "Back then," says Genesis 2, people experienced the world as a garden.

Understanding the garden in Eden in this way, we solve a puzzle that otherwise confronts perceptive readers of the Old Testament. It is a puzzle presented by texts that speak of living in the garden in Eden (or in the garden of God) as a feature of the *recent* human experience of *some* individuals or as a *possible* experience for human beings in the present or near future.

In Ezekiel 28, for example, the king of Tyre is described as residing in Eden, the garden of God, enjoying its privileges until "wickedness" is found in him (v. 15). He is then driven "in disgrace from the mount of God." In Ezekiel 31, the king of Assyria is described as a splendid tree with its top in the clouds and its roots fed by subterranean waters, provoking the jealousy of all "the trees of Eden in the garden of God" (vv. 8-9). These trees are also mentioned in the description of the downfall of the Egyptian pharaoh (vv. 16-18). Eden has, no doubt, been lost—but in these texts, it has been lost *recently*. Conversely, Isaiah 51:3 and other passages envision a partial restoration of Eden in the experience of the Israelite community in the near future:

> The LORD will surely comfort Zion and will look with compassion on all her ruins; he will make her deserts like Eden, her wastelands like the garden of the LORD.

In the Song of Songs, the garden experience can likewise be partially restored at the level of the individual male-female relationship, when true love and intimacy blossom between a man and a woman. Likewise, God promises in Leviticus 26:11-12, "I will walk among you and be your God, and you will be my people," recalling the reality described in Genesis 3:8. In the tabernacle, what was lost in Genesis 3 is to some extent restored.

Eden is not a "place" whose location has long been forgotten. It is the *experience* of being in right relationship with God and with creation. And what these various texts make clear is that, from the perspective of our biblical authors, "Eden" has not inevitably been entirely lost to the world. It can still be experienced, to some extent and in various ways. It is possible, for example, to get past the cherubim who guard the temple entrance and to meet with God. Tabernacle and temple both, in fact, represent in *microcosm* what the good, ordered world created by God is thought to be in *macrocosm*. They are sacred space. It is possible, also, to get past the brokenness of the male-female relationship that is described in Genesis 3 and to know something of human intimacy once again. Living in the garden, it is indeed possible, and our very human duty, to look after both the garden and the various other creatures that live in it—the sacred garden that does not belong to human beings but to the Creator. We shall return to these important matters in later chapters.

CREATION IS GOOD

Creation is not to be worshipped, then, for it is not divine. But, as we have seen, this does not imply a devaluing of creation. It is to be well looked after just *because* it is a creation—just because it is the temple-cosmos of the Creator God, where God dwells, and is filled with creatures that he has made. God is transcendent over creation, in biblical thinking, but he is also immanent within it. This is God's place.

As a sacred place in which God dwells, creation is also, for the authors of Genesis, a resolutely *good* place (Genesis 1:10, 12, 18, 21, and 25). It is a place where God's blessing is experienced by his creatures (Genesis 1:22, 28). It is a place not just of order but of beauty and of provision for material needs: the trees in the garden are said to be "pleasing to the eye *and* good for food" (Genesis 2:9). Like everything else in the cosmos, Genesis proposes that these realities do not arise as a result of chance or the work of impersonal forces. The Creator makes things this way—the Creator whose blessing rests upon the world from the beginning and whose ongoing care sustains it. This is recognized, among others, by the author of Psalm 65:

> You care for the land and water it; you enrich it abundantly. The streams of God are filled with water to provide the people with grain, for so you have ordained it. You drench its furrows and level its ridges; you soften it with showers and bless its crops. . . . The meadows are covered with flocks and the valleys are mantled with grain; they shout for joy and sing. (vv. 9-13)

The world that is created by the personal God is therefore never regarded by biblical faith as a problem to be overcome. It is good. There are problems that arise *within* the world, to be sure. *These* must be overcome.[50] The world itself, however, is not a problem to be overcome.

The World as a Problem in the East

This view stands in stark contrast to the views encountered in much Eastern thought, which shares the common ancient Near Eastern view that reality is ultimately impersonal. In the East, the world as we know it now, as persons, therefore *does* tend to be regarded as problematic. The world itself is an obstacle to the fulfillment of our human destiny, which is to merge once again with the impersonal. This is seen most clearly in the fundamental perspective that lies at the heart of the religious vision of India—namely, that our true human nature is somehow to be identified with what is ultimately sacred and real. Already in some of the later texts in the *Rig Veda* (around 1000 B.C.), the oldest and most important collection of Vedic Indian scriptures, we find Indian thinkers pressing behind the old gods toward this ultimate reality. This trajectory of reflection is continued in the later *Brahmanas* (around 800 B.C.) and *Upanishads* (starting around 600 B.C.).[51] In the end, it is established that the ultimate reality in question is unified, absolute, and impersonal. This is the truth about the cosmos; it is the truth also about us. The goal of those who embrace such a perspective is to bring this truth to realization. The transient phenomena of historical, personal existence are not of ultimate importance. Indeed, they obscure the truth about our destiny, which we can begin to fulfill only by withdrawing from attachment to the world as we find it. The old, personal gods *themselves* are caught up in samsara—an endless round of birth, death, and rebirth. Therefore worship of these gods cannot in the end enable the escape from samsara that we should be seeking. The world is a problem to be overcome, through religious (often ascetic) practice.

As we saw earlier, the stream of Hinduism that arises most directly out of this perspective and is regarded by some Hindus as the "highest" mode of the religion (classical Hinduism) holds that this ultimate reality is Brahman: an impersonal, eternal, and all-embracing oneness in contrast to multiplicity. Brahman is also formless, so that it cannot even be described. Any description would need to reduce Brahman to something else that does have form. It is this Brahman with which our true nature or real self (atman) is to be identified. Our real self is not the self that we think ourselves to be (whether that self be physical or an immaterial, individual soul). Our real human self is eternal and formless Brahman. It is the failure to realize this truth that lies at the root of the problems in human existence. The ultimate solution is to dispel the illusion that we are many rather than one. It is this illusion that creates desire and thus selfish action. The path of *liberation* is therefore ultimately the path of *knowledge*—seeing reality the way it really is.[52]

Siddhartha Gautama, the founder of Buddhism, turned away from the ideas of the eternal Brahman and the atman, and indeed from the authority of the Vedic scriptures. In Buddhism there is no "real self" that is Brahman—no *permanent* reality that can be referred to as the self, passing from one lifetime to the next. Gautama did, however, retain the Indian view of life as samsara—a series of lives, deaths, and rebirths caused by karma (the law that every action has an effect, so that actions performed out of desire have evil repercussions in the next lifetime). At the heart of this ongoing existence lies sorrow, which arises from clinging to the self. It is this clinging to the self that causes the wheel of existence to roll ever onward. Liberation (nirvana) is achieved when one ceases to cling to the self, and it is attained by following the Noble Eightfold Path (involving right understanding, intention, speech, action, livelihood, effort, mindfulness, and concentration). On this view, the human self, like everything else in the world (including the gods and Brahman), exists in a state of impermanence and flux. To recognize that I am, in fact, "no-self," a sum of ever-changing processes, is to grasp the highest truth. Ultimately, when right concentration is attained, all sense of self drops away. The illusion that "I am" is dispelled, and nirvana is experienced as "complete freedom from conditions and limitations."[53]

These differences between Hinduism and Buddhism noted, in both ways of thinking about the cosmos we find ourselves in a world that is itself an obstacle to the attainment of some greater good for which we should be striving. The world is a problem to be overcome as we strive toward something better. What is "real" is something other than the world that we experience through our senses. We may, in the first instance, *assume* that this world is "real," as we enter it at birth and grow up in it into adulthood, but our senses turn out to be unreliable guides to reality. To enjoy the order, beauty, and goodness of creation, assuming that what is personal is ultimately more important than what is impersonal, is to be ensnared in a trap. The point of existence is to gain one's freedom from this trap.

The World as a Problem in the West

This same basically suspicious and negative attitude toward "what appears to be the case" in the multifaceted universe, combined with a persistent search for the one truth or reality that lies behind it all, also turns up in different forms in the philosophy and religion of the West. In ancient Greece, as in ancient India, there developed an interest in getting "beyond" the traditional gods to the ultimate reality that might lie behind them, and behind everything. Interestingly, this development dates in origin to the sixth century B.C., precisely the century in which the Upanishads were being composed as the foundation of the Hindu perspective on the world and in which Siddhartha Gautama was founding the first Buddhist community. I have already mentioned the pre-Socratic philosophers Thales, Anaximander, and Anaximenes, who were looking for the one entity or substance out of which everything is derived and to which everything will ultimately return. For Pythagoras, the principle that unites all multiplicity is number. Mathematical relationships constitute the true nature of things. Pythagorean thought shares with Eastern thought a belief in the "wheel of existence," involving multiple reincarnations. It specifically shares those strands in Eastern thinking that imagine an essential human self or immortal soul. Like Eastern religionists, Pythagoreans practiced disciplines in pursuit of this soul's purification, in an attempt to escape from the "wheel." The greatest of these disciplines was "contemplation"—pure thought, as opposed to observation. For the Pythagoreans, thought was superior to sense, and intuition to observation, since the latter *involved* the senses. Observation was therefore regarded as an unreliable means of apprehending the eternal world, which was revealed to the intellect, not to the senses. Later still in Greece we meet Parmenides, who also rejected sense perception as misleading and advocated dependence on reason alone to access the truth of the cosmos. Reality, Parmenides suggested, bears no resemblance at all to the world we experience through our senses. It is unchanging, perfect, one, and continuous. The world as we sense it is a problem—a problem to be overcome on the way to the truth of the cosmos.[54]

In Plato, we see a somewhat weaker view (also expressed at different times by the complicated Parmenides), according to which the world of "appearances" (natural phenomena) is not *utterly* illusory. Nevertheless, there does exist elsewhere a "real," eternal, unchanging world, immeasurably superior to the world of our experience. To this real world human beings currently have only intellectual access. All human souls, Plato posited, lived at one time in this higher reality, before the union of each immortal soul with a body. We each recall this real world vaguely whenever we see something in the shadow world around us (the world that we see, touch, and smell) that reminds us of it. Philosophy, for Plato, consists in the effort to rise, through pure thought, from opinions about the appearance of things to knowledge of reality itself. In doing so, we propel ourselves along a path that, when reincarnations have ceased, will lead to the release of our immortal souls from their entrapment in the changing world.[55]

The problematic nature of the world with respect to human destiny is also an important tenet of the various forms of Gnosticism that arose soon after Plato's time, as it of the Manichaeism of the third century A.D. In Manichaeism, by way of example, the cosmos comprises Light and Darkness—the former currently under the sovereignty of the latter. Adam, "formed from the filth of matter," belongs to the kingdom of darkness, and he is "unaware that there is within him anything that pertains to the realm of Spirit and Light."[56] When a savior is sent to enlighten him about his soul's incarceration in the world, he laments that his soul is chained to his body. This "soul" is, in Manichaeism, an aspect of the divine substance, lost in the world, and in need of rescue. It needs to rejoin the Light. It is toward this goal that Manichaeism orients its adherents, urging an asceticism—a nonparticipation in the processes of the material world—that contributes to the escape of particles of Light from the Darkness. The material world is an evil to be overcome, as the soul finds its way back to the Light. Only Light will remain when Darkness is vanquished and the currently dualistic universe becomes One.

Creation Is Not a Problem

Biblical faith has often been associated, historically, with precisely these same kinds of negative or suspicious attitudes toward the material world—the world as we think we know it, through our senses, to be. In recent times, biblical faith has certainly been associated with such attitudes by advocates of dark green religion.[57] It must immediately be conceded that we can find many examples throughout the ages of people *claiming* to embrace biblical faith who have held such attitudes—influenced in many cases by precisely the Eastern and Western perspectives I have just described. The world has become for these people a problem; and the good things of the world—like food or wine or sex or simply the enjoyment of beauty—have become *part* of the problem.

Nevertheless, it should be clear by now that our *biblical authors* do *not* agree with those (either Eastern or Western) who hold such views. In Hebrew thought, the world is categorically not a problem to be overcome. It is not a mistake. It does not trap human beings in a place where they were never meant to be and in which they do not truly belong. It is not a place of shadows and illusions that only dimly, if at all, reflect a "real" world that exists somewhere else. Creation does not lack something in being experienced in personal terms by persons. Its physical, sensual pleasures are not traps set to ensnare the soul. On the contrary, in biblical faith the world is a wonderful place, created in such a way as to be exactly the right place—a good and a beautiful place— for the flourishing of the creatures, personal and otherwise, who have been created by the One who is personal. The Many do not obscure the One. On the contrary, in their multiplicity they tell of God's glory. As Psalm 19:1 puts it, "The heavens declare the glory of God; the skies proclaim the work of his hands." In biblical faith, the Many do arise from the One, in a sense, but they were never *aspects* of the One, and their destiny is not once again to *merge* with the One. Their destiny is, rather—at least in the first instance—to live out their lives in the world that the One has made, separate in being, but certainly in intimate communion with him in his temple-cosmos.[58] Their destiny is to live out a physical, material life in a physical, material, and good space. The Jewish perspective on life in creation captures this well:

Since God created all things good, humans have the obligation
to enjoy and enhance life. Good food, wealth, and sexual pleasure are all gifts of God, and should be enjoyed in the rightful
way.[59]

Any good gift of God can, of course, be abused and take human beings
off track. That is well understood in the biblical tradition, as it is in the
Abrahamic faiths. But the world that God has made is not intrinsically
problematic in any way with respect to human destiny.[60]

All of this is not to say that, from the biblical perspective, the destiny of God's creatures involves *nothing more* than life in the wonderful
world that we now experience.[61] It is to say only (but importantly) that,
in the biblical perspective, we do live, now, in a creation that is *good*.

A WORLD-AFFIRMING PERSPECTIVE

The broad outlines of the story that the book of Genesis tells about the
world are now clear. The order, goodness, and beauty that I find in the
world as I first encounter it as a child are there to be found because
the world is a creation of God, and it reflects his glory. It is this that
accounts for the astonishing fact that the world is (among other things)
"comprehensible"—to use Albert Einstein's word in the first epigraph to
this chapter. This God is, like me, personal; or more accurately, I, as a
person, am like God in being personal. God is to be found *in* the world
as a person relating to other persons, but he is not to be identified *with*
the world. Likewise, I, who am in the world, am not to be identified
with God in the present, nor is this my destiny in the future. In all, we
find in Genesis a world-affirming perspective. What is the world? It is
a sacred place, designed precisely as *the* place in which life, including
human life, can flourish. It does not represent an obstacle placed on the
path of human beings to some other, more satisfactory state of being. It
is the very place in which God's creatures are placed by God to live *out*
a (more than) satisfactory state of being.

3

SLOW TO ANGER, ABOUNDING IN LOVE, AND (THANKFULLY) JEALOUS
Who Is God?

As flies to wanton boys, are we to the gods. They kill us
for their sport.

Gloucester in Shakespeare's *King Lear*[1]

For, after all, put it as we may to ourselves, we are all of us from
birth to death guests at a table which we did not spread. The sun,
the earth, love, friends, our very breath are parts of the banquet.
. . . Shall we think of the day as a chance to come nearer to our
Host, and to find out something of Him who has fed us so long?

Rebecca Harding Davis[2]

From the very earliest moments in which human civilization began to
emerge (and possibly even earlier), human beings, as they sought to
make sense of the world, found a central place for deity. The question
was not so much whether deity existed—that was assumed. The question was who or what deity was.

Prior to the rise of "axial age" religions and philosophies, the way in
which people tended to construe this deity was fundamentally in terms
of multiplicity. This was certainly true of the ancient Near Eastern cultures that surrounded ancient Israel. The people inhabiting those cultures believed in "the gods," rather than in "God." Behind these many

gods there *was* typically a "One"—a primordial entity from which the many gods had once arisen. This One was, however, a shadowy entity, distant from the world in which we live, largely inactive in relation to it, and therefore not particularly relevant to life. It was the gods who actually *acted* in the cosmos, and were indeed *identified* with aspects of the cosmos, who mattered. This is true whether we are thinking of the gods of the sky (identified with sun, moon, planets, and stars), of the earth (identified with natural forces like storms), or of the netherworld (the world of the dead). Every aspect of the cosmos was associated with some deity in this way. The world of the ancient Near East was, then, a world of many gods.

Such a polytheistic and naturalistic view of the world was widely shared across many different cultures in ancient times, and it is still found in parts of the world today. It is reflected, for example, in the old Vedic hymns of India (prior to 1000 B.C.),[3] in the religion of China in the Shang period (1751–1111 B.C.),[4] and in the religions of ancient Greece and Rome.[5] It survives in the religion of contemporary tribal, indigenous peoples and of those modern Western people who self-consciously seek to resurrect older forms of religion under the banner of neopaganism.[6] Why has this perspective proved so attractive to so many down through the ages? One answer is hinted at in the words of the Earl of Gloucester in *King Lear* (in the first epigraph to this chapter). The world can appear to be so complex, and indeed so lacking in anything like uniform justice, that it requires deity (if it exists at all) to be multiple in nature. No one God can possibly be in control; there must be a pantheon of gods, each vying with the other and none especially interested in providing justice (much less mercy) to human beings. H. L. Mencken aligns himself with this perspective when he says, "It is impossible to imagine the universe run by a wise, just and omnipotent God, but it is quite easy to imagine it run by a board of gods."[7] In King Lear, Gloucester himself has every reason for holding to his own pessimistic polytheism. He has just been blinded by Cornwall and Regan, and he is understandably convinced that the cosmos is not characterized by good order. Human beings are merely pawns in the games of the gods. *King Lear*, as a whole, bears this out; the good die along with the wicked, and the widespread suffering that is endured seems beyond explanation.

As we shall see in chapter 7, biblical faith remembers the polytheistic environment out of which it emerged. But in its fundamental convictions about the nature of deity, it is very different from ancient Near

Eastern polytheism and indeed from other ancient and more recent polytheistic perspectives. For the biblical authors, the world is not the battleground or the sports field of the gods, each god having its own orbit of power, perhaps neglectful of the interests of mortal beings, and perhaps even vicious. Neither is the world a project governed by a board of gods, although that image is indeed suggested by some of our ancient Near Eastern nonbiblical sources themselves.[8] As we have already observed in chapter 2, our biblical authors see the world, marked as it is by order, beauty, and goodness, as the creation of one God. They see it, in the words of Rebecca Harding Davis (in the second epigraph to this chapter), as "a table which we did not spread," implying a host. Further, this one God has revealed himself to these ancient Israelites not just in creation but also in history. So they believed. In response, the biblical authors simply reject the many gods, and turn to the One.

In this rejection of the multiplicity of divinity, they do share something in common with the other "axial" religions and philosophies (both Eastern and Western) described in chapter 2—at least in their monistic and quasi-monotheistic forms.[9] It is a serious mistake, however, in noticing this fact, to fail to attend at the same time to what differentiates biblical faith from many of these "axial streams." When the founders and advocates of those religions and philosophies lose interest in the multiplicity of gods and look beyond them for the One, they frequently also look beyond personhood. The primordial divine entity that was irrelevant to life in the old religions *does* now become, in these new belief systems, the deeply relevant "ultimate" with which human destiny is bound up. This ultimate is, however, impersonal. The biblical authors agree with these thinkers that fundamental reality is singular, and not multiple. They insist, however, that the One who stands behind the gods as the ultimately Real God is, like the gods, personal. *They* are personal, many, and nonexistent. *He* is personal, one, and living. Indeed, he is not simply the One; he is Creator, and he is Host. The present chapter explores the various ways in which biblical faith in this one personal God is expressed.

GOD IS ONE

In any discussion of the God of the Bible, the best place to begin is with the notion of oneness itself, which becomes so important for each of the three Abrahamic religions that draw upon the Bible. The God of whom biblical faith speaks is one, and not many. There are no other gods in the heavens or on the earth or under the earth.

No Gods in the Heavens

This one God created the heavens and everything in them (Genesis 1:1, 6-8, 14-19). As part of the created order, neither the heavens themselves nor anything in them is divine. This is not the case in ancient Egypt. There the sky is represented by a goddess, Nut, who plays out her role in the cosmos by *means* of the sky.[10] Something similar is at work in contemporary indigenous tribal religion, where the sky deity (usually male) is often regarded as the supreme god, whose attributes are deduced from the attributes of the sky (e.g., he is distant and inaccessible).[11] In Genesis, however, the sky is neither god nor goddess but only an aspect of creation.

In the ancient Near East, two of the objects in the sky were especially significant—the sun and the moon. These were two of the most important gods in the pantheon. In fact, throughout most of Egyptian history, it was customary to associate the sun with the *supreme* god, variously called Atum, Re, or Amun. For one brief period, under Pharaoh Akhenaton (fourteenth century B.C.), *only* the worship of this sun god was permitted.[12] Sun and moon are also important in the ancient texts of the still-living indigenous Shinto tradition of Japan. In this Japanese way of thinking, all aspects of the cosmos are animated and overseen by supernatural beings called *kami*. In the heavens the *kami* are associated with aspects of reality like the moon and wind, and they are ruled by the sun goddess Amaterasu, who is said to have established the Japanese imperial line through her descendant Jimmu Tenno.[13] The authors of Genesis do not regard the sun and moon in such ways but simply as lights "to give light on the earth"—to illuminate God's temple-cosmos (Genesis 1:15; see our chap. 2). The stars, too, function in Genesis quite differently than in other religious traditions. In the ancient Near East, the stars were widely held to control human destiny; in contemporary tribal religion, they "are often considered to be manifestations or helpers of the sky god."[14] There are no such tasks assigned to the stars in the Old Testament. Like the sun and the moon, they become "disenchanted"—they become creatures, just like you and me. The ancient Israelites were commanded, therefore, neither to devote themselves to the worship of the heavenly bodies nor to fear them, for "the sun will not harm you by day, nor the moon by night" (Psalm 121:6).[15]

No Gods on the Earth

The God of the heavens is also the God of the *earth*, for he created the earth, and all that is in it (Genesis 1:1, 9-13, 20-31). Again, as part of the created order, neither the earth itself nor anything in it is divine. There are no gods to be found there, other than the God who creates all things. Other peoples in ancient Syria-Palestine thought differently. Among these peoples, the actions of the god Hadad (known as "Ba'al" in the Old Testament and as Adad and Haddu elsewhere) were considered to have important consequences for life on earth. Hadad was the son of the high god El and the consort of the goddess Anat—a storm god who was the source of the rains that brought fertility to the land and enabled the agricultural cycle to continue.[16] Adherents of Japanese Shinto still think along such lines. In Shinto, the earthly *kami* are immanent in the whole realm of nature and are seen (for example) in the growth, fertility, and productivity of plant life. They animate every aspect of earthly life.[17] Likewise, the indigenous Shoshoni of Wyoming in the United States still worship "Mother Earth"—the goddess who is "the sacred power of the earth, nourishing plants and animals." Many other peoples throughout history have also revered earthly gods in this way.[18]

However, the Old Testament sets its face against such worship. Genesis does know of nourishment for plants and animals; of growth, fertility, and productivity; of water and agricultural cycles. But Genesis attributes all of these to one creator God, who creates the conditions in which life can arise and who then oversees the functioning of the world to ensure that it flourishes. Genesis does not regard creation itself as sharing in divinity. Other parts of the Old Testament agree. Psalm 104, for example, describes God's ongoing creative care for the world in some detail. The hostility to Ba'al (Hadad) that is so evident in the narrative texts of the Old Testament arises directly from this perspective. It is particularly clear in the story of the prophet Elijah's confrontation with King Ahab and Queen Jezebel in 1 Kings 17–19. This entire story is a sustained polemic against the kind of religion that finds divinity in created things and specifically imagines that some gods other than God are involved in bringing fertility to the earth. The story begins in 1 Kings 17, when the one true God brings drought on the land of Israel— something only he can do. The Ba'al worshippers in the land naturally think otherwise, and a contest ensues on the top of Mount Carmel (1 Kings 18)—a contest that demonstrates beyond any doubt that the

LORD is God and that there is no other. Along the way, Elijah mocks Baʻal for being just too human to be taken seriously as a god. Observing his inactivity in the face of strenuous efforts by his worshipers to get him to do their bidding, he advises them, "Shout louder!... Surely he is a god! Perhaps he is deep in thought, or busy, or traveling. Maybe he is sleeping and must be awakened" (v. 27). Their response is to put more effort into the fertility rituals they are employing to get Baʻal's attention but to no avail: "There was no response, no one answered, no one paid attention."[19]

In biblical thinking, then, there are no other gods than God on the earth—no other gods who can create, sustain, and cause creation to flourish.

No Gods under the Earth

Only the netherworld, or underworld, remains—the world of the dead, known to the Hebrews as *sheʻol*. According to biblical faith, there are no gods there either. In the surrounding cultures, people certainly believed that there were gods inhabiting this world. In Mesopotamia, we read of Queen Ereshkigal, and her consort Nergal. In Egypt we encounter Osiris. In Syria we meet Mot, who is regarded in Ugaritic mythology as one of the enemies of Baʻal. As the god of the realm of death, Mot was thought to appear in the world each year prior to the life cycle restarting in the spring. The Greeks, later, also had chthonic deities of the underworld, in addition to heavenly and earthly (fertility) deities. Their pantheon included not just Zeus in heaven (the father of the gods) and Demeter on earth (the goddess of grain) but also Hades. Biblical faith, however, knows of no such netherworld deities. It confesses only (and even then occasionally) the presence of the Creator God himself in *sheʻol*: "If I make my bed in the depths (lit. *sheʻol*) you are there" (Psalm 139:8). Whereas Baʻal must submit to Mot each year as the annual cycles of nature run their course, Israel's Creator God certainly does not need to do any such thing. He has no divine competitors in the realm of death, just as he has none in heaven or on earth. This, too, is illustrated in the Elijah story. After announcing the drought on behalf of God—a drought that affects not only Israel but also the region of Sidon, which is the heartland of Jezebel's Baʻal worship—Elijah goes to this region himself. In a time of famine, he ushers in abundance and feeds a starving widow and her son. Later the son dies, and Elijah is able to bring him back to life (1 Kings 17). Right here, in enemy territory, it is made clear that Israel's God has no peers; neither Ba'al nor Mot exists.

Not Many, but One

Biblical faith leaves polytheism behind. God is One and not many—a belief that became fundamental in each of the three Abrahamic religions.[20] There *is* something of a divine assembly still apparent in some Old Testament texts (e.g., 1 Kings 22; Psalm 89; Job 1–2), and this assembly may also be implied in the curious plural of Genesis 1:26, "Let us make man in our image" (cf. also Genesis 3:22; 11:7).[21] The divine assembly is not made up of gods, however, and its members are not given any real authority or jurisdiction in the cosmos. They are merely God's advisors, referred to elsewhere in the tradition as "angels," who can be sent from time to time on errands on God's behalf. Even then, Isaiah disputes that God needs advice: "Whom did the LORD consult to enlighten him, and who taught him the right way?" (40:14). Human beings are not the only personal creatures in the cosmos. There are also "messengers." However, these messengers are indeed *creatures*, and not divinities. God is not many but One.

GOD HAS NO POINT OF ORIGIN
WITHIN THE COSMOS

This brings us directly to a second thing that must be said about God in biblical faith: that God has no point of *origin* within the cosmos.[22] Throughout the ancient Near East, deity was thoroughly integrated *into* the cosmos. All the gods had origins within the cosmos, and the primeval waters were an important (sometimes the ultimate) *point* of divine origin. The Egyptian text *Ritual of Amun* illustrates this well. Here, the first god arises out of the waters, separates himself from them, and then further divides internally into the "many."[23] These deities embody the various aspects of the natural world that comes into being along with them. The birth of the gods, then, is directly connected to the origins of natural phenomena. For example, the birth of the moon god coincides with the origin of the moon; neither functions nor exists without the other. This ancient Near Eastern idea of the gods originating as part of creation in a primordial watery chaos is also found in other ancient cultures. In China, this condition of chaos was referred to as *hundun*, which was thought ultimately to give way to a self-governing natural order overseen by a supreme deity called Shangdi or Tian, who ruled a pantheon of nature gods.[24] For the adherents of Japanese Shinto religion, the gods also emerged through spontaneous generation from the primeval divine chaos.[25]

Again, biblical faith disagrees. Neither in the book of Genesis nor anywhere else in the Old Testament is the creator God said to have an origin at all, much less an origin within the cosmos. This God is utterly distinct and separate from the creation that arises out of the primeval chaos. He is certainly *not* involved in bringing other gods into existence, whether through separation or procreation. He is, in fact, eternal, whereas the world he has made is not: "Before the mountains were born or you brought forth the earth and the world, from everlasting to everlasting you are God" (Psalm 90:2).

GOD IS SOVEREIGN OVER CREATION

God is one, and God is without origin in creation. The God of biblical faith is, third, completely sovereign *over* creation. Isaiah 40:26-31 makes this explicit. This passage begins by reminding us of God's creative acts:

> Lift your eyes and look to the heavens: Who created all these?
> He who brings out the starry host one by one, and calls them
> each by name. Because of his great power and mighty strength,
> not one of them is missing.

This is an all-powerful God, sovereign over both creation and history—a reminder that the Israelites, in this context, desperately need, because they are complaining about God's inactivity in the world.[26]

The gods of the ancient Near East are certainly not sovereign over creation. They do not even truly create at all. Rather, they find themselves in a cosmos that has already emerged, and whose basic characteristics have already been laid down as the gods themselves are coming into existence. These deities do have some ability and responsibility to order the cosmos in which they find themselves, but their actions must conform to rules that have already been established. Beyond this business of ordering, the gods are also tasked with *maintaining* the operation of the cosmos. They order, and they maintain, but they have no ultimate power over the cosmos or even (for that matter) over their own fates.[27]

The same is true, unsurprisingly, in all such naturalistic and polytheistic ways of thinking about the world. In such ways of thinking, the gods are inevitably limited in their individual and even collective powers with respect to a cosmos from which they themselves emerged. It is true, also, for the Hinduism that arises directly out of the Upanishads, where the gods (like humans) are caught up in samsara and need liberation from it. In earlier times the Vedic text *Rig Veda* had already asked, "Whence is this creation? The gods came afterward, with the creation of this universe. Who then knows whence it has arisen?" (10.129.6).[28] In the West, likewise, Aristotle's "unmoved mover," although it does exist outside the cosmos, is certainly not a creator with sovereign power *over* the cosmos. It is only the mind that brings the potentiality of pre-existing material into actuality—what Jonathan Barnes refers to as "a changeless source of change."[29]

In biblical faith, however, God is not merely the manager of a cosmic system whose fundamental parameters are already a "given" or the mover of what otherwise cannot move. God is the One who initiates *everything* in the cosmos. Whereas in the Sumerian version of the *Great Astrological Treatise*, the great gods Anu, Enlil, and Enki establish the lunar cycle in line with the given parameters, in Genesis 1 God simply speaks into being the heavens and the earth and everything within them.[30] God is sovereign in biblical faith—as he is in each of the Abrahamic religions that builds upon this faith or is deeply influenced by it.[31]

GOD IS INCOMPARABLE

The profound differences between God and the gods that we have begun to unpack in this chapter were not only well understood by our biblical authors but also explicitly commented upon by them. We have just read, in Isaiah 40:26-31, a description of God's sovereignty over creation. Importantly, this description is preceded by verse 25, which makes clear that the passage comprises part of an invitation to consider precisely how the one true God is so very different from all his competitors: "'To whom will you compare me? Or who is my equal?' says the Holy One." The question is, of course, rhetorical. The writer does not actually believe that there *is* any god who is comparable. This idea—that there is no other god worshipped in the ancient world who is the least bit like the God whom Israel knows—is explicitly expressed in the Old Testament on many occasions.

God Is Unlike the Gods

We encounter it, for example, in a song sung after the people of Israel have crossed the Red Sea during their escape from Egypt: "Who among the gods is like you, O LORD? Who is like you—majestic in holiness, awesome in glory, working wonders?" (Exodus 15:11). In the Exodus story, God reenacts the creation of dry land in Genesis 1:9-10. He separates the waters of the sea, and brings out of their midst dry land for the Israelites to walk upon. Which other God can do *that*? We encounter the same idea, in reference to the Exodus, in Psalm 77:13: "What god is so great as our God?" We also find it in Psalm 89:6: "For who in the skies above can compare with the LORD? Who is like the LORD among the heavenly beings?" In 1 Kings 8:23, King Solomon further proclaims, "O LORD, God of Israel, there is no God like you in heaven above or on earth below." The biblical authors would not have agreed, then, with Samuel Butler when he said, "There is no God but has been in the loins of past gods."[32] This comment suggests significant evolutionary continuity between various conceptions of deity across time. However, the biblical authors did not understand the living God as continuous with the gods at all. The God they knew was incomparable.

This great distance that exists between God, on the one hand, and the gods of the ancient world, on the other, inevitably results from the fact that God is one and not many. From a biblical point of view, the many who are worshipped as gods are not gods at all but simply aspects of creation. Deuteronomy 4:39 therefore instructs the Israelites to "acknowledge and take to heart this day that the LORD is God in heaven above and on the earth below. There is no other." Second Samuel 7:22 proclaims, "How great you are, O Sovereign LORD! There is no one like you, and there is no God but you." Isaiah 44:6-7 asserts, "Apart from me there is no God. Who then is like me?" There is but one God, the maker of all things and the Lord of the universe. The many "gods" are merely "man-made gods of wood and stone, which cannot see or hear or eat or smell" (Deuteronomy 4:28). They have no existence as gods beyond the images constructed for them in their temples by their worshippers.

God Is Unlike Human Beings

The other peoples of the ancient Near East, of course, would not have accepted such a characterization of their gods. For them, the gods were persons animating the images that were placed in their temples.[33] They were, in fact, rather similar to *human* persons. Like human beings, they had daily routines. They also possessed human-like inclinations, desires, and needs, and a human-like psyche and anatomy, which included the physical equipment for sex and childbearing. They experienced the whole range of human emotions, and they suffered their own particular limitations. They were certainly not morally superior to human beings. The gods were thus conceived as very much "like us," albeit on a grander scale—much as a king must have appeared to his subjects in the ancient world.[34]

This close paralleling of gods and humans is also found in other polytheistic systems. The Greek gods of Mount Olympus, for example, were also like human beings in many ways, while at the same time being immortal, powerful, and perfect in beauty. In fact, it was precisely this similarity to human beings that led some Greeks, over time, to doubt their real existence—to suspect that they were just products of the human imagination. Aristotle, for example, comments as follows:

> This explains why all races speak of the gods as ruled by a king, because they themselves too are some of them actually now so ruled and in other cases used to be of old; and as men imagine the gods in human form, so also they suppose their manner of life to be like their own.[35]

On this kind of view, humanity intuits genuine divinity (in nature) but misconceives of it; out of this misconception emerge human-like gods.

In biblical faith God is certainly personal, but he is not human. There *is* an analogy to be drawn between God's personhood and our own human personhood, for God created human beings "in his own image" (Genesis 1:27—we shall return to this matter in chap. 4). However, the distance that Genesis generally sets between Creator and creation already implies that we shall not find in Hebrew thinking the same level of correspondence between the personhood of God and the personhood of humans that we find more widely in ancient Near Eastern thinking or later in Greece. God is not, in Genesis, simply a superhuman aspect of the cosmos. God is the very Creator of the cosmos. So God is personal, but this does not mean that biblical faith attributes to God everything that is true of human persons. Analogy is possible, but wholesale association is not.

This "gap" in personhood between God and human beings is evident in many Hebrew texts. For example, the God of whom the Old Testament knows does not engage in sexual activity; he does not procreate. He neither slumbers nor sleeps (Psalm 121:4). He knows no shame or fear. He does not commit crimes or even misdemeanors. He *is* morally superior to human beings. As Numbers 23:19 says, "God is not a man, that he should lie." In all such respects, then, God is not only unlike the gods but also unlike *us*.

GOD IS GOOD—A GOD OF BLESSING

This leads us naturally to perhaps the most important thing that is claimed about God in biblical faith—next to the claims that he is one and not many, and does not originate with the cosmos but is sovereign over it. God is *good*. It is, of course, possible to conceive of one incomparable, sovereign, creator God who is malevolent or who is at least arbitrary, unpredictable, and untrustworthy. This is, indeed, what some people have claimed, historically, about the God of the Old Testament. A recent version of the claim is found in Richard Dawkins' book *The God Delusion*:

> The God of the Old Testament is arguably the most unpleasant character in all fiction: jealous and proud of it; a petty, unjust, unforgiving control-freak; a vindictive, bloodthirsty ethnic cleanser; a misogynistic, homophobic, racist, infanticidal, genocidal, filicidal, pestilential, megalomaniacal, sadomasochistic, capriciously malevolent bully.[36]

Others may not express themselves in quite so hostile a manner, but Dawkins' sentiments are, in general terms, broadly shared in post-Christian Western culture. A similar negativity about the biblical conception of God is certainly found among the advocates and practitioners of dark green religion.[37] The biblical God is an oppressive, chauvinistic sky god, deeply implicated in the calamity that has befallen Mother Earth. Sane, virtuous people do not worship such a god—most assuredly not people who care about the planet and about their fellow human beings.

The curious thing about this reading of God in the Old Testament is that it *does* claim to be a reading of the Old Testament. Yet it is perfectly clear that the authors who passed on to us these texts did not themselves believe what Dawkins and others believe about this God. They believed, on the contrary, that God is utterly good. This is one of their fundamental, overarching convictions. In what follows, I shall try to describe some of the ways in which they saw this goodness expressing itself, while at the same time offering what I think is a much more sober reading of the biblical texts than the "new atheists" offer. My conviction is that we should read these texts, in the first instance, as we may reasonably imagine their authors to have intended them—and not in ways that simply buttress our own prejudices. This means reading them *precisely* within the context of their authors' fundamental overarching convictions about reality, which is *precisely* what the new atheists have failed to do—and what many other modern readers apparently do not wish to do either.

Blessing in Genesis 1 and 2

The beginning of any story is important, of course, for getting hold of what an author is trying to say. Thankfully, we do not need to guess what, from the beginning, the biblical literature wants us to know. Genesis 1 tells us again and again that the creation is good (Genesis 1:10, 12, 18, 21, 25), indeed, that it is "very good" (Genesis 1:31). The goodness of creation implies (already) a belief among our biblical authors in the profound goodness of the God who created it—a goodness explicitly indicated in the same chapter, when they tell us that God's creating is bound up with his intention to "bless" his creatures. We meet this idea first in Genesis 1:22, where God is said to bless the sea creatures and the birds; we meet it again in Genesis 1:28, where God is said to bless human beings. This blessing is seen in the creation of a suitable environment in which God's creatures can live and in the gifts of the fertility and food that will ensure their ongoing life ("Be fruitful and increase in number"; "I give you every seed-bearing plant . . . every green plant for food"). In the case of human beings, God's blessing additionally involves ruling over the nonhuman creatures (Genesis 1:28—we shall return to this matter in chapter 9). Finally, at the end of the process by which creation first came into being, we are told that "God *blessed* the seventh day and made it holy, because on it he rested from all the work of creating that he had done" (Genesis 2:3).

It is at first sight strange, and in fact unusual in the Old Testament, that an inanimate object like a *day* should be said to be blessed. However, it is critical here to remember the close connection between temple and cosmos in the ancient mind and the marked similarity between ancient Near Eastern texts concerning the making of the world and those concerning the construction of temples. In both kinds of text, a story is told of the emergence of a stable and ordered environment in which divinity could find "rest," enjoying (along with his worshippers) the peace and security of the cosmos. The temple-dedication ceremonies that ended with this divine rest often lasted seven days. When we read in Genesis, then, that God blessed the seventh day, we are likely encountering this same ancient idea in a distinctively Hebrew form. God's initial burst of creative work has come to an end; creation has arrived at a state of blessedness—"very goodness"—in which God and his creatures may enjoy the wonderful creation that has resulted. As one writer puts it, "The seventh day is not actually blessed as an entity in itself; the day is blessed rather in its significance for the community . . . for the world and humanity."[38] What the seventh day signifies, among other things, is that God is good to all his creatures. This truth was embedded in Israel's ongoing life especially on the seventh day of each week (the Sabbath day), when human beings and other creatures that lived in immediate community with them rested from their work (Exodus 20:8-10). Obedience to the Sabbath commandment was, in fact, nothing less than an expression of *trust* in God's goodness, who was well able to provide for his creatures even though they did not work all seven days of the week.[39]

Ongoing Blessing

The Sabbath commandment clearly implies, of course, that God's blessing is regarded in biblical faith as being present and active in the world not only as it was *once* created by God but also as it *continues* to exist. Genesis itself already indicates this, as the story unfolds. Moral evil enters the world in Genesis 3–4, yet blessing evidently continues, for in Genesis 5:2 the authors remind us of God's blessing in creation just prior to providing an account of the way in which human fertility continued down through the generations from Adam to the sons of Noah. Such blessing does not cease even after the flood of Genesis 6–8, when watery chaos has temporarily reasserted itself over the ordered world. Genesis 9:1-11 repeats with modifications the basic ideas of Genesis 1, presenting the world as once *again* a suitable environment in which to live and a place in which fertility and food will once *again* ensure ongoing life.

A promise is given, in fact, that the order of the world will never again be disrupted in such a significant way by the reentry of chaos into the world: "never again will all life be cut off by the waters of a flood" (Genesis 9:11). Just previously, in Genesis 8:22, God has promised, "As long as the earth endures, seedtime and harvest, cold and heat, summer and winter, day and night will never cease." For the ancient authors of Genesis, then, the ongoing stability and the fertility of the world until the end of time is assured. God's blessing will sustain this world in the long term, even if evil has now entered into it and is working out its twisted ways within it.

God's intention to bless is then further powerfully communicated in Genesis 12:2-3, where the first steps are taken to create a special people, the Israelites, who will help to carry out God's good plans in the world:

> I will make you into a great nation and I will bless you; I will make your name great, and you will be a blessing. I will bless those who bless you, and whoever curses you I will curse; and all peoples on earth will be blessed through you.[40]

God commits himself to Abraham's descendants, but only as an aspect of his greater commitment to all the peoples of the earth. The later story in Numbers 22–24 suggests that this divine intention to bless cannot ultimately be frustrated. There, even a professional "curser," Balaam, finds himself blessing the Israelites—against his own will. Earlier in the same book of Numbers, we read the priestly words of blessing that were regularly used in Israelite worship: "The LORD bless you and keep you; the LORD make his face shine upon you and be gracious to you; the LORD turn his face toward you and give you peace" (Numbers 6:24-26).

In sum: although many modern readers of the Bible do not appear to comprehend it, it is clear that our biblical authors knew the creator God first and foremost as a God of blessing—a God who is good. It was something that they celebrated in song. "For the LORD is good and his love endures forever; his faithfulness continues through all generations," proclaims Psalm 100:5. Psalm 23:6 reveals an Israelite confident that "goodness and love will follow me all the days of my life." That entire psalm portrays God as precisely the excellent host whom Rebecca Harding Davis envisages at the beginning of our chapter, welcoming a weary traveler into his home and showering him with extravagant

hospitality: "You prepare a table before me in the presence of my enemies. You anoint my head with oil; my cup overflows" (Psalm 23:5).

God Is Good—a God of Love and Faithfulness and Deliverance

As Psalm 23:6 itself suggests with its reference to "love" (Heb. *khesed*),
blessing is not the only language used in the Old Testament to indicate
God's good intentions toward creation.

Love

The language of "steadfast love" (as some translations more helpfully
render *khesed*) is very commonly used of God in our biblical literature.
Khesed is the kind of love that is devoted and loyal. God's *khesed* is first
celebrated in Genesis 24:27, where it is directed toward Abraham. Later,
Abraham's grandson Jacob recognizes that it has marked his own life,
even though he is not worthy of it (Genesis 32:10). Such love also extends
to Jacob's son Joseph as he sits, falsely accused, in an Egyptian prison
(Genesis 39:21). Biblical faith often speaks of the abundance of this love of
God, as for example in Psalm 86:5: "You are forgiving and good, O Lord,
abounding in love to all who call to you." The earth is full of this love
(Psalm 33:5), and it overflows into the heavens (Psalm 36:5). "Because of
the Lord's great love we are not consumed, for his compassions never
fail. They are new every morning; great is your faithfulness" (Lamentations 3:22-23). It is, in fact, one of the constant refrains of the Old Testament that people ought to "give thanks to the Lord, for he is good; his
love endures forever (Psalm 106:1, and on twenty-five other occasions).

Two other Hebrew words, *rakham* and *rakhamim*, also capture
important aspects of God's love for his creatures. These words, both
referring to compassion, are closely related to another, *rehem*, which
means "womb." In 1 Kings 3:16-28, two women initially claim to be the
mother of the same child, but we read that ultimately the real mother
offers to give up her claim so that the child can live. The reason for
her action is that she is "filled with compassion for her son" (1 Kings
3:26). Compassion is the love of a mother for the child of her womb. It
is such compassion that is attributed to God in Jeremiah 31:20, where
God asks, "Is not Ephraim my dear son, the child in whom I delight?
Though I often speak against him, I still remember him. Therefore my
heart yearns for him [lit. "my womb," using Heb. *me'eh*]; I have great

compassion for him." In Isaiah 49:15, God's love for Israel exceeds even this deepest of attachments between two human beings: "Can a mother forget the baby at her breast and have no compassion on the child she has borne? Though she may forget, I will not forget you!" So profound is the biblical conviction about the love of God that the prophet Hosea can devote an entire chapter to this topic (Hosea 11).

Faithfulness

Steadfast love, and indeed a commitment to bless, implies *faithfulness*, which has just been mentioned in Psalm 100:5. This is another important word used with respect to God's goodness in the Old Testament. In Genesis 32:10, for example, Jacob acknowledges that the kindness and faithfulness of God have marked his life. Exodus 34:6 describes God as "abounding in love and faithfulness," while Deuteronomy 7:9 exhorts, "Know therefore that the LORD your God is God; he is the faithful God, keeping his covenant of love to a thousand generations of those who love him and keep his commands." Deuteronomy 32:4 affirms that "[God] is the Rock, his works are perfect, and all his ways are just. A faithful God who does no wrong, upright and just is he." Finally by way of example, Psalm 36:5 states, "Your love, O LORD, reaches to the heavens, your faithfulness to the skies."

Deliverance

God is a God of blessing, of love, and of faithfulness. The goodness of God is further experienced by the Israelites as *rescue from trouble*. God is a saving God. We see this theme, too, first articulated in the opening chapters of Genesis, where God rescues creation itself from destruction in the great flood. Creation is preserved, in microcosm, in the boat (Heb. *tevah*) that Noah has built, so that after the flood it may once again flourish (Genesis 8:15-17). This "macrocosmic" event in which all of creation is involved in Genesis is later replayed in the book of Exodus, at an individual, "microcosmic" level, in the story of Moses. In Exodus 2, Moses is saved from death by his mother, who places him in a boat (also Heb. *tevah*) and floats him downriver, where he is rescued by the pharaoh's daughter. The rescue of Moses, in turn, foreshadows the rescue of all Israel from Egypt in the Exodus itself—an event that was forever lodged in Israelite memory and that became foundational for their understanding of God as a rescuer or savior. "I have been the

LORD your God ever since the land of Egypt," proclaims God in Hosea 13:4. "You know no God but me, and besides me there is no savior."[1] From this point forward, Israel's story is marked by constant deliverance from enemies.

Individual Israelites located themselves consciously within this story when they prayed, as they often did, "Save me." Psalm 6:4 is representative: "Turn, O LORD, save my life; deliver me for the sake of your steadfast love." Psalm 22, prayed in deep distress, reminds God, "In you our ancestors trusted; they trusted, and you delivered them. To you they cried, and were saved; in you they trusted, and were not put to shame." Biblical literature also tells us, however, that God is not just interested in saving Israelites. God is intent, ultimately, on rescuing the entire world from its distress. Isaiah 49:6 reminds faithful Israelites of their own role in this salvation, which was first assigned to them (via Abraham) back in Genesis 12: "I will also make you a light for the Gentiles, that you may bring my salvation to the ends of the earth." Isaiah 45:22 addresses all the nations of the earth to whom this salvation is offered: "Turn to me and be saved, all you ends of the earth; for I am God, and there is no other."

I have deliberately quoted a number of different Old Testament texts in full in this brief review of aspects of God's goodness, for it is this literature with which Richard Dawkins claims to be interacting when he characterizes the God of the Old Testament as an "unpleasant character" who is "petty," "racist," "genocidal," and "sadomasochistic." Yet it is beyond any doubt that the authors of this literature did not think of God in any such ways. To the contrary, they proclaim that God is wonderful. They are captivated by his love, astounded by his faithfulness, and amazed by his willingness and his ability to rescue them, and ultimately the whole world, from trouble.

God for Us

In biblical thinking, then, God is good, and he intends good. He is, to quote the Apostle Paul in the New Testament, "*for* us" (Romans 8:31)— intent on blessing his creation, on loving it faithfully, and on rescuing it where necessary. Other than that God is one and that he is sovereign over the cosmos, this is the most fundamental thing that the Old Testament has to say about God. It represents the bedrock of the spirituality expressed within it. Even in deep distress the psalmist can say, "I am still confident of this: I will see the goodness of the LORD in the land of the living" (Psalm 27:13). It is consistent with this fact that the early chapters of the book of Genesis identify *distrust* in the goodness of God as lying at the heart of what is wrong with the cosmos—as lying at the heart of human alienation from God, from our fellow human beings, and from the rest of creation. The first step on the path to this alienation is the adoption of an uncharitable, suspicious, distorted view of God. We shall return to this topic more fully in chapter 5. I mention it now only because we are about to consider a few other aspects of God's character, as conceived by the biblical authors, which the modern mind sometimes has difficulty in reconciling with the goodness of God. But I propose that if we are not to misunderstand these aspects of God's character, then they must be considered precisely *as entirely bound up with his goodness.*

GOD IS GOOD—A HOLY GOD

First, God is *holy*—an attribute identified in Exodus 15:11 as one that sets him apart from the gods of the ancient Near East: "Who among the gods is like you, O LORD? Who is like you—majestic in holiness, awesome in glory, working wonders?" What is this holiness? Quite simply, it is goodness by another name—the goodness that listens to the cries of an oppressed people in Egypt and liberates them from the pharaoh. It is what differentiates God from human beings, insofar as human beings are *not* good. Hosea 11:9 makes this clear:

> My heart is changed within me; all my compassion is aroused.
> I will not carry out my fierce anger, nor will I turn and devastate
> Ephraim. For I am God, and not man—the Holy One among
> you.

A human being might well strike out vengefully against those who have betrayed him, but God's anger is constrained by his love, and this is an indication of his holiness.

Isaiah and Holiness

The conjunction of love and holiness is also evident in Isaiah 6:1-7, where we are told about a vision that came to the prophet Isaiah, in which he heard heavenly creatures cry out, "Holy, holy, holy is the LORD Almighty; the whole earth is full of his glory." Isaiah was distressed: "I am ruined! For I am a man of unclean lips, and I live among a people of unclean lips, and my eyes have seen the King, the LORD Almighty" (6:5). The holiness of God is God's pure goodness, casting light into the dark places of the human life. Naturally, such goodness *can* bring terrible destruction on God's creatures in the biblical story, when those creatures insist on treating God with contempt. For example, when Nadab and Abihu offer unholy fire before the LORD in Leviticus 10:1-3, they die. When some people of Beth-shemesh fail to respect the ark of the covenant in 1 Samuel 6:19-20, they also die. However, God's holiness is not characteristically associated in the biblical tradition with God's judgment. It is more commonly associated with salvation. This is exactly the case with Isaiah, whose confession of wrongdoing, prompted by his fresh grasp of God's goodness, is immediately followed by a "saving" event: "Then one of the seraphs flew to me with a live coal in his hand, which he had taken with tongs from the altar. With it he touched my mouth and said, 'See, this has touched your lips; your guilt is taken away and your sin atoned for'" (Isaiah 6:6-7). God's holiness is in search of a holy people, and God acts to achieve this end. His goodness may be problematic for human beings who are not good, but it is never a *great* problem, for God himself is at work to solve it.

The Israelites and Holiness

In the biblical story, God's work begins with the Israelites, for whom the call to holiness is a frequent command: "Be holy because I, the LORD your God, am holy" (e.g., Leviticus 19:2). The Israelites are to develop in themselves characteristics similar to God's own. Leviticus 17–26 identifies two qualities in particular as central to this quest for a holy life: justice and love. More generally, Leviticus outlines a ritual worship system, centered on the tabernacle, which is designed to aid the people of Israel in this endeavor (we shall return to this topic in chap. 10). Yet this worship system is designed not only to help them with the *pursuit* of holiness; it is also designed to deal with the problem of their *lack* of holiness in the meantime. It is, in part, a sacrificial system, and at its heart lies the idea of atonement. In the shedding of the blood of the sacrificial victim, peace is made between God and human beings. The central principle here is the principle of substitution, which is found throughout the biblical texts about sacrifice. This principle is well illustrated in the story about the institution of the Passover feast in Exodus 12:1-14. When God comes to execute justice on the land of Egypt, it is the blood of the sacrificial lamb on the doors and lintels of a particular

Israelite house that causes him to pass over that house. Whether it be Isaiah or the whole people of Israel, God does not just require holiness; he also takes steps to deal with its absence.

The World and Holiness

As with deliverance, so too with holiness: God's ultimate goal, in biblical faith, is not just the holiness of Israel, but the holiness of the entire world. In chapter 2 we saw that both tabernacle and temple represent in microcosm what God's good and ordered world is in macrocosm. They preserve sacred space in a world whose sacredness has been compromised by the entrance of moral evil. God still "walks" in this tabernacle- and temple-space as he walked in the garden. These sanctuaries not only *preserve* sacredness, however, but also *foreshadow* it. God has not given up on his temple-cosmos project and become content instead with much smaller, more manageable ones. Rather, these smaller projects point forward to a time when the whole temple-cosmos will be cleansed of evil, and (as the prophet Zechariah puts it), "Holy to the LORD will be inscribed on the bells of the horses, and the cooking pots in the LORD's house will be like the sacred bowls in front of the altar" (14:20). In other words, there will no longer be any distinction between the sacred and the profane. Holiness will embrace all. Whereas the glory of the LORD is so often said to fill the tabernacle and temple in the biblical story (e.g., 1 Kings 5:14), one day "the earth will be filled with the knowledge of the glory of the LORD, as the waters cover the sea" (Habakkuk 2:14). This is holiness; this is goodness.

Goodness and Holiness

The holiness of God, as we have learned, *can* be dangerous to human beings in biblical thinking, but this is not because God is not wholly good. It is because *human beings* are not themselves wholly good. Even so, God's holiness is not *characteristically* dangerous, because of God's love and compassion for all his creatures. In my view, C. S. Lewis captures the biblical perspective perfectly, when in *The Lion, the Witch and the Wardrobe* he describes Mr. Beaver telling his hearers for the first time of the lion Aslan: "'Then he isn't safe?' said Lucy. 'Safe?' said Mr. Beaver . . . 'Who said anything about safe? 'Course he isn't safe. But he's good.'"[42] Lewis understands the biblical literature here just as profoundly as Richard Dawkins misunderstands it when he characterizes the God of the Old Testament as "a vindictive, bloodthirsty ethnic cleanser." This is certainly *not* how our biblical authors thought of the holy, living God.

GOD IS GOOD—AN ANGRY GOD

One of the aspects of God's character that renders him "unsafe" in biblical thinking is his *anger*. Abraham fears it in Genesis 18:30, Moses experiences it in Exodus 4:14, and it is unleashed against the Egyptians in the Exodus, consuming them like stubble (Exodus 15:7-8). Later, it burns against God's own people Israel (Exodus 32:11). It is an often-mentioned reality in the Old Testament. Yet the anger of God is clearly understood by our biblical authors as also being bound up with God's goodness. How do they describe it?

Anger for Reasons

First, it is an anger that is not a matter of whim or caprice or spite. God does not get angry because his pride is hurt, or because he is envious of human beings. The anger of God is never arbitrary; it is always directed at what is evil. It is the anger of a good person outraged by the corruption of the world, as in Genesis 6:5: "the LORD saw how great man's wickedness on the earth had become, and that every inclination of the thoughts of his heart was only evil all the time." It is the anger of a person who is passionate about justice for those who are oppressed by others: "Do not take advantage of a widow or an orphan. If you do and they cry out to me, I will certainly hear their cry. My anger will be aroused" (Exodus 22:22-24). It is right that God should be angry about such things, our biblical authors believe—just as it is right that *human beings* should be angry about them (e.g., 2 Samuel 12:1-6). It is particularly good news that an *all-powerful* and *sovereign* God is angry about such things, because it gives grounds for hope—hope that justice will be done. God cares enough about his creation to *be* angry about evildoing and to take action against it. It is good news that he will not "leave the guilty unpunished" (Exodus 34:7) and that even if human beings themselves fail to deliver justice, justice will be done: "With righteousness he will judge the needy, with justice he will give decisions for the poor of the earth. He will strike the earth with the rod of his mouth; with the breath of his lips he will slay the wicked" (Isaiah 11:4). This is a wonderful promise.

Anger That Is Slow

Second, God's anger is not quickly or lightly expressed. It is anger that is slow to arise. It *is* true that God will not "leave the guilty unpunished" (Exodus 34:7), but it is also true that he is a "compassionate and gracious God, slow to anger, abounding in love and faithfulness, maintaining love to thousands, and forgiving wickedness, rebellion and sin" (Exodus 34:6-7). God is *for* his creation, and his anger is always constrained by his compassion and grace. This is why the world continues on its way at all, for, as the psalmist asks, "If you, O LORD, kept a record of sins, O Lord, who could stand?" (Psalm 130:3). All human beings are morally compromised, and if God's anger were not constrained by anything else, every human being would have a big problem. But as the psalm continues, "with you there is forgiveness" (v. 4). Even when faced with recalcitrant people, Nehemiah 9:17 reminds us that God remains "a forgiving God, gracious and compassionate, slow to anger and abounding in love." Because he is "compassionate and gracious, slow to anger, abounding in love . . . he does not treat us as our sins deserve or repay us according to our iniquities" (Psalm 103:8-10).

It is this very reality—that God's anger is slow—that becomes a sore point for the prophet Jonah when he is sent to announce God's judgment to Israel's hated enemies, the Assyrians. When the people of the capital city of Nineveh hear what God has to say to them, they turn away from their wickedness, and so God does not execute justice upon them. Jonah himself is furious. He already knew that God was "a gracious and compassionate God, slow to anger and abounding in love, a God who relents from sending calamity" (Jonah 4:2), but he cannot accept the outcome in the present case. Jonah is angry where God is not. Indeed, God chides him: "Nineveh has more than a hundred and twenty thousand people who cannot tell their right hand from their left, and many cattle as well. Should I not be concerned about that great city?" (4:11). God is concerned, but Jonah is not. God is slow to anger, but Jonah is quick.

Anger That Relents

Third, there is hope for those who *suffer* God's anger—and not just for those who wait (like Jonah) for it to fall on others. This is precisely because God's anger is constrained by God's love and compassion. There is hope that once an accounting has been made for wrongdoing, there might be a restoration. Thus, the author of the book of Lamentations reminds his readers, "Though [God] brings grief, he will show compassion, so great is his unfailing love. For he does not willingly bring affliction or grief to the children of men" (3:32-33). God is reluctant to bring affliction in the first place, and there is compassion to be found on the other side of it. The book of Isaiah comforts its readers with this thought: "For a brief moment I abandoned you, but with deep compassion I will bring you back. In a surge of anger I hid my face from you for a moment, but with everlasting kindness I will have compassion on you" (Isaiah 54:7-8).

Jealousy and Vengeance

Two often-misunderstood words that are closely associated with the idea of God's anger in the Old Testament are "jealousy" and "vengeance." Jealousy is essentially an intolerance of rivals, and throughout the Old Testament God is often said to be intolerant in precisely this way of other gods. The classic example comes from the Ten Commandments: "You shall not make for yourself an idol in the form of anything in heaven above or on the earth beneath or in the waters below. You shall not bow down to them or worship them; for I, the LORD your God, am a jealous God" (Exodus 20:4-5). In spite of such a commandment, God can later say of the people of Israel that they often "made me jealous by what is no god and angered me with their worthless idols" (Deuteronomy 32:21). Here, God is jealous of his right to be worshipped exclusively as the one and only God who created all things. From a biblical perspective, this is only right—there is, after all, only one God. Critically, God's jealousy is good news for his human creatures, for it is this jealousy that leads God to campaign against the false gods who can only do harm to those who devote themselves to them. "Worthless idols" cannot bless, or love, or rescue.[43] In the biblical perspective, God is, *thankfully*, jealous.

The goodness of God is likewise seen in the ultimate responsibility that God accepts for *vengeance*—the bringing of retribution on wrongdoers that ensures justice for the weak and oppressed. Psalm 94:1-3 cries out for this good thing:

> O LORD, the God who avenges, O God who avenges, shine forth.
> Rise up, O Judge of the earth; pay back to the proud what they
> deserve. How long will the wicked, O LORD, how long will the
> wicked be jubilant?

In a world in which the wicked are all too often "jubilant," there is need for one who will instead bring joy to their victims. It is a good thing, in the biblical perspective, that a person exists who is willing and able to do this.

Richard Dawkins could not misrepresent the Old Testament literature more egregiously, then, than when he describes the God portrayed in it as "jealous and proud of it" and as "a capriciously malevolent bully." Pride, capriciousness, and malevolence do not come into it. Quite the opposite is the case. Dawkins, however, completely fails to see the obvious connection made between the goodness and the jealousy of God in the biblical texts, referring to the latter as "maniacal."[44] He also fails to see the obvious connection between the goodness and the *vengeance* of God, insisting that when God's justice falls upon the ancient Canaanite cultures, as described in the biblical book of Joshua, this is "morally indistinguishable from Hitler's invasion of Poland, or Saddam Hussein's massacres of the Kurds and the Marsh Arabs."[45] This is spectacularly to miss the point. The Joshua narratives concern, precisely, the long-overdue judgment of a patient and merciful God on "jubilant" but corrupt human culture.[46] They have nothing to do with the kind of imperialistic conquest or ethnic cleansing that Dawkins' modern examples evoke. There is no idea in biblical literature that the Israelites had any "right" to the land of Canaan.[47] Nor has ethnicity anything to do with what happens, in this literature, to the Canaanites. They are driven out of the land (to the extent that they *are* driven out)[48] because they are wicked—just as the Israelites themselves are later driven out of the same land, for the same reason.[49] The Joshua narratives are, in the end, one kind of answer to the question of Psalm 94 ("how long?")— a persistent, biblical question.[50] How long will injustice be allowed to stalk the earth; how long will the cries of the oppressed go unheard? *Even-handed justice* lies at the heart of the matter—as it typically does, when biblical authors (and sometimes biblical characters) describe or reflect upon war. It is not by accident that the Judeo-Christian tradition that is grounded in this same biblical literature should have generated so much reflection on what a "just war" looks like; for when war is described in the Old Testament, reflection on justice is never very far away.[51] It is fundamentally the failure to grasp this important biblical framework for interpreting the texts touching on the conquest of Canaan, coupled with inattention to the obvious when dealing with some of the individual texts themselves,[52] that has led so many readers

—and not just Richard Dawkins—to misconstrue the Joshua narratives and their significance.[53]

GOD IS GOOD—A MERCIFUL GOD

The final aspect of the goodness of God I wish to consider here is already implicit in much of what I have said earlier. It is nevertheless best to be explicit about it. The God of whom the Old Testament speaks is a *merciful* and *forgiving* God. This is not, it seems, a perspective on biblical faith that many modern people understand very well. They just "know," somehow, that the Old Testament is a book of laws and anger and judgment, and not of love and mercy and forgiveness. This comes out in all sorts of ways, including throwaway comments like this one by Joseph Campbell (with respect to his computer): "It seems to me to be an Old Testament god with a lot of rules and no mercy."[54] Yet the biblical authors are *profoundly* convinced of God's mercy and claim that in this area, too, the one creator God is incomparable: "Who is a God like you," the prophet Micah asks, "who pardons sin and forgives the transgression of the remnant of his inheritance? You do not stay angry forever but delight to show mercy" (Micah 7:18). Notice: it is explicitly not anger in which God *delights*; it is mercy. Anger is a necessity, because of the darkness that exists in the world, but what lies deeper in God's heart is mercy. Mercy is a hallmark of God's character, in the biblical perspective, and the forgiveness that follows from mercy is to be celebrated: "Praise the LORD, O my soul, and forget not all his benefits—who forgives all your sins" (Psalm 103:2-3). How is it possible, then, for Richard Dawkins to allege that the God of the Old Testament is "a petty, unjust, unforgiving control-freak"? Is he even reading the literature that he so freely criticizes, or is he simply picking up his opinions about it secondhand?

THE GOOD GOD AND THE GODS

Who is God, then, in biblical thinking—beyond the truths that he is one and not many and does not originate with the cosmos but is sovereign over it? Answer: God is *good*, which is to say that God is holy. This goodness and holiness are seen in the blessing, love, faithfulness, rescue, anger, jealousy, vengeance, and mercy displayed by God in his interactions with his world. God is, in fact, *incomparably* good, according to the authors of the Old Testament. There is no other god like him. And these convictions have continued to be core convictions of the Abrahamic religions. All but one sura of the Qur'an, for example, begin with the words "In the name of Allah, the Most Merciful, the Most Compassionate."[55] This is, in Islam, the frame of reference within which everything else must be understood.[56]

The Gods

The biblical assertion about the incomparability of God in his goodness is certainly borne out by consideration of the various deities that were worshipped in the ancient Near East at the time the assertion was first made. There was, indeed, nothing like this God among these deities. It was not just that the other gods lacked the power to do good, although it was certainly true that their power was limited. While they did have more power than human beings (they were "superhuman"), they were nevertheless like human beings in living inside the cosmos rather than being sovereign over it; this itself limited their power. Such power as each possessed was then also constrained by the power of others: "In community, no god, even the head of the pantheon, can be truly omnipotent."[57] Their worshippers might hope for justice from the gods, then, but injustice might well arise that was beyond the gods' ability to prevent. Beyond all this, there was the question of whether the gods were good in themselves and intent on *doing* good to others. We saw earlier that the gods were not, in fact, regarded as morally superior to human persons, and although their worshippers might *hope* for good from them (and specifically for mercy and compassion), they could not be *sure* of it. Indeed, just as likely as pleasing the gods by one's actions was ending up on their wrong side completely accidentally and without ever knowing why—for the gods themselves did not clearly reveal what they were looking for from their worshippers.[58]

There was certainly no concept in this ancient Near Eastern way of thinking that the gods were *committed* in some way to the good of worshippers. The world was, after all, not set up in the first place with the good of nongods in mind. Most human beings entered the world, according to the Mesopotamian view, as the slaves of the gods.[59] The cosmos functioned *for* the gods and *in relation to* the gods; human beings were merely an afterthought. They were certainly not created to be the recipients of the blessing and love of the gods. The gods had, indeed, made no promises to humanity in general, and so there was no sense in expecting them to be *faithful*. On the contrary, the human task was to try to work out what the needs and desires of these somewhat fickle deities might be and then to try to satisfy them. Religion was about getting on with your job as an afterthought in the cosmos, hoping to stay out of trouble by doing this job well, and to derive some benefit from doing so. The character of this religion, focused as it was on gods who were not meaningfully or consistently "for us," is summed up well in these words:

> The divine, in its multiple, personalized presentations, was above all considered to be something grandiose, inaccessible, dominating, and to be feared . . . [the gods] were distant and haughty "bosses," masters and rulers, and above all not friends! One submitted to them, one feared them, one bowed down and trembled before them; one did not "love" them or "like" them.[60]

This has been the world of the gods not just in the ancient Near East but in other times and places as well. The immortal, powerful gods of the Greeks whom I also mentioned earlier were no different. They were not notably good either, nor were they notably committed to the good of mortal creation. The Greek gods were, in fact, famously fickle and easy to offend. Herodotus alludes to this when he has Amasis write to Polycrates in these terms:

> It is pleasant to learn that a friend and ally is doing well. But I do not like these great successes of yours; for I know the gods, how jealous they are, and I desire somehow that both I and those for whom I care succeed in some affairs, fail in others, and thus pass life faring differently by turns, rather than succeed at everything.[61]

We find a similar worldview coming to expression in a very modern context—in twentieth-century Vancouver (Canada)—in a story that Wayson Choy tells about his Chinese grandmother. In this story, Choy relates that his grandmother was always on the alert for occasions when children in the extended family were praised by other family members. She was concerned, Choy tells us, about the possibility of attracting the unwelcome attention of the kitchen god, with probably negative consequences.[62] The kitchen god liked to be the center of attention.

The Good God

Perhaps the new atheists are thinking of *these* gods when they write about the biblical God in the way they do. Perhaps they are reading various bits and pieces of the Old Testament through a polytheistic lens—if they are reading them at all. Be that as it may, this polytheistic lens is certainly not the one that *the biblical authors themselves* give us for reading the various individual sections of the Old Testament. *The biblical authors themselves* think of God as utterly unlike the gods of their ancient world. Goodness and holiness define this person; consistency of character marks him. He is not fickle, and he does not hide his will. It is possible to know what he expects, because he tells us; what he expects, it turns out, is that we should be like him. The cosmos itself was constructed with human beings centrally in mind. God did not create in order to meet his own needs. God's purpose in creating the cosmos was, in fact, to bless his creatures, to show them love and faithfulness, to rescue them from danger and distress, and to forgive and restore them when they falter. Being sovereign over the whole cosmos, God is able to deliver such things, just as he is able to deliver justice. This is the biblical God. If it really is *this* God that the new atheists and others despise, then I do not know what to say. But perhaps their problem is not with God but with the gods.

It is because our biblical authors believed such things that biblical religion was so different in character from ancient Mesopotamian religion and remains still so different from other religions that resemble it. Biblical religion is not about fearing a distant, dominating boss, whose real desires can never be fathomed, and trying to work out, somehow, how to extract a blessing from him. Rather, biblical religion is about entering gladly into the work of God in the world as a coworker with him, enjoying all the benefits that God freely gives to his creatures, while following the path through life that he has clearly and lovingly laid out. Whereas anxiety marks the spirituality of ancient Mesopotamia, then, biblical spirituality is marked by joy. "Rejoice in the LORD," urges the psalmist, "and be glad, you righteous; sing, all you who are upright in heart!" (Psalm 32:11).

4

OF HUMUS AND HUMANITY
Who Are Man and Woman?

What a piece of work is a man! How noble in reason!
How infinite in faculties!
In form and moving how express and admirable!
In action how like an angel! In apprehension how like a god!

Hamlet, in Shakespeare's *Hamlet*[1]

Man was made at the end of the week's work,
when God was tired.

Mark Twain[2]

"What is a human being?" (Psalm 8:4).[3] In asking this question the psalmist joins a very ancient conversation. For as long as human beings have reflected on the nature of the cosmos and have pondered the question of God, they have also (very naturally) asked questions about themselves. Indeed, every cosmology (a set of views about the world) and theology (a set of views about deity) is inevitably associated with an anthropology (a set of views about human beings)—where we came from, who we are, what our purpose is, and where we are going. Such an anthropology speaks not just to generalities but also to specifics— among other things, to the question of what it means to be female rather than male.

77

As we have already seen, in ancient Mesopotamia the cosmos was considered to have come into being along with and for the benefit of the gods.[4] The cosmos was fundamentally "where the gods lived." Its order was reflected, first, in the ordered life of cities, which were constructed for the gods, and, second, in the order and symbolism of the particular houses (temples) in which the gods lived. A cult image marked the presence of a particular deity in a particular temple—an image in which the god was embodied after special rituals had transferred him from the spiritual to the physical realm. By being present in the image, the deity was intrinsically bound up with the fertility, prosperity, peace, and justice of the city. The king himself was also a divine figure, representing the gods in his city-state.

If this is how the gods were thought of in ancient Mesopotamia, how were ordinary men and women conceived? Our Sumerian and Akkadian sources consistently portray human beings as having been created to work *for* the gods—to do "work that is essential for the continuing existence of the gods . . . that they have tired of doing for themselves."[5] In other words, ordinary human beings represented slave labor, created as a cosmic afterthought to meet the needs of deity. This involved participation in a highly stratified, hierarchical society with the divine king at its apex. Within this society, a few would have been involved in particular tasks with respect to the care of the king in his palace. For everyone, it involved participation in the economy of the city-state focused on the temple; for a few, it involved particular priestly tasks with respect to the care of the gods in the temples—feeding them and otherwise looking after their needs, in much the same way that the king was looked after by his own slaves. Put succinctly, the whole of human society was oriented toward the gods; the interests of temple and state were thoroughly intertwined. The religiosity that infused the entire system has been characterized by one author as involving

> a "centrifugal" feeling of fear, respect, and servility with regard
> to the divine . . . [that] was portrayed on the human model
> (*anthropomorphism*) and was spread out over a whole society
> of supernatural beings, gods (*polytheism*), whose needs people
> were expected to fulfill and whose orders were to be carried
> out with all the devotion, submission, but also generosity and
> ostentation that were thought to be expected by such lofty
> figures.[6]

Cosmology and theology are always and inevitably bound up with anthropology. The specific Mesopotamian example illustrates the general truth. Indeed, it reminds us that cosmology, theology, and anthropology are also always and inevitably bound up with politics—with the question of the good society. The organization *of* society is connected to the question of the nature of the human beings *in* that society and how that society is related to the gods in their relationship to the world. So it was in ancient Mesopotamia, and so it was in ancient Israel. We shall *begin* to reflect later in this chapter, from the perspective of biblical faith, on the question of the good *society* (the question of politics), although a full discussion of that topic must await chapter 10. For the moment I am interested in the anthropological question as such. What is a human being, biblically speaking?

Human Beings in Genesis 1–2

We begin again with the opening chapters of Genesis and with the following observation: although Mark Twain's comment about humanity (in the second epigraph to this chapter) alludes more explicitly than Hamlet's (in the first) to the Bible since it references the creation of human beings on the sixth day, in *fact* this comment reflects the anthropology of ancient Mesopotamia more than that of the biblical authors. For Twain, like his ancient Near Eastern counterparts, human beings represent something of an afterthought in the cosmos, created once the more important work has been completed. This final act of creation is not up to the high standards of God's earlier work but reflects in various ways a tired God's lack of energy and concentration. We are indeed lowly, secondary creatures in the whole scheme of things. God was not at his best when he made us.

A Cosmos Made for Its Creatures

The book of Genesis does not share this view of human beings. We are not created, so far as biblical faith is concerned, to meet God's needs. God does not *have* needs, and his presence in his temple-cosmos (or later in the tabernacle or the temple) does not depend on the satisfaction of any needs. Nor is the world created for the gods in the first place, in the book of Genesis. The world is created for *creatures*. These creatures do not need to feed the gods; rather, God blesses *them* with food (Genesis 1:11-12, 29-30). Moreover, no creature in Genesis is created as a slave of the gods. This includes human beings, whose position in creation is, in fact, an exalted one. They are not made on the sixth day because they come *late* in God's thinking, when he is tired, but because they represent the *high point* of the creation. One of the ways in which Genesis indicates this is precisely to move them out of the role of being *caretakers* of a divine image in a temple and into the role of *being* divine images in a temple themselves.

The Earthling, the Man, and the Woman

This reality is indicated, first, in an important verse in Genesis 1: "God created human beings in his own image . . . male and female he created them" (v. 27). Before we get to the "image," however, a word needs to be said about an interpretive and translational matter earlier in the verse. Where I have translated "human beings," many Bible translations have "man." It is important to underline that the Hebrew word (*'adam*) that lies behind this common translation does not have any connotation in terms of gender, as the remainder of verse 27 makes clear in defining "man" as both male and female. To be fair, the English word "man" has likewise not necessarily had any gendered connotation for much of its historical usage. It has, however, come to be regarded as intrinsically gendered in some modern discussions. This being so, it is wiser to avoid "man" in Genesis 1:26-27. "Human beings" is adequate. If it were not that science-fiction writers have already claimed the term for themselves, I would actually prefer "earthlings," for in Genesis 2:7, the Hebrew itself plays on the fact that the "earthling" (*'adam*) came out of the earth (*'adamah*, often translated as "ground"). The same translation (human being/earthling) is preferable in Genesis 2:5, 7-8, 15-16, and 18-21 (many Bible translations notwithstanding). It is only when we reach Genesis 2:22-25 that we find gender differentiation within the earthling. It is at this point, when we have two human beings instead of one, that it becomes possible for the first time in verse 25 truly to refer to "the man" (*'adam*) and "his wife."[7]

To put this in a different way, in most of Genesis 2 we are not dealing with what might be called a normal, fully created "man" out of whom a woman is then derived. We are dealing with an earth-being who is then sexually differentiated and produces a man and a woman. Only then does the residual "earth material," which is still called *'adam* (and also *'ish*, another Heb. word for "man"), become what we would recognize as a man. Only then does it become, as we shall see later in this chapter, a properly created human being. There is *continuity* between the earth-being and the man, indicated in the fact that *'adam* and *'ish* can be used for both, but they are not *identical*. The earth-being, prior to gender differentiation, in fact "contains" both the man and the woman—they make up one body. This is their past, and this is also their future, in marriage. In Genesis 2:24, although they are now separate beings, their destiny is once again to become "one flesh."[8]

Although this is not the interpretive stance with respect to *'adam* that many readers of Genesis have taken, there is one smaller, further indication that it is correct. In Genesis 2:17 it is the single earth-creature who is given the divine instruction not to eat from the tree of the knowledge of good and evil. However, this instruction is regarded in Genesis 3:2-3 as applying as much to the woman as to the man: "*We* may eat fruit from the trees in the garden, but God did say, 'You [plural] must not eat fruit from the tree that is in the middle of the garden, and you [plural] must not touch it, or you [plural] will die.'" The woman "heard" the instruction, even while she still "inhabited" the earth-creature.

THE IMAGE OF GOD IN GENESIS 1–2

I return now to the matter of the "image" mentioned in Genesis 1:27 and also in the preceding verse 26, where the creation of human beings in God's image is explained as creation in God's "likeness." Men and women are "like God"; they bear God's image. This is how they are in Genesis 1, and this is how they remain later in the book, even after moral evil enters their experience in Genesis 3, for Genesis 9:6 tells us, "Whoever sheds the blood of man, by man shall his blood be shed; for in the image of God has God made man." Once again "man" is *'adam* here, and once again there is no intention to specify males rather than females. In spite of the havoc wrought by evil throughout Genesis 3–8, in Genesis 9 human beings are still the image bearers of God. This reality is still fundamental to understanding them and to understanding how they should be treated.

What does the language of "image" and "likeness" signify? To understand it properly we must recall a number of things we have already discussed. Biblical faith, we remember from chapters 2 and 3, disputes the real existence of the many gods of the ancient Near East and characterizes their images in the ancient temples as merely "man-made gods of wood and stone, which cannot see or hear or eat or smell" (Deuteronomy 4:28). These images are as dead as the gods they allegedly embody. This is why the Israelites were forbidden to worship the many gods, including their imaged forms, for true divinity cannot be represented in any created thing (at least, that is the general case). This is also why the Israelites were instructed, "You shall not make for yourself an idol in the form of anything in heaven above or on the earth beneath or in the waters below. You shall not bow down to them or worship them" (Exodus 20:4-5). Israelite temples built and furnished in line with this commandment were therefore *aniconic*—they did not contain artifacts that attempted to "image" even the one creator God. The Old Testament pictures God in the inner sanctum of the Jerusalem temple as being enthroned on the cherubim whose wings covered the ark of the covenant (e.g., 2 Kings 19:15), but no image sat on that "throne," and God's imageless presence in the temple was not, in the final analysis, thought capable even of being expressed by way of human analogy (e.g., 1 Kings 8:27).

Creatures cannot image even the true God in biblical thinking, generally speaking. Nevertheless—and here is the extraordinary exception—there *are* "gods" in the world. There *are* images of God placed in a temple. These images are none other than the human beings—*all* human beings—whom God has created and set in his temple-cosmos:

> Against the canopy of space and the topography of earth— beating, swarming and lumbering with fertile and fantastic life—Adam stands in unique relationship with God. . . . No stone or wood chiseled into a godling's image, "the Adam" in two . . . is an animated, walking, talking and relating mediation of the essence, will and work of the sovereign creator God. As living image of the living God, Adam bears a relationship to God like that of child to parent.[9]

Whereas most created things cannot image the living God at all, God *can* be imaged by living, moving, thinking, breathing human creatures. He *is* imaged by them. Insofar as there are any "gods" in the world, then, human beings are those "gods." They image God, despite the fact that there are innumerable ways in which human beings are said in the Old Testament *not to be* like God (chap. 3). They are not *caretakers* of a divine image in a temple, then; they are *themselves* divine images in a temple. It is in fact no part of their created purpose, as living, personal beings who image God, to serve inanimate objects that cannot do so.

How, exactly, human beings (and not other creatures) image God is a natural question that arises, and it has been much debated throughout the ages. A number of suggestions have been made: the image resides in the capacity that human beings have to reason or more broadly in the intelligence they possess; in their ability to make moral choices through free will, rather than simply being driven by instinct and environment; in the fact of human self-consciousness itself. All of these aspects of "personhood" have been regarded as indicators of the "image."[10] As interesting and important as these various inquiries into the detail of the image are, however, we should not allow them to distract us from the main, astonishing, larger point: that in a biblical tradition that so stresses the great gulf fixed between Creator and creation, there should be any talk of human beings imaging God *at all*. We can only believe that the embrace of such risky language is absolutely necessary to capture the exalted position of human beings in the cosmos. Lowly, secondary creatures we are *not*, in biblical faith; slaves of the gods we are *certainly* not. Nothing less will do than to say that we are the very image bearers of God.

HUMAN DESTINY IN GENESIS 1–2

If human beings do not exist as slave labor for the gods, why are they created? Their destiny is first intimated in Genesis 1:26 and 28:

> "Let them rule over the fish of the sea and the birds of the air, over the livestock, over all the earth, and over all the creatures that move along the ground" . . . God blessed them and said to them, "Be fruitful and increase in number; fill the earth and subdue it. Rule over the fish of the sea and the birds of the air and over every living creature that moves on the ground."

Human beings are to "rule" the created order. In the ancient Near East, such rule was exercised by the gods through their temple images; they sat in their temples enthroned over the cosmos. Their authority was further delegated to the king—the one human being in the ancient world who was considered to be "like a god." To him the gods delegated rule over the parts of the cosmos he could affect (his city-state and such other regions as he controlled). An image of the king himself could, in fact, be placed in a temple beside the image of his god, giving symbolic representation to the idea that the king was the god's right-hand man.[11]

How like a God

In Genesis 1, in contrast, it is the destiny of *human beings* to rule over the cosmos; it is not the destiny of the ancient gods. It is, moreover, the destiny of human beings *all together* to rule; it is not just the destiny of the god-king of the city-state. Insofar as there are any "gods" other than God in the temple-cosmos, claims Genesis 1, all human beings are those "gods." Since every human is made in God's image, each embodies God's presence in his temple-cosmos and represents him there.

In Psalm 8, the psalmist reflects further on this theme, as he considers the heavens that an ancient contemporary from Babylon would have regarded as the home of the great gods. For worshippers of the one creator God, the heavens remain a majestic, awesome sight, even if these worshippers do not believe that the moon and the stars are gods (v. 3). It is this awesome sight that leads the psalmist to the question with which we began: "What is a human being?" (v. 4). The implied answer to this question—the answer from Mesopotamia—is "nothing or little." The psalmist's answer, set over against the Mesopotamian answer, is quite different: "you made him a little lower than God and crowned him with glory and honor" (v. 5). In this verse, the human being occupies a highly exalted position in the cosmos as a king, and he is crowned with two attributes of God himself: "glory" and "honor."[12] He is a divine king, this human being, and he plays a crucial role in the cosmos: "You made him ruler over the works of your hands; you put everything under his feet: all flocks and herds, and the beasts of the field, the birds of the air, and the fish of the sea, all that swim the paths of the seas" (vv. 7-8). The wonder of this leads the psalmist to end as he began: "O LORD, our Lord, how majestic is your name in all the earth!" (vv. 1, 9). He recognizes the extraordinary nature of the situation, and he praises God for it, for each and every individual human person has been raised to the status of *divinity and royalty* from the status only of a *slave*. "How like a god," as Hamlet affirms, is the human person, and in so affirming he stands closer to biblical faith than Mark Twain, even though Hamlet does not allude to the Bible—and even though he has personally lost any ability to take comfort from the perspective he articulates.[13]

It is thus evident just how inadequately new atheist Christopher Hitchens grasps the reality of biblical faith when he lists it among the "three great monotheisms [that] teach people to think abjectly of themselves, as miserable and guilty sinners prostrate before an angry and jealous god."[4] Clearly Hitchens has never spent much time with either Genesis 1 or Psalm 8.

The Necessary Gardener

The centrality of human beings, rather than the gods, to the cosmic story that begins to unfold in Genesis 1 is further explored, and at greater length, in Genesis 2. In this chapter, the story of creation is revisited, only now through a different lens. Rather than viewing it as a product of six days of creating, at the end of which human beings emerge as its rulers (Genesis 1), we see it as an organism that (over an indeterminate period of time) takes shape around the human beings, who are vital for its correct functioning (Genesis 2). This change of perspective is indicated first in Genesis 2:5-6. In the ancient Near East more generally, the natural world comes into being along with the gods, who embody its various aspects; human beings are an afterthought. In Genesis 2:5-6, conversely, the natural world comes into being only *along with* human beings, without whom it cannot function:

> No shrub of the field had yet appeared on the earth and no plant of the field had yet sprung up, for the LORD God had not sent rain on the earth and there was no man to work the ground, but streams came up from the earth and watered the whole surface of the ground.

We have already noted that, in ancient Near Eastern myth, everything in the world (including the gods) ultimately evolves out of primeval waters. These waters are present in Genesis 2:6 (just as they are in Genesis 1:2), yet with important differences. They cannot of themselves produce shrubs or plants.[15] Just as the rivers Tigris and Euphrates in Mesopotamia needed human beings to "rule" and "subdue" them—to bring order to them, under the direction of the god-king of the city-state, through irrigation—so also do these primeval waters.[16] So before vegetation can appear in Genesis 2, we need a human being to work the ground. We also need the rain cycle, which God has apparently delayed creating here until after human beings have been created. In other words, creation does not function, biblically, without the human beings who are placed within it to rule over it. It is only when the crucial human figure is in place, who can make use of both rain and groundwater to cultivate the "garden"—to keep it orderly and under control—that we can have shrubs and plants.

It is worth noting at this point that the edible plants in question (Heb. *'eseb*) are said in Genesis 1 to have been created on the third day (Genesis 1:11-12) *before* the creation of humans on the sixth day.[7] Whereas this food (Genesis 1:29-30) *precedes* human beings in Genesis 1, then, in Genesis 2 it cannot be created until human beings *already exist*. Clearly it is not the *order of events* in the process of creation that interests the authors of Genesis. It is the *significance* of the different aspects of creation in relation to each other and to God. Genesis 1 describes the world as a place designed by God in which life can flourish; Genesis 2 describes it as a place whose human population is essential to its flourishing. All things wait in Genesis 2, therefore, for a human being (*'adam*) to work the ground (*'adamah*). All things wait for the necessary gardener.

How like Dust

The gardener in question, we are told further in Genesis 2, is created just as the image of an ancient god might have been created. He is formed out of "the dust of the ground," from clay (Heb. *'afar min-ha'adamah*, Genesis 2:7), and then he is animated, just as other ancient Near East worshippers believed that the images in their temples were animated by the gods. God "breathed into his nostrils the breath of life, and the man became a living being." He becomes "a living being" just like other creatures God has made, be they the sea creatures (1:20) or the land animals and the birds (2:19). In Genesis 7:22 we read of the great flood destroying *everything* that had the breath of life in its nostrils. The solidarity of this particular "god"—the human being—with the rest of creation is thus made clear. This particular "image of God" is thoroughly terrestrial—a creature through and through, sharing with other animate life the breath of life in its nostrils. This double-sided presentation of the human being in Genesis 1–2 as both "god" and "creature" is characteristic of the rest of the Old Testament as well. From one point of view, humanity (*'adam*) is simply humus (*'adamah*). Humans are just as fragile as other creatures. Like them, they know a limited period of life, and they are vulnerable to threats on every side. Metaphors of dust and grass frequently describe them (e.g., Psalm 103:13-16; 104:29; Job 4:18-19). Job 34:14-15 solemnly remarks, "If it were [God's] intention and he withdrew his spirit and breath, all mankind would perish together and man would return to the dust." Yet, at the same time, human beings are "fearfully and wonderfully made" (Psalm 139:14) and "crowned with glory and honor" (Psalm 8:5). Like the images of the gods in the ancient world, human beings are, in biblical thinking, made from dust and yet destined for glory.

MALE AND FEMALE IN GENESIS 1–2

This brings us directly to the final way in which Genesis 2 revisits the story of creation told in Genesis 1. In Genesis 1, the image placed by God in his temple-cosmos to rule over it has two aspects to it, male and female. Genesis 2 now returns to this idea, describing the right relationship that ought to exist between the two image bearers in "the garden" (Genesis 2:18-25).

Solitude Is Not Good

As this part of the story of Genesis 2 begins, we immediately discover that we are at a point in the process of creation before God is able to pronounce it all "very good" (1:31). Here in Genesis 2, something is still not good: "it is not good for the man to be alone" (2:18). "Man" at this point in the story, it should be remembered, is not yet a male, but an earth-creature. As an earth-creature he exists in solitude, and this is "not good." It is not explicitly stated *why* it is not good, but we may surmise from what is said next that the earth-creature needs "help"—"I will make a helper suitable for him." This word "helper" is used most often in the Old Testament of divine assistance provided for human beings (e.g., in Hosea 13:9). It speaks, then, of a strength in the earthling that is insufficient by itself for the tasks that have been given to it. These tasks are, in the language of Genesis 1, to subdue and to rule over creation (1:26, 28). In the language of Genesis 2, they are to work the garden and take care of it (2:15). It seems that the human vocation in the cosmos can be fulfilled only in community, not individually. A human being needs "suitable" help—help that is literally (but awkwardly) in Hebrew "like opposite him" (*kenegdo*). The help must be both similar to him (like him) and yet also different from him (opposite, over against, at a distance from him).[18]

Animals and Birds Cannot Solve the Problem

In a passage that once again reminds us of the authors' lack of interest in the chronological process of creation, God now creates "out of the ground all the beasts of the field and all the birds of the air" (Genesis 2:19-20). The animals and birds come *after* the human beings (2:7), whereas in Genesis 1:20-26 they are created *beforehand*.[19] The logic of the progression within Genesis 2:18-20 implies, of course, that God has created all these other creatures to find out whether one of them might be suitable as a helper for the human being. Surprisingly (at first), this is not what the text explicitly says. Rather, we are simply told that God "brought them to the man to see what he would name them." Why is this?

This initially puzzling feature of Genesis 2 can be explained if we once again pay attention to its ancient Near Eastern background. Throughout the ancient Near East, "naming" was part of the process by which something came into existence and was assigned a function.[20] Thus an Egyptian text, *Ritual of Amun*, tells us that, prior to creation, "no god had come into being and no name had been invented for anything."[21] The Mesopotamian text *Enuma Elish* likewise speaks of the period when "no gods were manifest, nor names pronounced, nor destinies decreed."[22] In this ancient worldview, the birth of the gods is intrinsically bound up with the assigning of their functions and roles in the cosmos; more generally, to create something is to name it and to give it a function within an ordered world. With this background in mind, we quickly come to understand that, in naming the creatures in Genesis 2, *'adam* is joining with God in *creating the world*, not least by assigning the other creatures *roles* in the world. Their names speak not so much of what they *are* as of where they *fit* in the cosmos. Language itself, as in Genesis 1 (where *God* speaks), helps to order the world and to push back chaos. Here in Genesis 2, however, it is the language uttered by the *image* of God that accomplishes this, rather than the language uttered by God himself.

What was initially puzzling now comes into focus. As this first human being names and assigns functions to the other creatures, it becomes apparent that none of the animals or birds created by God is suitable as a partner. None *fits*; none is "like opposite him" to a sufficient degree. This is the case even though every creature shares with *'adam* an origin in the ground (Heb. *'adamah*, 2:19) and is, like him, a "living creature" (Heb. *nephesh khayyah*, 2:19; cf. 2:7). These other creatures are therefore "like" *'adam* to *some* degree, but language at this point is not an entirely reliable guide to the full reality. Just as the human being is both like and unlike God, so the animals and birds are like but also unlike the human being. This is a problem. Creation is apparently complete; all the creatures have found their place. The human being, however, remains "alone."

Unity in Community

The special place of human beings in the cosmos is in this way under-scored. Only another image bearer will suffice as a partner for *'adam*. Even though every animal and bird shares with *'adam* an origin in the ground and is a "living creature," none can supply equal, perfectly fit-ting community. And so the earthling is divided and becomes male and female. The divine commitment to aesthetics in the garden, sig-naled earlier in the "trees that were pleasing to the eye" (Genesis 2:9), is evidenced again in the aftermath of the division (2:21); God closes up the gap in the earthling's body through which the material has been extracted that becomes the woman. The body is returned to an attrac-tive state, now male. Two human beings now exist where previously there was one, and they exist in the closest possible relationship. She is, as the male affirms, "bone of my bones and flesh of my flesh" (2:23). Elsewhere in the Old Testament, this combination of "bone" and "flesh" refers to someone who is a member of one's family. In Genesis 29:14 Laban can say to his nephew Jacob, "You are my own flesh and blood" (literally, "my bone and flesh"). In Genesis 2 the language has an even more intimate significance, for the male and the female are destined to become again "one flesh" in marriage (Genesis 2:24)—to "return," as it were, to their original condition as the inhabitants of one body. The intimacy of this relationship is also indicated in the similar names given to the male and the female in Genesis 2:23. One is "man" (Heb. *'ish*) and the other is "woman" (Heb. *'ishah*). The animals and the birds have found their own places in the cosmos, bound up with their own names. Now the human beings have found their place too—in the clos-est proximity to each other, physically and linguistically. Now *'adam*, for the first time in Genesis 2, is properly and fully created, having moved from a state of "not good" to good. Human beings, Genesis tells us, are *intrinsically* both male and female—that is the communal reality that is "good." Only in community can humanity fulfill the human vocation.

The exalted position that women hold in the biblical story is by this point very clear. It is precisely the same high and exalted position that is occupied by men. Both men and women are made in the very image of God, and both are placed in the garden of God jointly to rule over it. They do this together as *'adam*, "humankind." They do it separately as *'ish* and *'ishah*—"man" and "woman." These latter names themselves indicate commonality as much as separation, however, and cooperation as much as individual action.

Failures of Reading

This conclusion about the nature and status of women in Genesis 1 and 2 appears to me to be obviously correct. Many other readers of Genesis throughout the ages, however, have not come to such a conclusion. In fact, Genesis has been widely associated, both by those who have read it as Scripture and those who have not, with very different perspectives on women—with strong ideas about the secondary character, even the inferiority, of woman in comparison to man and about the rightness of the subordination of women to men. To give just one example of an interpretation of Genesis 1–2 that runs in this direction, and which is very different from my own, let us consider the following words of the fifth-century A.D. Christian bishop St. Augustine, in which he considers the image of God in men and in women (pondering Genesis 1:26-27 and 1 Corinthians 11:7):

> The woman together with her own husband is the image of God, so that that whole substance may be one image; but when she is referred separately to her quality of help-meet, which regards the woman herself alone, then she is not the image of God; but as regards the man alone, he is the image of God as fully and completely as when the woman too is joined with him in one.[23]

In this passage from *De Trinitate*, Augustine proposes that the image of God is found fully and completely in the man, by himself as a man. It is not found in the woman, considered in her distinctiveness as a woman (as the man's "helper"). It is such readings of Genesis and other biblical texts that have convinced many feminists that Genesis, and the whole Bible, is a book that stands against the interests of women.[24] This is a marked theme, also, in the literature of dark green religion.[25] How is it that Genesis has come to be read in such ways? Of the many reasons that might be mentioned, I restrict myself here to three.

First, some readers have simply failed to recognize that the *order* in which things are described in Genesis 2 does not indicate anything about the relative *importance* of the man and the woman who live in the garden, and in particular does not indicate any kind of hierarchical relationship between them. Female comes after and "out of" male, the argument has gone, and this is *significant*.[26] But *even if* we were to regard the *'adam* of the early part of Genesis 2 as a male who exists prior to a female, it would be impossible to demonstrate from the chapter itself that this "ordering" *means* anything. One might as well argue that since *'adam* (as allegedly male) is formed out of the ground in Genesis 2, *'adam* is less important than the ground that precedes him and out of which he comes; or (taking an opposite but equally plausible stance) that woman, coming last in the sequence of ground-man-woman, must be considered to be the apex of the creative process as we move from lower to higher forms of life. But I have, in any case, offered cogent reasons for *denying* that the *'adam* of the early part of Genesis 2 is a male who exists prior to a female. I have also cast doubt on the idea that the authors of Genesis are interested in strictly chronological sequence in general.

Second, some believe that the naming of the female by the male in Genesis 2:23 indicates his claim to *authority* over her.[27] However, although naming is indeed often carried out in the Old Testament by those who have authority over others (e.g., parents), it cannot be demonstrated that the act of naming in itself *involves* the assertion of authority. A strong example that points in the opposite direction is Hagar's naming of God in Genesis 16:13. In Genesis 2:23 itself, the naming *certainly* carries no connotation of a claim to authority. The reverse is in fact true. First of all, the man names not only the woman (Heb. *'ishah*) but also himself (Heb. *'ish*). Does this imply that the male is taking authority over *himself*? Then again, the names he chooses themselves indicate the *mutuality* that exists between the two persons who were just beforehand one being. The names do not imply any kind of hierarchy. Finally, this naming must be read against the background of the earlier naming of the nonhuman creatures in Genesis 2:19-20. That naming is certainly not about taking "authority" either; it is about assigning a place in the cosmos to the creatures just created by God.

In Genesis 2:23 human beings also assign *themselves*, as newly created beings in the closest possible relationship to each other, a place in the cosmos. They do so as the two aspects of the *'adam* that is to rule the whole creation (Genesis 1:26-28). This is where men and women "fit" in the cosmos—together with each other and ruling over the kingdom they have been given to govern.[28]

Third, readers who know the remainder of the Old Testament story know that women often do not occupy within it the exalted status that my reading of Genesis 1–2 implies but characteristically live under the authority of, and in subjection to, men. Narrative coherence, many of them assume, requires us to read Genesis as legitimating this later world. However, this is to ignore the obvious point that Genesis 1–2 are followed by Genesis 3. It is to confuse the Genesis 1–2 *vision* of right relationships with the descriptions of *actual* relationships that follow in the remainder of the Old Testament, once moral evil has entered into human experience.[29] It is also to ignore the obvious point that Genesis 1 precedes Genesis 2. No reading of Genesis 2 about the creation of male and female can be accepted as correct, I suggest, that does not take seriously the claim of Genesis 1 that *'adam*, male and female, is created in the image of God and given *joint* dominion over creation. *That* is *also* a matter of narrative coherence.

The Nature of Human Society

To retrace our steps through this chapter thus far: the world in Genesis 1–2 (and indeed in Psalm 8) is not created for the gods but for creatures. Human beings are some of those creatures. They are "living beings" like many of the others—possessing the breath of life in their nostrils, even though they are made of clay, frail and vulnerable, mere dust and grass. What marks out human beings *from* these other creatures to whom they are so similar, however, is that each and every one of them, male and female, is made in the image of God. If there are gods in the cosmos apart from God, human beings are those gods—living, moving, thinking, breathing reflections of God's own personhood, created to share with God and the other creatures the sacred space of God's temple-cosmos and to rule over it and look after it on God's behalf. It is no part of the destiny of these images of God to be the slaves of the gods, including the human god-kings of the city-state. All are to rule the earth, not just one. It is not the intention of the authors of Genesis, either—having knocked god-kings off their high pedestals and insisted on the rule of all—to substitute for that kind of hierarchy a different one involving god-men and slave-women. If there are gods in the cosmos apart from God, they are women as well as men. The divine image that is to rule in the temple-cosmos is male *and* female.

At the beginning of this chapter I claimed that anthropology and politics are inevitably bound up with each other—that a particular understanding of the nature and destiny of human beings is always deeply connected to a particular vision of the good society. If it is now clear what the authors of Genesis 1–2 thought about humanness, can we say anything concerning their thinking about politics?

The way Genesis 2 ends does give us a hint in this direction—it shows us, indeed, that its authors did think that their vision of humanness *should shape* society in particular ways. We saw earlier that Genesis 2:24 envisages marriage as involving, metaphorically, a renewed sharing by the human pair of one body ("one flesh"). It also involves, however, a man leaving or forsaking his parents and setting up a home with his new wife—a "forsaking" that is no doubt *also* intended metaphorically. So far as we can tell, Israelite men (in common with those of other ancient Near Eastern societies) typically continued to live in or near the parental home after their marriages. They did not leave. Precisely because this is so, however, Genesis 2 makes clear that a man must *indeed* "leave" his parents in a very real sense and make his new wife his priority. He must "be united to" (or better, "cleave" or "stick" to) his wife. In Genesis 2, the honoring of the wife to whom the man is now united, in consistency with God's creation plan, is a higher duty than the honoring of one's parents. The woman is not created to be the lackey of her husband's extended family any more than she is created to be the servant of her husband. She is not a slave of the gods, and she is *certainly* not a slave of her husband or his family. She is a person made in the image of God, and, when arrangements are made for the ordering of society, her personhood must be respected. In this way, at least, it is already clear in Genesis 2 that a biblical vision of humanness *is* considered to have direct implications for politics.

Beyond this one *explicit indication* in Genesis 1–2 as to what the good society looks like when it is founded on a biblical understanding of the nature and destiny of human beings, two of the overall *emphases* of these chapters are also profoundly important for how the remainder of the biblical tradition works out the question of politics.

The first is the *humanistic* emphasis. The gods have been eliminated from the cosmos, and human beings have taken their place at its center. They live in a world designed for its creatures. It is not *only* the human creatures that God cares about; indeed, they have been placed in the world precisely to look after nonhuman creation. Still, the well-being of God's human creatures does lie at the center of his concern, and it is not just their well-being *in general* that he is concerned about. Each and every human life *in particular*, bearing as it does God's image, is deeply significant and is indeed inviolable.

What does this mean? It means, for example, that the good society is not to be ordered around an institution like human sacrifice, which is regarded as a heinous crime in the Old Testament. Human life is not to be wasted on such rituals, for human beings do not exist for the gods.[30] It also means that other *human beings* cannot take human life without just cause. To do so is also regarded as a terrible crime, and in Genesis 9:6 it requires a dreadful response: "whoever sheds the blood of man, by man shall his blood be shed; for in the image of God has God made man." Even a king cannot treat human life lightly.[31] It means, further, that even the weakest and most marginalized members of society must be looked after, and not simply abandoned to their fates.[32] It means that even enemies should be given hospitality and that even slaves have rights.[33] And it means much more than all of this, but these examples will suffice for the moment.

The second emphasis I have in mind is the (associated) *democratic* emphasis. This is already implied in the very fact that a king could *not* simply take a human life without proper cause and that slaves *did* have rights. *All* human beings are image bearers; *all* human beings share in the governance and care of the earth. All, and not just some, are to be treated as "gods"—women as well as men (and by implication, children as well as adults). This suggests that however the good society is to be organized, the ethos will be egalitarian. Indeed, whereas kingship elsewhere in the ancient Near East was intrinsic to the good society, having its origin in the realm of the gods, Israelite society lacks a king for a long time in the biblical story. When a king is eventually requested, it is regarded as a terrible sin on the part of the Israelites, and dire warnings are issued by the prophet Samuel about how the king will transform Israelite society for the worse (1 Samuel 8). The biblical *rules* about kingship themselves go out of their way to emphasize that the only good kind of king will be the one who takes on this leadership role as merely one among "brothers" (Deuteronomy 17:14-20).

We shall return to the themes of humanism and democracy when we come to our broader discussion of politics in chapter 10.

MAN AND WOMAN IN OTHER TRADITIONS

The understanding of man and woman that emerges from my reading of Genesis 1 and 2 represents a departure not only from the general view of human nature and destiny that we find expressed among the peoples of the ancient Near East, but also from the views that come to expression in many different cultures throughout the ages, whether in their literature or (sometimes more implicitly) in their societal practice.

In the West

We may begin to illustrate the point by referencing ancient Greece—in so many ways significantly influenced by the Near East, to which it looked from earliest times for inspiration in such matters as art, literature, and religion.[34] It is unsurprising, then, that in the important city-state of Athens we should find a society that, although in some key ways entirely different from its ancient Near Eastern counterparts, was in some ways quite similar to them. Athens has often been referred to as "the cradle of Western democracy,"[35] yet it was not especially democratic. Athenian society was, in fact, resolutely hierarchical. The only people fully involved in the political life of the city were the adult male citizens who had completed their military training. The majority of the population was excluded—among them women and also the huge number of slaves that was essential to the city-state's prosperity.

This was *not* the result of a failure to implement a societal vision of a more egalitarian kind. Instead, Athenian politics resulted from a particular anthropology—a particular understanding of the nature of human beings. The general Athenian (and Greek) sentiment was that slavery was a good and necessary institution, not least because it took serious account of the *nature* of slaves. As Aristotle puts it: "Slaves and brute animals . . . cannot [form a state], for they have no share in happiness or in a life of free choice."[36] With respect to women, the poet Hesiod (eighth century B.C.) had already expressed the view that they had been visited on men as a punishment because Prometheus, the champion of humanity, had stolen fire from the gods. Zeus "made women

mischievous in their ways and a curse for men."[37] By the time we arrive
at the period of Athenian ascendancy in the fifth century, belief in Hesiod's gods had been eroded by the assaults upon them by philosophers
and others, but the same negativity toward women remained. Beliefs
about the nature and role of women did not alter with the gradual dis-
placement of the gods, and this was not accidental. With the notable
exception of Plato, Athenian philosophers believed that women possessed strong emotions and weak minds. This was their *nature*. Their
position in Athenian society—excluded from political and economic
life and kept largely at home where they could do no damage to themselves or others—reflected this belief. For Aristotle, the relationship
of male and female was as follows: "the male is *by nature* superior, and
the female inferior; and the one rules, and the other is ruled."[38] The
ruling is, of course, for her own good. Again, "the male is *by nature* fit-
ter for command than the female" and "the inequality is permanent."[39]
Anthropology is bound up with politics, and convictions about the first
lead on directly to convictions about the second and thus to the actual
societal position of women in Athens, famously summed up in these
words: "we have courtesans for pleasure, concubines for the daily care
of our body, and wives in order to have legitimate children and a reliable custodian of our household."[40]

If we pass from the real Athens and the ideology that shaped (and
was shaped by) its society and we consider instead the ideal world of
Plato's *Republic*, what do we find? Interestingly, Plato assigns to women
in this ideal society a role nearly equal to that of men, because he questions the extent to which female nature is different from male nature.
For the good of society, he affirms, women should follow the same pur-
suits as men. This represents an egalitarianism of a kind. I say "of a
kind," because the position of most human beings in Plato's ideal society (male *and* female) remains subordinate with respect to the few who
run it. In the *Republic*, Plato grants political power only to an elite class
of "Guardians," chosen by a "Legislator." The republic is essentially a
totalitarian state. Beneath the Guardians (among whom may be num-
bered women) are the military, and beneath them the common people.[41] There may or may not also be slaves.[42] Women are nearly equal to
men, but most human beings are in no meaningful sense involved in
the governance of their world. All political decisions are made by the
Guardians—without reference to, and unaccountable to, the population at large. It is the Guardians who are intellectually in tune with the

Good; the majority has no direct access to it and need to be led toward it by others. It is the Guardians, then, who determine right belief and practice across the whole breadth of societal life and are responsible for maintaining the system of education that promotes the Good. The majority is allowed no independent judgment in such matters and certainly no independence of action.[43]

In all of this, there is little recognition of the equal status, dignity, and rights of each human person, and—despite the fact that Athens *is* often spoken of as the cradle of Western democracy—little serious commitment to the idea that responsibility for governance in the world lies with all human beings, not just with a few. The gods (and the god-kings) of the ancient Near Eastern city-states may have been displaced in Athens, but their places were filled by elites who behaved like gods without taking the name and who looked down from their exalted heights on the remainder of their fellow men and women. The male warrior-ideal dominated, and there was a correspondingly low view of family, including wives (not to mention courtesans and concubines). It was a society that built its economy on slave labor, with slaves being regarded as living tools whom the master could treat as he wished, much like animals. As Aristotle puts it, "The use made of slaves and of tame animals is not very different, for both with their bodies minister to the needs of life."[44] These slaves included among their number the preadolescent children who worked in the silver mines of Laurium. This was a society that did not aspire to the anthropological ideals of Genesis 1–2, and certainly did not reflect them. The governing anthropology of the Athenians *is* reflected in one of their central cultural activities: participation in the *symposion* or male drinking club, which often involved drunkenness, erotic entertainment provided by slave boys and girls, serial sexual encounters with friends and slaves, and often (at the conclusion) violent rampages through the streets.[45]

Western societies since those ancient times, taking their lead from Greece and then Rome (with something of a nod, at times, to the Old Testament), have not necessarily reflected biblical ideals any more clearly. It is sobering to consider, in this regard, the case of John Locke (1632–1704). Locke had a significant influence on the development of modern Western political theory, and therefore of modern Western states, and like Aristotle he was interested in how nature grounds one's position and participation in society. In his *Treatises on Government* Locke simply assumed the exclusion of women and the poor from the rights of citizenship—those who in the seventeenth century possessed no property. He also held that human beings captured in a just war were slaves by the law of nature. While opposing slavery in general elsewhere in his writings, he was both a major investor in the slave trade and a participant in the drafting of the Fundamental Constitutions of Carolina, which gave to slave owners in that part of the American colonies absolute power over their slaves. This is essentially an Athenian vision of the world, albeit tempered with a biblical perspective that holds that all human beings are at least *born* free and equal. In theory, Locke held that all human beings have the same liberties and rights by nature—just because they are human beings. In practice, the liberties and rights he defended were, in the end, only those of a few.[46]

In Islam

A similar tension is found in Islam. Hitherto in this book, I have tended to emphasize important commonalities among the so-called Abrahamic religions—striking similarities with respect to how they view God, the world, and God's relationship with the world. When we come to anthropology, there remain *some* similarities between biblical faith and Islam. The Qur'an does regard the human person in ways that are, in certain respects, similar to Genesis 1–2. In the Qur'an, as in Genesis, human beings are created out of the dust and animated by the breath of God, and they enjoy a close relationship with the rest of creation. Indeed, they are given dominion over the rest of creation by God—a reality underscored by the keyword *khalifa* (caliph). Human beings, in the Qur'an, are "caliphs of God" on the earth.

Yet, despite these similarities, Islam does diverge from the perspective of biblical faith in important ways with respect to the nature of human beings in general and the nature of woman in particular. Foremost in this regard is the fact that the Qur'an avoids any idea that human beings are made in the *image* of God. Islam's strong view of God's oneness and transcendence forbids any idea of humanity being "like" God in a way similar to the Old Testament conception. Like the Old Testament, the Qur'an places a great gulf between God and creation, but unlike the Old Testament the Qur'an makes no exceptions to this general rule. Human beings therefore do not possess the same exalted status in the Qur'an that they do in the Old Testament, as beings that, in a sense, are suspended *between* heaven and earth—"a little lower than God" (Psalm 8:5). In Islam, they stand resolutely on *this* side of the gulf, even though they *are* said to possess a few divine qualities: intelligence, free will, and the power of speech. There is no great emphasis in the Qur'an, either, on the human role in "tending" creation—in being the "gardener" of Genesis 2 and thus mediating God's blessing to creation. The predominant emphasis is not caring for but learning *from* creation. There is a sense in which all of nature is Muslim: "There is a natural, cosmic 'islam,'" claims Theodore Ludwig, in which all creatures "worship and serve God by conforming to the law of their being."[47] Human beings can learn from nature, and from all the signs within it that point to God, how to serve God well.[48]

The Qur'an also agrees with Genesis 1–2 that all human beings are equal under God. This is reflected in the absence within Islam (at least in principle) of any organized religious body that might govern the belief and practice of Muslims. Each person is expected to follow the path that her intelligence identifies as the right path. Islam is, in this respect, a radically individualistic religion; no "city, state, or any other institution [stands] between the individual and God."[49] Further, there are many verses in the Qur'an that make it clear that men and women, specifically, are equal before God:

> The text does not discriminate or show prejudice based on one's gender, but considers equality among all people to be something instilled in creation by God. The only distinction the Qur'an makes among people is based on belief, not biology.[50]

At the same time, however, "the text" contains various texts that call this equality into question. One of these is found in Sura 4, which is devoted to women. This sura has been understood historically to say in line 34 that "men are the managers of the affairs of women for that God has preferred in bounty one of them over another" and to allow a husband physically to abuse his wife if she is "rebellious."[51] It is a matter of debate within contemporary Islam how verses like this are to be understood in relation to the "equality" texts. Some argue that they are not part of "the eternal essence of the Qur'an that transcends time and space";[52] that "modern readers of the Qur'an should not consult 4:34 for guidance on marital relations," because "modern notions of what marriage is and how spouses should relate to one another differ significantly from seventh-century Arabia, where women were subjugated to men and physical abuse was permitted."[53] It is a question, however, whether the Qur'an itself, as the very speech of God that is unalterable and fixed for eternity, allows for this kind of move to be made.[54] There is certainly nothing in the Qur'an itself that provides readers with explicit help in distinguishing what is part of the eternal essence and what is not, and many Muslims would reject such a distinction out of hand. The Qur'an is not, after all, like the Bible, which has a narrative structure that helps its readers in precisely this manner, since there is a clear distinction within the biblical story between creation ideals, on the one hand, and the realities of a world gone wrong, on the other. We shall explore this matter further in upcoming chapters.

In the East

The understanding of man and woman that emerges from my reading of Genesis 1 and 2 represents a departure from much of the theory and practice not just of the Western and Islamic worlds but of the East as well. For Hindus, as we have seen, the world itself is an obstacle to the attainment of the greater good for which human beings should be striving. It is certainly not a sacred place created by a personal God. Speaking more specifically of Hindu anthropology, men and women are *not* persons made in God's image, destined to live in communion with God and to rule and look after the world in equality with each other. Indeed, one of the distinguishing marks of Hindu society historically, and one that is deeply rooted in Hinduism's ancient scriptures, is the caste system, which divides people into four or five classes and hundreds of castes. One enters both class and caste at birth. The highest class comprises the scholarly and priestly Brahmans, followed by the Kshatriyas (warriors and administrators), the Vaishyas (merchants, farmers, and artisans), and the Shudras (laborers), whose task it is to serve the other three. Beneath the Shudra are the untouchables or outcasts, the Dalits.[55] As in the case of ancient Greece, this Hindu social structure does not result from a failure to implement a societal vision of a more egalitarian kind but from core beliefs about the nature of reality. It arises out of convictions about the eternal order of things (dharma) that human beings *should* follow as they move (hopefully) toward liberation from the world of samsara.

In this world, cycles of life, death, and rebirth are caused by karma— the law that every action has its effect, so that actions performed out of desire have evil repercussions in the next lifetime. One is born into a particular class and caste precisely because of one's past karma. This is simply the way that the cosmos has always worked. It is the eternal order of things. Downward, backward movement in a future life is avoided by performing the duties currently assigned within one's present class and caste—*not* by seeking to rule and take care of the world on equal terms with others. As the *Bhagavad Gita* states, "Better to do one's own duty [dharma] imperfectly than to do another man's well; doing action [karma] intrinsic to his being, a man avoids guilt" (18.47).[56] One's focus should be on performing one's own dharma—whether as a warrior, a producer, a slave, or a woman. Hindu cosmology, therefore, is deeply connected to Hindu anthropology, and both are very different from the Genesis view. As in the ancient Near East and in ancient Greece, there can *in principle* be no recognition of the equal status, dignity, and rights of each human person. Quite the reverse is the case: "from the traditional Hindu perspective, the idea of human equality is patently false."[57]

This general difference in perspective between Hindu and biblical theology extends, in particular, to the place of women vis-à-vis men. Women have generally played a role subordinate to men in Hindu society. This is not surprising, since the Hindu scriptures, in presenting the ideal human life as comprising the four stages of student, householder, forest-dweller, and renouncer, have in mind directly only *men* of the *top three classes*.[58] The Shudra and Dalit classes cannot access this ideal life, and women do so only indirectly because they are related to the males of their families. "A woman does not deserve independence," states the *Law-Code of Manu*, traditionally considered to derive from Manu, the originator of human beings, and to provide guidance on dharma.[59] Women are

> ill-equipped for spiritual and intellectual development, which required great discipline of the mind and body. Because females were seen as pursuing pleasure rather than the disciplined spiritual life, it was essential for them to remain under the guard of the most important men in their lives.[60]

So it is that Hindu *boys* in the student stage have, traditionally, left home to be educated in the Vedic scriptures while girls have stayed at home to learn to be wives, mothers, and homemakers. So it is that during the householder stage a Hindu *girl* has, traditionally, been transferred from the domain of a father to that of a husband, often at a very young age. Her role in this new domain has been to be subject to her husband and to serve him—not eating, for example, until her husband has finished eating.[61] In the final stage of life, the "renouncer" (always a man) is meant to break all ties with normal life and to wander around by himself. Being entirely alone, as a man, is necessary to achieve spiritual perfection.[62]

In the eternal order of things (dharma), the woman's role is as supporter of the man. According to the *Law-Code of Manu*, the woman who serves her husband engages in work similar to that of Vedic study, while household work is equivalent to making the fire sacrifices (important rituals prescribed in the Vedas). These are the ways in which she fulfills her destiny.[63] The secondary status of women in relation to men is illustrated in a particularly powerful way by two long-standing customs in India. The first is *sati*—a practice whereby young widows, taking the idea of self-sacrifice for one's husband to its final conclusion, throw themselves onto their husband's funeral pyre. This practice is now rare in India, although for a long time attempts to ban it proved only partially successful. The second practice remains common—abortion or infanticide with respect to female children.[64]

It is worth noting in connection with Indian religion that although Siddhartha Gautama, the founder of Buddhism, significantly departed in some ways from a Vedic perspective on the world, he remained ambivalent on the question of the value and status of women in relation to men. He *did* reject the authority of the Vedic scriptures—setting over against the dharma of Vedic ritualism his own *dharma* (or saddharma, the true dharma)—and he *did* take a stand against divisions of caste, class, and gender among those walking on his path to liberation.[65] Nevertheless, he only reluctantly admitted women into monastic life, and he was gloomy about the consequences of their acceptance for the movement he had begun. His order of nuns was strictly subordinate to his order of monks, "so that even the most senior nun [was] inferior to the most junior monk."[66] It is unsurprising, then, that there arose in Buddhist societies, first, the widespread belief that women needed first to be reborn as men in order to achieve Buddhahood, and, second, the widespread decline of nuns' orders. *Human* destiny, on such a view of the world, is really only *male* destiny.[67]

This is also true to some extent in Jainism. Like Buddhism, Jainism "arose partly in reaction to the caste system of Hinduism."[68] Yet contemporary Jains inhabit the caste system, and they accept it as a way of organizing society. Their monastic orders are open to both men and women, but women in the Digambara sect are considered to be "incapable of practicing non-attachment to the degree of which a man is capable," since they wear clothing. In order to attain liberation from the wheel of existence, "a woman must await rebirth as a man."[69]

In sum: whether in the East or in the West, the biblical understanding of man and woman that emerges from my reading of Genesis 1–2 represents a significant departure from the understandings evident in the literature of many different cultures throughout the ages, and (sometimes more implicitly) in their societal practices. How any people-group views human nature is, as we have seen, inevitably bound up with how it views politics—with the accepted ideas as to what constitutes the good society and with the practices that are grounded in these ideas. The dominant understandings of anthropology and politics in many societies throughout the ages have not been good news for many members of these societies, including most women. The biblical story begins to move in a different direction from its very first pages, with its radical notion that all human beings are created in God's image. If this is so, it *is* good news for *both* men and women.

5

IT ISN'T NATURAL

Why Do Evil and Suffering Mark the World?

If there is a God, why is there evil?
And if there is no God, how can there be good?

Boethius[1]

How can I believe in God when just last week I got my tongue
caught in the roller of an electric typewriter?

Woody Allen[2]

The story so far: the authors of the book of Genesis believed that order,
goodness, and beauty exist in the world because it is the creation of
a personal God—a God who has created a sacred space in which life,
including human life, can flourish (chap. 2). God's purpose (as a thoroughly good person) in creating this world was to bless his creatures,
to show them love and faithfulness, to rescue them as necessary from
danger and distress, and to forgive and restore them as necessary when
they falter (chap. 3). The human creatures who stand at the center of
God's purposes are, each one, created by God in his image, equal in
standing *before* him and with a full part to play in the governance of
the cosmos in communion *with* him (chap. 4). The fundamentals of this

story are all expressed in Genesis 1–2, although in developing each one we have explored more broadly the remainder of the Old Testament.

The story so far has been upbeat. It is important now to emphasize, therefore, that our biblical authors were not naïve about the world in which they lived. They understood that life does not always, *in fact*, flourish in this world; the very fact that God must rescue human beings from danger and distress already implies this. Creation *suffers* in various ways, and so do human beings. This is an obvious aspect of existence, and all serious philosophies and religions have tried to account for it. For those who stand in continuity with the biblical tradition, it is a particularly challenging aspect of existence, precisely because they believe that there exists one God who is good. This is why so much has been written within the Jewish and Christian traditions, in different genres, on the "problem" of suffering—a "problem" precisely because suffering seems to call into *question* the existence of one good God. Woody Allen expresses the dilemma in a humorous (but still serious) way, in his account (in the second epigraph to this chapter) of his unfortunate experience with his typewriter.

Our biblical authors do not ignore the reality of suffering. How, then, do they account for it? To begin, we must turn in the first instance not to Genesis 1–2 but to Genesis 3. Here, as we shall see, the "accounting" is offered in terms of the embrace of evil by God's human (and other) creatures. It is the embrace of evil, our biblical authors claim, that explains much of the suffering that arises in the world.

SUFFERING . . . AND SUFFERING

I deliberately say "much" of the suffering, and not "all" of it, for it seems fairly clear that the book of Genesis is not interested in providing a *global, all-encompassing* explanation of suffering. As we shall see, it does not care to account for the suffering *as such* that is inevitably involved in bringing children into God's good world; it seeks to account only for the *increase* in suffering that evil produces (Genesis 3:16). Likewise, Genesis is not interested in accounting for the suffering *inevitably* involved in an occupation like farming, but only in understanding the *increased* suffering that results from the entrance of evil into the cosmos (3:17-19). Suffering as such—if we mean by this the hard work of bringing children into the world and raising them, or of planting and harvesting crops—is apparently not conceived of in Genesis 3 as incompatible with life in God's good creation. It does not need to be accounted for. It is intrinsic to living in the place where God has put us to live.

So also, it appears, is death. We did not pause to note this earlier, but it is interesting that when God first mentions death in Genesis 2:17, the earthling does not ask, "What do you mean, die?" He understands what is meant; he can apparently already make sense of it. As Genesis 3:19 tells us, indeed, it is his natural fate to die unless he eats from the tree of life ("For dust you are and to dust you will return"), and nothing in the first three chapters of Genesis implies that he has already eaten from this tree:

> The original human being shows no interest in the tree of life; indeed . . . he never eats of it prior to his expulsion from the garden, presumably because concern with death does not penetrate the consciousness of his simple soul.[3]

In sum: what needs to be accounted for in the book of Genesis is not suffering *as such*, for this does not challenge belief in a good world created by a good God. What needs to be accounted for, instead, is the suffering that arises from evil.

Two Kinds of Suffering

There is already here, then, an implicit distinction between two kinds of suffering. For the sake of clarity in what follows, I propose that we refer to these as "intrinsic suffering" (the suffering that is intrinsic to life in creation) and "extrinsic suffering" (the suffering that arises from embracing evil). Perhaps these are not the best terms to use, but I cannot think of a better way of encapsulating, briefly, what I want to say. In choosing this terminology I am deliberately trying to avoid a very unhelpful way of speaking about the two realities in question. Historically, among those who have wrestled with the problem of evil within a broadly Judeo-Christian context, it has been common to refer to *both* kinds of suffering as arising from "evil"—"natural evil," on the one hand, and "moral evil," on the other. Phenomena like earthquakes have been included under the first heading, and phenomena like torture under the second. Already in the adoption of this language, however, it is simply *assumed* that *all* suffering involves evil that needs to be accounted for. It is assumed that earthquakes, for example (and not just torture), represent a "problem" for those who assert that the world is the creation of a good God. This way of thinking can sometimes be taken quite far—so far that the precise relationship between the world as it was once created by God and the world as we know it now becomes uncertain. Consider the following quotation from the Renaissance Christian thinker John Calvin:

> For it appears that all the evils of the present life, which experience proves to be innumerable, have proceeded from the same fountain [i.e., the original embrace of evil by human beings]. The inclemency of the air, frost, thunders, unseasonable rains, drought, hail, and whatever is disorderly in the world, are the fruits of sin. Nor is there any other primary cause of diseases.[4]

It almost appears that whatever Calvin does not much care for in the world is attributed here to evil. This impression is by no means dispelled when he goes on to tell us that things like "the existence of fleas, caterpillars, and other noxious insects" derive from this same source. In this way of thinking, no space is permitted for suffering that is simply the inevitable outcome of the fact that the good God has made *this* world in *this* particular way, and not *another* world in some *other* way. All phenomena that human beings might *name* as "evil" are apparently to be considered *truly* evil. It is this way of thinking that Woody Allen is parodying when he reports his encounter with the typewriter. "Natural evil," on this view, is just as much of a "problem" for biblical monotheism as the problem of unrestrained human violence inflicted on fellow human beings, or indeed on other creatures.

Suffering Intrinsic to Creation

I propose that this is precisely what the book of Genesis does *not* lead us to assume, nor does the remainder of the Old Testament. I say again: what needs to be accounted for in Genesis is not suffering as such—suffering that arises simply from our physical, embodied existence in a physical, material world. We might not necessarily enjoy it, and we may even look for respite from it in the future. We might well consider it problematic—*for us*. But it does not necessarily raise any questions for our biblical authors about *God*.

The pain involved in bringing children into the world and looking after them, for example, is not a problem in this sense; indeed, such a "problem" is eclipsed in various biblical texts by great joy (e.g., Psalm 113:9). Suffering is a temporary, passing necessity on the way to something else: the enjoyment of children. Similarly, the pain involved in the labor of producing crops is only a necessary precursor to the enjoyment of food and of life generally (as in Psalm 128:2-3). It is indeed possible (and fitting) to find joy in the work itself even as one is engaging in it (Ecclesiastes 5:18). Then again, earthquakes are simply an aspect of the created order, just as wind and lightning are (1 Kings 19:11-12). Wind and lightning, too, can be destructive, but they are nevertheless aspects of the good creation that, in Psalm 148, is called to praise God. They are creatures in God's good world. Earthquakes *may* be associated, biblically, with God's judgment on moral evil (as may wind and lightning), but they *need* not be.

In biblical thinking, then, suffering that is intrinsic to life in creation does not require an accounting. The *problem* lies with the extrinsic suffering that arises out of evil—and indeed, with the presence of evil in the cosmos in the first place, which creates the very possibility that it might insinuate its way into the life of the world.

EVIL ENTERS THE WORLD

Genesis 3 opens by facing this reality directly: evil has, indeed, entered the world. It introduces us immediately and surprisingly to a creature of God who is apparently not under God's sovereign control nor under human dominion but who has apparently already "gone bad."

A Creature Gone Bad

This shadowy figure *is* a creature; he is one of "the wild animals the LORD God had made" (Genesis 3:1). But disturbingly he is also a "serpent"—a figure that was associated throughout the ancient Near East with the primeval chaos that Genesis 1 also tells us preceded the ordered creation (vv. 1-2). When Job alludes to the act of creation, he references the same figure: "his [God's] hand pierced the gliding serpent" (Job 26:13). In Egypt, Apophis (the enemy of the gods and the demon of chaos) was pictured as a snake, which represented the underworld through which the sun god Re had to travel in his combat with the forces of darkness.[5] On the Egyptian pharaoh's crown, one could find the snake image ("Uraeus") of Wadjet, who was the patron goddess of Lower Egypt. Throughout the ancient world, in fact, the serpent "was endowed with divine or semi-divine qualities . . . venerated as an emblem of health, fertility, immortality, occult wisdom, and chaotic evil."[6]

The authors of Genesis, then, are clearly alluding to an image that has deep roots in their cultural setting in the ancient Near East. The Genesis serpent is clearly not a *god*—that is explicit. Nevertheless, he does seem to represent dark, personal, but nonhuman forces that Genesis 1–2 has not led us to expect can exist in cosmos that is "good." In such a world, according to Genesis 1:3-9, even the primeval watery chaos has been put to useful, constructive work. We must immediately assume, then (although we do not yet have any explicit indication of this), that in the world that God has made it is possible for creatures to depart from the good and turn toward evil. There is free will in the cosmos, and, as Genesis 3 opens, at least one personal, nonhuman creature has exercised it—badly. This important truth will be explicitly confirmed later in Genesis 3, when the *first human beings* exercise their *own* free will. For the authors of Genesis, then, the existence of evil in the cosmos is to be attributed to the misuse of something that is *intrinsic* to the cosmos: the moral freedom of some of its creatures. This freedom is first misused by a creature that was presumably named by the earthling in Genesis 2 but whom the earthling was wise enough to see could not be his "helper." The question that now arises, as the serpent addresses the one whom the earthling *did* ultimately receive as helper, is whether human beings will *continue* to be so insightful.[7]

A Wise Villain

The serpent possesses his *own* wisdom; he is, we are told, "crafty" (3:1). The Hebrew here is *'arum*—a word that can also mean "prudent." Consider Proverbs 12:16, for example: "a prudent man (*'arum*) overlooks an insult"; or Proverbs 13:16, "every prudent man (*'arum*) acts out of knowledge." The word itself, then, indicates the potential for evil in what is good. *Prudence* is a virtue, but it is not virtuous to be *crafty*, as Job 15:5 makes clear: "your sin prompts your mouth; you adopt the tongue of the crafty (*'arum*)." It is a double-edged word. What *may* be a virtue may also become a vice—as in the case of the serpent. The question is, will the newly created human beings be able to discriminate between the two—between virtue and vice? The challenge is underlined by an interesting play on words in these opening verses of Genesis 3, when considered alongside the closing verses of Genesis 2. Through this device the authors explicitly link the serpent's craftiness to human nakedness: "the man and his wife were both naked (*'arummim*), and they felt no shame" (Genesis 2:25). Here human beings share an innocence that will shortly be shattered by the serpent's craftiness (*'arum*). When it is shattered, they will realize that they are naked (the closely similar *'eyrummim* [3:7] and *'eyrom* [3:10-11]), and they will seek to be clothed. Nakedness is lost by craftiness, which results in the *recognition* of nakedness.

The craftiness of the serpent is revealed in the question that he asks the woman: "Did God really say, 'You must not eat from any tree in the garden'?" (Genesis 3:1). At first glance this might appear to be a *friendly* question. The serpent is just trying to "help" the woman get things straight, perhaps so that she can then "help" the man. The allusion is back to Genesis 2:8-17, where we read that "all kinds of trees . . . pleasing to the eye and good for food" were to be found in the garden in Eden. Among these were "the tree of life and the tree of the knowledge of good and evil." The first human beings in Genesis 2 are "free to eat from any tree in the garden," except that they "must not eat from the tree of the knowledge of good and evil." When they eat of *that* tree, they will surely die. As we reread Genesis 2 in this way, we immediately understand *what* is "crafty" about the serpent's question in Genesis 3. God did *not* in fact say in Genesis 2, "You *must not eat* from any tree in the garden" (3:1). What God did say was almost exactly the opposite: "You *are free to eat* from any tree in the garden" (except the tree of the knowledge of good and evil, 2:16). The vocabulary of God in Genesis 2 indicates freedom and blessing. The vocabulary of the serpent in Genesis 3 indicates prohibition and restriction. The serpent's ploy is to suggest to the woman that God is really not so good after all. He shifts attention away from all that God in his generosity has provided for his creatures in creation and onto the one thing that God has for the moment explicitly withheld.[8]

A Fateful Conversation

An appropriate answer to the serpent's question would have been, "you are misquoting, and in the process misrepresenting, God; here's how things *really* are." The answer that actually appears in Genesis 3:2-3, however, is not so robust, and it already indicates that the woman is moving in the serpent's direction:

We may eat fruit from the trees in the garden, but God did say,
"You must not eat fruit from the tree that is in the middle of the
garden, and you must not touch it, or you will die."[9]

These words fail to represent God's generosity fully—she says only that
they "may eat fruit from the trees," not that they are "*free* to eat from
any tree." She then adds a prohibition—not present in Genesis 2:17—
with respect to the one forbidden tree: "you must not eat fruit from the
tree that is in the middle of the garden, *and you must not touch it*, or
you will die." The invitation of the serpent is to view God cynically and
untrustingly—to adopt an ungenerous and suspicious attitude toward
God. The woman, we see, is already moving in this very direction.[10]

The final step comes with the serpent's next response (Genesis
3:4-5): "you will not surely die." We are now beyond subtlety. This is
a direct contradiction to God's words in 2:17: "you will surely die." An
alternative vision is then presented: "your eyes will be opened, and you
will be like God, knowing good and evil." The woman buys into this
serpentine vision. She sets the forbidden tree on the same level as all
the other trees ("good for food and pleasing to the eye"; 2:9 and 3:6),
eats some of its good food, and gives some also to her husband. The
husband, of course, is not to be regarded as having left town on this
fateful day. He is "with her" (3:6), and, as the sequel shows, he is just as
much to blame for the misjudgment. He is present, but he says nothing
during the entire conversation. He just goes along with it all.

THE KNOWLEDGE OF GOOD AND EVIL

What kind of "knowledge" has now been acquired by human beings,
against God's will? We are not told, and it is in fact probably the wrong
question to ask. Certainly previous attempts to identify a particular
kind of knowledge in the passage have failed to convince.

Wise and Unwise Readings

For example, one tradition holds that it is *sexual* knowledge that has
been acquired in this transaction.[11] However, sexual knowledge is
already an aspect of the good creation (Genesis 1:28; 2:18-25). Nor is
it at all likely that the forbidden knowledge is *cultural*—the kind of
knowledge that enables civilization to emerge. This is, for example, the
assumption that lies behind Karen Armstrong's reading of the early

chapters of Genesis. She asserts that they present the rise of civilization that results from the forbidden knowledge as a disaster.[12] However, the rise and progress of human culture and civilization are already envisaged in the Genesis 1–2 description of the human vocation as ruling over creation and cultivating the garden. A third suggestion is that the new knowledge is *moral* in nature—the ability to make moral discriminations.[13] But moral knowledge, too, is already implicit in the very fact that God gives a command not to eat from the tree, and later holds the humans accountable for disobeying him. They "ought" to have known better—therefore they are considered to possess, already, moral sense. It is intrinsic to their creatureliness. All these kinds of knowledge are regarded, biblically, as good in themselves, and they are aspects of divine image bearing in the world. It is impossible to think of them, in the context of the Genesis story, as forbidden—and then acquired only as a result of human disobedience to God.

Genesis 3 itself does not encourage us to think of a *particular branch* of knowledge when it introduces the "knowledge of good and evil." It equates such knowledge, rather, with "wisdom" in general. When the serpent promises that the human beings will be "like God, knowing good and evil," the woman interprets this to mean simply "gaining wisdom" (3:5-6). The best starting point in understanding this idea is found in 2 Samuel 14:17-20. In this passage, a woman speaking to King David tells him that he is "like an angel of God in discerning good and evil . . . [having] wisdom like that of an angel of God—he knows everything that happens in the land." David knows "good and evil," which is another way of saying that he knows "everything." He possesses godlike wisdom. The point is not that he is literally omniscient but that he has remarkable insight, such that he is able to come to a correct judgment on any matter. In the Old Testament, this capacity for independent judgment is lacking in the very old (2 Samuel 19:35) and in the very young (Deuteronomy 1:39) or in those who *feel* themselves to be as inexperienced as the very young—people like King Solomon, in 1 Kings 3:7-9.[14]

Leaving Home

With the help of these texts, we see that in Genesis 3 the wisdom that makes one like God is the wisdom that is associated with adult independence from a parent. It is the wisdom that might enable a person to make his or her *own* judgments—autonomously.[15] It seems that the woman and her husband are not content with the knowledge that God has already *given* them—the knowledge that enables them to begin to fulfill their roles as divine image bearers. They want this other kind of wisdom too, and they are prepared to disobey God to get it. In doing so, they reveal that they have essentially decided no longer to be image bearers at all. They want to *be* gods, in the fullest sense, rather than *representing and mediating* God to creation. They want the autonomy that wisdom brings. The line between Creator and creation was sharply drawn in Genesis 1–2, but here in Genesis 3 human beings—desiring to be like God—try to blur that line. We encounter the same move in other Genesis passages—in chapter 11, for example, where the people of Mesopotamia seek to build "a tower that reaches to the heavens" (11:4). We also encounter it elsewhere in the Old Testament. In Ezekiel 28, for example, we hear God saying to the king of Tyre, who dwells in the garden in Eden,

> In the pride of your heart you say, "I am a god; I sit on the throne of a god in the heart of the seas." But you are a man and not a god, though you think you are as wise as a god. (v. 2)

It is not that wisdom, as such, is bad. Psalm 19:7-8 affirms that God himself grants wisdom, as people obey God and pursue wisdom only in dependence upon him. Other biblical texts tell us that it is "the fear of the LORD" that is "the beginning of wisdom" (Psalm 111:10)—the central proposition of Israelite wisdom literature like the book of Proverbs (9:10). Wisdom itself is not problematic—but *grasping* after wisdom out of a desire to be like God certainly is.

The biblical story of Solomon can be seen as an extended narrative reflection on this theme of right and wrong approaches to wisdom. Told by his father David that he must at all costs obey God's law if his kingdom is to flourish (1 Kings 2:1-4), Solomon asks God near the beginning of his reign for wisdom:

> I am only a little child and do not know how to carry out my duties. Your servant is here among the people you have chosen, a great people, too numerous to count or number. So give your servant a discerning heart to govern your people and to distinguish between right and wrong. (1 Kings 3:7-9)

With this wisdom from God, Solomon initially rules successfully over his kingdom. Over the course of time, however, we find him disobeying God's law in various ways, and eventually his accumulated indiscretions lead to outright rebellion against God (1 Kings 11:1-8). His wisdom is still on display in his exchange with the Queen of Sheba in 1 Kings 10:1-13, but it has degenerated by this point into a self-indulgent playing of games with words, which does his people no good at all. Wisdom and obedience to God are always in tension in the Solomon story, and ultimately they become completely divorced. Solomon becomes, in fact, the very picture of a typical ancient Near Eastern god-king. He is no longer the Israelite king of Deuteronomy 17, who keeps the law of God constantly beside him and does not turn from it "to the right or to the left" (17:20). Tragically, the inadequacies of and dangers inherent in a wisdom that is not "from God" are graphically on display in the Solomon story.[16]

THE CONSEQUENCES OF EMBRACING EVIL

The promise of the serpent in Genesis 3:4 turns out to be quite true, in a way. Human eyes *are* opened (3:7), Adam and Eve *do* become like God, knowing good and evil (3:22), and they *do not* die "when" (literally "on the day that") they eat the fruit of the tree (cf. 2:17). Yet this taking of their destiny into their own hands does not result in the wonderful new future they had no doubt envisaged.

Eyes Wide Open

With their eyes now open, the man and the woman realize that they are naked (3:7). This realization sends them into hiding—from each other and then from God (3:8). A disruption has clearly occurred in the relationship between God and his image bearers and between the image bearers themselves. This disruption has at least partly to do with the entry of shame into human experience, for just prior the human beings were naked and without shame (Genesis 2:25). The hiding of the body in clothes symbolizes the hiding of man from woman in shame. This is our first clue about what has happened. The extent of the disruption, however, runs deeper, as we discover when we hear the conversation in Genesis 3:10-13. Here the man blames both the woman and God for the trouble: "the woman *you* put here with me—she gave me some fruit from the tree, and I ate it." In turn, the woman shuffles the blame onto the serpent. Relationships have seriously broken down. Yet this is only the beginning. The extent of the disruption becomes *wholly* apparent only when we read Genesis 3:14-19. Here God "unpacks" for all the participants in the story the fuller dimensions of the relational breakdowns.

The Serpent Bites the Dust

What are these fuller dimensions? We read first of the consequences for the serpent—and indeed for the entirety of the animal world. Whereas to this point in the story God has been strictly a God of blessing, now we discover that God can also curse: the serpent is "cursed . . . above all the livestock and all the wild animals" (Genesis 3:14). The *serpent* thus certainly faces the consequences of his actions, although the wording of verse 14 (the serpent is cursed "above all") implies that all the *other* animals are also to some degree also affected by these actions. What this means for *wild* animals is ultimately clarified in Genesis 9:1-7 (as we shall see in our own chap. 9), and we may extrapolate from this passage what it means for *domestic* ones as well. In a world into which evil has entered, animal relationships with human beings will become strained; animals will suffer. The serpent's particular fate will be humiliation; this is the implication of "crawling on the belly and eating dust" (Genesis 3:14). One who thought himself wise and exalted will be brought low. Where kinship between humans and animals is the hallmark of the creation story in Genesis 1 and 2, enmity will mark the snake's world moving forward, as he strikes at human feet and human feet also strike at him (Genesis 3:15). At one level, this is an account of hostility between humans and snakes. At another level—remembering what the snake stands for in this story—it is an account of a long-term battle between human beings and the forces of darkness in the cosmos. These forces, themselves creatures of God who have turned bad, will seek to destroy human creatures by seducing and recruiting them. Human beings—at least when thinking more clearly than they do in Genesis 3—will strike back. At still another (third) level, we are reading here about broken relationships between human beings and animals more generally. The image bearers of God were to look after creation (including animal creation). Instead, they will find themselves at odds with creation.

Family Pain

After the serpent, God addresses the woman (Genesis 3:16). Unfortunately, our standard English translations do not help us to understand
well the first part of what he says to her, for they typically (and wrongly)
imply that the text concerns female pain experienced during the process of giving birth. The NIV, for example, translates Genesis 3:16a as
follows: "to the woman he said, 'I will greatly increase your pains in
childbearing; with pain you will give birth to children.'" However, the
Hebrew that stands behind the NIV's "pains" (*'tsb*) is never used in the
Old Testament to refer to pain experienced during the process of giving
birth. Birth pangs are referred to using quite different terms.[17] Moreover, the Hebrew word translated in the NIV as "childbearing" (*herayon*) clearly refers elsewhere in the Old Testament to conception or
pregnancy, not to childbirth.[18] The best way to translate Genesis 3:16a,
then, is as follows: "I will greatly increase your pain along with your
conception; in painful circumstances you will give birth to children."
The pain is not the pain of child*birth* but the painful family circumstances (Heb. *'itsabon*) in which the woman will now bring children
into the world. In Genesis 3:17, the man is likewise told that he will
now farm his land in the midst of pain (Heb. *'itsabon*, NIV's "painful
toil"). The double use of *'itsabon* in verses 16 and 17 emphasizes that the
woman's fate *mirrors* that of the man. Each will toil in painful circumstances, enduring not intermittent but ongoing pain.[19]

In other words, a change will come about in the circumstances
of both the man and the woman with respect to core aspects of their
human vocation. The man's creation-calling includes working the land,
and, as we shall see in 3:18-19, this now becomes marked by a new level
of struggle. The woman's creation-calling includes conceiving and giving birth to children. Genesis 3 does not suggest that before the entry of
evil into human experience this calling would have been without challenges; in Genesis 3:16 the woman is told that her pain will be greatly
increased, not that it will only now *begin*. Yet the calling now becomes
more problematic, in ways that it would not otherwise have been.

No doubt this reality for the woman (as for the man) is envisaged
partly as a matter of economics; it is a matter of agricultural produc-
tion. The double use of *'itsabon* in Genesis 3:16-17 implies this connection between the two, paralleling as it does the pain of the man and
of the woman. Family life will be tougher because life in general will

be tougher, as farmers struggle with an unresponsive earth. The new pain also arises, however, because the human pair's relationship is now fractured, so that they no longer face the world as "one flesh." This is starkly indicated in the second part of verse 16: "your desire will be for your husband, and he will rule over you." The dynamics of the male-female relationship have changed. In Genesis 1–2, men and women are created to work in partnership (1:27-28, 2:20-23); in Genesis 3, how-ever, the future of the woman is as a subject "ruled" by her husband (Heb. *mashal*). This verb refers to mastery or dominion, and it has not occurred previously in Genesis, although it *will* later (Genesis 4:7; 24:2; 37:8; 45:26). Most significantly for our present context, it also appears in Psalm 8:6-8:

> You made him *ruler* over the works of your hands; you put everything under his feet: all flocks and herds, and the beasts of the field, the birds of the air, and the fish of the sea, all that swim the paths of the seas.

What has become of the relationship between man and woman? These various occurrences of *mashal* make it clear that the man is envisaged in Genesis 3:16 as now relating to the woman as if she were *part of* the creation over which humans were given dominion, rather than being herself a coruler *over* creation.

For her own part, the woman is not envisaged as blameless when it comes to this increased dysfunction in male-female relations. Her "desire" will be for her husband. What does this mean? Our best clue is found in the nearby Genesis 4:7, where the same rare Hebrew word *tes-huqah* (desire) is used of sin's desire to gobble up Cain. In this text, evil is personified no longer as a serpent but as a wild animal of a larger and more dangerous kind, lying in wait for its victim and ready to pounce. Genesis 3:16 refers, then, to a female desire to control, even to consume, her husband. Intended for partnership, the human pair now find them-selves entangled *with each other* in a struggle for dominance, as they themselves both struggle for dominance over the *earth*.[20]

In summation of Genesis 3:16, then, the world of the family will be more painful for the woman than it would have been if the human pair had not turned away from God. The woman will experience fam-ily in the context of pain, for her relationship with her husband and their relationship with the earth is fractured. The kind of pain that children in such a dysfunctional world can cause will shortly be graphically illustrated in the story of Cain and Abel in Genesis 4.

A New Name

The change in the woman's situation is symbolized in Genesis 3:20 by the uttering of a new name. She is now called Eve (Heb. *khavvah*), which probably means "life." On one level this simply reestablishes what is already known from Genesis 1–2—that this woman will be "mother of all the living." The language of the text confirms this, for the Hebrew word for "living" (*khai*) is related to the Hebrew word for "Eve" (*khavvah*). According to Genesis 3, God's blessing of fertility will continue even in the midst of the problems that human beings have created by embracing evil. However, there is more to this name than simply confirming what is already known. The name Eve, along with the statement that "the man *named* his wife," echoes Genesis 2:19-20, where we learned that to name something in the ancient world was to assign it a *function*.

Back in Genesis 2, God brings every living creature to the earthling, who names each one. The Hebrew for "living" there is *khayyah*, which comes from the same verbal root as *khai*—the word that means "living" in Genesis 3:20. In Genesis 2 no living creature is suitable as a helper for the earthling, so God creates a coworker and wife for the earthling. The name given to this new creature reflects both her *difference* from the other living creatures and her *likeness* to the earthling. She is *'ishah* to his *'ish* (2:23). She is "(wo)man" to "man." She is not simply one "living creature" (*nephesh khayyah*) among many. The precise vocabulary used itself clarifies the nature of the relationships between the man, the woman, and the rest of creation. The *names* speak to the joint *function* that male and female have in creation; they are corulers and cogardeners of the rest of creation. The names define male-female relations in terms of unity in community.

It is this unity that is disrupted in Genesis 3, for here we are told that the man will now "rule over" (Heb. *mashal*) the woman as if she *were* simply one of the other living creatures after all. The second naming of the woman by the man in Genesis 3:20 reflects this change in relationship. In Genesis 2 her name (*'ishah*) reflects her *difference* from the animals, but in Genesis 3 her name (*khavvah*) *reminds* us of the animals (*khayyah*). Just as *'ish* and *'ishah* spoke of closeness between male and female, so now *'adam* and *khavvah* speak of distance between them. Which function is bound up with this new name for the woman? It is the function of motherhood. Essentially what has happened is this: the woman is now defined by the man in terms of only *one* of her original functions in the world. She is no longer defined in terms of her entire vocation, which is to rule over creation alongside the man. The *'adam* male and female (1:26) has now become an *'adam* (male) and a *khavvah* (female), who inhabit quite different vocational spheres—the world inside the home, on the one hand, and the world outside it, on the other.[21] Among other things, Adam's naming of Eve anticipates an important thematic development in the succeeding chapters, in which the fertile mother who responds to mortality by bearing children is juxtaposed with the "heroic" male who looks for immortality elsewhere than in home and family.[22]

Summing up the preceding paragraphs, then: God's ongoing blessing is evidenced in the name Eve. The blessing of fertility—of life—continues. But the name also reflects the newly disordered nature of the world in which God's blessing will now work its way out.

Labor Pain

The consequences for the *man* of this primal turning away from God are obviously bound up with the fate of the woman in the context of the family. However, there are additional consequences in the world outside the home.

It is *not* that there will now be work where there was none before. Work is already an aspect of the human vocation in Genesis 1–2. Human beings are created to work the garden and to take care of it (Genesis 2:15). They are made to rule and to subdue the earth (1:28). This would always have required effort, and indeed pain—just as there would always have been pain involved in the woman's birthing and raising children. Farming hurts, and it would have even in a world that lacked the "thorns and thistles" mentioned in Genesis 3:18. In the minds of the authors of Genesis 1–3, however, no such world in fact ever existed. Thorns and thistles are already part of the vegetation of the earth in Genesis 1–2, and they assuredly come under the heading of Hebrew *siakh*, the inedible plants described in Genesis 2:5 (and translated by the NIV as "shrubs"). They are not newly created in Genesis 3 any more than the "plants of the field" (Heb. *'eseb hassadeh*) that are good to eat. These latter plants are also already mentioned in Genesis 2:5, and they have previously been described under the heading "seed-bearing plants" in Genesis 1:11-12 and 1:29.

It is not, then, that there will be work now (because of the human embrace of evil) where there was none before. It is not even that there will be thorns and thistles now, where there were none before. It is just that work will now involve *more pain* than before. It will be experienced in a different way—as a struggle with an earth that is more reluctant to give up good things but insists instead on producing "thorns and thistles *for you*" (Genesis 3:18). The wording of this clause is strange, and it underlines that it is not the *world* that has changed, but people's *experience* of this world.[23] People and land now live under a curse. The land will still provide food, but only at greater cost. Both edible and inedible plants already exist, and both will continue to grow. But what Genesis 3 is keen to impress upon the reader is that much harder work will now be required to grow enough of the edible plants to survive.

Locked Out

It is in God's address to the man in Genesis 3:17-19 that we at last come across a reference to death—something for which the reader has been waiting since Genesis 3:6. "When you eat of it you will surely die," God said of the tree of the knowledge of good and evil in Genesis 2:16, but no death has yet occurred. Now we are told for the first time that it *will* occur, as human access to the tree of life is denied (Genesis 3:19, 24). Although not much is said about this second tree in Genesis 2, we may deduce from Genesis 3:22 that it offered the possibility of a different ending to normal human existence—that human beings were destined at some point to eat its fruit and become immortal. Such a state is not at all *natural* to them in the thinking of the Old Testament, but it is, in Genesis, considered to be a *potential* gift of God.[24] It is unthinkable to the good God, however, that the dysfunction and darkness that now characterize these "wise" human beings should last forever. Now, therefore, the normal processes of human life will be allowed to play themselves out. Instead of eating from the tree of life and gaining immortality, human beings will eat food only "until you return to the ground" (3:19). They will return to the very earth with which they have spent their whole working life struggling. The human destination is now the same as the human point of origin: "For dust you are and to dust you will return."

How does God ensure that this is so? He drives them out of the garden in which the tree of life is to be found. They are barred from this sanctuary by supernatural creatures ("cherubim"), whose representations are said elsewhere to adorn both tabernacle and temple (e.g., Exodus 25:18-22; 26:31; 1 Kings 6:23-29), and by a mysterious "flaming sword flashing back and forth" (Genesis 3:24). It is for the best that they are locked out in this way, for eternal life now would mean that evil and disorder were "locked into" the cosmos. The lockout is a blessing in disguise, even as it is also the final aspect of God's cursing.

THE BOOK OF GENESIS, EVIL, AND SUFFERING

Looking back on Genesis 3, then, we have discovered something of the Genesis authors' convictions about the presence of evil in the world, and the suffering that arises from its embrace. Almost from the beginning of human history, they propose, human beings have been seduced by evil and have failed to trust in the goodness and generosity of God. Recognizing the difference between themselves and the remainder of creation, they have nevertheless become confused about the significance of this difference. They have aspired, therefore, to be something other than God's image-bearing creatures. They have aspired to become autonomous gods, rather than to remain the servants of the one true God.

This human grasping after equality with God has not, however, produced the desired outcomes. It has indeed led to significant dysfunction in the human community. Creatures created to cooperate under God in the ruling of creation have instead, marked by guilt and shame, sought dominion as gods over each other. Thus disabled as image bearers of God, these creatures have been *unable* to rule over creation as they ought. The outcome has been an increase in suffering in the world. Human beings have also become locked into a long struggle with the forces of darkness to which they succumbed in turning away from God in the first place. Further, the possibility of immortality has been removed from them. This is ironic, for it is the very steps they have taken to become like God that have, in the end, resulted in the certainty that they *cannot* become like God—at least, not in terms of immortality. They no longer live in the garden in Eden—in that state of being described in Genesis 2 in terms of right community with God, with each other, and with the nonhuman creation. Apparently, they cannot live in this garden in the *future* either; it is barred to them. However, we shall return to "apparently" later.[25]

Outside the Garden

What does life look like outside the garden? This is graphically illustrated as Genesis 4 picks up the story. God's blessing of fertility certainly continues, as Cain and Abel are born into the human community. When the two boys grow older, however, Cain's offerings do not please God. This makes Cain angry—anger that results in the murder of his brother Abel. Cain himself is then exiled from his family and from their land. He moves further away from the garden, becoming "a restless wanderer on the earth" (Genesis 4:12). The expulsion of Adam and Eve from the garden did not disrupt human relationships in this way—they at least remained a functioning (albeit dysfunctional) family. Cain's murder of Abel, however, tears the family apart. Cain goes on to father a family line that evidences the same violent tendencies (4:20-22), and ultimately the whole human community slides into chaos and anarchy, and violence fills the earth (6:11-13). Here is the world that has turned away from God, our Genesis authors tell us, and has ultimately turned upon itself. The embrace of evil has spread like an infection, and the whole world has become sick. It is a world that has, in fact, come to the point of "uncreation," as the waters of chaos reassert themselves in the great flood of Genesis 6–8, and life on earth all but comes to an end.

Two Claims about Evil

In writing in this way, the authors of Genesis clearly mean to tell us at least two important things about evil in the world. The first is that evil is not an eternally existing reality alongside and equal to God—a "dark side of the Force" that balances its light side (as in *Star Wars*). Biblical faith is not dualistic. "In the beginning" there was not good and evil, but simply one omnipotent, transcendent, creator God who is wholly good (Genesis 1–2). The second thing that we are to know is that evil is not *created* by this one God as an intrinsic aspect of the cosmos. God is good and creates only what is good. To the question of the Christian author Boethius (A.D. 480–524/5), then, which opens this chapter (in its first epigraph), the authors of Genesis respond by affirming that the good in the world comes from God, but the evil in it comes from God's creatures, who turn away from what is good.[26] Evil comes from those who hide from God, distrusting his goodness and his generosity. Hiding from God in this way is all too easy, because there is free will in the cosmos. Therefore God does not coerce his creatures to come out of hiding, from the darkness into the light—although, as Genesis 3:9 suggests, he certainly *invites* them to do so.

BIBLICAL FAITH AND THE FAITHS

This explanation offered by the book of Genesis as to the existence of evil in the world and the connection that it forges between evil and much of the suffering that marks the world sets the biblical tradition apart from many other religious and philosophical traditions. To illustrate this point, I begin with ancient Near Eastern polytheism.

Ancient Near Eastern Polytheism

In the ancient Near East there were many gods, and the power of these gods to do good was limited, because the power of each was constrained by the power of the others. Godly power was also constrained by the cosmic parameters within which all the gods had to work, since they themselves had come into existence *with* the cosmos and were not sovereign *over* it. Moreover, these gods were not regarded as morally superior to human beings, so that although their worshippers might hope for good from them, they could not be sure of it. Given that the gods themselves did not clearly reveal what they wanted from mortal beings, their worshippers were just as likely to offend them completely accidentally, and without ever knowing why, as to please them. There was certainly no idea that the gods were *committed* in some way to the good of their worshippers. The world was not understood as being set up in the first place with human good in mind, and human beings were certainly not created to be the recipients of the blessing and love of the gods.

All of this being so, a couple of options arise for explaining evil and suffering. In the first place, evil could be imagined as being built into the very fabric of things—into the very parameters of the cosmos. The gods, who did not create these parameters, could do nothing about this evil, or the suffering arising from it.[27] In this conception, the problem is a lack of power; the gods are not powerful enough to deal with evil. Second, evil could be understood as resident in the gods themselves and as spilling over into the mortal realm. The gods were capable of malice, they were vain, and they were competitive among themselves.

They could also be incompetent, which is not the same thing as being wicked, but could nevertheless produce unwarranted, undeserved suffering.[28] Further, if we are also prepared to describe the *inscrutability* of these ancient gods as an evil (in that they did not reveal their requirements to their worshippers yet held them accountable for failing to abide by them), then we may also say that much suffering was understood in the ancient Near East as arising from the evil of inscrutability. Certainly ancient Near Eastern people often complained about this.[29] Whatever the precise explanation of evil and suffering in ancient Near Eastern polytheism, we are a long way in all of this from the biblical idea of evil (and related suffering) as arising in the world from creaturely abandonment of a right relationship with the one omnipotent, good, and self-revealing God.

Platonism

Dualistic systems of thought take a different approach to accounting for evil. Whereas in ancient Near Eastern polytheism the emphasis lies on how the many gods interact with the world of human experience, in dualistic ways of thinking the emphasis lies on the dual reality of good and evil that preexists these gods—if indeed there are "gods" at all.

The thinking of the Greek philosopher Plato, for example, appears to be dualistic in this way. He conceives of a universe in which "being" coexists eternally with "nonbeing"—a dualism of the kind found in all the ancient Greek philosophers in the absence of any idea of a God who genuinely *creates* (in the biblical sense). Being and nonbeing are the fundamental realities faced by the god who is referred to in Plato's *Timaeus* as "demiurge" or "craftsman" when he arrives on the scene and begins to craft the universe. The craftsman crafts on the basis of plans that already exist—an unchanging and eternal model ("what is and never becomes"). Following these good plans—the "Forms" that also appear in Plato's *Republic* as models for "crafting" the ideal state—the craftsman imposes order on a preexistent chaos, and he creates a material world that is as good as nature permits it to be. He does the best he can, but he is already constrained by the situation in which he finds himself. This is also the case with the lesser gods, to whom the craftsman then delegates the creation of human beings. It is these lesser gods who place individual souls in physical bodies, to the detriment of the souls' grasp of reality—which necessitates the human commitment to philosophy as the path by which the soul recovers both its understanding of the true nature of things and (ultimately) its release from bodily confinement.

There *are* gods in this account of the beginnings of existence, but these are gods constrained by preexisting realities. The cosmos comes into being as a result of (as the "offspring" of) a confrontation between a disorder ascribed to the power of "necessity," on the one hand, and the demiurge's intelligent causation, on the other.[30] The demiurge *is* able to craft the physical world, but disorder also remains, for it is beyond the capacity of the well-meaning "demiurge" to overcome it. Indeed, human beings themselves must still attempt to overcome this disorder, in pursuit of the Good:

> For them, as for the demiurge himself, goodness lies in the bringing of order out of disorder by imposing intelligence on necessity and sameness on difference. . . . However, the demiurge, being entirely good . . . orders not himself but everything else, while generated beings, being imperfect, must first bring order to themselves, so far as they can.[31]

Disorder is the residue that remains after the demiurge and the lesser gods have done their creative work in the cosmos. It has always and inevitably been "there," waiting to be confronted and overcome by those who pursue the Good.[32] Once again, we are a long way here from the convictions of our biblical authors about evil (and related suffering) as arising from our human abandonment of a right relationship with the one omnipotent, good, and self-revealing God.

Manichaeism and Zoroastrianism

In chapter 2 we pondered briefly the religion of Manichaeism that arose in the third century A.D. in the Persian Empire. In Manichaeism, the cosmos comprises Light and Darkness—the former currently under the sovereignty of the latter. As in Plato, so also in Manichaeism, currently embodied human souls have lost their grasp of reality. They need to be enlightened, so that they can rejoin the Light. However, whereas for Plato, matter is simply *problematic* for the soul's journey toward its destiny, for Mani (the founder of Manichaeism) matter is actually intrinsically *evil*. It is part of the Darkness. Whence comes this Darkness? It has always existed, in opposition to the powerful (but not omnipotent)

Good. Both Light and Darkness suffuse all reality, then, and they always have. The human being, in particular, is understood as a battleground upon which these cosmic powers fight. The evil that produces suffering has therefore always existed, inside and outside of the human being. It will remain this way until the end of time.

One of the major influences on Mani was Zoroastrianism, which emerged out of eastern Iran sometime in the centuries prior to its first appearance in recorded history in the work of the Greek historian Herodotus (mid-fifth century B.C.). A dualistic approach to the cosmos is also to be found in some strands of this religion. Zoroaster (also known as Zarathustra) taught that there is one supreme god, called Ahura Mazda. This god is eternal, uncreated, omniscient, and the creator of all that is good, including material creation. All the other gods that exist are subordinate to Ahura Mazda and have often been thought of in Zoroastrianism simply as attributes or helpers of Ahura Mazda. To the extent that this is so, Zoroastrianism's understanding of divinity is not dissimilar to the understanding of divinity found in the Old Testament (where God also has helpers in the divine assembly).

Yet there has also persisted a tendency in Zoroastrianism to regard some of these gods as divine powers *independent* of the supreme god. This is certainly true, for example, in the cult of Mithra, which later became popular throughout the Roman Empire. A particularly ambiguous figure in Zoroastrianism is the evil spirit Angra Mainyu (or Ahriman), who is locked in combat in this world with the holy spirit, Spenta Mainyu. Zoroaster himself was unclear on the question of whether Spenta Mainyu and Angra Mainyu, the originators of being and nonbeing, are *creatures* of Ahura Mazda or whether they are eternal principles. In Zoroastrianism, while Spenta Mainyu is often closely identified with Ahura Mazda, Angra Mainyu is certainly not, for he is Ahura Mazda's opposite. Angra Mainyu can, in fact, attain in some Zoroastrian texts a status almost equal with Ahura Mazda—an evil power versus a good one. When this way of thinking predominates, there is certainly the potential for a thoroughgoing cosmic dualism between good and evil. Yet Zoroastrianism even at its most dualistic has tended to believe in the ultimate triumph of good over evil, suggesting that its dualism is not in fact truly and innately eternal. Here the proponents of Zoroastrianism are in agreement with Mani, but not (apparently) with Plato.[33]

Confucianism and Daoism

Dualistic perspectives of West and East explain the existence of evil and suffering in the world in terms of the eternal coexistence (at least looking *backward* in time) of two interlocked forces, good and evil—two gods, or ultimate entities. Other religious and philosophical traditions of the East follow a very different path, for they do not begin their reflections on the human situation with any substantive idea of "gods" in mind at all—whether two or many. Consider, for example, Confucius' thinking, which developed against the background of the anarchy of the middle Zhou period in China.

The Zhou dynasty had come to power in the twelfth century B.C. and had created a society "remembered ever after as a model for the ideal Chinese society."[34] In this society, "Heaven" was considered to have given its mandate to rule to the righteous Zhou monarch ("Son of Heaven"), and society was organized hierarchically beneath this monarch in accordance with people's relationship to the royal family. The supreme deity authorized the supreme ruler, and cosmic order was maintained all the way down from this apex, symbolized in elaborate societal rituals. This picture reminds us in various ways of the situation in the ancient Near East. By the beginning of the ninth century B.C., however, this cosmic order was being disturbed. Independent states were emerging, each vying for power with the other, and inevitably questions arose in due course about the "Mandate of Heaven." If the Zhou rulers really were ruling in accordance with this mandate, why was there evil and suffering?

Confucius' answer to this question was that people (including rulers) had departed from the principles of harmonious life that had marked the early Zhou period, and he urged a return to them. The key principle was *li* (propriety or respectful ritual), the heart of which was filial piety directed toward parents and ancestors. Confucius taught that if his contemporaries would only perform the proper rituals and ceremonies, they would be transformed into people of humane goodness (*ren*). As the outer relationships came into order, so also would inner human nature. Confucius called his practice dao (way)—a term used in earlier times in China to designate a religious path. He was not particularly interested in gods and spirits, however, but primarily in human potential. What is it that inhibits human beings from reaching their full potential as individuals and as societies? It is not, in the end, the gods or the other spiritual forces—at least, not predominantly so. The problem lies within individuals and within societies. That is where evil and suffering really originate, as people turn away from the dao, and as society indeed fails to instruct them in the dao. Even then, it is not that human beings themselves are by nature evil or by nature inflict suffering. Human nature in Confucian thought is fundamentally good. The evil that exists in the world (as measured by its social effects) arises, in the end, only as a result of ignorance. It can be eliminated through self-transformation grounded in an education in the liberal arts.[35]

Confucian thought is, then, somewhat similar to biblical thought, in that the presence of evil in the world and the suffering that follows from it are understood as the result of a human departure from a prescribed "way" that is good. At the same time, the dao is not a personal, good, and transcendent God—or indeed anything or anyone that stands "outside" the human world. In addition, if dualism differs from biblical faith in raising evil to a power all but equivalent to God, Confucianism differs from it to the extent that it diminishes the importance of evil as a significant power external to human beings. To put it in the language of Genesis 3, Confucius knew of no serpent. Furthermore, the Confucian assessment of the level of intrusion of evil into human life is much more optimistic than in biblical faith. Our biblical authors do not believe that the human problem, in the end, is ignorance, nor that its resolution largely depends on education—although the removal of ignorance through education is certainly a good thing. In this respect, Confucianism shares the emphasis of much Eastern thinking and of the Eastern-influenced Western thinking of Plato (and Mani) that what humans most need in order to escape evil and suffering is *enlightenment*.

Essentially pragmatic rather than religious in orientation, Confucius did nevertheless still hold to the categories of good and evil. Classical Daoism as founded by Laozi, which developed in opposition to Confucianism, more radically questioned the very distinction between good and evil, at least in conventional terms.[36] According to the Daoist view, it is, in fact, a basic human problem that we make *judgments* about matters like good and evil, rather than simply "going with the flow" of our nature in harmony with the true dao. It is a basic human problem that all too often "conscious knowledge of right and wrong replaces spontaneous intuition."[37] The true dao is "the sacred principle immanent in nature, that which is the source of all and that to which all returns."[38] The greatest human good is to be in harmony with this dao—to be empathetic to and aligned with the alternating forces of yin and yang that are thought to characterize the eternal dao at its periphery (rather than at its ineffable core). Evil is, in fact, all that resists this pure nature. It is everything that prevents us from experiencing the natural rhythms of the universe itself. We get in harmony with the dao not by following Confucius' rules of propriety but (for example) by practicing weakness and passivity and living spontaneously without rules and plans in response to the movements of the dao. As in Confucianism, ignorance is closely allied with evil in Daoism. It is through ignorance that we lose harmony with the dao and consequently experience evil and suffering. Harmony with the dao, which is itself neither good nor evil, takes us *beyond* the categories of good and evil. We should above all seek union with the impersonal "One" that is prior to all multiplicity and is indeed identical with the primordial chaos out of which the world first evolved.

If Confucianism is similar to biblical thought in some respects, Daoism is certainly not. Here we have taken one step even further away from the biblical idea of the one transcendent, personal God who is in himself good, who defines what is good (and evil), and who calls his human creatures into conformity with his good character, rejecting what is evil.[39]

Hinduism and Buddhism

Mention of the impersonal "One" that is prior to all multiplicity reminds us of our earlier discussion of Hinduism and Buddhism, as does the close connection between ignorance and evil, which is also a feature of both religions from their beginnings. The universe in itself is neither evil nor good in Hindu and Buddhist thinking: like the dao in Daoism, it just "is." But human beings are ignorant of the nature of this universe and of who we are within it.

In classical Hinduism, suffering exists because, in the end, I am ignorant about my true identity as the eternal atman, which is identical with Brahman. I think that my empirical self—the living, breathing, thinking, desiring self—is my real self. This is a fateful illusion, which leads me to behave as an individual ego in relationship with the many other separate entities in the world. Above all, it produces *desire*, which births selfish action, which leads by the law of karma to endless reincarnations. This process is understood as one in which (if left to itself) suffering increases rather than decreases, for ignorance and desire compound over time, and the evil that is produced by desire continues to do its deadly work lifetime after lifetime. If, however, I can attain the knowledge that my true self is Brahman, the cycle can be arrested. There are, then, no separate things for me, as a separate ego, to desire. Multiplicity is revealed to be, in fact, One.

In the teaching of the Buddha, likewise, my whole existence involves suffering. There is suffering that is "associated with the changing conditions of physical life," suffering that arises from the impermanence of things, and suffering that arises from "unwholesome states of mind."[40] However, unlike Hinduism, the solution does not lie deep within myself, in the divine reality of the atman, for there *is* no permanent self or soul: "impermanence is not just a characteristic of the phenomena of the external world; it applies to oneself."[41] Failing to recognize this itself leads to selfishness and egoism—and to suffering. I must not hold onto the self in any way. By ceasing to cling to it, I can attain nirvana (liberation)—a state that may be achieved only by following the Noble Eightfold Path. This path is designed gradually to root out all clinging and to bring about the transformation of existence. Nirvana is the freedom from suffering that is attained when the causes of suffering are obliterated. It is "the cessation of greed, hatred and delusion."[42]

Although Hinduism and Buddhism are different from each other in many ways, in both worldviews evil and suffering are simply aspects of the illusory world that I am seeking to leave behind in favor of reality. My critical need is, once again, enlightenment: if only I could grasp the truth about existence, I would not be suffering.

Biblical Faith

From all such views about the place of evil and suffering in the world, biblical faith dissents. Good and evil do not exist simply as social constructs, and the words "good" and "evil" are not merely conventions of human speech; they are words that refer to objective realities. These realities are not simply realities as they *appear* to us, as if appearances were profoundly deceptive. The real world is in fact reliably (if not fully) communicated to us through our senses, and in this world good and evil really exist. "Good" refers to what is like God; "evil" refers to what is not. Although they are thus clearly distinct realities in biblical thinking, they are not *eternally* distinct. Evil has not always existed alongside

God and equal to God. It has arisen from within God's creatures, who have turned away from what is good and (in the case of human beings) have bequeathed this damaged inheritance to their descendants. Evil, thus understood as originating (first) in personal, nonhuman beings rebelling against God, (second) in the human failure to trust in the goodness and generosity of God, and (third) in the human desire to *be* a god, has led to suffering. Rather than cooperating together under God in the ruling of creation, human beings have instead sought to rule one another and have failed to complete their vital governance tasks. Widespread and devastating suffering has been the result. What are we to do about it?

6

ON LIVING IN A BLIGHTED WORLD
What Am I to Do about Evil and Suffering?

The only thing necessary for the triumph of evil is
for good men to do nothing.

Anonymous[1]

The small man thinks that small acts of goodness are
of no benefit, and does not do them.

Confucius[2]

In chapter 5 we saw that the book of Genesis does not shy away from the
reality of evil and the suffering it causes. The following question, then,
presents itself: What am I to do about such evil and suffering? Like
the questions addressed in our previous chapters, this too is a question
asked by all serious religions and philosophies down through the ages,
and so we pose it to our biblical authors here. We shall return to the
question of the suffering that is *intrinsic to living in creation*—the suffering that does *not* arise from evil—in chapter 9.

GENESIS AND FATE

It is helpful, in penetrating the heart of the biblical perspective on
suffering, first of all to underline what the authors of Genesis are *not*

saying about evil and its effects in Genesis 3–6. For the biblical authors, life "east of Eden" does *not* represent the way in which human life and society must *inevitably* develop now that evil has entered human experience. Human beings are *not* now fated or destined simply to live out this life, as if the consequences of the primal sin were now unalterable—the givens of human experience bequeathed to all of us by our first ancestors. According to Genesis, these realities do *not* represent the predetermined, God-ordained human lot in life.

Accepting the Curse?

This is, unfortunately, precisely how the Genesis story has been interpreted by many of its readers throughout history. On this view, Genesis 3 describes an irreversible "fall." The world in which we live has been indelibly marked by the sinfulness and stupidity of our first ancestors. We need simply to accept what we have inherited from them, since we would be rebelling against God if we were to seek to overcome the God-ordained curses that now characterize this fallen world. In these curses God has, as it were, "recreated" the cosmos so that it is a suitable place for fallen people to inhabit. While we should certainly try not to *add* to the evil and suffering of this world as we await our release from it, neither should we try to *change* much that is fundamental to its current (fallen) nature. That would be quite wrong.

This is why (for example) many Scots strongly opposed their countryman James Simpson when, in 1847, he advocated the use of anesthetics in childbirth. To use chloroform for the purpose of relieving a woman's birth pangs, they argued, was to seek to avoid one aspect of the primeval curse on woman. They argued the point with great vehemence, notwithstanding the fact that in Genesis 2 (as Simpson pointed out) God himself causes a deep sleep to come upon the earthling before performing the surgical operation that produces gendered human beings.[3] The same kind of approach to Genesis 3 also lies behind a long-commended approach to male-female relations in Western societies. On this view, the ruling of men over women that is envisaged in Genesis 3:16 is God ordained: it is not a *description* of how male-female relations *are often* ordered in the world but a *prescription* of how male-female relations *should always be* ordered.[4] In both examples, Genesis 3 tells us that we live in a world in which a mistake was once made and all of us must now pay the ongoing penalty. We do, in fact, pay for it, as we live out our days in a world where everything, in some way, has been touched and spoiled by the mistake. A hint of this view is contained in one modern writer's comment on Genesis 3:17, which describes the "toil" now associated with human work: "the toil that now lies behind the preparation of *every* meal is a reminder of the fall and is made the more painful by the memory of the ready supply of food within the garden."[5] The same view is explicit in this assertion by a commentator of a previous generation: "here certain fixed adverse conditions of the universal human lot are traced back to a primaeval curse uttered by Yahwe [the LORD] in consequence of man's first transgression."[6]

Everything has been affected by the primal sin—everything in creation at large and everything in human experience, including our relationship with God and our relationships with each other. To borrow the words of Abraham Durbeyfield to his sister Tess, in *Tess of the D'Urbervilles*, we live in a "blighted" world rather than a "splendid" one. God has made sure that this is so.[7]

Inevitable Trouble?

Later interpreters of the Old Testament may have understood Genesis 3 in such a way. Importantly, however, the Old Testament *itself* does not lead us to read the chapter in such a way.

It does not, first of all, view the events of Genesis 3 as having significantly affected the character of creation as *God's good creation*—a place blessed by God and entirely wonderful in character. As we read the Psalms, for example, we find them describing creation in exactly the same way as Genesis 1–2 describes it. This is the creation that the psalmists are *currently* experiencing, even *after* evil has entered the world. It is still a place in which the goodness of God is everywhere to be encountered. A good example of this is Psalm 147 (vv. 8-9 and 14-18):

He covers the sky with clouds; he supplies the earth with rain and makes grass grow on the hills.

He provides food for the cattle and for the young ravens when they call . . .

He grants peace to your borders and satisfies you with the finest of wheat.

He sends his command to the earth; his word runs swiftly.

He spreads the snow like wool and scatters the frost like ashes.

He hurls down his hail like pebbles. Who can withstand his icy blast?

He sends his word and melts them; he stirs up his breezes, and the waters flow.

In Psalm 147, then, the events of Genesis 3 have not visibly affected the nature of creation in general. It is still a splendid world.

Second, biblical faith does not view the events of Genesis 3 as inevitably leading to ongoing relational problems between God and *human beings*. Subsequent chapters in the Genesis story make this clear. Abel has a good relationship with God, and both Enoch and Noah are said to have "walked with God" (Genesis 5:24; 6:9)—a walk that is reminiscent of the experience of the first human beings in the garden in Eden (Genesis 3:8). Cain himself is clearly presented with a *choice* in Genesis 4:7. He might well submit to sin, which is pictured as a wild animal crouching at his door, *or* perhaps he will "master" it (Heb. *mashal*). There is nothing inevitable about his submission, as one whose human vocation is to "master" the created order in general.[8] Even while Cain is in fact submitting to sin and even after his murder of Abel, he is still described as living in God's presence and as talking with God. It is only later, in Genesis 4:14 and 4:16, that we hear of Cain *leaving* God's presence. So the expulsion of human beings from the garden does not mean, in Genesis, that they cannot "walk with God."

This communion with God in a "fallen" world, as we saw in our chapter 2, is given institutional expression in the Old Testament both in the Israelite tabernacle and in the temple. Both structures symbolically represent at least the partial reentry of humankind into the garden—into the ordered, good world created by God, where there is no evil or consequent suffering. Within these structures, too, it can be said that God walks among his people and is *their* God (Leviticus 26:11-12). Here, *sacred* space is preserved—the sacred space that the whole world ought to represent. These are the places from which the command is issued, "Be holy because I, the LORD your God, am holy" (Leviticus 19:2)—the places that foreshadow a world that will once again be completely holy. Beyond the tabernacle and temple, the garden in Eden can also be recovered to some extent *in human experience more generally*—when there is humility before God rather than godlike pride (Ezekiel 28; Isaiah 51:3).

Whatever results, then, from the entry of evil into the world in Genesis 3, it is not a fundamental change in the nature of creation nor inevitable, ongoing alienation between God and human beings. On the contrary, God continues to bless the world and the human beings who inhabit it—to walk among them and to commune with them.

THE CALL TO LIFE

All this being so, it is not surprising that the Old Testament does not regard the other consequences of the sin of Adam and Eve as inevitably defining human experience either.

Family and Work

In chapter 5 I mentioned in passing that although in Genesis 3:16 increased pain is associated with the bringing of children into the world, the predominant note struck in the remainder of the Old Testament when mothers and children are described is not pain but joy (Psalm 113:7-9). In chapter 5 I also suggested that the "increased pain" in question is partly bound up with the increased economic difficulties described in Genesis 3:17-19. To raise children is "painful," at least partly, because it is now more difficult to provide for them. I now add the observation that the remainder of the Old Testament does not regard these *economic* difficulties as something with which human beings must inevitably live. Consider, for example, Psalm 128, which promises the person who lives a reverent life before God that his life will be blessed (vv. 2-3):

> You will eat the fruit of your labor; blessings and prosperity will be yours. Your wife will be like a fruitful vine within your house; your sons will be like olive shoots around your table.

Biblical faith knows God above all as a God of blessing. Among other things, God blesses the land and the family, whether this is before or after the events of Genesis 3. The Old Testament does not consider it at all inevitable that "the toil that now lies behind the preparation of every meal is a reminder of the fall."[9] On the contrary, it knows of the possibility of joyous feasting in a thankful spirit, as a consequence of work carried out in a *joyful* spirit. This is surely the message of Ecclesiastes 5:18, which reminds us, "It is fitting to eat and drink and find enjoyment in all the toil with which one toils under the sun the few days of the life God gives us."

This same divine blessing on land and family is already evident in the immediate aftermath of the Genesis fall story. In Genesis 4 the birth of Cain is described. As Leon Kass notes, the chapter "celebrates the birth of a son, without report of pain or trouble to the woman, received joyously by his mother."[10] It also describes successful farming by Cain, without any mention of great difficulty or pain. Cain, we discover later in Genesis 4, does have a dark side, but as the chapter begins, he is farming with good results. Genesis 5 then proceeds to celebrate many births without mentioning pain or difficulty. Shortly thereafter, Genesis 9:20 describes Noah as "a man of the soil" (a farmer), and he is the first in the book to plant a vineyard. Noah's weakness of character is demonstrated in what follows (Genesis 9:21-27), but this should not blind us to the fact that he, too, is portrayed as a *successful* farmer. In fact, it is through his farming that Noah fulfills his father's hope that he would give human beings relief with respect to "the pain of our hands caused by the ground the LORD has cursed" (Genesis 5:29).[11] The cursing of the ground in Genesis 3, then, is not an unchangeable "fate." It *can* be "relieved."

Man and Woman

The struggle for supremacy in male-female relationships envisaged by Genesis 3:16 is also not inevitable. The biblical Song of Songs, for instance, paints a very different picture. The glory of springtime provides the background for much of this book, which constantly evokes in the reader's mind the lush garden of Genesis 2. New life springs forth from the earth, and God's creatures stir and renew their activity.[12] The lovers of the song identify themselves with this wider creation, reveling in it as they affirm each other with images drawn from the flora and fauna that they see around them. Each competes with the other as they try to find ways of extolling the other's beauty. There is no darkness in this. There is only joyous, mutual affirmation and a glorying in what is good. If Genesis gives us the male cry of delight when confronted by the woman ("bone of my bones, flesh of my flesh," 2:23), then the Song of Songs provides us with the reciprocal female cry ("My lover is mine and I am his," 2:16). The woman who in Genesis 3:1-6 takes the initiative and introduces alienation into the male-female relationship becomes in the song the woman who, still taking the initiative, draws the man into intimacy. Together they restore in their love what is fractured in Genesis 3. They meet face to face as equals; they are naked and without shame (Genesis 2:25).

A particularly important connection between Genesis and the Song of Songs, which helps to underline this point, is found in the rare Hebrew word *teshuqah* (desire), which appears in Genesis 3:16 and Song of Songs 7:10. In chapter 5, we saw that in Genesis 3:16 this word describes what happens when sex is wedded to power. Women, just like men, can use sex as a means to their own private ends, "desiring" to dominate their husband—just as sin "desires" (*teshuqah*, same word) to gobble up Cain in Genesis 4:7. The woman in Song of Songs 7:10, however, has given up all "desire" of this kind. She welcomes only the desire of her *lover* for *her*: "I belong to my lover, and his desire (*teshuqah*) is for me." The fallen reality of Genesis 3 is rejected in favor of the creation ideal of Genesis 1–2, and an abrupt halt is brought to the ever-expanding circle of alienation envisaged by Genesis 3–4. Desire is once again mutual and selfless. A connection with the story of Cain in Genesis 4 is also suggested by the phrasing of Song of Songs 7:11, where the woman offers to her lover this invitation: "let us go to the countryside" (Heb. *netse' hassadeh*). She wants to go there so that they can make love. An early version of Genesis 4:8, not reflected in our standard Hebrew text, finds Cain issuing this same invitation to Abel: "Let us go to the countryside" (*netse' hassadeh*).[13] Cain's purpose, however, is not to love his neighbor but to murder him. The two invitations represent two possible pathways through life. On one of these paths, human beings submit to evil, and on the other they do not.

According to the Old Testament, then, there is nothing inevitable about human beings living out the Genesis 3:16 description of male-female relations rather than the vision described in Genesis 1–2. On the contrary, the Song of Songs suggests that it is part of the human task as we live east of Eden to push back against the chaos that has entered the world because of evil and to cooperate once again with God in creating a world that is characterized by order and beauty.

The Human Community

This is true not just of *male-female* relations but also of *human* relations more generally. As it unfolds, the Genesis story describes a world in which terrible things can happen, like Cain's betrayal and murder of Abel in Genesis 4. The story of the world as Genesis tells it, and as it develops in Exodus, Leviticus, and beyond, is not for the faint-hearted. Its authors do not spare us in describing man's inhumanity to man. Yet, in the midst of the world east of Eden virtue is also to be found. There is friendship, loyalty, and self-sacrifice. There is life and not just death— life that can be spoken of in various places as eating from the tree of life. In the biblical book of Proverbs, this life is associated with wisdom, for wisdom is "a tree of life to those who embrace her" and "those who lay hold of her will be blessed" (Proverbs 3:18).[14] In this manner of life, "a longing fulfilled is a tree of life" (Proverbs 13:12) and "the tongue that brings healing is a tree of life" (Proverbs 15:4). Wisdom, a longing ful-filled, a tongue that brings healing—those who experience such things participate in the life of God. They know the blessing of God. To this extent, the tree of life that is found in the garden in Genesis 2–3 is still a matter of present human experience; it has not departed into the mists of ancient history. There is still access to Eden for the person whose life is centered upon God and upon God's dwelling in the tabernacle and in the temple (we recall that the tree of life is itself represented in the lampstands found in these sanctuaries).

To summarize the argument of this chapter so far, then: The Old Testament does not view the events of Genesis 3 as *cataclysmic* events that inevitably changed everything about the world in which we live. Indeed, when it comes to understanding the nature of our world, or how we should live in it in relation to God and to the rest of creation, the remainder of the Old Testament never again refers *back* to the events of Genesis 3 as important for human beings in the present.[15] The biblical authors certainly know that chaos and darkness are threats to creation and that they have been so almost from the beginning. They also know all too well that we are, each of us, born into the very *midst* of chaos and darkness because of the poor decisions of our ancestors and the ongoing poor decisions of our contemporaries. We are touched by these things simply by virtue of being born. There is a powerful sense in some biblical texts of the "baggage" we inherit from the past—the ways in which we are shaped and constrained by the darkness of those who have gone before us. The sins of our forefathers continue to wreak havoc even generations afterward, not least in the habits, customs, and traditions they pass down. There is also a powerful sense of the impact upon us *in the present* not just of individual evil but also of "structural" evil—the ways in which we are shaped and constrained by the darkness of groups and societal structures. Above all, our biblical authors know that we ourselves are far from passive recipients of all this evil—that human beings can, and do, embrace and participate in all the chaos and darkness. Evil, as well as the suffering it brings, has worked its way deeply into human existence. Of this our biblical authors are certain.

However, biblical faith does not regard it as inevitable that we must go on *living* in the world of Genesis 3. It does not hold that we must accept the world as we often find it simply as an expression of "God's will." Indeed, the Bible urges us *not* to do this but rather, by turning back to the creator God and reestablishing communion with him, to know a different world. That world, the biblical authors are confident, is in fact the world that the good God is *anxious* to provide for us. There is, then, no fatalism in the biblical perspective; there is, indeed, a pronounced opposition to fatalism.

CHOOSING OUR PATH

This opposition to fatalism is well illustrated in the way that the prophets Jeremiah and Ezekiel address their contemporaries in the aftermath of the fall of the city of Jerusalem in 587 B.C. to the Babylonian army.

Sour Grapes

Some of the prophets' contemporaries were evidently under the impression that, because of the sins of their ancestors prior to and in the early years of the rise of the Babylonian Empire, *their* "world" had now become cursed by God. A particular proverb was in circulation in the early sixth century: "the fathers eat sour grapes, and the children's teeth are set on edge" (Jeremiah 31:29; Ezekiel 18:2). Their ancestors had sinned, leading to the disaster of 587 B.C., and now they were (so they believed) living with the consequences—living as a people under God's ongoing judgment. It is possible that the proverb had arisen out of a misunderstanding of a passage like Exodus 34:6-7, in which divine punishment for wrongdoing is said to last for generations. Perhaps these Israelites had failed to notice that in this same passage God is said to be "the compassionate and gracious God, slow to anger, abounding in love and faithfulness, maintaining love to thousands, and forgiving wickedness, rebellion and sin." Wherever the faulty view of reality originated, Jeremiah and Ezekiel set out to correct it.

Ezekiel, for example, underlines the way in which God values each individual person and relates to each person as a moral individual, holding each accountable for his own life. Regardless of the circum-stances in which individuals find themselves, says Ezekiel, and even if these are *indeed* the result of God's judgment on their ancestors, God nevertheless expects individuals to make good decisions in the present, doing "what is just and right" (Ezekiel 18:5) and thus coming to know life. The fate of his contemporaries, says Ezekiel, lies in their own hands. It has not been decreed by God on the basis of their forefathers' actions in the past. God takes no pleasure even in the death of the wicked and is pleased when they turn away from their wicked ways (v. 23). Even an *individual's* past does not define what is possible going forward. Since this is the reality, Ezekiel urges his contemporaries to dispense with the misleading proverb—and with the excuse that it gives them to con-tinue in wrongdoing: "Turn away from all your offenses; then sin will not be your downfall. Rid yourselves of all the offenses you have com-mitted, and get a new heart and a new spirit" (vv. 30-31).

The Good God and Choices

Biblical faith does not regard human beings *in general* as fated by their ancestors' sins to live in a certain way, then; neither does it think that *particular* human beings are fated by the sins of their particular fathers. All of this is consistent, of course, with the fact that, in the biblical worldview (as we saw in chapter 3), there *is* only one God, and he is good. There is nothing that God's creatures could ever do, therefore, that *could* be cataclysmic either for the cosmos or for the history of a particular people. This obvious point has apparently been lost on many readers of the Old Testament through the ages, who have interpreted the fall in Genesis 3 as suggesting (virtually) that God has abdicated the throne of the cosmos and given control to some other, darker deity. In biblical thinking, however, God has not abdicated his throne. He con-tinues to bless creation, including human creation, even in the midst of disobedience, and his curses are not fates or destinies imposed upon a hapless humanity unable to do anything to mitigate or reverse them. These curses are, in fact, statements of consequence, bound up with a human being's next set of decisions. We are certainly given a picture in Genesis 3 of what life in a world of human autonomy looks like. From the perspective of biblical faith, however, the world of human auton-omy is not inevitable. We always bear responsibility for *choosing* that world, rather than choosing harmony with God and with the rest of the creation. There are, therefore, two pathways upon which we may walk in life. One involves obedience and blessing, and the other disobedience (autonomy) and cursing. As Deuteronomy 30:15-20 puts it, "See, I set before you today life and prosperity, death and destruction. . . . Now choose life." In this passage, obedience leads to a blessed life in the land, while disobedience leads to death, destruction, and expulsion from the land. This is *exactly* the choice that also lay before the first human beings in Genesis 3, at the macrocosmic level of the whole earth (Heb. *'erets*) that is inhabited by all peoples. Here in Deuteronomy, the choice is offered at the local, microcosmic level of *one* land (also Heb. *'erets*) that belongs to *one* people (the Israelites). In the aftermath of the events of 587 B.C., it was the same local choice that faced the same people of Israel who were addressed by Ezekiel. The message in all three cases—Genesis, Deuteronomy, and Ezekiel—is the same. There is no need to live under the curse. There is no need to live under God's judgment. Human beings must rather choose *life*.

King Ahab Gets to Choose

It is consistent with all of this that elsewhere in the Old Testament narrative, when God's judgment is announced ahead of time, it does not inevitably fall upon those to whom it was promised—if their next decision turns out to be a good one. This is true even of a very wicked person like King Ahab, who in 1 Kings 21:17-29 is told that he will die because of his crimes and that his royal line will die with him. Having heard these words, however, "he tore his clothes, put on sackcloth and fasted. He lay in sackcloth and went around meekly" (v. 27). What is God's response? "Because he has humbled himself, I will not bring this disaster in his day, but I will bring it on his house in the days of his son" (v. 29).[16] We are not told what would have happened if, in his son's day, the son (Joram) too had turned away from evil, but logic suggests a plausible answer. If the very wicked Ahab was able to choose his path, why not his less wicked son (2 Kings 3:2)?

God in the Midst of Suffering

It is also consistent with everything I have been saying thus far that even when God's judgment does fall on people, it is capable of being seen in retrospect as only the loving discipline of a parent who wants to bring his wayward child back onto the right path. This is the case, for example, in Deuteronomy 8:1-5, where the wanderings of the people of Israel in the wilderness are understood as God's "humbling" and "testing" of his people—as an opportunity to learn that "man does not live on bread alone but on every word that comes from the mouth of the LORD" (v. 3). The whole passage is summed up thus: "know then in your heart that as a man disciplines his son, so the LORD your God disciplines you" (v. 5). God may "bring grief" upon those who embrace evil, but "he will show compassion, so great is his unfailing love. For he does not *willingly* bring affliction or grief to the children of men" (Lamentations 3:32-33).[7] This suffering, then, is a consequence of the embrace of evil. Departure from evil ultimately brings relief from suffering. It is the good God's will that this should be so.

From the perspective of biblical faith it is also the good God's will, as far as possible, to bring good *out of* evil and its consequent suffering. The good might simply be the repentance just described, but it might also be something still larger, as in the case of Abraham's descendant Joseph. The story of Joseph (Genesis 37–50) is a story of betrayal—of the embrace of evil by Joseph's brothers, with terrible consequences for Joseph. The book of Genesis tells us, nevertheless, that in his later years Joseph was able to look back on his suffering and say, "You intended to harm me, but God intended it for good to accomplish what is now being done, the saving of many lives" (Genesis 50:20; see further our chap. 10). Then again, the good that comes from evil might be something larger still. In Isaiah 40–55 the suffering of the righteous is a means by which God reaches out and brings salvation to the world. In the climactic passage in Isaiah 52:13–53:12, we learn that *atonement* lies at the heart of this salvation. In chapter 3 we thought about atonement at the microcosmic level of the tabernacle: in the shedding of the blood of the sacrificial victim, peace was made between God and the Israelites—peace that was to lead to holiness. Here in Isaiah 52 and 53, however, atonement takes on macrocosmic proportions: "we all, like sheep, have gone astray, each of us has turned to his own way; and the LORD has laid on him the iniquity of us all" (53:6). Peace is now made between God and the entire cosmos, as God lays all human iniquity on a mysterious sacrificial victim (the "servant"), who breaks "the stranglehold that sin had maintained for countless ages over the human family . . . by bearing the sin of others and pouring himself out to death, the Servant has become the human vehicle through whom . . . others are healed."[8]

East of Eden

In the world east of Eden, then, we are called to choose the right path, in the confidence that evil in the world, and the suffering that follows from it, is not "fate." In choosing the right path, we can be sure that we are turning toward a God who has already turned toward us and stands with us, indeed, in the *midst* of our suffering. We can be sure that we are joining this God in a work he has already begun, leading his creatures on toward the light and abolishing their darkness.

This world east of Eden is one that is well understood, I think, by someone else who has written about it: John Steinbeck, in his novel *East of Eden*.[19] Inspired by the story of Cain and Abel and otherwise deeply influenced by biblical themes, Steinbeck describes a slice of human life in the United States in the late nineteenth and early twentieth centuries. Interestingly, in light of our discussion in chapter 2 about the strange geography of Eden, Steinbeck's story about life *east* of Eden is set in the *western* United States, in California—as far west as settlers could go! Distinguishing east from west is, in fact, a matter discussed early in the novel, and the "geography" of the land has important symbolic overtones throughout.

Steinbeck's world is a world in which there *can* be "thorns and thistles"; one of the central families in the story (the Hamilton family) farms land that is barren and unforgiving. In the course of the narrative, many of the characters make poor decisions, with serious consequences. Adam Trask invests his family fortune unwisely and loses almost all of it. His son Caleb goes off the rails, ultimately exploiting poor farmworkers in order to make his father's money back. His jealousy of his brother Aron leads in the end to his mother's suicide, which in turn leads to Aron's own death and to Adam's stroke. Evil works its way deeply into this family's life, not least in the mother, Cathy, who is heartless and cruel. Earlier in her life, she had killed her parents, and she ends the story as a prostitute who kills *herself.* In Steinbeck's world, Cathy functions as a kind of serpent figure, representing an evil that is deeper than what we find in the other characters.

Yet in this world east of Eden there is also a lot of good to be found. Samuel and Liza Hamilton may farm difficult land, but they are hardworking, good-hearted people. They are well loved by their neighbors, and they build a wonderful home life with their nine children. Samuel is an inventor, and inventors by definition are not defined by the world as they find it. Their daughter Olive becomes a very good mother, representing a stark contrast to the terrible mother, Cathy. In Olive and Cathy, then, we see represented the two ways of living that confront the reader throughout the book.

Indeed, right at the heart of the novel is the question of how far good and evil prosper as a result of choice—the question of free will. The story of Cain and Abel becomes the explicit lens through which this question is viewed, as Samuel, Adam, and the Chinese cook, Lee, discuss its meaning. Steinbeck affirms through these characters that to remain stuck in negative cycles of anger, revenge, and guilt is not inevitable. It is not inevitable, either, that sons and daughters will follow the example of their own parents. Lee's own studies of Genesis 4, we learn, have led him to see that God neither promises Cain that in time he will master sin nor commands him to do so but rather tells him that he *may* (Heb. *timshel*, from the verb *mashal*). Human beings have the ability to choose good over evil. Human beings (as this novel shows) have tremendous potential for love, kindness, and indeed greatness—*even as* they live east of Eden. They also have tremendous potential for depravity, self-destruction, and the destruction of others. They must choose their path. The novel ends with a measure of reconciliation within Adam's dysfunctional family, as he forgives Caleb and blesses him. Evil has been turned toward the good. The last word in this story is not the inheritance that Cathy has bequeathed her family. The last word is, literally, *timshel*—addressed by Adam to Caleb. It is a word of hope: "You may master."

THE PATH OF (AT LEAST) RESISTANCE

What am I to do about evil and suffering, then? Biblical faith proposes, first and foremost, that I am to resist evil, thereby cutting off at its root the tree of suffering that grows from its dark soil. I am not to capitulate to its seductions, and I am certainly not to accept its inevitability; I am instead to pursue steadfastly what is right. "See, I set before you today life and prosperity, death and destruction," says God in Deuteronomy 30:15. "Now choose life." The prophet Micah puts it in different words: "He has showed you, O man, what is good. And what does the LORD require of you? To act justly and to love mercy and to walk humbly with your God" (6:8). Pursuit of what is right begins with right thinking about God, which leads on to right thinking about our fellow human beings and ourselves and about the rest of creation. From this right thinking flow right relationships and right actions. To the extent that the human community walks this right path, refusing to accept that the world of their current experience is the only possible world, it is possible to know life in the garden in Eden. It is possible to flourish.

The extent to which *individual* persons and communities within the broader human community can know this life will, of course, always be deeply affected by what is going on around them. While admiring his desire to resist evil rather than to be passive in the face of it, I must therefore disagree with the words of the anonymous sage cited in the first epigraph to this chapter. It seems to me that human history is replete with instances in which evil has triumphed *even though* good men have done a substantial amount to oppose it. It would be truer to say, then, that *among* the things necessary for the triumph of evil is that good men should do nothing. But it is also true that among the things necessary for the triumph of evil, at least in the meantime, is simply superior numbers of bad men (and women). Thus it is that we find, in human history generally and in biblical thinking in particular, the reality of the righteous person or community that is seeking to walk the right path yet whose flourishing in the world is adversely impacted by a larger community that is not righteous.

The best example of this in the opening chapters of Genesis is Noah, "a righteous man, blameless among the people of his time," who "walked with God" (Genesis 6:9). The society around Noah, however, was terribly wicked—"corrupt in God's sight" and "full of violence" (Genesis 6:11). While Noah would be, in time, the means whereby God would bring redemption to this world, in the meantime he had to live in precisely this same world and to endure the catastrophe that engulfed it. This was not the garden in Eden. More generally, Psalm 106:3 affirms, "Blessed are they who maintain justice, who constantly do what is right." However, the blessing is not always very extensive in a world in which so many do what is wrong. This is why a text like Isaiah 56:1-2 can pronounce a person blessed who maintains justice and does what is right, and in the same breath speak about God's salvation being close at hand and his righteousness *soon* being revealed. Such a person is blessed because he stands on the side of the good God in the world, and (in biblical thinking) this is eventually the winning side. In the meantime, though, it is the wicked who often appear to be winning and the righteous who find themselves oppressed. The prophet Jeremiah can therefore tell God, "I would speak with you about your justice: Why does the way of the wicked prosper? Why do all the faithless live at ease?" The author of Psalm 37:35 likewise sees the wicked, and *not* the righteous, flourishing: "I have seen a wicked and ruthless man flourishing like a green tree in its native soil." Many biblical texts plead with God for an end to this reality. Among these are Psalm 7:9, "O righteous God, who searches minds and hearts, bring to an end the violence of the wicked and make the righteous secure," and Psalm 43:1, "rescue me from deceitful and wicked men."

It is not only men and women who oppose the righteous, however. As the book of Job reveals, the dark forces of the cosmos represented in Genesis 3 by the serpent are also hard at work trying to undermine those who walk on the right path. Like wicked people, these dark forces are given some leeway by God in their pursuit of this end—for reasons that are often completely hidden from the people who are suffering (as in Job's case).

Biblical faith, then, urges resistance to evil, but it does so with a clear-eyed realism about the prospects of success. It recognizes that the human pursuit of right relationships and right actions as a result of right thinking about God and creation may have only limited effects on a present world in which other persons exist who are intent on different goals.

THE PATH OF PATIENT ENDURANCE

It is because resistance to evil frequently itself *meets* resistance that our biblical authors so often urge their readers to be *patient* in pursuing the right path while *enduring* suffering. This is their second answer to the question we are discussing in this chapter. If the right path led us immediately and obviously to "the garden," there would be no need to urge us to keep on walking upon it. The fact is, however, that it does not; in biblical thinking, the triumph of good over evil is not easily achieved. It is not accomplished simply through personal discipline and virtue and certainly not through good organization. Kurt Vonnegut fondly imagines that it might be: "There is no reason why good cannot triumph as often as evil. The triumph of anything is a matter of organization. If there are such things as angels, I hope that they are organized along the lines of the Mafia."[20] To be fair, it is not just authors who have made this mistake throughout history but also bureaucrats and politicians. Be that as it may, it is certainly a mistake, in the biblical way of thinking.

In biblical faith, the right path does not lead humanity immediately and obviously to the garden, since evil and wickedness do not simply lay down their arms when confronted by good. It is possible for those who resist evil, therefore, to doubt their direction and to lose heart, as the author of Psalm 73 tells us with impressive honesty: "But as for me, my feet had almost slipped; I had nearly lost my foothold. For I envied the arrogant when I saw the prosperity of the wicked" (vv. 2-3). It is especially easy to lose heart given the seemingly overwhelming forces that oppose us in our frailty—to come to think of humble human actions in the cause of what is right as meaningless. This is surely what Confucius had in mind when he spoke of the human tendency to view humble actions as only "small acts of goodness . . . of no benefit" (the second epigraph to this chapter)—and therefore to refrain from doing them. It is because of this natural tendency toward despair in the face of evil that the psalmist exhorts us, "Be still before the LORD and wait patiently for him; do not fret when men succeed in their ways, when they carry out their wicked schemes" (Psalm 37:6). Psalm 37 advises, similarly, "Wait for the LORD and keep his way" (v. 34). In Psalm 38 this advice is taken seriously: "I wait for you, O LORD; you will answer, O LORD my God" (v. 15). We should resist evil, but the way is difficult. Therefore, patience in doing good is required—patience even while enduring the suffering that evil creates.

THE PATH OF PRAYER

The foregoing psalm reminds us that, so far as biblical faith is concerned, all that I have detailed so far—the pursuit of the good, resistance to evil, the patient enduring of evil and suffering that we are not currently able to do anything about—is to be carried out in the context of a right relationship with God. The right path through life, in other words, is not a path that humanity is supposed to walk *autonomously*. It can be walked only with God, and it involves conversation with God on the way—what is often called "prayer." This is the third answer given in the Old Testament to the question, what am I to do about evil and suffering? I am not to pray *instead* of acting, as if the doing of *any* good were entirely beyond me. I am, however, to pray in recognition (among

other things) of the *extent* to which the good is currently beyond me—
the extent to which evil forces currently have the upper hand. Indeed, I
am to pray recognizing that *I myself* need to be saved from these forces.
Again, we possess such a model prayer in the Psalms: "turn, O LORD,
and deliver me; save me because of your unfailing love" (Psalm 6:4).
This theme is found repeatedly in the Psalter:

> O LORD my God, I take refuge in you; save and deliver me from
> all who pursue me. (Psalm 7:1)

> Turn your ear to me, come quickly to my rescue; be my rock of
> refuge, a strong fortress to save me. (Psalm 31:2)

> Save me, O God, for the waters have come up to my neck . . .
> those who hate me without reason outnumber the hairs of my
> head; many are my enemies without cause, those who seek to
> destroy me. (Psalm 69:1-4)

Salvation, it is clear, does not come immediately; it can, in fact, take
a *long* time. Psalm 119:84, for example, asks, "How long must your servant wait? When will you punish my persecutors?" In Psalm 6:3 we read,
"My soul is in anguish. How long, O LORD, how long?" The problem of
wickedness, however, does not always lie on the outside. Sometimes the
Psalms recognize that the problem lies *inside* the person praying—that
it is the evil *within* that must be confronted for the praying person to
move ahead on the right path. So in Psalm 51, the psalmist asks God to
"wash away all my iniquity and cleanse me from my sin" (v. 2). Evil has
marked his whole life (v. 5), so he pleads, "Create in me a pure heart, O
God, and renew a steadfast spirit within me" (v. 10). Resistance to evil is
partial, if not futile, if it does not include resistance to the evil *within*.
Deliverance from evil is incomplete, if it does not include the evil that
lies in the heart.

THE PATH OF COMPASSION

We have now explored the first three aspects of the response of biblical faith to evil and suffering: pursuing the good that I am able to
pursue, enduring what I am not able to do anything about, and doing
both of these in the context of a right relationship with God. These
are well summarized in a prayer commonly attributed to the American
Christian theologian Reinhold Niebuhr (1892–1971): "God grant me the

serenity to accept the things I cannot change; the courage to change the things I can; and the wisdom to know the difference."[21] The *fourth* affirmation of biblical faith in response to evil and suffering is this: that I am to show compassion to those who bear their brunt. At present, I may not be able to defeat the evil forces ranged against me and others; the best I might be able to manage, as I walk with God and seek what is right, is patient endurance in the midst of prayer. Yet I *can* offer friendship and help to those who suffer. I *can* alleviate their suffering to the best of my abilities, even as I am unable to change their circumstances. Such compassion is frequently attributed to God himself in the Old Testament, as we saw in chapter 3—the "compassionate and gracious God, slow to anger, abounding in love and faithfulness" (Psalm 86:15), who is good to all and "has compassion on all he has made" (Psalm 145:9). This is a God who looks after people when they are in dire straits, as in the case of these wanderers in the wilderness:

> They will feed beside the roads and find pasture on every barren hill. They will neither hunger nor thirst, nor will the desert heat or the sun beat upon them. He who has compassion on them will guide them and lead them beside springs of water.
>
> (Isaiah 49:9-10)

Such is the compassion of God, and, since human beings have been created as his image bearers, it is not surprising that the same compassion is urged upon them:

> If you lend money to one of my people among you who is needy, do not be like a moneylender; charge him no interest. If you take your neighbor's cloak as a pledge, return it to him by sunset, because his cloak is the only covering he has for his body. What else will he sleep in? When he cries out to me, I will hear, for I am compassionate. (Exodus 22:25-27)

It would be better, of course, if there *were* no needy (Deuteronomy 15:4), but, since there are and since it is beyond my current capacity to change this fact, I must at least treat them with compassion. The biblical response to evil and suffering is not only personal, therefore, but also interpersonal—and indeed costly. I am to join God in showing compassion to my neighbor. It is just such compassion that Job's friends so signally fail to offer him in the midst of *his* suffering in the book of

Job. They prefer instead to hunt for reasons why God might be afflicting him. They see suffering as a theological puzzle to be solved, not as an opportunity to be "like God" to Job.

The Path of Hope

The fifth and final biblical answer to the question at the heart of our present chapter is this: that I am to *hope*. I am to hope for relief from my suffering, and beyond that I am to hope for the victory of good over evil. Beyond *that*, I am to dare to hope that what is bad in the world can somehow be turned to good, in some remarkable cosmic exchange of currency such as is suggested in the Joseph story. I am to dare to believe that even the darkest moments of my life have meaning in some larger, good plan of God for me. While resisting, enduring, praying, and displaying compassion, then, I am to hope—to hope for a world in which "nation will not take up sword against nation, nor will they train for war anymore" (Micah 4:3) and in which nothing will "harm nor destroy on all my holy mountain, for the earth will be full of the knowledge of the Lord as the waters cover the sea" (Isaiah 11:9). Such hope is not misplaced, from a biblical point of view, for the story of the Bible is the story of a God who continually provides relief, defeats evil, and turns bad to good. There is *reason* to hope. We shall return to this theme and explore it much more fully in chapter 11.

An Activist Path

What am I to do about evil and suffering in the world? I am to resist evil and pursue what is right. Where I cannot overcome evil, I am to endure it patiently in hope, while still pursuing what is right. In any event I am to pray that my fellow creatures and I will be rescued from it and to show compassion to others who find themselves the victims of it.

None of these responses, it should be noted, is a passive response. It is a common complaint in post-Christian Western culture (heard loudly in the circles of dark green religion) that at least the *Christian* adherents of biblical faith (leaving the Jews aside) are fundamentally *escapist* in their approach to the world. Christians mainly want to leave this world behind for another one, as soon as possible (the argument goes), and they are not very interested in doing much for *this* one in the meantime.[22] Although this is indeed true of some Bible readers, the Bible itself does not advocate such a stance; the Bible readers in question are simply not reading their Bibles very carefully. All the biblical responses to evil and suffering that I have catalogued in this chapter are responses of people who are convinced that evil, as well as the suffering that derives from it, is indeed a reality of the world in which we find ourselves and that this does make this world often unpleasant and sometimes truly awful. Yet these people are also convinced that evil and suffering are at odds with a deeper and more fundamental reality—the goodness that lies at the heart of the very being of God and of the world that he has created. A world without evil and its consequent suffering beckons such people—a world in which God and his creatures once again share completely sacred, holy space and all darkness and chaos are banished. Biblical faith calls people to inhabit such a world *now,* so far as we can and with God's help. This means taking up the fight, in various ways, against evil. It means refusing to believe that evil is here to stay as part of the fabric of the cosmos and that nothing can be done to change this (alleged) fact. Evil is not inevitable; it is, in the most fundamental sense, temporary. God's people—biblical people— live in the belief that this is so.

EAST AND WEST OF EDEN

It will not come as a surprise to those who have carefully followed the argument of previous chapters in this book that this biblical perspective on the right human response to evil and suffering differs markedly from what we find in many other religious and philosophical traditions. This difference is particularly noticeable in light of the "complaint" I have just described, for it turns out that many of these other traditions are *indeed* defined in terms of escape *from,* rather than change *within,* this world. Whereas the Old Testament calls us to inhabit, so far as we can, a world without evil and its consequent suffering, in these other perspectives we *are* called to depart from this world and to seek entry instead into another world that is already better. Human beings, on such views, are to commit themselves not to *helping rescue* the world from evil and suffering but to *being rescued from* such a world.

Plato

In the West, for example, we recall the Platonic idea of the "real," eternal, and unchanging world in which all human souls once lived. This world is juxtaposed to the shadow world in which we presently live—the world that we see, touch, and smell. The shadow world reminds us of the "real" world, but it is, in the end, only a reflection of it. We recall, moreover, that for Plato philosophy is the means by which one rises up via pure thought to the knowledge of reality. To walk the philosopher's path will, in the end, lead to the release of the immortal soul from its entrapment in the changing world. According to Plato, this process of disentanglement from our unfortunate brush with time and matter may be a long one. In the *Phaedrus*, it is suggested that "ten thousand years must elapse before the soul of each one can return to the place from whence she came."[23] In the meantime, the soul is reincarnated serially in new bodies, until it is embodied as a philosopher. After three successive lives of this sort, in which the philosophical soul retains its knowledge of the Good, it will escape our present world and attain salvation: "they choose this life three times in succession, then they have their wings given them, and go away at the end of three thousand years."[24]

It is not surprising that the Plato who believed all this should also have said that human affairs in this world are not worth taking very seriously.[25] This is only logical, given his overall understanding of the world. If there is no God at work in the world to redeem it, no God with whom I might ally myself in this task, nor any God to whom I might pray about this goal, then why *would* I seek to change the world? The *point* in Plato is certainly not to change it, but to escape it. Thus in the *Phaedo* (not to be confused with the *Phaedrus*),

> The philosopher is described as one who attempts to separate his soul from his body as much as he can, and in effect what this comes to is that he concentrates all his efforts on pure reasoning and pays as little attention as possible to the perceptions, desires, and emotions which arise only because he has a body. This is said to be practicing for death.[26]

The *point*, in Plato's thinking, is not even to pay much *attention* to the world—for example, by performing acts of compassion for those who suffer:

> The morality which our "true philosopher" lays claim to is thoroughly egocentric . . . to this one overriding ambition [escaping the cycle of reincarnation] *everything* else is subordinate, not only the demands of his own body but also all sympathy for

others, all concern for justice, and in short practically everything that we consider important to morality.[27]

None of this is surprising, for ethics and politics are always closely
bound up with cosmology, theology, and anthropology. Plato does not
share the Bible's perspective on the last three; it would be astonishing,
therefore, if he shared it on the first two.

Plotinus

The Neoplatonist philosopher Plotinus (c. A.D. 204–270), while following in the same line of thinking, radicalized Plato's escapism. In *The
Republic*, Plato tells us that even the philosopher can and must be compelled to take an active part in the governing of the city-state. It may
well be that our ultimate purpose and destiny are to escape the world,
but in the meantime there is civic duty to attend to. Human affairs may
not be worth taking very seriously, "but take them seriously is just what
we are forced to do."[28] This, however, is Plato. The quest for salvation in
Plotinus—a quest that will also involve many lifetimes—is undertaken
on a path that leads much more resolutely *away* from life in society.
Two other important philosophies of the Roman Empire, Stoicism and
Epicureanism, at least "had the merit of teaching men how to live in
this world."[29] In the Neoplatonism of Plotinus, however, we encounter
an inclination in Western philosophical thought toward "the contem-
plative and almost monastic ideal of the philosophic life . . . [making]
ethics a study rather of how to live out of society than in it."[30]

According to Plotinus, the practice of civic duty *is* a good *starting
point* from which to begin the quest for salvation, not least because
it teaches discipline and good judgment. The ascent of the soul truly
begins, however, with its purification—a process that involves constant
self-discipline (especially of the thoughts but also of the body). It is a
flight from the world, designed to liberate "the Soul from the cares and
pleasures of this life" and to render it "invulnerable against troubles
coming from outside."[31] Purification enables contemplation, then, of
what is "above" human existence, namely the Good. Salvation lies in
this "above":

> The Soul, whether from its own choice and love of adventure,
> or by the will of the higher powers, has exchanged the peace of

eternity for the unrest of time, and is or should be engaged on the return journey to our heavenly home.[32]

As with Plato, it stands to reason that a person holding such a view of the world will not be much interested in changing it. The important thing will be not to address the evil and suffering of the material world but steadfastly to fix one's gaze on the spiritual world. Unsurprisingly, then, Plotinus displays in his writing a marked indifference toward the world as we find it now. In fact, he shows himself quite capable of what William Inge calls the dispassionate "acceptance of monstrous acts of tyranny and injustice."[33] The philosopher *must* detach himself emotionally from the world in this way if indeed he is to render his soul "invulnerable against troubles coming from outside." All sympathy and pity for others *must* be suppressed, for they are dangerous to the soul's equanimity. It is only natural, then, that Plotinus responds to the many evils and sufferings of the world not by moving toward them in sympathy and (therefore) vulnerability but by withdrawing from them toward the simple "One" who is beyond being and who represents the ultimate goal of the human soul.[34] Such hardness of heart was, in fact, a notable mark of Greek and Roman civilization more generally. Their philosophers did not attempt to apologize for it but went out of their way to justify both the hardness and the resultant passivity with respect to what might nowadays be called "social injustice." The "good" person did not seek to change the world but only himself. In the end, it is no surprise that Platonism could do so little to regenerate the Roman society in which Plotinus lived. Even if the Neoplatonic philosopher could save himself (he thought), he certainly could not save his country.[35] It was not his intention even to try: "the call to seek and save that which was lost . . . the settled purpose to confront 'the world' . . . this call is but faintly heard by philosophers of this type, and they leave such work to others."[36]

Hinduism

This same idea—that the priority of the individual person is not to *help rescue* the world from evil and suffering but to be *rescued from* it— is found in the East as well as the West. In both Hinduism and Buddhism, the passing phenomena of historical, personal existence are not of ultimate importance. Adherents of these religions look (as Plato does) for what is ultimately real beyond the world as we find it. They try to withdraw from attachment to this world in an attempt to escape samsara—the wheel of existence. Within this worldview, there is no reason to seek to change the world as it presents itself to our senses. Indeed, there is—particularly in traditional Hinduism—every reason *not* to seek to change it, because the human beings who inhabit this world are understood to possess their particular stations in life precisely because of the law of karma. It is *just* and *right*, therefore, that each should be living the life that he is living. It is his bounden duty to live out this life—in his class and in his caste—and his progress in future lives depends upon doing this duty well. Any attempt to resist this pattern of life and to bring about social change runs contrary to these deeply rooted beliefs. This is *why* "the caste system in India . . . has not changed substantially in over two thousand years."[37] It is not an historical accident. It is precisely because "the samsaric realm is of little value when compared with the reality that transcends it."[38]

Even in those modes of Hinduism in which the One has come to be understood in personal rather than impersonal terms (e.g., as the gods Vishnu or Shiva) and in which direct access to the One is more broadly available across classes and castes, it is still escape *from* the world rather than transformation *of* the world that is central. The difference is simply that, in these cases, the path to liberation is understood as not so much involving *knowledge* (or in the meantime, the performance of duty) but *devotion* (bhakti) to the deity of one's choice. It is through self-abandonment to a god—turning all desires, wants, and needs to him or her—that I can be helped toward liberation. As Vishnu tells Arjuna in the *Bhagavad Gita* (8.16), "Even in Brahma's cosmic realm worlds evolve in incessant cycles, but a man who reaches me suffers no rebirth."[39]

To the extent that modern Hinduism takes a more activist approach to the world as we find it, this appears largely to be the result of the impact of the biblical worldview on India by way of the Western and Christian presence there before and during colonial rule. Active Christian compassion for those at the bottom of the Hindu social pyramid made a particular impression on people, from the time of the Jesuit Francis Xavier (sixteenth century) onward.[40] While the cosmology, theology, and anthropology of Hinduism "landed" in an ethical and political vision that could not resist evil or mitigate suffering, the impact of the biblical worldview (and its consequent ethical and political vision) was ultimately deeply felt in the Hindu reform movements of the eighteenth century and beyond.[41]

Buddhism

In Buddhism the theme of the renunciation of the world is even more central than it is in Hinduism. This has a lot do with the life of its founder, Siddhartha Gautama, who is central to Buddhist thinking as a model and guide. As a married householder with a child, Gautama was already following what Hindus call the "path of action," when at the age of about twenty-nine he abandoned his wife and child to become a wandering ascetic. In doing so, he turned his back on what Hindus regard as an essential stage in most people's personal spiritual development—the householder stage. In Hindu thought, only a few omit this stage and move on immediately to the renunciation of life in this world. Gautama, however, made immediate renunciation of the world the norm for those on his path to liberation. It was no longer necessary to wait for a lifetime, or many lifetimes, before moving out of "normal" life and seeking nirvana. The Noble Eightfold Path that leads to nirvana must, in fact, be walked *now*, he said, in community with others who have likewise withdrawn into monastic life. Importantly, this path could be walked by *all*, without regard for race or social status (and, to a lesser extent, gender; see chapter 4). The new monastic community transcended all other communities and thus transcended the caste system. To that degree, early Buddhism *was* a socially transformative movement. However, it was transformative only to a certain point, for one joined this community to be *liberated* from the world, not to *change* it. These early Buddhist monks did not, in fact, participate directly in society at all. They withdrew as far as possible, depending even for their subsistence on lay supporters who remained in the socially unchanged world.[42]

This distinction between monks and laity was later challenged by the Mahayana movement within Buddhism, which sought to open the path to Buddhahood to monks and lay supporters alike.[43] One of its innovations was to suggest that some beings who had previously reached nirvana had voluntarily remained in the samsara existence to help others along the way. These were known as bodhisattvas (beings in the process of becoming Buddhas)—some of whom were celestial beings who could be worshipped and asked for help in the hope of reducing one's time in samsara. In this reintroduction of personal gods into a monistic worldview we see a development parallel to, and influenced by, the bhakti development within Hinduism. Out of the Mahayana movement arose forms of Buddhism like Vajrayana (influential in

Japan and Tibet), with its emphasis on rituals and meditative practices that enable the achievement of Buddhahood within a single lifetime, and Pure Land Buddhism (popular in China), which focuses on the worship of the compassionate Buddha Amitabha and promises rebirth in the Pure Land paradise. Yet in these theistic forms of Buddhism we see the same fundamental perspective on human destiny as in theistic forms of Hinduism. It is always release *from* this world and not change *of* this world that is the aim; only the *means* differ. And once again, a more activist approach, which is out of step with Buddhism's deepest historical roots, arises only in the modern period when Buddhist societies are impacted by outside influences.[44] Detachment from the world lies at the historic core of this worldview.

Buddhism is, to be sure, famously associated with compassion—compassion for others and for all living beings. However, this compassion is not (and could not logically be) the compassion of which biblical faith speaks, involving the active alleviation of suffering in this present world as a good in itself. This is most evident in Buddhist discourse about "right thinking" and "right action." Right thinking (one aspect of the Noble Eightfold Path) does certainly entail "thoughts of compassionate aspiration for the well-being of all, tender thoughts of concern for all who are suffering, and the desire to bring goodness and freedom to all living things."[45] Yet when we come to "right action," it is significant that right thinking "lands" in "five ethical precepts," respected as a model for life by all Buddhists, which are framed in terms of *refraining* from certain things, not in terms of actively *pursuing* any.[46] In the end, these precepts have more to do with preserving one's dispassionate walk on the path toward nirvana than with articulating a genuine social consciousness. This is even more clearly the case in the ten precepts embraced by monks and nuns at their ordination. Here the vow takers commit to the five precepts just mentioned as well as five additional precepts, also involving "refraining."[47] Compassion in Buddhism is ultimately about achieving one's *own* release from suffering in the world—about entering into blissful harmony with the One. It is "an *attitude* of pity or empathy for oneself and others who are suffering. . . . [It] contains the *desire* to free all beings from pain."[48] It does not involve any commitment to actually transforming the (merely passing) world such that the suffering of others is lessened or removed. It is logical that this should be so, for in the Buddhist way of thinking, one can be "free of pain" only as one is liberated from samsara. Why, then, devote one's time and energy to the world of samsara? Gautama himself, speaking to his father just before leaving his wife and child to seek liberation, used the metaphor of a burning house to describe this present world: "it is not right to hold by force a man who is anxious to escape from a burning house."[49] Buddhist ethics and politics arise directly from Buddhist cosmology, theology, and anthropology.[50] It is inevitably so.

Islam

Although many people in today's world are confused on this point, including those who have embraced the modern stories introduced in our chapter 1, the biblical perspective on what I am to do about evil and suffering in this world differs markedly from all of the foregoing perspectives. It has a lot *more* in common, however, with a religion like Islam. Like biblical faith, Islam knows of a personal God—one who defines goodness (and therefore evil) and compassion. Like biblical faith, Islam understands that the presence of evil in the world results from a creaturely departure from the prescribed way that God has ordained and urges a return to this way. As in biblical faith, there are two paths, and human beings get to choose which one to take. This choice matters, for it will make a difference for what happens next, even though the ultimate victory of good over evil is in the end assured. There is no escapism in Islam, although there is a future hope. The primary human goal in a world marked by evil and suffering is to pursue change within it, not to escape from it. There is also no fatalism about evil in Islam, not least because Islam shares with biblical faith the conviction that, since there is only one God, the power of evil is limited. This comes out clearly in the retelling of Genesis 3 in the Qur'an, where Adam is said to repent after the primal sin and is then restored to favor as God's "caliph" and as the first of the prophets. Thereafter, each human being is free to obey God's commands and should in fact do so.[51]

In its treatment of evil and suffering, then, Islamic faith is similar to biblical faith in various important respects. The two faiths are not identical, however, and the Qur'an's retelling of the Genesis 3 story already hints at one significant difference between them. They do not agree on the scale of the problem of evil and on which steps need to be taken, and by whom, to deal with it. In Islam each person, individually, can and should turn to God. We may struggle with demons and with our own selves, but we each have the power to follow God's way: "humans have a divinely designed nature that has the capacity of realizing God's design."[52] There is a pronounced emphasis in Islam on individual power and responsibility. We do not find any great emphasis on the extent to which individuals are, in fact, internally compromised by evil or carry significant baggage from the past or face truly problematic structural evils in the present. In Islam, the scale of the problem of evil is not very large. Perhaps this is why Islam is unconvinced, too, about the need for radical divine action in the world (in redemption and atonement) to deal with evil. There is no need for a redeemer, nor for a vicarious atonement, to deal with evil in general and with each person's evil in particular. There is also no need to be inducted into a saving community. Allah has responded to evil simply by sending the Qur'an, and the problem of evil is solved to the extent that individuals turn to God and obey him (on the basis of the Qur'an), rather than going in a different direction. The human problem arose in the first place because individuals headed off in the wrong direction: "in one way or another, all the evils and troubles of the world have their origin in human unbelief."[53] There is, then, in Islam, a very high idea of the freedom of the will: "since sin is not of the essence of humans, it is possible to live in total submission to God's law—that is, it is possible for human beings to be perfect Muslims."[54] Islam is, in the end, about "self-transformation in harmony with God's design of felicity."[55] This transformation lies within the grasp of the committed believer who bends his will to the task.

There are similarities, then, between these two Abrahamic religions, when it comes to our primary question: What am I to do about evil and suffering? However, the similarities should not blind us to the fact that Islam and biblical faith provide fundamentally different answers to some important questions. How far are human beings compromised by evil in their attempts to do good? How significant is their struggle with the "dark forces" of evil in the world? How far does the removal of evil depend on particular actions of God, as well as on our own—on God *himself* taking steps to atone for evil and to redeem his creation? Is *self*-transformation really possible, and is it enough? Confucius would have agreed with Muhammad on such matters, despite their many other differences (see chap. 5). Biblical faith, however, agrees in the end with neither.

7

EVEN THE STORK KNOWS THAT

How Am I to Relate to God?

The great act of faith is when a man decides he is not God.

Oliver Wendell Holmes[1]

Man is born broken. He lives by mending.
The grace of God is glue.

Eugene O'Neill[2]

In the first part of this book I have outlined what I think the book of Genesis, in the context of the whole Old Testament, has to say about five central questions of human existence: What is the world? Who is God? Who are man and woman? Why do evil and suffering mark the world? What am I to do about evil and suffering? In answering these questions, I have sought to clarify the worldview that informs the biblical story by comparing and contrasting it with others—both Eastern and Western. What has gradually been emerging from this discussion is a unique biblical vision of how human life ought to be lived in the world. In the next five chapters I hope further to elucidate this vision. In chapters 8 and 9 we shall consider how Genesis and the rest of the Old Testament envision right relationships—both among human beings (chap. 8) and between human beings and the rest of creation (chap. 9).

In chapter 10 we shall explore more generally the question of the good society, and in chapter 11 we shall consider what it is that we are to hope for while living in that society. All of this rests fundamentally, however, on the answer to the question I pose in this chapter: How does biblical faith consider that I am to relate to God?

ON GIVING UP ON DIVINITY

The heart of the Genesis response to this question is well expressed in the words of Oliver Wendell Holmes cited in the first epigraph to this chapter: "the great act of faith is when a man decides he is not God." These words implicitly acknowledge that human beings have a habit of doing just the opposite—of capitulating to a desire to be "like God," rather than recognizing human creatureliness. We have already seen this reality illustrated in the story of Genesis 3, which traces the habit right back to the very beginnings of human experience in the world and understands it as lying at the heart of various human problems. In Genesis 3, the human pair is not content with the knowledge that God has given them so that they can fulfill their roles as image bearers of God. They want instead to *be* gods, in the fullest sense, rather than *representing and mediating* God to creation. They are prepared to disobey God in pursuit of this goal, blurring the line between Creator and creation that is sharply drawn in Genesis 1–2. Ironically, it is their very dignity as image bearers that enables this mistake to be made.

God Cannot Be Imaged

It is important to remember in this connection that, in general, biblical faith sets its face against *any* attempt to image God in something that is part of creation. The God who appeared to Moses in the burning bush and later rescued Israel from Egypt cannot even truly be *named* like a normal ancient Near Eastern god, and he certainly cannot be assigned a function in the cosmos.[3] God is simply "I am who I am" (Exodus 3:14). This is not so much a name as it is a statement of intent—the intent to be free in one's being and activity.[4] Nor can the God of the burning bush be captured in "an idol in the form of anything in heaven above or on the earth beneath or in the waters below" (Exodus 20:4). Unlike the religious faith of other ancient Near Eastern cultures, Israel's faith (when it really is Mosaic, biblical faith) is resolutely aniconic—it does not involve images of God. This is equally true of Islam. Here, too, "to liken God to anything created raises the danger of compromising God's oneness" and is to commit the grave sin of *shirk* (associating something else with God).[5] Walter Brueggemann refers to the significance of the aniconic nature of Hebrew religion in this way:

> If it is correct . . . that an imageless quality is [God's] distinctive characteristic, then we may see in the prohibition of images an assertion of the unfettered character of [God], who will not be captured, contained, assigned or managed by anyone or anything, for any purpose.[6]

The unseen God who speaks to Moses from the fire cannot be represented by any created thing. This God cannot be captured in any creaturely form.

It is this conviction that explains the caution exercised by biblical authors even when they attempt *linguistic* representation of God—lest they give the impression that God can be fully captured in human language. Perhaps the most notable example of this is found in Ezekiel 1, where the prophet Ezekiel receives a vision of God. It is no doubt a vision of *God*, but it is remarkable how God is described. In fact, the author goes out of his way, through the constant use of the language of analogy, to avoid the impression that God really *can* be described. He tells us about the *likeness* of things in God's realm—not about the things in themselves. What he sees, he tells us, *looks* like torches, like sapphire, like a human being. He does not, however, tell us what (exactly) is really there. Analogy piles upon analogy as we arrive at verses 26-28:

> Above the expanse over their heads was what *looked* like a throne of sapphire, and high above on the throne was a figure *like* that of a man. I saw that from what *appeared* to be his waist up he *looked* like glowing metal, as if full of fire, and that from there down he *looked* like fire; and brilliant light surrounded him. Like the *appearance* of a rainbow in the clouds on a rainy day, so was the radiance around him. This was the *appearance* of the *likeness* of the glory of the LORD.

God remains cloaked in mystery—even though he has certainly revealed himself to Ezekiel. Ezekiel has seen God, but human language cannot in the end *capture* what has been seen.

The unseen God cannot be represented by any created thing. This God cannot even be captured in the officially sanctioned structures of the Israelite worship system—even in the temple in which he has agreed to "dwell" (1 Kings 8:10-12), for in truth, "will God really dwell on earth? The heavens, even the highest heaven, cannot contain you. How much less this temple I [Solomon] have built!" (1 Kings 8:27). God's presence in the Jerusalem temple is real enough, as it was in the tabernacle beforehand, but God cannot be *captured* in either place.

The Worship of the Image

It is precisely because of all the voluminous material in the Old Testament that insists upon this clear distinction between Creator and creation that what is said about human beings as created *in the image and likeness of God* (Genesis 1:26-27) must be considered so remarkable.[7] If there *is* some created thing that can image God, our biblical authors tell us, it is this animated creature who is set apart from the rest of creation. And here is precisely where the human temptation lies. It is the temptation to view the image of God in human beings as something to be worshipped, just like other images in the ancient world existed to be worshipped. It is the temptation to turn from the worship of God to the worship of self—to pursue self-advancement, rather than the good of creation in service to God.

According to Genesis, it is this worship of the autonomous self as god that lies at the heart of what is wrong with the world. This is the fundamental idolatry. However, because human beings are *not*, in fact, gods, this worship of the self spawns still other idolatries. Because we are, in fact, incapable of supplying our own need for divinity, even as "gods," we look elsewhere. In biblical thinking, therefore, the abandonment of the living God is not followed by atheism but by polytheism. We elevate other aspects of the created order, along with ourselves, to divine status, and we offer these creatures, too, devotion and trust of which they are not worthy. In the ancient world out of which biblical faith emerged, the sun, moon, and stars were important deities of this kind, as were the gods associated with weather systems and fertility. All these deities "lived" in the world through the cult images placed in their temples, and their popularity, both inside and outside ancient Israel, can be gauged by how often their worship is attacked in the Old Testament (e.g., Isaiah 44:9-20; Jeremiah 10:1-10; Hosea 13:2).

From the perspective of biblical faith, however, worship of the gods is not the only way the distinction between God and creation can be obscured. The biblical authors also attack inappropriate human devotion to, or dependence upon, other *human beings*. Ezekiel 16:1-34, for example, provides us with a graphic and disturbing metaphorical account of Israel's history as God's "wife," who turned to adultery with Egypt, Assyria, and Babylon. Here the most common and well-developed metaphor in the Old Testament for idolatry—the sexual unfaithfulness of a wife to a husband—is employed in connection with political alliances with other nations. The same is true in Isaiah 31:1-3, where military reliance on Egypt is portrayed as akin to abandoning the true God and treating the Egyptians as if they were divine. In truth, however, "the Egyptians are men and not God" (v. 3). The ancient Israelites evidently had difficulty in maintaining this distinction, for time and again in the Old Testament it is Egypt—that richly fertile and very powerful country—to which they wish to "return" (e.g., Exodus 14:10-12) and that they are often tempted to imitate (e.g., Deuteronomy 17:14-20). Such texts make it clear that, in biblical faith, idolatry (misplaced worship) involves far more than the practice of a certain type of ritualistic religion. Idolatry is a matter of the whole orientation of a person's (or nation's) life. It is expressed not just in religious life but in social, economic, and political life as well.

The Destructiveness of Idolatry

In all of this biblical material, there is a powerful sense that idolatry is not only fundamentally wrong but also enormously destructive. It is not *only* that the worship of the creation rather than the Creator is offensive to God, and a perversion of the true nature of things (although it *is* both of these). It is also that in worshipping idols rather than God human beings do damage to themselves, to each other, and to the world in which they live. To turn from God to "gods" is to embrace a lie about reality. The serpent speaks with a forked tongue in Genesis 3 when he advocates this path. When humans respond to him by taking a half step toward divinity, it does not bring the wonderful life that he offers, but only alienation and separation from God. What results is the loss of any true sense of what it means to be a human being. This is because we are fated always to become like that which we worship, as our moral and religious compass swings to the magnetic pole of our idol. To go after false idols is to become false (2 Kings 17:15); to worship the works of human hands is to become like them (Psalm 115:8). When we forget who God truly is, the biblical authors propose, it is but a short step to forgetting who *we* are, who our *neighbor* is, and what the *world* is. All right knowledge depends upon the right knowledge (and worship) of the living God.

The book of Daniel works this out in a thoroughgoing way, picturing a world in which the worship of the one true God has all but disappeared. It is a world, Daniel tells us, that is governed by "beasts"—the beastly empires described in Daniel 2 and 7. It is a world, therefore, that has been turned upside down. The world created by God is one in which human beings should govern the animals (Genesis 1:26-30), but in Daniel, the "animals" govern the human beings. Here the idolatry of the self has been transposed into the idolatry of the state, and upon human beings who refuse such idolatry suffering falls, whether in fiery furnaces or in lions' dens or in some other way.[8] This is what happens when the emperor, in particular, comes to think that he is a god (Daniel 3). The book of Daniel illustrates well the general biblical point: that worshipping as a god anything that is not in fact God must ultimately have drastic consequences for human beings and also for the creation they are supposed to govern and care for on behalf of the Creator. It is not surprising that our biblical authors should take this view, for, as we have already seen in earlier chapters, cosmology and theology are always bound up with anthropology, and then with ethics and politics. What we believe about the nature of God and of the world is always closely bound up with our beliefs about human beings—how we should live, both individually and in society. Therefore, to exalt the created as divine; to make gods in the image of men, women, or animals; to substitute for God anything that is less than God—all of this, in the estimation of our biblical authors, can only lead to disaster.

That is why in the Old Testament idolatry is often described not so much as the infraction of a divine commandment but as the committing of an act of cosmic insanity. "Even the stork in the sky knows her appointed seasons, and the dove, the swift and the thrush observe the time of their migration" (Jeremiah 8:7), but the Israelites are too foolish, apparently, to know when the time has come to repent of idolatry. "The ox knows his master, the donkey his owner's manger" (Isaiah 1:3), but the Israelites constantly forget to whom they rightly belong.

In response, God appeals to his people to come to their senses (Isaiah 1:18). If the animals can recognize reality when they see it, surely the same must be true of God's image bearers, who have been granted the privilege of looking after his garden. In the Qur'an we find this same idea: that humanity, alone in creation, is out of step with God:

> Time and again, the Qur'an repeats the theocentric message that everything was created by God and is controlled by God. Most of nature accepts that situation and does not try to rebel or deny God's authority. Only humanity attempts to wrestle control from God and assert its independence . . . people must read the signs of creation to learn what true submission is.[9]

The "signs" must indeed be read, for to misread reality, to misplace our worship—in short, to be an idolater—is to court catastrophe.

Crossing the Line in Genesis 6

In Genesis the human desire to be "like God" is discovered not only in chapter 3 but also in chapters 6 and 11. In Genesis 6 we are two chapters removed from the story of Cain and Abel. Life continues outside the garden, and Cain's family line has reached its seventh generation—a number that, in accord with its typical use in the ancient world, represents the "fullness" or "perfection" of Cain's line. This perfection, however, is ugly. It is embodied by Lamech, who boasts to his wives of his excessive vengeance: "I have killed a man for wounding me, a young man for injuring me" (Genesis 4:23-24). With Lamech, the alienation of human being from human being that first occurs in Genesis 3 has become even more pronounced. In Genesis 3 the man is alienated from the woman—but they remain together and build a community. In Genesis 4, brother is alienated from brother (Cain from Abel), and the consequences are far more serious: death on one side and exile on the other. With Lamech, the alienation then extends into the broader community. As we transition into Genesis 6, it progresses still further outward.

Here we read that "the sons of God saw that the daughters of men were beautiful, and they married any of them they chose" (Genesis 6:2). The "sons of God" in this case are most likely angelic beings (as in Job 1:6), conceived of as intermarrying with human females in much the way that we commonly find in ancient Near Eastern texts.[10] To cross the boundary between earth and heaven is inappropriate, and this is immediately indicated by the language of Genesis 6:2, which parallels Genesis 3:6. The latter text tells us that when "the woman saw [Heb. *ra'ah*] that the fruit of the tree was good [Heb. *tov*] . . . she took some [Heb. *laqakh*]." In the former, "The sons of God saw [Heb. *ra'ah*] that the daughters of men were beautiful [Heb. *tov*], and they married [Heb. *laqakh*] any of them they chose." From the human side, the motivation behind such marriages seems to be the same as the one lying behind the eating from the tree—these people want immortality. I deduce the similar motivation from the similar consequence. Like the human grasping after divinity in Genesis 3, these marriages bring death: "my Spirit will not contend with man forever, for he is mortal; his days will be a hundred and twenty years" (6:3). In the aftermath of the intrusion of death into the world in Genesis 5, in chapter 6 human beings once again attempt to access the realm of immortality. They are met with a stern *reminder* of mortality, in the form of an abbreviation of the human life span." Shortly afterward we learn about the kind of world that results when such boundaries are crossed. In Genesis 1:10, God looks at the world and sees (Heb. *ra'ah*) that it is good (Heb. *tov*). When God looks at this very same world in Genesis 6:5, however, he sees (Heb. *ra'ah*) only the great magnitude of human wickedness (the similar-looking *ra'ah*, which is opposite to *tov*). As so often in the Hebrew language, the wordplay underlines the point that is being made: striving to change themselves into immortal beings, humans have succeeded only in changing the world—for the worse.

Crossing the Line in Genesis 11

The line is crossed again in Genesis 11, where we read of an attempt to build in Babylonia (literally "Shinar") "a city, with a tower that reaches to the heavens, so that we may make a name for ourselves and not be scattered over the face of the whole earth" (Genesis 11:4). The traditional Mesopotamian building method is envisaged—"brick instead of stone, and tar for mortar" (in Palestine, stone and mortar would have been used). What is the significance of the Tower of Babel (i.e., Babylon)? As we saw in chapter 2, the major temple complexes in ancient Mesopotamia featured (along with the temple) both a garden, symbolizing the fertility provided by the deity, and a pyramid-like ziggurat. The gods were thought to enter the earthly realm by way of the ziggurat, descending via its staircase to the temple at its foot to receive the gifts and worship of the people and to bring blessing, stability, and order to the community. It is no doubt a ziggurat that the Genesis authors have in mind in describing their "tower." Ziggurats are often said in Babylonian texts to have their "heads in the heavens," which is precisely the language used of the "tower" in Genesis 11:4—it "reaches to the heavens" (literally, "with its head in the heavens").

In Genesis 11, however, the building of the ziggurat symbolizes not piety in respect of the gods but opposition to the will of the one true God. It is associated with the idolatry of the corporate self. Commanded to "be fruitful and increase in number and *fill the earth*" (Genesis 9:1), the people described in Genesis 11 choose instead to settle down in one place. They refuse to be scattered "over the face of the whole earth," for they are intent on making "a name" for themselves. People possessing a name, in this sense, have already appeared in Genesis 6:1-4. They are the offspring of the aforementioned divine-human marriages— the "Nephilim," who are said to be "men of renown" (Heb. "men of the name"; Genesis 6:4).[12] Elsewhere in the Old Testament, however, it is only God who rightly makes a name for himself:

> Where is he who set his Holy Spirit among them, who sent his glorious arm of power to be at Moses' right hand, who divided the waters before them, to gain for himself everlasting renown.
> . . . This is how you guided your people to make for yourself a glorious name. (Isaiah 63:11-14)

For a mortal being to make a name for *himself*, then, is inappropriate. It is to seek to be "like God" in a wrong way—the "original sin" of Genesis 3.[13] This is the significance of the Tower of Babel. Its builders want to make a name for themselves, and they are prepared to disobey God to achieve this "heroic" goal.[14] Of course, their attempt at human solidarity in opposition to God, co-opting religion in the service of self-worship, is inevitably doomed, precisely because they are *not* God. "Let us make bricks," they say in Genesis 11:3 (Heb. *nilvenah*, "make"). God responds in verse 7 with "let us . . . confuse their language" (Heb. *navelah*, "confuse"), and it is confusion, not building, that occurs. The play on words, in this case, underlines not only who has the real power but also the appropriateness of his response: the idolaters receive poetic justice. Diversification of language, we are told, scatters them from

Shinar "over all the earth," and they stop building the city (v. 8). They become unable to cooperate in their disastrous project, and they begin to go their separate ways.

The name of the city that remains afterward is a *reminder* of what results from the idolatry of the corporate self—the community or the state. The Babylonians understood Babel to mean "gate of the god," but to the authors of Genesis its name signifies "confusion" (Heb. *balal*). It is not *blessing* on the human community that results from the building of this city and its ziggurat, they claim—the blessing that comes, in Mesopotamian thinking, from a god who passes through the gate to be with his people. What results is only the *fracturing* of true human community. Left to themselves, the peoples of the earth, with their "Mesopotamian" religion, would have built a corrupt civilization throughout the earth. The multiplicity of languages on the earth, then, is itself a blessing of God. It prevents monolithic, corrupt culture from developing unchecked in the world, just as the expulsion of Adam and Eve from the garden prevents the possibility of immortal, dysfunctional family life.

In the Genesis story, then, the true and living God does not enjoy a settled existence in Babylonia with a people whose primary interest is in their own reputation. The true and living God is rather to be found traveling with an obscure people, the family of Abraham, who embark on a long pilgrimage with God throughout the world, *leaving* Babylonia (and later Syria) because God tells them to (Genesis 11:31–12:5). This is what true image bearers of God *do*, in the biblical estimation. They travel with God. In the course of traveling with God, they bless other people, rather than building up their own imperial self-esteem: "All peoples on earth will be blessed through you," Abraham is told (Genesis 12:3).[15] Before speaking specifically of Abraham, Genesis tells us a little about his ancestors (11:10-32), the first of whom is named Shem. This is not accidental, for the Hebrew word *shem* means "name." God has a plan, which is to bless the entirety of creation. In executing this plan, he does not recruit those who are intent on making a name for *themselves*, but the descendants of someone who has been *given* a "name" (Shem). In the end, the name of Abraham itself *will* be great, but it will not be his own doing: "I will make your name great," God tells Abraham, "and you will be a blessing" (Genesis 12:2).[16]

The divine call to leave a polytheistic environment and to travel instead with the one true God to a new land is a recurrent feature of the biblical story that follows. In Exodus 3–15, Moses is remembered as being called by God to lead the Israelites out of the other great civilization of the ancient Near East—Egypt—in the midst of a mighty battle between the one living God and the allegedly divine Egyptian pharaoh. They leave Egypt and eventually end up (like Abraham) in Palestine. Later, Joshua exhorts the people, even after their entry into this promised land, to "throw away the gods your forefathers worshiped beyond the River [Euphrates] and in Egypt, and serve the LORD" (Joshua 24:14). Either they do not throw them away, or they later retrieve them, for it is the ongoing worship of the many gods of the ancient Near East that is ultimately responsible for the exile of the people of Israel from Palestine in the sixth century B.C., when they find themselves back in Mesopotamia (2 Kings 17:7-23). Again the Israelites find that they must leave a (polytheistic) foreign land, as some of them do in the books of Ezra and Nehemiah. By this point in the story, however, it has become clear that "leaving" is more about existential commitment than about change of location. The persistence of Israelite polytheism, *wherever* the descendants of Abraham live, leaves no room for doubt on this point. They are, it seems, always prone to "return" to "Egypt," in their life practices if not in their travels (Deuteronomy 17:14-20).

The Great Act of Faith

From the perspective of biblical faith, then, Oliver Wendell Holmes is right: "the great act of faith is when a man decides he is not God." It is when he agrees that he is instead a creature of God, called to walk with God and to do God's will. This involves departing from the worship of all other gods, including the worship of the self—whether individual or corporate. It involves acceptance of the difference between the Creator and the creation. There is one God, distinct from the cosmos he has created, and certainly not originating within it. There is one God, sovereign over this cosmos and incomparable with respect to anything else that might be worshiped as a god. How am I to relate to this God? First things first: I am to acknowledge that God is God and that I am not.

ON TRUSTING IN THE GOODNESS OF GOD

The second thing is to acknowledge that God is good. It is possible (as I pointed out in chap. 3) to conceive of one incomparable, sovereign, creator God who is malevolent, or at least arbitrary and unpredictable and therefore never to be trusted. Biblical faith, however, does not conceive of God in this way. Instead (as we saw in chap. 5), it identifies lack of confidence in the goodness of God as intrinsic to human alien-ation from God—as central to the brokenness of our right relationship with God.

Suspicion and Trust

The serpent's tactic in Genesis 3, we recall, is to suggest that God is arbi-trary—that God enjoys issuing unreasonable prohibitions rather than being primarily concerned with freedom and blessing. In making this proposal, the serpent attempts to shift attention away from all that God in his generosity has provided for his human creatures and onto the one thing that he has forbidden (viz., eating from the tree of the knowledge of good and evil). The human pair buys into this vision of God, choos-ing to view him ungenerously and suspiciously. They disobey him, and then they hide from him. But the disobedience is not the *beginning* of it all. The problems *begin* with the denial of God's goodness.

The person whose right relationship with God has been restored, by contrast, is the person who recognizes that, when God provides instructions for life, they are to be interpreted in the light of his good-ness; indeed, they represent an *expression* of God's goodness. Like the psalmist, she affirms that "the LORD is good and his love endures for-ever; his faithfulness continues through all generations" (Psalm 100:5). She acknowledges, "You are forgiving and good, O Lord, abounding in love to all who call to you" (Psalm 86:5). She responds gladly to the exhortation "give thanks to the LORD, for he is good; his love endures forever" (Psalm 106:1). She celebrates God's steadfast love (Heb. *khesed*), which she understands to be unceasing and abundant: "the steadfast love of the LORD never ceases, his mercies never come to an end; they are new every morning" (Lamentations 3:22-24; NRSV). She also cel-ebrates God's faithfulness, recognizing that God is "abounding in love and faithfulness" (Exodus 34:6) and that his "faithfulness [reaches] to the skies" (Psalm 36:5). She rejoices that God is "majestic in holiness, awesome in glory, working wonders" (Exodus 15:11), for she understands God's holiness as pure goodness in search of a thoroughly good world. She rejoices, too, in God's anger, which she understands is not a mat-ter of whim or caprice nor quickly or lightly expressed yet is a necessary aspect of the character of a good person faced with a corrupt world. She delights in the God who is "compassionate and gracious . . . slow to anger, abounding in love and faithfulness" yet who "does not leave the guilty unpunished" (Exodus 34:6-7). She is glad that this is a "God who avenges" (Psalm 94:1-3), bringing retribution on wrongdoers and ensuring justice for the weak and oppressed. She is glad that God is "a jealous God" (Exodus 20:4-5)—intolerant of rivals—and understands that this is good, not least because of the damage that idolatry does. She is very glad that this is a God who "pardons sin and forgives the transgression of the remnant of his inheritance" and who does not "stay angry forever but delight[s] to show mercy" (Micah 7:18).

All these aspects of God's goodness were rehearsed at greater length in chapter 3. I remind the reader of them here to make this one suggestion: that to relate rightly to God, in biblical faith, is to *embrace* all of them *as* aspects of God's goodness and to hold on tightly to this multifaceted goodness in all circumstances. Right relating to God, in fact, involves at its core a refusal to adopt *any* interpretation of our lives in this world (or, for that matter, any interpretation of the various parts of the Old Testament) that is inconsistent with this understanding of God as good. The righteous person begins not from a place of suspicion but from a place of trust.

Lament and Trust

The temptation to *distrust*—to adopt a false interpretation of God—is, of course, a strong temptation. Our biblical authors understand this very well and record many stories from Israel's past where such a temptation has arisen. To take one example, consider the immediate aftermath of the story of the exodus from Egypt. In Exodus 15, a wonderful hymn of praise to God proclaims confidently, "In your unfailing love you will lead the people you have redeemed" (v. 13). Exodus 15 is followed immediately, however, by Exodus 16, where the same Israelites sing a different "song": "If only we had died by the LORD's hand in Egypt! There we sat around pots of meat and ate all the food we wanted, but you have brought us out into this desert to starve this entire assembly to death" (v. 3). Here is the "return to Egypt" I mentioned earlier. The experience of hunger has quickly led these Israelites to a false interpretation of God (and their situation); they have come to doubt Moses' (and God's) good intentions toward them. *Rather than* trusting, they complain.

A different response to temptation is modeled in Psalm 73. The author of this psalm is certainly struggling to hold onto his own faith in God's goodness: "But as for me, my feet had almost slipped; I had nearly lost my foothold. For I envied the arrogant when I saw the prosperity of the wicked" (vv. 2-3). When the wicked prosper, it is all too easy to interpret their prosperity as indicating a deficiency in God's goodness; it is all too easy to feel foolish about continuing to trust: "surely in vain have I kept my heart pure; in vain have I washed my hands in innocence" (v. 13). The psalm does not ultimately take this view, however, and it is designed to help others who read it and pray it likewise not to take this view. As we move toward its conclusion, we find that in the course of his prayer the psalmist has processed his doubts, and has arrived at a renewed confidence: "my flesh and my heart may fail, but God is the strength of my heart and my portion forever" (v. 26).

This kind of prayer, often referred to as a "lament psalm," is one of the ways of rightly relating to God in biblical faith. God is good, yet his goodness appears to be absent in human experience right now. What is to be done? The answer advocated in the lament psalms is neither to give up on the goodness of God nor to pretend that things are better than they are. In the lament psalms, we see honest *confrontation* of the fact that there is a gap between theology, on the one hand, and experience, on the other. This gap is brought to God in prayer, and trust is renewed in God's goodness through the *process* of prayer. The psalms of lament are, therefore, regarded in biblical faith as being just as important for right relating to God as the psalms of praise. In these compositions, lament and trust go together; they are not alternatives. The challenging circumstances of life are neither ignored nor taken as a reason for turning away from God. They are fully described *before* God, and they issue characteristically in the prayer of those who still trust in his goodness: "turn, O Lord, and deliver me; save me because of your unfailing love" (Psalm 6:4).

Faith and Trust

This trust in God's goodness—in who God really is—is the essence of what the Old Testament considers as genuine *faith* in God. Faith is not merely *believing* certain things about God, nor is it simply *acknowledging* that God is good. Faith is *trusting* oneself to the goodness of God. In the book of Genesis, such faith is illustrated most clearly in the story of Abraham, who "believed the Lord, and he credited it to him as righteousness" (Genesis 15:6). Abraham trusted in God when God told him that, against all reasonable odds, he would have an heir—many descendants, in fact (Genesis 15:1-5). He trusted that God's good intention to bless him with these descendants would not be frustrated. Later, after his heir was born, Abraham trusted in God even when it appeared that God was going to take his child away (Genesis 22)—when it appeared, in fact, that God might not be good after all. Abraham's entire life, from his departure from Mesopotamia to his death in Palestine, can be seen as one long testing of his faith in God's goodness. Abraham did not just believe, intellectually, that God is good; he *trusted* himself and his family to the God whom he believed to be good, and he lived his life accordingly.

Later in the biblical story, King Hezekiah of Judah provides another example of this same faith. In his case, however, the choice to trust in God *rather than in idols* is perhaps even more striking. In 2 Kings 18:5, we are told that there was "no one like him among all the kings of Judah," who "trusted in the LORD" the way he did. In the story that follows, this trust is severely tested when the Assyrian king Sennacherib invades Judah and sends an army to besiege Hezekiah's capital city, Jerusalem (2 Kings 18:13-16). When the Assyrian emissaries arrive at his gates, they probe the basis of Hezekiah's "trust."[7] Does Hezekiah trust in human help from Egypt, as King Hoshea of Israel did before him, to no avail (2 Kings 17:4)? Such trust is misplaced, for Pharaoh is only the "splintered reed of a staff," unable to offer any genuine support (18:21). Do Hezekiah and his officials trust in God, then? But is it not God's sanctuaries in Judah (the Assyrians allege) that Hezekiah has just destroyed (v. 22)? Why would God help Hezekiah, under such circumstances? *Could* God help him, even under *different* circumstances? After all, no other god has hitherto been able to deliver "his land from the hand of the king of Assyria" (vv. 33-35). It will be no different, the Assyrian emissaries suggest, in the case of Judah and Jerusalem. If the Judeans persist in their rebellion, they will die, and if Hezekiah thinks otherwise, he is in fact being *deceived* by the God in whom he trusts (2 Kings 19:10). Under such great pressure to concede to what appears to be reality, Hezekiah chooses a different path—the continued path of trust and prayer (2 Kings 19:14-19). The God who has adopted Israel as a special people, he affirms, is not merely one god among many. He is God alone, Creator of "heaven and earth—God over all the kingdoms of the earth" (v. 15). It is undeniable that the Assyrians have known great success, destroying the gods of the various nations they have conquered. However, these were not truly gods. They were "only wood and stone" (v. 18). In order that all the kingdoms of the earth should know the difference between God and the gods, Hezekiah asks God to deliver

Jerusalem from the Assyrian's hand. Against all the odds, the city is duly delivered (19:35-36).[18]

What, then, do we learn from Abraham and Hezekiah about relating rightly to God? We learn that a deep-seated trust that God is good is fundamental to biblical faith. On this the Bible and the Qur'an agree: "If you tried to count God's blessings, you could never take them all in: He is truly most forgiving and most merciful" (16:18).

ON LOVING GOD

It is only out of this trust in the goodness of God—this fundamental conviction that God is *for* us—that there can arise the *love* for God that biblical faith also places at the heart of a right relationship with God. Such love would be impossible if God were a malevolent, arbitrary, or unpredictable person who could never be trusted. It is only the conviction that God is good—that God persistently and seriously loves his creatures—that can stir love in the human heart for God. It is precisely because God *is* such a God that the Israelites are *commanded* to love him, in words that are well known to many: "Hear, O Israel: The LORD our God, the LORD is one. Love the LORD your God with all your heart and with all your soul and with all your strength" (Deuteronomy 6:4-5).

The Hebrew verb here is *'ahav*—a common verb for "love" in the Old Testament. As such, it refers among other things to the attraction of an unmarried person to someone of the opposite sex (Genesis 29:18), to a husband's love for his wife (1 Samuel 1:5), to a parent's love for a child (Genesis 22:2), to the love of a daughter-in-law for her mother-in-law (Ruth 4:15), and to the love of a people for a hero (1 Samuel 18:16). It implies affection for, care for, delight in, and admiration for the other person. It also implies reverence and complete loyalty. As God has loved Israel "with an everlasting love" (Jeremiah 31:3), so the Israelites are to love God with the entirety of heart, soul, and strength. In Hebrew anthropology, the heart is the organ with which one thinks and makes moral choices; it includes what modern people would call the "mind." The soul is simply "the whole inner self, with all the emotions, desires, and personal characteristics that make each human being unique."[9] In the language of Psalm 103, it is "all my inmost being" (v. 1). Therefore, to love God "with all your heart and with all your soul" is to love God with the whole self, including rationality, will, and inner feelings and desires. To do so "with all your strength" is to put everything into it.

This love commandment is therefore closely linked in biblical thinking not only to the idea of God's goodness but also to the idea that God is one, and not many. Deuteronomy 6 itself implies the link, in its juxtaposition of this commandment to the preceding statement: "The LORD our God, the LORD is one." The implication is that there is a connection between the oneness of God, on the one hand, and the single-mindedness and wholeheartedness of the right human response to God, on the other.

This demand for single-minded devotion would have met with incomprehension, of course, in each of the cultures surrounding ancient Israel. In polytheistic cultures there are many gods among whom one's devotion must be distributed. This is not a problem, for a truly polytheistic system of belief is also intrinsically a pluralist system of belief. There are no false gods, as such, and therefore there can be no false religion. There can only be religion that does not work as well as another version. Repression of religion, therefore, where it did occur in the ancient Near East, was apparently a result of politics, not of religion as such—it was designed to deprive one's enemies of divine sustenance. Repression for *religious* reasons in a polytheistic system would have made no sense, for the gods themselves "would not be jealous of attention paid to other gods as long as their own needs were being met and their position was not in jeopardy."[20]

Biblical faith leaves polytheism behind, however, and strenuously denies that there are other gods in the cosmos—whether in the heavens or upon the earth or under the earth (chap. 3). The extent to which divinity is thus assigned exclusively to the one creator God and is removed entirely from the rest of the cosmos is well illustrated by Genesis 1:21, where "the great creatures of the sea" are only *creatures of the (created) sea*. Psalm 104:25-26 likewise refers to "the sea, vast and spacious, teeming with creatures beyond number" where lives "the leviathan, which you formed to frolic there." The significance of these texts becomes clear when we juxtapose them to the important Mesopotamian text *Enuma Elish*. In this text, the first gods are born from the union of Apsu and Tiamat, the primordial sea deities, through a mingling of their waters. Later, this primordial, divine sea becomes hostile to the gods, resulting eventually in a battle between Tiamat and Marduk, the champion of the gods. Marduk slays Tiamat and forms the cosmos from her corpse.[21] Genesis, of course, knows nothing of a *divine* sea at the beginning of time, even though it does know of a *primordial* one (Genesis 1:2). Still less does Genesis know of a primeval war among divinities out of which the cosmos emerged. The only sea monsters that Genesis allows into its creation story are *creatures*—creatures *of God*, which may be found frolicking in the oceans.[22]

If there is indeed no pantheon of gods but only one God (as biblical faith claims), then it follows quite logically that human devotion to divinity should *not* be "distributed." It should be focused, as Deuteronomy suggests, on the one God who is truly God, and not on other gods. It also follows that it should involve the whole self. The mind should not have one object of affection, and the emotions another. All of the heart and all of the soul and all of the strength should be directed toward the one, and not dispersed among the many. The Qur'an agrees: "Celebrate the name of your Lord and devote yourself wholeheartedly to Him. He is Lord of the east and west, there is no god but Him" (73:8-9). It is explicit about not distributing love among various gods: "there are some who choose to worship others besides God as rivals to Him, loving them with the love due to God, but the believers have greater love for God" (2:165). It is such single-minded and wholehearted devotion that the Bible also advocates.

ON OBEYING GOD

It is from this trust and love that another aspect of right relating to God arises. In Genesis 3, a *lack* of trust and love led to *disobedience*. Conversely, in biblical thinking, renewed trust in and love for God issues in renewed obedience. Deuteronomy 6 affirms this connection, for verses 4-5 with their love command are immediately followed by verses 6-9:

> These commandments that I give you today are to be upon your hearts. Impress them on your children. Talk about them when you sit at home and when you walk along the road, when you lie down and when you get up. Tie them as symbols on your hands and bind them on your foreheads. Write them on the doorframes of your houses and on your gates.

The command to obey follows naturally, then, from the command to love. The God who saved the Israelites from Egypt did not save them so that they could wander around in the wilderness without direction or purpose. He saved them so that they could live a particular kind of life—the life bounded by God's "commandments," which are always to be front and center in Israelite consciousness. These commandments are to be found in their homes and upon their persons. They are to be reflected upon at every stage of the day. They are to be passed on with serious intentionality to the next generation.

The Deuteronomic vision for Israel is a microcosm of what is also true in a larger way for the whole of creation. God has not created *human beings* to wander about *creation* without direction or purpose. He has created them to live a particular kind of life—the kind of life represented by someone like Noah, whom Genesis 6:9 describes as "a righteous man, blameless among the people of his time, [who] walked with God." Noah trusted in and loved God and followed the right path through life—the path of obedience to God's commandments. It was indeed because "Noah did everything just as God commanded him" (Genesis 6:22; see also 7:5, 9, 16) that life on earth was able to continue after the great flood. While we are not explicitly told about the spirit in which Noah obeyed God, it stands to reason that those who trust in and love a *God* who is good are bound to view his commandments as being good *for his creatures*. The righteous person obeys these commandments, then, not out of fear of reprisals (as a slave might obey a master), nor out of a grudging sense of duty (as a self-centered child might obey a parent he cannot yet escape), but with a sense of gladness.[23]

It is precisely this gladness that we often encounter in the Psalms when God's commandments are mentioned. The psalm that introduces the entire book of Psalms begins, in fact, with this central affirmation: "blessed is the man . . . [whose] delight is in the law of the LORD . . . on his law he meditates day and night" (Psalm 1:1-2). In this text "delight" in God's law is bound up with the blessed life, which is compared in verse 3 to that of a fruitful, ever-flourishing tree. Later, in Psalm 19:7-8, we are told that "the law of the LORD is perfect, reviving the soul; the statutes of the LORD are trustworthy, making wise the simple; the precepts of the LORD are right, giving joy to the heart." Still later, Psalm 119:20 reveals a worshipper whose "soul is consumed with longing for your laws at all times"—so much so that he rises at midnight "to give you thanks for your righteous laws" (v. 62). "Oh, how I love your law!" he exclaims in verse 97; "I meditate on it all day long." And again: "your righteousness is everlasting and your law is true" (v. 142). In biblical faith, God's commandments are not the impositions of a mean-spirited god intent on spoiling life by curtailing human freedom, as the serpent suggests in Genesis 3. They are instead signposts on the path to blessing, placed there by One who desires his creatures to find their way. The one "who fears the LORD, who finds great delight in his commands," then, is the one who finds blessing (Psalm 112:1), for in the Psalms, obedience to God is associated not with the *curtailment* of human freedom but with *true* freedom to live as we ought and as is good for us: "I will always obey your law, for ever and ever. I will walk about in freedom, for I have sought out your precepts" (Psalm 119:44-45).

Along with humility, trust, and love, then, obedience lies at the heart of right relating to God. This is true not only of biblical faith but also of Islam: "knowledge achieved by intelligence [*iman*, or faith] on the basis of God's guidance, then submission chosen by free will—this is the path of Islam."[4]

AN IMPOSSIBLE TASK?

How am I to relate to God? I begin by acknowledging that God is God, and that other "gods" (including myself) are not. I commit myself to the truth that God is good. I entrust myself to his goodness, I seek to love him with all my heart and soul and strength, I gladly obey him, and I pray to him, in thanksgiving, praise, and lament. This is the heart of the matter, from the perspective of biblical faith.

Not Easy . . .

Is this easy? It would be fair to say, I think, that our biblical authors regard it as simple but not easy, for "man is born broken" (Eugene O'Neill, in the second epigraph to this chapter). We are born into a world that has already in many ways turned its back on the true and living God, misunderstanding his nature and character. Much of society at large appears to have little interest in trusting, loving, obeying, and praying to God, and quite likely the habits and traditions of my own family—the "baggage" that I have been handed from the past—do not tend in this direction either. In such a world, in which other people's "truth" is so challengingly different from biblical truth, it is difficult to arrive at, and to maintain clarity of mind on, what is true. Even if one does arrive at clarity, it is difficult to live consistently with the truth, when so many are not even attempting to do so. The temptation *not* to relate rightly to God is strong, and it comes at us not just from society in general and from our own families in particular but also from dark forces that are not even human (see chaps. 5–6).

Relating rightly to God, then, is *not* easy; the challenges come from various directions.

The difficulty is well reflected in the various narratives of Genesis and of the remainder of the Old Testament. Even Abraham, who in so many ways "gets it right," still displays at times a lack of trust in God. In Genesis 12, God promises Abraham that he will make him "into a great nation" (v. 2). By Genesis 15, however, Abraham and Sarah are still childless, and Abraham, weary of waiting for the single heir who must be born if further descendants are to follow, adopts into his family his servant Eliezer (vv. 2-3). God then confirms that Abraham's heir shall come "from his own body"—it will not be someone like Eliezer (v. 4). This only leads to a second, wrongheaded strategy by Abraham to progress the promise. He takes Hagar as a concubine (16:2-4)—a move that leads to great unhappiness. Unhappiness is characteristically the outcome in the Genesis story when Abraham and Sarah act on their own initiative, independently of God. Hagar causes marital friction between husband and wife, and, when Sarah treats her harshly (16:6), the pregnant Hagar ends up fleeing the family home. Once again God attempts to put Abraham back on the right path (chap. 17), making clear that the promised son is not Hagar's son Ishmael, as Abraham would prefer. Ishmael is certainly "from Abraham's own body," but he is not the heir. Isaac, whom Sarah herself will bear, is the promised heir (17:18-19). Throughout this story, then, Abraham is asked to trust God. To some extent he is able to do this, but to some extent he is not. This is evident not only in his strategizing about the heir but also in his strategizing with respect to Sarah, when he is confronted by powerful men who desire her (Genesis 12:10-20; 20:1-18). Abraham is apparently not beyond telling a lie, or at least a half truth, to save his own skin.

. . . But Not Impossible

Relating rightly to God is not easy, for all sorts of reasons. Yet it is not impossible, either—not least because God himself, in this biblical story, is in the business of "mending" what is broken (to quote O'Neill again). God is more than willing to supply the "glue" for this task, which is "the grace of God." This grace is God's ongoing commitment to show goodness and love to his creatures even while they are unable to respond to him as they ought. Over time, in the biblical perspective, this grace can be restorative, as God himself works in the world to bring goodness out of evil.

We see this most clearly, perhaps, in the case of Jacob, Abraham's grandson. In Genesis 25:19-34, as his story begins, Jacob does not possess a faith like Abraham's. Unlike his grandfather, he finds it very hard to trust God. His obedience is halting—less spectacular and more marked by failure than Abraham's. His name in Hebrew—*ya'aqov*—is connected with the noun *'aqev*, which means "heel." Jacob is so named, we are told, because he was born clutching the heel of his twin brother Esau (Genesis 25:26). *'Aqev*, however, is in turn a play on the verb *'aqav*, "to cheat." As we might expect in light of what we have seen in earlier chapters in Genesis, the name predicts the person Jacob becomes; it relates to his function in the first part of his story. In Genesis 27 we shall find Esau saying that Jacob has cheated him twice (v. 36), first taking his birthright and then his blessing. It is this cheating that leads to Jacob's hasty flight from the promised land and to his long residence abroad in order to avoid Esau's revenge. Later, as he returns to the promised land, Jacob receives a different name from God—the name "Israel" (Genesis 32:29; 35:10). This name informs us about Jacob's role both as God's chosen one and as the father of many descendants—the "children of Israel." With the new name, Jacob has found a new place in the cosmos—a new function.

The story of Jacob that is built around these two names is a story of redemption. It is a story of God's *grace* in rescuing Jacob—grace that is explicitly signaled in Genesis 28:10-22. Here, in a dream, Jacob sees a ziggurat stairway (often unhelpfully referred to as a "ladder") connecting earth and heaven. He observes God's servants ("angels") coming and going on this stairway to heaven, occupying themselves with the business of God. The main interpretive question in this story is where *God* is to be found. Does the beginning of verse 13 tell us that Jacob sees the LORD standing *above* "it" (the stairway)? This is how the line is often translated (e.g., in the NIV main text). In this case, God is in heaven, ready to receive the angels who report back to him after patrolling the earth.[25] If this reading is correct, the text speaks of "the sovereign ruler of heaven and earth, who is ministered to by angels constantly. This is 'the LORD, the God of Abraham . . . and the God of Isaac' who addresses Jacob. This heavenly vision gives the promises that follow a majestic authority and weight."[26] However, the particular combination of the Hebrew verb and preposition here (*nitsav* plus *'al*) usually means in the Old Testament "to stand beside."[27] It never means specifically "to stand above." Most likely, then, God is standing not above the ladder but "beside *him*" (Jacob, as the NIV footnote allows).[28] The story, then, is not about the majesty of a God who sits in the heavens but about the love of a God who descends the stairway to be with Jacob where he is—about a God who looks for friendship with Jacob in the midst of his current circumstances. Before Jacob turns away from wrongdoing in his life and before he has even the faintest notion that his whole life journey lies in the hands of God, God is found *with* Jacob, where he is. And God gives Jacob a remarkable promise—a promise of land, of descendants, and of God's presence protecting Jacob and ultimately returning him to the land of Canaan (28:13-15).

This is a story, then, about God's grace in the midst of a journey—a journey that was only necessary in the first place because Jacob made some very bad choices within a highly dysfunctional family context. His bad choices notwithstanding, God is present when Jacob leaves Canaan, and God is also present twenty years later when Jacob returns. On this second occasion God "wrestles" with his broken servant by the river Jabbok (Genesis 32). Jacob loses the wrestling match—a loss that is symbolic of the death of the person he *has* been and the birth of the person he *is* to be. The point of the entire struggle is apparently to teach Jacob, once and for all, that God is really God and that Jacob is not. The good God is stronger than the only partly good Jacob—thankfully so, from a biblical point of view.

Possible, with God's Help

Relating rightly to God, from the biblical perspective, is not easy, but it is possible—not least because God himself is in the business of mending what is broken. This mending is not just a matter of walking alongside lost individuals and turning evil to good in their lives; it is also a matter of God's wider work in dealing with evil and its consequences in the whole cosmos. What this work entails, precisely, is not yet explicitly clear in the Abraham and Jacob stories. It begins to become clear, however, as we come to the story of Moses and we read about sacrifice and atonement in the tabernacle. Sacrifice, we noted in chapter 3, is designed to deal with the problem of the Israelites' lack of holiness "in the meantime"—while they, like their forefather Jacob/Israel, are becoming the people they should be. The Israelites are called to be a holy people—a people who have given up on divinity, who trust in God's goodness, and who love and obey their God. In the meantime, however, there is a need for atonement. God does not just *require* holiness and does not just walk alongside people *encouraging* it. God also takes steps to deal with its *absence*. That is a central feature of Israel's sacrificial system. In the same way, God reaches out to the *entire world* through the suffering of the righteous "servant" of God in Isaiah 40–55 (see our chap. 6). As God lays all iniquity upon this mysterious sacrificial victim, peace is made between God and humanity. Atonement is one aspect of how God "helps" us to relate to him rightly. It is an aspect of the goodness of God in which the righteous human being is called to trust.

RELATING TO THE ONE, AND RELATING TO ALLAH

This biblical view of right relating to God is not one that we find reflected at all in many other religious and philosophical traditions. Even in Islam, which as I have demonstrated does bear some similarity to biblical faith in important respects, we find key distinctives.

Relating to the One

In comparing the biblical view of right relating to God with other traditions, I leave aside entirely polytheistic systems of thought, where God is not *one* person to whom I *might* relate. These traditions quite obviously do not reflect the biblical view at all.

The same is true of those religions and philosophies that possess no idea at all of a single, ultimate deity who is *personal*. In these traditions there *is* "One" to which human beings, in a sense, are supposed to "relate," but the relationship is not one that exists between *persons*. The Brahman of classical Hinduism, for example, is resolutely impersonal. In the end I cannot even separate Brahman from myself, because my true identity is the eternal atman, which is identical with Brahman. In classical Buddhism, there is also an "ultimate," but it is dharma—a universal ordering principle that is present everywhere. Confucianism, likewise, knows of an ultimate principle in the cosmos that holds things together, but it is not a person. This point is underscored by John and Evelyn Berthrong, who say of their seventeenth-century representative Confucian, Dr. Li, that he "had always thought that there was something mysteriously profound about the ultimate nature of the Dao, but he was not prepared to accept that the Way was a person. That seemed a step too far."[9] In classical Daoism, too, the dao—the eternal source of all reality—is impersonal. Finally, Plato's ultimate reality—the highest idea of the good, the beautiful, and the true—is also not a person, nor is Aristotle's "unmoved mover."

It stands to reason that in all such traditions human life cannot involve, at its core, a relationship with one transcendent, personal God. Within these traditions, it makes no sense to give up on divinity in the biblical sense, for there *is* no such divine Person before whom to relinquish it. It may even be that the whole notion of a distinction between myself and any ultimate reality is fundamentally misguided. It also makes no sense in these traditions to trust in God's goodness, as if there existed an ultimate Person who intended good toward us. The biblical notions of love for and obedience to God likewise become incoherent, for they imply a loving, transcendental Person who has given humanity guidelines and laws to follow. These other traditions cannot set at the heart of human life such trust, love, and obedience. Instead, they place there a striving for harmony with, or absorption into, the One. They possess no conception of a God who, in the midst of human striving, is acting in the world to rescue the lost, to guide them back onto the right path, and to atone for their sins. Rather, it is for human beings to *achieve* harmony with the One—through the performance of duty, the adoption of proper rituals and practices, or meditation and contemplation. Optimism with respect to the human capacity for self-transformation thus marks these traditions—an optimism that is well illustrated in Confucianism.

In some ways, Confucianism is more similar to biblical faith than traditions like Hinduism and Buddhism. From previous chapters we recall that Confucius understood the presence of evil in the world and the suffering that follows from it as arising from a human departure from a prescribed "way" that is good. He advocated a return to this way, such that society could renew itself, and he valued even small actions in pursuit of resistance to evil and suffering. There are two paths in Confucianism, and we (both individually and corporately) get to choose which one to take. Our choices make a difference as to what happens next, and we can indeed hope for the ultimate victory of good over evil. There is no fatalism in Confucianism nor any escapism. These represent similarities with biblical faith.

Yet precisely because Confucianism shares with Hinduism and Buddhism the absence of one personal, transcendent God, it also shares with them (and *not* with biblical faith) an optimistic view of the human capacity for self-transformation. For Confucius, the execution of proper rituals and ceremonies would ultimately transform people into people of humane goodness. As outer relationships were brought into order, so also would inner human nature become ordered, and in this way everything would ultimately become harmonious. In this way of thinking, what is wrong with the world can be put right through good education and then through good behavior by the educated. Man is not broken, and does not need God to mend him in any way. There is, after all, no God who is in the business of mending. Human beings must, and *can*, get on with the business of improving the world by themselves.

Relating to Allah

Relating to Allah is, of course, different than relating to the "One" in the aforementioned traditions. Islam turns its back on any kind of monism, as well as on all forms of polytheism. God is one and personal and must absolutely not be associated or confused with anything in creation. Islam agrees closely with biblical faith in such respects, and with biblical faith it sets at the heart of human life a right relationship with God that involves giving up on divinity, trusting in the goodness of God, loving God, and obeying God. It does not necessarily *weigh* these aspects of the relationship in the same way. There are perhaps questions to be asked, for example, about whether the theme of *love* for God is as central in Islam as it is in biblical faith. Although a recent open letter from prominent Muslims to the Christian world identifies love for God as one of the "foundational principles of both faiths," it must be admitted that references to love for God in the Qur'an are very few.[30] Yet, broadly speaking, Islam and biblical faith do approach the matter of right relating to God, *in these respects*, in similar ways.

However, Islam differs markedly from biblical faith, just as Confucianism does, on the question of how broken human beings are, and how much mending God must do (and is doing) in the world. It also differs on how much divine help is required for human beings to maintain a right relationship with God. In Islam (as in Confucianism), man is *not* born broken, and has no need of the "glue" that is represented by God's gracious work with broken people in the Old Testament story. For Muslims, it is not an aspect of God's goodness to provide this kind of help, for it is not required. God does help human beings, to some extent, to walk the right path—to overcome their baser desires and so on. This is not, however, the kind of fundamental help that biblical faith envisages. From the very beginning to the very end of a human life "it is possible," in Islam, "to live in total submission to God's law. . . . It is possible for humans to be perfect Muslims."[31] Islam is about "self-transformation in harmony with God's design of felicity."[32] Allah does not seek out the lost and redeem them; he does not "descend the ziggurat" to meet with his people even before they turn to him; he does not take the initiative to deal constructively with their sins.

It is significant in this respect that, when the Qur'an retells the stories of Abraham and Jacob, it omits the parts of these stories that suggest that God *does* do such things. In the Qur'an, Abraham is the perfect Muslim and a model for others to follow. Jacob is the faithful prophet of God—he never cheats, and he certainly does not meet God, while lost, at the bottom of a "ladder."[33] In general, the intimacy between God and human beings that the biblical "ladder" passage implies is not a very marked feature of the Qur'an. It tends to picture God in terms of power, majesty, and greatness—the God at the top of the ladder, not the God at its foot. When it does speak more generally of God's love, it does not portray it in terms of God seeking the lost and the broken. It tells us of a God who loves those who do good (2:195), who are mindful of him and pure (9:4; 9:108), who are evenhanded (49:9), who are steadfast and trust him (3:146; 3:159), and who love him, follow his prophet Muhammad, and fight in his cause (3:31; 61:4). The Qur'an never states that God loves someone who has not loved him first—never implies that God loves someone who has not already turned toward righteousness. In fact, on many occasions Allah is said *not* to love such people. God *is* loving, forgiving, and merciful in Islam, but human beings experience these things only in the context of their submission to God. As the prophet Muhammad puts it,

> If you love God, follow me, and God will love you and forgive you your sins; God is most forgiving and merciful . . . but if they turn away, [know that] God does not love those who ignore his commands. (3:31-32)

These references to God's love in the Qur'an are themselves not many, and neither is God's love a characteristic highlighted in the ninety names of God known to Muslims. This being so, it is perhaps not surprising that references to human love *for God* in the Qur'an are also so few in number. If love does not lie at the heart of who God is, there is no reason why it should lie, either, at the heart of the right human response to God.

Biblical faith envisions a different relationship between God and his human creatures, ordered *most fundamentally* by love—first, the love of God for his creatures and, second, their love in return. At this crucial point the Christian and Islamic traditions diverge. In biblical faith, right relating to God is possible only because God, in his love, makes it so.

8

LOVE ALL, TRUST A FEW, DO WRONG TO NONE

How Am I to Relate to My Neighbor?

A rule is a rule. And let's face it. Without rules there's chaos.

Cosmo Kramer[1]

Love thy neighbor—and if he happens to be tall, debonair and devastating, it will be that much easier.

Mae West[2]

How am I to relate to my neighbor? The groundwork for an answer to this question has already been laid. In chapter 4, we learned that in biblical faith the world is created not for the gods but for creatures, including human beings. Each and every human life is deeply significant; indeed, each one is inviolable. The biblical worldview is thus profoundly humanistic, and in important ways democratic. All human beings are image bearers of God, share in governance over the cosmos, and have the same rights. All, and not just some, are to be treated as "gods." In chapter 5, we discovered how the Genesis authors see this humanistic and democratic world being impacted by the embrace of evil. The relationships between God and the image bearers and between the image bearers themselves, have become damaged. The question of this chapter, then, takes on added importance: how am I to relate to my human neighbors *now*, in this broken world, east of Eden, that is nevertheless still the creation of God?

AM I MY BROTHER'S KEEPER?

The beginnings of an answer to this question are found in the story of Cain and Abel in Genesis 4. Before we get to the matter of neighbor-keeping, however, it is important to sketch some of the religious background to the Cain-Abel conflict, since (typically for a biblical text) the author certainly wants the reader to understand what goes wrong in Cain's relationship with Abel in the light of what has already gone wrong in Cain's relationship with God.

As Genesis 4 opens, we discover, first of all, that God's intention to bless his creation has not been disturbed by what has just happened in Genesis 3. Human beings are still being fruitful, and are still increasing in number (Genesis 1:28). The first evidence of this is the birth of Cain. His name *qayin* sounds somewhat similar to the verb *qanah*, which commonly means "to acquire or buy" but most likely in this context means "to create."[3] It is a play on these two words that lies at the heart of what Eve says in Genesis 4:1, the second part of which should be translated as follows: "I have created a man with the LORD." This is the only place in the Old Testament where *qanah* is used of a human being creating anything; everywhere else God is the subject of the verb. The full significance of this fact comes to light when we consider that in Genesis 3 it is precisely the blurring of the lines between Creator and creation (the human desire "to be like God") that is the problem. Here, right at the beginning of Genesis 4, the "confusion" between Creator and creature becomes acute. The question is: who is responsible for human life? Eve's claim is not just that she has created Cain with God's *help*, as many translations render the line—that would be astonishing enough—but that she has been a *cocreator* with God in the creation of Cain! Her newfound "godlikeness" has gone to her head. Just as God created a man in Genesis 2, so now (with God) Eve creates another one. The name Cain, therefore, speaks of the human tendency toward self-divinization.[4]

The name Abel (Heb. *hevel*) speaks, in contrast, of the reality of a human being's existence as mortal. *Hevel* means "breath" or "breeze" (e.g., Isaiah 57:13) and thereby refers to what is insubstantial or fleeting or to actions that are in vain or to no purpose—futile or pointless endeavors whose effects do not last. Everything to do with mortal existence is said in the Old Testament to be "ephemeral" or "fleeting" in this way. Representative is Psalm 39:5: "You have made my days a mere handbreadth; the span of my years is as nothing before you. Each man's life is but a breath (*hevel*)."[5] Where the name Cain speaks of grasping after divinity, then, the name Abel signifies the transient nature of human existence.

The Religion of Cain

The opening verses of Genesis 4 find both Cain and Abel exercising dominion over the created order, caring for animals and for the land. They are doing this successfully, under the blessing of God (the curse on the ground in Genesis 3 notwithstanding). They are also doing it in communion with God: they offer the fruits of their labor to God "at the end of the year" (4:3).[6] A problem arises, however (vv. 3-5). Its nature is never explicitly described, but it certainly cannot be that sacrifice itself is problematic, for both brothers sacrifice but only one is blamed. Furthermore, both kinds of sacrifice are said to be valid elsewhere in the Pentateuch (Leviticus 2; Deuteronomy 15:19-23).[7] However, it is likely that at least one dimension of the problem does involve a difference in the *quality* of the sacrifices. Whereas Cain brings to God only "some of the fruits of the soil," Abel brings "fat portions [i.e., the best cuts] from some of the firstborn of his flock."[8] In other words, Abel brings his best to God, and Cain does not. The remainder of the Old Testament makes clear that sacrifices are not really sacrificial if they do not cost the worshipper much (e.g., Malachi 1:8). One should not hold back the best for oneself, as the wicked priests at Shiloh did in 1 Samuel 2:12-17. The story of Cain reminds us of these other cases. It may also have reminded an ancient, literate person of the Greek poet Hesiod's Prometheus, who sets a precedent among the Greeks for keeping the sacrificial meat for themselves and offering the gods only bones wrapped in fat.[9]

What follows in Genesis 4 suggests, however, that there is more to this business than merely the quality of the sacrifices. A worshipper who behaves like Cain is clearly not relating to God as he should. There is a deeper problem, exemplified in Cain's response to God's unfavorable reaction to his sacrifice: "so Cain was very angry, and his face was downcast" (4:5). The anger implies a prior posture. The anger implies that Cain thinks he has certain "rights" with respect to God—that a sacrifice *ought* to lead to divine "favor." Herein lies the problem: Cain's view of God and of sacrifice represents the typical ancient Near Eastern (and later Greek) attitude toward religious ritual. These ancient peoples "expected their gods to show them favor in their various endeavors. They were therefore very interested in how to attain the favor of the gods."[10] As one ancient Babylonian text counsels its readers, "Every day worship your god. Sacrifice and benediction are the proper accompaniment of incense. . . . Offer him daily, and you will get your reward."[11] Sacrifice, in this way of thinking, is about giving in order to receive; it is nothing other than a form of bribery. This is the mindset of Cain:

> Cain's display of anger reveals retrospectively his state of soul in making the sacrifice. Because he had sought to place God in his debt by means of his gift, Cain feels slighted by what he takes to be God's unjustified rejection of his offering.[12]

This attitude toward sacrifice is not limited to the ancient Near East or ancient Greece. Concerning the ancient Vedic *shrauta* sacrifices in India, for example, Mark Muesse writes that "in return for pleasing songs sung in a *deva*'s or *devi*'s honor and offerings of meat, Soma, and other sumptuous foods, the gods were believed to grant the sacrificer's wishes."[13] As Indo-Aryan religion developed, its rituals became unattached even to these gods and came to be merely about power: "The rites were no longer performed to persuade or prompt the gods to act on human behalf; rather, the rite itself . . . came to be seen as the true agent of control." The gods may pass away, but the human desire for control through ritual always remains. For many modern Hindus, of course, the gods have by no means passed away, and they still require pleasing and appeasing through sacrifice and offerings. This has involved in the past, and can still involve today, the "highest" form of sacrifice—human sacrifice. As Muesse reminds us, until the nineteenth century the worship of the goddess Kali involved weekly human sacrifice, and "even today, on extremely rare occasions, there are reports of human sacrifice or self-immolation in honor of the goddess."[14] Such events are rare *not* because the fundamental nature of Kali worship has changed over the centuries but because of external pressures. After all, the *Puranas* (second-order Hindu scriptures) themselves make clear that although Kali is content for a limited time with animal sacrifices, "a human sacrifice pleases her for a thousand years."[15] Human sacrifice, then, is a central idea in this kind of religion. Through such sacrifice, the gods are appeased, and humans benefit in return.

Of course, this notion that the gods must at least sometimes be bribed with human sacrifice is not solely a feature of Indian religion. It is found in polytheistic traditions elsewhere as well—both in ancient times (e.g., in the Near East, Greece and Rome, and China) and in more modern times (e.g., in the Americas).[16] It makes perfect sense—that is, if one first grants the truth of the governing beliefs concerning the nature of the gods, the world, and human beings. The sacrifice of one human being is a relatively small price to pay to ensure that cosmic order is maintained: that the rains fall, that the crops grow, and that the gods cooperate with human beings instead of opposing them.

The Religion of God

This religious background, then, explains Cain's anger: he believes that he has done his part, but God has not returned the favor. It also highlights the extraordinary nature of God's response to him. As Cain offers the sacrifice, even though it is not a very wholehearted sacrifice, he possesses certain expectations. It is not the wholeheartedness or the lack of it, however, that God is concerned about. It is that Cain is not walking in the "right" way (Genesis 4:7); he is (more literally) not "doing good."[7] In other words, he is not living according to God's creative intent; he is living against the "good" grain of creation. Perhaps this divine challenge comes as a surprise to Cain, as Leon Kass suggests: "The god Cain encounters is not the god he expected. This one does not just make rain or grow crops; He cares for life, for individuals (including one's rivals), and for right."[8] In God's response we see the outline of what will, in the remainder of the Old Testament, become a fuller picture of the biblical view of both sacrifice and "right."

Biblical sacrifice is not about feeding the gods. The incomparable God who created the whole world does not need to be fed. Psalm 50:12 ridicules this very notion: "if I were hungry I would not tell you, for the world is mine, and all that is in it." In Genesis 8:21, we note, God is said only to *smell* the pleasing aroma of Noah's sacrifice. This stands in marked contrast to the gods in the Mesopotamian *Epic of Gilgamesh* who, having been deprived of human sacrifices for a while, smell the aroma of Utnapishtim's sacrifice and gather like flies around the altar. The gods may be very hungry; God, however, is not.[19]

In biblical thinking, furthermore, God cannot be *bribed* with sacrifices. Indeed, God is not at all interested in the "order" that sacrifices supposedly restore to the cosmos. God is interested in what is *right*, and this right is not reducible to mere order. In the ancient Near East, "right" *was* order. Even the gods had to conform themselves to this order. Human beings were then expected also to "fit in," and they did so through both ritual and ethical performance. There should be no disturbance to the harmony of things—conformity was everything. When it came right down to it, indeed, ritual performance was *more important* than ethical performance. Looking after the gods was much more important than behaving in a civil manner toward one's neighbor:

> Everything in the universe, material or immaterial, human or divine, was laid down by decrees. Man's duty was to conform to these regulations. The contrast was not . . . between morally right and wrong, but between order and disorder.[20]

In biblical thinking, however, the *fundamental* contrast is between morally right and wrong, as defined by the character of the one God who creates everything. *Doing what is right* is more important than promoting social harmony. Jeremiah's rugged nonconformity in the face of the many false prophets who were pursuing "peace" is a good example (e.g., Jeremiah 8:8-13). Peace is not a good thing if it comes at the expense of what is morally right and good. Furthermore, doing what is right is more important than *sacrifice*. The prophet Isaiah is clear about this when he urges people, in God's name, to *stop* sacrificing so long as they are indulging in violence and injustice (Isaiah 1:10-17). Sacrifice is all very well, so long as its significance is not misunderstood, but God is not ambiguous, in a litany of Old Testament passages, about its relative importance:

> I desire mercy, not sacrifice, and acknowledgment of God rather than burnt offerings. (Hosea 6:6)

> Even though you bring me burnt offerings and grain offerings, I will not accept them . . . but let justice roll on like a river, righteousness like a never-failing stream. (Amos 5:22-24)

> To do what is right and just is more acceptable to the LORD than sacrifice. (Proverbs 21:3)

Sacrifice will not persuade God to turn a blind eye to moral evil. This is, according to Jean Bottéro, "one of Moses' great revolutions in Israel: to replace the purely material maintenance of the gods with the single and sole 'liturgical' obligation in life to obey a moral law."[21] It is not that ancient Mesopotamians lacked any kind of ethical code, he continues, but that ethic was solely concerned with the promotion of order and the avoidance of the harm that follows from disorder.

Two Ways

So it is that Cain, with his typically ancient Near Eastern attitude toward sacrifice and his presumption about the benefits due to him in the "trade" that he is brokering, is confronted by God with the question of moral right. God who is good and does what is good (Heb. *tov . . . hetiv*; Psalm 119:68) asks Cain whether he intends to be and to do the same. Two ways now open up before Cain, as they had previously opened up before his parents. The first way leads him back to God (and to his brother). He can recognize his fault, he can acknowledge his anger as irrational and wrong, and he can begin to "do what is right" (Genesis 4:7). If so, he will be welcomed back and be able to remain, as it were, "at home." The second path leads Cain out of his home and into an ambush, for "sin is crouching at your door; it desires to have you, but you must master it" (Genesis 4:7). Evil waits like a wild animal outside Cain's door, ready to pounce on him as he *leaves* home. This evil beast, we are told, "desires" Cain (Heb. *teshuqah*)—a word we last came across in Genesis 3:16, where it spoke of the woman's desire to control her husband. Cain must "master" the beast (Heb. *mashal*), exercising his dominion over *this* "animal" just as he should exercise it over *all* animals. God is asking Cain, in other words, to live as he was created to live: to be a "ruler [*mashal*] over the works of [God's] hands" (Psalm 8:6). The second path, then, is the path that leads away from God and into the dysfunction and chaos of evil that has already been described in Genesis 3. Because this path leads away from God, it also leads away from family. Even though Cain has done wrong, however, he still has a chance to avoid this path, for it is not individual wrongs, in biblical thinking, that propel one along the path away from God. It is the refusal, in the midst of such wrongs, to be reconciled with God, followed by a settled determination to keep on walking. In the early verses of Genesis 4, Cain's conscious decision has not yet been made. Cain and God are still in conversation.

The decision is not long in coming, however. Cain wants to define his relationship with God on his own terms. Like his parents, he covets the life of the autonomous self, so he steps out further on the path of ancient Near Eastern fertility religion. Evil consumes him, and he murders his brother Abel. Perhaps he does this out of jealousy; perhaps he does it to present God with a more powerful sacrifice and to see whether, after all, he can get God to do his bidding. One way or another, the story illustrates the common biblical view: a departure from the one true God inevitably leads to injustice, and indeed to bloodshed, in human society. We have now arrived specifically at the question that is central to this chapter, but by way of situating it in its proper context. Once people abandon right relating to God, as Cain has done, the abandonment of right relating to one's fellow human beings will surely follow.

Loving the Neighbor

The nature of right relating is clarified in what comes next—a dialogue between God and Cain that parallels the previous dialogue between God and Adam and Eve. The human embrace of evil is followed first, in both cases, by a question from God. In Genesis 3 it was "where are you?" (3:9). In Genesis 4 it is "where is your brother Abel?" (4:9). The question provokes, next, a lie. In Genesis 3 it was "I was afraid because I was naked" (3:10), but the truth was that Adam was afraid because he had disobeyed God. In Genesis 4 the lie is "I don't know" (4:9), but the truth is that Cain knows very well. The lie is followed, then, by an evasion of responsibility. Back in Genesis 3 the man blames the woman for the problem, the woman blames the snake, and the snake (as one wit once famously put it) does not have a leg to stand on (3:12-13). In Genesis 4 we find a different kind of evasion, one that gets us to the heart of the matter concerning right relationships. In response to God's question, Cain, the son of the mother who confidently regarded herself as God's equal, brazenly poses a question of his own: "Am I my brother's keeper?" (4:9).

The question is never explicitly answered, because it does not need to be. From the perspective of biblical faith, the answer is obvious. Yes, if you have been created to work the garden and take care of it (literally to "keep" it, Heb. *shamar*; Genesis 2:15), you are certainly also to "keep" (*shamar*) your brother. Just as the good God "will keep you [*shamar*] from all harm—he will watch over [*shamar*] your life" (Psalm 121:7), so also a righteous image bearer of God will watch over the life of his fellow image bearer. That is the core of right relating to my various neighbors: to "keep" them.

The Cursing of Cain

Cain's decision to do the opposite leads to dreadful consequences. As in Genesis 3, the evasion of responsibility is followed by a divine curse. Structurally, the curse in Genesis 4:11 is very similar to the one in Genesis 3:14. In the latter, God says (literally), "Cursed are you *from* [i.e., above all] the livestock" (*'arur 'attah mikkol-habbehemah*). In the former, he says (literally), "You are cursed *from* the ground" (*'arur 'attah min-ha'adamah*). The parallelism suggests that the sense of Genesis 4:11 is that "you are *more* cursed than the ground." It is not just the ground that is now cursed by God (3:17); it is a human being. When Cain now works the land, "It will no longer yield its crops for you" (4:12). Neither of these was true back in Genesis 3. Tragically, the disruption between the human and the land is now greater, because the wrongdoing is greater and the land has become polluted with Abel's blood (4:11).

The idea of blood pollution is not uncommon elsewhere in the Old Testament.[22] Any illicit act of killing brings pollution to the land and bloodguilt to the murderer's community. If the blood of the victim is not dealt with, its negative effects in terms of physical, economic, and social decline may linger on through generations. Blood, therefore, must be "removed," in one of several ways. The first, the payment of monetary compensation to the victim's family, is not common in the Old Testament (although it was common in the rest of the ancient Near East).[23] The second, exile from the community, appears in biblical legal and ritual texts as a temporary solution in the case of *accidental* homicide.[24] Neither option suffices, however, in cases of *premeditated* homicide.[25] In such cases, only a third option may be taken: "atonement cannot be made for the land on which blood has been shed, except by the blood of the one who shed it" (Numbers 35:33). Genesis 9:6 says something similar in a narrative context and provides the reason: "whoever sheds the blood of man, by man shall his blood be shed; for in the image of God has God made man." Human life is precious, so, in cases of premeditated murder, the murderer must be handed over for justice to "the avenger of blood" (as Deuteronomy 19:12 calls him). This is the closest male relative of the victim, whose responsibility it is to avenge the murder—if that is what the family desires. The role of a court in such an ancient societal setting was confined to placing limits on familial vengeance; courts did not themselves *enact* vengeance. This is why in the *legal* texts of the Old Testament we find no discussion of cases where a family decides for whatever reason *not* to seek such vengeance. Such a decision would have lain outside the purview of the court. We do, however, find one *narrative* example where such a case is described.

This is the case of David's son Absalom, who is exiled by his father because he murders his brother Amnon (2 Samuel 13:34–14:33). In exile, Absalom is essentially "dead" to David. Interestingly, however, this "death" is not regarded as inevitably lasting forever. If the family that has been wronged simply decides in favor of reconciliation, "death" comes to an end. The woman of Tekoa urges David in precisely this direction in 2 Samuel 14:4-17. In making her argument, she refers to *God's* way of dealing with human beings as a model for David's own behavior: "God does not take away life; instead, he devises ways so that a banished person may not remain estranged from him" (14:14). Because God works for reconciliation, so should David. To the other three remedies for the spilling of blood, then, we must now add a fourth: forgiveness and reconciliation. In one way or another, however, "blood" must be dealt with. It cannot simply be ignored.

We must read Genesis 4 against this background. A murder has occurred, and it needs to be dealt with. In the case of Cain and Abel, however, there is no evidence that Adam desires to exact vengeance on Cain. Why lose a second son when you have already lost one?[26] Neither is there any evidence in Genesis 4, however, that Cain either acknowledges wrongdoing or desires reconciliation—which would be crucial for forgiveness to be meaningful. His intention simply to leave "home" is, from Genesis 4:8 onward, a firm one. He does not accept responsibility for the murder (4:9), and when informed that he shall become "a restless wanderer on the earth"—a punishment that describes only the life he himself chose the moment he *left* "home"—he does not respond with penitence but with a complaint: "my punishment is more than I can bear" (4:13).

It is a self-focused response. Cain fears that to be sent into exile is virtually to *be* sentenced to death, for he will be living in a place where he may be killed by anyone without fear of retribution. The normal constraints placed upon human behavior by fear of an "avenger of blood" will not apply in a land far from his familial home: "whoever finds me will kill me" (4:14). Cain's response is deeply ironic. He is concerned about whether *he* can expect justice to be done in the future if he is murdered. He is entirely unconcerned about whether justice has been, or will be, done with respect to *Abel*. Incredibly, he does not even notice how lenient, given the circumstances, is God's punishment of exile. He complains, rather, about its harshness. Here is someone apparently devoid of any fellow feeling—incapable of loving his neighbor, even when it is his own brother. Human community has arrived at a dark place. The expulsion (Heb. *giresh*, 3:24; NIV's "drove out") of Adam and Eve from the garden did not disrupt human relationships in this way—that family remained as a functioning family. The expulsion (Heb. *giresh*, 4:14; NIV's "driving me") of Cain from the land is far more catastrophic. Family relationships are now *severely* disrupted, and so also is the divine-human relationship. Until this point in the story, human beings have always lived in God's presence, even if not in the garden. For the first time, with Cain, we see a human being leaving this presence (4:14, 16).

The Care of Cain

Even in exile, however, God looks after Cain. He keeps him, even though Cain would not keep his brother. He promises him justice, even though Abel did not receive justice. He even goes so far, apparently, as to promise that *he* (God) will be Cain's avenger of blood: "If anyone kills Cain, he will suffer vengeance seven times over" (4:15). That is to say, any murderer of Cain will suffer the full measure of vengeance.[27] Furthermore, God "put a mark on Cain so that no one who found him would kill him." Whatever this "mark" or "sign" (Heb. *'oth*) is, exactly—and it is not further described in the story—it indicates, in the context of the book of Genesis, God's blessing and goodwill.[28] The word has previously occurred in Genesis 1:14, where we read of "lights in the expanse of the sky . . . [that] serve as signs to mark seasons and days and years." We meet it again later in Genesis 9:13 (the rainbow is the *sign* of the covenant), and in 17:11 (circumcision is the *sign* of the covenant). The mark is, then, a symbol of God's promise to look after Cain. A murderer who deserves to die is instead only exiled, and in his exile he remains an object of God's continued blessing. He is treated, still, as part of God's family. In the land of "Nod" ("wandering") Cain is watched over by God as Cain *should* have watched over Abel but did not.

The Age of Heroes

This continued blessing is immediately seen in Genesis 4:17-22, where Cain produces a family line responsible for many wonderful aspects of human culture. It is not a blessing, however, that results from any tangible virtue in Cain. Cain himself, we note, builds a city in the land of wandering. In light of the Tower of Babel incident yet to come, we are entitled to wonder about this project. By building a city, Cain has, in fact, refused the life of wandering God has prescribed. City building under these circumstances suggests that once again Cain is self-reliant, not someone who trusts in God's goodness and in his ability to protect.

God's continued blessing is also not the result of virtue in Cain's *descendants*. In chapter 7 I mentioned the "ugly perfection" of Cain's line, represented by Lamech, who boasts to his wives that "I have killed a man for wounding me (Heb. *petsa'*), a young man for injuring me" (Heb. *khabburah*; 4:23). The disproportionate, unjust nature of the action is underlined by his astounding claim, "If Cain is avenged seven times, then Lamech seventy-seven times" (Genesis 4:24). Even God's promise to avenge Cain moved extravagantly beyond what later became proportionate justice in Israel. In cases of injury, Exodus 21:23-25 limits retribution, should it be desired, to exact equivalence: "if there is serious injury, you are to take life for life, eye for eye . . . wound for wound [Heb. *petsa'*], bruise for bruise [Heb. *khabburah*]." Retribution is not to be excessive; it is to be just. God had promised Cain a special level of deterrence in his case as a vulnerable outsider to organized society. A heavy price would be exacted from any community that killed him.

Lamech now transforms this special provision of God for Cain into something dark and self-indulgent, taking to himself godlike powers. Lamech has not been killed, and he is not being avenged by anyone. He is certainly not being avenged by *God*. He is only taking refuge behind God's promise to Cain in order to justify his own excessive and murderous act. He then appears to extend the "principle" into the future, promising that disproportionate revenge will become his rule. He will be eleven times more vengeful than God promised to be—a greater god, when it comes to vengeance, than God himself. This new approach to matters of life and death, we note, is "celebrated" in a poem (Genesis 4:23-24)—a poem whose stylistic beauty lies in stark contrast to its disturbing content.[29] Beauty and self-glorifying barbarism walk hand in hand in Cain's line. It is consistent with this negative portrayal of

Lamech that it is he who is said to have "married two women"—the first mention of polygamy in the Old Testament. The Genesis authors no doubt regard this as another negative development; nothing in the story so far encourages us to think otherwise. The process by which ancient and powerful men collect women as possessions has begun.

Lamech represents the culmination of Cain's chosen path—the destination to which wickedness eventually leads. Leon Kass plausibly suggests that we should see him as representing the flowering of the heroic ideal in the ancient world. At the heart of this "heroism" lay an exaggerated sense of self-worth and a wounded self-esteem constantly in search of "satisfaction." Everyone punished "the contempt shown him in a manner proportionate to the stock he set by himself, vengeance became terrible, and men bloodthirsty and cruel."[30] It is not transcendental "right" that tells the hero what is "proportionate," we note—it is the self-regard that we see already in Cain and then in sharper focus in Lamech. Kass understands this as a distinctively male response to the problem of death and to the removal of the possibility of immortality. It is a response that matches Eve's earlier, female response:

> For Eve, bearing a child may satisfy the human desire for immortality; "creating" life may satisfy the human wish to be as God. But her man-child Cain and his male descendants have to seek such satisfactions by other means, not by giving life but by threatening it, especially in heroic encounters. Cain and Lamech are neither the last nor the greatest of those who pursue the heroic option. But . . . the Bible wastes no time in calling attention to the problem their conduct represents . . . [Genesis 4] surely paints a vivid picture of the bloody indecency connected with the way of Cain and the pursuit of human self-sufficiency and heroism.[31]

"Bloody indecency" is right. So it always is, claim our biblical authors, when people think of themselves as gods, rather than as image bearers of God. When human beings fail to relate rightly to God, fellow image bearers suffer.

A Different Way

It need not be this way. As we follow the story of Genesis 4 through to its end, we discover a third son of Adam and Eve—Seth (4:25-26).

This son is neither dead nor exiled as the story ends, and he signals a brighter future for the human race. It is surely significant, now that we have read Cain's story, that in Seth's case Eve does not repeat her claim to the cocreation of a child. Her words reflect a new humility: "God has granted me (appointed for me, put into my hands) another child in place of Abel." This child is definitely a gift from God: "Chastened regarding . . . her own pride in Cain's birth, she feels only gratitude in the birth of Seth. . . . Tragedy has humbled parental pride."[32] This is the correct way of looking at things from the point of view of the authors of Genesis, and it is no surprise to find them associating the birth of *this* child with a revival of worship of the true God throughout the earth. The path followed by Cain, away from God, has been fully described, with its consequences traced through many generations. The other path, rejected by Cain, is now seen as the one along which his younger brother leads the righteous.

It is interesting to note that, in the family tree of Genesis 5, neither Cain nor Abel is mentioned. It is Seth who carries the human race forward, and he does this as someone who is explicitly described using the language of image and likeness, in continuity with Adam (5:3). Here is someone wearing the right linguistic clothing, coming after a brother whose actions demonstrate that these clothes are not to his liking. Furthermore, Seth names his own son Enosh (4:26)—the same word used of human beings in Psalm 8:4, where the question is asked, "What is a (mere) human being?" The name suggests acceptance of the *difference* between God and human beings—rejection of the parity that "heroes" might claim. Finally, it is noteworthy that those who begin to turn away from Cain's way in Seth's time *do not sacrifice*. They do only what is centrally required: "At that time men [i.e., people] began to call on the name of the Lord."[33] The way of Cain is not inevitable. It is possible to walk on the way of Seth—in right relationship with God and neighbor.

Rules of Engagement

How am I to relate to my human neighbors in this broken world that nevertheless remains the good creation of God? The story of Cain and Abel proposes at least two answers to this question. The first is that we are to look after our neighbors—we are to keep them. This is perhaps the more obvious of the two answers, arising from the way in which Cain does *not* treat Abel. Less obvious, but I think implicit in the way that God *does* treat Cain, is the idea that we are to be generous to our neighbors even when they are our enemies and even when they live dark lives that breed further darkness. Both these answers are also given to our question in other parts of the Old Testament.[34]

God's Good and Righteous Law

One of the most important biblical passages to consider in this context is Exodus 20:1-17, which describes what are often called the Ten Commandments. Just prior to this passage, the story of Israel's escape from Egypt is recounted. It is the story of an almighty, cosmic battle between the pharaoh, the "god" of Egypt, and the God who spoke to Moses out of the burning bush. Ten plagues, followed by the exodus itself, make the point clearly: it is Moses' God, and not the pharaoh or any other Egyptian god, who is the God of fertility and blessing, and (in the end) the God of life and death (Exodus 12:12). It is Moses' God who is the only true God—the one who has ultimate power over both creation and history.[35] As the Israelites leave Egypt and cross the sea in Exodus 14, God's acts of creation are, in fact, being replayed. Dry land once again emerges out of the watery chaos, as the Spirit-wind sweeps across the earth (Genesis 1:1-10; Exodus 14:21-29). The ten plagues of Egypt are then superseded by the ten "words" or "commandments" in the desert, as the Israelites arrive at Mount Sinai to hear from God what it means for them to be his people. Such words are necessary, for as Genesis 3–11 has amply illustrated, and as Cosmo Kramer humorously reminds us (in the first epigraph to this chapter), "without rules there's chaos." Daoism may advocate living spontaneously without rules and plans, but biblical faith is more inclined to agree with Aristotle: "man, when perfected, is the best of animals, but, when separated from law and justice, he is the worst of all."[36] So it is that in biblical faith, when watery chaos gives way to God's order, there are always rules. So it is in Exodus 20.

The first three words concern the Israelites' relationship with God. The true God is a God of freedom rather than oppression. He is the one "who brought you out of Egypt, out of the land of slavery" (Exodus 20:2), as opposed to the Egyptian "god" who inflicted upon the Israelites brutality, exploitation, and death. Because of his character, the Israelites are now to have "no other gods before me" (20:3) nor to construct any representations of deity for the purposes of worship (20:4-6) nor to misuse God's name (20:7)—probably a prohibition (among other things) of attempts to manipulate God through chanting the divine name in magical spells.[37] God will not be treated as an object—as a power to be harnessed in pursuit of human goals and agendas. God will not look favorably on the religion of Cain, with its manipulative sacrifices.

These first three commandments, delineating the right way of relating to God, are then followed immediately by seven more concerning the right way of relating to human beings. God's ten words, then, reinforce what we have seen earlier: our vision of the nature of the cosmos as a whole is intimately connected with our vision of humanness and society. Living well with God is bound up with living well with our fellow creatures. In Exodus 20:8-17, the God who will not be treated as an object to be exploited also demands that human beings not treat their neighbors in this way. The God who insists on being addressed as "Thou" rather than "It" also insists that mortal beings should not disregard their neighbor's personhood. The God who will not allow mortal beings to use him for their own purposes also sets limits on the human tendency to use others—to grasp after what our neighbor needs.

As described in Exodus 20:8-11, the Sabbath is the central symbol of the difference between the good society ordained by God and the oppressive society ordained by the gods. The good world created by God has at its heart a seventh day of rest, in which there is space for all creatures to remember that life is more than work and that the universe is more than an object to be manipulated in pursuit of gain. The world of the pharaoh of Egypt, in contrast, is marked not by rest but by feverish productivity (Exodus 1–2). As one writer puts it, the Sabbath command envisions

> a human community . . . peaceably engaged in neighbor-respecting life that is not madly engaged in production and consumption, but one that knows a limit to such activity and so has at the center of its life an enactment of peaceableness that bespeaks the settled rule of [God].[38]

In the Sabbath, God's people receive an "alternative to the exploitative ways of the world that begin in self-serving idolatry and end in destructive covetousness."[39]

After the word about the Sabbath, we encounter six further words about right relating to our neighbors. It involves honoring one's parents, and avoiding murder, adultery, stealing, and giving false testimony against a neighbor (Exodus 20:12-16)—the rejection of neighbor destroying and the embrace of neighbor keeping activities. The last of the commandments is the most fundamental (20:17); it concerns coveting (i.e., desiring or yearning for something belonging to someone else).[40] This is nothing less than a warning, in *human* relationships, against that attitude that is responsible for the fracturing of the *divine-human* relationship. In Genesis 3, evil first enters the world because of a human desire to possess something (divinity) that belongs to God; in Exodus 20, evil continues to enter the world because of a human desire to possess things that belong to our neighbors. We see this illustrated in Genesis 4. It is, after all, Cain's anger about not possessing (and his desire for) Abel's good reputation that takes him on the path that ultimately leads to murder. Later in the biblical story, in 2 Samuel 11–12, we find David desiring the wife (Bathsheba) of another man (Uriah). This desire leads to profound moral evil as he first commits adultery (which is a form of stealing) and later facilitates what is essentially a murder, when during a battle he has Uriah deliberately positioned where he is very likely to be killed. Still later, in 1 Kings 21, King Ahab, who has abandoned God and led Israel into the worship of other gods, covets the property of one of his subjects (Naboth). Covetousness leads to false testimony, murder, and the theft of Naboth's property. Abrogation of the opening commandments about worshipping the true God leads to abrogation of the later commandments about treating one's neighbor in the right way.

It is wrong *desire*, these texts suggest, that lies at the heart of a dysfunctional community—desire for the wrong gods and desire for the wrong things. We want things without regard for the other persons with whom we are in relationship, whether God or other human beings. That is why there are murders and adulteries and the other features of human life described in the "ten words" of Exodus 20:1-17. That is, in fact, why there need to be laws in place that will deal with relational breakdowns, as the remainder of Exodus 20–23 indicates (as, e.g., in Exodus 21:15-17, which deals with the case of a son who strikes or abuses his father or his mother, thus failing to honor them).

Love and the Law

These seven commandments concerning neighbor keeping in Exodus 20:8-17 are not to be regarded as an exhaustive account of the human duty toward fellow human beings, from a biblical perspective. They represent only some of the important principles involved in good relationships. These commandments are, after all, largely negative in character. They concern some things that we should not do; they do not tell us what we *should* do. They tell us, for example, that we should not steal, but they do not tell us what our duty is to others who have less than we have, or indeed have nothing at all. We need, then, other passages from the Old Testament to help fill out the picture. For example, we discover elsewhere that one of the major ethical values of biblical faith is generosity (Deuteronomy 15:7-11; Psalm 112:5; Proverbs 11:25; 22:9). Generosity is not commanded in Exodus 20, however—only the avoidance of covetousness.

Taken together, these various other Old Testament passages tell us what Exodus 20 by itself does not. They tell us that we are not to covet other people's possessions but *rather* to be generous toward them. Against the wrong and selfish desire that lies at the heart of coveting, the Old Testament sets a different kind of desire. It is the desire to move out toward the neighbor with openheartedness, seeking the neighbor's good. This outward-moving desire is referred to in Leviticus 19:18 as "love." It is the counterpart, with respect to fellow human beings, to the love that a person ought rightly to have for God: "love the LORD your God with all your heart and with all your soul and with all your strength" (Deuteronomy 6:4-5). Leviticus 19:18 urges the same healing movement toward one's neighbor, employing the same language (Heb. *'ahav*): "love your neighbor as yourself." That is, we are not to put our own interests ahead of those of our neighbor but to consider them at the same time as, and alongside, our own. Here is the higher principle that lies behind the principles of neighbor keeping that we find articulated elsewhere in the Old Testament, including those in the Ten Commandments. It is love for neighbors, displacing covetousness, that allows us to avoid dishonoring parents, murder, adultery, stealing, and false testimony. It is love for neighbors that produces generosity toward them. I put myself in my neighbor's shoes, and I ask, "How would I like to be treated in these circumstances?"; then I act. In deciding on this course of action (contra Mae West in the second epigraph to our chapter), the desirability of the neighbor is irrelevant. What is relevant is only that neighbors *are* neighbors, and that we should desire their good.

WHO IS MY NEIGHBOR?

Who, then, is my neighbor? The Hebrew word is *re'a*—a word that can refer to various persons. It can refer to a friend (Genesis 38:12), to a lover (Song of Songs 5:16), or to a husband (Jeremiah 3:20). It can refer simply to another person in one's proximity (1 Samuel 15:28). Most strikingly, perhaps, the neighbor in the Old Testament includes the enemy. The immediate context of the command to love the neighbor in Leviticus 19:18 makes this clear. If I am wronged by someone, and find myself tempted to "seek revenge or bear a grudge against one of your people," I am *not* to do so but instead to love. Proverbs 25:21-22 unpacks this further: "If your enemy is hungry, give him food to eat; if he is thirsty, give him water to drink. In doing this, you will heap burning coals on his head, and the LORD will reward you." It is for God to bring vengeance on the enemy if he persists in being an enemy; it is not for human beings to do so. The cycle of heroic vengeance, described by Leon Kass earlier, is thus broken. This theme is central to the David/Saul story in 1 Samuel. Time and again David finds himself in a position to do harm to Saul, thereby preventing Saul from doing harm to *him*. He refuses to take advantage of these situations, however, leaving vengeance to God (1 Samuel 24:11-13).

The book of Job also picks up the theme of right treatment of enemies. In the midst of massive questions about why he is suffering, Job spends an entire speech detailing his understanding of the virtuous life (Job 31:1-40). He has not, he says, looked lustfully at a girl (v. 1), or "lurked at my neighbor's door," preying on his wife (v. 9). He has not denied justice to his slaves, because his slaves are made in God's image just like him (vv. 13-15). He has not "denied the desires of the poor or let the eyes of the widow grow weary" (v. 16) nor kept bread to himself rather than sharing it with orphans (v. 17). And here are the specifically important lines: Job claims that he has not "rejoiced at my enemy's misfortune or gloated over the trouble that came to him" (v. 29), nor has he "allowed my mouth to sin by invoking a curse against his life" (v. 30). Job is virtuous; he has loved his neighbor as himself—including his enemy.

LOVE GOD AND LOVE YOUR NEIGHBOR

It is these two injunctions, then—to love God and neighbor—that lie at the heart of the Old Testament understanding of the right way to live in the world. These principles provide the framework within which more specific instructions like "do not steal" and "be generous" make sense. These are, in fact, the principles according to which *all* specific rules about how we should live are to be understood, as we shall see further in chapter 10. Behind and beneath all such rules are *relational* realities. I should relate rightly to *God*, acknowledging that God *is* God, entrusting myself to his goodness and seeking to love him, obey him, and pray to him; and I should relate rightly to my fellow *human beings*, seeking their good, "keeping" them, and avoiding covetousness and all the wrongs that arise from it.

The two "loves" in question are intimately related to each other. From the perspective of biblical faith, it is only as I grow increasingly in a right relationship with God that I can possibly grow increasingly in right relationships with my neighbors and do difficult things like refusing to hold a grudge or to seek vengeance. Just as in Genesis 3 the *fracturing* of human relationships is the product of a fractured relationship between humans and God, so also the healing of the human relationship with God, and the fresh perspective that this gives upon life, is bound up with the *healing* of relationships within the human community. The latter healing cannot happen without the former. Like the former, it is simple but never easy, for (we must again remind ourselves) "man is born broken." We emerge into a world that is already marked by deep fractures within communities: families are dysfunctional, tribal and societal relationships have broken down, and entire societies are in conflict with each other. These dysfunctions are global, and they are generational: there is a long history behind each of them. In such a world, our biblical authors concede, it is difficult to love one's neighbor, even if the neighbor is literally one's own brother. Change is possible only because the God who created the world is a God of grace—one who mends the relationships that have become broken.

In Genesis these truths are best illustrated in the story of Jacob and Esau. Like Cain and Abel, they are brothers. Unlike Cain and Abel, their broken relationship is healed, as God moves in mysterious ways to bring about a reconciliation. The breach is initially caused by Jacob cheating Esau out of his rights as the firstborn son (25:19-34). It is compounded when, in Genesis 27:1-40, Jacob's mother Rebekah convinces him to deceive his father into bestowing the patriarchal blessing on him instead of Esau. At stake now is not simply how much *property* each son will get but who will be the "top son" overall. Favoritism drives the plot, reflecting deep dysfunction within the family: "Isaac . . . loved Esau, but Rebekah loved Jacob" (25:28). Clearly, the curse of Genesis 3 is impacting this family. There is no love of "neighbor" here—only self-interest and partisan affection. And once again in Genesis, a son is ultimately driven into exile, as Jacob leaves town to escape his brother's fury (27:41–28:5).

Reconciliation takes a long time to occur. To reach it, Jacob in particular has to learn some important life lessons, as he encounters situations that gradually lead him back to God (and therefore to Esau). In exile, Jacob lives with Rebekah's brother Laban, and in Laban he meets his match in terms of cheating. After working seven years to get Laban's daughter Rachel as his wife, he is deceived and gets the elder daughter Leah instead. He has to work for seven more years to get Rachel (29:14-30). He spends a considerable amount of time in the story that follows caught in the cross fire between these two wives, contributing to the family pain with his own favoritism, learned perhaps from his mother: "Jacob . . . loved Rachel more than Leah" (29:30). The favoritism is reflected in the names given to some of Leah's children (29:32-34).[41] Rachel, loved by Jacob, is nevertheless childless, unhappy, and jealous. She resorts to surrogate motherhood as a solution to her problems, and Leah responds by doing the same (30:1-24). The childbearing contest eventually kills Rachel (35:18). Jacob has a family, but at great cost. The consequences of deceit are perhaps more visible to him now, away from home, than they were when he was living at home. The perpetrator has become the victim—an experience from which he no doubt learns.

It is this learning experience, combined with the wrestling match with God that is described in Genesis 32, that provides the context for reconciliation between Jacob and Esau. God has been working on Esau too. When they eventually see each other, Esau runs to meet Jacob and embraces him (33:4). The breach has been healed; enemies have once again become friends, and neighbors. At the heart of it, for Jacob, is his newfound ability, as a result of being cheated, to understand what his own cheating of his brother-neighbor meant. He has acquired the human empathy that is essential to loving another "as oneself"—an empathy that Cain never achieved.

LOVE, PROPRIETY, AND SELF-INTEREST

In sum: I am to love my neighbor. By "neighbor," I mean every other human being who is, like me, made in God's image, whose life is inviolable and whose general vocation and whose human rights are the same as mine. I am not to think of myself as a higher, more special being than anyone else or indeed as a lesser, less special being. We are all "gods," in a way, but we are all named "Abel" as well: we are, at the same time, "like God" and yet also "fleeting." We are not called to be heroic—to leave our mark on the world (and inevitably the mark of our boot on others). We are not called to control life or to evade death; attempts to do so often just result in the control and death of others. We are called only to be human—just like everyone else. Everyone else includes our enemies. These, too, are our neighbors.

By "love," I mean "keeping" other persons. I am to look after them actively and to look out for their interests, as best I can and as often as the opportunity presents itself. I am to do this in line with God's own character and actions in the world, and in light of God's own specific commands about what love entails, rather than making the mistake of thinking that I can myself, without God's help, "know good and evil." I am to imitate and obey God, rather than falling for the heroic myth that we human beings ourselves, as individuals and groups, are the measure of what "right" means. Precisely because God is God and we are not, *true* love for God and neighbor will entail obeying God *rather than* conforming to society, where necessary. It may even entail *opposing* the ordered society, in all its sophistication, its artistic expression, and its collecting of beautiful objects and people. Loving my neighbor, moreover, involves both negatives and positives. It involves refraining from such neighbor-harming activities as favoritism, cheating, oppressing my workers in pursuit of gain, failing to honor my parents, murdering, committing adultery, stealing, and providing false testimony. At the root of all such evil is covetousness, and from this too I must refrain. Positively, neighbor love involves taking stringent action, with God's help, rightly to order my desires. Beyond that, it involves virtues like generosity and the deliberate cultivation of empathy, without which it is impossible even to *conceive* of how to love my neighbor as *myself.*

It should already be obvious to the reader who has read thus far in the book that other religious and philosophical traditions, differing markedly from biblical faith in so many other ways, cannot understand the human duty with respect to other human beings in this biblical way. It would be unreasonable to expect them to do so, for as I have taken care to remind the reader on various other occasions, ethics and politics are inevitably, thoroughly, and *always* bound up with cosmology, theology, and anthropology. Our understanding of the story in which we find ourselves inevitably shapes our suppositions about, and imperatives regarding, how I should relate to others. In that sense, the question of Genesis 3 ("Where are *you*?") is always connected with the question of Genesis 4 ("Where is *your brother*?"). It is also connected with important further questions, like "Who is your brother?" and "What do you mean by 'brother'?" Supposing that I *do* wish to do "right" by my brother or sister, what does that look like? *What* is right, and *why* is it right?

So it is that in this very chapter we have seen that, for many societies down through the ages, it has been considered quite "right" that human beings should be sacrificed to maintain good order in the cosmos. Biblical faith does not consider this to be right at all. At the heart of this differing evaluation is a disagreement about the nature of right (in relation to order) and ultimately a disagreement about who God is in relation to the world. Such disagreements do not always lead to *great* differences of opinion about how I should relate to my neighbor. At the level of individual ideas, in fact, we find many similarities across traditions in this regard. Nevertheless, the individual ideas are rooted in larger stories about the world that *are* quite different from each other, and inevitably the precise understanding of an idea and the weight given to it in a particular tradition are both deeply affected by this larger context. This is why even ideas that at first appear similar can often be seen, upon careful reflection, not to be so similar after all.

Love of Neighbor in the West?

Precisely because ethics *are* inevitably part of a larger "package," we would be foolish to read Plato (for example) expecting to find him commending anything like a biblical love of neighbor. For Plato (we recall from chap. 6), "the morality which our 'true philosopher' lays claim to is thoroughly egocentric."[42] The main business of life is to separate the soul from the body, and the rest is about good order. "Justice" is, indeed, merely the will to fulfill the duties of one's station in society, and not to interfere with the duties of others in *their* stations. Similarly, we should not expect to find the biblical idea in the Neoplatonist Plotinus, for it was his mission in life to render the soul invulnerable to external troubles. This is not consistent, either, with a generous, outward-moving love for one's neighbor.

The philosophy of the Greco-Roman world more generally is likewise bound to disappoint. It is true, as Inge claims, that Stoicism and Epicureanism, in contrast to Neoplatonism, "had the merit of teaching men how to live in this world."[43] But what did they teach? Epicurus teaches that individual pleasure is the highest good and that "the highest sort of pleasure is tranquility, freedom from fear and anxiety."[44] The ethic that follows from this is fundamentally self-interested: I am to indulge easily satisfied desires, "thereby gaining self-sufficiency and the confidence regarding the future that accompanies it."[45] Epicurus embraces only such virtues as "are needed in order to live an untroubled life."[46] Among these virtues is justice: "a disposition . . . to adhere to the agreement neither to harm nor be harmed" and "to do so for the right reason" (i.e., because it contributes to a pleasant life).[47] Even friendship is important primarily for the security that it provides *me*. There is no biblical love of neighbor here. Nor is there in Stoicism. Although there are *elements* of biblical-like thinking in the Stoic ethic (a commitment, for example, to honesty and equity in dealing with others and to honoring one's parents), as a whole this philosophy tells a very different "story" from that of biblical faith. Biblical faith cannot, for example, consider pity, grief, or sorrow—those outward movements of the person in compassionate concern for others—as deformations of the soul, as Stoics do. Nor does biblical faith agree with Stoicism at all that dispassionate reason should be the guiding principle to which we should cling in our relationships—whether with God or with our fellow human beings.

Love of Neighbor in the East?

The situation is no different in the East. We should not expect to find a biblical love of neighbor commended in classical Hinduism, for example, for whereas biblical faith requires me to identify with the suffering image bearer at the foot of the societal hierarchy—to regard her and treat her as I do myself—classical Hindu faith requires exactly the opposite. The person at the bottom of society deserves to be there. When I come across a poor man begging at the temple, I may have a limited duty to lessen his suffering, but I display such benevolence as a person who continues to stand further up the chain of being than him.

I remain superior to him. Those at the bottom of the hierarchy *rightly* serve those at the top, and the former are certainly not as important or as valuable as the latter. Among the "lower people" under consideration here are women—including very young women—whose lives are not believed to be as important as those of men (as the widespread practice of female infanticide in India illustrates).

Classical Buddhism also knows little about the biblical love of neighbor. It *does* regard men and women as (more or less) equal in value, and it *does* teach compassion for all. Many of the individual elements of the Buddhist ethic, to be sure, are compatible with biblical faith. As we have seen, however, the fundamental aim of the Buddhist is to achieve his own *release* from suffering in the world, rather than *engaging* with the suffering world out of love for neighbor. Ethically, the Buddhist's goal is to *refrain from increasing* suffering, rather than to act positively *to lessen or remove* suffering. Fundamentally the focus is on the self: how do *my* actions impact *my* own spiritual journey? Right actions produce "a positive condition of mind and body . . . one that is ultimately conducive to the attainment of Nirvana."[48] Ethics is all about escaping Gautama's "burning house" (already described in chap. 6).

Submission and Love in Islam

Two further examples will suffice: Islam and Confucianism. Islam does share significant similarities with biblical faith, and the open letter from prominent Muslims that I mentioned in chapter 7 ("Common Word") identifies loving one's neighbor *as* one of these similarities. Love for neighbor is, indeed, presented in this letter as one of the foundational principles of Islam. Yet I cannot see that this is actually the case.

It is intriguing, first, that in writing their (very short) introduction to this theme in Islam, the authors do not, at the beginning, cite the Qur'an in establishing Muhammad's commitment to the principle, but instead refer to two "traditions" (*hadith*) from the second tier of the Muslim canon. When they do later refer to the Qur'an, the texts they cite do not, in fact, speak of love for neighbor as the motivating force for the various righteous activities that are mentioned therein (e.g., giving money to orphans, the needy, travelers, and beggars). This is not surprising, because "love between human beings . . . is mentioned only a handful of times in the Qur'an," and it is never appealed to as a motivation for neighbor keeping.[49] This, in turn, is not surprising, since love is not central to the Muslim concept of *God* nor to the Muslim idea of the right human response to God. Transcendent power, on the one hand, and submission, on the other, are the governing ideas.

If the Qur'an does not explicitly tell believers to love their neighbors, however, it certainly does tell them explicitly *not* to love some of them. Muslims are exhorted, for example, *not* to love outsiders to the faith, who are considered to be both God's enemies and theirs (60:1). This is logically consistent with the fact that among the various people in the Qur'an whom God *himself* does not love are the unbelievers (the *al-kafireen*; 2:276; 3:32; 30:45). Here "neighbors" and "enemies" are in two different camps, divided along confessional lines; love is to be offered to the one but not to the other. The Qur'an, then, does not exhort love for the enemy. Indeed, the concept of *jihad* (struggle) is very important to Muslims: "The world is divided into two mutually hostile camps: the sphere of Islam (*dar al-islam*) and the sphere of War (*dar al-harb*). Enemies will convert, like the polytheists, or submit, like the Christians and the Jews."[50] Once again, power and submission are the governing ideas; love is reserved for those who have submitted to power and are obeying Allah's laws. Obedience to God, rather than love for neighbor, is the key concept in the Muslim view of how to relate rightly to one's fellow human beings.

Propriety and Love in Confucianism

Confucianism, like Islam, is similar to biblical faith in some ways, and Confucian thought is often mentioned as possessing parallels to the biblical idea of loving one's neighbor. There are, indeed, surface similarities between some of the sayings of Confucius and some biblical injunctions. In the *Analects*, for example, Tzu-kung asks Confucius, "Is there a single word which can be a guide to conduct throughout one's life?" Confucius replies, "It is perhaps the word '*shu*' [reciprocity]. Do not impose on others what you yourself do not desire" (15:24).[51] This negative injunction, however, falls some way short of the positive biblical requirement to love one's neighbor as oneself. In other places, Confucius enjoins a general benevolence toward one's fellow men, and in one place the injunction is directly followed by another to "employ the labour of the common people only in the right seasons" (1:5).[52] Confucius thus advocates wise and just treatment of one's workers. This is certainly one aspect of a biblical love for the neighbor, but it is *only* one aspect. Immediately following this, general benevolence ("love") toward the masses is contrasted with the cultivation of friendship with one's "fellows" (1:6).[53] Biblical faith, however, requires more than just general benevolence toward the majority of human beings who are neither our workers nor our friends. It requires active love.

In the end, in truth, what Confucius is really interested in is *propriety*, and not love—that everyone should know his place in the cosmic order of things and should behave appropriately in that place. For Confucius, the same close association exists between cosmic order and right that we see in ancient Near Eastern religion, and ethical behavior is the behavior that contributes (along with the performance of ritual) to the maintenance of order. In fact, the same Chinese word, *li*, is used in Confucian thought for both ritual and ethical behavior in pursuit of order. People should strive for conformity, through ritual and ethical performance, with the pattern of reality laid down in the cosmos as a whole, which is mirrored in ideal human society. They should play out, as well as they can, their assigned roles as dutiful father or child or ruler or subject. *Filial* love lies at the heart of this order—love appropriate to the relationship of a child to a parent—as a model for other "appropriate" loves. Propriety is the key.[54]

The distinction between propriety and biblical love is well illustrated in Chinese history itself, in the outrage with which Confucians greeted the teachings of the fifth-century B.C. philosopher Mo Tzu (Mozi). Mozi was highly critical of the selective and partial love that he saw arising out of the Confucian emphasis on filial piety as the fundamental paradigm for social relationships. Believing in one good and supreme power who loves all people impartially and altruistically, Mozi taught that "unequal treatment of others must be replaced by 'universal love', loving all others as oneself, equally and impartially, showing the same respect for their lives and possessions as for one's own."[55] This biblical-sounding view of things was not well received: "Confucians were not uninterested in love, but . . . such lack of discernment of social location meant that we were liable to forget the levels of obligations we owed to different people."[56] In other words, love was disruptive of the proper order of things.

A Global Ethic?

The case of Confucianism is instructive, not least because it illustrates well the problem in assuming that any particular religion or philosophy is similar to another in its overall teaching just because it happens to possess certain apparent similarities in the details. This problem has unfortunately not been noted by many modern people. In fact, it is quite commonly believed nowadays that the biblical idea of loving one's neighbor as oneself, often referred to as "the Golden Rule" or "the ethic of reciprocity," is a staple of religious and philosophical life throughout time and space, found in many cultures at many different times. Evidence that this belief has, indeed, pervaded the popular mind (and culture) may be found in that great bastion of popular wisdom—Wikipedia. In its entry on the Golden Rule, the "rule" is "found" to be important in an impressive array of religions and philosophies, including all the cases in which I have just taken pains to *distinguish* biblical faith from others.[57]

Such a "Wikipedia belief" about the historical and geographical pervasiveness of the Golden Rule is untenable. In order to adopt such a position, the reader of the various texts in question must ignore significant differences not only among the texts themselves but also among the overall contexts in which they are found—the worldviews within which their ideas are expressed and within which their true significance must be appreciated. Such a reader, in fact, must employ precisely the kind of reductionist strategy that we routinely find employed in the writings of believers in an axial age like Karen Armstrong, who tells us that

> at their core the Axial faiths share an ideal of sympathy, respect, and universal concern. . . . Regardless of their theological "beliefs"—which, as we have seen, did not much concern the sages—they all concluded that if people made a disciplined effort to reeducate themselves, they would experience an enhancement of their humanity . . . an alternative state of consciousness.[58]

The "core" to which Armstrong alludes here is, of course, an illusion. It can "exist" only to the extent that people ignore the fundamental differences among the faiths in question. For example, theological beliefs very much *did* concern the biblical "sages," and they were fundamental to their ethics.[59] The same reductionist strategy is also apparent in much of the work of the Parliament of the World's Religions, an organization deeply influenced by axial age thinking. Consider, for example, its publication "Towards a Global Ethic: An Initial Declaration" (1993). There are many affirmations with which it is easy to agree in this document, but the following is not one of them: "that a common set of core values is found in the teachings of the [world's] religions, and that these form the basis of a global ethic."[60] This statement is, in fact, patently absurd, as any honest reading of the situation (and of this book) must surely demonstrate.

9

On Keeping the Earth

How Am I to Relate to the Rest of Creation?

While I know myself as a creation of God, I am also obligated
to realize and remember that everyone else and everything
else are also God's creation.

Maya Angelou[1]

Thank God men cannot fly, and lay waste the sky
as well as the earth!

Henry David Thoreau[2]

In chapter 8 we have seen that the question of Cain—"Am I my brother's
keeper?"—is answered by biblical faith in the affirmative. Yes, I am my
brother's keeper. I am indeed to love my neighbor. But what about the
rest of creation? Am I to love it too? Do I have duties and responsibilities toward it, of the kind that I have toward my fellow humans beings?
I once saw a cartoon in which an ape in a zoo is looking out through
the bars of his enclosure at the person preparing his food and thinking,
"Am I my keeper's brother?" What is the answer to *that* question, and
does it change if the ape is not in captivity? In short, how am I to relate
to the rest of creation?

I have already articulated the beginnings of a response in chapters 2 and 4, where I discussed, first, the nature of the world in general and, second, the nature of human beings in particular. Creation, we recall, is a temple-cosmos, and human beings are the divine images who are supposed to look after it. Their task is to

> rule over the fish of the sea and the birds of the air, over the live-stock, over all the earth, and over all the creatures that move along the ground . . . [to] be fruitful and increase in number; fill the earth and subdue it." (Genesis 1:26, 28)

Every human being, made in God's image, embodies God's presence in his temple-cosmos and participates in his rule there. In Genesis 2, in fact, the natural world is conceived of as coming into being only *along with* human beings, without whom it cannot function. This dependence runs in both directions, for the human being is one with creation in being *created*; she is one of the creatures into whose nostrils God has "breathed . . . the breath of life" so that she becomes "a living being" (2:7). This same term (a living being) is used of the sea creatures (1:20) and the land animals and birds (2:19), and in Genesis 7:22 the flood destroys everything that has "the breath of life in its nostrils." The solidarity of this particular "god" (the human being) with the rest of creation is thus clear. This particular image of God is thoroughly terrestrial—a creature through and through, sharing "the breath of life" with other animate beings. Yet it remains a person who is like God in ways that other creatures are not. This double-sided presentation of the human being in Genesis 1–2 as both "god" and creature, I have affirmed—both as part of creation and yet "over" it—is characteristic of the rest of the Old Testament also. We must now explore this presentation further.

A Common Life

We begin with texts that emphasize the *oneness* of human beings with the rest of creation. In Genesis 1–2, when God's creation is first described, we read that the earth is at first "formless and empty" (Genesis 1:2). God provides both form, giving the cosmos a particular structure and shape, and content, making an empty place full of life. All the creatures that fill this new holy space are said in Genesis 1 (in a recurring refrain) to have been created "according to their kinds"—distinct from each other, in an ordered environment. A God-given dignity, then, is already implied of each individual member of the various families of creation—a dignity that is *not* dependent upon human beings, even though they have their own role to play within the cosmos. All creatures are God's creatures, whatever their "kinds." Indeed, human beings are resolutely *part* of the creation in Genesis 1. They do not have a day of creation to themselves but instead share the sixth day with the other land creatures. In Genesis 1, then, the emphasis lies on the human commonality with, not difference from, the rest of the animal creation.

Genesis 2 underlines this commonality by telling us that humans are "produced" from the earth in the same way as the other animals (Genesis 2:7, 19). Humans are humus (as I explained in chap. 4)—only one subset of God's "living beings" into whom he has breathed the breath of life. The psalmist recognizes this: "when you send your Spirit, they [i.e., all creatures] are created, and you renew the face of the earth" (Psalm 104:30). Human beings are wonderfully created (Psalm 139:13-16; Job 10:8-12) but no more so than other creatures. Psalm 104:10-23 makes this clear: all creatures have their own purposes and destinies under God independent of their relationships with us. The book of Job returns to this same theme in its closing chapters (38–42), as a suffering Job is pressed to recognize that his is not the only show in town. God has many creatures (other than humans) to look after, each living its life quite independent of Job and not sharing Job's concerns. It is significant in relation to this point that the conclusion to the creation week in Genesis 1:1–2:4 occurs not on the sixth day with the creation of human beings but on the seventh day, when God "rested." It is Sabbath rest, not the creation of humanity, that completes creation and brings it to its fullness.[3] This Sabbath rest was later observed weekly in Israel, and on that day it was again the *commonality* of all creatures that was emphasized:

> On it you shall not do any work, neither you, nor your son or daughter, nor your manservant or maidservant, *nor your animals,* nor the alien within your gates. For in six days the LORD made the heavens and the earth, the sea, and all that is in them, but he rested on the seventh day. (Exodus 20:8-11)

From the beginning of the biblical story it is clear: the human being is one creature among many, and should not think of herself, inappropriately, as a "god" over against the remainder of creation. Solidarity with creation should mark her worldview and her practice. The biblical authors would therefore agree with Maya Angelou (in the first epigraph to this chapter): "while I know myself as a creation of God, I am also obligated to realize and remember that everyone else and everything else are also God's creation."

Priests and Kings

It does not follow for these authors, however, that human beings are just the same as other creatures. They are not. They are creatures made in the image of God, with a task given to them with respect to the rest of creation.

Earth Keeping

In Genesis 2 the task is defined in terms of "earth keeping." As we saw in chapter 2, the world is portrayed here as a garden—an enclosed parkland, where human beings live in harmony with their kin (the animals) and with God, who walks in the garden in the cool of the evening. The image of the garden is itself the image of a sanctuary. It is not surprising, then, that the human being is placed in the garden by God "to work it and take care of it" (Genesis 2:15)—or more literally, "to serve it [Heb. 'avad] and keep/guard it [Heb. shamar]." This is priestly language (Numbers 3:7-8). It is *religious* work, this work of the human being in God's world. It is *holy* work, looking after the garden—a garden that does not belong to us but to someone else. As Psalm 24:1 reminds us, "The earth is the LORD's and all that is in it." We are simply the tenants, tasked with serving the garden (and its creatures) and keeping it—or, in more modern language, "conserving" it.

In the Genesis story itself, our earliest extended picture of what this looks like is provided by Noah, who (as one writer puts it) is "portrayed as uniquely righteous in 6:9 . . . [and] also [as] the arch-conservationist who built an ark to preserve all kinds of life from being destroyed in the flood."[4] Noah understands that he is to look after the earth on behalf of its owner—a theme later developed outside of Genesis in a text like Leviticus 25:23, which reminds the Israelites that "the land is mine and you are only tenants." The land of Israel, in other words, is to be regarded as a microcosm of creation. The Israelites are to take care of *it* as people *should* take care of the whole earth. Elsewhere in the Old Testament, the land is explicitly described, along these lines, as a gift from God. It is not a land owned by inalienable right because of Israel's activity in possessing it (Deuteronomy 8:7-10; 11:10-12; 26:9), nor was it earned through virtue (Deuteronomy 9:4-5). It might, in fact, be lost if the Israelites failed to act justly while living in it (Hosea 12:9; Amos 7:17).

Ruling and Subduing

In Genesis 1 the human task is defined not in terms of earth keeping, but in terms of "ruling" (Heb. *radah*; 1:26, 28) and "subduing" (Heb. *kavash*; 1:28). These are both verbs that echo Old Testament language elsewhere about kingship and military conquest. We read of the land of Canaan being "subdued" (*kavash*) before God and his people (Numbers 32:22, 29; Joshua 18:1) and of David "subduing" all the nations (2 Samuel 8:11). To use *kavash*, then, is to use the language of conquest. *Radah*, on the other hand, represents the language of government. It is used elsewhere in the Old Testament of kings governing their subjects (e.g., 1 Kings 4:24) and of other kinds of ruling as well (Isaiah 14:2; Psalm 49:14; Jeremiah 5:31). It is often associated with ideas of force or harshness (e.g., in Ezekiel 34:4). The language used of human rule over the earth in Genesis 1, then, is fierce—even disturbingly graphic—language. It is perhaps unsurprising that historically some have taken it to legitimate aggressive, exploitative, and rapacious human actions with regard to the rest of creation. It is for this reason that Paul Watson, the cofounder of Greenpeace, urges his readers to abandon biblical faith (along with the world's other dominant religions), claiming that it promotes anthropocentrism and focuses (with the others) "exclusively on the superiority and divinity of the human species."[5] Yet to read the Genesis language in this way is certainly to wrench the words out of their proper context.

People Keeping

In the first place, the vocation of kings *in the context of the ancient world* involved not only ruling and subduing but also looking after the welfare of their subjects and ensuring justice for all. To denote human beings as "kings" over the earth, therefore, does not of itself imply that these rulers have permission to exploit and ravage the earth. This is especially the case, second, *in a literary context* (Genesis 1–2) in which it is made clear that human "kingship" is derived solely from the one God who alone is truly King. The earth is the LORD's, in biblical thinking, and only insofar as this sovereign God invites us to do it may we *participate* with him in *his rule* over it. Genesis does not envision absolute and unfettered power, which human beings can exercise with no moral restraint. Humankind's responsibility is rather to exercise "rule" *on behalf of* the God in whose world they live—a just, peaceable dominion, of the sort that is described for us in Psalm 72. It is clear from all of this that the dominion given to human beings by God in Genesis 1 cannot be understood as a *lording it over* the rest of creation. Particularly when Genesis 1 is read alongside Genesis 2, it becomes apparent that dominion is much better understood as a sacrificial *looking after* creation. It is an aspect of our being created in God's image that human beings should imitate God in his creativity and in his providential care for creatures. Human dominion, rightly exercised, is for the benefit of all creation. The ruling king of Genesis 1 is at the same time the priestly servant of Genesis 2. He is a steward of God's world, accountable always and in every respect to the Owner of the garden, the Creator.

A Challenging Task

As the language of Genesis 1:26-28 reveals, however, this human vocation—the responsibility to govern, serve, and conserve creation—is evidently not regarded by our biblical authors as an easy one. From their perspective, the world does *require* ruling and subduing, along with serving and keeping. This is not, in Genesis 1–2, because evil is to be found in the world, for evil does not enter the world until Genesis 3. Rather, it is because the good world that God has made is a *wild* world. As human beings explore it and settle it, they will *need* to be proactive, rather than passive, if it is to "work" in an optimal way.

What this means, precisely, is not made explicitly clear in the book of Genesis, but it does not take much imagination to guess what it *probably* means. In chapter 5, I suggested that Genesis 3, when it details the entrance of evil into the world, is not interested in providing a *global, all-encompassing* explanation of suffering in terms of evil. Suffering is inevitably involved, I argued, in bringing children into God's good world and in working the land. This kind of suffering is not, for the Genesis authors, incompatible with life in God's good creation; indeed, it is *intrinsic* to living such a life. Although God has created a *good* world, it is not devoid of challenges and problems that we must over-come in order to live a blessed life in it—and indeed to bring blessing to creation itself.

It is this reality that is alluded to, I suggest, in the Genesis 1 reference to ruling and subduing. God's good world will always need to be *controlled* and *shaped* in various ways if life is to flourish. Jungle and forest will need to be pushed back and kept back for human settlement and agriculture to take place. Wild land animals (Heb. *khayyat ha'arets*; 1:24-25) will need to be kept away from domestic ones ("livestock," Heb. *behemah*; 1:24-25). Rivers will need to be contained and directed if they are to provide water for crops and be beneficial (rather than destructive) to all life—to bring life rather than death. This is just the way the world is. The earth does not just need to be kept, but also controlled; it needs further *shaping*, beyond what God has done in the original creative moments of the cosmos. The human relationship with the remainder of creation, therefore, is inevitably a relationship marked by struggle as well as by harmony—from the beginning. This is not the case simply because human beings have embraced evil, although inevitably this makes the struggle more intense. The struggle is already built into the fabric of things. It is intrinsic to the good world that God has created.

WAR ON CREATION

Evil does later enter the world, of course, and the human embrace of it inevitably impacts the human relationship with creation, just as it has impacted the human relationship with God and with other human beings. The impact on animal creation in particular, first introduced in Genesis 3:14 (where the serpent is "cursed . . . above all the livestock and all the wild animals"), is more fully explored in Genesis 9:1-7. Here, after the great flood, the human race receives once again the original creation mandate of Genesis 1:28: "be fruitful and increase in number and fill the earth" (9:1). Genesis 9:1-7 opens and closes by alluding to these earlier words.

However, whereas Genesis 1 and 2 marry the development of human society to the task of looking after the rest of creation, Genesis 9 now envisages human society as developing *in tension* with that task—specifically its governance of *animal* society. In Genesis 2, all the animals pass before human eyes to be named, as a search is made for the earthling's partner (Genesis 2:19-20). As this happens, the animals find their place in the scheme of things, in relation to human beings and to each other. Kinship and friendship between animal and human creation are the keynotes of Genesis 2. In Genesis 6, likewise, the birds and the land animals come to Noah to be kept alive on the ark (6:20); once again the emphasis lies on friendship and on a shared destiny. The atmosphere of Genesis 9, however, is very different. While it is the same Genesis 1 command that (re)starts creation—"be fruitful and increase in number and fill the earth"—*this* time the command is accompanied neither by an instruction to keep nor by an instruction to rule animal creation. It is accompanied, rather, by words that tell of fear and conflict in the human-animal relationship: "the fear and dread of you will fall upon all the beasts of the earth and all the birds of the air, upon every creature that moves along the ground, and upon all the fish of the sea; they are given into your hands" (Genesis 9:2, NIV). I shall object to one aspect of this translation ahead, for it brings into the frame more animals than are probably envisaged by the text. For the moment, though, let us allow it to stand. The animals (or many of them) are now envisaged as looking upon their human counterparts not as their keepers nor even as their rulers but in the way that the residents of a land might look upon a conquering army.

That is what the language of "fear and dread" implies, as a text like Deuteronomy 11:25 makes clear: "No man will be able to stand against you. The LORD your God, as he promised you, will put the terror and fear of you on the whole land, wherever you go." This verse refers to the Israelite conquest of Canaan, in which God gave Israel's enemies "into their hands" (e.g., Deuteronomy 20:13, using the same language as Genesis 9:2). Human beings are thus envisaged in Genesis 9 as having abandoned their God-given responsibility to exercise just and appropriate dominion over the earth. Instead, war has been declared on animal creation. The multifaceted nature of human kingship is reduced to one aspect—conquest. In essence, the dimensions of the curse of Genesis 3 on the animal world are now being more fully revealed, as evil works its way deeply into creation. Here, indeed, are the (fallen) men who, if they could fly, would "lay waste the sky as well as the earth" (Thoreau, in the second epigraph to this chapter).

VEGETARIANS AND CARNIVORES?

What are the implications of this newly declared "war" on animal creation? One of them is made explicit in Genesis 9:3: "Everything that lives and moves will be food for you. Just as I gave you the green plants, I now give you everything." Once again, I have an objection to aspects of this translation, but let it stand for the moment. The allusion here is to Genesis 1:29-30, where God provides plants and trees that give both human beings and animals food to eat—language that has sometimes been interpreted as indicating that the author of Genesis 1 thought of the original creation as a vegetarian place, unmarked by predation.[6] On this view, there were no carnivores in the pristine creation; meat eating became a facet of life on earth, whether in the human or the nonhuman world, only at some point after human beings embraced evil. Genesis 9:3, on this view, identifies the point. It is in this verse (it is argued) that God explicitly gives human beings permission to move from a vegetarian to a carnivorous state, and it is here (implicitly) that some other animals also fall into such a state. This, however, represents an implausible reading of Genesis 1–9.

Animal Sacrifice in Genesis 1–8

In the first place, there are various indications throughout Genesis 1–8 that the authors, before we get to Genesis 9, already think of animal sacrifice as an important aspect of human life. Genesis 3:21 refers to garments of skin being provided for human beings by God, which certainly involves at least animal *death*. Genesis 4:2-4 tells us of Abel's sacrifice of sheep. In Genesis 7:2-3, Noah is instructed to take "two of every kind of unclean animal, a male and its mate" into the ark, but also "seven of every kind of clean animal, a male and its mate, and seven of every kind of bird, male and female." He needs sufficient animals to allow *both* conservation of species *and* also sacrifice (for which ritually "clean" animals are required). All of this implies a functioning sacrificial system prior to Genesis 9, and in the Old Testament a considerable amount of sacrificial ritual involves the eating of the sacrificial victim. Sacrifice and eating go together. The authors of Genesis, then, clearly do *not* regard Genesis 9 as the beginning of the human carnivorous state.

Carnivores and "Creeping Things"

Nor do they say anything that implies that carnivorousness entered the *animal* world only as a result of the human embrace of evil. To the contrary, in detailing the sixth day of creation in Genesis 1:24-25, they clearly portray God's original creation as already including three different categories of land animals. Their Hebrew "labels" are *behemah*, *remes*, and *khayyat ha'arets*. The first of these is easy to translate: "livestock." These are the animals that human communities raise and look after as part of their domestic economy (e.g., cows, sheep, goats). The third is also easy: "wild land animals" (lit. "beasts of the earth")—animals that do not form part of the domestic economy. To categorize the world of land animals in this way, as including both the domestic and the wild, is already to imply predation; it is to root in the original creation the reality of the world that was known to the Genesis authors, in which many wild land animals were certainly predatory. More than this, it is plausible to interpret the distinction between the second and third terms, *remes* and *khayyat ha'arets*, as being drawn on the basis of predation and nonpredation within the class of these wild animals.

In order to see this, we must first be clear that the *remes* (sometimes translated as "creeping things") *are* indeed wild. A translation like the NIV does not help us here, since it translates *remes* as "creatures that move along the ground," reserving the adjective "wild" only for its translation of *khayyat ha'arets* (wild animals). As we review other occurrences of *remes* in Genesis 1–11, however, we find that this noun is used in various texts, just like *khayyat ha'arets*, to refer to wild land animals as an entire class. In Genesis 1:26, for example, the *remes* are the only such animals mentioned: human beings are to rule over all the earth—that is, over "fish . . . birds . . . livestock . . . *remes*." The same is true in Genesis 6:7, where God vows to wipe out all "livestock . . . *remes* . . . birds," except those found on the ark.[7] In both cases, *remes* includes what is elsewhere indicated by *hayyat ha'arets*. The opposite is the case in Genesis 9:9-10, where God makes a covenant "with the birds, the livestock and all the wild animals [*khayyat ha'arets*]" *on* the ark. Only the *khayyat ha'arets* are explicitly mentioned here, but the covenant certainly includes the *remes*. Both *khayyat ha'arets* and *remes*, then, can refer to wild land animals as an entire class. However, this obviously cannot be the case when they are used together, as they are in Genesis 1:24-25. Here, a distinction of some kind is clearly intended—a distinction *within* the world of the wild. This understanding of the sixth day of creation fits well with what we read of the fifth (Genesis 1:20-23). Here, two categories of animal life are initially described (sea life and birds, v. 20), but they soon become three, because a distinction is drawn (in v. 21) between "the great creatures of the sea" and "every living and moving thing with which the water teems" [Heb. *ramas*]. The "living and moving things" form a subset within sea life. In the same way, in Genesis 1:24-25 *remes* most likely refers to a subset within wild land animals.

Which animals *are* these? They have often been understood, historically, as *small*, wild land animals (e.g., mice, reptiles, insects) as opposed to *large* ones. This is, however, nothing more than a guess arising from the alleged nuance of the verb *ramas* (to creep, move lightly), which has *suggested* smallness to some interpreters.[8] The implausibility of this guess becomes evident, however, when we consider Psalm 104:20, where "all the animals of the forest [*kol khayto-ya'ar*] prowl [*ramas*]." It is not only of *small* land animals, then, that *ramas* is used in the Old Testament; *all* wild land animals can "prowl" (or creep). The distinction often drawn between *remes* and *khayyat ha'arets* in terms of small and large animals is, therefore, unconvincing. Much more plausible is the distinction that has sometimes been proposed between predators and nonpredators. Following this proposal, we should read Genesis 1:24-25 as distinguishing between domestic animals (*behemah*); wild, nonpredatory land animals (*remes*); and wild, predatory land animals (*khayyat ha'arets*). It is then *particularly* clear that the Genesis authors did not believe that predation entered the animal world only as a result of the human embrace of evil. It was a feature of life from the beginning.

Carnivores and the Goodness of Creation

There is, in fact, no positive evidence *anywhere* in the biblical tradition that its authors believed in an original vegetarian state of creation, either in the human or in the animal realm. A prophetic passage like Isaiah 11:6-9, with its vision of a day when predatory and nonpredatory animals will lie down together in peace, has sometimes been cited as if it had something to contribute to our understanding of the biblical perspective here. This idea arises, however, only from the (faulty) logic that insists that everything that is true about the *future* in biblical thinking is also true about the *past*.[9] Conversely, a text like Psalm 104 stands firmly against the idea that creaturely eating habits now are very different from those in the past. Here the psalmist celebrates God's many creative acts, from the beginning of time to the present. All of God's creatures look to God "to give them their food at the proper time" (v. 27), and this applies as much to the "lions [that] roar for their prey" (v. 21) as to any other creature. Here is a wonderful creation functioning as it should under God's sovereign care: "in wisdom you made them all" (v. 24; including carnivores). For the psalmist, then, one of God's most praiseworthy creative acts is the creation of a carnivorous lion. As one commentator has rightly said, "The predatory lions are not an evil (unless they prey on the flock!)."[10]

Where the Wild Things Are

If Genesis 9:3 cannot plausibly be interpreted as marking a transition from a vegetarian to a carnivorous human state, to what *does* it refer? We can make significant progress toward an answer to this question, first of all, by offering a better translation than the NIV of Genesis 9:2. The NIV text reads as follows:

> The fear and dread of you will fall upon *all the beasts of the earth* and all the birds of the air, upon every creature that moves along the ground and upon all the fish of the sea.

However, the Hebrew behind "the beasts of the earth" (*khayyat ha'arets*) is exactly the same as the Hebrew we find in Genesis 1:24-25, which the NIV itself correctly translates as "*wild* animals," *not* as (land) animals in general.[11] The NIV also offers the same (correct) translation of the term in Genesis 9:10. It is baffling, then, that the translator offers us in Genesis 9:2 "beasts of the earth." The reader is thereby misled into thinking that the verse refers to *all* land animals, not just to a particular *class* of land animal. We *ought* to translate the verse in this way:

> The fear and dread of you will fall upon all the wild (predatory) land animals and all the birds of the air, upon all the wild, non-predatory land animals ["every creature that moves along the ground," Heb. *ramas*], and upon all the fish of the sea.

The Lost Sheep (and Cows)

This translation allows us to notice something rather striking when Genesis 9:2 is compared with Genesis 1:24-25 and Genesis 9:10. In Genesis 9:2, one class of animals is not mentioned at all—the *behemah*, "livestock." Genesis 9, we thus realize, is concerned only with animal life in the *nondomestic sphere*: the predatory wild land animals, the birds, the remaining wild land animals (*remes*), and the fish. It is *wild* creatures, and not creatures in general, that now live their lives in fear and dread of human beings. The livestock *already* "belong" in human hands, from the perspective of Genesis. We may go further: the animals explicitly singled out in Genesis 9:3 as being given over to humans now for food are not *animals in general* but only some of the *wild land animals*: "Every wild but nonpredatory land animal [Heb. *remes*] that is living shall be food for you. As I gave green plants to you—everything" (Genesis 9:3; my translation). Why are these particular animals (e.g., deer) singled out? Most likely it is because they are to become a much *more important* food source for humans than the others mentioned.[12]

Hunters and Warriors

We can now say confidently that Genesis 9:2-3 is not a passage about human beings beginning to eat animals. It is a passage about a change in the human relationship with the animal world, whereby wild creatures of land, sea, and air become targets of human aggression rather than subjects of human governance and care. They become first and foremost menu items. The authors of Genesis already know of human beings as meat eaters prior to Genesis 9. Human beings sacrifice and eat the domesticated animals that they have themselves raised (as Genesis 3:21; 4:2-4; and 7:2-3 imply). Nothing is thought to be amiss with this practice, nor is there any indication in Genesis that the hunting of wild animals is itself intrinsically problematic.[13] Meat eating is not itself a problem, insofar as it is practiced out of human need and in an overall context of creation care.

What Genesis 9:2-3 envisages, however, is the replacement of a care mind-set with a conquest mentality. This new mentality conceives of wild creatures as an enemy people that needs to be subjugated—a kingdom to be conquered so that the victor may benefit from the collected spoils. It is an exploitative, rapacious approach to the wild. Human need would not of itself require people to move much beyond the domestic

economy in pursuit of food, and if need were determinative, the hunting that did occur beyond those confines would have minimal impact
on the world of wild creatures. Genesis 9 envisages a world, however,
in which such distinctions between the domestic and the wild have
been obliterated. There is no longer any order to the world; there is only
chaos. Another boundary has been breached, in a biblical book that is
replete with examples of such boundary infringements. It is now open
season on all nonhuman creatures, insofar as they might possibly satisfy human desires. The force of Genesis 9:3 in this context is *not* "just
as I gave you plants, now I give you animals"; it is "just as I gave you
plants that you had not cultivated, now I give you wild creatures that
you have not domesticated." These are some of the fuller dimensions
of the curse on the animal world that is first pronounced in Genesis
3. Creation is not right; even the animals are being deeply affected by
human dysfunction.

ANIMAL AND HUMAN RIGHTS

In the biblical perspective on this newly cursed world in which relations between human beings and wild creatures are now defined in
terms of hunter and hunted—and not keeper and kept or sovereign and
subject—it is important to note that the inhabitants of animal world
still have rights. Even in warfare, biblically speaking, there are rules of
engagement.[14] This is signaled in the very curious wording of the first
part of Genesis 9:3, which the translation of the NIV obscures: "everything that lives and moves will be food for you." The translation I have
just offered reads instead, "every wild but nonpredatory land-animal
that is living shall be food for you." The Hebrew wording that I have
thus tried to represent reminds us that all the creatures of God are
indeed "living" beings. Nonhuman creatures are *like* human beings in
this respect (Genesis 2:7), whether they be sea creatures (Genesis 1:20)
or land animals or birds (Genesis 2:19). Every creature of God has "the
breath of life in its nostrils" (Genesis 7:22). This is an important truth,
which from a biblical perspective must be embodied in the human relationship with wild animals, *even as* those animals become human food.

Shepherds and Wolves

For this reason, the *statement* about wild creatures now becoming
human food (Genesis 9:3) is immediately followed by an *instruction*

that prohibits any eating of "meat that has its lifeblood still in it" (9:4). That is, the animal must be definitely and completely dead before it is eaten, which is assured by draining its blood from its carcass. Even in the world of "fear and dread," there are still rights and wrongs when it comes to the treatment of the victims of hunting. In biblical thinking generally, the life force (the blood) of an animal does not belong to any human being but to God. According to Deuteronomy 12:23, "The blood is the life and you must not consume the life along with the flesh." Leviticus 17:11 agrees that "the life of the flesh is in the blood. I have consigned it to the altar on your behalf to atone for your lives, because the blood, in its value as life, makes atonement." In Leviticus 17:3-4, in fact, any Israelite who sacrifices an animal "in the camp or outside of it instead of bringing it . . . as an offering to the LORD . . . shall be considered guilty of bloodshed; he has shed blood and must be cut off from his people." Exceptions appear to have been made for wild land animals that were clean in sacrificial terms, like deer, and for clean wild birds. In these cases the blood was buried. The main point is, however, that the taking of animal life must be sanctioned by God and carried out in the presence of God in order to be legitimate. It cannot be done casually. In these later biblical texts, as in Genesis 9, law enters the story to control, if it cannot eradicate, the evil that has entered the world. Its purpose is to order, even if it cannot restore, the broken relationships between humans and animals. Human beings may have relinquished many aspects of their ordained task of being rulers of the world—of being "shepherds" of their flock. As Leon Kass aptly puts it, however, "The shepherd is not—and must not become—a wolf. He can and must abide by the restriction on eating 'flesh with the blood thereof.'"[5]

Sacred Killing

Animals have rights, just as human beings have rights. The connection between these two topics—the taking of animal life and the taking of human life—is evidently already in the minds of our Genesis authors, because in Genesis 9:4-6 they move on without pause from the one to the other. The logic progresses in three steps: humans must respect animal life even while taking it away (v. 4); animals must also respect human life, and are not *permitted* to take it away (v. 5);[6] and finally, humans are to respect human life and to respond to its destruction decisively and appropriately: "whoever sheds the blood of man, by man shall his blood be shed; for in the image of God has God made man" (v. 6). All of God's creatures have rights, which God takes steps to protect in a world that has been damaged by evil. The story of Cain in Genesis 4 illustrates this truth on the *human* side of things. A curse falls on Cain, and he finds himself in a dangerous world. He fears for his life, because there is no one who can function as his "redeemer of blood," ensuring that justice will be done in the event of his death. God himself, as we have seen in chapter 8, guarantees this justice. Similarly, the consequences of the curse that falls on the *animals* in Genesis 9 are mitigated by the "rule of law" that God institutes in Israel's sacrificial system. In a world in which wild animals are victimized by conquering human beings, it is made clear that the taking of animal life is a religious act. This is good news, for it limits the human ability to act rapaciously toward creation. Indeed, later in the biblical story many of these animals, including all the carnivorous ones, are entirely forbidden to the Israelites as food, Genesis 9 notwithstanding (Deuteronomy 14:1-21; Leviticus 11).

GENESIS 9 AND FATE?

One important question remains to be asked of Genesis 9:1-7: Are we to regard God's words in this passage as defining the inevitable path that human beings must follow in relating to wild animals in a fallen world? Are we to understand that the exploitative, rapacious approach to the animal world that is envisaged here is not only a path that *might* be adopted by human beings but also a path that will and *should* be adopted, because God has ordained it so? The question here is similar to the one I posed in chapter 6 regarding the curses in Genesis 3. There, I noted that many have understood Genesis 3 in the following way: that because we live now in a fallen world because of the sinfulness and stupidity of our first ancestors, we must simply accept what we have inherited from them. The curses are God-ordained curses in which God has (as it were) "recreated" the world as a place suitable for fallen people. The proper response to evil, and to the suffering that arises from its embrace, is to live in this God-ordained world without seeking to change it. On this view of things, to seek to change the world would be, in fact, to rebel against God.

Remembering Genesis 3

In answering my own question now about Genesis 9:1-7—a passage that merely unpacks the significance of the curse of Genesis 3:14—I begin by repeating what I said in chapter 6 regarding the wrong interpretation of Genesis 3. The authors of Genesis are *not* saying that life east of Eden represents the way in which human life and society *must* now inevitably develop. God's curses are not regarded in biblical thinking as fates or destinies imposed upon creatures who can do nothing now to reverse them. God's curses represent, rather, statements of consequences that are bound up very much with a human being's next set of decisions. There are two pathways presented to readers by the biblical literature—two ways in which its readers might go. One involves obedience and blessing. The other involves disobedience (autonomy) and cursing. It is up to the reader to choose. The same is true, I propose, with respect to Genesis 9. Its authors are not saying that human beings are *fated* to abandon a relationship of care with the animal world and adopt a conquest mentality instead—that a world marked by a conquest mentality is *God ordained*. They are simply describing a second path that *may* be chosen, alongside the path that is described in Genesis 1–2.

In pursuing my argument in chapter 6, I pointed out the various ways in which the remainder of the Old Testament does not view the events of Genesis 3 as cataclysmic. That is, it does not view them as inevitably changing everything about the world in which we live. The Old Testament (I noted) does not ever again even refer *back* to the events of Genesis 3 as important for human beings in the present, when it comes to understanding the world in which we live or how we should live in relation to God and the rest of creation. It knows that chaos and darkness are threats to creation. It knows that human beings can and do embrace chaos and darkness and become implicated in them. But our biblical authors urge us *not to live* in the world of Genesis 3. They urge us, in turning back to God, to know a different world. This world, they tell us, is in fact the world that the good God is anxious to provide for us. In chapter 6, I cited various biblical texts relevant for a proper understanding, along these lines, of the curses relating to *the man and woman*. It is not difficult, similarly, now to cite texts relevant for a proper understanding of the curse relating to *the animals*—texts that reflect expectations of human beings that are more in line with Genesis 1–2 than with Genesis 3 and 9.

The Present Imperative

One such text is Hosea 4:1-3. In this passage, the prophet Hosea brings against the Israelites an indictment from God:

> There is no faithfulness, no love,
>   no acknowledgment of God in the land.
> There is only cursing, lying and murder,
>   stealing and adultery;
> they break all bounds,
>   and bloodshed follows bloodshed.
> Because of this the land mourns,
>   and all who live in it waste away;
> the beasts of the field and the birds of the air
>   and the fish of the sea are dying.

Here as elsewhere in biblical thinking, the abandonment of God by human beings leads on first of all to fractured relationships among them ("lying and murder, stealing and adultery;" v. 2). There is a further consequence, however: since the earth keepers are now unable to function as *they* should, the *rest of creation* also suffers. Clearly, Hosea's view (God's view) is that none of these things should be happening. The Israelites *ought* to be worshipping God, looking after their human neighbors, and justly ruling the animal creation. People keeping and earth keeping are thus closely related in this passage. The animals are certainly laboring under a curse, but only because their keepers are not living as they should. They have forgotten their vocation, which is to look after a world full of other creatures that belong not to them but to God. As God says in Psalm 50:10-11, "Every wild animal of the forest is mine, the cattle on a thousand hills. I know all the birds of the air, and all that moves in the field is mine." Animals both domestic and wild belong to God, and in their own way they worship God: "Wild animals and all cattle, creeping things and flying birds . . . let them praise the name of the LORD" (Psalm 148:10).

It is only the wicked who live like Hosea's contemporaries. The righteous remember their vocation, and that is why "the righteous know the needs of [or, better, "care for"] their animals" (Proverbs 12:10). *These particular* animals are, of course, domestic ones (Heb. *behemah*), which are not the focus of interest in Genesis 9 but which do appear among the "cursed" creatures of Genesis 3:14. The implications of the curse for these *domestic* animals are never explicitly described in Genesis, but they may reasonably be assumed to involve the same kind of mistreatment at the hands of human beings that Genesis 9 envisages for *wild* animals—the kind of mistreatment, in the domestic sphere, that we could still catalogue all too easily in the world of today. Proverbs 12:10 urges not acceptance of this curse but creation care. So, too, does the passage concerning the Sabbath in Exodus 20:8-11 (already quoted earlier), in which it is clear that domestic animals are some of the "neighbors" we are to love by allowing them to rest, along with us, on one especially holy day of the week. Whatever the effects of the curse on the animals in Genesis 3 and 9, then, the present imperative in biblical thinking is clear: human beings remain rulers, and should care for animal creation.

RESPECT AND INTERVENTION

How am I to relate to the rest of creation? I am to relate to it as one creature among many, refusing to regard myself as God in relation to it. Yet I am to recognize that I am unlike other creatures, in that I am made in the image of God. As such, I am to view myself as an earth keeper, working and taking care of God's garden. I am also to view myself as a ruler, ruling on God's behalf, looking after the welfare of my subjects, and ensuring justice for all. This demanding vocation, I am to recognize, is greatly complicated by the human embrace of evil. Even in the best-case scenario, evil disables the human community from properly carrying out its divinely sanctioned tasks. At worst, it leads the human community to declare war on the animal world (in particular). Yet, from the perspective of biblical faith, it remains my task actively to pursue my vocation. To return to where we began: it remains my task to regard the ape as my brother, my fellow creature— one of those that I am called to serve and to keep, as well as to rule and subdue. Indeed, part of what needs to be mended in us by the grace of God is what is broken in this respect—namely, our willingness and ability to commit to the task of cooperating with God in governing the cosmos well.

A Limited Perspective

The book of Genesis, then, read in the context of the whole Old Testament, provides a clear answer on the generalities of how human beings ought to relate to the rest of creation. It does not, however, answer every specific question about this matter—just as it does not answer every question about what it means to love one's human neighbor. In particular, we are left to wonder about the following question: How far should human rule over God's good world involve *changing* the world, and how far should it involve only *maintaining* the world as we first find it?

Earlier in this chapter, I mentioned three examples of changes that human beings must inevitably make (and have made) to the world in pursuit of creational flourishing: they must push back and keep back (at least to some extent) both jungle and forest, keep wild animals away from domestic ones, and contain rivers, directing them to productive ends. These are the kinds of things, I imagine, that are implicit in God's command in Genesis 1:28 to "be fruitful and multiply, and fill the earth and subdue it; and have dominion over the fish of the sea and over the birds of the air and over every living thing that moves upon the earth." Although God has created a *good* world, it is not devoid of challenges and problems that human beings must overcome to live a blessed life in it while also blessing creation. Jungles and forests, wild animals, and rivers present some of these challenges. It is difficult, in fact, to imagine how a burgeoning human population could ever have survived, and then flourished, *without* changing its environment in such ways (and others), and there is no evidence that the biblical authors themselves *tried* to imagine this. It must have been as obvious to them as it is to us that if one is going to keep domestic sheep in ancient Palestine, one is going to have to fight off lions and bears (1 Samuel 17:34-37). It must have been as obvious to them as it is to us—much more obvious, in fact—that if one is going to survive at all in such an environment, the problem of access to usable (and indeed drinkable) water will need to be solved.

But what are the *limits* placed upon human beings by the divine commands to serve and to keep, as well as to rule and subdue? What are the *constraints* upon their actions with respect to jungles and forests, wild animals, and rivers, even as they are compelled to subdue them and even as they engage in deliberate environmental change? The biblical authors do not explicitly tell us.

Plague and Passivity

They do not tell us, for example, exactly how the righteous human being ought to respond to disease, which is certainly an aspect of "the world as we find it" and does not obviously originate in the human embrace of evil but nevertheless causes human suffering rather than flourishing. Biblical authors *do* look to God as a healer of disease (Exodus 15:26; Deuteronomy 32:39; Ezekiel 34:16; Malachi 4:2), just as they understand God as working out his purposes of justice and redemption through the medium of disease (among many such media). Further, they do consider it a good thing that God's prophets possess healing gifts (1 Kings 17:17-23; 2 Kings 20:1-7). From the perspective of the biblical authors, then, it is not intrinsically impious to resist and seek to overcome disease, although they are naturally critical of those who look to human beings *rather than* to God for healing (Jeremiah 46:11; 2 Chronicles 16:12). The trajectory of these biblical texts is well summed up in the deutero-canonical text, Wisdom of Sirach (38:1-14).[17] Here, the author advises his readers to honor doctors, whose ability to heal comes from the God who himself created medicines and gave human beings knowledge of them. In earlier times, it could very well have been part of King Solomon's purpose in describing plant life to catalogue their healing properties.[18]

So it is clear that biblical faith does not encourage a fatalistic attitude toward disease nor even a passive one. The biblical attitude is not that of Father Paneloux in Camus' *La peste*, who when he becomes ill chooses to trust God *rather than* calling a doctor.[19] In fact, the biblical texts suggest an active rather than a passive or fatalistic response to disease—and not just the action of prayer, which is, of course, everywhere commended and modeled in cases of illness and other troubles in the Psalms. All of this is clear. However, the biblical literature does not allow us to know which constraints its authors might have placed *around* such an active response, given their overall worldview.

The Need for Wisdom

The Old Testament does not answer every specific question, then, about how human beings ought to relate to the rest of creation. It invites the reader, instead, into the way of wisdom and discernment, guided by two familiar imperatives: remember that you are *one creature among*

many (and not, therefore, a "god" in relation to others); remember that
you are made in the image of God (and are, therefore, an earth keeper
and ruler of creation). These imperatives will inevitably require that,
to some extent, we intervene in and change aspects of creation as we
find it, especially when it causes suffering. But these same imperatives
will also lead us to respect and accept creation as we find it, *even when*
it causes suffering. I do not imagine for a moment, for example, that
our biblical authors would have thought it right to launch a killing
campaign against all bears and lions in ancient Palestine just because
occasionally a bear or a lion caused the human population suffering.
Nor do I imagine that they would have advocated the abolition of cliffs
in ancient Palestine just because human beings occasionally fell from
them, rivers because they occasionally drowned in them, or fire because
it occasionally burned them—even if such things could have been abolished. These are all just aspects of how the world works. There is a
"givenness" about creation in biblical thinking that requires that we
approach it with respect and acceptance. And then there is (yes) the
imperative to "rule and subdue." Wisdom lies in knowing when and
how to accept certain aspects of creation as given, and when and how
to "push back" and to change.

ON ESCAPING, ACCEPTING, AND TRANSFORMING THE WORLD

As in previous chapters, our understanding of the biblical perspective will inevitably be sharpened and clarified if we compare and contrast this perspective with others. A convenient way of organizing our
thinking here is to group these other perspectives under three headings. I shall consider first of all religious and philosophical traditions
that emphasize the importance (and even the centrality) of *escaping*
"the natural world," then a couple that emphasize *acceptance* of it, and
finally one that emphasizes *transforming* it.

Escaping the Natural World

For reasons that will become clear in a moment, I shall focus here on
Plato. For Plato, we recall, the natural world that we perceive with our
senses is only a shadowy version of a more "real" world in which our
ultimate human destiny lies, as our souls escape our bodies and fly back
to their true home. The embodied, physical world is therefore not very

important; it is, indeed, a "problem" for us. This does not mean that for Plato the material world, in itself, is *bad*, as it was for the Gnostics and the Manichaeans who came afterward. On the contrary, the craftsman who crafted it made it as good as it could possibly be, given its physicality. The material world does *reflect* the world of the Forms (the ideal world); it does *reflect* "the Good." For Plato, then, we can learn *something* about the Good by studying the natural world. To this extent, the natural world is important and worthy of note. It is only so, however, as an aid to the rational soul's movement up and away from this material world to the "real" world. For this reason, Plato did not consider even *human* affairs in this world as worthy of being taken very seriously. We should not expect to find, therefore, that he took *nonhuman* affairs very seriously either. Everything in this way of thinking about the world is bent toward the individual philosopher escaping the earth. It *cannot* be a central human concern to be an earth keeper, and it *is* not.[20] If Plato only reluctantly conceded that a philosopher should be involved in ruling over *human* society, we can be sure that there was no idea in his mind that human beings should be involved in ruling *nonhuman* society—especially not on behalf of a personal God.

There is one important respect, however, in which Plato's thinking about the natural world is somewhat similar to biblical thinking, so long as we are prepared to make some important distinctions. The similarity lies in what Plato has to say about his craftsman making the best possible world *given its physicality*. This idea in Plato is often referred to using the phrase "the recalcitrance of matter." According to Plato, the craftsman works to a plan, represented by the Forms. He tries to make his material conform to the plan, but he is hampered by the very nature of the material itself—the very properties of earth, water, air, and fire. There is purpose in his work (a "teleology"), but the world that actually emerges in the end is the result not only of teleology but also of "necessity." The craftsman simply cannot achieve everything he wants to achieve. The physical material with which he is working is "recalcitrant."[21]

The overall picture here of a frustrated craftsman failing to deliver on his plan is not at all similar, of course, to the biblical idea of the God who creates the world. There is no idea in the biblical literature that God intended to create something else but had to settle for what he eventually got. God purposed to create this world, and God did so. Still (and restating Plato somewhat), the notion that physicality inevitably imposes constraints even on the almighty creator God is certainly consistent with the biblical idea that there is suffering that is intrinsic even to a creation that is said so forcibly in Genesis 1 to be *good*. That is to say: given that God *purposed* to create a world in which human beings, as well as wild animals, cliffs, rivers, and fires, are as they are and also *purposed* that his creatures should genuinely be free, it is indeed inevitable ("necessary") that from time to time human beings will be eaten, fall from great heights, drown, and be burned. These are the necessary correlates to the joy of being alive in a world such as this: to the amazement with which we greet the lion in the savanna, to the thrill that we get from climbing a mountain or swimming across a bay, to the contentment that arises when we sit by a blazing fire in the hearth. It is not that matter is "recalcitrant." It is just that it is matter.[22]

Hinduism shares with Platonism an emphasis on *escape* as the fundamental human priority with respect to the natural world. Brahman pervades everything in nature, of course, and so everything becomes a potential point of access to the sacred for human beings. Plants and rivers can be manifestations of the sacred, and it is well known that Hindus regard the cow as especially sacred among the animals. But as in Platonism, the natural world is, in the end, of interest in Hinduism only as a window into another world into which Hindus hope, as soon as possible, to enter. The natural world is illusion. There are, therefore, none of the emphases in classical Hindu faith that we find in biblical faith concerning the intrinsic goodness of the material world and the primary human duty actively to care for it, or indeed to subdue it. The material world is not important as such and in its own right but only as a place in which divinity manifests itself and in which other souls, in various forms, are currently "stuck." I myself might become further stuck in this world if I behave in ways that disrespect the sacred (including subduing it).

So it is that even the sacred Ganges can be allowed to become one of the most polluted rivers in the world. Bathing in the Ganges at the present moment is "one of the most auspicious acts a Hindu can perform,"[23] and at the same time a dangerous thing to do in terms of physical health. Strictly from the perspective of classical Hindu faith, this is not very problematic, for the body, in the end, does not matter and neither does the pollution of the Ganges, *as a river*. The Hindu is not called to keep the body or the river—only to encounter, in his currently embodied form, the divinity in the river's waters and in so doing perhaps to move a few more steps closer to release. When Hindus protest about the state of the Ganges, then, they typically do so not because of the pollution of the river as such but because disrespect has been shown toward divinity. Many Hindus do not protest at all and indeed find it impossible to believe that bathing or drinking in this sacred place can possibly do them any harm. Whether in its monist or more polytheistic and animistic forms, then, Hinduism does not very much resemble biblical faith in its understanding of how human beings should relate to the natural world, even though the two traditions agree that the world is indeed sacred space.[24]

Accepting the Natural World

This brief discussion of Hinduism has illumined an interesting reality—namely, that people will not necessarily possess strong commitments to look after the natural world just because they hold it to be sacred in various ways. This can be true even where people do *not* understand the primary human goal in terms of escaping from the world, but rather *accept* it, as they find it, as the very environment in which they are to live out their lives. It is well known, for example, that premodern Native American tribes tended (in common with indigenous peoples elsewhere in the world) to place great emphasis on the "intrinsic value and sacredness of nature."[25] Yet the Montagnais people of Canada still attempted, on their beaver hunts, to kill every beaver they encountered; the Plains Indians, on their buffalo hunts, typically killed many more buffalo than they needed; and white-tailed deer were hunted "to extreme scarcity and even to local extinction" by various Indian tribes.[26] To these polytheistic and animistic peoples, the world was to be accepted, as they found it, as sacred, and the primary goal was to live well in it rather than to escape from it. However, the popular notion that this worldview led such peoples to a particularly strong commitment to look after the natural world is not well founded. Much more could be said on this topic, but space prevents it in the present context.[27]

Instead, we turn our attention to a very different religious tradition, Islam, in which *acceptance* of the natural world is nevertheless still the fundamental posture. As we have seen in previous chapters, the similarities between Islam and biblical faith are significant. With biblical faith, Islam shares the idea that we live in a world that is sacred space and that was created by one personal, merciful, and compassionate God. The role of human beings *in* creation is also somewhat similar; human beings are creatures of the dust, closely related to God's other creatures and yet standing apart from them in important ways. In chapter 4 we saw that in Islamic thinking human beings are the "caliphs of God" on earth. We may now add that there are at least hints in the Qur'an, somewhat similar to what we found earlier in Hosea, that the manner in which these caliphs live their lives can affect the rest of creation.[28]

There is similarity, but, as we have also seen, there is significant difference. Islam's overriding commitment to God's oneness and transcendence forbids any idea of human beings as image bearers of God who share his likeness. There can, then, be no great emphasis on the human role in looking after creation. The predominant emphasis in the Qur'an, when it comes to right relating to the natural world, is *learning* from that world. The natural world is already in submission to the almighty Allah who created it, serving God by conforming to his laws. Everything in that world, from molecules to animals, functions exactly as it should within the design and purpose of the one, omnipotent God. It is, therefore, a world replete with signs that point to God, and human beings can learn from these signs about how they themselves should submit to God.

Creation does not require subduing in Islam, then. The natural world is already subdued; it is in exactly the right state of submission to Allah, and everything in the natural world already happens just as Allah wills. Nor does this world really need looking after or active keeping—it is doing just fine as it is. What the natural world really needs, in fact, is to be left alone:

> The prohibition [in Sura 30:30] against altering creation is at the heart of the Qur'an's view of the natural environment. It is God's creation, not humanity's. To modify or somehow interfere with creation is to usurp God's role and to set oneself up in God's place. Consequently, those who abuse and harm the environment are guilty of the unforgiveable sin of *shirk*, or associating themselves with God.[29]

In biblical thinking, conversely, although the creation does indeed belong to God and not to humanity, human beings *are* rightly "associated" with God in the governance of the cosmos. They are called, in fact, not only actively to keep the natural world but also to participate in its subduing. It does not function in an optimal way independently of human participation in the governance of the cosmos. To "interfere with creation," then, is not to "usurp God's role" but to do precisely what God has asked us to do as his image bearers. This also means, incidentally, that in biblical thinking the natural world does not present us with unambiguous "signs" that tell human beings how to live before God. We can learn *some* things from observing nature, in biblical thinking, but learning is not the only (or even the main) human task with respect to the natural world.

Again, we encounter here a recurring theme in this book: that the answer given to any one of the important individual questions about life, the universe, and everything is inevitably bound up with the answers given to all the others. Even in the case of traditions that are quite similar to each other in various respects (Islamic and biblical faith), significant differences in cosmology, theology, and anthropology inevitably lead to significant differences on thinking about right relating to nonhuman creation. On cosmology: Are there aspects of creation that need "subduing"? On theology: Does the nature of God rule out the possibility of his being "associated" with creatures in governing the cosmos? On anthropology: Are human beings called to participate with God in *shaping* the cosmos or only to submit to God *in* the cosmos? Is there such a thing as *righteous* human intervention in, and changing of, creation as we find it? Is there, indeed, such a thing as a righteous degree of *human autonomy* in interaction with the natural world, in which human wisdom gets to decide when and where intervention and change should occur?[30]

The differences are even more stark when we turn to other traditions in which the natural world is, again, accepted precisely as it is given to us but in which there is no belief in a personal God who has revealed important things independently of nature—for example, that human beings are called to be caliphs, or image-bearers of God. Consider the ancient Stoics, for example, with their goal of living in agreement with what reason finds nature to be. The Stoics accepted nature as the reality to which one should conform oneself, but there is no idea in Stoicism that one has any particular responsibility toward the nonhuman aspects of nature.[31] Stoic thinkers are, indeed, decidedly anthropocentric in their thinking. So it is that in *The Nature of the Gods*, Cicero can tell his audience, "It remains finally for me to show in my peroration that all things in this universe of ours have been created and prepared for us humans to enjoy."[32] And William Stephens, describing the view of Epictetus, says that "animals are born to serve humans; they are not born for their own sake."[33] There is nothing here approaching the biblical sense of human responsibility for a natural world that exists for its own sake. Reason, it seems, finds nonhuman nature to exist, conveniently, for *us*, and animal rights do not exist. Even *human* rights are limited in this worldview. Whereas those embracing the biblical tradition have historically looked with horror on both abortion and infanticide as involving the destruction of an image bearing creature of God, the Stoics were happy to endorse both practices as "reasonable." In the first case, they held that what nature teaches us about ethics is taught by the tree and its fruit. A baby is part of the mother's body, just as the fruit belongs to the fruit tree, until both (fruit and baby) "fall." Therefore, up to the point of birth, the mother could do anything she pleased to the baby.[34] In the second case, babies with mental or physical defects were judged "useless" as opposed to "sound," and like all useless things they were to be discarded by reasonable people.[35]

Transforming the Natural World

Beyond religious and philosophical traditions that emphasize the importance of *escape* from the natural world or *acceptance* of it, I mention, finally, one that emphasizes *transforming* it. This is a decidedly modern way of looking at the world, and it is exemplified in the writings of the seventeenth-century English philosopher Francis Bacon.

Bacon lived at a time (1561–1626) when what we now think of as the modern scientific worldview was first being shaped. Like the Stoics, "reason exploring nature" was, for him, everything—reason unencumbered by any previous form of tradition, philosophy, or religion. Rigorous empirical inquiry into the nature of this world, with experimentation at its heart, was the method. The pursuit of truth must begin, Bacon thought, with the destruction of false ideas—the idols of the tribe (which we worship because of human nature), of the cave (emerging out of education or custom), of the marketplace (arising from public communication), and of the theater (deriving from traditional philosophical systems). The goal was total knowledge of nature—not in order to live in *agreement* with it but in order to *master* it. Knowledge was power; complete knowledge would result in complete mastery,

Bacon thought, and would be followed (as science produced technology) by the transformation of the world. Bacon's view was utopian, distantly informed by certain biblical texts concerning the coming of the kingdom of God. He believed that the effects of the curses in Genesis 3 could not only be mitigated but also abolished. His view was also, like Stoicism, thoroughly anthropocentric. For Bacon, the natural world existed fundamentally for human use and benefit.[36]

It is with the faith of people like Francis Bacon that I believe people like Lynn White (mentioned in chap. 2) are confusing biblical faith. This confusion is generally rife within the circles of dark green religion. Biblical faith does not advocate (or indeed justify) the bending of everything in nature to human ends, any more than it advocates or justifies an escapist or a passive approach to the natural world. It advocates a wise balancing of earth keeping and earth subduing, accompanied by people keeping as well, as we live out our lives in the good world in which the good God has placed us.[37]

10

I Saw the New Jerusalem

Which Society Should I Be Helping to Build?

Political life revolves around disputes over authority: who may
legitimately exercise power over others, to what ends, and under
what conditions. In such disputes it might be enough to appeal
to something in human nature that legitimizes the exercise of
authority, and leave the matter there. But . . . any reflection about
human experience has a way of traveling up the chain of causes,
first to the cosmos, then to God.

Mark Lilla[1]

Each constitution has a vice engendered in it and inseparable
from it. In kingship it is despotism, in aristocracy oligarchy, and
in democracy the savage rule of violence; and it is impossible,
as I said above, that each of these should not in course of time
change into this vicious form.

Polybius[2]

In chapters 7–9 we have explored the *moral vision* of the Old Testament—the vision that human beings are called to pursue in light of
what is true about God, the world, human beings, and evil and suffering.
In the present chapter we turn to the question of *politics*. Which society
should I be helping to build? What attitude should I strike toward what

the ancient Greeks called the *polis* (from which we get "politics")—the city-state, or its modern-day equivalents? Which kind of polis should I be advocating for and striving to bring into being?

Perhaps the very question will surprise some readers—not least because of some of the things I have already said in this book. In chapter 4 I argued that in biblical faith, the right way of thinking about the nature and calling of human beings ought to have real implications for life in society. It ought to impact the way women and slaves are treated, how matters of life and death are handled (e.g., in cases of sacrifice and murder), and how the weakest and most marginalized members of society (even our enemies) are regarded. In chapter 6 I further claimed that biblical faith requires people to be activists—to resist evil and pursue what is right, refusing to acknowledge that evil is here to stay and that nothing can be done to change this (alleged) fact. Biblical faith forbids us to adopt the kind of passive stance toward the world that we find in other religious and philosophical traditions, in which the primary human goal is to escape *from* rather than pursue change *within* the world. It must be clear, finally, from chapters 7–9, that our biblical authors think of love for God, neighbor, and the rest of creation not as interesting theological abstractions with no "street value" but as relational commitments that require *action* in the real world.

All of this being said, is it not *obvious* which kind of polis I should be pursuing? Surely biblical politics arises directly from the biblical moral vision? The building plans for the New Jerusalem have been provided.[3] The human task is simply to build it, insofar as it lies within our power to do so, and to build it as quickly as we can. Isn't that the biblical perspective?

Perhaps surprisingly, the answer to this question is no. Our biblical texts do *not* draw a direct line of connection between theology and ethics, on the one hand, and politics, on the other. They suggest, rather, a much more pragmatic perspective—a perspective that is informed, in a serious way, not only by hope that in the future the world will be different than it is now but also by the nature of the world *as we actually find it*. The hope of the New Jerusalem *informs* this politics, but there are other dimensions to the politics as well. In important ways, the biblical moral vision is, in fact, *accommodated* in the biblical tradition to the circumstances of history and culture, rather than *imposed* upon history and culture. God himself is not understood as imposing the biblical moral vision on society—even though, if anyone has the power to do it, it is presumably God. If God does not do so, then it follows that human beings are not to do so either, since we recall that we are urged on many occasions in biblical texts to try to be like God—to "be holy as I am holy." In sum: biblical faith does not advocate passivity with respect to politics, but it does not advocate, either, a utopian approach. It charts a middle path.

GOD AT WORK IN THE WORLD (GENESIS 1–36)

That God, who is perfectly and incomparably good, is not himself interested in short-term utopian political schemes is clear, first of all, from the biblical narratives concerning the primeval world, as well as from the stories about the first three patriarchs (Abraham, Isaac, and Jacob). In Genesis 1–36, God certainly *calls* his human creatures toward the same goodness that he displays; in fact, he commands it. However, God certainly does not *coerce* it—as if human beings were created to be (as in Mesopotamian belief) the slaves of the gods. God *commands* it, knowing that it is for his creatures' own good that they should obey the command, but he allows his creatures, nevertheless, to exercise moral freedom in choosing whether to obey. Moreover, the human failure or *refusal* to obey the command does not bring the world to an end, nor does it lead to divine disengagement from the world. What happens instead is that God, who is perfectly good, finds ways of continuing to *work* for the good in a world now compromised by evil. He does not reject the world, or even stand aloof *from* the world; he takes the world as he now finds it, and he actively works with what he finds. God *pursues* the good; he does not, by fiat, *impose* it. He turns the world as much toward the good as he can, while respecting the moral freedom of the human creatures who inhabit it.

In Genesis 3 and Genesis 9

We see this first in the story of Genesis 3. Before human beings embrace evil in the garden, they are "naked but not ashamed" (2:25). When they turn away from God, however, they experience shame, and this shame leads them to a hasty and ill-thought-out attempt at clothing, so that their nakedness will not be exposed (3:7). They make "loincloths" for themselves—a word used elsewhere in the Old Testament for "belts." It suggests a very inadequate attempt at a cover-up. The fig leaves used in this cover-up are themselves not ideally suited for manufacturing clothing.[4] The picture painted here is of very limited human success in "fixing" the situation in which they now find themselves. Into this broken situation, however, steps God, who is intent on providing a more lasting solution to the problem. He makes "garments" for them (3:21)—a word used elsewhere in the Old Testament for the main ordinary garment of a person in ancient Palestine (a long, knee-length or ankle-length shirt). If there must be clothing, at least it shall be proper clothing. God has essentially accommodated himself to the new reality of shame in the world, and he has become actively involved in finding the best way forward, given all the circumstances. From the perspective of the biblical authors, God remains the God who is "for us," even in the midst of our wrongdoing and shame. When moral evil enters God's good creation, he does not abandon his creatures but comes closer, accommodates himself further, and helps them to deal with these new realities. He aids them in finding a way to continue their journey in the fallen world, in which physical nakedness has now become problematic because of evil.

Shortly thereafter, Genesis 9:20-23 tells a story related to this same theme, in which Noah becomes drunk and lies naked in his tent. He has been "exposed," both physically and in terms of his intemperance. The proper course of action, attributed to his sons Shem and Japheth in the story (but not to Ham), is to turn one's eyes away and "cover" the nakedness. There need to be rules, as the human story unfolds, about the circumstances in which nakedness may be exposed. Passages like Exodus 20:26, Exodus 28:42-43, and Leviticus 18 eventually articulate some of these rules—rules that are necessary because human beings can no longer deal with God in their nakedness; they would be consumed by God's goodness. They cannot deal with *each other* either; they would be consumed by their mutual darkness, evidenced in guilt, shame, wrong desires, and loss of respect for self and other. In such circumstances, clothing helps to keep human relationships in some kind of good order. According to our Genesis authors, *God himself* is involved in the construction of such order. He brings order out of chaos, just as he first did in the creation of the world itself.

In Genesis 4–6

Between Genesis 3 and Genesis 9, we see other examples of the same kind of divine interaction with the world. In Genesis 4, for example, God "keeps" the murderer Cain, even though Cain would not "keep" his brother Abel. God promises to be Cain's avenger of blood, and puts a "mark" on Cain, so that no one who finds him will kill him (4:15). God creates structures—in a sense, he creates *society*—so that things will not become worse than they already are. This is not an ideal society, but it *is* one in which there is at least some good. God's continued blessing on Cain is seen immediately in what follows in Genesis 4 where, even in the midst of societal darkness, various significant cultural achievements are described (4:19-21).

It is instructive to compare and contrast this section of Genesis with its Mesopotamian counterparts, in which we find a resolutely upbeat account of the evolution of ancient human culture. Mesopotamian tradition tells us of seven superhuman sages who arose from the sea before the great flood and taught humanity the arts of civilization (writing, agriculture, and city building). The oldest of these sages is called Adapa, and he is associated with the city of Eridu—generally regarded in Mesopotamian tradition as the first city to be founded. In Mesopotamian thinking, then, civilization is made possible *by the gods*, and it is rooted in the divine will; it is an undiluted good. This upbeat picture of civilization is also found in later writers like Aristotle, for whom "the city is the first truly self-sufficient community; it comes into being for the sake of life, but it exists for the sake of living well."[5] The biblical picture is rather different. God's blessing of Cain is certainly foundational to the building of human civilization, but civilization is not an undiluted good. Whereas in Mesopotamia it is rooted straightforwardly in the divine will, in Genesis it is able to arise as much because God *redeems* it as because God *wills* it. Human progress and cultural advancement are much more ambiguous entities in Genesis than they are in Mesopotamian (and indeed Greek) tradition, because they arise in the midst of assertions of autonomy from God, acts of defiance against God, and acts of barbarism with respect to human beings (Genesis 4:23-24). The human polis, then, while in a sense good (and capable of good), is also problematic.

In Genesis 6–9

This same kind of interaction of God with the world is seen in the flood story in Genesis 6–9. At the outset, God sends a flood upon the earth because of humanity's great wickedness—because "every inclination of the thoughts of his heart was only evil all the time" (Genesis 6:5). When the floodwaters recede, we find that that nothing has changed in the human condition: "every inclination of his [the human person's] heart is evil from childhood" (Genesis 8:21). Yet in Genesis 8, God promises that he will "never again curse the ground because of man," and that He will "never again . . . destroy all living creatures" (8:21). In fact, "As long as the earth endures, seedtime and harvest, cold and heat, summer and winter, day and night will never cease" (8:22). In the perspective of our biblical authors, fallen humanity is not about to change in its general approach to God, the neighbor, and the world at large. Therefore, God announces a change in his *own* approach to humanity and to the world at large. God accommodates himself to the reality of things. Even though human beings are still wicked, God will never again respond to human wickedness by (almost) turning the ordered world back into a watery chaos. The order that has once again been brought *out* of chaos in Genesis 8 will endure, so that God's creatures may flourish in it. As Walter Moberly puts it,

> The text's overall emphasis remains YHWH's [the LORD's] resolution to sustain life on earth in the future. This resolution, however, is a paradoxical expression of merciful divine forbearance in the face of recognition of human life post-Flood as no improvement on human life pre-Flood. Humanity remains undeserving of the gift of life in a regular world order, but the gift will be given nonetheless.[6]

In Genesis 12–36

This characteristic of God as One who "works with what he finds" in the world, first intimated in the opening chapters of Genesis, is subsequently revealed more expansively in the stories of Abraham, Isaac, and Jacob. Abraham and Sarah are far from ideal characters. Abraham is capable of lying when it suits him (Genesis 12:10-20; 20:1-18), and Sarah is capable of being cruel (to the concubine Hagar, 16:1-16). Both are portrayed as failing to trust God for the son that God had explicitly promised them. They take matters into their own hands in an entirely questionable way, using a concubine to get a son who is *not* the son of the promise (Genesis 16). This is far from the ideal society, but God works within the framework of the societal disorder that results from people's faults and failings, and he turns it back toward order (and toward the good). In the course of the Abraham story, we learn that God would even have gone on working with the very wicked societies of Sodom and Gomorrah, if only a few righteous people had been found in them (18:22-33). Unfortunately, they could not be found. Later in the Genesis story God works with Jacob, Leah, and Rachel, even though their society is *also* deeply flawed. It is a society in which brother deceives brother (e.g., 27:1-40; 29:15-30)—in which Esau (who is famously "a hairy man") is outdone by Jacob (who is a "smooth" man, 27:11). The Hebrew adjective is *khalaq*, which refers at one level to Jacob's physical appearance but elsewhere in the Old Testament is also used of deceptive speech. In Proverbs 26:28, for example, "A lying tongue hates those it hurts, and a flattering ['smooth'] mouth works ruin." This is a society in which there are "smooth operators." It is also one deeply corrupted by favoritism (Genesis 25:28; 29:30), in which it is possible to say of Rebekah that Jacob is "*her* son" and of Isaac that Esau is "*his* son" (Genesis 27:5-6) and also that "Jacob . . . loved Rachel more than Leah" (29:30). It is an unhealthily competitive society that brings death to its members (29:31–30:24).

GOD AT WORK IN THE WORLD (GENESIS 37–50)

The society of *Jacob's children* is similarly flawed, as the family baggage is passed on from generation to generation. We learn this from the long story in Genesis 37-50, which focuses on Joseph but in which other family members are also prominent—people like Reuben and (especially) Judah.

The Dreamcoat and the Pit

As the story opens, we meet Joseph as a favorite of his father and as a teller of tales about his brothers (Genesis 37:2-3). Jacob prefers Rachel's child over Leah's, as he had previously preferred Rachel over Leah herself (30:30). He pampers this favorite son, giving him a coat that is evidently not a working coat and allowing him to live a protected life at home while his brothers are out in the fields.[7] The coat appears to go to Joseph's head. He dreams—of a future in which he is elevated above his brothers, as well as his parents—and he *shares* these dreams with others. He is either very naïve or deeply insensitive—or both. He provokes his brothers' hatred, and hatred hardens into an intention to murder and then to hide the body in a water cistern (37:18). Reuben, dissenting from this plan, plays for time and proposes that Joseph should instead be flung into the cistern alive. The strategy works, but not in the way that Reuben intended. In his absence, the others (prompted by Judah) decide to sell Joseph to some passing Midianite traders (37:25-28).[8] Reuben returns to find the cistern empty. He subsequently goes along with the others' plan to explain Joseph's disappearance in terms of an encounter with a wild animal (37:31-33). No one comes out of this opening section of the story very well. Jacob creates an unhealthy environment in the family to begin with; Joseph pours fuel on the flames; the brothers are a murderous bunch. Judah persuades them not actually to murder but only because there is no profit in it, whereas selling Joseph will make them some money. Reuben comes out best, but even Reuben does not directly confront his brothers about their wickedness, and later he certainly does not tell Jacob the truth about what has happened.

Joseph's Triumphs

As we follow the remainder of the story in Genesis 39–50, Joseph remains a deeply flawed character. He does, of course, have his moments of triumph, and we must not underemphasize these. Sold by the Midianites into the household of Potiphar, an Egyptian who is one of the pharaoh's high officials, he attracts the attention of Potiphar's wife.[9] He resists her, because to submit to her demand for sexual intimacy would be to break faith with both God and Potiphar (39:8-9). It would represent a failure both to love God and to love his neighbor. We notice here that Joseph displays precisely that "fear of the LORD" that the book of Proverbs commends and that is the beginning of wisdom (e.g., Proverbs 1:7). Later in Proverbs, it is one aspect of this wisdom that a young man should not succumb to the charms of an adulteress (Proverbs 6:23-26; 7:10-20). Joseph does the right thing.

It does not do him any good in the short term. Fleeing the would-be adulteress, he leaves a garment in her hand (Genesis 39:12); Joseph is not a lucky man where clothing is concerned. The first garment stripped from him was used as evidence of his "death" (Genesis 37); the second is used as evidence of his "lust" (Genesis 39). Lying in the woman's hand, the garment represents the extent to which *Joseph* is also "in her hand"—the phrase that commonly refers in Hebrew to being in someone's power. As we track the exercise of power in Genesis 39, "hand" is actually a key word, although it is not always represented in the English translations of the various verses. Joseph begins the chapter in the hand of the Ishmaelites (i.e., the Midianites; 39:1). In Potiphar's house, however, God prospers Joseph's hand (39:3), so that everything belonging to

Potiphar is given *into* Joseph's hand (39:4, 6, 8). In a way, Joseph refuses to exercise this power by refusing to sleep with Potiphar's wife. The consequence is that *he* falls into *her* hand, and this leads to a spell in prison.

God's power is greater than anyone else's, however, and it is God's character to display "steadfast love" (39:21); in the longer term, therefore, Joseph again prospers.[10] First, the other prisoners are given "into the hand" of Joseph (39:22); he is put in charge of the other people in the prison. He exercises this newfound power so well that the warden gives no thought to anything "in his hand" (39:23); he can depend on Joseph's competence. Ultimately, Joseph's prospering is seen in his elevation to the highest administrative position in Egypt (Genesis 41:41-45).[11] At this point in the story, Pharaoh himself takes a ring from his own hand and transfers it to the hand of Joseph (41:42).[12] He also dresses Joseph in garments of fine linen. At last, Joseph once again possesses the clothing of nobility—clothing he has not possessed since the "coat" in Genesis 37.

Joseph's Dark Side

Joseph does have his moments of triumph, then. However, what are we to make of his actions once he becomes the highest administrator in Egypt? His wisdom is already in doubt as his service to the pharaoh begins, for we are told that he marries an Egyptian wife—Asenath, who is said to be "daughter of Potiphera, priest of On" (Genesis 41:45). The high priest of On (Heliopolis, seven miles northeast of modern Cairo) was an important person, for this city was an ancient seat of the worship of the sun god Ra. From one point of view, this means that Joseph has married well; his resistance to the wife of Potiphar has led to his reward in the daughter of Potiphera—one more play on words, among many, in the Joseph story. From the biblical point of view, however, it is not so straightforward. The reader of the biblical story remembers the seriousness with which Abraham approached the matter of getting a wife for Isaac from among his *own* people (24:1-4). She also remembers Deuteronomy 7, which forbids intermarriage with foreigners because of the danger of apostasy that such marriages bring with them, as well as 1 Kings 1–11, where Solomon marries an Egyptian princess (and later *many* foreign wives) and actually *commits* apostasy. The Joseph story has a biblical context, and in that context questions are bound to be asked about his marriage to an Egyptian, especially a woman so closely associated with an Egyptian god. The "reward" of the daughter of Potiphera is ambiguous, at best. This is precisely why, in some later traditions,

Asenath is represented as a *Jewish orphan* (not an Egyptian), adopted previously by the eunuch Potiphera as a daughter. Another possibility is explored in the romantic novel "Joseph and Asenath," written in Greek at some point after the second century B.C. In this story, Joseph first *rejects* (the Egyptian) Asenath as a suitable wife and marries her only after she repents of her idolatry and converts to true religion. These are simply different strategies for "rescuing" Joseph from the problem that Genesis raises: at this point in the story, Joseph is just too assimilated to Egyptian culture for comfort.

Beyond the question of the marriage, however, there is also the question of Joseph's behavior as (essentially) the governor of Egypt during the seven years of abundance and the seven years of famine (Genesis 41). Joseph's plan is a good one: during the years of abundance, to put away food that can later function as a reserve, "so that the country may not be ruined by the famine" (41:36). However, it is important to note that this food is afterwards *sold* to the Egyptian people by Joseph (41:56). He *gives* food to his family when he resettles *them* in Goshen, but he *sells* it to the Egyptians and to the Canaanites (47:11-14). When the Egyptians' money is gone, he then *gives* them food *in exchange for* their livestock, and when their livestock are gone, he *gives* them food *in exchange for* their land, making them serfs of the pharaoh (47:15-21). The people are grateful enough to be alive (47:25), but, in truth, these are very oppressive arrangements. This is, in fact, exactly the sort of oppression from which God will shortly rescue the Israelites in the exodus; it is exactly the sort that the prophet Samuel describes in 1 Samuel 8, when picturing the Israelites under a king who rules as the kings of other nations do. Such oppressive societies bear no relation to the *good* society envisioned in the Old Testament. Joseph cannot be assessed positively, then, in his role in *producing* this oppressive Egyptian society, especially when we remember the calling of Abraham's descendants in Genesis 12 to be a blessing to the Gentile nations. Joseph fails to bless *any* Gentile in this part of the story, with the exception of the Egyptian god-king himself.[13]

God's Presence in the Joseph Story

Jacob's children are flawed individuals, then.[14] However, as he does in the earlier sections of Genesis, God *works with* these far from ideal characters; he is active in their world. This is not equally apparent at all points in the story. For example, God is curiously absent from the opening scenes of the story in Genesis 37 (and indeed in Genesis 38, about which I shall say more in a moment). God's activity *is* explicitly described, however, in Genesis 39. Here Joseph is still the flawed character of chapter 37, but God is involved in his life:

> The LORD was with Joseph and he prospered, and he lived in the house of his Egyptian master. When his master saw that the LORD was with him and that the LORD gave him success in everything he did, Joseph found favor in his eyes and became his attendant. . . . From the time he put him in charge of his household and of all that he owned, the LORD blessed the household of the Egyptian because of Joseph. The blessing of the LORD was on everything Potiphar had, both in the house and in the field. (Genesis 39:2-5; see also vv. 21-23)

This passage *does* remind us of the promise to Abraham. Here Joseph *has* become a means by which the blessing of God falls on the Gentiles—and, on this occasion, on more than just one.

In the end, we discover that God has been working in and through *all* the lives of the members of Jacob's family *all the way through* the Joseph story, no matter how wicked those family members may have been. The wickedness is alluded to in Genesis 45:4, when Joseph unveils himself to his brothers, ominously, using these words: "I am your brother Joseph, the one you sold into Egypt!" Is this to be the moment for revenge? No, Joseph has managed to attain a larger perspective. His brothers did sell him into Egypt; they failed to love their brother, and they did not "keep" him. But even in their *crime* God was at work in the world, nudging it toward the good: "It was to save lives that God sent me ahead of you. . . . God sent me ahead of you to preserve for you a remnant on earth and to save your lives by a great deliverance" (45:5-7). In a very real sense, Joseph affirms, "It was not you who sent me here, but God" (45:8). As one commentator has written, "God's will makes use of all human action," even though God's will is "domesticated or limited by no human choice."[5]

We encounter the same idea a second time in Genesis 50:15-21. After Jacob's death, the brothers are concerned that Joseph's generosity toward them might evaporate. But Joseph reassures them that it is not his task to judge them; this is God's task. As I pointed out in chapter 8, from a biblical perspective this is precisely what a virtuous person is *supposed* to think and say concerning those who have wronged him. More than this, however, Joseph is convinced—even though his brothers did intend him harm—that the evil that *they* intended *God* intended for good: "You intended to harm me, but God intended it for good to accomplish what is now being done, the saving of many lives" (50:20). The Joseph story begins in hatred and envy; it ends in harmony. Why does this happen? It happens because God has turned evil to good. Many of the Psalms lead us to expect that he *will* characteristically do this; God is one who overturns the plans of the wicked (e.g., Psalms 33:10-11; 35:4; 140:1, 4).

GOD AT WORK IN THE EXODUS STORY

At the heart of the good society, according to the book of Genesis, is the God who pursues the good, overcoming what is evil. Nevertheless, by the end of the book we have progressed only a little further along the road to the fulfillment of God's promise to Abraham—the promise that our biblical authors are convinced lies at the *heart* of God's good purposes for the cosmos. Abraham had been promised as many descendants as the stars of heaven or the sand of the sea (Genesis 15:5; 22:17), but Genesis 46:27 tells us that all the persons of the house of Jacob that came into Egypt were only seventy. Abraham had also been promised a land—the land of Canaan. As the book of Exodus opens, however, his descendants are still living in Egypt. The promised land is still almost entirely in the possession of the Canaanites, with the exception of the burial plot bought by Abraham and the piece of land bought by Jacob (23:17-20; 33:19). Apart from these tokens, there *is* no possession of the land by the descendants of Abraham. Abraham had been promised, finally, that his family would be a blessing to the Gentiles. As we have seen, not many Gentiles have been blessed thus far in the story. The blessings have been mixed. As the book of Genesis ends, the promise appears to have run aground in the sands of a foreign country.

In the book of Exodus, in response to this problem, we find once again the pattern of redemption in the midst of judgment that we found earlier, in Genesis 1–11. The people of God are again led out of a foreign land—Egypt, this time, rather than Mesopotamia—and onward toward their destiny. In the Exodus, God takes his flawed people out of the land of oppression and back toward Canaan, redeeming them in the midst of his destruction of all the might of the Egyptian pharaoh (Exodus 7–12). The central human character in the story is Moses, who is himself saved in the midst of destruction in Exodus 1–2. The crucial element in the process of Israel's rescue is the ten plagues that fall on Egypt, as the pharaoh refuses to let the people go. To the Egyptians, we recall, their ruler was a god. Therefore, the plague sequence is essentially a contest between the living God and a false god, designed to reveal who it is that truly controls creation. This is why the plagues mainly consist of environmental disasters—a polluted river, plagues of insects, diseased animals, hail, and darkness. The final plague of the firstborn in Exodus 12 reveals who has control over human life itself. The "contest" is a rout, and the one true God leads his people out of their bondage, and toward the land of promise.

A significant question now arises: Are the people who leave Egypt of a different character than their ancestors? Are they more inclined than their forebears to ally with God in his pursuit of the good in the world? I could cite various examples from the book of Exodus to illustrate that this is *not* the case, but one striking one shall suffice. As we arrive at the point in the book where God himself introduces Israel for the first time, as an entire people, to their special calling to be the people of God (Exodus 19–24), right at that moment, we discover in a dramatic way that Abraham's descendants have not changed. While Moses is at the top of Mount Sinai receiving God's law—about which we shall think in more depth in just a moment—we find the people at its foot, committing apostasy. "Come," they say to Aaron, "make us gods who will go before us" (Exodus 32:1). The people, disastrously, have not changed.

Has *God* changed, in his commitment to these people and to the world? For just a moment it appears that his commitment, at least to the Israelites, is wavering; he announces his intention to be done with them, on the ground that "they are a stiff-necked people" (Exodus 32:9). Moses asks God, however, to bear with them *even though* they are "a stiff-necked people" (Exodus 34:9)—and God agrees. The parallel with the flood story in Genesis 6–9 is noted by Walter Moberly, who says this about it:

> This narrative analogy suggests a deep theological vision. God deals with the world in general in the same way as with Israel in particular. If both Israel and the world show themselves to be faithless at the outset and to be continuingly faithless . . . then their continued existence is similarly to be understood in

terms of the merciful forbearance of God toward those who do not deserve it. Life for both Israel and for the world is a gift of grace.[16]

From all of this it is clear that, in the biblical way of thinking, God does not deal with the world in an all-or-nothing way. He works with the world as he finds it, and (indeed) he accommodates himself to the world as he finds it, so that the world—and human society—may continue. When it comes to the new Jerusalem, God is a gradualist. He nudges the world slowly *in the direction of* this great city, rather than dropping it from heaven directly *upon* the world.

THE GOOD SOCIETY IN GOD'S LAW

This truth is further illustrated in the guidelines that God gives to Israel *at* Mount Sinai, described first in Exodus 19 through Leviticus 27 and later amplified in the books of Numbers and Deuteronomy. Here, for the first time in the biblical story, we find a comprehensive set of rules guiding the Israelites as to how their society should function. Traditionally, these rules have been referred to as biblical "law" (Heb. *torah*), and that is the shorthand designation that I shall also use, while recognizing its limitations.[17] Here is the good society, then, ordained for Israel by the good God. What is particularly striking about this good society, however, is that it is evidently not the *ideal* society. Ideals are certainly plentiful in these biblical texts; the moral vision of the Old Testament certainly *informs* the law in a fundamental way, and the humanistic and democratic emphases I mentioned back in chapter 4 are everywhere encountered. Yet there is much more expressed in this divinely originated and instituted law than moral ideals. In many places, indeed, moral ideals are not expressed at all. Biblical law is designed not just to set the biblical moral vision before the Israelites but also to achieve other ends. Even the God who is entirely good does not "help to build" a society based only on the moral vision of the kingdom of God. He "helps to build" a society that *also* takes serious account of people's moral failings.

Laws Concerning Slaves

It is easy to illustrate this important point. Consider, first of all, the rules concerning slaves in ancient Israelite society—those people, both native and foreigner, who were deprived of their freedom, at least for a time, and could be bought and sold as the property of a master. Men and women could find themselves as slaves in Israel for various different reasons.[18] Biblical law does not set out to question the *institution* of slavery, but it does set out to regulate it. If a slave is blinded or his tooth is broken, he is to be set free as compensation (Exodus 21:26-27). If a man beats his slave to death, he is to be punished (Exodus 21:20). Slaves are to share in the Sabbath rest (Exodus 20:10) and to take part in sacrificial meals (Deuteronomy 12:12, 18). The rights of female slaves who become concubines are protected (Exodus 21:7-11). If a slave has escaped from his master and has sought refuge with someone else, Deuteronomy 23:15-16 forbids that person to hand the slave back. Slaves of Hebrew descent are to serve for only a limited period of time, and then they are to be released, unless they choose to stay with their master (Exodus 21:1-6; Deuteronomy 15:12-18).

There is, in all of this, a clear sense of the *humanity* of slaves. They are regarded as part of the family of the master, sharing in the family's worship and in its weekly rest from labor, and they also have certain legal rights with respect to the master. To a certain degree, there is a more generous attitude to slaves here than we find in some comparable ancient Near Eastern literature. For example, as yet we know of nothing in other ancient Near Eastern law codes that is comparable to the Deuteronomic prohibition concerning the fugitive slave who has sought asylum from a master.[19] The provisions for debt slavery in the case of Israelites, in particular, are not very harsh.[20] With all this said, however, it remains the case that in Israelite law slaves are certainly *not* considered in any way *equal* in their humanity to their masters. This is particularly clear in Exodus 21:29 and 21:32, where we learn that if an ox gores a free man or woman and thereby causes death, the owner of the ox is to be put to death. However, if the ox gores a *slave*, the owner need only pay a compensatory sum of money to the master. Moreover, if *debt slavery* for *Israelites* was short lived (by statute), this was not true for *slavery in general*. Slaves acquired through purchase from neighboring nations, for example, were considered to be the absolute property of their owners, and their status as slaves was permanent.

How does such a society qualify as "good"? Where *is* the "good"? It consists in this: that if there are going to be slaves in a society, there should at least be laws regulating their treatment. That such laws were absolutely necessary in ancient Israel is obvious from the many texts that describe people ignoring them. Slaves were not supposed to work on the Sabbath, yet biblical texts often describe and condemn the breaking of the laws about the Sabbath (e.g., Ezekiel 23:38). Hebrew slaves were to be released after six years of service, but Jeremiah 34:8–22 tells us that the Israelites had often previously ignored this law and were breaking it also in Jeremiah's day. There was, it seems, no natural predisposition on the part of many ancient Israelites to treat slaves well. It is good, in such a context, that laws were introduced whose aim was to ensure that slaves enjoyed a certain degree of protection from those who wished to exploit them. God himself is described as the source of such legislation and as the ultimate guarantor of its enactment. In Jeremiah 34, it is the failure to release slaves in accordance with the law that leads ultimately to God's judgment falling on the southern part of the kingdom of Israel (Judah). In the law, God engages with human society where he finds it, and he takes steps to leave it *better* than he finds it.

There is, evidently, a relative good in all of this. The *ideal* society of the biblical moral vision is not, however, captured by these legal texts. In the biblical moral vision, men and women are called to keep their neighbors, moving out toward them with openhearted generosity and love, and seeking their good. I am to put myself in my neighbor's shoes and ask, How would I would like to be treated in these circumstances? I am to love my neighbor as myself. This "neighbor" is the person in my proximity, including the stranger and the immigrant, and indeed the enemy. Should not the slave, then, be regarded as my neighbor? Job 31, where Job describes the virtuous life, certainly suggests that *he* thought so. Importantly, virtue is clearly defined in this passage in terms that *exceed* what is required in the law. The law forbids adultery (Exodus 20:14), but Job claims not only to have avoided adultery but also to have refrained from looking lustfully at a girl (Job 31:1). Not only has he refrained from stealing (Exodus 20:15) but he has also not "denied the desires of the poor or let the eyes of the widow grow weary" (31:16), nor has he kept bread to himself rather than sharing it with orphans (31:17). Most importantly for our present purposes, Job has not denied justice to his slaves whenever they have brought a "complaint" against him (31:13). This is to move far beyond the terms of the master-slave relationship that are laid down in the law; it is to treat the slave as a neighbor. Indeed, the *basis* for Job's approach is explicitly the common humanity of both the master and the slave (Job 31:15). Both are fashioned by God in the womb; in the language of Genesis 1, both are created in the image of God.

This does not, apparently, imply for Job that the institution of slavery should be abolished. Nevertheless, there is an evident egalitarian tendency in his thinking here. If followed through logically it must suggest that slavery, if it is to exist *at all* for reasons of economic hardship, will be temporary for all slaves (and not just Hebrew ones). Certainly Genesis 1 and 2 do not imply *at all* the kind of permanent hierarchy in social relationships that an institution like slavery often involves. Genesis 1 and 2 know only of *all* men and women exercising joint dominion over the whole earth. Moreover, when in the biblical prophetic writings the ideal society of the future is pictured, it is a society in which *everyone* has an equal stake—in which *everyone* is able to sit under his own "vine and fig tree" (Zechariah 3:10; cf. 1 Kings 4:25).

It is clear from the example of slavery, then, that the purpose of law in the Old Testament is not only to promote the biblical moral vision. Part of its purpose is simply to bring some degree of order—some degree of justice—to the world as God finds it. It is to prevent things from being worse than they otherwise might be. The Old Testament, I suggest, does not *promote* slavery; it simply *recognizes* that slavery exists. *While* it exists, biblical law seeks to regulate it in a way that is appropriate to the historical and cultural circumstances at hand, measuring what is realistically possible in those circumstances. *All* societal law must pay such due attention to what is possible given the circumstances—including the circumstance noted by George Bernard Shaw, when he asserts, "The ordinary man . . . is an anarchist. He wants to do as he likes. He may want his neighbor to be governed, but he himself doesn't want to be governed."[21] Often, perhaps even typically, people prefer to be left alone to do what they like. If law does not take circumstances into account and does not take seriously how far people can be expected to obey it, it can do no good. There is, indeed, little point in creating any law, in any society, that most people will refuse to obey. Therefore, all law must involve concessions to the very evils that it seeks to restrain:

> The emergence of law . . . [is] a response to the evils that lurk
> in the hearts of men. To control these evils, law must not only
> accept their unavoidable existence; it must also offer them

concessions and, moreover, even enlist their aid in support of civil peace.[22]

Civilization superimposes itself, in the form of law, upon a state of nature in which might is always right; it forces upon all, even the mighty, some degree of submission to a rule of law that stands above all. To that extent, biblical law does reflect (and promote) the biblical moral vision.[23] However, all law must *pay attention* to nature even while demanding this submission, which is why biblical law does not *always or entirely* reflect the biblical moral vision.[24]

Laws Concerning Women

Other realities of life are recognized in biblical law and regulated in a similar way. The authors of Genesis 1–11 propose, for example, that each and every human being, male and female, is made in the image of God and rules equally over the world—that each and every human life is deeply significant and inviolable. Biblical *law* recognizes, however, what the remainder of the Genesis *story* already recognizes: that in the fallen world of the ancient Israelites, women were not widely *regarded* as the equals of men and could indeed be treated very poorly, or even appallingly, by men.

As to the story, rather than the law, consider again the section of Genesis that concerns Jacob's children, and specifically Genesis 38. Here, for a moment, the focus of the story shifts away from Joseph and onto his brother Judah. Why this should be so is not made explicitly clear. My own view is that it is one aspect of a more general "move" made by the authors of Genesis, as a result of which "the Joseph story" (as it is often called) turns out to be, more importantly, "the Judah story." Although it is Joseph who dreams about lordship over his brothers in Genesis 37 (and who certainly experiences *some* fulfillment of that dream), ultimately in the book of Genesis it is Judah who truly *inherits* the dream. In Genesis 49:8, it is of *Judah* that it is said, "Your brothers will praise you; your hand will be on the neck of your enemies; your father's sons will bow down to you."[25] This is why Judah is important and why the question of Judah's line of descent is important—which is what Genesis 38 first and foremost concerns. Judah's line is in danger of extinction in this chapter; it is saved by his resourceful daughter-in-law, as two dead sons are replaced with two living twins.

Be that as it may, what is important to my present purpose is the way in which Genesis 38 portrays male-female relationships. Judah marries a Canaanite wife, we read—the daughter of Shua, who is not named, does not speak, and is hardly a character at all in her own right.[26] The actors in these opening verses are the men; the woman is passive (38:1-3). The wife of the first son, Er, although she *is* named (Tamar), is likewise described in verses 6-10 in a way that makes her life appear quite derivative of her husband's. Tamar exists to bear Er's child, even though he is dead (38:8). When Er's brother Onan takes advantage of the situation, pretending to fulfill his brotherly obligations (to continue Er's line) while really just having sex with Tamar, society does not intervene to punish him. It is only because *God* takes action that Onan is prevented from carrying on in such a way.

Perversely, Tamar is then held responsible by Judah for the deaths of both of his sons (38:11). She is, to Judah, a bad-luck charm, so he removes her to a safe distance. He promises that this is only a temporary measure until his third son grows up, but he is lying (38:14). Judah has no intention of fulfilling his responsibility to Tamar as the head of the household and arranging for her remarriage. Again, there is apparently no legal recourse open to Tamar, as a woman, to right this wrong. She takes matters into her own hands, therefore, dupes Judah into sleeping with her, and becomes pregnant (38:12-19). She has lived respectably as a widow to this point; now she dresses in the way that a prostitute might. Judah, who is apparently not quite so concerned as Tamar to honor *his* dead spouse, thinks that Tamar *is* a prostitute and gladly takes the opportunity to have sex with her. It is another indication that, in this story, women live simply for the benefit of men— indeed, that the women are not really *persons*, so far as the men are concerned. Judah does not ask who Tamar is; she is simply an available woman by the roadside. He certainly does not recognize her, even though she has been a member of his own family for some time. In due course, Tamar's pregnancy becomes public knowledge, and she is accused of prostitution (38:24). Judah accepts the charge at face value and orders that she be burned to death. At this point in her story, as at earlier points, Tamar appears to have no legal rights—certainly none of the kind that we later read about in Deuteronomy 24:13-21, where a person's *claim* about what has happened must be tested, in case he is lying. Tamar, despite her lack of rights, *does* escape death, but only because *she* has been wise enough to obtain proof that Judah is the father of her children (Genesis 38:25).

Clearly, the Genesis 1–2 vision of male-female relations does not govern human behavior in this story. We see in Genesis 38 a very different world—a world in which men treat women badly and in which women possess few resources for dealing effectively with this reality. I do not imagine for a moment that our biblical authors mean us to think well of this disfigured world; indeed, a proper reading of Genesis 1–2 *itself* sets us up to think badly of it, and reading Genesis 37 prior to Genesis 38 sets us up to think badly, in particular, of Judah. This is the same Judah who has just been centrally involved in selling his own brother into slavery for profit. In other words, we know already the kind of person with whom we are dealing. When we read in Genesis 38, therefore, about Judah marrying a non-Israelite woman and sleeping with (someone he thinks is) a prostitute—something every reader of the Old Testament knows should be avoided—our opinion of him is not likely to improve. Nor is this likely when we read of his double standards (he condemns a widow for having sex, even though he as a widower has just done so) and of his hypocrisy (he takes responsibility for Tamar late in the story, as the head of the house who will have her executed, even though he has not taken responsibility earlier, as the head of the house who should have arranged her remarriage). All the indications are that Judah is being portrayed by our biblical authors in Genesis 38 as a thoroughly nasty piece of work. As much as anyone else in this story, Judah needs to be changed.

The biblical *story*, then, recognizes that in the fallen world of the ancient Israelites, women were not widely regarded as the equals of men and that men could treat them appallingly. Biblical *law* also recognizes the sorry state of male-female relationships in the world east of Eden, the vision of Genesis 1–2 notwithstanding. That is to say, from the perspective of biblical faith, *God* (who gives the law) understands full well the nature of the world with which he is working, as he seeks to lead it ever more steadily toward the good. Quite evidently, *God* does not set out in biblical law to change this reality by way of legislation. He restricts himself to a number of rules about male-female relations that offer women *some* protection and *some* justice, in an historical and cultural context in which they have *none*—in which they have become unequal to and in fact the property of men.[27] Deuteronomy 22:13-21 provides a good example of such rules, as well as revealing quite a bit more about the society to which the rules were given. No equality under the law for women is envisaged in this text. It does not set out to *challenge* the state of affairs that it seeks to regulate. It restricts itself to ensuring that there is *some* legal remedy available to a woman in the case described and that, if she is falsely accused, she retains in perpetuity both her status as a wife and the economic security that goes along with it. It is not difficult to define the "good" that is being pursued here. It is the "good" of reputation, security, and provision. It is equally clear, however, that it is only this *limited* good that is being pursued. What is *not* being pursued is the moral vision of the Bible with respect to male-female relationships, and especially (in this case) marriage. Along the same lines, we should note that biblical law allows for, but regulates, divorce (Deuteronomy 22:19; 24:1-4). This does not mean that divorce is considered compatible with the biblical moral vision. Malachi puts the matter bluntly, when he records God himself as saying, "I hate divorce" (2:16). Divorce is, nevertheless, *permitted* in biblical law; a legal framework is created in which marital breakdown can be negotiated.

Order Rather Than Chaos

One of the purposes of biblical law, then, is simply to bring some degree of order—some degree of justice—to the world of chaos in which ancient Israel lives. This is true not only of what we might call, in modern terminology, "civil" or "criminal" law (the cases described earlier) but also of what we might call *ritual* law—rules concerning such things as sacrifices, foods, and clothing. In fact, it is clear that this kind of biblical law is focused much *more* on order than on justice.

It is true that some of the sacrifices authorized in Israelite ritual law are designed to deal with moral wrongdoing and with the broken relationships that result from it. In Leviticus 6:1-7, for example, the person who has injured his neighbor in some way (e.g., by robbing him) is required to put this right not only with his neighbor (through restoration and compensation) but also with God (through sacrifice). To that extent, ritual law is *somewhat* similar to civil and criminal law. It is a response to what is broken in society, offering a remedy for it. If there were no evil in the world, such sacrifices would not be necessary; there is evil, however, so they *are* necessary.

Yet it is equally clear that much of what we find in Israelite ritual law does not operate in moral categories at all. Its purpose is to deal not with what we commonly refer to as moral faults but with entirely other kinds of "faults" or problems. In Leviticus 12:1-8, for example, a sacrifice is required shortly after a woman has given birth to a child. This is not because there is anything morally wrong with childbearing.[28] The issue is, rather, one of "cleanness" and "uncleanness"—that is, ritual purity and impurity. This is a major concern in biblical law. It is also expressed in the immediately preceding Leviticus 11, where rules are laid down about which "living things" the Israelites may and may not eat—which animals, birds, and sea life are clean and unclean from a ritual point of view. These rules are certainly regarded as *important*, because they are some of the means by which Israel is to be holy, as God is holy (11:45). However, they are not premised entirely (or perhaps even mainly) on *moral* considerations. Israel's ritual rules are all envisaged as playing their part in orienting the chosen people toward God in obedience, but the individual laws are not necessarily themselves about right and wrong moral action as such.[29]

God, the Good, and the Ideal

In summation, it is not the purpose of law in the Old Testament only to promote the biblical moral vision. The society that is built around the law is certainly *called to pursue* the moral vision. The fundamental commands to love God and neighbor are themselves embedded in the law, and these commands are worked out in all sorts of practical and detailed ways in the same law. In *torah*, however, what is ideal is always balanced with what is already "there"—in human beings and in human society—and the ideal is often *accommodated* to the reality. *God*, in biblical thinking, accommodates *himself* to ongoing reality, so that *human society itself* can continue. To put this in a different way: in biblical thinking, even God does not attempt to legislate the kingdom of God into being. It follows, then, that human beings, who are constantly exhorted in the biblical tradition to "be like God," should likewise not attempt to do so.

In his interactions with the world, then, whether in law or in story, we find an enormous degree of pragmatism attributed to God in the Old Testament. We also find a very pragmatic view taken of human society. From the beginning, God does not relate to the world in an all-or-nothing way. God does call all people to worship him, to treat all their neighbors well, and to look after his garden. There can be no question about what God is looking for in his world; there are certainly ideals to be pursued. In the biblical perspective, however, God does not impose these ideals. This means that worshippers of God must think hard as they form their own view of the polis and must consider precisely *how* their reflections travel up "the chain of causes, first to the cosmos, then to God"; they must think critically about what it *is*, exactly, that God "authorizes" in terms of "who may legitimately exercise power over others, to what ends, and under what conditions" (Mark Lilla, in the first epigraph to this chapter). As Lilla says later in his book, "For many believers in the biblical religions, today as in the seventeenth century, sundering the connection between political form and divine revelation means betraying God, whose commandments are comprehensive."[30] If my own observations and arguments in this chapter are correct, however, *sundering* this connection is not the only thing that believers should be concerned about. There is more than one way of "betraying God," and one of them involves forging *too close* a connection between political form and—not divine *revelation* but—the Bible's *moral vision*. To seek to impose (legislate) the kingdom of God on society when even God himself does not do so is a mistake; it is naive; it is, according to the Bible, to depart from the will of the good God who deals (and wants believers to deal) with reality.

BIBLICAL FAITH, PASSIVITY, AND UTOPIANISM

We turn now to consider the perspectives of various nonbiblical religious and philosophical traditions on the topic of "politics" in order to sharpen our sense of what the biblical literature is and is not saying. As we do so, I need to register my debt to the work of Shmuel Eisenstadt, who provides us with a helpful typology of such perspectives so far as axial traditions are concerned. Throughout his work, Eisenstadt argues that the common denominator in axial breakthroughs was "the emergence, conceptualization and institutionalization of a basic tension between the transcendental and mundane orders."[31] In all of these traditions, the belief emerges (or is radicalized) that there is another dimension beyond our (mundane) political realm, a "higher transcendental moral or metaphysical order which is beyond any given this- or other-worldly reality."[32] The differences among the traditions that enjoyed a "breakthrough," Eisenstadt thinks, have to do with the following question: How (if at all) should this belief be translated into new institutions, projects, and practices "on the ground"? He distinguishes between "otherworldly" axial civilizations, like those dominated by

Buddhism and Hinduism, "this-worldly civilizations" that have not been monotheistic, like Confucian China, and the monotheistic civilizations shaped by Judaism, Christianity, and Islam. I am indebted to this typology in what follows.

A Passive Approach to Society

In "otherworldly civilizations," Eisenstadt notes, the political arena has not been viewed, historically, as the primary arena in which the transcendental vision should be realized; we find no "strong alternative conceptions of the social and, in particular, the political orders."[33] The transcendental vision in classical Hinduism and Buddhism, as we have seen in previous chapters, leads not to any proposals for (or activism with respect to) the transformation of the larger society but rather to principled passivity. The ultimate point of human endeavor is to escape the world, not to change it. Clearly, this "principled passivity" does not square well with the approach advocated in biblical faith. Biblical faith, as Eisenstadt himself well understands, calls its adherents to participate in the reconstruction of the mundane, political world in the light of the transcendental vision.[34] The one, transcendent God who created the world commands that society should substantially reflect the kingdom of God. Society in its current form falls well short of this vision, and the gap must be closed. God calls the world toward this vision, and obedience to this call requires that society should be changed.

In a "this-worldly civilization" like Confucian China, Eisenstadt continues, the political arena *has* been seen as the primary locus within which the transcendental vision should be realized. Nevertheless, this has not led "to far-reaching institutional reconstruction of the political centers of the society."[35] This is because Confucius was fundamentally interested in *retrieving the harmonious past*, not in creating *new* institutions, projects, and practices in society. In spite of the language that Eisenstadt himself uses, the Confucian vision was not truly "transcendental" at all; it came not from "outside" Chinese society but from its past. There was no God "outside the system" summoning Confucius (or the political powers he was addressing) into conformity "on the ground" with a genuinely transcendental vision. The political institutions of his day, Confucius believed, had broken down because of a failure of people on all sides to behave with propriety. Propriety must be restored, especially in the ruler and the ruling classes. What was required, above all, was not changes to the structures of society nor indeed even legislation to restrain evil *in* society but (rather) the inculcation and maintenance, through ritual practice, of virtue in the ruler and in the aristocracy. The possession of such virtue would allow the ruling classes to rule without recourse to coercion, as their good example trickled down to the masses.

The ultimate point in Confucianism is not to escape the world, but neither is it to change the world very much. We are dealing here with a *relatively* passive approach to society.[36] It is *people* who need to change, conforming themselves to revered and traditional customs. Biblical faith agrees that people need to change, of course, but not just by conforming themselves to custom within their assigned roles in a given society. As we have seen in previous chapters, biblical faith calls for a more radical change. More than this, holding individual societies accountable to a genuinely transcendental standard, biblical faith looks for changes not just in *people* but also in societal *structures*.

A Utopian Approach to Society

The tendency in Eisenstadt's third category of axial traditions is not passivity, principled or otherwise, but utopianism. Here there exists a *strong* and *urgent* call to reconstruct the mundane, political world on the basis of a God-given transcendental vision. In the modern world, fundamentalist Islam (or "Islamism," as some prefer) illustrates this tendency well. For adherents of this ideology, "it is the task of the Islamic state to enforce obedience to the revealed law of Islam—the Shari'a," which is "a timeless manifestation of the will of God, subject neither to history nor circumstance."[37] Like the Hebrew *torah*, Shari'a applies "to much more than law in the strictly legal sense. It includes the details of ritual, as well as a whole range of customs and manners." Yet there is "no ultimate distinction between religion and morality, law and ethics. All are seen as proceeding directly from the command of God."[38] All people, in all times and places, are called to submit to this timeless manifestation of the will of God, and it is the task of the Islamic state to ensure that they do, establishing the kingdom of God on earth. The gap between the transcendental vision and the earthly reality should be closed *speedily*, and it should be closed *completely*. This utopianism has manifested itself in a particularly strong form in modern Iran, where it has taken on explicitly messianic dimensions. Shi'ite Muslims await the Twelfth Imam, who will return at the end of time to save the world; Ayatollah Khomeini, who took power in Iran in 1979, "allowed himself to be referred to by the title Imam," implying that he was this messiah.[39] In this way of thinking about the Islamic state, it is the sovereignty of God that the state should incarnate. Therefore, religious authorities may well be the best wielders of political power (as Khomeini certainly believed), since other "sovereigns" (e.g., kings or "the people") may lack the expertise or the commitment to fashion society entirely in accord with the Shari'a. What is being demanded in Islamism is the genuine "vice-regency of man under God's sovereignty," right now.[40]

Such utopianism is not an inevitable component of Islamic thinking, and Muslims dispute just how far it is deeply rooted in Scripture, tradition, and history. In reality, the Shari'a itself "represents the compromise made in the first two centuries [of Islam] between the moral perfectionism of the early Muslim communities such as the Kharijis, and the demands of an expanding Islamic community that aimed to be inclusive and universal."[41] In addition,

> no Islamic society, even during the high tide of Islamic civilization, was governed exclusively according to Islamic law. There was always a gap between the theoretical formulations of the jurists and the *de facto* exercise of political power. Moreover . . . Islamic law was everywhere supplemented by local customary laws.[42]

Historically, it has been the task of the *political* authorities, who have not typically been the clergy, to decide how far and in which ways the clergy's interpretation of the Shari'a is to be implemented.[43] It has been the prior task of the religious authorities to reconcile the demands of Shari'a with the demands of everyday life. In practice, historically, "the idealism of the Shari'a" has been "mitigated by a humane and humanistic pragmatism."[44]

Such pragmatism has been required on all sides not least because, although the Shari'a is regarded as the timeless manifestation of the will of God, it is not always clear how best to understand and to apply it. Some of the difficulty is due to the fact that, as in the case of the Old Testament, there are *tensions* within the Shari'a itself that need to be resolved—not least between moral vision and legal permissions or realities. In chapter 4 I noted one such tension—namely, that in Islam women are represented both as equal to men under God yet as unequal to men under the law. Then again, *all* human beings are theoretically equal under God in Islam, yet Islamic law provides for slavery. More-over, divorce is permitted in Islam, yet according to Muhammad, "Among the things permitted by God, the most detestable is divorce."[45] It is not just a matter of *applying* the Shari'a; the Shari'a must itself be *interpreted.*[46]

Beyond the question of interpretation, there is also the question of how far, in Islam, it is even the business of other people to tell the individual Muslim what to think and to do. The Qur'an states that "there is no compulsion in religion" (2:256), and, on one interpretation of this verse, "no Muslim is required to accept anything as true just because other Muslims have found it to be true."[47] Needless to say, *Islamists* do not accept this view, tending to prefer verses like the following: "struggle against the disbelievers and the hypocrites and be tough with them" (9:73). Yet historically, the *freedom* to submit (or not) to God's will has been an important emphasis in Islam, and it has been believed that

> only God can judge the extent to which an individual's activities conform to the jurists' schema. Law in the narrower sense is restricted to dealing with those activities that are explicitly forbidden (*haram*) or to adjudicating between competing claims of individuals.[48]

Historically, there have been limits to compulsion in Islam, arising from the belief that no "city, state, or any other institution [stands] between the individual and God" and that the individual Muslim must get on with the business of being a Muslim, by himself and in community with other Muslims.[49] In some Islamic thinking, this belief results in a principled distinction between the religious and political spheres.[50] Even in Iran, many senior Islamic clergy, both during the Khomeini regime and after his death, remained "opposed to Khomeini's idea that the clergy should take an active role in politics."[51]

A Measured Approach to Society

The utopian approach to the world that we have just been discussing, whether deeply rooted in Islamic history and tradition or not, is certainly not one that is shared by biblical faith. There is, in biblical faith, a transcendental vision to which earthly reality is called to conform. But there is no idea that the gap between these two should, or can, be closed speedily and completely. Biblical faith also holds, as some

Muslims do, that a messiah will one day come to bring about the trans-formation of our mundane political realm (as we shall see in chap. 11). However, it does not hold that such a person will come to rule over a particular, secular, modern state or that he will necessarily come any time soon. Nor does it hold that, in the meantime, some kind of ideal, temporal form of government ought to be instituted—a government comprising religious authorities, perhaps—in order to *bring in* God's kingdom. Instead, our biblical authors are prepared to settle, in the meantime, for *ordinary* forms of government, and they portray God as settling for these as well.[52] Even though the opening vision of the book of Genesis respecting human governance of the cosmos is *democratic*—all are image bearers, and all govern—biblical law does not advocate for democratic governance as such or indeed for *any* particular kind of governance. It merely *allows* for various forms of governance, includ-ing kingship (Deuteronomy 17). Having allowed for kingship, it puts all its efforts into *constraining* this institution by placing around it such severe limitations that the "king" is *relativized* and is placed on a level similar to that of the people. It is, again, a pragmatic, not a utopian, approach to the polis—informed no doubt by sentiments similar to those in Polybius (in the second epigraph to this chapter), that *all* insti-tutions of government can go wrong in human hands and that the ones that bear the greatest weight of utopian expectation are likely to go most badly wrong of all.[53]

In sum: biblical faith does not advocate passivity with respect to politics, but it does not advocate utopian politics either. It neither accepts the polis as we find it nor insists that it must be founded four-square, and by Wednesday, on the vision of the new Jerusalem. Biblical faith charts a middle way when it comes to the organization of human society, just as it does when it comes to the human approach to the natural order (chap. 9). Like God, biblical faith looks for a society that promotes righteousness in the world as much as is realistically possible, while at the same time restraining and minimizing evil as much as it can—and even redeeming evil, where it can, and turning it toward the good. It is this "middled" society that I should be helping to build, as I participate (with God) in nudging contemporary society ever more closely toward the good.[54]

A Bird Perched in the Soul

What Am I to Hope For?

Exiles feed on empty dreams of hope. I know it. I was one.

Aegisthus in Aeschylus' *Agamemnon*[1]

Hope is a longing for a future condition over which you have no agency. It means you are essentially powerless. . . . When we realize the degree of agency we actually do have, we no longer have to "hope" at all. We simply do the work.

Derrick Jensen[2]

In chapter 6 I argued that one of the "paths" that biblical faith exhorts us to follow when faced with evil and its consequent suffering is the path of hope. I am to hope for the victory of good over evil, and beyond that, that what is bad in the world can somehow be turned to good. I have also mentioned hope in other chapters of this book—most recently in chapter 10, concerning hope as the context within which we pursue the good society. However, I have not yet fully explored what the biblical authors say about *what* I am to hope for. That is the theme of the present chapter.

HOPE IN THE BOOK OF GENESIS

In the primeval garden of Genesis 2, we recall, two particular trees are described, among the many that are "pleasing to the eye and good for food" (Genesis 2:9). One of these is the tree of life, and the other is the tree of the knowledge of good and evil. The latter stands for wisdom grasped in independence of God—the penultimate source (after a lack of trust in God's goodness) of all the evil in the world. The former stands for immortality—to eat from it is to live forever (Genesis 3:22). In Genesis 3, this immortality is denied to human beings because of their lack of trust in God's goodness and their independent grasping after wisdom. The problem is that they might eat from the tree of life and, as fallen beings, "live forever." The solution is exile: "so the LORD God banished him from the Garden of Eden . . . [and] he placed on the east side of the Garden of Eden cherubim and a flaming sword flashing back and forth to guard the way to the tree of life" (Genesis 3:23-24). Human beings are excluded from perfect communion with God in his sanctuary; the possibility of becoming immortal has, for the time being, disappeared.

A Beginning in Hope

Immortality itself, we must be clear, has not been *lost*. That way of putting things would imply that human beings once possessed it. There is a long tradition of reading Genesis 1–3 in just this way: once we were immortal, and now we are not. However, there is *nothing* in the Genesis story to suggest that human beings, before the serpent shows up, already possess immortality—that they are already eating the fruit of the tree of life. On the contrary, Genesis 3:22 implies otherwise: "The man has now become like one of us . . . he *must not be allowed to* reach out his hand and take also from the tree of life and eat, and live forever."[3] He *might* now eat fruit from the tree; therefore, he *must* be prevented.

Therefore, we should read the tree of life as speaking to the question not of intrinsic human *nature* but of human *destiny*. The *hope* of immortality is certainly present in the garden. Had God's injunctions about the tree of the knowledge of good and evil been heeded, we imagine, the human pair would have been allowed to eat from the tree of life; otherwise, its very existence would be puzzling. However, there is no hint in this story—nor anywhere else in the biblical tradition—that human beings *are already* immortal prior to the "serpent incident."

The ancient Christian author Athanasius reads the story correctly on this point, when he says that "man is by nature mortal, inasmuch as he is made out of what is not" and then goes on to state that it was only the *destiny* of human beings to escape "their natural state, had they remained good."[4] Readers of Genesis who have thought otherwise, I suggest, have been more influenced than they probably imagine by Pythagoras and Plato, and their notions of preexisting, immortal human souls.[5] They have failed to pay attention to the evident difference, in this matter of innate human nature, between the Hebrew and the Greek worldviews.

The human beings of Genesis 1–2 are mortal beings, then, who *may eventually* be given the gift of immortality. In Genesis 3, this possibility is removed. Human destiny is now that which is natural for a creature of the dust; it is to "return to the ground, since from it you were taken; for dust you are and to dust you will return" (Genesis 3:19). The human condition is marked almost from the beginning, says Genesis, by dysfunctional relationships with God, our neighbor, and our fellow creatures. It is marked by a kind of wisdom, but it is also marked by death; we "return to the ground." This unfortunate turn of events should not blind us, however, to the reality that the book of Genesis evidently *begins* in hope. Hope is already bound up with the good creation that God has made—and not just with creation after the entrance of evil. There is a future with God, in this creation story, and it is bright with promise. The gateway to this future is the tree of life.

The book of Genesis begins in hope; human beings are born looking forward to something they do not yet possess. This beginning in hope is typically obscured by those who assume that the first humans *already* possess what, in fact, they have only been promised.

Hope for Creation

Readers who make this mistake typically make a number of related assumptions that are equally poorly grounded in biblical evidence. These assumptions, about the nature of God's original creation more broadly, in turn affect how they read many of the "hopeful" biblical texts *outside* the book of Genesis.

The readers I have in mind tend to think of human immortality as only *one aspect* of what was perfect about the original creation. For them *the entire creation* was an originally perfect entity, created by a

God who is himself perfect. On this view, it is not just human beings who exist in the original creation in their optimal (immortal) state. The *whole of creation* is ideal and already exists in its optimal state. As the story of creation begins, therefore, it is not just *human beings* who have nothing for which to hope; *nonhuman* creation has nothing for which to hope, either. This is because hope implies change, and creation (on this view) *needs* no change, either in human or nonhuman terms. This is not a world that is "going anywhere." It is a static, perfect entity, mirroring the nature of the eternal, perfect God who also never changes.

Consequently, when these Bible readers encounter biblical texts that speak of *future* changes in the world order, they cannot think of these changes as being intrinsic to God's original plan in creation. A perfect creation *needs* no change. Change (and hope) can therefore be connected only with life in the world *after* Genesis 3—after the fall, when perfection has been lost. Therefore, when biblical eschatological texts speak about events like God eventually creating new heavens and a new earth (e.g., Isaiah 65:17-25), these texts are assumed to be speaking about changes necessary in the cosmos *only because* the original creation has been touched by evil. Only a creation that has become less than perfect *needs* to be changed. What does it need to be changed *to*? Well, it needs to be changed *back* into its original state. Therefore, these eschatological texts are read as predicting a *future* perfection that is, in reality, only the restoration of an *original* perfection. After all, the world in this way of thinking cannot become more perfect in the future than it was in the past. So the perfect God must simply be set on fixing, in the future, what went wrong in the past (the loss of perfection), when Adam and Eve messed up and the whole world became messed up with them. God is intent simply on taking his creatures back to the perfect garden.[6]

This has (naturally) implied to these same Bible readers that we can discover, from the eschatological texts in the Bible, much more about the original creation than Genesis 1-3 explicitly tell us. If the perfect future is really just a return to the perfect past, then we can safely reconstruct the *past* from what the Bible says about the *future*. So if (for example) we are told in Isaiah 65:19 that when God creates the new heavens and the new earth, "the sound of weeping and of crying will be heard in it [Jerusalem] no more," we may safely deduce that, in the original creation, there was no weeping and crying.[7] Furthermore, if we are told in Isaiah 11:6 that, in the future, "the wolf will live with the lamb [and] the leopard will lie down with the goat," we may deduce that in the original creation there was no predation.[8] This logic is already reflected in the Bible-reading tradition as early as the second century A.D., when Theophilus of Antioch writes,

> The animals are named wild beasts from their being hunted, not as if they had been made evil or venomous from the first— for nothing was made evil by God, but all things good, yea, very good,—but the sin in which man was concerned brought evil upon them. For when man transgressed, they also transgressed with him. . . . When, therefore, man again shall have made his way back to his natural condition, and no longer does evil, those also shall be restored to their original gentleness.[9]

The future perfection mirrors the original perfection, and the original perfection can be reconstructed from its mirror image in the future.

I propose that there is no good reason to make any of these assumptions. First, there is no reason to interpret the "goodness" of creation in Genesis 1–2 as involving a static perfection or as precluding change or movement over time—as precluding the notion of a greater destiny for creation.[10] I certainly laid great stress in chapter 2 on giving proper *weight* to the idea of the goodness of creation in biblical thinking, and I noted various ways in which this idea differentiates the biblical world-view from others. In that context, I was concerned that we might take "goodness" to mean *less* than our biblical authors intend it to mean. In the present context, I am more concerned that we might invest the biblical notion of goodness with much *more* content than is actually intended—in fact, that we might import into it entirely wrong ideas.

When our biblical authors tell us that creation is good, they mean that it is a wonderful place, created in such a way as to be exactly the right place—a good and a beautiful place—for the flourishing of God's creatures. They do not mean that, in this original state, creation has already arrived at its final destination. To the contrary, they tell us in Genesis 1–2 that change is built into the very fabric of creation from the beginning, as its human creatures set out on their quest to multiply, to rule and to subdue, and to keep and to serve. Along with these divine image bearers, nonhuman creation also sets out on a journey; its destiny is bound up with theirs. It is not yet explicitly clear where the great journey will *end* for all these creatures. However, it is reasonable to assume, as we have just seen, that for the image bearers it is intended to end in the eating of the fruit of the tree of life; this is the human destiny.[11] Given the close identification of human with nonhuman creation, it is further reasonable to assume that nonhuman creation will share in this glorious destiny. This is, indeed, what our later eschatological texts make *explicitly* clear: all of creation, not just humanity, has a future. "Good" does not preclude "even better" in Genesis 1–2 or anywhere else in the Bible—any more than the existence of the (wonderfully good) chrysalis precludes the ultimate emergence of the (spectacular) butterfly. Creation can be good and at the same time be destined to be something even better.

If this is true, it follows (second) that we *cannot*, in fact, assume that biblical texts that speak about great changes in the cosmos in the future are always speaking about changes necessary because the original creation has been touched by evil. Often, as we shall see ahead, it appears that this *is* the reason for the change. It is not *necessarily* the reason, however. It also follows, third, that we cannot assume that eschatological texts predicting a *future perfection* in the cosmic order are reliable guides to what their authors thought about the *original state* of creation. In other words, we cannot use the vision of even better to deduce what must have been true about the original good. If we *do* try to read passages like Isaiah 11:1-9 and 65:19 in this way, in fact, we immediately run into significant difficulties. We are then forced to the view that our biblical authors considered the original creation to be free of intrinsic suffering and predation.[12] Yet I have given reasons in chapters 5 and 9 for questioning both ideas, and I am not the only reader, historically, to have done so. The ancient Christian bishop Augustine, for example, did not think that predation began after the fall, nor did the noted medieval theologian Thomas Aquinas, who said this:

> In the opinion of some, those animals which now are fierce and kill others, would, in that [original] state, have been tame, not only in regard to man, but also in regard to other animals. But this is quite unreasonable. For the nature of animals was not changed by man's sin, as if those whose nature now it is to devour the flesh of others, would then have lived on herbs, as the lion and falcon.[13]

It makes much more coherent sense of the entire Old Testament tradition if we do *not* "read into" Genesis 1–2 ideas taken from eschatological texts like Isaiah 11:1-9 and 65:19—as if our biblical authors thought they were dealing with a God who could never do anything new.[14] It makes much better sense to read these texts as concerning quite *new* realities.

If this is correct, then the book of Genesis begins in hope not just with respect to *human beings* but with respect to *the whole of creation*. Creation is going somewhere; there is movement (and trajectory) knit into its fabric from the beginning. Hope is already bound up with the entirety of the good creation that God has made—and not just with the creation after evil has entered it. However, this hope has been obscured by interpreters who have made *assumptions* about the biblical view of such matters, rather than paying careful attention to actual biblical texts. Preferring to depend on what they think *must* have been the case about God's original creation (that it was perfect), rather than explore what the biblical authors actually say about it, they have imported ideas into the biblical texts that are not, in fact, there. They have made the same mistake about creation in general that they make about (the supposed immortality of) human beings in particular. They have read the biblical authors as believing that creation, from the first, already possessed what was, *in fact*, only part of God's future plan for it.

Hope in the Midst of Evil

This is the train of thought with which Genesis opens, then—that at the end of the journey that God has embarked upon with creation, something even better awaits. As we already know, however, the train is no sooner out of the station than it gets derailed. Does hope die in the wreckage? It does not. There is hope to be found, not only in Genesis 1–2 but also in Genesis 3. It is not to be found, however, in the place where many readers have historically looked for it.

From ancient times, readers of Genesis 3 have looked for it in Genesis 3:15. In this verse the serpent is told by God, "I will put enmity between you and the woman, and between your offspring and hers; he will crush your head, and you will strike his heel." Many have found here a *promise* that humanity will one day vanquish the powers of evil. The early Christian bishop, Irenaeus of Lyons, was one of these:

Christ completely renewed all things, both taking up the battle against our enemy and crushing him who at the beginning had led us captive in Adam, trampling on his head, as you find in Genesis that God said to the serpent, "I will put enmity between you and the woman, and between you and the seed of the woman." From then on it was proclaimed that he who was to be born of a virgin, after the likeness of Adam, would be on the watch for the serpent's head.[15]

In all honesty, however, this reading of Genesis 3:15 is a dubious one. The NIV translation just cited lends it support in the way that it renders the last two verbs: the human descendant will "crush," and the snake's descendant will "strike." In this translation, it sounds as if the snake *merely* strikes the human whereas the human *decisively* crushes the snake. When one considers the Hebrew of the verse, however, one finds no such distinction. In fact, the verb in each case is the same verb (Heb. *shuf*)![16] In other words, the antagonists *each* strike the *other*. The strike in each case is potentially fatal, but not necessarily so. This is a text, then, not about the ultimate human triumph *over* the powers of evil, but about the ongoing battle throughout history *between* these two opponents. There is nothing overtly hopeful about this text.[17]

This does not mean, however, that the authors of Genesis, as "men in exile," did not "feed on dreams of hope" (Aeschylus, in the first epigraph to this chapter). On the contrary, there *are* grounds for hope to be found even in Genesis 3. They lie in the mere fact (if it *is* "mere") that God continues to pursue a relationship with human beings even after they embrace evil. They eat from the forbidden tree, and immediately God comes looking for them in the garden with the simple question, "Where are you?" (Genesis 3:9). He still walks in the garden, and he still talks to his image bearers. *This* is a ground for hope. Then again, God is actively involved in this chapter in helping the human pair deal with their "nakedness" in what is now a fallen world. He is actively involved in finding the best way forward for human society, given all the circumstances. This also suggests that God has not given up on the world. It may not yet be clear what all this means for the destination that lies at the end of the journey, but at least the journey continues.

In chapter 10 we saw various other ways in which God's willingness to continue on this journey is indicated throughout Genesis 4–11: in his care of the exiled murderer Cain; in his blessing of Cain's family line, even in the midst of significant moral failings; in his rescuing of Noah (and all of creation, in miniature) in the midst of the great flood; and in his long-term commitment to bless creation in the aftermath of the flood, as he makes "an everlasting covenant . . . [with] all living creatures of every kind on the earth" (Genesis 9:16). This term "covenant" (Heb. *berith*) is an important one. It is used in a number of ways in the Old Testament to describe human relationships—of a treaty or an alliance (e.g., between Abraham and Abimelech in Genesis 21:25-34), a constitutional agreement between king and subjects (e.g., between David and Israel in 2 Samuel 5:1-5), a pledge of friendship (e.g., between David and Jonathan in 1 Samuel 18:3; 20:8; 23:18), or a marriage (e.g., Proverbs 2:17; Malachi 2:14). A covenant is an agreement between two parties in which a relationship is forged involving moral obligations on each side. It is this term that is taken up here in Genesis 9 and used of God's ongoing commitments with respect to creation. The relationship continues, even though it has become strained.

God has not given up on his plan to bless creation. Nor has he given up, specifically, on the part of the plan that involves having human beings "be fruitful and increase in number; fill the earth and subdue it" (Genesis 1:28; see also 9:1). This is evident in Genesis 11. When humanity decides to settle down in Mesopotamia, God frustrates their plans and scatters them "from there over all the earth" (11:8). Moreover, in response to their attempt to "make a name" for themselves in Mesopotamia, we recall, God calls a family *out of* Mesopotamia, one of whose ancestors is (appropriately enough) named Shem (the Hebrew word for "name"). Human beings *will* "fill the earth"; God ensures that this is so.

Hope Founded in Covenant

It is at this point in Genesis that the plan of God for the cosmos takes on more definition. To the covenant with *all living creatures* in Genesis 9, God now adds a covenant with Abraham that has implications for *all human beings*. Abraham is promised, as one aspect of this covenant, that he himself will have his name made great (alluding back to Genesis 11).[18] God's agenda, however, does not concern only Abraham; it is also true that "all the families of the earth shall be blessed." Abraham's *family* is to be blessed by God in order that all the *nations* shall be blessed by God. Abraham is to be given a land (12:1) in which this blessing can be worked out, so that Abraham may do *in a particular place* what all human beings are called to do *on the earth*—to be fruitful and multiply

(Genesis 1:28). The multiplication of Abraham's descendants into a "great nation" is a microcosm of the larger human reality. So whereas in Genesis 1:28 all human beings are the recipients of God's blessing, being fruitful and multiplying throughout the earth (Heb. *'erets*), in Genesis 12 it is *Abraham* who in the first instance is to receive this blessing and inherit a land (also Heb. *'erets*), filling and governing it as a great nation. One fragment of the human race is taken up and given a promise of land and nationhood, to the end that all the earth may still receive God's blessing, as God originally intended. The people of God—the descendants of Abraham—are called out by God for a mission, and the mission is cosmic in its implications, involving the fulfillment of God's promise to bless his creation.

This is a story that is still going somewhere. The presence of evil notwithstanding, there is hope in this story that God will still fulfill the plans he had in mind in creating the cosmos in the first place. We saw in our chapters 8 and 10 how this biblical conviction concerning God's ongoing work in the world, even in the midst of evil, is expressed not just in the story of Abraham but also in the stories of Jacob and of Joseph. The promise to Abraham survives, somehow, the problem of childlessness, which is a prominent theme throughout the book of Genesis (Genesis 11:30; 25:21; 29:31). It survives famine (12:10; 26:1; 41:54). It survives, in Abraham's case, the danger to Sarah from powerful men like the pharaoh of Egypt (12:10-20; 20:1-18). Most fundamentally, it survives the threat posed by the all-too-often poor moral character of God's people themselves. It survives because the covenant is a covenant with God. The promise is the promise of God. And God, in biblical perspective, is determined to see his creation flourish.

HOPE IN THE REMAINDER OF THE BIBLICAL NARRATIVE

It is the promise to Abraham in the covenant that occupies center stage for most of the remainder of the Pentateuch. When Abraham's descendants end up in Egypt, it is this covenant that God remembers (Exodus 2:23-25), leading to the great escape from Egypt we know as the exodus. The exodus eventually results in the partial fulfillment of the promise: the promised land is occupied, and the Israelites settle down to live there.

Hope Founded (Again) in Covenant

God not only *remembers* covenant *in* Egypt, however; he also *intends* covenant, in bringing Israel *out of* Egypt. The book of Exodus makes this clear. God's purpose in liberating his people is not to set them loose in the desert but to take them to Mount Sinai to make a covenant once again. In Exodus 19:3-6 they are urged, as God's particular possession among all the peoples, to keep this new covenant, which involves keeping God's law. This is a covenant fundamentally concerning one people, then. If the Noah covenant is about *all* living creatures, and the Abraham covenant is about *all* nations, the Sinai covenant is focused much more closely on the *one* nation, Israel. But Israel is still called, in this covenant, to a much larger task:

> Now if you obey me fully and keep my covenant, then out of all nations you will be my treasured possession. Although the whole earth is mine, you will be for me a kingdom of priests and a holy nation. (Exodus 19:5-6)

The whole earth remains God's domain, and the task of God's people, as a "kingdom of priests," is still to mediate God's blessing to it. That is what priests do.[19] Covenant may have narrowed down here, then, in one sense: from all living creatures, to all human beings, and now to one people-group. The narrowing, however, is still with an eye to the larger agenda, which is the blessing of all creation.[20]

The book of Deuteronomy, which closes the Pentateuch, is itself *constructed* according to the model of an ancient covenant treaty; that is its literary form.[21] Deuteronomy defines *the essential relationship* between God and Israel in terms of the Sinai covenant. This covenant is not, however, restricted to the original "parties" involved. Deuteronomy quite explicitly recognizes the ongoing (present) nature of covenant, since Moses' words here are addressed to the second generation of Israelites, after the wilderness wanderings, who had not themselves participated in the events at Mount Sinai. *These* Israelites are assured that God's covenant with Israel applies just as much to them as to their forebears. It is, in fact, one of the concerns of Deuteronomy that each generation should—through ritual, reflection, and education—relive their connection with this covenantal past and so make the past real in their present time.

Hope Founded in the Monarchy

In the narrative that follows Deuteronomy, just as much as in the one that precedes it, God works actively in the world to pursue his good ends. As in the Pentateuch, he does so in the midst of significant dysfunction and wickedness even among the people he has called to help him. The story in the first book of Samuel about how Israel eventually came to be ruled by kings illustrates this truth in a striking manner.

As the prophet Samuel moves into the closing years of his life, we discover (1 Samuel 8), the Israelites are unhappy with the way they are being governed. They ask Samuel for "a king to lead us, such as all the other nations have" (8:5). This request is represented in the story as a rejection of God's own kingship—as yet another attempt by the Israelites to evade their calling to be God's own people (8:7). It is also represented, however, as something that will result in great damage to Israelite society itself. A king "such as all the other nations have," Samuel tells them, will centralize all power around himself and erode the freedoms and rights that the Israelites possess as a result of being the covenant-people of God:

> This is what the king who will reign over you will do: He will take your sons and make them serve with his chariots and horses, and they will run in front of his chariots. Some he will assign to be commanders of thousands and commanders of fifties, and others to plow his ground and reap his harvest, and still others to make weapons of war and equipment for his chariots. He will take your daughters to be perfumers and cooks and bakers. He will take the best of your fields and vineyards and olive groves and give them to his attendants. He will take a tenth of your grain and of your vintage and give it to his officials and attendants. Your menservants and maidservants and the best of your cattle and donkeys he will take for his own use. He will take a tenth of your flocks, and you yourselves will become his slaves. (1 Samuel 8:11-17)

God's law may well accommodate itself to human frailty and folly (our chap. 10), but it nevertheless does prescribe a view of society that is radically different from the one that Samuel here outlines to the Israelites. This is clear not least in the provisions that are made in the law for kingship in Israel:

> When you enter the land the LORD your God is giving you and have taken possession of it and settled in it, and you say, "Let us set a king over us like all the nations around us," be sure to appoint over you the king the LORD your God chooses. He must be from among your own brothers. Do not place a foreigner over you, one who is not a brother Israelite. The king, moreover, must not acquire great numbers of horses for himself or make the people return to Egypt to get more of them, for the LORD has told you, "You are not to go back that way again." He must not take many wives, or his heart will be led astray. He must not accumulate large amounts of silver and gold. When he takes the throne of his kingdom, he is to write for himself on a scroll a copy of this law, taken from that of the priests, who are Levites. It is to be with him, and he is to read it all the days of his life so that he may learn to revere the LORD his God and follow carefully all the words of this law and these decrees and not consider himself better than his brothers and turn from the law to the right or to the left. Then he and his descendants will reign a long time over his kingdom in Israel. (Deuteronomy 17:14-20)

The king, in this passage, must be an Israelite ("from among your own brothers"). He must understand "from the inside" the history and traditions of the people, and he must be able and willing to govern in line with them, rather than introducing alien ideas from the outside world. He is also not to *behave* like one of the semidivine kings of the surrounding cultures, accumulating horses, wives, or large amounts of silver and gold. Ancient Near Eastern kings are not to be his role models. Instead, he is to remain, in all respects, as one among his "brothers"—both in behavior and in attitude (he will not "consider himself better than his brothers"). He will be able to be this sort of king if, like his brothers, he follows God's law, remembering the character of the one true God. Then he will be able rightly to order his kingdom—under God. Given all of the foregoing, it is quite obvious that the "king" in Deuteronomy is hardly a king at all—if we measure kingship by its historical expressions from the ancient Near East all the way down to relatively modern times. The institution of kingship is *allowed for* in Israel by Deuteronomy 17, but what is really *described* here is the leadership of one person among equals. The "democratic ideal" embedded in the biblical moral vision constrains the political reality of kingship.

It is not this Deuteronomic kingship that the Israelites have in mind in 1 Samuel 8. They are looking instead for the kind of king that was commonly found among Israel's ancient Near Eastern neighbors—the divine god-king of the despotic city-state. The society they are seeking to build, then, is not a society that reflects God's kingship over the earth but one that stands against it. Yet remarkably, albeit quite consistently with the biblical view of God's relationship with the world that we encountered in our chapter 10, God works with what he finds in this story. He does not stand on his dignity and simply refuse the people's request. They may have rejected *him* (1 Samuel 8:7), but he has not rejected *them*.

God accedes, in fact, to Israel's demand for kingship "such as all the other nations have," even though it is foolish and wrong: "Listen to them and give them a king," he tells Samuel in 1 Samuel 8:22. Samuel does then provide them with a king, who appears to be exactly the kind of king they desire. They want a king to "lead us and to go out before us and fight our battles" (1 Samuel 8:20), and this is what King Saul does in 1 Samuel 11, leading the Israelites to victory over the Ammonites. From this point onward in the biblical story, kingship becomes central to God's own plans for both Israel and the whole world; it becomes a ground for hope. Israel herself has kings for as long as she retains national independence (i.e., until first Israel, and then Judah, is conquered by a foreign power and assimilated into an empire). Drawing on the language of kingship, the biblical literature then looks forward to a kingdom of God that will one day arrive, at the heart of which will still be a human king. I shall have more to say about this future hope in a moment. The institution of kingship is, as I say, accepted into the divine plan—not temporarily but eternally. God does not spend his time in the biblical story fighting against it. He simply seeks, throughout the story, to take what has begun in wickedness and foolishness and turn it toward the good.

The Significance of David

In the books of Samuel, this "turning toward the good" is already illustrated in the story of David, who is presented as *God's* choice for king (in contrast to *the people's* choice, Saul). God first gives the Israelites the kind of king they *want* (Saul) but later the kind of king they *need* (David). David is the person they need because, at least initially in this story, he is "a man after [God's] own heart" (1 Samuel 13:7). He is the kind of man that is envisaged in Deuteronomy 17:14-20. From the Goliath incident onward, he fights the battles of the LORD, not his own (1 Samuel 18:17; 25:28; 30:26). The Israelites wanted someone to "fight *our* battles," but for David the battles are always God's—God is the warrior, and David fights at his side (while Saul stays at home: 1 Samuel 18:12-16; 2 Samuel 5:2). David is also a person of exemplary moral character in this part of his story. Saul treats David very badly, whereas David treats Saul and his family well at all times (1 Samuel 18:10-30; 19:8-10; 24:1-7; 2 Samuel 4; 9). David does not stand on his dignity as a king; in fact, he holds the office lightly. When he moves the ark of the covenant up to Jerusalem in 2 Samuel 6:12-23, we find him dancing in front of it all the way. Michal, Saul's daughter, clearly thinks that David's behavior is inappropriate for a king, and she is contemptuous of him, but he has no time for her view of kingship. He is first and foremost a worshipper of God, and only then a king. His piety is further expressed in 2 Samuel 7, where he asks the prophet Nathan whether he may build God a temple. He seeks permission from one of God's spokesmen; he does not simply proceed because he has the power to do so. God is nudging the institution of kingship toward the good, and in David he finds a willing partner. David rules Israel with justice and equity, doing what is "just and right for all his people" (2 Samuel 8:15).

It is in the David story that we read about another covenant—a covenant between God and David himself:

> When your days are over and you rest with your fathers, I will raise up your offspring to succeed you, who will come from your own body, and I will establish his kingdom. He is the one who will build a house for my Name, and I will establish the throne of his kingdom forever. I will be his father, and he will be my son. When he does wrong, I will punish him with the rod of men, with floggings inflicted by men. But my love will never be taken away from him as I took it away from Saul, whom I removed from before you. Your house and your kingdom will endure forever before me; your throne will be established forever. (2 Samuel 7:12-16)

Here, God makes a covenant with an individual Israelite, who is promised an everlasting royal house. Inevitably (and rightly), we read this passage in the context of the biblical story as we have explored it to this point. We are therefore bound to understand the covenant with David in the context of the Sinai covenant, the Sinai covenant in the context of the Abraham covenant, the Abraham covenant in the context of the Noah covenant, and the Noah covenant in the context of what has happened in the opening chapters of Genesis. We now appreciate, then, that the hope for the world that is articulated in the Noah and Abraham covenants has come to involve a royal line within Israel. It has come to involve a son of David. Covenant "narrows down" as we move along in the Old Testament story, involving first the whole of creation, then all humans, then just Israel, and now, finally, one Israelite. However, it always narrows down in the context of a larger plan; God calls one people, and ultimately one person, to live in a right relationship with him and to bring blessing to the whole earth in doing so. David now finds his own particular place within this great plan.

A Phoenix from the Ashes

The unconditional, long-term nature of the promise enshrined in this covenant with David is important for what comes later in the biblical literature. David himself proves to be a disappointment; his commitment to the good does not last. He falls spectacularly from grace in 2 Samuel 11 and the following chapters, not only committing adultery with Bathsheba but also, to cover up his affair, arranging for her husband (Uriah the Hittite) to be killed. This represents yet another notable failure by an Israelite to bless a Gentile—a notable failure to mediate God's kingdom to the world. David's son Solomon, after a rocky start where justice is concerned (1 Kings 1–2), seems to be on the right path in 1 Kings 3–4, receiving wisdom from God and governing justly and well. By the end of his reign, however, he has broken every rule that Deuteronomy 17 articulates about kingship. He multiplies horses, wives, silver, and gold, and he turns to other gods (1 Kings 4:26; 10:14-29; 11:1-6). Subsequently, the kingdom is divided into a northern part (Israel) and a southern part (Judah). There are very few high points for the monarchy thereafter. Hezekiah does appear in 2 Kings 18–20 as a kind of second David, trusting and listening to God (see especially 2 Kings 18:5-8), and Josiah appears in 2 Kings 22–23 as a kind of second Moses, determined to obey God's law. In the end, however, the monarchy of Israel fails to express the kingship of God to such an extent that it is swept away. Israel's kings, like the first human beings, go into exile.

What survives? Has all the hope that was grounded in the monarchy entirely dissipated? The answer is no; hope remains. The monarchy
may have originated in a wicked desire to evade the rule of God; it may
have failed to express the rule of God for most of its history; and it
may have come to an end under the judgment of God. However, hope
remains, because God has committed himself to the descendants of
David. There are already hints of this hope in the way that the story
of the later monarchy is told in the books of Kings.[22] The hope is fully
expressed, however, in the prophetic literature of the Old Testament.
Like a phoenix from the ashes, the Davidic monarchy arises in this literature as an important aspect of biblical hope for the future. Here,
the biblical authors, for the first time in the biblical story, lay fully bare
their convictions about the extent of God's commitment to his original
creation purposes, and they clarify what these purposes are.[23]

HOPE IN THE BIBLICAL PROPHETS

The prophets presuppose the broken state of creation that is described
elsewhere in the Old Testament and that is explicitly articulated in
Genesis 3 in terms of three broken relationships: the human relationship with God, the human relationship with other human beings, and
the human relationship with the rest of creation. They look ahead to
a time when these various relationships will be healed—and, beyond
that, to an entirely new order of being in the cosmos. The forces of
cosmic darkness will be defeated, they tell us, and all the suffering they
have initiated will be abolished. More than this, creation itself will be
transformed, and, as an aspect of that transformation, immortality will
be gifted to human beings after all. The journey with creation upon
which God set out "in the beginning" will be completed. There will be
redemption of what has gone wrong, but there will also be the fulfillment of the plan that would have been enacted (it seems) even if *nothing* had gone wrong. And this will involve, among other things, an end
to *all* suffering, no matter how it has arisen in the world—suffering
both "intrinsic" and "extrinsic" (our chap. 5).

The Focus of Prophetic Hope

In the Old Testament, the focus of this prophetic hope is the city of
Jerusalem. I hope not to be misunderstood here. I do not mean physical, historical Jerusalem—the city that existed back in biblical times,

and still does today. In the case of the prophets, the Jerusalem I have in mind is actually a larger-than-life Jerusalem. It is not so much a physical place as a metaphor for the redeemed world in which God once again dwells fully and intensely in his (now transformed) temple-cosmos. It is Jerusalem as a restored garden in Eden—and then something more.

This is the Jerusalem already pictured in the book of Psalms—the place that God has chosen as his dwelling place (e.g., Psalms 78:68; 132:13), and whose inhabitants share in his blessings forever (Psalms 23:6; 132:13-18; 133:1-3). The Psalms use this language even though the physical temple in Jerusalem was obviously not considered biblically to "contain" God (1 Kings 8:27), and no worshipper, historically and physically, would have dwelled there forever. Likewise, Jerusalem is greatly exalted in the Psalms as the "highest point on the earth" (e.g., Psalms 2:6; 68:18; 87:1; 99:9)—even though the physical Mount Zion was (and remains) quite a small hill. In the Psalms, Jerusalem is also the source of life-giving springs of water and the place where the living God defeats the waters of chaos (e.g., Psalms 46:2-4; 93:3-4). So far as we know, however, the water systems of physical Jerusalem have only ever produced quite mundane waters, and no physical waves have ever smashed into Jerusalem's foundations—the city lies well inland from the sea. Moreover, Jerusalem, in the Psalms, is a place that God unfailingly protects from enemy attack (e.g., Psalms 48:3-7; 76:1-12), but the biblical texts themselves tell us that the physical Jerusalem was destroyed by the Babylonians in the sixth century B.C. (2 Kings 25).

In the Psalms and in the Prophets, then, "Jerusalem" stands for something more than the physical city. It represents something much bigger: being forever in communion with God, forever safe with God in his "high mountain fortress," forever nourished by God, and given life by God. It is the city on the mountain that stands at the very center of the cosmos—and, as such, it is the city to which God will gather Israel from exile and to which, ultimately, Gentiles will also come to seek the LORD of Hosts.[24] That is the biblical prophetic hope, and "Jerusalem" is its focal point. We may describe this hope more expansively under three headings that speak directly of transformation.

The Transformation of the Human Person

The biblical prophets hope, first, for the transformation of the human person in relation to God. Genesis tells us that the intimate communion that first characterized the divine-human relationship has been lost, and alienation has taken its place. When the prophets address this issue, they speak, first, of God bringing his own people, Israel, to a new level of awareness of sin and to a new experience of cleansing from sin, which makes it possible to leave the past behind and to enter into a new era:

> I will take you out of the nations; I will gather you from all the countries and bring you back into your own land. I will sprinkle clean water on you, and you will be clean; I will cleanse you from all your impurities and from all your idols. I will give you a new heart and put a new spirit in you; I will remove from you your heart of stone and give you a heart of flesh. And I will put my Spirit in you and move you to follow my decrees and be careful to keep my laws.[25] (Ezekiel 36:24-27)

From a biblical perspective, there is such a thing as "eschatological forgiveness." The sins of the past will be washed away. Connected to this resolution of problems in the *past* is a transformation that relates to the *future*—a new heart is provided, and a new spirit. If the new age that is being envisaged here is to be truly new, it will be possible only if people's motivations and aspirations are different from what they were before—if they cease desiring the wrong and begin to desire only the right. Therefore, there is not only *forgiveness* but also *transformation*. These are the personal aspects of a new creation that experiences more broadly the new kind of fertility we shall discuss shortly. In this situation God's judgments are no longer necessary, since there is no longer wrongdoing:

> You will live in the land I gave your forefathers; you will be my people, and I will be your God. I will save you from all your uncleanness. I will call for the grain and make it plentiful and will not bring famine upon you. I will increase the fruit of the trees and the crops of the field, so that you will no longer suffer disgrace among the nations because of famine.
>
> (Ezekiel 36:28-30)

The last two Bible passages cited come from the book of Ezekiel. We find a similar scenario in the book of Jeremiah, where we are told of a new *covenant* written on the heart. In this scenario, God's law now becomes part of the very fabric of the human person, and obedience comes naturally. Here, too, we are told about the forgiveness of sins:

> "The time is coming," declares the LORD, "when I will make a new covenant with the house of Israel and with the house of Judah. It will not be like the covenant I made with their forefathers when I took them by the hand to lead them out of Egypt, because they broke my covenant, though I was a husband to them. . . . This is the covenant I will make with the house of Israel after that time. . . . I will put my law in their minds and write it on their hearts. I will be their God, and they will be my people. No longer will a man teach his neighbor, or a man his brother, saying, 'Know the LORD,' because they will all know me, from the least of them to the greatest. . . . For I will forgive their wickedness and will remember their sins no more."
>
> (Jeremiah 31:31-34)

The eschatological phenomena described here are, of course, described with respect to *Israel* in the first instance. The reconciliation with God that is envisaged in the prophetic writings is not, however, limited to Israel. It is a universal reconciliation, in a time when God pours out his spirit on *all* flesh (Joel 2:28-29), and the result is as follows:

> In that day there will be a highway from Egypt to Assyria. The Assyrians will go to Egypt and the Egyptians to Assyria. The Egyptians and Assyrians will worship together. In that day Israel will be the third, along with Egypt and Assyria, a blessing on the earth. The LORD Almighty will bless them, saying, "Blessed be Egypt my people, Assyria my handiwork, and Israel my inheritance." (Isaiah 19:23-25)

The transformation is universal, and it is radical. It goes to the very roots of the human person. It restores, seemingly, what the human pair possessed in the garden in Eden before the serpent came—intimate knowledge of God, unspoiled by wrongdoing. Perhaps these texts recall a time when "the man and his wife heard the sound of the LORD God as he was walking in the garden in the cool of the day," but they did not hide. One might well imagine that this was already a time (as Jeremiah 31:34 puts it) when there was no need that "a man teach his neighbor, or a man his brother, saying, 'Know the LORD,'" because everyone knew

God. Yet these prophetic texts also press beyond the *restoration* of a right human relationship with God and on to something new. They appear to envisage that, in the future, there will no longer be the possibility of evil reentering the human story. Something fundamental changes in the future; God's law is now found written on the heart, and God's spirit is found "in" the human being, leading her to "follow my decrees and be careful to keep my laws."[26] What is envisaged here is not *simply* a return to the past. A new day has dawned.

The Transformation of Human Society

The biblical prophets hope, second, for the transformation of human society. Near its beginning in Genesis, the biblical story provides us first with an account of human community and then with an account of human community disrupted. Human beings become alienated not only from God but also from each other. Israel's prophetic eschatology, conversely, pictures human society redeemed and reconciled. In the first instance, the prophetic hope is focused on the restoration of community in Israel itself—the reunification of a people formerly divided:

> The word of the LORD came to me: "Son of man, take a stick of wood and write on it, 'Belonging to Judah and the Israelites associated with him.' Then take another stick of wood, and write on it, 'Ephraim's stick, belonging to Joseph and all the house of Israel associated with him.' Join them together into one stick so that they will become one in your hand."
> (Ezekiel 37:15-17)

Ezekiel anticipates here the reunification of Israel and Judah after the Babylonian exile has come to an end. Various prophetic texts then incorporate into their vision of the restored community the idea of a righteous king who will govern it. If human society is to function as it should, a just government is required, as outlined in Psalm 72:1-2. Here the author pleads, "Endow the king with your justice, O God, the royal son with your righteousness. He will judge your people in righteousness, your afflicted ones with justice." It is in relation to this righteous king that the "son of David" idea is developed in our prophetic literature, building on the Davidic covenant described in 2 Samuel 7. Ezekiel himself envisages such a king when he writes about a future time in which God the Shepherd will gather his flock and set over the flock a shepherd who is "my servant David" (Ezekiel 34:22-24). Among other texts in which this Davidic ruler also appears we may mention Jeremiah 33:15, Zechariah 9:9-10, and also Isaiah 11:1-5, which reads as follows:

> A shoot will come up from the stump of Jesse; from his roots a Branch will bear fruit. The Spirit of the LORD will rest on him—the Spirit of wisdom and of understanding, the Spirit of counsel and of power, the Spirit of knowledge and of the fear of the LORD—and he will delight in the fear of the LORD. He will not judge by what he sees with his eyes, or decide by what he hears with his ears; but with righteousness he will judge the needy, with justice he will give decisions for the poor of the earth. He will strike the earth with the rod of his mouth; with the breath of his lips he will slay the wicked. Righteousness will be his belt and faithfulness the sash around his waist.

The righteous king, we note here, will deliver the needy and the poor from the hands of those who oppress them; the enemies of God will need to be dealt with decisively if a just human society is to exist. This is a prominent theme in the prophetic literature. Indeed, the transformation of human society can truly be *human* rather than simply *Israelite* only when God's rightful reign over the whole earth is established in such a way. The transformation of human society, therefore, inevitably involves bringing the enemies of God into submission (e.g., Zechariah 12:1-9). The long-term goal is not *destruction*, however, but *construction*—that Israel and all the nations will live in harmony, all worshipping the only living God:

> This is what the LORD Almighty says: "Many peoples and the inhabitants of many cities will yet come, and the inhabitants of one city will go to another and say, 'Let us go at once to entreat the LORD and seek the LORD Almighty. I myself am going.' And many peoples and powerful nations will come to Jerusalem to seek the LORD Almighty and to entreat him." This is what the LORD Almighty says: "In those days ten men from all languages and nations will take firm hold of one Jew by the hem of his robe and say, 'Let us go with you, because we have heard that God is with you.'"[27] (Zechariah 8:20-23)

The Transformation of Creation

The biblical prophets hope, third, for the transformation of creation itself. Genesis tells us initially of a close relationship between human and nonhuman creation but later of human beings becoming alienated from the animal and from the natural world. Unsurprisingly, biblical eschatology speaks of the overcoming of this alienation. Ezekiel 36 is again one of the key passages, interweaving hope for the restoration of fertility and agriculture with other aspects of the anticipated future transformation (vv. 8-9, 11, 29-30, 34-35). Another key passage is Hosea 2:18, which describes God making a covenant with the animals: "In that day I will make a covenant for them with the beasts of the field and the birds of the air and the creatures that move along the ground. Bow and sword and battle I will abolish from the land, so that all may lie down in safety." Part of what will characterize the new age, it seems, is safety for the animals from human predation. This idea of safety pervading the entirety of creation is also developed in Isaiah 11:1-9, where the vision of the son of David delivering the needy and the poor from their oppressors is immediately followed by a vision of cosmic peace.

In these various passages, the human relationship with other creatures, and with the earth itself, is healed. But more than this, the cosmos is radically transformed. In the created world as we know it, no wolf would ever cohabit with a lamb; no leopard would ever lie down with a goat (Isaiah 11:6). This is an entirely new order of things—a new heavens and a new earth (Isaiah 65:17-25; 66:22-23; Ezekiel 47:1-12). Only in such a new world could it possibly be that the sound of weeping would never be heard (Isaiah 65:17) and that everyone could be guaranteed to live to a ripe old age (65:20). Indeed, only in such a new world could death itself conceivably be swallowed up forever (Isaiah 25:8); only there could it be true that "multitudes who sleep in the dust of the earth will awake: some to everlasting life, others to shame and everlasting contempt" (Daniel 12:2). Here, in the end, we discover that the possibility of immortality has not, after all, disappeared from biblical hope. It is still very much alive. The expectation expressed by Job is not without wider biblical support, and his yearning is not futile: "And after my skin has been destroyed, yet in my flesh I will see God; I myself will see him with my own eyes—I, and not another. How my heart yearns within me!" (Job 19:26-27). Job hopes—and other biblical authors claim that he is not foolish in hoping—that in his own person, after death, he will encounter God. It had appeared that humans beings east of Eden could hope only for death, but, in fact, "your dead will live, their bodies will rise" (Isaiah 26:19).

ON VALUE AND ACTION

From the perspective of biblical faith, all of this is what I am to hope for. We may well live in a present world order in which there is an enormous amount that is wrong. People do not worship God but worship idols instead. There is an immense amount of injustice, as well as neglect toward, and damage of, God's creation. This is true both within individual societies and also in the international arena. God is at work in the world, however, turning things toward the good; God has always been at work in the world in this way. A day is coming when God will bring justice to the world—he will bring to account those who oppose him, whether they affirm that they are his people or whether they do not. This will also be a day of salvation, in which universal peace will be established in a new world order. This is the biblical vision. In some ways, it is a vision that concerns a return to Eden. It is also a vision that moves us beyond Eden, however, and into a reality in which human beings have never lived before—the reality of the new Jerusalem. It involves astonishing realities like the bodily resurrection of the dead and the swallowing up of death forever. It is not so much a return to the beginning of God's story, then, as an arrival at the ending that was always going to *be* the ending. What was promised by the presence of the tree of life in Eden now becomes, in this prophetic vision, a reality. The ending, it turns out, was never in doubt—only the path taken to arrive there. God's story has been a story of many twists and turns—from the first twist in the garden through the many turns in the subsequent narrative and on to the final destination. The destination, however, has always remained the destination.

This biblical answer to the question "What am I to hope for?" has often been misunderstood—as if hoping for such a future inherently devalues the present *in relation to* the future and inevitably encourages passivity "now" while we *wait* for "then." It is not likely that anyone who has carefully read this book will hear the biblical authors in such ways, but since many *have* done so, there is a need to consider the matter explicitly. Do our biblical authors wish their readers to possess a hope for the future that leads to a devaluing of the world as we presently know it? Moreover, do they advocate "waiting" as our dominant mode of being in the present world, as opposed to active engagement?

The answer to both questions is no. Biblical faith requires of us, first, a very high valuing of the present world as God's good world (albeit touched by evil). It is God's temple-cosmos, his garden, and his kingdom—over which he is already King. God lives here, with us, and provides for us and blesses us here, along with all God's creatures. God is also present in particular ways to Israel, through the tabernacle and the temple in which he also "lives"—those microcosmic realities that represent the truth about the macrocosm that is the cosmos. God is not somewhere else *rather than* here in biblical thinking, and we are not called to *live* somewhere else *rather than* here. We are certainly to live *here*, in this good world, with God—taking good care of the world as we encounter it.

We are, to be sure, heading for something even *better*—better not least because this current version of the world is touched by evil and by death, and biblical hope points us forward to a time when evil and death exist no more. But this "better" is *indeed truly* only another "version" of what we already know in our present experience. It is not "somewhere else"; it is in fact only some*when* else. *Time* must pass before the world eventually becomes what it is destined to be—before the kingdom becomes fully God's and everything arrives at the destination that God planned for it in the beginning. *Time* must pass, but we are not envisaged as changing our *space*. We do not, in biblical faith, fly off into some other realm, becoming spirits instead of material beings. The new heavens and the new earth are exactly that—still a *heavens* and an *earth*. The new earth is a place inhabited not by disembodied souls but by resurrected bodies (and their souls). In biblical thinking, then, what comes next will be deeply continuous with what we know now, even if it will also be discontinuous in some ways. It will certainly still involve matter, even if it is transformed matter. There is, in all of this, no devaluing of the present world. There is only a yearning that this world should become, as quickly as can be, the world that it was always destined to be. There is only a yearning that the present world should quickly birth its offspring that, like all offspring, will be both like and unlike its parent.

Second, biblical hope is certainly not a passive hope. It is certainly not the kind of hope that Derrick Jensen has in mind in the lines quoted in the second epigraph to this chapter—a hope that removes human agency, engendering "waiting" as our sole or main occupation in the world. In biblical thinking, entirely the opposite is true. Hope is what keeps one *going*, living a good and a just life in the midst of very real challenges—hope, and also faith. Faith holds that God *does* still live in his temple-cosmos—that God *is* still at work here and now in this present world, drawing it toward the good. Faith insists that God *himself* is good. It holds that God's kingdom is not simply future but now and that God is continually blessing his creatures in this kingdom *now*. To have faith, then, is to participate actively in this work of God in the world, as we live out our vocation as kings and priests.

From a biblical perspective, hope is what enables us to keep going in this work of mediating God's blessing to the world, even when we fail spectacularly to deliver. Hope is what enables us to keep going even when we find ourselves to be David, who so spectacularly failed to bless the Gentile Uriah. Hope tells us that success is *possible* in the here and now, because in cosmic terms it is *inevitable*. Those captivated by biblical faith therefore keep on pursuing the prophetic vision now, because they know that one day it will come to pass. They keep on pursuing the Song of Songs vision of marriage, because they know that one day everything that interferes with it will be destroyed. They keep on resisting the evildoer, because, although they nearly lose their footing when they see "the prosperity of the wicked" (Psalm 73:2) and although they fear that they have kept their hearts pure and have washed their hands in innocence for nothing (73:13), they trust that finally "those who are far from you [God] will perish" (73:27).

"Hope" is *not* the opposite of "agency" in biblical thinking; it is its very wellspring. Hope is what allows love to persevere, as *it* perseveres in what Emily Dickinson charmingly pictures as its perpetual birdsong:

> "Hope" is the thing with feathers—
> That perches in the soul—
> And sings the tune without the words—
> And never stops—at all.[28]

Hope is, in fact, love's servant, rather than something that undercuts love's incentive. As one famous interpreter of the Old Testament once said, "And now these three remain: faith, hope and love. But the greatest of these is love" (1 Corinthians 13:13). Hope is not the greatest thing;

love is the greatest thing. And any hope that undercuts (active) love is not a biblical hope.

HOPE IN OTHER TRADITIONS

We should not expect that religious and philosophical traditions that differ so greatly from biblical faith in so many other ways should now be found to be similar when it comes to the matter of future hope. Indeed they are not, with the exception (to some extent) of Zoroastrianism and Islam. Like biblical faith, Zoroastrianism holds that "there will be an ultimate ending of time, with a general resurrection of all dead. The final cosmic battle will lead to the banishment of evil forces forever, the earth will be purified in a great conflagration, and a restored world will endure forever."[29] Islam also looks for the bodily resurrection of the dead and envisages both an accounting for all evildoing and rewards for righteousness, as well as conceiving of the afterlife as being lived out in a "garden" that is somewhat like the gardens of present experience.[30]

Some of the other traditions express very little future hope of any meaningful kind at all. In the naturalistic polytheism of ancient Mesopotamia, "hope" was restricted for most people, realistically, to a kind of undisturbed shadow existence in the underworld, which was an unpleasant place.[31] In ancient Egypt, there was a greater possibility for happiness in the afterlife, but attaining and maintaining that state were nevertheless arduous exercises, involving (among other things) the ability to remember and to be able to recite material from the Book of the Dead. In ancient Greece, a person needed gold in order to cross the first hurdle in Hades (the River Styx), and it was possible for those who had lived well then to enter the restful fields of Elysium. The idea of reward and punishment exists in some of this mythology, but nothing approaches the biblical idea of the one creator God, who is taking the whole of creation on a journey into new time and transformed space and who remains so committed to matter that he resurrects the dead.

Such biblical ideas are also absent in the Greek *philosophical* tradition. We recall that Plato looked ultimately for souls to escape the material world and to fly back to the stars. This negativity toward matter is reflected even more intensely in the Gnostics and Manichaeans who followed him. There is no hope for the transformation of the material world or even for its redemption; we may hope only to escape. Outside the Platonic tradition, Epicurus taught that souls released from their bodies dispersed like smoke. The Stoics believed that some souls survived a bit longer, until everything was consumed by fire and the cycle of existence began once again. In the case of *these* souls, there really was no smoke without fire. It is not surprising, then, that when the Christian missionary Paul was attempting in Athens to communicate his message about "Jesus and the resurrection," the Epicurean and Stoic philosophers could not comprehend what he was talking about (Acts 17:18-34). Indeed, the notion of physical resurrection caused some of the gathered crowd to "sneer" (17:32). This story underlines the profound difference between biblical faith and Greek philosophy when it comes to hope.[32]

In the East, too, hope typically takes a form very different from its biblical counterpart. In Hinduism, we recall, the body is only the shell inside which the soul resides in the course of its onward journey toward salvation. As in Plato, salvation is conceived of as escaping the material world. The escape, though, is *into* the "One"; it is a *merging* with the One. The Many do not get saved *as* the Many, and certainly not as *persons* (much less as *embodied* persons). Instead, when one of the Many gets to a point in the reincarnational cycle where he is discharging only good karma, he ceases to *be* one of the Many. This is the hoped-for "afterlife," prior to which there is no judgment offered by the one, good, creator God but only the punishments entailed in all the past lives of the individual soul. The "future hope" of Buddhism is similar, even though in other ways Hinduism and Buddhism are very different from each other. In neither case (obviously) are there resurrected bodies or an eternal community of persons and other creatures that is "like" but also "unlike" the communities we experience now.

Nor is there any such eternal community in Sikh thought. Sikhism differs in various ways from Hinduism and Buddhism: there *is* one creator God, who is personal (or, at least, has personal dimensions), and the world in which we live *is* real, rather than illusory. Yet it is still the soul, and not the body, that is the "real" self—an immortal spark from the fire that is God, destined to return to God after the many reincarnations in human and other bodies that result from bad karma. When the soul returns to God, eventually, it does so as part of a creation that is an emanation of God's being, not a separate entity. Unsurprisingly, then, the soul's destiny is not to dwell in communion with God as one of the eternal Many but to be absorbed back into the One; it is to "attain complete absorption into God's being like water blending with water."[33]

Theodore Ludwig characterizes the Sikh tradition thus described as "a religious perspective that specifically integrates elements" from the Abrahamic and the prior Indian religions.[34] As readers of our previous chapters will immediately realize, however, Sikhism is in reality a fusion, not of *Abrahamic* and Indian thought, but of *Greek* and Indian thought.

In sum: there is no future hope of a remotely biblical kind to be found in most of these other religious and philosophical traditions. Biblical faith stands resolutely at odds with much of what they have to say. Moreover, *what* they have to say does not provide much of a foundation for meaningful human action that aims to make this world a better place. The Old Story, by contrast, calls us to hope for a better world and at the same time to act in this one to nudge it toward the kingdom of God. Indeed, in its articulation of biblical hope, it gives us reasons to keep going in pursuit of present good, even when we despair that good can ever be achieved.

FURTHER UP AND FURTHER IN

New Dimensions in the Old Story

Do not think that I have come to abolish the Law or the Prophets;
I have not come to abolish them but to fulfill them.

Jesus in the Gospel of Matthew, 5:17[1]

Therefore, since we are surrounded by such a great cloud of witnesses, let us throw off everything that hinders and the sin that
so easily entangles, and let us run with perseverance the race
marked out for us. Let us fix our eyes on Jesus.

Letter to the Hebrews, 12:1-2[2]

In the first chapter, I explained why, in answering my ten questions,
I would restrict myself initially to the literature that forms the older
part of the Old Story—the Old Testament. My intention, however, was
always to return at a later point to what is, from a Christian point of
view at least, the *newer* part, the New Testament—a body of literature
that, because of some core convictions that its authors share about the
significance of Jesus of Nazareth, develops biblical faith in a particular
direction. We have now arrived at that later point; it is time to discuss
this "particular direction," to which I shall refer in what follows as "New
Testament faith."

My strategy in this chapter will be to return to each of the questions we discussed earlier and suggest what the outline of a "fuller" answer to each question looks like when we take account of the New Testament materials.[3] Just as we previously read the Old Testament story in the context of its beginning in Genesis 1–3, so now we shall read the New Testament in the context of its "beginning" in the Old Testament. This is what the New Testament authors themselves invite us to do, and indeed what they portray Jesus of Nazareth as inviting us to do as well. Throughout his life, they tell us, Jesus constantly pointed his hearers back to the older part of the Story, indicating where truths were written in the Old Testament that were important for a proper understanding of him, his work, and other matters as well (e.g., Matthew 21:13; 26:31). His overall posture toward the Old Testament is well illustrated in the quotation from chapter 5 of Matthew in the first epigraph to this chapter. Furthermore, after his resurrection (the New Testament writers claim), Jesus attempted to dispel the confusion of two of his disciples by reminding them of their Old Testament Scriptures (Luke 24:13-27). Later, the Apostle Paul (one of Jesus' most influential early followers), wishing his young friend Timothy to continue steadfast in his faith, reminds *him* of

> the holy Scriptures, which are able to make you wise for salvation through faith in Christ Jesus. All Scripture is God-breathed and is useful for teaching, rebuking, correcting and training in righteousness, so that the man of God may be thoroughly equipped for every good work. (2 Timothy 3:15-17)

These "holy Scriptures" are the *Old Testament* Scriptures. The New Testament was at this time only in the process of formation and did not yet exist as a collection of Scriptures; only the Old Testament, the foundation upon which it was built, existed. According to the New Testament authors, it is in the *Old Testament* that the Christian will find the older and larger part of the great Story in which she is still caught up, telling her of the "great cloud of witnesses" that surrounds the one who is still "running the same race" (Hebrews 12:1-2, our second epigraph).

WHO IS GOD?

The most central of the convictions about the significance of Jesus of Nazareth that drive the development of New Testament faith is that he is *divine*. It makes sense, then, to switch the order of our two opening "questions" in chapters 2 and 3 and, before turning to the question "What is the world?" to ask again the question "Who is God?"

God Is One

New Testament faith continues to hold that God is One. There are still no other gods in the heavens or on the earth or under the earth. In the book of Acts, one of the early followers of Jesus, Stephen, faces charges that he uttered "words of blasphemy against Moses and against God" (6:11). He responds by retelling a significant portion of the Old Testament story, reminding his listeners of the time when their forebears at Mount Sinai asked Aaron to "make us gods who will go before us" (7:40; cf. Exodus 32:1). Stephen agrees with the Old Testament authors that what happened next was idolatry, and he suggests that God himself, in fact, "gave them [the forebears] over to the worship of the heavenly bodies" (7:40-43).

Later, after the healing of a man in the city of Lystra (14:8-18), the bystanders hail the Apostle Paul and his colleague Barnabas as incarnations of the Greek gods Hermes and Zeus, and they try to offer sacrifices to them. Paul and Barnabas react with horror, urging their worshippers instead to turn to "the living God, who made heaven and earth and sea and everything in them" (14:15). Later still, the silversmith Demetrius of Ephesus expresses concern that Paul has been too successful in persuading people that "man-made gods are no gods at all" (19:26). As a consequence, Demetrius warns, the goddess Artemis "will be robbed of her divine majesty" (19:27).

God is One in New Testament thinking—and there is no other. Acknowledging to the Christians in Corinth that "so-called gods, whether in heaven or on earth," *are* worshipped by many, Paul nevertheless asserts that "for us there is but one God, the Father, from whom all things came and for whom we live" (1 Corinthians 8:5-6). In his letter to the Christians in Galatia, Paul reminds them that *they* were once "slaves to those who by nature are not gods" (Galatians 4:8). Now, however, all people are called to worship the one and only God.

God Is Good

New Testament faith also continues to hold that God is good and, indeed, that God is the "only One who is good" (Matthew 19:17). This good God gives good gifts to those who ask him and also to those who do not.[4] The Apostle Peter urges the Christians to whom he is writing to grow up in their faith, "now that you have tasted that the LORD is good" (1 Peter 2:3). The second letter of Peter envisages Christians as being "called . . . by his own glory and goodness" (2 Peter 1:3). In the New Testament, as in the Old Testament, the goodness of God is expressed in God's blessing. Jesus reminds his hearers of the reality of this blessing in creation itself: "he [God] causes his sun to rise on the evil and the good, and sends rain on the righteous and the unrighteous" (Matthew 5:45). In Acts 3:25, speaking to Jewish worshippers in the Jerusalem temple, Peter recalls the blessings promised in God's covenant with Abraham, reminding them that they are the very heirs of "the covenant God made with your fathers [when he] said to Abraham, 'Through your offspring all peoples on earth will be blessed.'"

The goodness of God is expressed in the New Testament not only in blessing but also in love, faithfulness, and deliverance. John's Gospel famously links love and deliverance when it proclaims, "God so loved the world that he gave his one and only Son, that whoever believes in him shall not perish but have eternal life" (3:16). Paul's opening remarks in his letter to the Christians in Rome remind them that they "are loved by God and called to be saints" (Romans 1:7). In the *closing* remarks to his second letter to the Christians in Corinth Paul describes God as "the God of love and peace" (2 Corinthians 13:11). Paul himself had many experiences of the deliverance of the loving God from "deadly peril" (2 Corinthians 1:10-11), and he certainly came to think of God as "faithful; [one who] will not let you be tempted beyond what you can bear" (1 Corinthians 10:13).[5] Indeed, even if human beings are faithless, Paul asserts that "he [God] will remain faithful, for he cannot disown himself" (2 Timothy 2:13). This is a God who, in Paul's mind, is "for us." This being so, we are in a good place, for "if God is for us, who can be against us? He who did not spare his own Son, but gave him up for us all—how will he not also, along with him, graciously give us all things?" (Romans 8:31-32).

New Testament faith continues to hold that God is also good in other ways. For example, 1 Peter 1:15-16 emphasizes the holiness of God and exhorts its readers likewise to be holy: "But just as he who called you is holy, so be holy in all you do; for it is written: 'Be holy, because I am holy.'" In Revelation 4:8, the worship of God is pictured in such a way as to remind us of Isaiah 6, as we hear the cry, "Holy, holy, holy is

the LORD God Almighty, who was, and is, and is to come." God's goodness, then, according to New Testament faith, can be seen precisely
through his blessing, love, faithfulness, deliverance, and holiness. It
can also be expressed through anger. The beginning of Paul's argument
in his letter to the Roman Christians describes this anger of God, which
is "being revealed from heaven against all the godlessness and wickedness of men who suppress the truth by their wickedness"; they suppress
it, not least, in worshipping gods that are not gods at all (Romans 1:18-
23). As it is in the Old Testament, God's anger in the New Testament is
still "anger for a reason" (righteous anger), which involves both jealousy
and vengeance (1 Corinthians 10:22; Romans 12:19). It is nevertheless
anger that is slow, because God is "patient with you, not wanting anyone to perish, but everyone to come to repentance" (2 Peter 3:9). Here,
we learn also that God's anger relents when people respond to him in
the right way and turn toward the good. This underlines a final point of
continuity with the Old Testament: that, in New Testament faith, "the
LORD is full of compassion and mercy," delivering people "not because
of righteous things we had done, but because of his mercy" (James 5:11;
Titus 3:5).

The Father and the Son

In the New Testament, God remains one, and God remains good. In
affirming such truths, New Testament faith does not differ at all from
the *Jewish* faith that also builds on the faith of Abraham, Isaac, and
Jacob. Both faiths stand in continuity with what has gone before. They
diverge sharply from each other, however, in their answers to the following question: "Who is Jesus of Nazareth in relation to this God?"
In Judaism, Jesus stands in the same relation as the rest of us; he is a
creature of the one God who was known already to Abraham, Isaac, and
Jacob. In New Testament faith, however, Jesus himself *is* this one God.
He is not a creature of God—not even a special one like a prophet—but
in fact God. This remarkable claim is made, for example, in John's Gospel. Here, Jesus' claim to be the light of the world (8:12) leads to a long
reflection on who Jesus' father is and who the father of his conversation
partners might be. *Their* first claim is that their father is Abraham, but
Jesus tells them that this cannot be so, because they do not behave as
Abraham behaved (8:39). Then they claim that God himself is their
father, and Jesus rejects this idea as well: "if God were your Father, you
would love me, for I came from God and now am here" (8:41-42). In

reality, Jesus suggests, they are children of the devil (8:44). Although Jesus has just appeared to differentiate himself from God who is his father, he then presents *himself* as the person who can give others eternal life (8:51). He finishes with an audacious claim: "before Abraham was born, I am!" (8:58). Jesus is alluding here to the revelation of God to Moses in Exodus 3:14, where we are told that "God said to Moses, 'I AM WHO I AM.'" In referencing this verse from Exodus, Jesus is evidently claiming to be God. This is confirmed by the people's response to his words: "they picked up stones to stone him" (John 8:59), for they regarded this claim as blasphemous.

The language of "Father" and "Son," which is used here to distinguish two persons who are nevertheless both one God, reappears elsewhere in the New Testament. It reappears, for example, in the introduction to many of Paul's letters to the churches, where he wishes "grace and peace to you from God our Father and the Lord Jesus Christ" (e.g., Galatians 1:3). Sometimes this language is used in conjunction with the language of "Holy Spirit," which is deployed to indicate a third person who is *also* one with the other two in being God. We see this, for example, in Matthew 28:20, where Jesus' followers are sent out to make other disciples, "baptizing them in the name of the Father and of the Son and of the Holy Spirit." The early Christians believed that God is one, but they also believed that God is three. They felt that they were pressed to this paradoxical conclusion by the events in which they had been recently caught up, which allowed for no other explanation. How exactly to *say* that God is one and yet three, without making mistakes—without falling back into polytheism, for example, or into a "simple" oneness in God that did not make room for Jesus' full divinity—then became a matter of considerable discussion in the early postapostolic church. It led ultimately to the formulation of various "creeds" (official statements of belief in the church) that tried to speak well about the "one-in-three" reality (the Trinity) and to guide Christians in how *not* to speak about it (or believe it).[6]

New Testament faith does not just diverge from *Judaism* on this matter of the God who is three in one. It diverges also from all the other religious and philosophical traditions we have described in this book. Among the Abrahamic religions, it differs just as much from Islam as it does from Judaism, for in Islam the oneness of God *is* a simple oneness, and no allowance for "three" can possibly be made. The Qur'an therefore affirms that Jesus was "nothing more than a messenger of God" and urges Christians to stop speaking of a Trinity (4:171). God is One, and far above having a son, so Christians should not claim that Jesus is the Son of God (9:30-31). To do so is, in fact, to commit the unforgiveable sin of *shirk* (associating anything with Allah). From a Christian point of view, of course, this last assessment misses the mark, since orthodox Christian faith does not *associate* a human Jesus with a divine Father but holds that the one God, who is truly one, *is also* three.[7]

WHAT IS THE WORLD?

As in the Old Testament, so also in the New Testament: the world is the creation of the one personal God. As such, it has a beginning and an end, and it is not eternal. Its end is pictured in Revelation 21:1, where "the first heaven and the first earth [have] passed away." Its beginning is mentioned in Ephesians 3:9, with its reference to "God, who created all things" and is further pictured in the prologue to John's Gospel:

> In the beginning was the Word, and the Word was with God, and the Word was God. He was with God in the beginning. Through him all things were made; without him nothing was made that has been made.[8] (John 1:1-3)

John begins his Gospel by clearly echoing the language of Genesis 1, but now interpreting the creation story in light of Jesus. The God who creates the world is now seen to be Triune (three), for the "Word" mentioned here is also the person who in John 1:14 "became flesh and made his dwelling among us. We have seen his glory, the glory of the One and Only, who came from the Father, full of grace and truth." This is Jesus— the same one (we recall) who later claimed, "Before Abraham was born, I am!" The ordered creation that Genesis 1 envisions as coming into being through the words of God turns out, in the New Testament, to have been created with the participation of the Word. Colossians 1:16-17 develops the same idea:

> By him [Jesus] all things were created: things in heaven and on earth, visible and invisible, whether thrones or powers or rulers or authorities; all things were created by him and for him. He is before all things, and in him all things hold together.

The One Who Calms the Sea

The identification of Jesus with the creator God is also made in the New Testament in more subtle ways. Consider, for example, the story of Jesus stilling the storm on the Sea of Galilee, as it is told in Matthew 8:23-27. Matthew does not place this story in the same position as Mark and Luke; he associates it directly with other miracle stories that underline Jesus' Godlike power.[9] He also leads into the story differently. He prefaces it with two of Jesus' sayings about discipleship: a warning against an unconsidered decision to follow Jesus and a summons to radical *decisiveness* in following him (8:19-22). Just after these sayings, Matthew inserts a statement unparalleled in the other two gospels: "he [Jesus] got into the boat and his disciples *followed* him" (8:23). Matthew wants us to understand the journey of the disciples with Jesus in the boat and the stilling of the storm in terms of discipleship ("following"). This is a story, therefore, not only about Jesus' immediate disciples, in a boat with Jesus, but also about Matthew's readers, who are (as it were) "in the same boat."

On the lake itself, a storm blows up, of which Jesus is unaware, because he is asleep. Matthew calls the storm, literally, "an earthquake"—a word that commonly occurs in the Bible when apocalyptic horrors are being described.[10] Understandably, the disciples are scared by this apocalyptic storm, and they address Jesus in significant language: "Lord [Gk. *kurie*], save us" (8:25). "Save us" is the language that is often addressed to God in the Psalms, not least when people are threatened by water.[11] The word *kurios* means "Lord," and it has divine connotations in Matthew's Gospel and elsewhere in the New Testament.[12] The disciples, then, are talking to God and looking to him for deliverance. Jesus responds by rebuking the wind and the waves, and everything becomes calm. "What kind of man is this?" the disciples ask. "Even the winds and the waves obey him!" (8:27). They know from their Scriptures, of course (e.g., Genesis 1), that only God can govern the chaotic waters. It is only the creator God, as Psalm 89 reminds us, who is able to "rule over the surging sea; when its waves mount up, you still them." Astonishingly, then, it is the creator God who is in the boat with those disciples and who will shortly disembark on the other side of the lake to heal two demon-possessed men, and to forgive the sins of a paralyzed man (8:28–9:8).[13] The sea, however, as always in biblical thinking, is simply the sea—merely one of the aspects of the creation of the one

God "who created the heavens and all that is in them, the earth and all that is in it, and the sea and all that is in it" (Revelation 10:6). Like the sea in the book of Genesis, Matthew's sea is not divine, and it has no divinities in it. It is easily calmed—by God.

The Goodness of Creation

Is creation still good, in New Testament faith? In 1 Timothy 4:4-5, where Paul opposes people who advocate ascetic practices with respect to food and sex, he explicitly claims that it is: "everything God created is good, and nothing is to be rejected if it is received with thanksgiving, because it is consecrated by the word of God and prayer." Similar sentiments are expressed in 1 Corinthians 10:25-26, where Paul quotes Psalm 24:1: "eat anything sold in the meat market without raising questions of conscience, for, 'the earth is the LORD's, and everything in it.'" Jesus' own teaching leans in the same direction. He is remembered in Mark's Gospel, for example, as teaching that "nothing that enters a man from the outside can make him 'unclean.' . . . It doesn't go into his heart but into his stomach, and then out of his body" (Mark 7:18-19). Created things, in themselves, are good. Creation itself *functions* in a good way, displaying to those with eyes to see it the ongoing providential care of God (Matthew 5:45). This is a world in which the good God still looks after all his creatures—the birds as well as the humans (Matthew 6:26). The New Testament perspective is still a world-affirming perspective. Indeed, Jesus himself sometimes got into trouble with his contemporaries because they saw his teaching and lifestyle as *too* world affirming. He *could* be characterized by others as "a glutton and a drunkard" (Matthew 11:19).

WHO ARE MAN AND WOMAN?

In New Testament faith, as in the preceding faith upon which it builds, human beings possess a highly exalted status. They are the image bearers of God. The point is implicit in Matthew 22:15-22, where Jesus is asked, "Is it right to pay taxes to Caesar or not?" In response, he requests to see a Roman coin and asks whose "image" and inscription are found on it. Hearing that it is Caesar's, he tells his audience that they should "give to Caesar what is Caesar's, and to God what is God's." The point is that while the coin belongs to Caesar and should rightly be given to Caesar, the *self* should be given to God. All human beings, bearing the image of God, belong to God and should obey and serve God: "loyalty to Caesar must always be set in the larger context and thus be relativized by the full submission of the self to God."[4] It is not only Caesar, however, who is relativized by this "image-bearing" reality. In Colossians 3:8-11, Paul urges his readers,

> You must rid yourselves of all such things as these: anger, rage, malice, slander, and filthy language from your lips. Do not lie to each other, since you have taken off your old self with its practices and have put on the new self, which is being renewed in knowledge in the image of its Creator. Here there is no Greek or Jew, circumcised or uncircumcised, barbarian, Scythian, slave or free, but Christ is all, and is in all.

In this passage, the image of God that has been fractured by the human embrace of evil is now, in Jesus Christ, being restored. This process must, of course, involve the image-bearers in *departing* from evil. The "knowledge" in which the image is being renewed is the knowledge of God, by which is implied a right relationship with God.[15] The evil described appears to be in large measure bound up with "ethnic, cultural, and social distinctions" in Colossae.[16] In the humanity that is now being renewed, says Paul, all such distinctions have been abolished. Even the barbarous Scythians, "reputed by the Romans to be the wildest, most uncivilized, people living," are not to be regarded as lying beyond the Christian's sphere of obligation, when it comes to treating properly other image bearers of God.[17]

The New Humanity

In the early chapters of Genesis, the trajectory of human relationships moves from unity to disunity. The story of the Old Testament, in multiple ways, traces the growing dysfunction in human relationships that results from the fracturing of the divine-human relationship. In the New Testament, the trajectory moves in the opposite direction as Paul sees those who are "in Christ" as increasingly embodying "one new humanity." He addresses this theme in two key passages. In 1 Corinthians 12:13, he reminds the Christians in Corinth, "We were all baptized by one Spirit into one body—whether Jews or Greeks, slave or free—and we were all given the one Spirit to drink." He goes on to exhort each person in the "body" to play her own part well, exercising the gifts she has been given; members might serve as apostles, prophets, teachers, workers of miracles, healers, helpers of others, administrators, or speakers of different kinds of tongues (12:28). Everyone stands on equal terms in Christ, and has been given a gift, but the purpose of the gift is not self-exaltation; it is that the *community* should function well. Unfortunately, this is not currently the reality "on the ground" in Corinth, and that is the underlying problem that Paul is addressing. In Galatians 3:26-28, however, the problem is that the equality *itself* is under threat. Paul therefore reminds the Christians in Galatia,

> You are all sons of God through faith in Christ Jesus, for all of you who were baptized into Christ have clothed yourselves with Christ. There is neither Jew nor Greek, slave nor free, male nor female, for you are all one in Christ Jesus.

Image bearers of God who are having their image restored in Christ are on equal terms with each other. They possess an "equality that has both spiritual and social dimensions."[8] They are not to behave in any manner toward each other that belies this fact, whether in denying others equality or in failing to contribute properly to the *community* of equals.

All Are Equal

We see very clearly in these various texts the humanistic and democratic emphases of biblical faith that we first encountered in chapter 4— emphases that are found elsewhere in the New Testament literature as well. James expects, for example, that those possessing New Testament faith will display an impartial attitude (expressed in actions) toward both rich and poor (James 2:1-4). If one man comes to a Christian meeting "wearing a gold ring and fine clothes" and another comes "in shabby clothes," his readers are not to treat them in accordance with this social difference. They are equals before God. Paul, likewise, expects that what he has to say to the Galatians about there being "neither Jew nor Greek" will lead to changes in the way that they view the world and in the ways that they conduct themselves. Jews have no privileges over Gentiles, and the latter are not to conform to Jewish law. Nor, on the other hand, are Gentiles to use their freedom from the law for any purpose other than to serve other people. Paul also expects that the fact that there is "neither slave nor free" in Christ will make a difference to the slave owner Philemon, whom he urges to receive back the runaway slave Onesimus, "no longer as a slave, but better than a slave, as a dear brother" (Philemon 16).

In line with the truth that there is "neither male nor female" in Christ, we discover that women are regarded as "sisters" within the New Testament church, just as slaves are "brothers" (e.g., Romans 16:1). This reflects Jesus' own democratic affirmation of women in general, as he ministered to the needs of all, as well as his acceptance of them in particular as disciples who were, like the men, capable of instruction.[19] Women held positions of authority in the early church: in Paul's letter to the Romans, Phoebe is noted as a deacon of the church in Cenchrea, and Junia as an apostle (Romans 16:1, 7).[20] Women also actively participated in church meetings, both praying and preaching ("prophesying"), just like the men (1 Corinthians 11:5).[21]

WHY DO EVIL AND SUFFERING MARK THE WORLD?

As in the Old Testament, so also in the New it is recognized that there is evil in the world, and consequently suffering. The serpent of Genesis 3 shows up here, too, in the form of Satan—the one who tempts human beings and deceives them, the enemy who masquerades as a friend.[22] He is still a creature of God and not a god, however, so his power in the world remains limited, and in the New Testament perspective it has, in fact, been broken by Christ. Satan is, therefore, heading for ultimate destruction.[23] Nevertheless, he has gained some power in the world, and he has become something of a "prince of this world" and a "god of this age," as human beings have given in to his wiles (John 14:30; 2 Corinthians 4:4).[24] To *this* extent, "the whole world is under the control of the evil one" (1 John 5:19), which means that, recalling Genesis 3:15, the "mutual bruising" of the serpent and the human community continues into the present: "our struggle is not against flesh and blood, but against the rulers, against the authorities, against the powers of this dark world and against the spiritual forces of evil in the heavenly realms" (Ephesians 6:12). Yet although this struggle is real, the gates of hell "shall not overpower" the advancing church of Jesus Christ as it looks to bring in fully the kingdom of God (Matthew 16:18).

The Embrace of Evil

There is evil, and then there is the human embrace of evil. As in the Old Testament, this involves in the New Testament heart and mind, as well as actions:

> Out of the overflow of the heart the mouth speaks. The good man brings good things out of the good stored up in him, and the evil man brings evil things out of the evil stored up in him.
>
> (Matthew 12:34-35)

The first problem is the "sinful, unbelieving heart that turns away from the living God" (Hebrews 3:12). This results in the substitution of other gods for God. Then, from out of the heart flow "evil thoughts, murder, adultery, sexual immorality, theft, false testimony, slander" (Matthew 15:19). The human being is no longer living in line with God's character and laws. She is living the autonomous, "wise" life that the serpent facilitates in the garden (James 3:14-15). To the extent that she remembers God at all, she misremembers who God truly is and lives (accordingly) in a suspicious and defensive way. This "Genesis reality" is reflected in the New Testament in different places, including Jesus' parable about the talents (Matthew 25:14-30). A man goes on a journey, leaving his servants some money to use while he is away. One of them refuses to use the money to make more. Instead, he digs a hole in the ground, and he hides the money in it. When confronted by the returning master, the servant tells him that he did this because he "knew" the master to be "a hard man, harvesting where you have not sown and gathering where you have not scattered seed. So I was afraid and went out and hid your talent in the ground" (25:25). His failure to live in accordance with the way God really is becomes his downfall—as it does also in the case of the wicked servant in Matthew 18:21-35, who receives mercy from his master but refuses to show that same mercy to his fellow servant and instead has him thrown into a debtors' prison.

Man's Inhumanity to Man

As this last story illustrates, the human embrace of evil leads to suffering, as God's image bearers neglect, oppress, and damage each other. Romans 1:18-32 graphically outlines the progression, as human beings are alienated from God and then from each other. By observing creation, they can grasp something of who God is, suggests Paul, but the history of humanity is characterized by the suppression of this truth. Claiming to be wise, "they became fools and exchanged the glory of the immortal God for images made to look like mortal man and birds and animals and reptiles" (1:22-23). They began to use each other sexually in wrong ways, and they have now become "full of envy, murder, strife, deceit and malice. . . . They are senseless, faithless, heartless, ruthless" (1:29-31). The New Testament offers many such catalogues of man's inhumanity to man—the suffering that arises from the embrace of evil. There is no end to the "biting and devouring each other" that human beings so greatly enjoy (Galatians 5:15; James 4:1-4).

Suffering Intrinsic to Creation

There is suffering that arises from evil, in the New Testament, but as in the Old Testament there is also suffering that arises for other reasons entirely. This is clear in John 9:1-9, where Jesus is asked a question by his disciples about a man who was born blind. The question reveals their own convictions about the close connection that must exist between evil and suffering: "Rabbi, who sinned, this man or his parents, that he was born blind?" (9:2). For the disciples, there are only two alternatives, and both of them involve someone committing evil acts. Jesus' response, just prior to healing the man, is significant: "neither this man nor his parents sinned, but this happened so that the work of God might be displayed in his life" (9:3).

Again, in Luke's account of Paul's journey by sea, as a prisoner, from Caesarea to Rome in Acts 27–28, we read that even at its beginning the journey was difficult, because of strong headwinds; it was, in fact, "dangerous" (27:9). Later, things became worse, because a storm arose and the ship took "a violent battering" from this storm (27:18). In fact, Paul and his companions gave up "all hope of being saved" (27:20). Ultimately, they became shipwrecked on Malta, where Paul, in the course of putting some brushwood on a fire, was bitten by a snake (28:3). There is much suffering in this account, but it is not said to arise because of evil. If it arises for any "reason," it is the poor judgment that leads those in charge of the expedition to persevere in sailing in dangerous conditions. The storm is simply doing what a storm does. For that matter, the snake is simply doing what a snake does. Human suffering arises, in each case, from being in the wrong place at the wrong time. The

Maltese people themselves do not understand this. They first assume that Paul must be a murderer; he managed to escape from the sea, but the snakebite reveals that "justice has not allowed him to live" (28:4). When Paul does not, in fact, die, they change their minds and proclaim him to be a god (28:6). Like Jesus' disciples in John 9, they have two alternative explanations in mind for what they see before them, and both are wrong. Paul is neither a criminal nor a god; he is simply someone, like them, who from time to time gets caught up in the suffering that is intrinsic to the way in which God's good world works.

WHAT AM I TO DO ABOUT EVIL AND SUFFERING?

In chapter 6 I described how biblical faith is convinced that evil and suffering are at odds with the deeper reality of goodness that lies at the heart of the being of God and of creation, and how it refuses to acknowledge that they are here to stay as part of the fabric of the cosmos. I noted, indeed, the various ways in which human beings are called upon to take up the fight, with God's help, *against* evil and suffering. These same convictions and imperatives are to be found in the New Testament. As in chapter 6, we may best discuss them in terms of various "paths" that are laid out before the faithful person.

Resistance

The first of these is the path of resistance. I am to resist evil, thereby cutting off at its root the tree of suffering that grows from its soil. I am not to give in to its seductions but to pursue steadfastly what is right. In New Testament thinking, this involves, first, resisting the tempter Satan, as Jesus does in Matthew 4:1-11. The one who tempts Jesus in this passage knows (as the serpent in Genesis 3 knows) what God has said, and he knows how to mislead people about *what* has been said and what it means. In two of the three temptations described in this passage, he quotes Scripture to Jesus, and Jesus responds with other Scriptures, which reveal that Satan is twisting their meaning. This wise response is very different from the response offered by the human beings in the garden in Eden. Resistance to evil lies also at the heart of Ephesians 4:26-27, which urges readers not to "give the devil a foothold" by allowing anger to be unresolved overnight, and Ephesians 6:10-18, which urges them on four occasions to "stand" (primarily a term of resistance) against the evil one, having donned the very armor of God.[25] James 4:7-8 advises Christians to "resist the devil, and he will flee from you," and instead to "come near to God, and he will come near to you." First Peter 5:8-10 likewise instructs believers to resist the devil, who "prowls around like a roaring lion looking for someone to devour." These believers are suffering, but it will last only a short time, and then "the God of all grace, who called you to his eternal glory in Christ . . . will himself restore you and make you strong, firm and steadfast."

As well as resisting the Evil One who is on the *outside*, the New Testament also urges the faithful to resist the evil desires that lie on the *inside* and that express themselves in actions (James 1:13-15). They are to "struggle against sin" (Hebrews 12:4) or, in Paul's language in Romans 8:13, to "put to death the misdeeds of the body," which refers in this context to the person the believer used to be, before beginning to walk on the right path. Paul returns to the same idea in his letter to the Colossians:

> Put to death, therefore, whatever belongs to your earthly nature: sexual immorality, impurity, lust, evil desires and greed, which is idolatry. Because of these, the wrath of God is coming. You used to walk in these ways, in the life you once lived. But now you must rid yourselves of all such things as these: anger, rage, malice, slander, and filthy language from your lips. Do not lie to each other, since you have taken off your old self with its practices and have put on the new self. (Colossians 3:5-10)

Resistance to evil in New Testament faith does not imply a thoroughgoing judgment *on* evil in the short term. It is recognized that such judgment rests with God alone and therefore will not fully come to pass until the end of time (Matthew 7:1-5; 13:24-30). Paradoxically, resisting evil may involve, in the short term, *not* resisting the evildoer, and this may, in turn, involve not resisting the governing authorities, even when they have become, in some respects, evil (Matthew 5:38-42; Romans 13:1-7). At the same time, however, the early Christians were themselves quite capable of resisting evildoers, including the governing authorities (Acts 4:18-20). I shall come back to this point, in a larger context, in our discussion of the good society.

Endurance and Prayer

The New Testament urges resistance to evil and its consequent suffering. Along with the Old Testament, however, it also recognizes that the human pursuit of the good may have only limited effects on the present world in which other people are intent on achieving different goals. And so New Testament faith also urges *patience* in pursuing the right path, while *enduring* suffering. The triumph of good over evil is not easily achieved in biblical thinking. In Luke 8:15 Jesus commends his followers who hold fast to his words and, like plants deeply rooted in good soil, "persevering produce a crop." Perseverance is necessary. Paul promises in Romans 2:7 that "to those who by persistence in doing good seek glory, honor and immortality, he [God] will give eternal life." In Romans 12:12 Paul exhorts the Roman Christians to "be joyful in hope, patient in affliction, faithful in prayer." He hopes that the Christians in Colossae may have "great endurance and patience" (1:11).

The right path through life is also represented in New Testament faith as a path of prayer. The very form of prayer that Jesus taught his disciples envisages that they will regularly ask God, "Your kingdom come, your will be done, on earth as it is in heaven" (Matthew 6:10). It is only when God's kingdom fully comes that evil will be finally defeated. It is only then that believers will not also need to pray, "Deliver us from the evil one" (Matthew 6:13). In the meantime, prayer is itself a precaution against temptation (Matthew 26:41; 1 Corinthians 7:5). Therefore, instructs Paul, "Pray in the Spirit on all occasions" (Ephesians 6:18).[26]

Endurance and prayer, then, recognize and affirm two important realities that emerged in our chapter 6—namely, that judgment on evil belongs, fully and finally, to God, and that this God is understood, in biblical faith, as being utterly good. It makes sense, then, for the person who trusts in such a God to endure and to pray, for this good God is constantly seeking to turn the evil toward the good.

Compassion and Hope

The fourth aspect of a biblical response to evil and suffering mentioned in chapter 6 was compassion. I may not be able to defeat the evil forces ranged against me; the best that I can manage may simply be patient endurance in the midst of prayer. Yet I can offer friendship and help to those who suffer and in this way imitate the God who "has compassion on all he has made" (Psalm 145:9). Jesus himself, as God among us, is marked in the Gospels by this same compassion.[27] From the perspective of New Testament faith, it is certainly one of the marks of the *disciple* of Jesus.[28] The author of the letter to the Hebrews reminds his readers of how this compassion used to mark *them*:

> You stood your ground in a great contest in the face of suffer-
> ing. Sometimes you were publicly exposed to insult and per-
> secution; at other times you stood side by side with those who
> were so treated. You sympathized with those in prison and joy-
> fully accepted the confiscation of your property, because you
> knew that you yourselves had better and lasting possessions.
>
> (Hebrews 10:32-34)

The final aspect of a biblical response to evil and suffering that we discussed in chapter 6 was hope. Among other things, I am to hope that what is bad in the world can somehow be turned to good—that even the darkest moments of my life have meaning in some larger, good plan of God. It is about this hope that Paul speaks in his letter to the Romans:

> We know that in all things God works for the good of those who
> love him, who have been called according to his purpose. . . .
> If God is for us, who can be against us? He who did not spare
> his own Son, but gave him up for us all—how will he not also,
> along with him, graciously give us all things? . . . Who shall
> separate us from the love of Christ? Shall trouble or hardship
> or persecution or famine or nakedness or danger or sword? . . .
> I am convinced that neither death nor life, neither angels nor
> demons, neither the present nor the future, nor any powers,
> neither height nor depth, nor anything else in all creation, will
> be able to separate us from the love of God that is in Christ
> Jesus our Lord. (Romans 8:28-39)

As we saw in chapter 11, such hope does not negate human agency. We must still resist, endure, pray, and have compassion. But for the New Testament authors, we *should* hope as well, for a better world is coming.

HOW AM I TO RELATE TO GOD?

In Genesis 3 the earthlings are not content with being image bearers of God. They want to *be* gods, in the fullest sense, rather than *representing and mediating* God to creation, and they are prepared to disobey God in pursuit of this goal. They blur the line between Creator and creation that is sharply drawn in Genesis 1–2.

The Image Bearer Who Is God

Astonishingly (and for many people offensively), the New Testament literature itself blurs this line, by speaking of one image bearer of God who was and is, in fact, God. It speaks of "Christ, who is the image of God," and Christ, "the image of the invisible God . . . [by whom] all things were created" (2 Corinthians 4:4; Colossians 1:15-16). This is not, however, a human being who desires (wrongly) to be God and grasps after this divinity. For the New Testament authors, this is a God who *willingly became a human being,* laying down aspects of divine prerogative to deliver people from evil. The movement is opposite to the one made by the first human beings; it is downward, rather than upward. The first human beings grasped at equality with God for their own eternal benefit; Jesus, for the eternal benefit of others, let it go. The Apostle Paul urges his readers in Philippi to pattern their lives on Jesus in this same respect:

> Do nothing out of selfish ambition or vain conceit, but in humility consider others better than yourselves. Each of you should look not only to your own interests, but also to the interests of others. Your attitude should be the same as that of Christ Jesus: who, being in very nature God, did not consider equality with God something to be grasped, but made himself nothing, taking the very nature of a servant, being made in human likeness. And being found in appearance as a man, he humbled himself and became obedient to death—even death on a cross!
>
> (Philippians 2:3-8)

Trust

The consequence of this identification in the New Testament of Jesus of Nazareth as God Incarnate is that the question of right relating to

God becomes at the same time the question of right relating to Jesus. Human beings are still exhorted in the New Testament to *trust* in God's goodness and to hold on to it, in all its aspects, in all circumstances—to ground themselves in God's steadfast love for them. However, it is not only the steadfast love of the *Father* in which they are to trust but also that of the *Son*. It is the "love of Christ" from which Paul is confident we cannot be separated in Romans 8—the love that can also be described there as "the love of God that is in Christ Jesus our Lord" (8:39). It is the love of Christ—in all its width, length, height, and depth—that Paul hopes the Christians in Ephesus will grasp (Ephesians 3:18). Likewise, we are to trust in the *faithfulness* of the Father but also of the Son. The Father, "who has called you into fellowship with his Son Jesus Christ our Lord, is faithful" (1 Corinthians 1:9), and the Son, repeatedly in the New Testament, is also seen as faithful to his mission to redeem and save the world, even to the point of death. John envisions him in the book of Revelation as a rider on a white horse who "is called Faithful and True" (Revelation 19:11). Then again, God is still a *rightly angry* God in the New Testament (Romans 1:18-19), and this is true not only of the Father but also of the Son. Evildoers cry out at the end of time to the mountains and the rocks, imploring them to "fall on us and hide us from the face of him who sits on the throne and from the wrath of the Lamb!" (Revelation 6:16). Finally, the *mercy* of God is still a reality in the New Testament. It is at the same time the mercy of Jesus Christ (Ephesians 2:4; 2 John 3).

In the New Testament, then, God has not changed in being good, but he *has* changed in taking on human flesh. Relating rightly to God still means trusting in God's goodness, but this goodness is now expressed centrally in Jesus Christ. It still means (as it does in the Old Testament) trusting in God's goodness even in the midst of suffering and the lament that suffering evokes. Now in the New Testament, however, it is clearer just how much God suffers *with* his creation, rather than simply empathizing with suffering and lament from the outside. The God to whom people are called rightly to relate in New Testament faith is the God who "laid down" divinity and "became obedient to death" (Philippians 2:8). He knew a life of suffering.[29] From the New Testament perspective, then, when followers of Christ suffer, they know that God deeply understands their suffering, and they trust, indeed, that as Paul says, "We share in his sufferings in order that we may also share in his glory" (Romans 8:17).[30]

Love

Beyond trust, biblical faith also places at the heart of a right relationship with God a *love* that arises out of a conviction about God's goodness. Human beings are supposed to love God (Deuteronomy 6:4-5).
When asked by the Pharisees in Matthew 22:34-40 about "the greatest
commandment in the Law," Jesus identifies it as this same Deuteronomic commandment. Love for God in the New Testament is the same
single-minded and wholehearted response to God that we find in the
Old. This is illustrated, for example, in Matthew 6:24: "No one can serve
two masters. Either he will hate the one and love the other, or he will be
devoted to the one and despise the other. You cannot serve both God
and Money." Love for God is, of course, love for the Son as well as for the
Father. The close connection between these two is illustrated in Jesus'
own words to his disciples in John 14:20-21:

> I am in my Father, and you are in me, and I am in you. Whoever
> has my commands and obeys them, he is the one who loves me.
> He who loves me will be loved by my Father, and I too will love
> him and show myself to him.

Obedience

This same chapter in the Gospel of John illustrates that *obedience* also
remains at the heart of right relating to God in New Testament faith—a
glad obedience, offered to both Father and Son:

> If anyone loves me, he will obey my teaching. My Father will
> love him, and we will come to him and make our home with
> him. He who does not love me will not obey my teaching. These
> words you hear are not my own; they belong to the Father who
> sent me. (John 14:23-24)

Jesus himself becomes, in New Testament thinking, "the source of
eternal salvation for all who obey him" (Hebrews 5:9). The centrality of
obedience, along with love, is indicated also by these words in the First
Letter of John:

> We know that we have come to know him if we obey his com-
> mands. The man who says, "I know him," but does not do what
> he commands is a liar, and the truth is not in him. But if anyone

obeys his word, God's love is truly made complete in him. This is how we know we are in him: whoever claims to live in him must walk as Jesus did. (1 John 2:3-6)

Is It Easy?

Is relating rightly to God *easy* in New Testament faith? As in the Old Testament, it is simple, but it is not easy, since "man is born broken." However, God is still in the business of mending what is broken, and central to this "business," in the New Testament as in the Old, is atonement. In chapter 6 I drew attention to the mysterious "servant" figure of Isaiah 40–55, whose suffering is a means by which God reaches out and makes peace with the whole world. This is part of how God "mends"; it is an aspect of the goodness of God in which the righteous human being is called to trust. In the New Testament, Jesus identifies *himself* as this "servant." In Mark 10:45, for example, he proclaims that "the Son of Man did not come to be served, but to serve, and to give his life as a ransom for many."[31] His crucifixion, where he is indeed "obedient to death," is understood in terms of atonement—as a central way in which "God was reconciling the world to himself in Christ, not counting men's sins against them" (2 Corinthians 5:19). This is why John can write, as the context for his comments in 1 John 2:3-6 about the centrality of obedience, the following words:

> I write this to you so that you will not sin. But if anybody does sin, we have one who speaks to the Father in our defense— Jesus Christ, the Righteous One. He is the atoning sacrifice for our sins, and not only for ours but also for the sins of the whole world. (1 John 2:1-2)

Trust, love, and obedience remain at the heart of right relating to God in the New Testament, but everything that this means is affected in some way by the convictions of the New Testament authors about Jesus—who he is and what he has done. A central element of right "trust" in God is now trust in the great atoning sacrifice that lies at the heart of the entire human story, as a result of which human beings who "fall short of the glory of God" are clothed with a "righteousness from God [which] comes through faith in Jesus Christ to all who believe" (Romans 3:22-23).

HOW AM I TO RELATE TO MY NEIGHBOR?

In exploring the theme of right relating to neighbor in the Old Testament in chapter 8, we began with the story of Cain and Abel, and it is instructive to observe the way in which the Cain and Abel story is appropriated in the New Testament. Cain and Abel appear here as representatives of two paths through life. Abel stands on the side of faith: it was by faith that "Abel offered God a better sacrifice than Cain did," according to the writer to the Hebrews (11:4). His blood, crying out to God from the ground (12:24), is only some of the blood of the righteous that has been spilled through the ages by "hypocrites" and "vipers," according to Jesus (Matthew 23:29-36). Upon their heads will come all this blood, "from the blood of righteous Abel to the blood of Zechariah son of Berekiah" (v. 35). The "way of Cain," by contrast, is the way of "godless men, who change the grace of our God into a license for immorality and deny Jesus Christ our only Sovereign and Lord" (Jude 4, 11). It is the path moving in the opposite direction from love for one's neighbor:

> This is the message you heard from the beginning: We should love one another. Do not be like Cain, who belonged to the evil one and murdered his brother. And why did he murder him? Because his own actions were evil and his brother's were righteous. Do not be surprised, my brothers, if the world hates you. We know that we have passed from death to life, because we love our brothers. Anyone who does not love remains in death. Anyone who hates his brother is a murderer, and you know that no murderer has eternal life in him. (1 John 3:11-15)

Here, in essence, is the New Testament answer to the question "How am I to relate to my neighbor?" I am to love her, and this will involve both my interior life as well as my actions.[32] This is, we recall from chapter 8, "the religion of God," which prioritizes doing what is right over mere religious ritual. In the words of James, "Religion that God our Father accepts as pure and faultless is this: to look after orphans and widows in their distress and to keep oneself from being polluted by the world" (James 1:27). In the words of John, "Anyone who does not do what is right is not a child of God; nor is anyone who does not love his brother," and "anyone who does not love his brother, whom he has seen, cannot love God, whom he has not seen" (1 John 3:10; 4:20).

Jesus' Teaching

The love of neighbor that is commended in these New Testament texts is first commended by Jesus himself. When asked in Matthew 22:34-40 about "the greatest commandment in the Law," Jesus follows up his reference to loving God immediately with this observation: "And the second [commandment] is like it: 'Love your neighbor as yourself.' All the Law and the Prophets hang on these two commandments" (vv. 39-40). Elsewhere, Jesus addresses the question of who the neighbor *is*. In Luke 10:25-37, he is explicitly asked this question by "an expert in the law." In response, Jesus tells a story about a man going down from Jerusalem to Jericho who falls into the hands of robbers, who leave him for dead. Two religious "professionals," in turn, pass him by, ignoring his plight. Finally, a Samaritan, "a member of a community hated by the Jews" and with whom "relations . . . were especially bad at this time," arrives on the scene, and he rescues the victim.[33] "Which of these three do you think was a neighbor?" asks Jesus, and the expert in the law replies, "The one who had mercy on him." Jesus tells him, "Go and do likewise." The enemy can be the neighbor. Indeed, Jesus' own teaching was that although *some* might wrongly interpret the Old Testament as saying, "Love your neighbor and hate your enemy" (Matthew 5:43), *his disciples* should "love your enemies and pray for those who persecute you, that you may be sons of your Father in heaven. He causes his sun to rise on the evil and the good, and sends rain on the righteous and the unrighteous" (5:44-45). By loving in such a way, the disciples would be imitating God—as they *should*: "be perfect . . . as your heavenly Father is perfect" (5:48).

This is evidently not love for neighbor that offers itself hoping for a return. It is not self-interested love, offered out of a desire for release from the wheel of suffering or for "heaven" or some such ulterior thing. It is not the kind of love that the ancient Roman poet Horace commends when he advises, "'Tis your own safety that's at stake, when your neighbour's wall is in flames, and fires neglected are wont to gather strength."[34] What we see commended in the New Testament Gospels is, rather, self-giving, other-focused love, which loves just because love is good. What is commended is love that knows that it is right to care about your neighbor's house regardless of whether your own safety is at stake, and even if it is positively dangerous to help him.

Jesus' Life

However, Jesus did not just *teach* that people should love their fellow human beings in this openhearted and nonpartisan manner. He also *lived* in this way. He himself was "perfect as [his] heavenly Father is perfect." He treated everyone he met as an image bearer of God—no matter how *others* might have regarded them or which stratum of society they inhabited or how "unclean" or marginalized they might be. Women were his neighbors, for example, even though one ancient Jewish text says, "He that talks much with women brings evil upon himself and neglects the study of the Law and at last will inherit Gehenna [hell]."[35] So were the tax collectors, even though to stay in such a person's home was essentially to share in his sin.[36] The ritually unclean lepers and the social outcasts in general, often described in Bible translations as "sinners," were also his neighbors (Mark 2:15-17; Luke 5:13). The entire life of Jesus Christ is remembered in the Gospels as a period of "gracious activity, directed especially to the sinful and despised people in Israel and even to gentiles," which "aroused suspicion and downright opposition from the Pharisees and their scribes."[37] Jesus is also remembered as loving these and other *enemies* and eventually as laying down his life for them. God, who promises in Genesis 4 to be his enemy Cain's avenger of blood and puts a mark on him so that no one will kill him, becomes in the New Testament the God who himself *lays down his life* for his enemy out of love for him.[38]

So it is that the imitation of *God* in the Old Testament becomes also the imitation of *Christ* in the New Testament, as we are urged not to pursue the "heroic ideal" discussed in chapter 8, but to pattern ourselves instead on Jesus: "be imitators of God, therefore, as dearly loved children, and live a life of love, just as Christ loved us and gave himself up for us as a fragrant offering and sacrifice to God" (Ephesians 5:1).[39] For our New Testament as for our Old Testament authors, the Ten Commandments tell us something about this "life of love," but they do not exhaust its demands (Romans 13:8-14; Galatians 5:13-15). In the end, we are called to be nothing less than "like God"—to be like Jesus. Like Jesus, Christians are to *love* their fellow human beings, with an open heart and without partiality (Romans 12:9-21; 1 Corinthians 13).

HOW AM I TO RELATE TO THE
REST OF CREATION?

The whole world remains, in the New Testament, God's world. "From him and through him and to him are all things," writes Paul in Romans 11:36, "the earth . . . and everything in it," he adds in 1 Corinthians 10:26 (quoting Psalm 24:1). In his vision in the book of Revelation, John sees worshippers saying of God, "You created all things, and by your will they were created and have their being" (4:11). In line with the core convictions of New Testament faith about the divinity of the Son, Paul can say much the same about *Jesus* in his creative role: "there is but one God, the Father, from whom all things came and for whom we live; and there is but one Lord, Jesus Christ, through whom all things came and through whom we live" (1 Corinthians 8:6). God created "all things," and as we saw earlier in this chapter, continues to care for "all things," feeding the birds as well as looking after the grass of the field (Matthew 6:26-30; 10:29-31).

The Image and the Creation

In chapter 9, when exploring the relationship of human beings to the rest of creation in Genesis, we looked extensively at the human vocation to rule over God's temple-cosmos as his image bearers—a rule that is ultimately for the health and proper functioning of creation. In the New Testament, we meet the ultimate image bearer—the one in whom this human vocation comes to a climax. This is Jesus—"the image of the invisible God," of whom Paul says, "all things were created by him and for him . . . in him all things hold together" (Colossians 1:15-20). Since Jesus *is* this ultimate image bearer, it is not surprising that he is also said in other New Testament texts to be "the ruler of God's creation," the one in whom proper human dominion over creation has been restored (Revelation 3:14; Hebrews 2:8). The writer to the Hebrews looks back specifically to Psalm 8, which itself expresses the human vocation in terms reminiscent of Genesis 1 and 2: "you crowned him with glory and honor and put everything under his feet" (Psalm 8:7-8; cf. Hebrews 2:8). He then goes on to speak of "Jesus, who was made a little lower than the angels, now crowned with glory and honor because he suffered death, so that by the grace of God he might taste death for everyone" (Hebrews 2:9). In this way he links Jesus with the Genesis (and Psalm 8) vision of the human-creation relationship. As one writer has said of this passage,

"In Jesus we see exhibited humanity's true vocation. In an extraordinary way he fulfills God's design for all creation and displays what had always been intended for all humankind, according to Ps 8."[40]

Cosmic Redemption

As we might expect, the redemption of God that is so central to New Testament faith is the redemption of "all things," just as it is in the Old Testament. Colossians 1:19 tells us,

> God was pleased to have all his fullness dwell in him [Jesus], and through him to reconcile to himself *all things*, whether things on earth or things in heaven, by making peace through his blood, shed on the cross.

The redemption that Jesus initiates is *cosmic* in its scope—as broad as the original creation.[41] It is a new heavens and a new earth that New Testament faith anticipates, just as it is in the Old Testament. Peter explicitly says so in 2 Peter 3:13: "In keeping with his promise we are looking forward to a new heaven and a new earth." This is also what John sees in his vision in the book of Revelation:

> I saw a new heaven and a new earth, for the first heaven and the first earth had passed away, and there was no longer any sea. I saw the Holy City, the new Jerusalem, coming down out of heaven from God, prepared as a bride beautifully dressed for her husband. And I heard a loud voice from the throne saying, "Now the dwelling of God is with men, and he will live with them. They will be his people, and God himself will be with them and be their God." (Revelation 21:1-3)

Another important passage on this theme of cosmic redemption is Romans 8:18-23. Here Paul, in the context of "present sufferings," looks forward to the coming of the new age, when human beings will be adopted into God's family and their bodies will be redeemed (8:23). However, it is not just human beings who look forward to this new age. Nonhuman creation, too, waits "in eager expectation for the sons of God to be revealed"; it is "groaning as in the pains of childbirth," waiting for the new heavens and the new earth to be born (8:19, 22). Currently "subjected to frustration" (8:20)—it does not function properly because the human beings tasked to look after it have not been doing their job—it looks for freedom from this frustrated condition once human beings themselves are fully redeemed.[42] Given the intimate relationship intended to exist between human and nonhuman creation in the Genesis vision of the world, it should not surprise us that the redemption of each is bound up with the other in the epistle to the Romans. As human beings experience freedom from the curse of Genesis 3, so also will creation itself. The NIV describes this newfound freedom of creation in terms of its being "liberated from its bondage to decay" (Romans 8:21). This is not helpful if it makes us think of freedom from physical, material processes. It is, rather, liberation from *corruption* that is in mind. The verb that is related to the noun behind the NIV's "decay" (Gk. *phthora*) first appears in the Greek translation of Genesis 6:11-13, where it describes the way in which the earth has become corrupt and filled with wrongdoing. Human beings have gone wrong, and they have brought creation "down" with them. It is to this reality of being (unwillingly) implicated in human evil that Paul refers in Romans 8:20, when he says that "the creation was subjected to frustration, not by its own choice."[43] The passage as a whole captures well the New Testament perspective: "Creation is to be redeemed, not redeemed from. Just as the resurrection hope is hope of a resurrection body, so resurrection life is to be part of a complete creation."[44]

Earth Keeping

All of this implies that nothing has changed in the New Testament with respect to the human duty to care for the rest of creation.[45] God still cares for all of it, and New Testament faith calls for the imitation of God. Christ, specifically, holds all of it together, has redeemed all of it, and exercises righteous dominion over it as the quintessential image bearer of God. New Testament faith calls for the imitation of Christ, in whom the image of God in his disciples is being restored, so that they can turn from evil and live as they were created to live. Earth keeping is one aspect of this creation calling, just as destroying the earth represents a grievous departure from it.[46] In the book of Revelation, the redeemed are, indeed, described in precisely the language of kings and priests that is used of human beings in Genesis 1-2 to describe their calling: "you have made them to be a kingdom and priests to serve our God, and they will reign on the earth" (Revelation 5:10). Kings and priests they were created to be, in the first creation; kings and priests they remain, in the new creation. The present reality may be passing away, and it may indeed be destined for "fire" (Hebrews 1:10-12; 12:26-29; 2 Peter 3:7-13). It is, nevertheless, the reality *in which* human beings are called by New Testament faith to live righteously. It must pass through "fire" only to become a more purified version of itself, in which (resurrected) kings and priests are still needed.

WHICH SOCIETY SHOULD I BE HELPING TO BUILD?

In chapter 10 I argued that we find an enormous degree of pragmatism attributed in the Old Testament to God in his interactions with the world, and we also find a very pragmatic view taken of human society. God calls all people to worship him, to treat all their neighbors well, and to look after his garden. But, in the biblical perspective, God does not impose these ideals. This is clear from both Old Testament story and law. The law promotes a moral vision, but it also accommodates the ideals of the moral vision to circumstantial reality. I illustrated this point especially with respect to the position of women and slaves under the law. In biblical thinking (I argued), even God does not attempt to legislate the kingdom of God into being; therefore, neither should human beings.

The Kingdom of God Is Here

New Testament faith proclaims that the kingdom of God (or the kingdom of heaven, as it is sometimes called) has in fact come, in Jesus Christ. In Matthew 21:31, for example, the kingdom is something that the tax collectors and the prostitutes are already entering, and in Luke 17:21 it is something that is within (or among) people. This conviction about the present reality of the kingdom of God in New Testament faith leads inevitably to an insistence that people should live *in* that reality. Addressing a problem among the Christians in Rome concerning what Christian faith has to say about eating and drinking (are certain foods "unclean"?), Paul affirms this:

> The kingdom of God is not a matter of eating and drinking, but of righteousness, peace and joy in the Holy Spirit, because anyone who serves Christ in this way is pleasing to God and approved by men. Let us therefore make every effort to do what leads to peace and to mutual edification. (Romans 14:17-19)

Paul expects the fact that these Roman Christians are living in the kingdom of God to make a difference in how they behave, individually and in community.[47] We saw earlier in the chapter just how insistent this demand for character and integrity is in the New Testament. We also saw something of just how radical it is. It relativizes the demands of the state and confronts religious, ethnic, cultural, and social distinctions. It requires of all the disciples of Christ that they love all their fellow image bearers as Christ loves those image bearers, without reserve and without partiality.

The Kingdom of God Is Not (Fully) Here

The kingdom of God has come. At the same time, it is equally clear that in New Testament faith the kingdom of God has not yet *fully* come; it remains to come in the future. As we saw earlier, Jesus teaches his disciples to pray, "Your kingdom come, your will be done on earth as it is in heaven" (Matthew 6:10). The kingdom of God is something that emerges only gradually in the world, like a field in which both wheat and weeds are currently growing. Both are allowed to go on growing until the "harvest" (the Day of Judgment), when the weeds will be burned and the wheat taken into the barn (Matthew 13:24-30). The kingdom of God is also like a mustard seed, which must grow until it "becomes a tree, so that the birds of the air come and perch in its branches" (Matthew 13:31-32). From the New Testament perspective, the kingdom of God has begun to take root in the present world, but it must still be "entered" in the future by the righteous: "not everyone who says to me, 'Lord, Lord,' will enter the kingdom of heaven, but only he who does the will of my Father who is in heaven" (Matthew 7:21).

It is this reality of the kingdom of God that is both "now" and "not yet" that explains, I believe, those various passages in the New Testament where the radical edge of the commandment to live "in the kingdom" is apparently lost or has become at the least dulled. If the disciples of Christ are forbidden, no less than their Old Testament forebears, to adopt a passive stance toward the world, they are also forbidden (like them) to opt for a utopian approach. The metaphor of growth is indeed important for the way that biblical faith looks at the world. The kingdom of God needs to emerge; it cannot just be made to appear. It comes by stealth, and not by revolution.

On Changing and Not Changing the World

So it is that in the New Testament, in line with verses like Galatians 3:28, we find Paul asking Philemon to receive back Onesimus "no longer as a slave, but . . . as a dear brother." The kingdom has come. Yet the apostles of the early Christian church do not insist that all slave owners should release their slaves or (more than this) that the institution of slavery should be abolished.[48] The kingdom is not yet here. Likewise, women are regarded as "sisters" within the New Testament church, hold positions of authority therein, and can be found both praying and preaching in Christian meetings. Yet, at the same time, Paul can apparently be found arguing that these image bearers are not really image bearers in the same way that men are and that (in fact) the man is the "head" of the woman (1 Corinthians 11:2-16). This "headship" is elsewhere cited as the reason "wives should submit to their husbands in everything" (Ephesians 5:22-24; see also 1 Peter 3:1). Furthermore, in 1 Timothy 2:11-12, Paul says that "a woman should learn in quietness and full submission. I do not permit a woman to teach or to have authority over a man; she must be silent." The kingdom has come, but is not yet fully here. Finally, the claims of the state upon human beings are certainly regarded as being relativized in the New Testament, yet Paul still instructs the Christians in Rome as follows:

> Everyone must submit himself to the governing authorities, for there is no authority except that which God has established. The authorities that exist have been established by God. Consequently, he who rebels against the authority is rebelling against what God has instituted, and those who do so will bring judgment on themselves. (Romans 13:1-2)

There is no demand in this passage that the Roman state should be reformed in line with biblical principles. The kingdom has come, but the rule of godless kings persists.

Accommodation

These are all examples, I suggest, of the accommodation of the biblical moral vision to the realities of the world as the early Christians found it. There was, in truth, no prospect that these early Christians *could* realistically have reformed the Roman state nor engineered the abolition of the institution of slavery nor even have got away with being the catalyst behind a movement to emancipate individual slaves or to transform the institution of marriage. They lived in a society of a type that was similar in many ways to the older ancient Near Eastern city-states. Order was everything, and disorder was suppressed ruthlessly and violently. The early Christians were hard pressed during most of the first three centuries of the Church's existence even to find "space" within which they themselves could *exist*. For most of that time they were a minority movement, radically out of line with the surrounding culture in their core perspectives on the gods and the world (quite apart from anything else) and actively persecuted by the state just for their insistence on worshipping one God and not also the emperor.

In such a context, it is understandable that often in the New Testament Christians are exhorted to live within the cultural norms of their time and place and are not encouraged to exercise what New Testament faith overall implies to be the full extent of their Christian liberty. Paul himself is recorded as being quite capable of conforming to other people's religious and cultural norms when the situation demanded it, even on an issue upon which he took a fiercely principled stand elsewhere.[49] Peter is explicit in 1 Peter 3:1-2 that he is exhorting wives to be submissive to their husbands precisely "so that, if any of them do not believe the word, they may be won over without words by the behavior of their wives, when they see the purity and reverence of your lives." Just prior to this, Peter is also clear that he is advocating submission by everyone to "every authority instituted among men" because he wants to "silence the ignorant talk of foolish men" (2:13-15). These are just two aspects of Peter's wider concern that his readers should "live such good lives among the pagans that, though they accuse you of doing wrong, they may see your good deeds and glorify God" (2:12). Paul expresses the same concern about slaves in Titus 2:9-10: "Teach slaves to be subject to their masters in everything . . . so that in every way they will make the teaching about God our Savior attractive."

What we find in the New Testament, then, is the same sort of accommodation of the biblical moral vision to political and social reality that we find in the Old Testament. There are ideals to be pursued by those who inhabit the coming kingdom of God, but they must be pursued within constraints. Only in this way is it possible to understand the real tension within the New Testament literature between the ideals, on the one hand, and some of the practical advice given to Christians about how to live their lives in the Roman Empire, on the other.[50]

Subversive Advice

The *advice* is itself *subversive* advice, of course, as is the theology that informs it. In the long term, first, if Philemon really takes seriously Paul's exhortation to treat Onesimus "as a dear brother," he is going to have considerable difficulty treating him as a slave. The same is true of Paul's reminder to slave owners in Ephesians 6:9 that they share with their slaves one Master in heaven, "and there is no favoritism with him."[51] If masters continue to treat slaves as slaves, they are in for a rude awakening when they meet *their* Master. In the long term, second, if husbands really take seriously Paul's advice to "love your wives, just as Christ loved the church and gave himself up for her" (Ephesians 5:25), questions are inevitably going to arise about what it really means that the husband is the "head" of the wife and that the wife ought to "submit" to the husband. This is especially so since Paul himself says in Ephesians 5:21 that *all* Christians ought to "submit *to one another* out of reverence for Christ." Moreover, if it really is the case that *all* image bearers of God are to be regarded as possessing "an equality that has both spiritual and social dimensions"[52] and if the Christian's contribution to the Christian community is really to be determined not by things like gender or race but only by gifting, then the question is bound to be asked whether the instructions of 1 Timothy 2:11-12 really apply to all Christians in all times and places. Finally, in the long term, the idea that the claims of the state upon the image bearers of God are only *relative*, in respect of the *absolute* claims of God, when combined with the idea of the equality of all image bearers, is inevitably going to raise questions about how far obedience to Caesar should go and even about whether there should be a Caesar at all. The apostles themselves already confronted the first of these questions about the state early on in the story of the church, and they chose to *disobey*—not Caesar, admittedly, but certainly the legitimate authorities (Acts 4:18-20).

The apostolic advice is subversive and presses toward the kingdom of God.[53] Unfortunately, its subversive nature is often missed by those who are overly impressed by the force with which the apostles argue their case for accommodations with society, *even while* pressing toward the kingdom of God. Such people see the biblical accommodation, but mistake it for the biblical moral vision. Also missed, often, is just how curious is some of the apostolic Scripture reading in pursuit of these accommodations. The apostles are not, apparently, reading the Old Testament in a very straightforward manner, and Paul's letters, in particular, "contain some things that are hard to understand" (as his colleague Peter once affirmed; 2 Peter 3:8).[54]

Which Society?

In sum: in answer to the question "Which society should I be helping to build?" the New Testament tells us the same thing as the Old. I should be helping to build a society that promotes righteousness in the world as much as is realistically possible, while at the same time restraining and minimizing evil as much as it can—and even redeeming evil, where it can, and turning it toward the good. It is a "middled" society that I should be helping to build, even as I participate (with God) in nudging that society ever more closely toward the good.[55]

WHAT AM I TO HOPE FOR?

In chapter 11 we explored the Old Testament answer to the question "What am I to hope for?" We noted there that, according to Genesis, creation had a "beginning in hope"—minimally, the hope of human immortality. This hope is apparently removed in Genesis 3 yet restored in the prophetic literature. It had appeared that humans beings east of Eden could hope only for death, but, in fact, this is not so. The New Testament agrees with the Old that immortality could only ever have come as a gift to mortal humanity and could not have been innate, for it knows of "God, the blessed and only Ruler, the King of kings and Lord of lords, who *alone* is immortal and who lives in unapproachable light, whom no one has seen or can see" (1 Timothy 6:15-16). Yet the New Testament also agrees that the hope of immortality has been restored, and that it makes sense for humans beings to "seek glory, honor and immortality . . . eternal life" (Romans 2:7). At the end of time the perishable will be clothed, in many cases, with the imperishable and the mortal with immortality:

> When the perishable has been clothed with the imperishable, and the mortal with immortality, then the saying that is written will come true: "Death has been swallowed up in victory."
>
> (1 Corinthians 15:53-54)[56]

The Possibility of Immortality

How is this possible? It is possible because Jesus "has destroyed death and has brought life and immortality to light through the gospel" (2 Timothy 1:10). In New Testament faith, he is only the first of the "multitudes who sleep in the dust of the earth [and] awake: some to everlasting life, others to shame and everlasting contempt" (Daniel 12:2). He is only the first of those of whom Isaiah says, "Your dead will live, their bodies will rise." He is the first to experience the bodily resurrection that such texts foresee and that God's general commitment to matter in the Old Testament would in any case lead us to expect. His body is missing from the tomb on Easter morning, and after the resurrection it still bears the scars that he received on the cross (John 20:1-9, 24-31). Those who follow Christ can, then, hope for a similar bodily resurrection leading to eternal life. As Jesus himself promises in John 6:40, "Everyone who looks to the Son and believes in him shall have eternal life, and I will raise him up at the last day." Jesus can promise this because he has dealt with the evil in the cosmos in which human beings have become implicated and that has alienated them from God. Death, rather than immortality, lies at the end of the road that begins with sin, but death no longer reigns. God's *grace* reigns, so as "to bring eternal life through Jesus Christ our Lord" (Romans 5:12-21). Paul describes this reality further in his letter to the Colossians:

> When you were dead in your sins and in the uncircumcision of your sinful nature, God made you alive with Christ. He forgave us all our sins, having canceled the written code, with its regulations, that was against us and that stood opposed to us; he took it away, nailing it to the cross. And having disarmed the powers and authorities, he made a public spectacle of them, triumphing over them by the cross. (Colossians 2:13-15)

Hope Founded in Covenant

We also discussed in chapter 11 the way in which, in the Old Testament, hope is founded in covenant: the covenant with all *living creatures* in Genesis 9, with Abraham (and all *human beings*) in Genesis 12 and 15, with the *Israelites* as "a kingdom of priests and a holy nation" in Exodus 19, and with *David* and his descendants in 2 Samuel 7. Ultimately, we recall, the prophetic literature speaks of a "new covenant" written on the heart, in which God's law becomes part of the very fabric of the human person. This covenant is associated with the forgiveness of sin and with the restoration of intimacy with God. As we have just seen in the Colossians passage, for our New Testament authors, it is this "eschatological forgiveness" that God offers to people in Jesus Christ. Indeed, they tell us, Jesus already offered this forgiveness during his own earthly lifetime—which is one of the things that provoked opposition. "Take heart," he says to a paralyzed man in Matthew 9:1-3. "Your sins are forgiven." At this, "some of the teachers of the law said to themselves, 'This fellow is blaspheming!'" Only God can forgive sins, in biblical thinking, so Jesus is indeed either God or a blasphemer.

The atoning sacrifice that lies behind this eschatological forgiveness is understood in the New Testament as being offered in Jesus' crucifixion, in advance of which Jesus himself takes up the theme of the new covenant in his teaching. At a meal with his disciples, he says of the cup that he is holding that it is "the new covenant in my blood, which is poured out for you" (Luke 22:20). In New Testament faith, this is where the redemptive plan of God that is woven throughout all the biblical covenants finds its focal point. The events of Easter week are the very events that bring redemption to all human beings and to all living creatures.

Hope Founded in Monarchy

The covenant with *David* is specifically evoked in the New Testament in a number of ways. One of the titles by which Jesus is known in the Gospels is "Son of David" (Matthew 1:1; 21:9). He is also described as "king of the Jews" by the wise men who attend his birth (2:2), and he acknowledges this to be true when pressed about it later by Pontius Pilate (27:11). Later, the same title is used in mockery by the Romans (27:29, 37). So far as our New Testament authors are concerned, however, the wise men are wiser than the Romans; they get it right. Crucified by the Romans, Jesus nevertheless rises from the dead, and John sees him in his vision in the book of Revelation as "the Lion of the tribe of Judah, the Root of David, [who] has triumphed" (5:5). John goes on to say that "the kingdom of the world has become the kingdom of our Lord and of his Christ, and he will reign for ever and ever" (11:15). Jesus is Son of David, and he is King. At the same time, he is presented in the New Testament as being very much the *humble* king of Deuteronomy 17, and not the lordly king of the ancient Near Eastern city-state. He is, in fact, a servant-king, "obedient to death" (Philippians 2:6-8). It is only after he first relinquishes his power that we read that

> God exalted him to the highest place and gave him the name that is above every name, that at the name of Jesus every knee should bow, in heaven and on earth and under the earth, and every tongue confess that Jesus Christ is Lord, to the glory of God the Father. (2:9-11)

Jesus Christ is the king who stands at the heart of the kingdom of God, anticipated in the Old Testament and announced in the New. The monarchy in Israel has, indeed, been "turned toward the good," and David's line has delivered God's redemption.

Hope for Creation

Finally, in chapter 11 we discussed the Old Testament's "hope for creation" as a whole. We do not need to discuss this theme in the New Testament much more than we have already done. Suffice it to say that the hope that in Genesis 1–2 is already bound up with the entirety of God's good creation is *still* the hope that is on display in the New Testament. Moreover, the New Testament, like the Old, continues to use Jerusalem as a metaphor for talking about this hope. We see this in Revelation 21:1-4, where the new order of things, anticipated in passages like Isaiah 65:17-25 and 66:22-23, is unfolded. In a way, it represents a return to the garden from which human beings were banished when they left "home" (Revelation 22:1-5); it is not *only* that, however. It also represents the goal to which the whole of creation was always being drawn, even before the serpent had yet slithered and even before Adam and Eve had yet succumbed to his smooth voice.

New Testament Hope

What am I to hope for, according to New Testament faith? I am to hope for all the things that the people in the Old Testament hoped for—with the exception of the things that have already happened, because Jesus has come. And in the meantime, I am (as before) not only to wait but also to act. I am to live the life that I am called by God to live. Hope is the wellspring of agency in New Testament thinking, as in Old Testament thinking. The very reason that John communicated his vision in the book of Revelation to his early Christian contemporaries was *not* so that they could puzzle over its esoteric details (which is ironic, in light of the way the book has often been read). It *was* so that they would stand fast in their faith, continue in their hope, and persist in living in the right way (Revelation 1–3).

NOT A NEW STORY

As the various sections of this chapter have all conspired together to reveal, the New Testament does not tell a new story. It only takes an older story further—further up and further in. The ancient Christian writer Augustine was so struck by the extent to which this is true—the extent of the continuity of the two parts of the Christian Bible as making up one Story—that he offered these thoughts about it, with which we close the chapter:

> In it [the Old Testament] . . . there is so great a proclamation and prediction of the New Testament that no commandment and promise is found in the teaching of the gospel and of the apostles, however difficult and godly, that is not present in those old books.[57]

On the Judicious Closing of the Mind

The Question of Truth

The ideas of economists and political philosophers, both when
they are right and when they are wrong, are more powerful than
is commonly understood. Indeed the world is ruled by little else.
Practical men, who believe themselves to be quite exempt
from any intellectual influence, are usually the slaves
of some defunct economist.

John Maynard Keynes[1]

He was so often nearly right. . . . But I think he thought that the
object of opening the mind is simply opening the mind. Whereas
I am incurably convinced that the object of opening the mind, as
of opening the mouth, is to shut it again on something solid.

G. K. Chesterton on H. G. Wells[2]

I hope that in chapters 2–12 I have done a decent job of explaining biblical faith. If so, it should at least be clear how the Old Story told in the
two Testaments of the Bible answers the enduring human questions
we have been exploring. If that is the case, then I have at least rescued
the Old Story from the violence that has threatened to silence it, and it
has been allowed to speak for itself. We understand, at least, what the

biblical story *claims* about the world in which we live—about how it came to be, what the human place in it is, and how we should live here.

ON TRUTH AND DANGER

We are now in a position to return to where we began. We are ready to return to Thomas Berry's charge (in chap. 1) that "the old story, the account of how the world came to be and how we fit into it—is no longer effective." The Old Story, I acknowledged in that chapter, is in fact routinely regarded nowadays, on all sides, not just as ineffective but also as problematic and even dangerous. Implicit or explicit in that judgment is the further judgment that the Story is untrue. It does not correspond to the way things were, or are. That is why it is problematic and even dangerous, as we look toward the future. It is not a reliable guide to reality, and those who think that it *is* will inevitably do damage as they *engage* with reality.

Of the two questions that arise here—is the Story true, and is it dangerous?—the first is logically prior. Unless people believe the Story to be true, it cannot be problematic or dangerous. It is only as I find myself to be part of this Story and as this discovery then leads me to act (or to fail to act) in certain ways, that there arises anything that might be worth someone else "worrying about." The issue of the truthfulness or untruthfulness of the Story is therefore paramount. Is it coherent? Is it true to the facts, and does it make sense of them? Is it truer to the facts, and does it make better sense of them than competing stories? These are important inquiries to make of *any* governing story (metanarrative) in human life, given that so much hangs on the outcome of the inquiries—my sense of who I am, where I should be heading, and what I should do next. The surprising thing is just how infrequently these inquiries *are* nowadays made of the Old Story, or indeed of *any* similar stories. I can discern at least three reasons for this general lack of curiosity.

The War of Myths

The first is that many people do not appear to be aware of *the disputed nature of reality*. They are not aware of the way each of us is inevitably caught up in a "war of myths."[3] Among these naïve folks are to be included the "practical men" described by John Maynard Keynes in the quotation in the first epigraph to this chapter. These are people who "take the world as they find it" and simply get on with life, assuming that what is true about reality is self-evident and that right and wrong are more or less self-evident as well. They are often suspicious of, and hostile toward, those who suggest otherwise—"impractical" men, like philosophers or religious teachers. They do not ask questions of their own story, because they do not *see* it as a story. They see it simply as the way things are.[4]

The fact of the matter, however, is that each one of these practical men lives in a world that has been profoundly shaped by other people's ideas concerning what is true about reality and concerning what is right and wrong. It could be the ideas of economists and political philosophers, or it could be the ideas of ancient, inherited religion. Whichever it is, no one is "exempt from . . . intellectual influence," or indeed from moral influence. There is no one who does not live inside an (inevitably disputable) story. Human beings are always "storied," regardless of whether they reflect upon this fact, just as they are always "political," regardless of whether they vote. "The world is ruled by little else" than powerful ideas, "both when they are right and when they are wrong." We can do no other than find ourselves in a story. The only question is, Are we going to make any effort to ensure that we are governed by *right* ideas rather than *wrong* ones? Or are we simply going to remain "slaves" to *inherited* ideas, without engaging in any critical reflection on them?[5]

Truth and Harmony

The second reason I can discern for the general failure to ask difficult questions regarding the truth of individual metanarratives is that, among many of those people who *are* aware of the disputed nature of reality, there is a marked reluctance to acknowledge the *extent* of the dispute. Among many of the advocates of a historical axial age, for example—one of the currently influential stories about the world that I described in chapter 1—there is a strong desire to affirm what is allegedly common among various religious and philosophical traditions and to downplay what differentiates them. In this way of thinking, *affirmation* is the correct mode of approach to metanarratives—or at least, to the metanarratives that are considered acceptable (which is an interesting point all by itself). Evaluative questions concerning the coherence of this or that tradition or whether what it claims is really true to the facts and makes sense of them—such questions are not on the agenda, because they tend toward disharmony. This is especially true when we get to asking whether *this* tradition is truer to the facts than *another* one or makes better sense of the facts than another one. In this "axial" way of thinking, that which is true is not as important as that which promotes harmony.

Yet, as we have seen throughout this book, the extent of the dispute about reality among our religious and philosophical traditions is not trivial but enormous. It is beyond question that the Old Story is quite distinctive when compared with other stories and that these stories are considerably different from each other as well. They differ not only on matters of belief about God, the world, and the nature of humanity but also on matters of right and wrong—how human beings should treat each other, for example, and what the good society looks like. These various metanarratives, each vying for our attention in a veritable marketplace of metanarratives, claim *very* different things about who I am and about what I should do next. I cannot see, then, that questions about truthfulness can be avoided. They are pressed upon us by the data. Here I agree with Christopher Hitchens: "since all of these revelations, many of them hopelessly inconsistent, cannot by definition be simultaneously true, it must follow that some of them are false and illusory."[6] Not all of these competing stories can be true, even though each may contain some truth. Which ones *are* true, then? Or which *one* is true? These are very important questions. It is certainly a good and important thing to open up our minds, moving beyond the limits to thinking that are accepted by the practical man. It is certainly important to understand the genuine complexity of the world and the various claims that are made about it. To quote Chesterton (in the second epigraph to this chapter), however, surely it is not the case "that the object of opening the mind is simply opening the mind." Surely "the object of opening the mind, as of opening the mouth, is to shut it again on something solid." It is to decide, after due consideration of what the mind has discovered, what is likely to be true. We do not want to become (I suggest) like the bishop in C. S. Lewis' *Great Divorce*, for whom the ongoing discussion of ideas had become more important than the truth and the spiritual journey more important than the destination.[7] In our pursuit of the truth about the world, we need to weigh the competing claims that are before us, and we need to come to a decision. The inquisitive opening of the mind needs to be followed, at the appropriate time, by an at least partial (yet judicious) closing of it.

Faith and Reason

My comment about the mind brings me, however, to the third reason why it is not common nowadays for truth questions to be asked of individual metanarratives. It is precisely because these are *rational* questions, and faith (it is often said) is not something that is rational. Faith is often perceived, in fact, as being the very opposite of reason. Theodore Ludwig claims the following, for example, about how many Muslims view Christians: "Muslims point out that Christians often see 'faith' as a believing without knowing why, accepting without rational certainty, a 'leap of faith' even against the testimony of reason."[8] I do not actually know whether this view of faith is any more or less common among Christians than among Muslims. It seems to me that setting faith at odds with reason is a fairly typical response of religious people of all kinds to facts, or alleged facts, that threaten their current grasp of their faith. Beyond this, it is a fairly typical *human* response to facts, or alleged facts, that threaten someone's current metanarrative. It is not a strictly religious impulse. It is the impulse (for example) of the practical man, confronted suddenly by something that he cannot account for in his world. He seeks sanctuary from the relentless march of logic, lest he be compelled to convert to a different worldview (the very existence of which he has only just discovered). He seeks sanctuary in "faith."

I propose, however, that every human being *should* be held accountable to reason when she says she believes something and *should* be expected to be able to say *why* and *in which* ways that belief accords with reality. Where this accountability is lacking, bad things can happen, although not all of them are *equally* bad. People can leap in faith into a relatively harmless pit of self-delusion, which is very sad from the individual point of view but not of great significance societally. I am thinking here, for example, of those confused souls in mental institutions who believe themselves to be Jesus, Napoleon, or some other figure of historical importance. However, people can also leap into the abyss of abandonment to dark powers—for example, those who threw themselves so enthusiastically into the "faith" bound up with Adolf Hitler in the 1930s. If faith really is "believing without knowing why . . . a 'leap of faith' even against the testimony of reason," then reason cannot help me to decide in whom or what to invest my faith, and why. I must simply leap blindly, and whether I am giving myself to the devil or to God, who can really say? The problem is that we can all too easily see the dangers of this approach to life when *others* are doing the "leaping" (into cults, for example, or into devotion to "the great leader"). We are not so perceptive when it is we ourselves who are behaving in this lemming-like fashion.

Over against this irresponsible approach to life, I commend my foregoing truth questions as questions to be asked of *any* story presenting itself as a true story. Is it coherent? Is it true to the facts, and does it make sense of them? Is it truer to the facts, and does it make better sense of them, than competing stories? "The heart has its reasons which reason does not know," claims Pascal, and that may well be.[9] Yet reason had better be consulted in its proper domain, or trouble will follow. In the excellent Topography of Terror museum in Berlin, built on the site of Nazi-era buildings belonging to the Gestapo and the SS, there are many photographs that illustrate the terrible consequences that follow from leaping, along with the crowd, into religious and political devotion in particular. Without good reasons otherwise, why *not* follow the crowd? It is certainly safer than the alternative. In this same museum, however, there are also photographs that tell of a different possibility—of standing back from the crowd, with a critical gaze, even at great risk to oneself. One of the most striking of these dates from 1936 and was taken in a shipyard in Hamburg, following an address to a crowd by Hitler himself. Everyone in the photograph has a hand raised in the Nazi salute—except one man. This man (probably ex-Nazi Party member August Landmesser) stands with his arms folded. He has critical distance; he possesses independent thought. He has his wits (as well as his virtue) about him; he is skeptical. Perhaps he has observed, among other things, that the man who has just spoken to the crowd and whose racial theory exalts (at the top end of the hierarchy) Aryan human beings who are tall, long-legged, slim, and blond, is himself a dark-haired, unattractive man of medium height and build. This is the kind of thing that critical minds tend to notice.

Therefore, although I do not agree with "new atheist" Sam Harris on a considerable number of issues, I do agree with him on this point:

> Nothing is more sacred than the facts. No one, therefore, should win any points in our discourse for deluding himself. The litmus test for reasonableness should be obvious: anyone

who wants to know how the world is, whether in physical or spiritual terms, will be open to new evidence.[10]

This focus on "reasonableness" and "evidence" is, in fact, entirely consistent with a biblical and Christian understanding of faith, despite what Muslims may think about Christians—and despite what Richard Dawkins thinks, too, about faith as "blind trust, in the absence of evidence, even in the teeth of evidence."[11] As others have pointed out, this "is not a Christian definition of faith but one that Dawkins has invented to suit his own polemical purposes."[12]

The Truth of the Story

I accept, then, the need for *inquiries* to be made of the Old Story, just as they ought to be made of all similar stories. This Old Story is said by many modern people to be untrue. Many others (among whom I number myself) hold it to be true. I accept the obligation to explain *why* and *in which* ways my belief accords with reality. Indeed, I think that the biblical tradition itself requires this kind of explanation from me.[13] And then (since now the observer *does* perhaps have something to worry about), I accept the further obligation to try to explain why this belief is not problematic or dangerous with respect to the present and the future. I accept the obligation to justify what I said in chapter 1: that when the biblical story is properly understood, it provides a point of departure for precisely the path out of trouble and into a better future, for humankind and for the planet, for which its detractors are often looking.

In what follows in the final two chapters of the book, then, we shall retrace our steps through the content of chapters 2–12, examining once again the answers given by biblical faith to our ten questions. These answers will now be clustered under a smaller number of headings, however, and the focus will be not upon description but upon justification. I shall discuss first the question of truth (chap. 13) and then the question of danger (chap. 14). First of all, then: Can the Old Story still be regarded as a *true* account of life, the universe, and everything?[14]

ON THE NATURE OF THE WORLD

In chapters 2 and 12, we examined what this ancient Story has to say about the *world*. The question now becomes: Is it *plausible* in what it says, when considered from a modern point of view? I believe that it is.

The Cosmic Story

The world is not eternal, the ancient Story claims. Indeed it is not, agrees modern science (for the most part).[15] The universe had a beginning in time, and it will end.[16] Consistent with the biblical perspective, modern science tells us that we are midway through a complicated cosmic story whose telling embraces (and this the biblical authors do not, of course, tell us) such startling realities as novae explosions. It is these explosions that first scattered throughout the galaxies the dust of the stars out of which we are all made. We are stardust—that is how the carbon, iron, phosphorous, and calcium in our bodies were formed. The time that thus began and then moved on flows in only one direction (forward)—a remarkable cosmological oddity, much pondered by cosmologists, astrophysicists, and mathematicians, because everything else in the universe is potentially symmetrical. Time, however, flows in only one direction, and not all the science fiction stories or "back to the future" movies in the world will make it do otherwise. Story (beginning, development, and end) seems to be built into the very structure of the universe. Rowan Williams has said that this new understanding of the universe

> has put back into our understanding of the universe elements of narrative, elements of biography. The universe has a biography, a story of life. This is a story which moves forward, which accumulates, which points ahead. The stories that are visible in the lives of individuals are not some kind of aberration in a universe which basically goes round in circles.[17]

The universe does not run on eternally, in endless cycles of existence, as some religious and philosophical traditions suggest. It began, it is developing, and it will end. We inhabit a story.

The Finely Tuned Universe

In its current shape, the universe also displays order—another of the marked emphases in the Old Story. There is an order to the cosmos that allows life to flourish on earth. The *precision* that is necessarily involved in this ordering is perhaps not sufficiently appreciated. We live in what scientists sometimes refer to as a "finely tuned" universe. If any one of various fundamental physical constants in this finely tuned universe were even slightly different from what it is, life on earth would be impossible.[18] For example, if the ratio of the strength of the electrical forces and the strength of gravity were different or if the ratio of the mass of the galaxies and the gravitational energy required to pull them apart were other than it is, then life would not exist. Now it is *possible* that such fine tuning happened simply by chance, but this does not seem to me a very *plausible* explanation for the way things are. I am more of Voltaire's opinion, when he writes, "The universe puzzles me, and I cannot imagine that this clockwork can exist and not have a clockmaker."[9] To choose a better analogy, borrowed from the eighteenth-century English poet Edward Young, it makes little sense to me to attribute the artistry of the universe to anything other than an artist.[20] Nor does this apparently make sense to those who propose, in all seriousness, that the universe is the creation of aliens, who substitute in modern science fiction for the ancient gods we have read about in earlier chapters.[21] This, too, seems to me an implausible idea. However, at least its proponents recognize the even greater implausibility of attributing the order of the universe to chance.

All of this is to say that the existence and nature of the cosmos in which we live imply, to me, a personal creator God of the kind that biblical faith proclaims.[22] The cosmic story in which we are bound up implies a Storyteller—someone who is weaving the story together into a coherent tale. Writing of the moment when he himself began to make this connection, G. K. Chesterton tells us,

> I had always vaguely felt facts to be miracles in the sense that they are wonderful; now I began to think them miracles in the stricter sense that they were *wilful*. I mean that they were, or might be, repeated exercises of some will. In short, I had always believed that the world involved magic: now I thought that perhaps it involved a magician. And this pointed a profound emotion always present and sub-conscious; that this world of ours has some purpose; and if there is a purpose, there is a person. I had always felt life first as a story: and if there is a story there is a story-teller.[23]

The facts that Chesterton felt to be miracles in 1908 have been shown by the developments in modern science since his time only to be even more miraculous. It has only become clearer the extent to which the universe has come about by design, with life on earth (including the creation of human persons) being the central focus of this design.

Faith and Science

A word of clarification is necessary at this point, since I have just used a word ("design") that carries "baggage" in contemporary discussions about faith and science in different parts of the world. It is often deployed by people who want to set up in opposition God's design of certain aspects of the world, on the one hand, and natural processes, on the other. In this way of approaching the world, this or that aspect of the created order is said to be explicable *only* in terms of God's design, and *not* in terms of natural (especially evolutionary) processes.[24] I need to be clear, then, that I do not mean by my own use of the word "design" to imply any such opposition and that, in fact, I do not believe that biblical faith requires or commends any such opposition. I am convinced, with many scientists, that "the science of Darwinism is fully compatible with conventional religious beliefs" and with biblical thinking itself.[25] For example, in chapter 9 we had reason to look at Psalm 104. It is significant that in this psalm God's work in the world is undertaken *in and through* natural processes, and not *separately* from them. All of God's creatures look to God "to give them their food at the proper time" (104:27), and God does so. This does not mean, however, that the "lions [that] roar for their prey" (104:21) are sitting around under a tree with their arms folded, waiting for manna (or antelopes) to fall from the sky. Rather, God is providentially involved in the world *in and through* what is natural and instinctual (i.e., hunting). Likewise, a baby grows naturally in its mother's womb; it *evolves* therein. It is of this same process, however, that the psalmist can say, "You knit me together in my mother's womb. I praise you because I am fearfully and wonderfully made" (Psalm 139:13-14). It is of the human being that began life as a single cell inside its mother's body that Psalm 8 claims, "You made him a little lower than the heavenly beings and crowned him with glory and honor" (8:5). There *is* natural process, but it is all part of a grand design. Order emerges in, through, and at the end of natural process—an order in which lions, as well as human beings, have their assigned places.

The mistake that has so often been made in discussions about science and faith is to think that this design cannot involve natural processes and, conversely, that if natural processes can be demonstrated, then the idea of design is threatened. On the one hand, then, we find religious people, noting that in Genesis 1 God makes all creatures "according to their various kinds," denying that there could be "natural processes by which new species emerge from preexisting species, through descent and modification."[26] On the other hand, there are scientists who appear to think that Darwin's discovery of natural processes signals an end to notions of a natural order.[27] Both are confused, I think. The first group is confused in believing that "kinds" cannot arise through a divinely ordained *process*—to which my response is, "Why not?" The second group is confused in holding that the process cannot result in (divinely ordained) "kinds." Leon Kass points out, however, that whatever our theory of how our current species of life on earth came into being, there *is* obviously an order of things in which there *are* separate species:

> In reproduction, like still mates with like, and the progeny are, for the most part, always like their parents in kind. Genealogy may explain lines of descent or kinship of genotypes, but existent organisms behave largely true to their type. Is not your average rabbit much more impressed by the difference between a rabbit and a fox than he is by the fact that they have the same genetic code or that they are mutually descended from a common mammalian forebear? Species, however mutable, still make sense.[28]

Order exists, in the animal world as much as in the rest of the world, and it needs to be accounted for.

Design is not antithetical to process, nor process to design. More generally, biblical faith need not be conceived of as the enemy of modern science, nor modern science as the enemy of biblical faith.[29] In fact, modern science itself arose only as biblical faith gradually displaced, over the course of European history, what had previously been believed about the physical world under the influence of, first, ancient Near Eastern and then Greek thought. What *had* been believed was that the main importance of the physical world lay in the access it provided to a world beyond it—the world of the gods (in ancient Near Eastern thought) or the world of Forms (in Plato). The new understanding that began to emerge in the course of the Renaissance, deriving ultimately from biblical faith, was that the world as a creation of God, separate from God but possessing an order imprinted upon it by God (and therefore obeying laws), was a legitimate object of inquiry *in itself*. It was only as this new understanding gained ground that modern science became possible.[30] Its current practitioners have unfortunately all too often forgotten, just as completely as its current antagonists, this close family connection.

The Sense of the Sacred

The cosmic story—albeit a much longer and more complicated story than our ancestors could possibly have imagined—implies a Storyteller. It implies the kind of personal creator God that biblical faith proclaims. It is this Storyteller, I suggest, who has been encountered throughout history, in all parts of the world, by human beings in all cultures and in all stages of life, giving rise to the ubiquitous human phenomenon of religion—which is otherwise a difficult phenomenon to account for. Are we actually to imagine that there is nothing real to which religion responds—that the experience of the world as "sacred space," which is so fundamental to human experience all through the ages, is simply a commonly shared human delusion? Some may find this easy to believe; I must say that I do not. Human beings are fundamentally religious beings, it seems to me, and we always have been. We are drawn to worship, as a moth is drawn to the flame. Why is that? An important aspect of this worship is thankfulness—a sense of gratitude for the world, and for our lives in it and for those we love. Why do we feel thankful? Do such intuitions correspond to *nothing* outside our heads and hearts? For myself, the existence of a Storyteller makes good sense of these intuitions in a way that nothing else does. I agree with Christina Rossetti: "Were there no God, we would be in this glorious world with grateful hearts, and no one to thank."[31] To have "grateful hearts, and no one to thank"—*that*, to me, makes *no* sense.

Of course, the human encounter with the sacred has not necessarily always been *explained* by people using the language of encounter with a personal creator God. Nevertheless, it is perfectly plausible to view it as having *involved* such an encounter, regardless of whether people themselves explained it in this way. Even in the great world religions where deity has been understood by some in impersonal terms, it is significant that many adherents of those religions have found themselves unable to believe in such deity. The widespread worship of personal gods has reemerged from (or has simply continued) within these very same religions.[32] It does not appear easy, then, for human persons to think of deity in impersonal terms. It is certainly incoherent to be *thankful* to a deity that is not personal, although this has not prevented people from speaking in such terms—of being thankful to such entities as "Nature," for example. G. K. Chesterton addresses precisely this case, arguing that if someone "can manage to be thankful when there is nobody to be thankful to, and no good intentions to be thankful for, then he is simply taking refuge in being thoughtless in order to avoid being thankless." He goes on to suggest that "Nature" is nothing other than a "fairy godmother" in a "fireside fairytale." He points out, however, that "there can only be fairy godmothers because there are godmothers; and there can only be godmothers because there is God."[33]

A Good World

We shall return to the gods, and God, under the next heading. The significance in our present context of the human bias toward personal gods lies in what I think it has to say about the deep plausibility of the Old Story in its world-affirming perspective. Surely it cannot be true—when so much *trouble* has apparently been taken to ensure the existence of a physical world in which life, including human life, can flourish—that this world is only of secondary importance with respect to some other kind of existence? Surely it cannot be true that our human personhood itself is unimportant? Surely it cannot be the case that matter, so long in the making, does not in the end matter? Everything about the finely tuned universe suggests otherwise. Biblical faith also suggests otherwise. Both together tell us that we are supposed to take this good world very seriously. The world was not created as a puzzle to be solved nor as a problem to be overcome, but as a wonderful and good place to be enjoyed.

Is the Old Story plausible, then, in what it has to say about the world, when considered from a modern point of view? I believe that it is—once it is conceded, of course, that we are not dealing in this Story with a modern scientific textbook but with ancient philosophy, and that we cannot expect it directly to answer *all* of our modern questions, even if it still speaks to some very important ones. In particular (and to pick up on an earlier point), we must be clear that this Old Story is much more interested in *design* (and what this signifies) than in *process*—that process is, in fact, of comparatively *little* concern to its authors and that reading this concern into the Story is certain to result in a *misreading* of it.[34] It is also certain to produce an entirely unnecessary conflict between biblical faith and modern science, which *is* deeply interested in the processes by which things come to be and has discovered huge amounts of information about these processes.[35] Yet although modern science can tell us much, it too cannot tell us everything we need to know. In particular, it cannot tell us about the most important things. One of the greatest of modern sociologists, Max Weber, talked about this reality in a lecture delivered at the University of Munich in 1918:

> Who—apart from certain overgrown children, who are indeed to be found in the natural sciences—still believes today that a knowledge of astronomy or biology or physics or chemistry could teach us anything at all about the *meaning* of the world? How could one find clues about such a "meaning," if there is such a thing? . . . Tolstoy gave us the simplest answer to the only important question: "What should we do? How should we live?" The fact that science does not give us this answer is completely undeniable.[36]

The Old Story, as ancient philosophy, cannot be expected to speak directly to all of our modern questions, but neither can modern science. Both together are required if we are to come to a comprehensive understanding of the world in which we live and of our place and purpose in this world.

ON THE NATURE OF GOD

In chapters 3, 7, and 12, I tried to clarify the broad outlines of biblical faith with respect to the personal God who is implied by the personal creation—the one and only, sovereign and good God, whom Israelites in the Mosaic tradition claim to have encountered in the world throughout their extraordinary history. Millions of others throughout history have also come to believe, like them, that this is the only true God.

One and Not Many

They have agreed, on the one hand, with those who, from at least the sixth century B.C. onward, in different parts of the world, have concluded that the One and not the Many should rightly be the focus of human devotion. This represents a decision *in favor of* the One precisely because the nature of the world is believed to imply one, and not many, gods; it also represents a decision *against* the Many, who as time has passed have been judged to be implausible divinities. We see this process clearly at work in ancient Greece, for example. The poet Xenophanes (born around 580 B.C.) already mocks his sixth-century contemporaries for supposing "that the gods are born (as they themselves are), and that they have clothes and speech and bodies like their own." He criticizes his predecessors Homer and Hesiod, who "attributed to the gods everything that is a shame and reproach among men, stealing and committing adultery and deceiving each other."[37] According to the plays of another Greek, Euripides (485–406 B.C.), these are gods focused upon the enjoyment of their own lives, and certainly not on human well-being. They are indifferent to human beings at best and destructive of them at worst—irrespective of human virtue and sometimes simply because the humans get caught up in divine quarrels. These gods are certainly not good. In *Hippolytus*, for example, Aphrodite and Artemis are such vile characters that no right-thinking worshipper could possibly admire them. In *Heracles*, Amphitryon rightly says of Zeus himself, "Your love is even less than you pretended; and I, mere man, am nobler than you, great god. . . . You are a callous god or were born unjust."[38] The ancient Greek gods have not survived well the passage of time, nor have the ancient gods as a class. There are many fewer naturalistic polytheists in the world today than there used to be.

A Person and Not Impersonal

These millions of believers in the God of biblical faith have, on the other hand, *disagreed* with those who from the sixth century B.C. onward, rejecting the worship of the *many personal* gods, have come to regard the One as *impersonal*. These millions have found it impossible to believe that the complicated cosmic story in which we are involved lacks a Storyteller and that the finely tuned ordering of the world in which we live came to exist without a Tuner. They have found it impossible to believe that our own sense of self as human persons living in this wonderful world is, in the end, an illusion and that the material world, in the end, is unimportant. It has not seemed to them very much of an advance, having rejected as the focal point of their personal lives the many personal gods who are not "for us," to embrace an impersonal deity who is likewise not "for us" or for the world.

Basil Mitchell, for many years a professor of philosophy at the University of Oxford, writes of his own disillusionment as a young man with this "monistic" philosophy of the One, which he regards as failing "to attach enduring importance to individual persons; to the institutions that molded them and enabled them to flourish; to the historical processes that had formed them; and to the natural world that nourished them."[39] The destiny of human souls, he came to believe, "was such that it could be realized only in a community, both in this life and beyond, a community in which they could be known and loved."[40] His own personal life, involving the experience of being known and loved, strongly suggested to him that this was the right way of looking at things. The human bias toward personal gods, even in religious traditions in which there is a strong monistic emphasis, suggests that this has been true for many others as well, even if they have not embraced the God of whom *biblical faith* speaks. Human persons typically appear to need a more world-affirming, and person-affirming, perspective than monism can offer.

Thus it is that in the "epic" era of Hinduism (stretching from the fourth century B.C. until the fourth century A.D.), for example, we find a marked interest in the worship of the many gods that is not reflected in the earlier Upanishads but now comes to be nourished by the *Ramayana* and *Mahabharata* epics. These texts speak of Vishnu, creator and preserver of the universe, and his incarnations Rama and Krishna; they speak of Shiva, the creator of all beings, and of Durga, the virgin goddess. They foreshadow a great flowering of devotional cults in India in the succeeding centuries, provoking in turn (in modern times) reform movements such as the Arya Samaj, which called for a return to ancient tradition, and for a rejection of a devotional Hinduism that was focused on the many popular gods.[41]

Buddhism, likewise, developed after Gautama's time into two separate streams, one of which (Mahayana Buddhism) chose as its supreme spiritual model not the one who reaches nirvana and stays there but the bodhisattva. The bodhisattva is a person who has reached nirvana but has chosen to remain within samsara (the wheel of suffering) to help others. Some of these bodhisattvas, like Avalokiteshvara ("an omnipresent savior rich in love and compassion"), are regarded as celestial beings who can be approached in worship and prayer.[42] The Buddhism that rooted itself in China in the early centuries A.D. included a "Pure Land" Buddhism that was centered upon another compassionate god,

Amitabha Buddha. This god was thought to have created a paradise open to all who recited his name "with a concentrated and devout mind."[43] Devotees, even sinful ones, could hope to be reborn there, because Amitabha Buddha had promised to save all beings. This apparently very distant relative to the Buddhism of Gautama "soon became the most popular form of Buddhism in China," eclipsing for a time both Daoism and Confucianism, and later became popular also in Japan.[44] Human beings, it seems, cannot easily do without personal gods.

One and Personal

Like the "millions," I find the many "gods" to be too much like us to be believable or (indeed) to be deserving of any human devotion or imitation. I do not, in fact, believe that they exist. I also find it impossible, however, to believe in the ultimacy of an impersonal One, with its consequent requirement that I must devalue so many things about the world that appear to be true and good. "It isn't a very cheerful philosophy that everything is illusion," the Irish poet W. B. Yeats once said (while holding, himself, to that philosophy).[45] I agree; I find it neither cheerful nor plausible, and I lend it no credence. Yet as Leo Tolstoy once suggested, we should not "spurn" the concept of God just "because of absurdities that have been attached to it."[46] For myself, I am drawn (like the millions) to the God who is neither impersonally One nor personally Many and in whom I perceive no absurdity (although I do see plenty of mystery). This is the kind of God who is implied by the good world in which we live, as it is revealed to our senses as well as to our science (which depends to a large extent, of course, on the reliability of our senses). It is the God of biblical faith—the God whom we are like in important ways but who is not like us, in equally important ways; who is perfectly good, in ways that I am not; and who, in his goodness, is "for us" and "for creation."

However, my convictions about the "right answer" to the question "Who is God?" do not arise only from reflection on the nature of the world—indeed, not even *mainly* from this source. Long before I knew that anyone actually used to *worship* the exciting gods of Greece whom I encountered in my childhood books and long before I knew what "monism" was, I became familiar with the New Testament Gospels. I read there about a most extraordinary person, Jesus of Nazareth, who appeared in so many ways to be admirable and worthy of imitation, and yet also to be quite mad—or perhaps even wicked, beneath the goodness. Here was a man who claimed to *be* God. This is not something that ever seems very likely to be true when a person first encounters it. Yet some of the people who were the least likely in the ancient world to think it true—Jews of the first century A.D., so deeply rooted in worship of the one God and so profoundly "wired" to oppose the polytheism of their surroundings—came to believe it. It was they who first became convinced that Jesus *was* God, and many others then became convinced too—because they could not explain him in any other plausible way. If Jesus was not God but nevertheless claimed to be so (as C. S. Lewis has famously put it), he must have been mad (deluded) or bad (deceiving).[47] He certainly could not have been good and at the same time sane. As I read the Gospels at that time, however, and as I read them now, I encounter someone who is supremely good and supremely sane. Therefore, I am obliged to take his astonishing claims about himself deeply seriously—as even doubting Thomas was ultimately obliged to do (John 20:24-31). Here, in the end, is the God who is One and not Many. Here is One, who is also a Person.

ON MAN AND WOMAN

In chapters 4, 8, and 12, we considered what biblical faith has to say about humanity—the image bearers of God who live in God's temple-cosmos. There, we discussed the ways in which biblical faith presents human beings (male and female) as *being like* the other creatures ("living beings") as well as the ways in which they are presented as *standing apart* from these other creatures, having responsibilities for ruling and keeping. We further considered the humanistic and democratic emphases of the biblical material, rooted in the notion of the sanctity of each and every human life.

On Humanism

The idea that every human being is created by a personal God in his image, equal in standing *before* him and with a full part to play in the governance of the cosmos in communion *with* him, has not been central to most cultures throughout the ages, and it is not central to numerous cultures at the present moment either. Yet it *is* an idea, nonetheless, that millions of people throughout history have found compelling and that (at least in part) they have embraced as their own. They have found in this idea an explanation of their own deep sense that they are part of creation, *similar* in so many ways to other creatures, and yet at the same time entirely *different* from them in so many others.

Human beings are very similar, in particular, to the other higher primates (monkeys and apes). Scientists sequencing the genome of the chimpanzee have discovered that the overlap in DNA in this case is between 95 percent and 98.77 percent, depending on how exactly one counts. Yet a chimpanzee remains a chimpanzee (just as a fox remains a fox, and a rabbit a rabbit). A chimpanzee is not a human being. It does not possess a highly developed brain capable of abstract reasoning, language, or problem solving. It does not possess a desire for self-expression, and the appreciation for beauty that produces cultural innovations like art and music. It does not have an ability to understand and to influence the world around it through the development of tools, leading to such distinctively human innovations as building fires, cooking food, and making and wearing clothes. These are just observable facts. As Leon Kass has rightly said, "Human beings really are different from and higher than the other animals," and he gives us his own description of the ways in which this is so:

> Human beings, alone among the creatures, speak, plan, create, contemplate and judge. Human beings, alone among the creatures, can articulate a future goal and use that articulation to guide them in bringing it into being by their own purposive conduct. Human beings, alone among the creatures, can think about the whole, marvel at its many-splendored forms and articulated order, wonder about its beginning, and feel awe in beholding its grandeur and in pondering the mystery of its source. . . . These self-evident truths do *not* rest on biblical authority. Rather, the biblical text enables us to confirm them by an act of self-reflection.[48]

There is, then, an obvious distinction to be made between human beings and other creatures. Many have found in the Old Story an explanation of this distinction. In its humanistic dimensions, biblical faith separates humans from the rest of creation while at the same time exiling from creation the unbelievable (and even reprehensible) ancient gods that humans used to serve as slaves. As people throughout history have encountered this faith, many have found it not only to be plausible but also to correspond to their deepest yearnings—their deepest hopes about what might be true about the world and about themselves. Certainly I myself find the biblical view congruent with reality in just these ways.

On Democracy

The same is true of the biblical idea about humanity in its democratic dimensions. It is one thing to exile the *unseen* gods from creation. It is quite another to exile the gods who are *seen*—those other humans beings with whom one is, in practice, unequal and who (like the unseen gods) oppress and enslave. The biblical idea that every single human being is made in God's image and is to be respected as such—that everyone is to have a full share in the governance of God's world, rather than merely servicing those who govern it—has therefore spoken powerfully to humanity throughout history. It has spoken especially powerfully to those who find themselves at the bottom of society's social and political pyramid. It has (for example) fueled the hope of the common poor, governed by rich aristocracies, that there might one day be a more just society in which they would possess a genuine stake. A famous case where this was so is the Peasants Revolt in England in 1381. During an open-air sermon in the course of this revolt, the Christian priest John Ball uttered these words:

> When Adam delved and Eve span, Who was then the gentleman? From the beginning all men by nature were created alike, and our bondage or servitude came in by the unjust oppression of naughty men. . . . Therefore I exhort you to consider that now the time is come, appointed to us by God, in which ye may (if ye will) cast off the yoke of bondage, and recover liberty.[49]

The biblical idea of humanity has likewise touched a deep cord in women, historically. It has done so where they have felt their human identity trampled upon in oppressive social structures, in which they have been bought and sold by men who have considered women to be only and merely the means of fulfilling various male needs for pleasure, children, and service. It has done so where women have been deprived of any role in public life and where they have not had equal rights under the law. The biblical idea of humanity has seemed to these women to be the very foundation of a vision of a better world.[50]

I agree with them. I find that the biblical vision of human existence explains convincingly who I am and what I am to do. The world has indeed become a better place to the extent that this vision has already taken hold of it—a much greater extent than many people, without a profound sense of the past, have been able (or willing) to see. It has become a better place precisely to the extent that the intrinsic value and human rights of all human beings have been recognized—be they men, women, or children—and to whatever tribe, ethnicity, or religion they may belong. The world would be a better place still, I contend, if this biblical vision in its entirety—humanistic and democratic, and centered on the one, personal, and good God—were to be widely embraced. Moreover, since coherence is one measure of truthfulness, it is clear that the biblical vision of humanity coheres well with what biblical faith also has to say about the cosmos itself and about God. It is surely right that the God who is "for us" in creation is for *all* of us, and not just some—for females as well as males, for children as well as adults, for the poor as well as the rich, and for the powerless as well as the powerful. It follows that *we too* should be "for all," and not just for some, and that *we too* should commit ourselves to loving *all* of our neighbor human beings as ourselves—considering their interests and protecting their dignity and rights along with our own.

In making this last point, I do not believe that I would find much opposition from many of those who are otherwise antagonistic to biblical faith yet who themselves embrace a humanistic and democratic vision of humanity. The question that remains to be asked, however, is this: Is it really possible to sustain such a vision if it is divorced from a broader story in which its coherence is evident? I believe that it is not. The vision in question is intrinsic to the Old Story, does not make sense without it, and cannot long survive its rejection. "Secular" humanism, when it truly is secular and not simply a decaying—but not yet quite dead—form of biblical humanism, is certainly not up to the task. We shall return to this matter in our final chapter.

On Evil and Suffering

To the extent that one has already embraced what biblical faith has to say about the nature of the world, the nature of God, and the nature of human beings, one is bound to embrace, to the same extent, its explanation (and not the competing explanations described in chaps. 5, 6, and 12) as to why evil and suffering mark the world. It would be logically inconsistent to affirm that the cosmic story in which we are involved is being written by the biblical God, who has created the kind of world that biblical faith describes, and then to adopt the perspectives on evil and suffering that are found in, say, Hinduism or Buddhism.

Monism, Dualism, and Biblical Faith

Such Eastern views are inevitably implausible to those who hold the world that we see and feel to be the real world in which God has placed us to live. They will be implausible even to people who may not believe in the personal God of biblical faith but who merely accept the world as they find it *as* the real world. Earlier, I mentioned Basil Mitchell's disillusionment with monism precisely because of its failure to attach enduring importance to individual persons, institutions, historical processes, and the natural world. It also fails to attach sufficient weight, in my view, to the evil and suffering we encounter in the world. Faced with awful reality, it turns its gaze elsewhere—to a world that is *said* to be more real. Why we should believe in such a "real" world, however, so very different from the world of our ordinary experience, is entirely unclear.

Dualism, by contrast, takes evil and suffering much more seriously. However, it does so to the extent that we can have no ground for hope that good will overcome evil and that we will make sense, in the end, of suffering. Perhaps to hope for the overcoming of evil is to be delusional, but such hope is certainly a deeply rooted aspect of the human psyche. We are innately hopeful and not only worshipful beings, it seems to me. Why is that?

Over against these monistic and dualistic ways of thinking about the cosmos, the biblical account allows us to live in the real world yet also with hope. It explains how there can be one perfectly good and personal God who is "for us" and yet at the same time a creation in which terrible evil and suffering are to be found. There is free will in the cosmos, claims biblical faith, and many of God's creatures choose badly (chaps. 5 and 8–9). *That* is why there is so much suffering. As an observer of the ways of the world, I find this explanation convincing. Most of the suffering in the world is *indeed* the result of bad moral choices made by human beings. The story of man's inhumanity to man is *indeed*, above all (as biblical faith asserts), a story of human beings aspiring to be gods and heroes rather than to be good neighbors. In this story, the temptation to pursue heroic divinity is *indeed* fundamental—a temptation that appears to be very powerful and to derive not only from "inside" human persons but also from "outside." That is to say: it does not seem possible to account for moral evil (empirically) simply in terms of moral human actors (evil that is "inside"). Moral evil is a larger and darker reality than can be contained merely within the human soul. So, at least, has it seemed to many who have encountered it.

Suffering Intrinsic to Creation

The biblical account of things also allows us to live in the real world, with hope, in a second way. It does so precisely because it does not present us with a *global, all-encompassing* account of suffering in terms of moral choices. It would be impossible to accept biblical faith as true if it *did* tie all suffering to moral evil in such a manner, since it is perfectly obvious that some suffering in the world arises simply from the fact that the world is the way it is, and not otherwise. It is also perfectly obvious that the world already had this nature long before human beings lived here. Certainly the suffering that arises from being the victim of torture while held captive by enemies arises from the embrace of evil by human beings; moral considerations are involved. However, the same cannot be said for suffering that arises from accidentally placing one's hand too near to a naked flame; moral considerations do not come into it. It is simply *in the very nature* of fire that it burns and that my hand will inevitably hurt if I place it in or near the flame. It is, in fact, *good* that my hand hurts; if it did not, I would not withdraw it, and the fire would do even more damage.[51] Likewise, the water that is so essential to life on this planet possesses certain properties that will cause suffering, and perhaps even death, to those who accidentally fall into rivers. Again, one of the fundamental laws of physics is the law of gravity. This law is essential to the proper operation of the universe as we know it, and we are generally glad that it exists. In a world in which the law of gravity operates, however, it is certainly the case that if I step off a high cliff I am going to fall a great distance and cause myself suffering or even death. This is not the result of evil. A significant amount of suffering in the world is of this kind. It arises out of the very fact that the world *is* finely tuned to allow life to flourish here. That which makes the world "good" (to use the language of Genesis 1) is precisely that which makes it dangerous. Some suffering in this world is inevitable.

Three further examples will serve to underline the point. First, the earth's crust is made up of tectonic plates that float on a molten interior, moving and interacting with each other. This molten interior is essential to life on the planet, because it is responsible for the shield around the earth that protects it from radiation (which is itself a product of nuclear fusion, which is necessary for life). It was tectonic activity that first formed (among other things) land masses and ocean basins, making the earth habitable. It is continuing tectonic activity that keeps the earth habitable, by preventing the land masses from returning to the oceans through erosion. All of this is good. Yet in this same good world, volcanic eruptions, tsunamis, and earthquakes are sooner or later inevitable, as the tectonic plates run into each other. They do not result from *evil*, although they *can* cause suffering.[52]

Tropical storms arise, second, because tropical areas possess warm waters. They do so because of the way the earth is heated by the sun, which is precisely the way it *needs* to be heated to optimize habitable conditions on earth. Moreover, storms in general (not just tropical ones) are good for life on earth, replenishing its resources. They are not the result of evil, although they can certainly cause suffering.[53]

Finally by way of example, we may consider diseases. Some diseases are the result of random genetic mutation, which appears to be inevitable for any reproducing biological species. Others are caused by bacteria, which are necessary to our existence in *many* ways. They become harmful to us only when they mutate and before we adapt to them. Disease, it seems, is simply intrinsic to the created order. It does not arise from evil, although it can and does cause suffering.[54]

Terence Fretheim sums up the situation well:

God has created a dynamic world; earthquakes, volcanoes, storms, bacteria, and viruses have their role to play in the becoming of the world—in both a pre-sin and a post-sin world. These creatures function in an orderly process in many ways, but randomness also plays a role; in the words of Ecclesiastes 9:11, "Time and chance happen to them all." Because humans are part of this interconnected world, we may get in the way of the workings of these creatures and be hurt by them. This potential for "natural evil" was present from the beginning of the creation.[55]

A Persuasive Account

I find the biblical account of suffering persuasive, then, to the extent that it does explain *much* suffering in terms of moral evil but does not attempt to explain *all* suffering in this way and does not call all suffering evil. This does leave me, of course, with the question "Why has God chosen to create precisely this *kind* of world and not some other kind?" Biblical faith does not answer this question, but it is not difficult, I believe, to come up with answers that are *congruent* with such faith. At the heart of any such answer would be the conviction that the God who is good has good purposes in creating *this* kind of world and that precisely *this* kind of world (including the possibility of evil arising within it) is the one in which God's purposes were and are going to come to fruition.[56] My main concern in this section, however, has not been to answer such a question. It has been to clarify, at the very least, that *given* that this is the kind of world that God, *in fact*, chose to create, some suffering is inevitable. A world in which suffering were not possible would not be the world that we know, and, indeed, it would not be a world that could support *life* as we know it. We cannot have the good of this world without some suffering.[57]

On Human Beings and the "Natural" World

In chapters 9 and 12, which build in turn on chapters 2 and 4, we considered what biblical faith has to say about a right human relationship with nonhuman creation. We considered the human duties of both keeping the earth and of ruling and subduing the earth, and we thought about the close connection, biblically, between people keeping and earth keeping. We also thought a little more about the difference that moral evil does, and does not, make to how creation as a whole functions and to the human relationship with creation specifically. This last theme we also pursued briefly in chapter 11. Clearly these various ideas are *coherent* with the broader biblical perspective and follow quite naturally from the ideas that the world is God's temple-cosmos and that human beings are divine image bearers placed there to look after it. Are these ideas also congruent with reality outside the text? I believe that they are.

They are, first of all, congruent with *historical reality*—with what we know of the world before human beings existed. Earlier I stated that it would be impossible to accept the biblical story as a true account of reality if it did not allow for "intrinsic suffering," including suffering that predates human existence. The suffering that arises from predation certainly comes into that category. So far as we can tell, nature has always been (as it is now) "red in tooth and claw."[58] There has always been a food chain in which there have existed carnivores and herbivores; there have always been ecological systems in which both carnivores and herbivores can live and reproduce in balance. This, too, is part of the good order of the world. Without carnivores, herbivores would reproduce until they consumed all their food sources, leading to mass starvation. Starvation is a much more painful end for a deer, in fact, than being killed and eaten by a wolf. For that matter, it is a much more painful end for a hadrosaur than being killed and eaten by a Tyrannosaurus rex, or a bison by a saber-toothed tiger—both of which deaths would have occurred (by any reasonable assessment of the evidence) well before human beings existed on the planet.[59]

The biblical ideas are also congruent, second, with the order of the world as we find it *now*. As we saw earlier, in this order of things human beings, similar in so many ways to other creatures, are nevertheless also entirely different from other creatures in many ways. Moreover, "man is the only animal that *decides* how other animals *should* be treated."[60] It is to such empirical realities that the biblical ideas correspond. As a matter of *fact*, human beings exercise dominion over the earth, and they do so because of the personhood that biblical faith describes in terms of "image bearing." As rational and moral beings, they *decide* what *should* happen. No other creature has this capacity or senses such a calling. This is simply one of the various ways in which ancient theological theory seems to correspond to experience. One does not need to be particularly "theological" to see that this is the case; it is self-evident.[61]

There is a related respect in which the biblical ideas also fit with the world as we find it now, and this has to do with the question of why things are *wrong* now. I said earlier that I find the biblical view of evil plausible. There, it was the story of man's inhumanity to *man* that I had in mind—a story of human beings aspiring to be gods and heroes rather than good neighbors. It is equally the case, however, that biblical faith roots the story of the human failure to look after *nonhuman* creation in the same aspiration. This, too, is plausible. It is the heroic ideal that has traditionally taken men out of the home and the local community and into the wider world, as they look to make a name for themselves and to leave a mark on the world. It is the heroic ideal that leads men to respond to the human lack of immortality not through "ordinary" means like fathering children but through "the pursuit of power, dominion, and (especially) glory in battle."[62] This is what it means to be godlike. It is not enough to be an ordinary, mortal man, living in one's neighborhood, loving one's neighbors (including one's wife and children), and looking after "the garden." Instead, one must go forth in pursuit of immortal fame, earned on the field of battle *or in the hunt*—which is why so many ancient kings spent so much time hunting, and recording their hunts on lavish wall reliefs in their palaces.[63] It is as human beings pursue divinity and glory in this way that creation suffers—as the egotistical desire to "leave a mark" on the world does *in fact* badly mark and scar it. Precisely because human beings are image bearers and *not* just like the other animals, they can do incalculable damage when they cease walking in God's ways and start walking in their own. Is there any question, then, that biblical faith accords in this area with reality "on the ground"? Creation suffers because human beings neglect their fundamental task to care for God's good world.

ON POLITICS

In chapters 10 and 12, we considered the question of politics: which kind of polis should I advocate for, and strive to bring into being? There, I resisted the idea that biblical politics arises directly from the biblical moral vision—that the human task is simply to build the new Jerusalem. Biblical faith (I argued) displays a pragmatic perspective when it comes to politics. It is informed in a serious way by *both* the nature of the world as we actually find it and the hope that, in the future, the world will be different than it is now.

Such an approach to politics is consistent with the biblical view of God's patient work in the world more generally, and it makes sense. First, it makes sense of a deeply rooted human instinct that our political lives, as well as our personal lives, ought to be lived in accordance with some greater pattern in the nature of things. It makes sense of the notion that there is right and there is wrong and that we ought to conform ourselves to what is right. There are other accounts of right and wrong that do *not* make sense. Most notably, there is the view that right and wrong do not exist as objective realities. On this view, "right" and "wrong" refer only to the customs of society, and they are entirely constructed *by* society. They correspond neither to nature nor to the character of God. Yet while such a view is widely held in theory, it is not so commonly practiced. I observe, for example, that when people accuse others (often with great passion) of wrongdoing, they typically appear to be claiming much more than that certain social proprieties have been breached. Their cry is not that "killing that child breached some of our social conventions" but that "killing that child was *wrong*." The language we typically use in such cases indicates a belief that individual and political life *ought* to be lived in accordance with some greater pattern of things. Many people intuitively understand this. Historically, even those who have been convinced that the Old Story must be displaced from a dominant position in political life have often, nevertheless, accepted that the polis must be built upon *some* greater pattern. This includes important philosophers like Jean-Jacques Rousseau and Immanuel Kant.[64]

The biblical approach to politics makes sense to me, second, because, while it presses toward moral ideals in this way, it also takes account of reality on the ground. It takes account of limitations in human wisdom and virtue, and it takes account of outright moral failure. The biblical approach is not utopian. I am persuaded that this resistance to a utopian approach to the polis is right and that it is rooted in a sound assessment of human nature. History itself teaches me to be suspicious of utopian politics, regardless of whether they are directly rooted in religion. When and where people who adopt such approaches to the polis have gained sufficient power to enact their utopian plans, great suffering among their subjects has typically resulted. Noble ideals have often lain at the heart of such plans, but they have foundered on the rocks of human reality—including the reality that power corrupts even the well intentioned. There are famous, overtly religious examples of this phenomenon, such as what happened in sixteenth-century Münster, Germany, when some radical Anabaptists proclaimed that city to *be* the new Jerusalem.[65] There are also famous nonreligious examples, such as what happened in eighteenth-century revolutionary France or in twentieth-century postrevolutionary Russia and China.[66] People set out to change the world and to bring in "the kingdom of God" or its secular equivalent, and they *did* change the world, but not necessarily for the better. It was precisely some of the bloodshed and chaos resulting from these various utopian endeavors, specifically in the post-Reformation period in the sixteenth century, that caused the thoroughgoing reassessment of the role played by the Old Story in European politics that I mentioned just a moment ago—and it was right for this reassessment to be demanded.

I am drawn, then, to a politics that grounds itself in a vision of the kingdom of God, while taking proper account of the limitations that are placed on the attainment of that kingdom in our present time. I find deeply plausible a politics that insists that political life (as well as individual life) *ought* to be lived in accordance with some greater pattern of things, while urging caution and wisdom in how, and how quickly, that pattern is given political expression. Caution and wisdom are particularly necessary given the reality that there may well be principled disagreement *within the polis* about the precise nature of the vision that is to be pursued. Utopian politics must always ride roughshod over such disagreement in pursuit of absolute conformity to the beliefs about the Good of those who possess the power. Pragmatic politics, however, recognizes the need for negotiation. For the common good, it seeks to preserve legitimate "space" between the moral vision and the political reality and, indeed, between freedom of action and coercion. Caution and wisdom are also necessary because there is no political *system*, as such, that is not capable of foundering on human reality—including the reality that power corrupts even the well intentioned. All political systems are capable of failing those who most need them to succeed—those for whom the ideology or theology informing any particular system is, in fact, of little relevance. As Gandhi once asked,

> What difference does it make to the dead, the orphans, and the homeless, whether the mad destruction is wrought under the name of totalitarianism or the holy name of liberty or democracy?[67]

ON HOPE

In chapters 11 and 12 we discussed the hope of a better world that, in part, drives a biblical politics. In biblical faith, we noted, hope is bound up with the story of the cosmos right from the beginning. The Old Story has always been a story that is going somewhere, and the "somewhere" has always been better than what we know about now.

The plausibility of biblical hope is bound up, I think, with the plausibility of the other aspects of biblical faith that we have been exploring in this book and in this chapter. If indeed we are caught up in a Story (as I think we are) and if the Story has at its heart a finely tuned universe created by a good Storyteller who has very specific goals in mind in his storytelling (which I think it does), then the idea that the Story has a happy ending that still *involves* a carefully constructed universe is certainly not incredible. Indeed, if we *have been* created as physical beings destined for immortality, it is not incredible that the happy ending *involves* embodied immortality. If the death of the Son of God was *followed* by a resurrection, then it is not incredible that we ourselves might attain our immortality *through* a resurrection. The truly incredible thing would actually be if the Story, with all of its beauty and order, goodness and love, attention to detail, and all of its diversity and apparent purpose, were found to be going *nowhere*. The truly incredible thing would be if all our self-denial in pursuit of the common good, all our self-sacrifice on behalf of our fellow creatures, all our patient suffering in the hope of relief, and all our efforts to make things better were to meet (finally) with no reward. The truly incredible thing would be if all the love we pour out on others throughout our lives and all the wisdom that we gain in the process of living were to have no continuing reality or purpose.

I believe that the minds and hearts of most human beings intuitively reject such incredible ideas. It requires considerable repression of our intuition, in fact, to make them appear plausible. We are "wired" for happy endings, in which good overcomes evil, just people are rewarded and wicked people are punished, the goods of the world are fairly distributed, and what is dead comes to life again. Many of the stories that human beings have told through the ages, and still tell (whether in books or in movies or in some other medium), reveal the extent to which this is the case. We are wired for hope, just as we are wired for worship and thanksgiving. We aspire to "live happily ever after." In a 1939 lecture delivered at the University of St. Andrews in Scotland, J. R. R. Tolkien, with whom we began our reflections in this book, employed the term "eucatastrophe" to refer to the way that so many of our human stories *give* us such an ending.[68] The Greek prefix *eu* (as in "utopia") means "good"; a "eucatastrophe" is a sudden turn toward the good. Tolkien proposed that the biblical story essentially weaves various threads of eucatastrophe found in other, smaller stories into one large Story:

> The Gospels contain a fairy story, or a story of a larger kind which embraces all the essence of fairy stories . . . , and among the marvels is the greatest and most complete conceivable

eucatastrophe. . . . The Birth of Christ is the eucatastrophe of Man's history. The Resurrection is the eucatastrophe of the story of the Incarnation. This story begins and ends in joy. It has preeminently the "inner consistency of reality." There is no tale ever told that men would rather find was true, and none which so many skeptical men have accepted as true on its own merits. For the Art of it has the supremely convincing tone of Primary Art, that is, of Creation. To reject it leads either to sadness or to wrath. . . . Art has been verified. God is the Lord, of angels, and of men—and of elves. Legend and History have met and fused.[69]

What other stories hint at, says Tolkien, the Old Story—the True Story—articulates fully.

Biblical hope is plausible, I suggest, even if it speaks of things that are astonishing. It is a hope that reason can offer justification for embracing. It is not the hope of which Greek tragedy speaks. Greek tragedy describes Prometheus, before he gives human beings the gift of fire, as providing them with "blind hopes" that keep them "from being preoccupied with death" and free them "from gloom about the future."[70] Biblical hope is not, however, blind hope, any more than biblical faith is blind faith. It is not hope that is embraced against the evidence just because it "carries us on pleasantly to the end of life."[71] It is, instead, hope with its eyes wide open.

14

RISK ASSESSMENT

Is the Story Dangerous?

A creed can only be absolute in its historical existence, not
universally valid for all. . . . The claim to exclusive possession of
truth, that tool of fanaticism, of human arrogance and
self-deception through the will to power, that disaster for
the West . . . can be vanquished by the very fact that God has
manifested himself historically in several fashions and has
opened up many ways toward Himself.

Karl Jaspers[1]

A prudent man sees danger and takes refuge,
but the simple keep going and suffer for it.

Proverbs 22:3

I have argued in chapter 13 that the biblical story about how the world
came to be, what the human place in it is, and how we should live here
is plausible. Is it at the same time dangerous? As the biblical book of
Proverbs observes, a prudent person will always want to avoid danger.
Is there danger, then, in biblical faith, from which we might wish to
"take refuge," rather than "keep going and suffer for it"? My argument
in this chapter, in brief, will be as follows: there is *some* danger, but not

of the kind that people often imagine. Biblical faith is dangerous only in promoting the good.

ON GOD AND THE WORLD

Biblical faith insists on the devotion of the whole person to the one creator God (Deuteronomy 6:4-5; John 14:6), and it is routinely claimed nowadays that this *is* dangerous—that it leads inevitably to narrowness of thought, dogmatism, violence, and even war. This is certainly what proponents of the axial age hypothesis have typically believed; Karl Jaspers invented this "age" precisely to counter this perceived threat. As the quotation in our first epigraph reminds us, he was convinced that human beings need a larger and more generous story than the biblical one, which he connected directly with the barbarism and the dark passions of his own period of history (mid-twentieth-century Germany). We need a story, he claimed, with which *all* human beings can identify, whatever their own traditions might be.[2] Likewise, the proponents of dark green religion, who tend to be hostile toward monotheistic religion in general and favor instead a "preaxial" spirituality that is local and pluralistic, have been forthright on the dangerous nature of the biblical story. They associate monotheism, and especially Christian monotheism, with imperial agriculture, authoritarian nationalism, violence, bigotry, and anthropocentrism (and thus the rape of the planet). For Derrick Jensen, for example, biblical faith legitimates the conquest of all other cultures *and* the planet. Beyond these two groups of critics, we find Marc Ellis arguing that "monotheistic religions . . . are born in a cycle of violence" and that violence inevitably continues within them and between them.[3] We also find Regina Schwartz writing a book that concerns, as her subtitle tells us, "the violent legacy of monotheism" and advocates a return to the pluralism that monotheism has suppressed.[4] Just how far such ideas have taken root in popular, post-Christian, Western culture can easily be gauged simply by carrying out an Internet search for the phrase "Christianity is dangerous."

The Character of God

Is the biblical view of God dangerous, then? At least two things must be said in response to this kind of claim. It seems to me, first of all, that it is not belief in the *oneness* of God that, of itself, results in the terrible things that monotheism's detractors associate with it. Rather, it is a particular view of the *character* of the one God and what this means for how I should live—what this one God's *will* is. For example, if the one God is not "for" *all* creatures, but only "for" human beings, and he wills that I should live in a manner consistent with this "truth," then it may well be that nonhuman creation will suffer. Again, if the one God is not "for" *all* human beings, but only "for" me and my tribe or my state, and he wills that I should live in a manner consistent with *this* "truth," then bigotry and violence toward other human beings may well follow. If, however, the one God is the kind of person that I have described in this book, such consequences do not *at all* follow. In this case, I find myself obliged to imitate a God who is generous to all of his image bearers, and who cares for all of his creatures, human or not. I am obliged to "keep" both neighbor and garden. In this case, belief in the one God is the very thing that will *forbid* me from living as an authoritarian nationalist, a violent bigot, or a planetary rapist.

Historically, it is belief in *this* one God that has, *in fact*, prevented many believers from taking such perverse paths. These believers have not, *in fact*, read their Bibles in the way that Regina Schwartz reads hers. They have read it, fundamentally, in the way that I read mine. If anyone doubts that this is so, I fear that they have not made it their business to become acquainted with the facts of history; they have opted instead for hearing about them only secondhand, from others. Indeed, one of the tiresome routines that often accompanies the condemnation of biblical faith nowadays is the rehearsal of various carefully selected, and often not well understood, "facts" of history that are said to "prove" its dangerous nature. It is not difficult, of course, to find instances in the past where people claiming to possess biblical faith have indeed erred, sometimes grievously and with terrible consequences. The contemporary enthusiasm for identifying such abuses is unfortunately not typically accompanied by any evident desire to publicize the various ways in which biblical faith, conversely, has shaped the world very much for the better. In fact, the enthusiasts appear all too often to be entirely ignorant of such realities, even though there are many books that provide excellent access to them.[5]

A case in point is the way in which the medieval European "Crusades" (1095–1291) are often deployed in assaults on biblical faith, as writers seek to catalog all the many instances of "the grievous harm religion has inflicted on society, from the Crusades to 9/11" (as the book jacket to Richard Dawkins' *The God Delusion* puts it). On the one hand, the assailants often display woeful levels of ignorance about the Crusades themselves, which Rodney Stark has recently undertaken to address in his book, *God's Battalions: The Case for the Crusades.*[6] They typically appear to be unaware, on the other hand, of the extent to which, for many Christians in medieval times, involvement in military conflict was not their chosen manner of response to Islam. These writers do not tell their readers about Francis of Assisi, for example, who in the course of the fifth Crusade visited the camp of Malik al-Kamil, the sultan of Egypt not to try to kill him but to talk to him.[7] Perhaps overinfluenced by a "clash of civilizations" model of Islamic-Christian relations, the critics do not typically remind their readers, either, that during the period of the Crusades there were still large indigenous Christian populations living under Muslim rule not just in Palestine but in many other places as well.[8] *Their* biblical monotheism was not innately dangerous to others. Indeed, there were periods prior to the eleventh century during which Christians were well integrated into the social fabric of politically Muslim societies. The case of the ninth-century Nestorian Patriarch Timothy, an Arabic-speaking Christian living in Baghdad, the seat of the Abbasid Caliphate (750–1258), illustrates the point. Of Timothy, Philip Jenkins says,

> [He] lived in a universe that was culturally and spiritually Christian, but politically Muslim, and he coped quite comfortably with that situation. As faithful subjects, the patriarch and his clergy prayed for the caliph and his family. The catholicos [head of the church] was a key figure at the court of the Muslim caliph.[9]

The Character of the "Gods"

Just as belief in the one God of biblical faith, as such, is not the problem at the heart of what is wrong with the world, so too (second) the abandonment of this belief is far from being the solution. As Walter Moberly says of Regina Schwartz's perspective in particular,

> One can readily understand—even sympathize—with Schwartz's dislike of aspects of our world. But whether the remedy is to see them as rooted in the Bible, and escapable if only one could truly break free from the Bible's lingering influence, raises basic issues about one's worldview and how one forms it.

. . . Getting rid of talk of the Bible and talk of God will not solve the problems.[10]

By way of example, people inflicted violence on their neighbors and displayed a lack of care for the environment long before the rise of monotheistic religion. Murder, as Lawrence Weschler so perceptively put it in a 1997 review of Schwartz's book,

> has found many other traveling companions besides monotheism. Pagans—whether Homeric Greeks or Vedic Aryans—weren't exactly slouches at constructing transcendental rationales for their earthly depredations. When it comes to genocidal mayhem, surely the Iliad and the Mahabharata can match Exodus blow for blow.[11]

Violence is as old as the human race. Likewise, we should dismiss the romantic and false idea that, before there was monotheism, there was ecological sensitivity and care. There is no reason at all to believe that ancient, nonmonotheistic peoples were any more capable than we are of living within the population carrying capacity of their environments and not damaging the earth or its various animal populations. In fact, Thomas Neumann (writing in particular of American, precontact native peoples) suggests that it is

> important to surrender the image of the aboriginal peoples living in idyllic harmony with host ecological systems, at least if by that is meant living in a way that conformed to current notions of ecological propriety.[12]

Writing of the *modern* native peoples who are often used by scholars as the basis for reconstructing what the distant native *past* "must" have been like, Michael Alvard says that

> the appearance of balance between traditional native groups and their environment has more to do with low human population densities, lack of markets, and limited technology than it does with any natural harmonious relationship with nature.[13]

The problems of violence and lack of care for the environment long predate the rise of monotheistic religion. They have also *remained* problems long after monotheistic religions have largely been rejected, as the history of the bloody and polluted twentieth century graphically illustrates. Indeed, as alternative beliefs have come to predominate, and the *constraints* provided by belief in one God to whom all people are accountable have been removed, these problems have become *worse* than they were before. Among these, we may mention a growing belief in the absolute supremacy of the nation-state or "the people"—a belief that arises when the state/people is no longer regarded as accountable to God.[14] That is a belief that is not merely *allegedly* but *genuinely* dangerous.[15] Consider, also, the characters in ancient texts capable of being considered as appropriate role models, once people have decided no longer to imitate the one God of the Bible. One alternative, for example, is the heroic warrior Arjuna from the *Mahabharata*—a sacred text within the *pluralistic* Hindu tradition, which tells stories of "the heroes of old who provide models for the Hindu way of life."[16] Heinrich Himmler, the man responsible in the German Third Reich for implementing the Final Solution with respect to inferior, non-Aryan races, was significantly influenced by Hinduism in various ways, and he once told his chiropractor Felix Kersten that he always carried with him a copy of one of the *Mahabharata*'s chapters, the *Bhagavad Gita*. In this chapter, Arjuna is reluctant to fight on the battlefield, because it will cause great suffering. However, the god Vishnu (in the form of Krishna) urges Arjuna to overcome his reluctance. Arjuna must remember (Vishnu tells him) that it is the atman (soul) that is important, and not the body. He must get on with his duty, which is to kill, while remaining emotionally detached from his actions and thus remaining at peace. Himmler viewed himself very much in the same way: as a man with caste duties to perform, in the larger context of the karma that belonged to the Germanic peoples as a whole—a man who must set aside sentiment and emotion in pursuit of those duties. "Performance of duty detached from passion was indeed what he continually sought from his staff at the death camps."[17]

The French philosopher Jean-Jacques Rousseau believed that "human beings living in society cannot remain moral for long without understanding how their actions relate to something higher than themselves."[18] The case of Heinrich Himmler reminds us, however, that our very definition of "moral" is intrinsically bound up with what we believe to be *true* about what is "higher" than ourselves. Himmler's "god" was a god who justified unspeakable atrocities, and this particular case well illustrates my general point. Belief in the one God of biblical faith is not, as such, the problem that lies at the heart of the human condition, nor is the abandonment of this belief, as such, the solution.

ON HUMANITY

Is the biblical view of *humanity* dangerous, then? Certainly it is. It is dangerous to anyone who does not wish to think of every other human being as their image bearing "neighbor" or to love him or her as such (chap. 8). It is dangerous, for example, to everyone who wishes to "assimilate man without remainder to the rest of nature," insisting that (after all) there is nothing very special about human beings as a class, and certainly not as individuals.[19] Biblical faith is also dangerous to those who have become confused about where the boundaries between science and philosophy lie and who think that because human beings are, in some sense, products of a great evolutionary struggle in which only the fittest survive, society itself should be organized on that same basis.[20] Biblical faith is dangerous, moreover, to those among the powerful who would like to be left alone to use and oppress the weak and to those among the rich who would like to be left alone to use and oppress the poor. Such faith threatens all those for whom the current social order is everything or for whom individual human beings are merely dispensable flotsam and jetsam on the great sea of inevitable social change. It challenges every "ends justifies the means" and every "greatest good" argument. It confronts any idea that anyone is too young or too old, too black or too white, too sick, too different, or too foreign to have the same rights as everyone else, including the right to life. It opposes any diminution of the importance of the individual person out of regard for the convenience of other family members, the health of the economy, the good of the state, or the well-being of the planet. The biblical idea about the human being is, in truth, *very* dangerous.

Self-Evident Rights?

The danger that lies at the heart of this revolutionary idea does not worry me at all, however. I am much more concerned about the danger that lies in the erosion of it. Many in the post-Christian, Western world appear to believe that it is self-evident that "human rights" should be accorded to human beings. There is, however, nothing self-evident about it—as history reveals to anyone who pays it serious attention. Every anthropology, I must again assert, is bound up with a cosmology and a theology. Therefore, my view of what a human being *is* and what her *rights* might be is inevitably bound up with the much larger set of convictions I hold about the nature of the world and of God. What is often thought of as the "Western" view of human rights is intrinsically connected with the Story that has historically shaped Western culture—the story in which all human beings, from conception to the grave, are image bearers of God. Such a view of human rights did not mark the ancient Near Eastern environment out of which this Story emerged or the Greco-Roman environment in which it developed into its fuller shape.[21] Nor has this view of human rights dominated in other great civilizations, like those in India or China.[22] Moreover, this same "Western" view has been progressively *abandoned* in the West (rather than merely inconsistently held) as this or that nation-state has abandoned the Old Story. One need only cite many of the actions of both the German and the Russian states, their armed forces, and many of their citizens before, during, and immediately after the Second World War to establish the point. We do not find in these many actions any great regard for human rights, and this is entirely predictable given the nature of the governing metanarratives in Russia and Germany at that time. The prevailing metnarratives did not provide any *basis* for universal human rights.

The Erosion of Rights

It is not surprising, then (although it is still shocking), that even in the contemporary Western states that so bitterly opposed either the German or the Russian states (or both) throughout much of the twentieth century, we should now be seeing a similar erosion of the biblical idea of the human being. This phenomenon, in countries like the United Kingdom, the Netherlands, and Canada, is directly related to the erosion of the Old Story in these countries. Human life is becoming cheaper. Life in the womb is very cheap indeed, and it is routinely traded off against the convenience, or merely the wishes, of the parents.[23] Life at the other end of the spectrum is also becoming cheaper, as legal means have been created to allow people easily to end their own lives, if they wish, and to allow others to help them. Who is really doing the "wishing" is, of course, a serious question. There is ample opportunity, in such situations, for pressure to be brought to bear on the elderly by family members, medical professionals, and ultimately the resource-poor state, so that the elderly conveniently "wish" in the "correct" direction.[24] The disabled also experience this pressure:

> I've lived so close to death for so long that I know how thin and porous the border between coercion and free choice is, how easy it is for someone to inadvertently influence you to feel devalued and hopeless—to pressure you ever so slightly but decidedly into being "reasonable," to unburdening others, to "letting go." Perhaps, as advocates contend, you can't understand why anyone would push for assisted-suicide legislation until you've seen a loved one suffer. But you also can't truly conceive of the many subtle forces—invariably well meaning, kindhearted, even gentle, yet as persuasive as a tsunami—that emerge when your physical autonomy is hopelessly compromised.[25]

Since these attitudes to abortion and suicide represent nothing other than a return to a pre-Christian, Stoic view of humanity, it is not surprising that we are also seeing, now, serious public discussion as to whether infanticide (the killing of young children) is really so wrong.[26] The Stoics considered infanticide to be entirely unproblematic. In sum: in the post-Christian West, the right to life is evidently deeply in question at present. The questioning of other rights has already begun, and more questioning cannot be far behind.[27] It is inevitable that this should be so, because the foundation upon which the rights have been built has been eroded. People need a good reason to respect other people as genuine equals, especially when it is against their own interests to do so. Vague unease about treating others badly, or about other people treating them badly, will not suffice for more than a short time in preserving rights. As G. K. Chesterton once put it in relation to his own contemporaries,

> Many of them held, and still hold, very noble and necessary truths in the social and secular area. But even these it seemed to me they held less firmly than they might have done, if there had been anything like a fundamental principle of morals and metaphysics to support them. . . . Their hearts were in the right place; but their heads were emphatically in the wrong place.[28]

People need a good reason to respect other people as genuine equals and to protect their rights. For those who hold to biblical faith, *this* is the "good reason": "God created man in his own image, in the image of God he created him; male and female he created them." Strip away this foundation, and what exactly remains as the "reason"?

ON EVIL AND SUFFERING

The third question I want to address in this chapter is this: Is the biblical account of evil and suffering dangerous? On the contrary, I assert, sharing biblical convictions about such matters has certainly led many people to embrace a way of life that is unquestionably good. It *must* lead them in such a direction, I believe. As we saw in chapters 6, 8, and 12, those who seriously follow a biblical pathway through life must be realistic about the existence and the nature of evil, and about just how deeply compromised the world is by it. Yet they cannot be fatalistic about it. They must resist evil and oppose it wherever they find it. They must do this patiently over the long term, understanding that the triumph of good over evil is not easily or quickly achieved. They must do it prayerfully and dependently upon God, recognizing the extent to which the problem is actually far too large for them—the extent to which, as Felix Adler puts it, "We stand, as it were, on the shore, and see multitudes of our fellow beings struggling in the water, stretching forth their arms, sinking, drowning, and we are powerless to assist them."[29] Seriously biblical people must do all this while displaying great compassion and while offering friendship, neighbor-love, and help to others who suffer (including their enemies). They must do it all hopefully, trusting that God's good purposes for the world will indeed, one day, come to fruition. They recognize, with Abraham Heschel, that

> a religious man is a person who holds God and man in one thought at one time, at all times, who suffers harm done to others, whose greatest passion is compassion, whose greatest strength is love and defiance of despair.[30]

They *recognize* this, and, however imperfectly, they *practice* this kind of religion. No one could possibly do otherwise who has genuinely come to understand God and the world in the way that biblical faith understands them.

I ask, then, How could *this* perspective on our (necessary) human response to evil and suffering possibly be seen as dangerous? I do not personally believe it to be dangerous at all, except (of course) to those who promote and benefit from evil and suffering. However, I *do* think that some of the *competing* accounts of evil and suffering that we considered in chapters 5 and 6 are dangerous.

Fatal Fatalism

They are dangerous, first, insofar as they encourage a fatalistic approach to evil and suffering. Whereas biblical faith urges us to make *this world* a better place, some of these competing accounts encourage us to depart from this world and to strive to enter *another world* that is already better. This makes Plato and Plotinus dangerous; it makes Hinduism and Buddhism dangerous as well. As we saw in chapters 6 and 8, such philosophies encourage significant passivity in our approach to the ills of the world, and they discourage the active alleviation of suffering in it. They are fatalistic with respect to the world at large, even if they are not entirely fatalistic with respect to what individuals can achieve in their own lives. It is, of course, understandable that people looking at our often massively suffering world might be *tempted* to try to escape it, rather than seek its transformation. Who has not been tempted to fatalism? Who has not been tempted to despair? Yet, in the biblical way of thinking, it is inexcusable to succumb to such temptations—not least because it leaves those who are suffering exactly where they presently are, and it leaves unchallenged the evil that *causes* their suffering.

Alarming Amorality

The competing accounts are dangerous, second, insofar as they question the objective reality of good and evil. Daoism, for example, urges us to reject this distinction as artificial and, following our intuitions, to get in harmony with the eternal dao that is the sacred principle immanent in nature. Evil is only that which resists pure nature—that which prevents us from experiencing the natural rhythms of the universe itself. How do we get in harmony with the dao? We must practice weakness and passivity and live spontaneously, without rules and plans, in response to its various movements. A modern proponent of such a view in the West is Hans-Georg Moeller, a specialist in Chinese philosophy. Writing in the conclusion to his book *The Moral Fool*, and while conceding that "it is probably neither possible nor desirable to be a complete moral fool as envisioned by some Daoists," Moeller writes as follows:

But I think it is quite possible, natural, and healthy to be an imperfect [fool], someone who, most of the time, does not really believe that she knows what is really good or bad, and who does not even use such terms in an absolute sense.[31]

This relativist approach to good and evil, he believes, is much safer than an absolutist one. Earlier in the book, in fact, Moeller offers his opinion that "morality—or ethics—can be dangerous."[32] My response is this: whatever dangers lie in morality, they surely pale into insignificance when compared with the dangers of amorality. Who in their right mind would wish their family, their community, or their state to be run by people living spontaneously without rules and plans, and following only their intuitions about what is "natural"? Who in their right mind would wish such a person to have *any* power or responsibility with respect to themselves, or those they love? This is especially so when what is "natural" is such a disputed matter and when it is so unclear why what is *descriptively* natural should have any kind of *prescriptive* impact on how we live. Leon Kass gets to the heart of the matter:

Not only is nature silent about right and justice; [but] absolutely no moral rules can be deduced from even the fullest understanding of nature. . . . The cosmos can have nothing at all to say or teach about all the important questions of human beings *living with other human beings*.[33]

In other words, even if we are really clear (which we are not) about what "is," we cannot move directly from what "is" (in nature) to what we "ought" to do (as human beings). It is a dangerous delusion to think otherwise, and when these kinds of ideas have been taken seriously in human history, they have only ever caused significant suffering to human persons and societies, not to mention the rest of creation.

Who is more dangerous, then? Is it the person who "suffers harm done to others, whose greatest passion is compassion, whose greatest strength is love and defiance of despair" (Abraham Heschel)—the person who holds that good and evil are not simply conventions of human speech but words that refer to objective realities? Or is it the person who "does not really believe that she knows what is really good or bad, and who does not even use such terms in an absolute sense" (Hans-Georg Moeller) but simply "goes with the flow"?

Perilous Naïvety

The "big stories" about evil and suffering that compete with the Old Story are dangerous, finally, insofar as they underestimate the power of evil and its depths. In my estimation, this is true of both Confucianism and Islam. We recall that these two perspectives on life, the universe, and everything share an optimistic view of the human capacity for self-transformation. What is wrong with the world can be put right, in Confucius' teaching, by good education and then by putting such education into practice. Man is not much "broken," on this view, and he does not need God to "mend" him in any way. He can and must mend himself, and it is not very difficult to do this. Islam takes a similar view, although it is a genuinely theistic philosophy in a way that classical Confucianism is not. Human beings should (and can) gain right knowledge of Allah, and then they should submit to him. This brings about a complete transformation in human life. The path is difficult neither to find nor to follow.

For my own part, I believe that such views display a perilous naïvety about evil and about what needs to be done to overcome it. Right knowledge, of itself, *evidently* does not bring about moral transformation in human beings—even supposing that right knowledge is something we are predisposed to desire in the first place.[34] It is possible to be highly educated and at the same time morally depraved. There is, in fact, a certain kind of moral depravity that only the highly educated can attain, because it requires sophisticated skills of rationalization and self-deception. Both Confucianism and Islam, however, place a high degree of confidence in education as a solution to the problem of evil. If you know what is good, you will do it. It is not surprising, perhaps, that there should be such confidence, since both philosophies are premised on an understanding of the good that is far more limited than biblical faith suggests it ought to be. They consider the good to be achievable because they begin with a narrow idea of what it entails. This is clear in the Confucian idea that what is required of human beings is only a return to some ancient Chinese attitudes and customs. It reveals itself also in the Islamic idea that "God does not require anything of us that is beyond our capabilities."[35] Since the good is so narrowly defined, there is (correspondingly) no robust understanding of evil—the absence of the good—or of the difficulty involved in conquering it.

If, however, one accepts the strenuous demands of biblical faith concerning love of God, our neighbor, and planet as defining the good—as the genuine moral imperatives that are laid upon us—and if one measures what is evil against those standards, then one is bound to find the Confucian and Islamic perspectives problematic. One is bound to think, *then*, that it is *well* beyond our capabilities to be good and that the belief that we can save ourselves from evil is, in fact, a dangerous delusion. This is especially the case when we consider the huge question of what is to be done, in the presence of a good God, about all the evil in which we have *already* participated, even *before* we turned back to the right path. Is that evil really so trivial that it can simply be swept under the rug, now that we have decided to turn in a different direction? In short, the adherent of biblical faith is bound to find unconvincing any proposal about solving the problem of evil and suffering that does not include the idea of atonement—of making right what is wrong.

On Human Beings and the "Natural" World

Our fourth question is this: Is it dangerous to understand in a biblical way the human role with respect to nonhuman creation? The proponents of dark green religion certainly think so. For them, biblical thinking on this topic is an example of "Abrahamic anthropocentrism, which . . . separate[s] humans from nature."[36] It is one aspect of "the religions of imperial agricultures, whether Abrahamic or Vedic," all of which fail to promote "feelings of reverence toward and belonging to nature."[37] For them, both "the humanist concept of sustainable development and the Christian concept of stewardship are flawed by unconscious hubris."[38] Biblical faith is typical of "the world's dominant religions . . . [which] promote and justify violence, bigotry, and anthropocentrism and focus 'exclusively on the superiority and divinity of the human species.'"[39]

Foolish Generalizations

If this book accomplishes anything worthwhile among its readership, I fervently hope that among its accomplishments will be a decrease in the number of foolish, sweeping generalizations about religion of the kind I have just cited. It helps clarity of thought not one bit when words like "Abrahamic" and phrases like "Abrahamic or Vedic" and "the world's dominant religions" are tossed around in such ways. It simply contributes to preventing people from seeing what is actually there, in specific, individual religious traditions. I, for one, see no danger in biblical faith of the kind that the critics commonly identify—*when I consider what the biblical tradition actually says*. I see no danger precisely because I do not understand the "anthropocentrism" of this tradition as separating human beings from nature. I do not understand it as failing to promote "feelings of reverence toward and belonging to nature." I do not think that it *does* focus exclusively "on the superiority and divinity of the human species." These are all simply mistakes of reading. On the contrary, I read the Old Story as obliging me to imitate the God who is generous to all of his creatures and to look after *his* garden as I *should*, as his image bearer. There is no hubris in this. There is only a deep sense of responsibility, rooted both in the Story itself and in my sense of the facts on the ground. The facts on the ground are these: that as a human being, I can impact the natural world either for good or for evil. The one choice that is not open to me is *not to impact it at all*. If the Old Story *is* dangerous, it is not dangerous to nonhuman creation but only to those who do not want to acknowledge any human *responsibility* for nonhuman creation and would like to be able to treat it simply as "product" with which human beings can do as they please.

A Necessary Foundation

Not only do I disagree that the biblical Story represents a danger to the "natural" world, I actually believe that something very much like this Story is required as a necessary *foundation* for the care of that world. It is not just the protection of *human* rights that requires such a foundation; it is also the protection of the rights *of the rest of creation*. People need a good reason not only to respect other people as genuine equals but also to accept genuine responsibility for nonhuman creation— especially when it is against their own interests to do so. Vague unease about treating creation badly will not suffice, nor will arguments about our long-term and general interests, especially when we have pressing short-term and particular needs—when the economic realities of today loom much larger in the mind than the predicted environmental realities of tomorrow. There need to be *reasons* for creation-care, and they need to be compelling—rooted in a story that people hold to be absolutely true. This is what Thomas Berry acknowledges when he tells us that we need "a story that will educate us, a story that will heal, guide, and discipline us."[40]

Where is this story to be found? Is it to be found in the various nonbiblical traditions discussed toward the end of chapter 9? Will it be found in traditions with an escapist bent, like Platonism or Hinduism, or more world-affirming ones like Islam or in a modernist ideology like Francis Bacon's? I profoundly doubt it. So, it seems, do many dark green religionists; they prefer, like Thomas Berry, a *new* story. The problem is that the new story that dark green religionists tell is patently untrue. There never was an Eden-like, dark green golden age in the Paleolithic period of human history, as they imagine. There never was an era prior to the rise of civilization that was marked by peace, equality, and ecological wisdom. This is a myth—a story that is not true. Stories that are untrue cannot ultimately help us, even if (like the stories told to children about monsters under the bed) they may be capable for a short while of altering our thinking and behavior.[41]

So where is the story to be found that will "educate us . . . heal, guide, and discipline us"? I humbly beg to differ with Thomas Berry in his dismissal of the Old Story and his advocacy of the new. I think that the Old Story is precisely the sort of story that we need. This Story gives me very good reasons to be an ordinary mortal being, living in family and community, rather than a hero or a god looking to leave my mark on the world. It tells me, indeed, that it is *only* as I live in this ordinary way that I shall inherit the immortality I may be seeking—*only* as I refuse to regard myself as divine and insist instead on doing my duty as an earth keeper (working and taking care of God's garden) and also as a ruler (looking after the welfare of my subjects and ensuring justice for all).[42] This demanding vocation, I must recognize, is greatly complicated by the human embrace of evil, which even in the best-case scenario disables the human community from properly carrying out its divinely sanctioned tasks in creation. At worst, it leads human beings to declare war on creation. The Story is realistic about such things, and transparently so. Yet from the perspective of biblical faith, it remains my task, nevertheless, actively to pursue my image bearing vocation. The Story is realistic but also idealistic, and persistently so.

It is this kind of Story, I believe, that we need to inhabit if we are to "save the planet"—not least because it makes *equally* strenuous demands upon us *both* to love our human neighbors *and* to love the nonhuman creation. Dark green religionists are quite right to draw attention to the ways in which imperatives about the latter have often been ignored. There *is* such a thing as a humanism that is not very "green." However, it is not difficult to find "green" approaches to the world, both historically and in the present moment, that are profoundly nonhumanist and are even disturbingly casual (at best) about human rights and interests.[43] It is not much of an improvement in the overall state of things, I suggest, if a lack of love for nonhuman creation is simply replaced with a lack of love for its human population. We need to hold together love of neighbor and love of creation. That is, indeed, what the Old Story demands of us.

ON POLITICS

Fifth, is a biblical *politics* dangerous? It certainly is to at least three groups of people, because in various ways it undermines their own "stories."

Hostile to the Status Quo

The first group comprises those who either do not wish to change society at all or do not wish to change it very much. They may or may not possess what Shmuel Eisenstadt refers to as a "transcendental vision" (chapter 10), but if they do, they do not view the *political* arena as the primary arena in which the vision should be realized. Their stories do not require much (if anything) in the way of political activism. This results in either a *principled* passivity (Hinduism) or *relative* passivity (Confucianism) in respect to the polis. A *biblical* politics challenges both the passive stance and the truthfulness of the stories that justify it. Biblical faith proposes that we *should* all be participating, as far as we reasonably can, in the reconstruction of the mundane, political world in the light of the larger biblical vision of the kingdom of God. Biblical faith is, therefore, dangerous to the passive. For myself, I am not very concerned about this fact, because I believe that the passive approach to politics that biblical faith confronts is far *more* dangerous. Indeed, I believe that it would be a very good thing if the moral vision offered by the Bible, as I have described it in this book, were to make even more of an impact on Indian and Chinese societies than it already has—if the biblical view of humanness (for example) informed politics in these and other societies much more significantly than it already does. It is a genuinely dangerous politics, I believe, that offers so little to those at the bottom of the caste system in India or allows such a casual attitude to human rights as we find in modern China. A biblical politics, conversely, has resulted historically in huge (and beneficial) social changes in the societies where it has been seriously embraced. It will always impel to such transformation all those who take it seriously.[44]

Hostile to Utopia

The second group to whom a biblical politics is dangerous comprises the utopians, of whichever ideological stripe they might be. This would include those who still pursue a Marxist-Leninist vision of the world and look for radical change, at any cost, to bring about conformity in society to that vision. It would also include people of a deeply capitalist and right-wing persuasion, such as the Christian Reconstructionists presently found in significant numbers in the United States, who would like to see the government of that country operate in submission to biblical moral principles and law.[45] It would certainly also include Islamists, for whom (we recall from chapter 10) "it is the task of the Islamic state to enforce obedience to the revealed law of Islam—the Shari'a."[46] On this view, Muslims are to found the Islamic state in every possible location, because all people in all times and places are called to submit to the timeless manifestation of the will of God that is the Shari'a. All such utopians stand at the opposite end of the political spectrum to the passive types. They possess a transcendental vision (although, in the case of Marxist-Leninism, no gods are involved), and they are determined to reconstruct the mundane, political world on the basis of that vision, closing the gap between vision and reality as quickly as possible.

A biblical politics again challenges both the stance and the truthfulness of the stories that justify it. Certainly it would be a very good thing if the biblical moral vision were to impact all sorts of societies more than it already has. Certainly the biblical vision of *the kingdom of God*, and not *some other* vision, should inform our reconstruction of the mundane, political world. Biblical faith certainly proposes *this*. However, it also proposes that caution and wisdom must be exercised in how it is done, because the kingdom is both "now and not yet." Biblical faith itself raises serious questions about the authoritarian, antidemocratic, repressive, totalizing tendencies of utopian politics of all stripes and about its tendency to blur important distinctions between morality and politics, between morality and law. This is no less true of quasi-Christian utopianism than of any other kind.[47] History itself, right down to the present, testifies to the way in which religion, for

all the good that it can do, "can also express darker fears and desires
. . . destroy community by dividing its members . . . inflame the mind
with destructive apocalyptic fantasies of immediate redemption."[48] A
biblical politics is dangerous to utopians, then, and this is a good thing,
since the politics that biblical faith confronts in utopianism is far *more*
dangerous.

Hostile to the Naked Public Square

The final group for whom a biblical politics is dangerous comprises
those who, like the utopians, take an activist approach to politics but
reject the idea that biblical faith, or any religious faith for that matter,
should have any role to play in politics. With one eye firmly on the utopians and concerned that the polis should be pluralistic and peaceable,
they set out to exclude the divisive forces of religion from public space
and to make (and keep) religion a private matter. To use a commonly
employed metaphor, they advocate for a "naked public square" when it
comes to public discourse.[49] All (at least theoretically) may enter the
public square, but each must check her religious identity at the gates
and operate within the square only as a citizen. This response to the
utopian determination to reconstruct the mundane on the basis of the
transcendental is, as it were, "nuclear." It is to insist on an absolute *disjunction* between the mundane and the transcendental. On what, then,
is the polis to be founded?

The options are essentially two. The first is that the polis should
be founded on the *will*. The good society is to be whatever its human
inhabitants (some or all) want it to be. There is no objective, transcendental "pattern" in reality that the polis should approximate. We are
on our own, and we must decide. This argument is at least as old as
the Greek Sophists of the fifth century B.C. (men like Protagoras and
Thrasymachus), who challenged the Athenians and others about the
objectivity of their own politics. As Protagorus himself put it (according to Socrates, according to Plato), "Man is the measure of all things."[50]
The second option is that the polis is to be founded on what is *natural*. There is no objective *transcendental* pattern to reality according
to which the polis should be built, but there *is* a *natural* pattern. The
polis should be founded on what nature reveals to be true and good.
This argument is well illustrated in the opening lines of the American
Declaration of Independence:

> When in the course of human events, it becomes necessary
> for one people to dissolve the political bands which have con-
> nected them with another, and to assume among the powers
> of the earth, the separate and equal station to which the Laws
> of Nature and of Nature's God entitle them, a decent respect to
> the opinions of mankind requires that they should declare the
> causes which impel them to separation. We hold these truths
> to be self-evident, that all men are created equal, that they are
> endowed by their Creator with certain inalienable rights, that
> among these are life, liberty and the pursuit of happiness.

God "shows up" in these sentiments as the one who created "Nature,"
but it is from *Nature*, and not God, that we learn what we need to know
in order to build the polis. The crucial truths are not revealed directly
by God, but are "self-evident" to those who ponder the cosmos.

A biblical politics is dangerous to those who hold to either of these
two views, for while it resists utopianism just as firmly as they do and
places (as they do) a high value on peaceable order in society, a biblical
politics insists that faith should (and must inevitably) have a role to
play in politics. Those who embrace biblical faith are compelled, then,
to reject the popular idea in modern Western thinking that religion
is a private matter. They must insist, indeed, that there cannot be an
absolute disjunction between a mundane political order and the transcendental vision of the kingdom of God. All societies must measure
themselves against (and *will* ultimately be measured against) this transcendental standard, and all societies must strive for conformity with
it. Biblical politics is, therefore, dangerous to those who hold these two
alternative views. Yet I am not very concerned about this danger; I am
much more concerned about the danger in the two alternatives.

The Will of the "People"

Is the polis really to be founded on the *will*? Then justice itself can be
nothing other than what people *will* it to be; the *law* can be nothing
other than what people will it to be. Who are the people who are doing
the "willing"? Perhaps it is the majority of the inhabitants of the polis,
in which case they can decide with impunity what is to be done with
everyone else. There can be no appeal to any higher authority, because
none exists. As Thrasymachus argued long ago, "justice" itself can be
nothing other than obedience to the laws of society, which the majority

itself has just invented; the mob rules.[51] Of course, the phrase "the will of the people" is usually just a nice piece of rhetoric in such societies, designed to disguise who is *really* doing the willing. As Thrasymachus also understood, the people who *really* make the laws are the strongest political groups in society, and they make them not in the interests of the majority but only in their own. "Justice" represents nothing other than the interests of the powerful; might is right. The mob does not even come into it, unless they possess high-quality weapons and genuine access (somehow) to decision making—*then* there might be some constraint on the powerful elites from below. There can certainly be no constraint from above, however, for there *is* nothing above. There is no Good with which they must concern themselves, other than the good of their own continued hold on power. One of the earliest modern thinkers to grasp this point with great clarity was Niccolò Machiavelli, who suggested (in 1513, in Italy) that "it is necessary for a prince, if he wants to preserve himself, to learn how not to be good, and to use this knowledge and not use it, as necessity dictates."[52] Here, it is *one* person who is doing the willing, and what he is mainly exercising is the will to power of the "outstanding man who uses extraordinary means in order to transform a corrupt matter [i.e., "the people"] into a good matter [i.e., the kind of society he desires]."[53] A short time later in England, Thomas Hobbes, in his influential book *Leviathan* (1651), also demonstrated that he had grasped the point. Hobbes envisaged an all-powerful, unconstrained state exercising godlike power.[54] The state could be god in this way, of course, precisely because no god above existed to constrain it.

This is a *truly* dangerous politics, I propose, which has been responsible for some dark passages in human history. It is the politics at the heart of Marxist philosophy, in which law is an instrument of the state, not a limitation upon those who make policy. The law's very purpose is to eliminate the political power of the bourgeoisie and to educate citizens "properly" so that the desired communist social order can be achieved. What this has meant for "the people" in states where Marxism has become the dominant ideology is well illustrated by the recent history of both Russia and China. The politics of the will is also the politics at the heart of Fascism, one of the great enemies of Marxism in the twentieth century. In National Socialist Germany, for example, we see Machiavelli, by way of Friedrich Nietzsche and his famous "overman" or "superman" (German *Übermensch*), feeding the politics of Adolf Hitler and his friends, as well as their approach to law and their treatment of those whom they considered *Untermenschen* ("under men"). Law became, in Nazi Germany, "whatever the people/the state decides." This understanding of law was precisely what encouraged many German lawyers of the time to take a passive stance with respect to Nazi barbarism, on the ground that *Gesetz ist Gesetz* (the law is the law).[55] There *could* be no appeal, *beyond* the law, to what was right. If the polis is really to be founded on the will, not *all* of us are necessarily in a lot of trouble, but *many* of us are. We are in trouble not least because (ironically) an approach to politics first developed in order to avoid utopianism, by getting rid of the transcendent, has in fact proved to be highly productive *of* utopianism. It is a utopianism, however, in which there is no God to inhibit the pretensions of "the gods" (a.k.a. powerful men). This is, of course, partly why it has resulted in so much more bloodshed than the overtly religious politics it was designed to replace.

Conformity to Nature

If the polis cannot be founded on the will, can it be founded instead on what is *natural*? Here, we encounter the problem identified earlier: How are we to arrive at a consensus on what is "natural," and, even if we do, how can we move from what is *descriptively* "natural" to what we *should* do? Suppose we can describe what "is"; have we thereby resolved the question of "ought"? These are difficult problems. In spite of what the American Declaration of Independence claims, it is quite obviously *not* self-evident, if Nature is to be our guide, "that all men are created equal, that they are endowed by their Creator with certain inalienable rights, that among these are life, liberty and the pursuit of happiness." In retrospect, this bold claim can be seen to be nothing more than an outrageous bluff. The writers were able to pull it off only because the majority of the people they were addressing already inhabited, to some extent, a biblical Story in the context of which this kind of claim made sense. As we saw in one of our earlier chapters, it is not necessarily self-evident to a *Hindu* that all men are created equal. Again, to many *Japanese* in the period prior to the Second World War, getting into harmony with nature meant getting into line with the will of the divine emperor and offering him unquestioning obedience.[56] This was "self-evidently" the right thing to do. So who gets to say what is "natural"? Who gets to say what this means for life in the polis? Most importantly, what is the *real* basis for this assertion of "meaning," if it is indeed not self-evident?

Whether it is admitted or not, the answer must be that what is truly decisive in deciding what "natural" means is the "big story" that the decision makers hold to be true—the story they (often covertly) inhabit. The appeal to what is natural is simply a sleight of hand.

This implies, however, that the naked public square is not as naked as it is sometimes made to appear. There is lot of clothing being worn, even if it is disguised under apparent nakedness. So who gets to wear her clothing, and who is required to check his at the door? Why is religious clothing forbidden (in the minds of some, at least), but other kinds are not? Is not this notion of the naked public square, in the end, a delusion, at best—or just another piece of rhetoric in the pursuit of power, at worst? I believe that this is indeed the case. Whether we are *dealing* with delusion or something worse, we are certainly dealing with something that is dangerous. It is dangerous to the extent that it maintains the privilege of some stories over others without allowing a proper and healthy criticism of the *privileged* stories, which are not even *understood* as stories but simply as collections of neutral "facts." The idea of the naked public square is also dangerous to the extent that it does not allow proper and appropriate consideration of the de-privileged stories and of what they might have to say that is of value for public life.

The Clothed Public Square

Is *biblical politics* dangerous to those who defend the "naked public square" in these terms? It is. However, I, for one, am happy about that. I do not believe in the naked public square; I do not think that it exists. I do believe, however, in the *nonnaked* public square. I do believe in a "place" where all competing metanarratives are open for inspection and critique, in a respectful and constructive manner, so that the citizens of the polis can freely debate their merits and decide together on the best way forward in pursuit of what is good. For this to happen, however, a Muslim must be able to stand in the public square as a Muslim, a Christian as a Christian, a Hindu as a Hindu—and a secularist as a secularist and an atheist as an atheist. They do need to agree that reason and debate will be the means of engagement, and not violence and war. They do need to agree that there can be no prior censorship of views expressed in the square and that no ideas (religious or otherwise) are to be protected from criticism. They do need to agree that the process of reasoning must be accessible to all those present, and not only to fellow believers. However, they absolutely do *not* need to agree—and they *should* not agree—to pretend to be people they are not or to speak only in ways that give this impression.

In particular, they should not be asked to believe what they believe *any less firmly* than they do, *unless* they are genuinely persuaded otherwise. They should be not asked to be nonabsolutist in their belief. Absolutism is one of the great "monsters" that many defenders of the naked public square want to keep outside the gates, since they identify it with intolerance.[57] Yet everyone (including each defender of the naked public square) is an absolutist in his core convictions about what is true and good and beautiful.[58] To ask for nonabsolutism is to ask only that someone *else* should be less serious about his or her core convictions than I am. It is specifically to ask that someone else should not be as serious about his or her *religious* convictions as I am but should instead participate in the dishonest game of painting all religions as essentially believing the same things and having the same kind of vision of the world. It is a game in which the other is diminished so that I may feel comfortable. This is not a game that I would like to see played out in the public square. An axial age nonabsolutism cannot help us to build a robust and enduring polis. What we need instead is genuine dialogue between people who genuinely disagree about lots of things, not least because their stories are so different from each other. *Tolerance* will be required—tolerance of debate, of criticism, and indeed of conversion (since real debate can change people's minds). *Liberalism* will be required, in the old-fashioned political (not religious) sense of that word. It will be the genuine tolerance (and liberalism), however, of those who possess strong convictions and who think that other people are wrong (and even wicked). It will not be the pseudo-tolerance and false liberalism of those who care little about much of what they themselves say they believe and even less about the beliefs of others. In the end, we need genuine pluralism, not pseudo-pluralism—the kind of genuine pluralism that many of the defenders of the naked public square, for all their rhetoric about pluralism and tolerance, apparently cannot tolerate.[59]

The creation of such a nonnaked public square is, in my view, a necessity if the notion of public space is not itself to become increasingly repressive, even in societies that proudly regard themselves as liberal and democratic. This tendency toward repression is already clear in some of the world's leading liberal democracies, as the allegedly neutral territory of the naked public square is being expanded and expanded and is coming closer and closer to home. The citizens of these societies have shorter and shorter distances to walk before they arrive at the gates at which they (but not others) must check their "private" identities. More and more of life is being defined as "public" space, in which "private" beliefs, moral opinions, and customs cannot appropriately (or sometimes even legally) be expressed.[60] The very notion of private space itself is under threat.[61] Ironically, once again, it is precisely an approach to politics first developed to curb utopianism that is now, in successive "utopian spasms," producing a polis in which hard-won freedoms are being so visibly eroded—without many people apparently noticing or caring.[62] The state is striving to "fix" things—to make people safer, to compel them to treat each other in better ways, to engineer virtue. The state is committed to bringing in the new Jerusalem, and only politicians who *promise* to try to achieve this can even get elected. In the wake of these utopian spasms, unfortunately, comes significant erosion of moral and other freedoms, including the freedom to criticize the behavior or the religion of my neighbors or even to criticize the state itself. In this emerging world, if we want freedom, we need to stay at home. Even *there* it is not clear that freedom will be permitted.[63] Effective resistance to such politics will require a Story that refuses the idea that the polis should be founded on the will to power, or on what is allegedly natural. Effective resistance will require a Story that leads us to found the polis, instead, upon far more solid, eternal realities. Crying loudly about how our own or our neighbors' "rights" are being eroded, when we have no convincing idea about where these rights come from, is not going to help.[64]

In sum: biblical politics is dangerous to those who are committed to the status quo, utopian in their political programs, or in love with an allegedly naked public square. I see biblical politics as implying not the "third way" of doing politics in the modern world that is represented by a bankrupt nineteenth-century liberal theology but a "fourth way"—the way of orthodox and appropriately conservative (and appropriately radical) religion, combined with a genuinely liberal (but also passionate) politics.[65] If the biblical faith that leads us on this fourth way is dangerous to those who possess inadequate (and dangerous) views of politics, however—and who can regret that?—it is certainly not dangerous to the polis itself. The path of which I speak, in fact, leads only in the direction of the common good.

ON HOPE

Lastly, is biblical *hope* dangerous? As we saw in chapter 11, some have thought so, on the grounds that it leads to a devaluing of the present in relation to the future and that it encourages passivity *in* the present while we *wait* for the future. I do not dispute that we can find such devaluing and passivity in the thinking and writing, both fictional and nonfictional, of some who have regarded themselves as standing in the biblical tradition.[66] As I demonstrated in chapter 11, however, the allegation of danger rests upon a misunderstanding about the nature of biblical faith. Real biblical faith requires of its adherents a very high valuing *of* the world as it is now, as well as active work *within* the world to make it better. Biblically, hope is what keeps one going in the work of mediating God's blessing to the world, even in the face of great challenges that might tempt one to despair. Sometimes it seems that Albert Camus must be right when he offers the opinion that those who hold out hope for the human condition are mad.[67] However, it is precisely the hope that God's kingdom will indeed one day arrive that strengthens the believer in pursuing the prophetic biblical vision in the present, even though it might seem impossible that it should ever become a reality. Hope is what allows love to persevere.

Such hope is not dangerous. Its absence is, however, very dangerous. Human beings are wired to hope, and they *need* to hope. Our innate human curiosity itself "breeds hope, about improving our condition and perhaps about the existence of a benevolent God. It can also breed despair if we think our hopes are groundless."[68] It can breed more than just despair, however: "Take hope from the heart of man, and you make him a beast of prey," claimed Marie Louise Ramé.[69] Leon Kass agrees:

> Civilized life, in which human beings live partly for posterity, depends upon hope for the future. Absent such hope, human beings, always seeing doom before their eyes, would be little inclined to do much of anything. Most likely living for the moment, they would hardly be inclined to accept the restraints of law or the obligations to do justice.[70]

We need hope in order to live well, for visibly "man does not live—or live *well*—by bread alone, not even by bread and circuses."[71] Hope is indeed one of the key things that is required to prevent us from becoming Friedrich Nietzsche's "last man" (the antithesis of his "overman")—the man who simply accepts what "is" and focuses all his energy not on changing anything but only on his own comfort and entertainment. This is the man who is

> the lowest and most decayed man, the herd man without any ideals and aspirations, but well fed, well clothed, well housed, well medicated by ordinary physicians and by psychiatrists.[72]

This is man once God has been abolished and all hope has gone with him—someone who is entertaining himself to death. This is man "living for the moment"—and, in the process, defining the future, which now looks bleak. It is *hope* that gets us out of our armchairs to try to do something about what is wrong with the world now and to make it better in the future. It is *hope* that leads us to make sacrifices in the present for the sake of that future. The abolition of hope is the abolition of man. It is for this reason that Derrick Jensen is so very wrong (and dangerous) when he writes,

> A wonderful thing happens when you give up on hope, which is that you realize you never needed it in the first place. You realize that giving up on hope didn't kill you, nor did it make you less effective. In fact it made you more effective, because you ceased relying on someone or something else to solve your problems— you ceased *hoping* your problems somehow get solved, through the magical assistance of God, the Great Mother, the Sierra Club, valiant tree-sitters, brave salmon, or even the Earth itself—and you just began doing what's necessary to solve your problems yourself.[73]

The footnote to these lines reads, "Kind of like a belief in a Christian God or a Christian heaven." I quite agree that is sensible to give up on hope in "the Great Mother, the Sierra Club, valiant tree-sitters, brave salmon, or even the Earth itself." I even agree that it is sensible to give up on hope in "magical assistance" from God. To give up on hope in *God*, however, is madness—particularly given the profoundly challenging, even overwhelming, problems that face the world, which can and do often tempt us to hopelessness. To give up on hope in God—now that is dangerous.

POSTSCRIPT

Biblical Faith for a New Age

·Perhaps every generation believes that it has reached a turning
point of history, but our problems seem particularly intractable
and our future increasingly uncertain.

Karen Armstrong[1]

The crisis is real, and it is upon us.

David Suzuki[2]

We live in turbulent, quickly changing times. Some people think that
these are pivotal times. For religious historian Karen Armstrong, we
are at a "turning point of history"; for ecologist David Suzuki, we are
in a "crisis." It is to help us find guidance in the midst of such circumstances that each of these writers has participated in the telling of a
particular story about the past. Karen Armstrong believes that we can
find the guidance we need by looking back to a previous "axial age"—to
another "crucial turning point in history," as Karl Jaspers referred to the
period 800–200 B.C.[3] For Armstrong, we shall find the right path in our
own *second* "axial age" by drawing the right conclusions about the *first*.
David Suzuki looks further back for wisdom—to preaxial, indigenous
societies that possessed a "sense of *relationship* with the natural world,

from which flow very different environmental values and responsibilities [than our own]."[4] Indigenous nature-wisdom foreshadows a certain kind of future "by its historic precedent of sustaining a long-term ecological equilibrium with the natural world."[5] I am grateful that both writers have written, and I admire many aspects of their vision for the future of our world.

I do not believe, however, in a historical axial age, and I do not believe in a dark green, Paleolithic, golden age. As I have tried to show in a different book, both stories are fundamentally untrue.[6] These past "ages" exist only in the mind and only because they are needed to ground the message their creators wish to proclaim about what we should all believe and do, now and in the future. I also do not believe that we *are* necessarily at a turning point in history, although we may well be in a crisis. Only time will tell. Regardless of whether we are, I do believe that, to know how to live in the face of *any* of life's challenges (or crises or turning points), each one of us needs to be able to answer the question with which we began our inquiries, in this book, into life, the universe, and everything: "Of what story or stories do I find myself a part?" Only then can any one of us answer the following question: "What am I [then] to do?"

In the course of these enquiries, I have examined various proposals about the story in which we find ourselves and about the ethic (how we should live) that flows from them. I have explained why I do not find most of these stories persuasive, although at various points I do find truth in some of them. I have done all of this in the course of reexamining at length the much-maligned Old Story with which many of the world's other "big stories" have vied for a long time and which more recent, modern, Western stories have now sought to displace—including those told by Karen Armstrong, David Suzuki, and the "new atheists." In spite of widespread contemporary agreement that this Old Story is untrue, I have argued that there remain excellent reasons for believing it to be true. There remain excellent reasons for continuing to affirm this Old Story as the most coherent overall account available to us of the way things are and will be. Furthermore, in spite of widespread contemporary agreement that the Old Story is also dangerous, I have argued that it is *good* and not dangerous—or more precisely, that it is good in *being* dangerous.

It is this Old Story, I propose, into which we still need to read ourselves even in these late modern or postmodern times, as many have done in earlier times if we want to understand who we are and how we ought to live. In fact, it is this Old Story that provides the most secure foundation upon which to build the better future for humankind (and for the planet) for which many of its detractors are looking. It is an Old Story that is big enough and deep enough and long enough to ground a New Age—whether that age is "axial" or not.

NOTES

CHAPTER 1

1   David Suzuki, *The Legacy: An Elder's Vision for Our Sustainable Future* (Vancouver, B.C.: Greystone, 2010), 86.

2   Thomas Berry, *The Dream of the Earth* (San Francisco: Sierra Club, 1988), 123–24.

3   Douglas Adams, *The Hitchhiker's Guide to the Galaxy* (London: Pan Books, 1979).

4   This section of chapter 1 and much of what immediately follows draws to a significant extent on Iain Provan and Loren Wilkinson, "'Unscripted, Anxious Stutterers': Why We Need Old Testament (Hi)story," *Sapientia Logos* 1 (2008): 12–36. That essay in turn depends heavily for its opening paragraphs on a lecture originally written by Loren Wilkinson, whom I gladly acknowledge, therefore, as the source of much of my text to this point and as the inspiration for my thinking.

5   J. R. R. Tolkien, *The Lord of the Rings* (London: HarperCollins, 1991), 738–39.

6   The phrase "inextricably middled" was coined by David L. Jeffrey, "The Self and the Book: Reference and Recognition in Medieval Thought," in *By Things Seen: Reference and Recognition in Medieval Thought*, ed. David L. Jeffrey (Ottawa, Ont.: University of Ottawa Press, 1979), 1–17 (2) (throughout the notes, page numbers in parentheses refer to the specific pages cited).

7   Dante Alighieri, *The Comedy of Dante Alighieri, the Florentine,* Cantica I, *Hell,* trans. Dorothy L. Sayers (Harmondsworth, U.K.: Penguin, 1949), 71.

8   Alasdair MacIntyre, *After Virtue: A Study in Moral Theory* (Notre Dame, Ind.: University of Notre Dame Press, 1981), 216.

9   Karl Jaspers, *The Origin and the Goal of History*, trans. M. Bullock (New Haven: Yale University Press, 1953).

10 John Hick, *An Interpretation of Religion: Human Responses to the Transcendent,* 2nd ed. (New Haven: Yale University Press, 2004); and Karen Armstrong, *The*

Great Transformation: The Beginning of Our Religious Traditions (New York: Knopf, 2006).

11 Bron Taylor, *Dark Green Religion: Nature Spirituality and the Planetary Future* (Berkeley: University of California Press, 2010).

12 Berry, *Dream*; Suzuki, *Legacy*; and Derrick Jensen, *Endgame*, vol. 1, *The Problem of Civilization* (New York: Seven Stories, 2006).

13 Note the following books, for example: Richard Dawkins, *The God Delusion* (New York: Houghton Mifflin Harcourt, 2006); Daniel C. Dennett, *Breaking the Spell: Religion as a Natural Phenomenon* (New York: Viking, 2006); Sam Harris, *The End of Faith: Religion, Terror, and the Future of Reason* (New York: Norton, 2004); and Christopher Hitchens, *God Is Not Great: How Religion Poisons Everything* (New York: Twelve Books, 2007).

14 This quotation greets one immediately on the home page of the new atheists website: "The New Atheists," accessed October 26, 2012, http://newatheists .org/.

15 See "Atheist Bus Campaign," accessed October 11, 2013, https://humanism.org .uk/about/atheist-bus-campaign/.

16 I have given substantial attention of this kind to the stories of the axial age and the dark green golden age in my book *Convenient Myths: The Axial Age, Dark Green Religion, and the World That Never Was* (Waco, Tex.: Baylor University Press, 2013). For responses to "new atheism," see, e.g., David Berlinski, *The Devil's Delusion: Atheism and Its Scientific Pretensions* (New York: Crown Forum, 2008); Terry Eagleton, *Reason, Faith, and Revolution: Reflections on the God Debate* (New Haven: Yale University Press, 2009); and William Lane Craig, ed., *God Is Great, God Is Good: Why Believing in God Is Reasonable and Responsible* (Grand Rapids: InterVarsity, 2009).

17 Berry, *Dream*, 123.

18 See Pew Forum on Religion & Public Life, "U.S. Religious Knowledge Survey," Pew Research Center, accessed October 26, 2012, http://www.pewforum .org/U-S-Religious-Knowledge-Survey.aspx. E.g., respondents were asked to identify which prohibition on a list of four is not found in the Ten Commandments and which biblical figure is associated with the Exodus.

19 Two Bible questions set in a recent Canadian survey were of a level similar to the ones in the Pew study. Teenagers were asked whether they knew the names of the founding father of Judaism and of the person who denied Jesus three times; 10 percent knew that the first was Abraham, and 22 percent that the second was Peter. Even among adults the latter figure only rose to 42 percent. See Reginald W. Bibby, *The Emerging Millennials: How Canada's Newest Generation Is Responding to Change and Choice* (Lethbridge, AB: Project Canada Books, 2009), 93.

20 Leon R. Kass, *The Beginning of Wisdom: Reading Genesis* (New York: Free Press, 2003). I was pleased to come across this book after my own project was well under way, and quotes from it now litter my own. The reason I could so effortlessly overlook such a large book is that Kass is not a specialist in biblical studies, but a distinguished researcher in molecular biology and bioethics. In the specialized academic world as it now exists, it is all too easy for such a book by a "nonspecialist" not even to cross the bibliographical radar screen of the specialist.

21 Kass, *Wisdom*, 1.

22 I have also refrained, for the reader's sake, from offering in my footnotes exhaustive lists of authorities for the various points I make about nonbiblical traditions. I have instead restricted myself to a small number of easily accessible and

readable sources, so that interested readers can at least follow up their interest to some small extent. I am entirely satisfied, nevertheless, that the authorities I do cite do not mislead us in what they have to say.

23   Agatha Christie, *The Murder of Roger Ackroyd* (London: Collins, 1926).

24   This is exemplified, e.g., in Robert Alter's *Genesis: Translation and Commentary* (New York: Norton, 1997).

25   This is true to such an extent that it makes sense to some to reconstruct modern science so that it coheres with their reading of the Genesis text. See further Arthur McCalla, *The Creationist Debate: The Encounter between the Bible and the Historical Mind* (London: Continuum, 2006).

26   Iain Provan, V. Philips Long, and Tremper Longman III, *A Biblical History of Israel* (Louisville, Ky.: Westminster John Knox, 2003).

27   C. S. Lewis, *The Last Battle* (Harmondsworth, U.K.: Puffin, 1964), 124–35. Lewis displays here, in what is overtly a children's story, a profound grasp of the difficulty faced by the ideologically committed in altering their worldview, even when confronted by what is plainly reality.

CHAPTER 2

1   Quoted in Benjamin Gal-Or, *Cosmology, Physics and Philosophy* (New York: Springer Verlag, 1981), 166.

2   Quoted in Arthur Frank Wentheim, *Radio Comedy* (New York: Oxford University Press, 1979), 203.

3   These turn out to be (to put the matter in its simplest terms) the most basic building blocks of our world.

4   Here I must make a few things initially clear for the sake of readers unfamiliar with Bible reading and indeed with the nature of our biblical texts and their translations. When I say "Genesis 1:1," this is shorthand for "the first chapter of Genesis, and the first verse of that chapter." All biblical citations will take such a form in what follows. When I say that the opening line of Genesis is "in the beginning God created the heavens and the earth," I mean that this is how the line is translated in the New International Version (NIV) translation of the Bible, which I shall use for the sake of convenience throughout my succeeding chapters. The actual *text* of Genesis 1:1 (and most of the rest of the Old Testament) is written in ancient Hebrew. For the most part the NIV is a reliable guide to the content of this ancient Hebrew text. However, I shall often refer to the actual Hebrew text in what follows to bring greater clarity to our reading of Genesis, and sometimes I shall refer to the Hebrew to correct what I consider to be mistakes in the NIV's translation.

5   This is an example of merismus—a way of speaking found in many languages whereby one can "describe the totality of something in terms of its extremes, e.g., 'good and bad', 'big and little', etc. Here we have an example of this usage to define the universe." Gordon J. Wenham, *Genesis 1–15*, WBC 1 (Waco, Tex.: Word Books, 1987), 15.

6   The verse does not necessarily mean to say that nothing existed prior to God's creation of our cosmos. Genesis 1:2 may indeed reasonably be understood to describe *what* existed prior to this reality. Nevertheless, the cosmos as we know it had a beginning. For a discussion of the issues of translation and meaning in Genesis 1:1-2, see (among others) Claus Westermann, *Genesis 1–11*, BKAT 1 (Neukirchen-Vluyn: Neukirchener Verlag, 1974), 130–41, and Wenham, *Genesis 1–15*, 11–15. The situation is apparently similar in the Qur'an: Allah does not necessarily call creation as we know it into being out of nothing. See John Kaltner,

Introducing the Qur'an for Today's Reader (Minneapolis: Fortress, 2011), 48–49. What biblical (and indeed Muslim) faith certainly disallows, however, is any kind of eternal dualism in the cosmos, whereby entities like the "darkness" coexist for all time alongside God. It may not be entirely clear *in Genesis 1:1-2* that God also *created* the darkness (and the water) that were present before our cosmos took shape, but this is certainly the plain implication of many *other* biblical passages that affirm that there is only one God and none who is like him.

7   For example, centrally important to the revelations first received by Mohammed in Mecca was the idea that a judgment day is coming and that human beings need to turn away from idolatry and polytheism and follow the one God. To clarify the word "Abrahamic" in this context, I shall continue in this book the practice that others have initiated of referring to the three religions mentioned using this word. I use it only as shorthand, however, to refer to these monotheistic traditions that "bear certain 'family likenesses'" in a way that none of them does with (say) Hinduism or Buddhism. R. Walter L. Moberly, *The Theology of the Book of Genesis* (Cambridge: Cambridge University Press, 2009), 200. These three traditions are at the same time very different from each other, as we shall see, and "it is hardly meaningful to appeal to the Abrahamic *apart from* its subsequent transformation and appropriation" therein (220). "Abraham" does not stand for the same things in these traditions, even when it comes to the question of who the god of Abraham actually is, and there is "no reason to single out Abraham as the characteristic category in light of which the three religions can best be described." Alon Goshen-Gottstein, "Abraham and 'Abrahamic Religions' in Contemporary Interreligious Discourse: Reflections of an Implicated Jewish Bystander," *Studies in Interreligious Dialogue* 12 (2002): 165–83 (173).

8   Theodore M. Ludwig, *The Sacred Paths: Understanding the Religions of the World*, 4th ed. (Upper Saddle River, N.J.: Pearson Prentice Hall, 2006), 91.

9   Mark Muesse, *The Hindu Traditions: A Concise Introduction* (Minneapolis: Fortress, 2011), 125, 127.

10   Jeffery D. Long, *Jainism: An Introduction* (London: I.B. Taurus, 2009), 83.

11   Jonathan Barnes, *Aristotle: A Very Short Introduction* (Oxford: Oxford University Press, 2000), 100.

12   At the same time there have, of course, been tendencies in these "Abrahamic" religions, historically, to stress the transcendence of God so much that the personhood of God is all but lost (along with his creatorship). This is particularly the case where and when the Abrahamic religions have been heavily influenced by religion and philosophy (e.g., Indian or Greek) in which the personal nature of ultimate reality is problematic. Neoplatonism has played a particularly significant role here, and not just in Christianity (where its influence is large and well known). Malise Ruthven notes an early trend in Islamic philosophy "towards an utterly remote, unknowable God who does not even create." *Islam: A Very Short Introduction* (New York: Oxford University Press, 1997), 62–63.

13   Gerasimos Santas, "The Form of the Good in Plato's *Republic*," in Fine, *Plato*, 249–76 (250).

14   Barnes, *Aristotle*, 104.

15   Sikhism represents something of an exception, in that here we encounter an emphasis on a "creator of the universe . . . transcendent far beyond it . . . [and] personal." Ludwig, *Paths*, 193–94. However, there is more to it than this, and in the end, "the Sikh experience of God as ultimate reality includes monistic and monotheistic, impersonal and personal dimensions."

16   Ludwig, *Paths*, 144–45.

17   Ludwig, *Paths*, 179.

18   Long, *Jainism*, 2. Elsewhere, Long writes, "What Jains deny is that there is a *creator* God" (90).

19   Ludwig, *Paths*, 236.

20   Ludwig, *Paths*, 237.

21   Livia Kohn, *Introducing Daoism* (London: Routledge, 2009), 23.

22   Muesse, *Traditions*, 131–33. The same complexity is found, e.g., in some traditional African religions, where "the concept of a supreme God operates as a principle of ultimacy that gives underlying unity to the multiplicity of deities and spirits: the Many powers are understood to be aspects of, or intermediaries for, the One God." Benjamin C. Ray, *African Religions: Symbol, Ritual, and Community*, 2nd ed. (Upper Saddle River, N.J.: Prentice Hall, 2000), 27.

23   Ludwig, *Paths*, 147–48.

24   Kohn, *Daoism*, 117. For the many other gods of popular Daoism, see more generally pp. 116–31.

25   In the case of the Indian religions, for example, this is true for both Hinduism and Buddhism, where it has apparently not proved easy for many fully to embrace the uncompromising monism (all are really One, and the rest is illusion) that lies at the heart of each. The situation is somewhat different in Jainism, where "the One" is already many, in the sense that "the unity of souls . . . is a unity of *nature* or *essence*" and "their numerical distinctiveness is not illusory," whatever else might be. Long, *Jainism*, 91.

26   Blaise Pascal, *Mémorial*, accessed September 30, 2013, http://www.users.csbsju .edu/~eknuth/pascal.html.

27   Barnes, *Aristotle*, 104.

28   The Hebrew behind the various English translations of these words (*tohu va bohu*) itself communicates, by way of a wordplay, the close connection between the "formlessness" and the "emptiness." The phrase is sometimes left untranslated in modern translations so that this effect is not lost. See, e.g., the German translation of Andreas Schüle, *Die Urgeschichte (Genesis 1–11)*, Zürcher Bibelkommentare (Zurich: Theologischer Verlag, 2009), 27.

29   I employ the male pronoun in accordance with long-standing convention. However, I do not mean to imply by its use that God is portrayed in biblical thinking as male rather than female. It is already clear from Genesis 1 itself (vv. 26-27) that this is not so, for it is male *and* female human beings together who are said to "image" God. I shall have more to say about this in chap. 4.

30   Sikhism, by contrast, thinks of the world as God's creation but *also* as "an emanation of God's being." Ludwig, *Paths*, 194.

31   For a more extensive description of these societies, see chap. 8 of my *Convenient Myths*. "Complex" societies are those in which we find cities containing thousands of people, rather than just villages containing a few hundred, and in which (among other things) these people occupy specialized roles, rather than simply being (all of them) farmers. Such societies begin to emerge in Mesopotamia and Egypt as we enter the period of the Bronze Age civilizations that arise in the fourth millennium B.C.

32   John Walton, *Ancient Near Eastern Thought and the Old Testament: Introducing the Conceptual World of the Hebrew Bible* (Grand Rapids: Baker Academic, 2006), 87–112.

33   The Hebrew is literally "a voice/sound, a barely audible whisper." To be fair, this "voice" is not explicitly associated with God either, but the connection is clearly

implied in the way that the sequence is structured ("wind . . . not in the wind; earthquake . . . not in the earthquake; fire . . . not in the fire; gentle whisper"). It is also implied in the fact that it is not "the word of the LORD" that comes to Elijah in v. 13 (contrast v. 9) but a "voice" (the same word as in v. 12). It is clearly God who is speaking—as it is also in Genesis 3:8, when the "voice" of God is heard in the garden in Eden.

34   Lynn White, "The Historical Roots of Our Ecologic Crisis," *Science* 155 (1967): 1203–7. This essay is conveniently reproduced in *Western Man and Environmental Ethics*, ed. I. G. Barbour (Reading, Mass.: Addison-Wesley, 1973), 18–30, and the quote comes from the latter (25).

35   See further my *Convenient Myths*, chap. 9.

36   See further my *Convenient Myths*, chap. 8.

37   We find this in pictorial form, for example, in an eighteenth-century B.C. fresco from the city of Mari and in a thirteenth-century B.C. ivory inlay from the city of Asshur in Assyria. Walton, *Thought*, 122.

38   We should not necessarily confuse "rest" with "leisure after work." A more important connotation of "rest" in such a context involves a god taking up residence in a temple in order to *rule* in an orderly manner. See Walton, *Thought*, 114.

39   E.g., Exodus 35:14, 28; 39:37; Numbers 4:9.

40   The Hebrew is very similar: *vayikal moshe 'et-hammela'kah* (Exodus 40:33), and *vayikal 'elohim mela'kto* (Genesis 2:2).

41   See further my *Convenient Myths*, chap. 8.

42   This same idea is perhaps expressed in one of the second-tier texts of the Muslim canon (the hadith), cited in Kaltner, *Qur'an*, 47, where Muhammad says, "The whole earth is a mosque that is a place to worship." However, this may say less about the world being sacred and more about the freedom of the Muslim to choose any place (outside or inside) to pray, because this is acceptable to Allah. It is interesting that the Qur'an itself avoids any mention of God "resting" after creating, although it does know of God ruling. It is apparently anxious to avoid any idea that God was wearied after creating (Sura 50:15). Islam also has no (associated) idea of a weekly Sabbath rest for *people* (Ludwig, *Paths*, 475), which is interesting given that Muhammad copied many other aspects of Judaism (e.g., praying regularly during the day, praying toward a sacred center, and keeping the Day of Atonement).

43   On both see, e.g., John Skinner, *Genesis*, 2nd ed., ICC 1 (Edinburgh: T&T Clark, 1930), 59–66.

44   See also Kass, *Wisdom*, 59n4.

45   Walton, *Thought*, 122–23.

46   For the former, see "Gilgamesh," trans. Benjamin R. Foster, in Hallo and Younger, *Context of Scripture*, 1.132:458–60; hereafter COS. For the latter, see "Enki and Ninhursag: A Paradise Myth," trans. S. N. Kramer, in *Ancient Near Eastern Texts Relating to the Old Testament*, ed. J. B. Pritchard (Princeton: Princeton University Press, 1969), 37–41; hereafter ANET.

47   It is interesting to note in connection with this question of geography the implication of the mention of "good" (i.e., pure) gold and onyx in connection with the land of Havilah in Genesis 2:12. In Ezekiel 28, the garden of God is itself a place of precious stones (v. 13). Pure gold was much used in covering the furniture in the holiest parts of the Israelite tabernacle, and later it was also used in the temple (e.g., 1 Kings 6:20-22). Onyx stone is otherwise mentioned in the Old Testament *only* in connection with the decoration of the tabernacle and temple and with the clothing of the high priest (e.g., Exodus 25:7). Although the land

of Havilah at first appears to be *outside* the garden in Genesis 2, it is in fact apparently *inside* it—a situation that is possible in cosmic, but not in physical, geography!

48 Note, e.g., Isaiah 2:5, in the context of the cosmic order that spreads out into the world from the temple in Jerusalem, and Psalm 36:9, in the context of benefiting from the fountain that sends forth life-giving waters from this temple.

49 The relevant part of Isaiah 45:21, e.g., reads, "Who foretold this long ago, who declared it from the distant past?"

50 We shall return to this topic in chaps. 5–6.

51 Ludwig, *Paths*, 76–78.

52 Ludwig, *Paths*, 96–100.

53 Ludwig, *Paths*, 148–55. Jainism also retains the basic ideas of karma as a universal law, suffering existence within samsara as the basic human problem, and liberation from the karmic cycle as the ultimate human goal.

54 See further on the pre-Socratics and the Pythagoreans, W. K. C. Guthrie, *A History of Greek Philosophy*, vol. 1, *The Earlier Presocratics and the Pythagoreans* (Cambridge: Cambridge University Press, 1962).

55 Eric Voegelin, *Plato* (Baton Rouge: Louisiana State University Press, 1957).

56 David J. Levy, "The Religion of Light: On Mani and Manichaeism," in Arnason, Eisenstadt, and Wittrock, *Axial Civilizations and World History*, 319–36 (333).

57 Consider, for example, the first volume of Derrick Jensen's *Endgame*, which sees biblical faith as (1) legitimating the conquest of the planet, since its primary texts include one that commands human beings to subdue the earth and have dominion over it (233); (2) teaching that God's home is not primarily of this earth and as presenting us with a God who cannot provide us with a workable this-worldly ethic (32); and (3) encouraging in its adherents the killing of the planet, because it will hasten "the ultimate victory of God over all things earthly, all things evil" (226). It is important that we believe to the contrary, he says, that "the material world is primary . . . that spirit mixes with flesh" (301).

58 As Charles S. Peirce puts it, "The movement of love is circular, at one and the same impulse projecting creations into independency and drawing them into harmony." *Collected Papers*, vol. 6, *Scientific Metaphysics*, ed. Charles Hartshorne and Paul Weiss (Cambridge, Mass.: Harvard University Press, 1935), 191 (6.288). I am grateful to Paul Teel for drawing my attention to this.

59 Ludwig, *Paths*, 389.

60 It is, however, not just among those who claim to hold to biblical faith that we find beliefs and attitudes that appear to call the goodness of creation into question. Islam is strikingly world affirming in the main, and there is in its basic teaching no idea that creation is intrinsically problematic with respect to human destiny; see, e.g., Ruthven, *Islam*, 103–4. Nevertheless, tendencies toward world negation can be found, for example, in some strands of Sufism, with its ultimate aim of union with God and its ascetic practices (including very Eastern practices, like yogic breathing); see Ruthven, *Islam*, 64–69; and Ludwig, *Paths*, 461–63. Even in Sufism, however, asceticism is not the main focus in the quest for union with God. The spiritual guides who are adopted by their followers are, in fact, often worldly-wise and quite rich, participating very much in "the good life," and there is a strong emphasis on their importance in assuring their disciples of success and happiness, often in world-affirming ways (material success, children, and so on).

61 We shall return to this matter in chap. 11.

CHAPTER 3

1   William Shakespeare, *King Lear*, 4.1.36–37. References are to act, scene, and line.
2   Maud Van Buren, *Quotations for Special Occasions* (New York: H. W. Wilson, 1938), 176.
3   Ludwig, *Paths*, 73–76; and Muesse, *Traditions*, 40–57.
4   Ludwig, *Paths*, 206–7; and Kohn, *Daoism*, 1–4.
5   Ludwig, *Paths*, 331–33; Robert Parker, "Greek Religion," in Boardman, Griffin and Murray, *Greece and the Hellenistic World*, 254–74; and Mary Beard, John North, and Simon Price, *Religions of Rome*, 2 vols. (Cambridge: Cambridge University Press, 1998).
6   Ludwig, *Paths*, 34–68; and Taylor, *Religion*, passim.
7   H. L. Mencken, *Minority Report* (Baltimore: Johns Hopkins University Press, 2006), 63.
8   The gods of Ugarit in Syria and of Mesopotamia *were* pictured as making major decisions as a group, gathering in a divine assembly chaired by a high god. In the earliest Sumerian literature the chair is Anu. In later Mesopotamian literature, it is Marduk in Babylonia and Asshur in Assyria. In Ugaritic literature, it is El. See Walton, *Thought*, 92–97, and particularly his comments on the "board" of gods on pp. 103–4.
9   For a brief explanation of monism, see chap. 2.
10 Walton, *Thought*, 168–69, 181.
11 Ludwig, *Paths*, 39–40.
12 Daniel C. Snell, *Religions of the Ancient Near East* (Cambridge: Cambridge University Press, 2011), 72–79.
13 Ludwig, *Paths*, 293–95; and C. Scott Littleton, *Shinto: Origins, Rituals, Festivals, Spirits, Sacred Places* (New York: Oxford University Press, 2002), 23–36.
14 Jean Bottéro, *Religion in Ancient Mesopotamia*, trans. Teresa Lavender Fagan (Chicago: University of Chicago Press, 2001), 62–63, 181–82; and Ludwig, *Paths*, 41.
15 For the prohibition of astral worship, see, e.g., Deuteronomy 4:19: "When you look up to the sky and see the sun, the moon and the stars—all the heavenly array—do not be enticed into bowing down to them and worshiping things the Lord your God has apportioned to all the nations under heaven."
16 For a brief introduction to this god, see Iain Provan, "2 Kings," in *1 & 2 Kings, 1 & 2 Chronicles, Ezra, Nehemiah, Esther*, Zondervan Illustrated Bible Backgrounds Commentary 3, ed. John Walton (Grand Rapids: Zondervan, 2009), 110–219 (117).
17 Ludwig, *Paths*, 293–95; and Littleton, *Shinto*, 23–36.
18 Ludwig, *Paths*, 41.
19 On the details of the story, see Iain Provan, *1 & 2 Kings*, Understanding the Bible (Grand Rapids: Baker, 1995), 132–50. It is, of course, belief in the fundamental connectedness of everything—the continuity of gods or spirits, the land, and ourselves—that lies at the heart of the idea that rituals correctly performed will produce the desired results. Note by way of analogy what Ronald M. Berndt says about Aboriginal religion in the Australian north and northwest: "The great fertility cults . . . are designed to activate—through a combination of male and female elements—the natural forces surrounding man. Life is a continuing process of birth and re-birth, decay and revival, in nature, and in man. To ensure that this process is not jeopardized, spiritual intervention is necessary." *Australian Aboriginal Religion* (Leiden: Brill, 1974), fasc. 4, p. 26. Note further Muesse's comments on Vedic ritual (*Traditions*, 50–57).

20 Islam itself can rightly be said to have "emerged" out of polytheism, both in the sense that it emerged out of a culture marked by polytheistic belief and in the sense that Muhammad himself may have taken some time after beginning to receive his visions to leave polytheism behind fully. That is the implication of the now-infamous "Satanic verses" concerning three Meccan goddesses, transmitted by such early Islamic scholars as Muhammad's first biographer Ibn Ishaq (d. A.D. 767) and the annalist Tabari (d. 923). See further Ruthven, *Islam*, 35–36. In turn, Muslims typically think of Christians as polytheists because in the Christian belief system God is not only one but also three. The Qur'an expressly states that God "has not begotten, and has not been begotten, and equal to Him there is not anyone" (112). The various inscriptions on the Dome of the Rock in Jerusalem underline the point. The Islamic "oneness" of God is absolute, and to associate anything else with God is to commit the grave sin of *shirk*.

21 For a good, brief discussion of the phrase, see Wenham, *Genesis 1–15*, 27–28.

22 This is also true in Islam, to such an extent that the Qur'an itself, being the very speech of God, is regarded as uncreated. Ruthven, *Islam*, 23, 60–61. The oneness and transcendence of God are not understood in biblical faith, conversely, as requiring that Scripture is uncreated. It is understood to be God's Word but at the same time to have emerged out of genuinely historical and human circumstances by way of genuinely participating authors.

23 Walton, *Thought*, 88–89.

24 Ludwig, *Paths*, 232.

25 Ludwig, *Paths*, 293–94.

26 Other passages along the same lines are Isaiah 42:5-17 and 43:1-7.

27 Walton, *Thought*, 97–99.

28 The text is cited in Ludwig, *Paths*, 76. For a fuller discussion of it in context, see Muesse, *Traditions*, 44–45.

29 Barnes, *Aristotle*, 102.

30 Walton, *Thought*, 191–95 (esp. 192).

31 In Islam, e.g., "the oneness of God means . . . that all power belongs to God. There is no other source of power, since God has no competitors. It follows, then, since God is the only creator of the world, that everything that takes place in the created world results from God's will." Ludwig, *Paths*, 473.

32 Geoffrey Keynes and Brian Hill, eds., *Samuel Butler's Notebooks* (New York: E. P. Dutton, 1951), 232.

33 See further chap. 8 of my *Convenient Myths*.

34 Walton, *Thought*, 103–5.

35 Aristotle, *Politics*, trans. H. Rackam (Cambridge, Mass.: Harvard University Press, 1944), 1.1252b.

36 Dawkins, *Delusion*, 51.

37 Note by way of example the comments of Derrick Jensen (*Endgame*, 1:160) on the jealousy of the biblical God and its role in producing the hegemony of the gods of modern science, capitalism, and civilization.

38 Westermann, *Genesis 1–11*, 237 (my translation).

39 The story of the manna in Exodus 16 illustrates the same point.

40 The precise sense of the verb "bless" in the last line here is disputed, but the translation offered here is, I believe, sound; see further our chap. 7.

41 I follow here the New Revised Standard Version translation.

42 C. S. Lewis, *The Lion, the Witch and the Wardrobe* (New York: HarperCollins, 2009), 80.

43   On the whole theme of idolatry in the Old Testament, see further Iain Provan, "To Highlight All Our Idols: Worshipping God in Nietzsche's World," *Ex Auditu* 15 (2000): 19–38.

44   Dawkins, *Delusion*, 246.

45   Dawkins, *Delusion*, 247.

46   Notice the deliberate emphasis in various biblical texts upon just how dark this culture was and just how long it had been so (e.g., Genesis 15:16; Leviticus 18:24-26; Deuteronomy 9:4-5). Notice, further, the same kind of emphasis on the war in Canaan as *God's* (and not the Israelites') war. The Israelites are only God's vassals, summoned to help him fight (e.g., Amos 2:9; Psalm 78:53-55). When the Israelites are being faithful, in biblical thinking, they always fight God's battles in this way, and not their own. Their request for a human king in 1 Samuel 8:7-20 is indeed portrayed as wicked precisely because, in general, it represents a rejection of God's kingship and, in particular, it involves the raising of a standing army for the king's own use, such that the Israelites "will be like all the other nations, with a king to lead us and to go out before us and fight *our* battles."

47   The promised land, in biblical thinking, is fundamentally a gift. It is not something that Israel owns by inalienable right, because of her own activity in possessing it; it belongs to God and it is given to Israel in pursuit of God's long-term (and good) plans for the world (e.g., Genesis 12:1-3; 15:1-16; Deuteronomy 8:7-10; 9:4-5; Amos 2:9-10). Indeed, it is a gift that can be taken away if the Israelites do not handle it properly (e.g., Amos 7:17), precisely because, in biblical thinking, God can fight *against* Israel as well as on her side. Indeed, in a very real sense, God *never* fights on Israel's side at all; the question is always whether Israel is going to fight on God's side—on the side of justice and righteousness. Thus in 1 Samuel 4, e.g., when Israel tries to manipulate God into fighting against the Philistines by bringing the ark of the covenant into the camp, God demonstrates his independence of them by seeing to it that they are routed. We find the same idea in passages like Isaiah 10:5-6 (where the Assyrians are described as the rod of God's anger against Israel) and Jeremiah 25:9-11 (where Nebuchadnezzar is the vehicle of God's anger against Israel).

48   Some biblical texts give the impression that the conquest of the land of Canaan was complete and that all the original inhabitants were wiped out; e.g., "Joshua subdued the whole region. . . . He left no survivors. He totally destroyed [Heb. *khrm*] all who breathed, just as the LORD, the God of Israel had commanded" (Joshua 10:40-42; cf. Deuteronomy 7:1-6 and 20:16-18). Other texts, however, lead us to reconsider this first reading of such passages. In the first place, the predominant way of referring to the conquest of Canaan in the Old Testament is in terms of expulsion, not killing (e.g., Leviticus 18:24-28; Numbers 33:51-56; 2 Kings 16:3)— just as the Israelites, later, are said to have been expelled from the land because they sinned in the same way as the Canaanites (2 Kings 17:7-23). Second, there are clearly many Canaanites still living in the land in the *aftermath* of Joshua's victories who are not ultimately even *expelled* from the land, much less killed (e.g., Judges 1:1-3:6; 2 Samuel 24:7; 1 Kings 9:15-23). Clearly, then, there is something very strange about the language of Joshua 10 (and associated passages). It seems, in fact, that we are dealing here with hyperbolic language that is fairly typical of ancient Near Eastern conquest accounts and that we should not interpret it as claiming anything more than that Joshua won comprehensive military victories. See further K. Lawson Younger Jr., *Ancient Conquest Accounts: A Study in Ancient Near Eastern and Biblical History Writing*, JSOTSup 98 (Sheffield: JSOT Press, 1990).

49 Texts like Deuteronomy 4:25-28, 1 Kings 14:15-16, and 2 Kings 21:11 look ahead to this reality, and various other texts describe it retrospectively (e.g., 2 Kings 17:7-23). That it is wickedness and not ethnicity that leads to the divine command to *khrm* ("totally destroy") people is underlined by the case in Deuteronomy 13, where *Israelites* worshipping other gods are consigned to this same fate (v. 15).

50 Psalms 6:3; 13:1-2; 35:17, and numerous other occasions.

51 We see this in narratives like Judges 11, where before we even get to the fighting, there is a long preamble (in vv. 12-28) that has to do with the *justice* of the case, in the course of which God is called upon as impartial judge in the dispute (cf. 2 Chronicles 20:6-12). War is intrinsically a *judicial* business. We see it, too, in biblical law—in the very idea that there are *rules* of war concerning such matters as proper regard for the land when a siege is taking place (20:19-20) and proper treatment of prisoners of war (21:10-14).

52 I do not suggest that the *solution* to the problem of the strange language in Joshua 10 (and related texts like Deuteronomy 7:1-6 and 20:16-18) should have been obvious to these readers, since only modern scholarly research has made this solution clear. However, the strangeness itself should have been obvious to any Bible reader who knows what God's justice typically looks like in the remainder of the Old Testament; who is aware, specifically, of the way in which combatants and noncombatants are typically distinguished in warfare therein (e.g., Exodus 22:24; Numbers 14:3); and who is further aware that children, in particular, are not held morally accountable for wrongdoing and are not to be caught up in their parents' wrongdoing (Deuteronomy 1:39; 24:16—in the very book of Deuteronomy that speaks about the Canaanite wars). It should also have been obvious to any Bible reader who reads past the book of Joshua into the book of Judges and finds so many surviving Canaanites there and to any careful reader of Deuteronomy 7:1-3, which (curiously), after telling the Israelites that God is "driving out" the current inhabitants of the land, then urges them to "destroy them totally" (Heb. *khrm*, as in Deuteronomy 20:17 and Joshua 10:40), and *then* tells them not to intermarry with them. All of this, already, raises real questions about the proper understanding of *khrm*, long before we get to the matter of the typical language of ancient Near Eastern conquest accounts.

53 Notice, for instance, the easy manner in which the biblical narratives about the conquest of Canaan were co-opted by some early settlers in the Americas to justify their actions (as "Israel") against the indigenous peoples ("Canaanites, Ammonites," and so on). A good example is Cotton Mather, *Soldiers Counseled and Comforted: A Discourse Delivered unto Some Part of the Forces Engaged in the Just War of New England against the Northern and Eastern Indians, Sept. 1 1689* (Boston: Samuel Green, 1689).

54 Joseph Campbell, *The Power of Myth* (New York: Anchor Books, 1991), 24.

55 Ludwig, *Paths*, 474.

56 It should be noted, however, that in Islam (unlike biblical faith) there is little exploration of what these names might signify in terms of relationality. In Islam, Allah is, in fact, defined more by what he is not than by what he is—i.e, Allah has many names (including these two), but the names reveal little about Allah's *nature*.

57 Walton, *Thought*, 105.

58 Walton, *Thought*, 142–45.

59 See further chap. 4 ahead, as well as my *Convenient Myths*, chap. 8.

60 Bottéro, *Religion*, 37.

61 Herodotus, *Histories* 3.40.2, trans. A. D. Godley (Cambridge, Mass.: Harvard University Press, 1920).

62 Wayson Choy, *All That Matters* (Toronto, Ont.: Doubleday Canada, 2004). More generally, but briefly, on traditional Chinese religion, see Ludwig, *Paths*, 225–26. It is intriguing that Islam, which rejects the multiplicity of gods, nonetheless also shares *something* with ancient Near Eastern polytheism in understanding (the singular) God still as an inaccessible and dominating master and a ruler, and most definitively *not* as a friend.

CHAPTER 4

1 William Shakespeare, *Hamlet*, 2.2:303–6.

2 Mark Twain, *Mark Twain's Notebook*, ed. Albert Bigelow Paine (New York: Harper & Brothers, 1935), 381.

3 The Hebrew word '*enosh* is commonly translated "man," but the translation is open to misunderstanding in modern times, in which the issue of gendered language has become so important. There is no evident intention in the text to refer just to males. It is humanity in general that is in view (as it is when '*enosh* is used in verses like Deuteronomy 32:26 and Job 36:25). See further my comments ahead on the Hebrew word '*adam*.

4 See further chap. 8 of my *Convenient Myths*.

5 Walton, *Thought*, 215.

6 Bottéro, *Religion*, 6.

7 It is only at this point that the authors apparently begin to use the word '*adam* to mean the same thing as the word '*ish* ("man") that appears in v. 24 ("a man will leave his father and mother"). *At this point*, and only at this point, are maleness and femaleness now front and center. Just prior to Genesis 2:24, in v. 23, the word '*ish* is itself used to refer to the undifferentiated earth-being ("she was taken out of man," v. 23). On a related matter, the proper name Adam that appears as a translation of '*adam* in various translations of the Bible at different places throughout chapters 2 and 3 is best avoided until Genesis 3:20. Only here does it become sensible, with the naming of the woman as Eve, to understand '*adam* as a personal name for the man.

8 In all of this I agree in significant ways with the reading of Genesis 2 offered by Phyllis Trible in *God and the Rhetoric of Sexuality*, Overtures to Biblical Theology 2 (Philadelphia: Fortress, 1978), chap. 4.

9 "Adam," in *Dictionary of Biblical Imagery*, ed. Leland Ryken, James C. Wilhoit, and Tremper Longman III (Downers Grove, Ill.: InterVarsity, 1998), 9–14 (9).

10 For a good brief discussion of the reading tradition and a bibliography, see Wenham, *Genesis 1–15*, 26–32; and, further, J. Richard Middleton, *The Liberating Image: The Imago Dei in Genesis 1* (Grand Rapids: Brazos, 2005).

11 Walton, *Thought*, 278–86.

12 For "glory" (Heb. *kavod*) in this sense, see, e.g., Exodus 33:18 and Ezekiel 1:28; for "honor" (Heb. *hadar*), see Psalm 96:6 (NIV's "majesty") and Psalm 145:5 (with *kavod*).

13 His speech concludes thus, in lines 308–10: "And yet to me what is this quintessence of dust? Man delights not me—nor woman neither, though by your smiling you seem to say so."

14 Hitchens, *God*, 73.

15 "Shrub" represents the Hebrew word *siakh* (probably referring to nonedible plants), and "plant" represents '*eseb* (probably referring to edible plants or plants that provide edible food).

16   Mesopotamia was and is dominated by the twin river system of the Tigris and Euphrates, which run south from the southern Caucasus Mountains through arid land. It is only their waters that made life possible in this region in ancient times, but the same rivers brought death as well. They were snow fed, and they could (and did) flood, sometimes washing out whole cities. They had to be "tamed" if they were to be useful to the inhabitants.

17   The Hebrew word *siakh* does not appear in Genesis 1 and occurs on only three other occasions in the Old Testament (Genesis 21:15; Job 30:4, 7), so its precise connotation is uncertain.

18   Kass (*Wisdom*, 73) adds the interpretations "boldly in front" and "in his face."

19   The NIV implausibly tries to negate the difference in "chronological" arrangement between Genesis 1 and 2 with respect to animals and humans by translating Genesis 2:19 in the pluperfect. God has just said, "I *will* make a helper suitable for him" (v. 18); in v. 19, he then goes on to form out of the ground a number of possible candidates. The NRSV is much better: "So out of the ground the LORD God formed every animal of the field." On the order of events in Genesis 1–2; see further Kass, *Wisdom*, 30, 54–56.

20   Walton, *Thought*, 87–92, 188–90.

21   Walton, *Thought*, 88.

22   Walton, *Thought*, 90.

23   Augustine, *The Trinity* 12.7.10, trans. Arthur W. Haddan (Buffalo, N.Y.: Christian Literature, 1887), 159.

24   In this, they follow the view of early feminist pioneers like Elizabeth Cady Stanton, who may rightly be called the founder of modern feminist interpretation of the Bible and who was the inspiration behind *The Woman's Bible* (1895 and 1898). Elizabeth Cady Stanton, *The Woman's Bible: A Classic Feminist Perspective* (New York: Dover, 2002).

25   Note, e.g., Jensen's convictions (*Endgame*, 1:283) about the violence that is endemic to civilization, nurtured by axial age religions: "This violence . . . is widely accepted, because from birth we are individually and collectively enculturated to hate life, hate the natural world, hate the wild, hate wild animals, *hate women*, hate children, hate our bodies, hate and fear our emotions, hate ourselves" (emphasis added). The standard line in dark green religion is then to argue that the period prior to the rise of axial age religions was one unmarked by such problems—one that was marked, to the contrary, by peace, equality, ecological wisdom, and useful religion. For a full description and critique of this view, see my *Convenient Myths*, chaps. 4–6.

26   Consider, e.g., the following post: "Why Was Eve Created Second? (Women in Church Leadership, Part 7)," *Passionate Follower's Journal*, October 2, 2007, accessed October 26, 2012, http://thepfjournal.wordpress.com/2007/10/02/why-was-eve-created-second-women-in-church-leadership-part-7/.

27   So, e.g., Wenham, *Genesis 1–15*, 70: "Though they are equal in nature, that man names woman (cf. 3:20) indicates that she is expected to be subordinate to him."

28   See further Kass, *Wisdom*, 74–75. Later in Genesis, Eve apparently names Cain, and again the naming is not about taking *authority* but about where Cain "fits" in the story (4:1; see further our chap. 8).

29   This overall tension in the Old Testament between what is and what might or should be when it comes to society—between moral vision and pragmatic reality—we shall explore in greater depth in chap. 10.

30   Note, e.g., the negative biblical references to the practice in such verses as 2 Kings 16:3; 17:17, 31.

31   Ahab discovers this after the judicial murder of Naboth in 1 Kings 21:1-26.

32   Note the instructions, e.g., in Deuteronomy 14:28-29, and the condemnation in Job 22:5-11.

33   See Proverbs 25:21 and Job 31:13-15.

34   See further chap. 8 of my *Convenient Myths*.

35   This is such a well-known descriptor for Athens that it can be (and regularly is) deployed in modern media without any further explanation. E.g., John Lichfield, "Disbelief and Anger in the Cradle of Western Democracy," *Independent*, May 8, 2010, accessed June 20, 2013, http://www.independent.co.uk/news/world/europe/disbelief-and-anger-in-the-cradle-of-western-democracy-1968232.html.

36   Aristotle, *Politics* 3.9.1280a 32–34, trans. Benjamin Jowett (New York: Random House, 1943), 142.

37   Hesiod, *Theogony*, 9.600-2, trans. Norman O. Brown (Indianapolis: Bobbs-Merrill, 1953), 70. Kass describes a further Greek tale from Plato's *Symposium*, which also understands women as something of a curse laid upon men (or at least a distraction): "Zeus tries to remedy a dangerous tendency of original human beings to storm heaven by halving their strength and giving them some other desire to occupy them" (*Wisdom*, 101). The "halving" turns the original human being into man and woman; the desire is erotic longing for "the other half." Sex distracts humans from the pursuit of divinity.

38   Aristotle, *Politics* 1.5.1254b 13 (trans. Jowett), 59 (emphasis added).

39   Aristotle, *Politics* 1.12.1259a 40 (trans. Jowett), 75 (emphasis added).

40   Pseudo-Demosthenes, *Against Neaera by Apollodorus*, in *Legal Speeches of Democratic Athens: Sources for Athenian History*, ed. Andrew Wolpert and Konstantinos Kapparis (Indianapolis: Hackett, 2011), 187–226 (224).

41   Julia Annas refers to Plato's view as follows: "Women who have natures suitable to be Guardians should . . . be appropriately trained." "Plato's *Republic* and Feminism," in Fine, *Plato*, 747–61 (749).

42   Most scholars think that there were, but see Brian Calvert, "Slavery in Plato's *Republic*," *Classical Quarterly* 37 (1987): 367–72.

43   The Stoics also embraced "egalitarianism of a kind." Stoicism was about conforming the will to the course of the history that is fated to occur in line with the will of impersonal Nature, identified with the god Zeus of popular Greek religion. This meant, for the Stoics, living in line with innate reason, which is our own special human "nature." In principle, all human beings with the capacity to reason were thus on an equal footing. This did not mean, however, that even in Stoic *ideals*, much less in social *practice*, women and slaves were in fact treated as equals. See David M. Engel, "Women's Role in the Home and State: Stoic Theory Reconsidered," *Harvard Studies in Classical Philology* 101 (2003): 267–88. In other words, the Stoic "universal brotherhood of man" had definite limits; see further our chap. 9.

44   Aristotle, *Politics* 1.5.1254b 24–25 (trans. Jowett), 59.

45   Oswyn Murray, "Life and Society in Ancient Greece," in Boardman, Griffin, and Murray, *Greece and the Hellenistic World*, 204–33 (224–26).

46   See, e.g., David Armitage, "John Locke, Carolina, and the *Two Treatises of Government*," *Political Theory* 32 (2004): 602–27.

47   Ludwig, *Paths*, 475.

48   Ludwig, *Paths*, 474–76; and Kaltner, *Qur'an*, 70–73.

49   Ludwig, *Paths*, 479–80; and Ruthven, *Islam*, 75–92 (91).

50   Kaltner, *Qur'an*, 108–112 (112).

51 Ruthven, *Islam*, 96. He follows here the translation of Arthur J. Arberry in *The Koran Interpreted* (Oxford: Oxford University Press, 1983).

52 Kaltner, *Qur'an*, 107.

53 Kaltner, *Qur'an*, 121, 122.

54 Ruthven, *Islam*, 97. This belief *would* of course allow for proposals to *translate/interpret* a text like Sura 4:34 differently, and it is interesting in this respect to note that the new translation of the Qur'an offered by M. A. S. Abdel Haleem in the Oxford World's Classics series does so in part: "husbands should take good care of their wives with [the bounties] God has given to some rather than others" (Oxford: Oxford University Press, 2005). The reference to the abuse of the wife remains, however. It is to this new translation that I refer in the remainder of the book when quoting the Qur'an.

55 Ludwig, *Paths*, 117–18; and Muesse, *Traditions*, 72–82.

56 Ludwig, *Paths*, 119.

57 Muesse, *Traditions*, 74.

58 Ludwig, *Paths*, 118–23 (120).

59 Ludwig, *Paths*, 120.

60 Muesse, *Traditions*, 86.

61 This happens in some Muslim households as well. One of my teaching assistants once spent a month living with different Muslim families in Southeast Asia, and, in a few of these households, the men would eat alone with their guests while the women (who had prepared the meal) watched. The women and children in this scenario would typically eat later.

62 Ludwig, *Paths*, 120–21.

63 Ludwig, *Paths*, 113.

64 See further Ashok Prasad, "Harsh Reality of India's Unwanted Girls," *BBC*, October 22, 2007, accessed October 26, 2012, http://news.bbc.co.uk/2/hi/programmes/this_world/7050657.stm; and her "India's Missing Girls," *BBC*, October 18, 2007, accessed October 26, 2012, http://news.bbc.co.uk/2/hi/programmes/this_world/7039681.stm. An earlier study reported in *The Lancet* (2011) estimated that between four and twelve million girls were aborted in India over the preceding three decades. Prabhat Jha et al., "Trends in Selective Abortions of Girls in India: Analysis of Nationally Representative Birth Histories from 1990 to 2005 and Census Data from 1991 to 2011," *Lancet* 377, no. 9781 (2011): 1921–1928, accessed December 29, 2012, http://www.thelancet.com/journals/lancet/article/PIIS0140-6736%2811%2960649-1/abstract.

65 The Buddha's different construal of dharma was only one element in an overall strategy in early Buddhism *semantically* to turn the old Vedic world upside down—to take what was familiar and to do something quite different with it. See Sheldon Pollock, "Axialism and Empire," in Arnason, Eisenstadt, and Wittrock, *Axial Civilizations and World History*, 397–450 (402–4).

66 Ludwig, *Paths*, 167; see also Donald W. Mitchell, *Buddhism: Introducing the Buddhist Experience* (New York: Oxford University Press, 2002), 27–28.

67 We find this same idea (that men stand higher up the reincarnational chain of being than women) expressed by Timaeus in Plato's work of that name (even though in the *Republic* Plato himself regards men and women as being on equal terms). For Timaeus, each human soul began life on a star, before being born into the material world, and "he who lived well during his appointed time was to return and dwell in his native star, and there he would have a blessed and congenial existence. But if he failed in attaining this, at the second birth he would pass into a woman, and if, when in that state of being, he did not desist from

evil, he would continually be changed into some brute who resembled him in the evil nature which he had acquired, and would not cease from his toils and transformations until he helped the revolution of the same and the like within him to draw in its train the turbulent mob of later accretions, made up of fire and air and water and earth, and by this victory of reason over the irrational returned to the form of his first and better state." *Timaeus* 42b–c, in *Timaeus and Other Dialogues*, vol. 3 of *The Dialogues of Plato*, trans. Benjamin Jowett (London: Sphere Books, 1970), 246–47.

68 Long, *Jainism*, 16.

69 Long, *Jainism*, 17.

CHAPTER 5

1 Boethius, *The Consolation of Philosophy* I.4.12, trans. Richard Green (Indianapolis: Bobbs-Merrill, 1962). Here, Boethius is quoting Epicurus, who is himself quoting Lactantius.

2 Woody Allen, "Selections from the Allen Notebooks," in *Without Feathers* (New York: Random House, 1975), 5–6.

3 Kass, *Wisdom*, 62. Kass' earlier comments on this page clarify: "unless and until fear of death is accompanied by something like self-conscious *knowledge* of death as a *badness*, the creature will have no interest in trying to overcome death by seeking immortality from the tree of life."

4 John Calvin, *Commentaries on the First Book of Moses Called Genesis*, 2 vols., trans. John King (Edinburgh: Calvin Translation Society, 1847), 1:177. I was alerted to this reference by my student Bethany N. Sollereder, whose unpublished Regent College master's thesis on evolutionary theodicy has provided me with more than one useful lead in my own work. "Evolutionary Theodicy: An Evangelical Perspective" (Master's thesis, Regent College, 2007).

5 Lowell K. Handy, "Serpent (Religious Symbol)," in Freedman et al., *Anchor Bible Dictionary*, 5:1113–16 (hereafter *ABD*).

6 Nahum M. Sarna, *Genesis* (Philadelphia: Jewish Publication Society, 1989), 24.

7 Kass, *Wisdom*, 80–81.

8 The tree of life is not explicitly withheld, although it seems that the humans do not eat of its fruit anyway. I discuss this further ahead.

9 It also indicates that she is confused, because in the Hebrew text of Genesis 2:9 (as opposed to the NIV) it is the tree of life that is in the middle of the garden, not the forbidden tree. Kass, *Wisdom*, 85.

10 Similarly Wenham writes, "The woman corrects the snake, but not quite accurately. . . . The creator's generosity is not being given its full due, and he is being painted as a little harsh and repressive" (*Genesis 1–15*, 73).

11 Robert Gordis, "The Knowledge of Good and Evil in the Old Testament and the Qumran Scrolls," *JBL* 76 (1957): 123–38 (130–36).

12 Karen Armstrong, *A Short History of Myth* (Toronto, Ont.: Knopf, 2005), 60. Dark green religionists possess their own version of this allegedly biblical argument; consider, e.g., John Zerzan's *Twilight of the Machines* (Port Townsend, Wash.: Feral House, 2008), which finds the roots of our contemporary human difficulties in the new knowledge that created the possibility of the Neolithic agricultural revolution and the domestication of animals. This led in due course to "civilization," which soon took "an iron grip" on the human spirit—note the title of his fourth chapter, "The Iron Grip of Civilization: The Axial Age."

13 Gordis, "Knowledge," 124–25.

14 For a further discussion of wisdom in 2 Samuel 14 and its wider context in Samuel–Kings, see Iain Provan, "On 'Seeing' the Trees while Missing the Forest: The Wisdom of Characters and Readers in 2 Samuel and 1 Kings," in *In Search of True Wisdom: Essays in Old Testament Interpretation in Honour of Ronald E. Clements*, ed. Edward Ball, JSOTSup 300 (Sheffield: Sheffield Academic, 2000), 153–73.

15 Kass, *Wisdom*, 63–64.

16 For a detailed analysis of the Solomon story along these lines, see Provan, *1 & 2 Kings*, 23–102.

17 The one possible exception is found in 1 Chronicles 4:9, which describes the pain of the mother of Jabez, but further analysis proves this not to be an exception after all. See further Iain Provan, "Pain in Childbirth? Further Thoughts on 'An Attractive Fragment' (1 Chronicles 4:9-10)," in *Let Us Go Up to Zion: Essays In Honour of H. G. M. Williamson on the Occasion of His Sixty-Fifth Birthday*, ed. Iain Provan and Mark Boda, VTSup 153 (Leiden: Brill, 2012), 285–96.

18 See, e.g., Hosea 9:11, where "Ephraim's glory will fly away like a bird—no birth, no pregnancy, no conception [*herayon*]."

19 There is no true mirroring if *'itsabon* is understood as "birth pangs," for then the man's pains are daily and ongoing, whereas the women's pains (albeit significant) are temporary and short lived. Kass understands this without following through on the point (*Wisdom*, 116).

20 So also Victor P. Hamilton writes, "Far from being a reign of co-equals over the remainder of God's creation, the relationship now becomes a fierce dispute, with each party trying to rule the other." *Genesis 1–17*, NICOT (Grand Rapids: Eerdmans, 1990), 202. This understanding of the verse is perhaps reflected in the curious report in the Talmud (*Tamid* 32b) that Alexander the Great rediscovered the entrance to the garden of God in the parts of Africa that were said to be governed by women.

21 "There is division of labor, defined relative to work: the one gives birth, the other tills." Kass, *Wisdom*, 94.

22 Kass, *Wisdom*, 119. As an interesting extrabiblical example of the "heroic" male, he later cites the Trojan Hector in Homer's *Iliad* (198 n. 1). See further our chap. 8 ahead.

23 Here I disagree with commentators like Umberto Cassuto, *A Commentary on the Book of Genesis I, from Adam to Noah: Genesis 1–6:8*, trans. Israel Abrahams (Jerusalem: Magnes, 1978), 168–69. More helpful is C. John Collins, *Genesis 1–4: A Linguistic, Literary and Theological Commentary* (Phillipsburg, N.J.: P & R, 2006), 164: "The account never implies that that 'the ground' did not produce 'thorns and thistles' prior to this point; it instead indicates that working the ground is to be the arena of 'pain'—and this is due not to a change in the properties of the ground but to the change in humanity and to God's providential purpose of chastisement."

24 Among those who get this right is Wenham, who comments on the wording of Genesis 3:22: "'Take from the tree of life' seems to imply that while he was in the garden man could have eaten of the tree, but he had not" (*Genesis 1–15*, 85). Wenham stands in a long tradition of reading at this point, which includes the thirteenth-century Jewish exegete Ramban, who argued that since Adam's sole objective before the fall was to serve God, he had no motivation to eat from the tree of life.

25 See further our chap. 11, on hope in biblical faith.

26   Some have recently disputed whether Boethius really was, or remained to the end, a Christian. I find these arguments entirely unpersuasive.

27   Walton, *Thought*, 107. This kind of suffering could also be attributed to demons (306).

28   Walton, *Thought*, 305–6.

29   Walton, *Thought*, 306–8.

30   Plato, *Tim.* 47e–48a.

31   James L. Wood, "Is There an *Archê Kakou* in Plato?" *Review of Metaphysics* 250 (2009): 349–84 (378), referring to *Tim.* 30a, 35a, 48a.

32   Having cited Wood's words in support of this reading of Plato, however, I must acknowledge that he himself holds (nevertheless) that "in the *Statesman* and *Timaeus* . . . what seems to be a competing principle of evil" indeed only *seems* to be ("*Archê Kakou*," 350) and that "in a strict sense there is no metaphysical or divine evil in Plato, because evil metaphysically conceived reduces to pure negativity or indeterminacy, which as such lacks independent reality" (349). Whether evil has indeed *actually* "always and inevitably been there," from Plato's perspective, can thus be disputed.

33   Ludwig, *Paths*, 337–40; and Jenny Rose, *Zoroastrianism: An Introduction* (London: I.B. Tauris, 2011).

34   Ludwig, *Paths*, 208.

35   Ludwig, *Paths*, 210–13, 241–42.

36   Ludwig, *Paths*, 213–15, 234–41; and Kohn, *Daoism*, 23–28.

37   Kohn, *Daoism*, 26.

38   Ludwig, *Paths*, 214. A similar idea turns up in the thinking of the Neoplatonist Plotinus, whose philosophy we shall consider in chap. 6.

39   We are also some distance away from biblical faith in the case of Japanese Shinto, where good and evil are defined only in terms of *wa*, the "benign harmony" that is intrinsic to nature and human relationships. Anything that disrupts *wa* is by definition bad, and anything that promotes it is good. Conformity with the natural and societal order is the important thing, not conformity with a transcendental and personal Good. See Littleton, *Shinto*, 58–65.

40   Mitchell, *Buddhism*, 36–37.

41   Mitchell, *Buddhism*, 37.

42   Mitchell, *Buddhism*, 60.

CHAPTER 6

1   This quotation is often falsely attributed to Edmund Burke—an eighteenth-century British politician. Its true origin remains shrouded in mystery.

2   *I Ching: Book of Changes*, trans. James Legge (New York: Bantam, 1969), 391.

3   See further Linda S. Schearing, "Parturition (Childbirth), Pain, and Piety: Physicians and Genesis 3:16a," in *Mother Goose, Mother Jones and Mommie Dearest: Biblical Mothers and Their Children*, ed. Cheryl Kirk-Duggan and Tina Pippin, SemeiaSt 61 (Atlanta: Society of Biblical Literature, 2009), 85–96.

4   This was, indeed, an aspect of the reading tradition to which the earliest feminist writers from the seventeenth century onward believed they had to give particular attention as they sought to carve out space for women in the public realm. See Hennie J. Marsman, *Women in Ugarit and Israel: Their Social and Religious Position in the Context of the Ancient Near East* (Leiden: Brill, 2003), 1–12. E.g., when Judith Sargent Murray wrote an important essay in 1790 on the equality of the sexes, the context was one in which "for her opponent, and to a large extent

most of American society, the Scriptures contained only one meaning, in the case of Gen. 3:16 one that justified woman's subordination to man" (4).

5   Wenham, *Genesis 1–15*, 82.

6   Skinner, *Genesis*, 78.

7   Thomas Hardy, *Tess of the D'Urbervilles* (London: Octopus, 1986), 37. Abraham himself does not, however, attribute our human predicament to God but to bad luck; given that there are in this cosmos many splendid and only a few blighted worlds, "tis very unlucky that we didn't pitch on a sound one, when there were so many more of 'em."

8   I discussed this same verb *mashal* back in chap. 5, noting that it is employed in Psalm 8:6 of human rule over creation.

9   Wenham, *Genesis 1–15*, 82.

10   Kass, *Wisdom*, 125.

11   Hamilton, *Genesis 1–17*, 321, correctly writes, "That Noah even was able to plant a vineyard that produced lush growth is testimony to the lifting of the curse on the ground (8:21). Noah is not pictured as eking out a miserable, hand-to-mouth existence as he works among thorns and thistles." Noah's father is Lamech (Genesis 5:28-29), who is quite unlike his namesake in Genesis 4, to whom we shall return shortly (our chap. 8). The elder Lamech is "heroic" and bloodthirsty, in line with other men in the fallen world of Genesis 3–4. Noah's Lamech represents the other way through life—one of submission to God (and to mortality) and of hope for the future through family. See Kass, *Wisdom*, 145–48, 153–54, 158n8.

12   See further Iain Provan, *Ecclesiastes and Song of Songs*, NIV Application Commentary (Grand Rapids: Zondervan, 2001), passim.

13   Wenham, *Genesis 1–15*, 94.

14   As Duane A. Garrett rightly states, "The words hold the promise of escape from the curse of death." Strangely, though, he thinks of this as a promise of the end-times, rather than as a reality of the present. See his *Proverbs, Ecclesiastes, Song of Songs*, NAC 14 (Nashville: Broadman & Holman, 1993), 82.

15   The comment of Robert Sacks (quoted in Kass, *Wisdom*, 203n9) with respect to the entire "primeval history" in Genesis 1–11 is of interest here: "The origins of the whole must be stated in some form, but they must also be forgotten. From a Biblical point of view they may not be hearkened back to either as a paradigm or as a way of understanding." Although he greatly overstates the point, he is certainly onto something.

16   See further on this passage Provan, *1 & 2 Kings*, 157–60.

17   See further on this passage Iain Provan, *Lamentations*, NCB (London: Marshall Pickering, 1991), 96–97.

18   Paul D. Hanson, *Isaiah 40–66*, Interpretation (Louisville, Ky.: Westminster John Knox, 1995), 161.

19   John Steinbeck, *East of Eden* (New York: Viking, 1952).

20   Kurt Vonnegut, *The Sirens of Titan: A Novel* (New York: Dial Press Trade, 2009), 167.

21   Robert McAfee Brown, ed., *The Essential Reinhold Niebuhr: Selected Essays and Addresses* (New Haven: Yale University Press, 1987), 251.

22   Derrick Jensen, e.g., characterizes such people as follows: they believe that God's home is not primarily of this earth, and they welcome the killing of the planet because it will hasten "the ultimate victory of God over all things earthly, all things evil" (*Endgame*, 1:226).

23   Plato, *Phaedrus* 247a, in *Timaeus and Other Dialogues*, vol. 3 of *The Works of Plato*, trans. Benjamin Jowett (New York: Tutor, 1937), 407.

24   Plato, *Phaed.* 247a.

25   Plato, *Laws* 7.803b–804c, trans. Trevor J. Saunders (New York: Penguin, 1970), 291.

26   David Bostock, "The Soul and Immortality in the *Phaedo*," in Fine, *Plato*, 886–906 (891).

27   Bostock, "Soul," 898.

28   Plato, *Laws* 7.803b–804c.

29   William R. Inge, *The Philosophy of Plotinus*, 2 vols. (London: Longmans, Green, 1918), 2:163.

30   Inge, *Plotinus*, 2:163.

31   Inge, *Plotinus*, 2:172.

32   Inge, *Plotinus*, 2:185.

33   Inge, *Plotinus*, 2:175. For one striking passage, see 2:188.

34   In Plotinus' resolutely hierarchical worldview, all of reality is bound up either in "emanation," which is movement from the upper levels of reality down through the lower (involving ever greater diversity), or "return," which is movement from the lower levels of reality up through the higher (involving ever greater unity).

35   I am paraphrasing here Inge, *Plotinus*, 2:174.

36   Inge, *Plotinus*, 2:190.

37   Muesse, *Traditions*, 81. Interestingly, it continues to resist change, even as the modern state makes serious efforts to reform it through strong laws about discrimination and quotas.

38   Muesse, *Traditions*, 81.

39   The text is cited in Ludwig, *Paths*, 103.

40   See Dick Kooliman, *Conversion and Social Equality in India* (New Delhi: South Asia, 1983). Note what Muesse says about this in terms of the contemporary scene: "Because of their ambiguous status [at the bottom of the caste system], Dalits often debate whether or not they are truly Hindus. In modern times, many have converted to other religions, particularly Christianity and Buddhism, because they have felt little benefit in identifying as Hindus" (*Traditions*, 78). Islam has also made its own particular impact historically in India, of course, not least in helping to produce Sikhism (also in the sixteenth century), which has also turned its back on passivity with respect to the world as we find it, as well as on the Hindu caste system. Ludwig, *Paths*, 188–203.

41   Ludwig, *Paths*, 86–88.

42   Ludwig, *Paths*, 128–33.

43   Ludwig, *Paths*, 134–37.

44   Ludwig, *Paths*, 141–43.

45   Mitchell, *Buddhism*, 54.

46   Buddhists are to refrain from taking life, stealing, wrongful sexual behavior wrongful speech, and the taking of drugs or alcohol. Ludwig, *Paths*, 169–71. Avoiding such things will certainly reduce the amount of evil and suffering *added* to the world, but it will not *alleviate* the suffering that already exists.

47   Monks and nuns are to refrain from eating after noon; from watching shows, singing, and dancing; from using adornments of garlands, perfumes, and ointments; from sleeping in a high bed; and from handling gold and silver. Ludwig, *Paths*, 171.

48   Mitchell, *Buddhism*, 79 (emphasis added).

49   Ludwig, *Paths*, 129.

50 Jainism is similar. There is indeed a noticeable commitment in the Jain community to charitable acts (Long, *Jainism*, 99). However, the fundamental posture is escape from the world, not transformation of it, and (as Long himself also points out) the charitable acts are themselves "ultimately in the service of spiritual liberation."

51 Ruthven, *Islam*, 26–28. Zoroastrianism also resists any idea that the correct response to evil and suffering is "withdrawal from the world into some ascetic frame of life." The world remains a good place, and "believers are enjoined to participate fully in the maintenance of life," freely choosing "whether to be a follower of the Truth or of the Lie" (Ludwig, *Paths*, 345). The same is true of Sikhism: "the overall existence of the world is good and beneficial, and accordingly Sikhism does not advocate asceticism or withdrawal from the world" (194).

52 Ludwig, *Paths*, 478.

53 Ludwig, *Paths*, 478.

54 Ludwig, *Paths*, 477.

55 Ludwig, *Paths*, 478. The same is essentially true of Zoroastrianism ("humans have the freedom to choose between good and evil and, thus, determine their ultimate destiny. . . . The Good Religion empowers those who hear and accept to transform their minds and their hearts"; 340), and Sikhism ("the path of transformation is above all to focus on the word of the guru . . . for in this way one can attune one's inner being to the harmony and grace present in the divine name"; 196).

CHAPTER 7

1 Oliver Wendell Holmes, *The Mind and Faith of Justice Holmes: His Speeches, Essays, Letters and Judicial Opinions*, ed. Max Lerner (Boston: Little, Brown, 1946), 416. The quotation is from a letter written to William James on March 24, 1907.

2 Eugene O'Neill, *The Great God Brown*, in *The Plays of Eugene O'Neill*, 3 vols. (New York: Random House, 1954), 3:318.

3 This is consistent with what I said in chap. 4, that throughout the ancient Near East naming was part of the process by which something came into being. Naming went along with the assigning of a function in the cosmos. This is as true of the gods as it is of any other aspect of the cosmos.

4 See John I. Durham, *Exodus*, WBC 3 (Dallas, Tex.: Word Books, 1987), who says of the verbs in God's reply to Moses that they are "first person common qal imperfects of the verb היה 'to be', connoting continuing, unfinished action: 'I am being that I am being', or 'I am the Is-ing One', that is, 'the One Who Always Is'. Not conceptual being, being in the abstract, but active being, is the intent of this reply" (39).

5 Ludwig, *Paths*, 473.

6 Walter Brueggemann, *Theology of the Old Testament: Testimony, Dispute, Advocacy* (Minneapolis: Fortress, 1997), 184–85.

7 See, further, chap. 4.

8 See further Iain Provan, "Daniel," in the *Eerdmans Commentary on the Bible*, ed. John W. Rogerson and James D. G. Dunn (Grand Rapids: Eerdmans, 2003), 665–75.

9 Kaltner, *Qur'an*, 66.

10 The Gilgamesh who appears in the Mesopotamian *Epic of Gilgamesh* is, e.g., the product of such a marriage. It is not plausible, given the way Genesis 6 is written, to understand the "sons of God" as human beings of the line of Seth, as argued by many of the church fathers, or human kings, as argued by Meredith

Kline, "Divine Kingship and Genesis 6:1-4," *WTJ* 24 (1962): 187–204. Admittedly the vocabulary itself is used elsewhere in the Old Testament of human kings (e.g., Psalm 2:7; Psalm 82) as well as of angels. But the contrastive "sons of *God* . . . daughters of *'adam*" implies what the rest of the language in connection with Genesis 3 also suggests that we are dealing here with the crossing of a divine-human boundary. We recall the emphasis in the creation story that everything in creation should reproduce "according to its kind," and the later biblical prohibitions of various kinds of "mixing," especially in the sexual realm—the crossing of set boundaries as illustrated in such practices as sexual intercourse with animals (Leviticus 20:16) or with human beings of the same gender (Leviticus 20:13). Here in Genesis 6, it is an even more fundamental boundary that has been crossed.

11   Kass, *Wisdom*, 152–54. I agree with Kass that what happens in Genesis 6 is that "human beings react . . . to the discovery of their unavoidable finitude" (154). I disagree that it is "especially the men" (the part of the quote I have omitted), because I do not agree that the "sons of God" are human beings.

12   These Nephilim show up again in Numbers 13:33, where the majority of the spies who were sent by Joshua to spy out Canaan report giants whom they call by this name. This period in history is part of the "afterward" alluded to in Genesis 6:4, where these mighty warriors are said to have been "on the earth in those days—and also afterward." Goliath was likely regarded as one of the last of these people, and his story illustrates what Genesis 6 and 11 are really all about—human quests for immortality always fail; even Nephilim die.

13   Note the interesting parallel in the case of the legendary Mesopotamian hero, Gilgamesh: "Should I fall," he proclaims (in the *Epic of Gilgamesh*), "I shall have made me a name." *ANET*, 79.

14   On the "heroic ideal" of manliness, see further our chap. 8 ahead.

15   As I intimated in chap. 3, the precise sense of the verb "bless" in the last line is disputed, but I stand by the translation. The verb's rare form (referred to in Heb. as a "niphal") does make certainty difficult. Some have therefore doubted whether it refers to all peoples on earth being blessed through Abraham (including Moberly, *Theology*, 121–61). However, the larger narrative context certainly favors my interpretation. Abraham is called out to mediate the blessing of God that is bestowed on all creation in Genesis 1 and ultimately produces a people who are likewise called to mediate this blessing to other nations (Exodus 19:3-6; see further our chap. 11). The apparent progression within Genesis 12:1-3 also favors this interpretation: Abraham is blessed (v. 2), his name will be used as a blessing (v. 2), those who bless Abraham will be blessed (v. 3), and, finally, all nations will find blessing in Abraham. For further discussion, see Wenham, *Genesis 1–15*, 274–78; and Christopher J. H. Wright, *The Mission of God: Unlocking the Bible's Grand Narrative* (Downers Grove, Ill.: InterVarsity, 2006), 199–208.

16   The same promise is made much later in the story to King David: "Now I will make your name great, like the names of the greatest men of the earth" (2 Samuel 7:9).

17   The same Hebrew word, *batakh*, appears in vv. 5, 19, 20, 21, 22, and 24 of 2 Kings 18—disguised in our English translations under phrases like "basing confidence on" and "depending on."

18   See further on Hezekiah, Provan, *1 & 2 Kings*, 252–65.

19   Christopher J. H. Wright, *Deuteronomy*, NIBCOT 4 (Peabody, Mass.: Hendrickson, 1996), 99.

20   Walton, *Thought*, 111–12 (112).

21   See "Enuma Elish," trans. Benjamin R. Foster, *COS*, 1.111.390–402.

22   Interestingly, this kind of myth *is* alluded to in such texts as Isaiah 27:1; 51:9; Psalm 74:13; and Job 7:12. Here, our biblical authors do not spend time disputing some of the fundamentals of the story told about the world by their neighbors but content themselves with reorienting the ancient myths around the one true God.

23   On Noah's righteousness, contrasted with the wickedness of the people of "heroic" temperament in the Genesis story, see Kass, *Wisdom*, 151–67. That chapter also has a helpful account of significant differences between the biblical and Mesopotamian flood stories, not the least of which is that "unlike Utnapishtim, Noah is not elevated to divine status at the end of his ordeal . . . he remains as mortal as before" (167).

24   Ludwig, *Paths*, 480.

25   This is how the KJV, NASB, and NIV (in its main text) interpret the words; compare 1 Kings 22:19-22; Job 1:6-8, 2:1-3; and Zechariah 1:10.

26   Gordon J. Wenham, *Genesis 16–50*, WBC 2 (Waco, Tex.: Word Books, 1994), 222.

27   This is its meaning on two preceding occasions in Genesis (18:2 and 24:13).

28   As E. A. Speiser, *Genesis*, AB 1 (Garden City, N.Y.: Doubleday, 1964), 218, correctly writes, "This is the established meaning of the Heb. phrase."

29   John H. and Evelyn Nagai Berthrong, *Confucianism: A Short Introduction* (Oxford: Oneworld, 2000), 137.

30   See "A Common Word between Us and You," *A Common Word*, accessed October 26, 2012, http://www.acommonword.com/the-acw-document.

31   Ludwig, *Paths*, 477.

32   Ludwig, *Paths*, 478.

33   On the whole matter of common but in the end quite different narratives in the Old Testament and the Qur'an, see further Michael Lodahl, *Claiming Abraham: Reading the Bible and the Qur'an Side by Side* (Grand Rapids: Brazos, 2010).

CHAPTER 8

1   Larry David, "The Big Salad," *Seinfeld*, season 6, episode 2, directed by Andy Ackerman, aired September 29, 1994 (Culver City, Calif.: Sony Pictures Home Entertainment, 2005), DVD.

2   Autumn Stephens, *Drama Queens: Wild Women of the Silver Screen* (Berkeley, Calif.: Conair, 1998), 4.

3   This is likely also its meaning in Genesis 14:19, 22, and Proverbs 8:22, and certainly its meaning in Deuteronomy 32:6 and Psalm 139:13. In this last passage, the writer says, "You created my inmost being; you knit me together in my mother's womb." The objections of Collins to this rendering of *qanah* in at least the last two passages are unconvincing (*Genesis 1–4*, 194–97).

4   Kass, *Wisdom*, 126, also references the medieval Jewish commentator Rashi to this effect.

5   See also Psalm 144:4; and Proverbs 31:30.

6   The NIV translates this unhelpfully as "in the course of time." It is the end of the agricultural year that the author has in mind.

7   Here, I believe that Collins (*Genesis 1–4*, 199–200, 212) is correct, and that Kass (*Wisdom*, 132–37) is mistaken. Kass lays much weight on the idea that sacrifice "is of human origins. God neither commands nor requests it." Yet it seems to me that sacrifice is already implicitly introduced by God in Genesis 3:21. It is from

such animal sacrifices that later, in the book of Leviticus, the priests likewise get skins for clothing (Leviticus 7:8). Regardless of whether this is correct, Genesis 4 certainly does not give the impression that there is something questionable about sacrifice as such.

8   Here Collins (*Genesis 1–4*, 199–200, 212) is mistaken and Kass (*Wisdom*, 135–36) is correct. Collins underestimates the significance of the contrastive way in which the sacrifices are described in Genesis 4:3. Certainly it is "the condition of Cain's heart [that] is . . . the problem," but this condition also leads Cain to offer less to God in sacrifice. Cassuto gets the point: "Apparently the Bible wished to convey that whilst Abel was concerned to choose the finest thing in his possession, Cain was indifferent" (*Genesis*, 205).

9   Hesiod, *Theogony* 9.534–42.

10   Walton, *Thought*, 143–44.

11   Quoted in Walton, *Thought*, 144.

12   Kass, *Wisdom*, 138.

13   Muesse, *Traditions*, 54.

14   Muesse, *Traditions*, 161.

15   Muesse, *Traditions*, 161.

16   Just within the last few decades the frozen body of a young girl, the so-called Inca Ice Maiden, was discovered on Mount Ampato in Peru—a girl sacrificed as an offering to an Inca mountain god sometime between A.D. 1450 and 1480. For a photograph see http://www.nationalgeographic.com/inca/inca_culture_1.html, accessed June 21, 2013.

17   The word used here is the Hebrew *hetiv*, which comes from the same root as the word frequently used for "good" in Genesis 1.

18   Kass, *Wisdom*, 135.

19   *Gilgamesh*, ANET, 93.

20   Wilfred G. Lambert, "Destiny and Divine Intervention in Babylon and Israel," *OtSt* 17 (1972): 65–72 (67), quoted in Walton, *Thought*, 152. See further the entirety of Walton's pages 149–61.

21   Bottéro, *Religion*, 169.

22   We find it, e.g., in Numbers 35:33; 2 Samuel 21:1-14; and Hosea 4:2-3.

23   It does turn up in 2 Samuel 21:1-9, where David is looking for a solution to the famine that has arisen in the land as a result of Saul's bloodguilt. Here the Gibeonites appear to have the options of financial compensation or the death of Saul's sons. Note also the case of the negligent owner of an ox (Exodus 21:29-30) and compensation as a social reality more generally, presupposed by Proverbs 13:8: "The ransom of a man's life is his wealth."

24   See Exodus 21:12-14; Numbers 35:9-34; and Deuteronomy 19:1-6. In these texts, a killer is given the protection of asylum pending trial, either at an altar (Exodus) or in designated cities of refuge (Numbers, Deuteronomy). If the homicide is found to be unpremeditated, he remains there until the death of the high priest (Numbers 35:25), partly to protect him from the dead person's family and partly to deal with the issue of blood pollution.

25   Deuteronomy 19:11-13 and Numbers 35:31-34 make this clear.

26   It would perhaps be surprising if we were to discover in ancient Israel *more generally* a desire within families for such vengeance. The case of David and Absalom indicates at least one case in which things were otherwise.

27   The number seven, in biblical thinking, indicates fullness. See Psalm 79:12: "Return sevenfold into the bosom of our neighbors the taunts with which they taunted you, O Lord!"

28 In the entire history of asking the wrong kinds of questions of Genesis 1–11 and thereby missing the point, the discussion about "the mark of Cain" occupies a prominent position. Readers who are nevertheless interested in the history of the discussion should consult Ruth Mellinkoff, *The Mark of Cain: An Art Quantum* (Berkeley: University of California Press, 1981).

29 See Wenham, *Genesis 1–15*, who writes of the poem, "Its disciplined form only accentuates the barbarity of the message: Lamech is even more depraved than his forefather Cain" (114).

30 Kass, *Wisdom*, 138–39. He is quoting Rousseau at this point.

31 Kass, *Wisdom*, 148. Later in the book (pp. 155–56), Kass also connects the heroic male response to death with art (the creation of beautiful things that will hopefully last) and with the possession of beautiful women: "the love of Helen and the love of glory are twin faces of heroic ambition" not just in Greece but also in many cultures worldwide. It is relevant to this point not only that Lamech utters a poem but also that he "fathers" different arts—not only that he marries two wives but also that one of his wives is named Adah, which in Hebrew means "ornament" (145–46).

32 Kass, *Wisdom*, 149. The theme of "life as a gift from God" is further developed later in the Genesis story in the various accounts of mothers who are barren for a time (Kass, *Wisdom*, 148n33) and who, indeed (in the case of Sarah), bear a child when they are well past typical childbearing years.

33 For all three points, see Kass, *Wisdom*, 149–50.

34 They are also reflected in the well-known words of the Countess of Rousillon to Bertram that form the title to our present chapter: "Love all, trust a few, do wrong to none." William Shakespeare, *All's Well That Ends Well*, 1.1:61-62.

35 On the "creation conflict" in the opening chapters of the book of Exodus and the echoes here of the Tower of Babel story in Genesis 11, see Gordon McConville, *God and Earthly Power: An Old Testament Political Theology, Genesis–Kings*, LHBOTS 454 (London: T&T Clark, 2006), 52–54.

36 Aristotle, *Politics* 1.3.1253a 31–33 (trans. Jowett), 55.

37 For a discussion, see Durham, *Exodus*, who says, "This commandment prohibits a lack of seriousness about Yahweh's Presence in Israel, demonstrated through a pointless, misleading, or even false use of his name. . . . Its range is broad enough to cover even the magical usage argued by Mowinckel . . . [It] is couched in language deliberately chosen to permit a wide range of application, covering every dimension of the misuse of Yahweh's name" (287–88).

38 Brueggemann, *Theology*, 185.

39 Brueggemann, *Theology*, 185.

40 The Hebrew is *khamed*, which in a context like Exodus 20:17 means "inordinate, ungoverned, selfish desire." F. Brown, S. R. Driver, and C. A. Briggs, *A Hebrew and English Lexicon of the Old Testament* (Oxford: Oxford University Press, 1907), 326.

41 "She named him Reuben, for she said, 'It is because the LORD has seen my misery. Surely my husband will love me now.' . . . 'Because the LORD heard that I am not loved, he gave me this one too.' So she named him Simeon. . . . 'Now at last my husband will become attached to me, because I have borne him three sons.' So he was named Levi."

42 Bostock, "Soul," 898.

43 Inge, *Plotinus*, 2:163.

44 Tim O'Keefe, *Epicureanism* (Berkeley: University of California Press, 2010), 117.

45 O'Keefe, *Epicureanism*, 117.

46   O'Keefe, *Epicureanism*, 130.

47   O'Keefe, *Epicureanism*, 143.

48   Mitchell, *Buddhism*, 43. On the similarity of Jainism, see further my comments in chap. 6.

49   Kaltner, *Qur'an*, 77.

50   Ruthven, *Islam*, 119–20.

51   Confucius, *The Analects*, trans. D. C. Lau (New York: Penguin, 1979), 135.

52   Confucius, *Analects*, 59.

53   Confucius, *Analects*, 59–60; see also p. 116.

54   This is also true of the Shinto perspective in Japan: "at the core of Shinto theology lies the idea that *wa* ('benign harmony') is inherent in nature and human relationships, and that anything that disrupts this state is bad." Littleton, *Shinto*, 59. Littleton continues later, "Anything that contributes to *wa* is by definition, good; those things—behavior, emotions, desire, and so on—that disrupt it are perceived as being fundamentally evil" (61). Among the things that contribute to *wa* are the many rituals of Shinto, including such apparently nonreligious rituals as the removal of one's shoes before entering a house. Among the atoning rituals that restore *wa* when it is disrupted are bowing low and (in more extreme cases) suicide.

55   Ludwig, *Paths*, 215–16.

56   Berthrong, *Confucianism*, 60.

57   "Golden Rule," *Wikipedia*, accessed October 26, 2012, http://en.wikipedia.org/wiki/Golden_Rule.

58   Armstrong, *Transformation*, 390–91.

59   For a full discussion and critique of the "axial age hypothesis," see further my *Convenient Myths*, chaps. 1–3, 7, and 9.

60   Council for a Parliament of the World's Religions, "Towards a Global Ethic: An Initial Declaration," *Urban Dharma*, accessed October 26, 2012, http://www.kusala.org/udharma/globalethic.html.

Chapter 9

1   Maya Angelou, *Wouldn't Take Nothing for My Journey Now* (New York: Bantam, 1994), 34.

2   Henry David Thoreau, "Journal XIV: August 1, 1860—November 3, 1861," *The Journal of Henry David Thoreau* (Boston: Houghton Mifflin, 1906). The entry is for January 3, 1861, and can be read at http://www.walden.org/documents/file/Library/Thoreau/writings/Writings1906/20Journal14/Chapter%206.pdf (accessed October 11, 2013).

3   We recall from chap. 8 that this is what the number seven indicates symbolically in the Old Testament—the notion of fullness or perfection.

4   Wenham, *Genesis 1–15*, 33.

5   Quoted in Taylor, *Religion*, 99. For a similar critique, see Peter Knudtson and David Suzuki, *Wisdom of the Elders* (Toronto: Stoddart, 1992).

6   See, e.g., Hamilton, *Genesis 1–17*, 313: "The opening chapter of Genesis was quite explicit that in the beginning man and the animals were vegetarian." Also Kass, *Wisdom*, 48, 177–80.

7   See also 1 Kings 4:33, where the NIV's "animals and birds, reptiles and fish" should be "livestock and birds, wild animals [*remes*] and fish."

8   E.g., Wenham, *Genesis 1–15*, 25.

9   See further our chap. 11, where we return to the matter of reading Isaiah 11 well.

10   Collins, *Genesis 1–4*, 165. Collins also draws attention to Psalm 147:8-9, where the

text moves seamlessly from a description of God supplying the earth with rain and making grass grow to his provision of food for cattle and for ravens alike. The latter certainly eat meat. Again, this is just how creation *is*.

11   The NIV makes the same mistake in Genesis 1:30. The focus of concern in this text is how the land animals in the nondomestic, nonhuman sphere will eat. Domestic animals (Heb. *behemah*) do not need to worry about this, because they are looked after directly by human beings.

12   Engaging our imaginations about why this might be so, we could suggest that predatory wild animals are often dangerous (as well as being forbidden as food by later Israelite law), that birds are more difficult to catch and offer less "gain" for effort than, for example, deer, and that at least some fishing involves boating on the sea, which the ancient Hebrews were famously reluctant to do. *Remes* in Genesis 9:3 *could*, of course, mean to refer to *all* wild land-animals, given the "fluidity" of its usage in Genesis 1–11, but nothing important in my argument hangs upon this point.

13   Hunting is first mentioned in Genesis 10:9 with respect to Nimrod, who hunts "before the LORD" (which certainly does not imply disapproval of the practice), and later it is mentioned with respect to Esau in Genesis 25:27-28, where no evaluation of it is apparent.

14   This is certainly true in human warfare. Notice the rules of war listed in Deuteronomy 20, e.g., including the interesting rule (in the context of a discussion about creation care) concerning trees: "When you lay siege to a city for a long time, fighting against it to capture it, do not destroy its trees by putting an ax to them, because you can eat their fruit. Do not cut them down. Are the trees of the field people, that you should besiege them? However, you may cut down trees that you know are not fruit trees and use them to build siege works until the city at war with you falls" (vv. 19-20). Trees, and not just animals, have rights.

15   Kass, *Wisdom*, 178. "Shepherd" was, in fact, a common epithet for the ruler in the ancient Near East, as is reflected in biblical texts such as 2 Samuel 5:2; Isaiah 44:28; and Ezekiel 34:23.

16   Compare the case of the goring ox in Exodus 21:28-29, which is put to death because it kills a human being.

17   "Deutero-canonical" is one way of referring to books that are not held in common with other biblical texts as fully and equally "scriptural" within the Christian tradition. Protestant Bibles do not typically include the Wisdom of Sirach, but Roman Catholic ones do.

18   1 Kings 4:33. None other than the Roman Jewish author Josephus suggests this in *Antiquities* 8.2.5.

19   Albert Camus, *La peste* (Paris: Gallimard, 1947).

20   This has not prevented some from advocating a "Platonic politics of consciousness" in pursuit of a modern attempt to live in harmony with nature. See William Ophuls, *Plato's Revenge: Politics in the Age of Ecology* (Cambridge, Mass.: MIT, 2011).

21   For a larger discussion of Plato's natural philosophy, see Thomas Kjeller Johansen, *Plato's Natural Philosophy: A Study of the Timaeus-Critias* (Cambridge: Cambridge University Press, 2004).

22   Here I do not quite agree with the interesting comments of Kass, *Wisdom*, 49–50.

23   Muesse, *Traditions*, 112.

24   The same can be said of Jainism, in spite of recent attempts to reconceive of it as a "green" religion. Its fundamental orientation is toward a negative evaluation

of the natural world and a consequently ascetic approach to it—as is also the case in Buddhism. See further Christopher K. Chapple, *Nonviolence to Animals, Earth, and Self in Asian Traditions* (Albany: State University of New York Press, 1993); and idem, ed., *Jainism and Ecology: Nonviolence in the Web of Life* (Cambridge, Mass.: Harvard University Press, 2002).

25 Taylor, *Religion*, 147 (who is summarizing an argument of the ecologist David Suzuki at this point).

26 Shepard Krech III, *The Ecological Indian: Myth and History* (New York: Norton, 1999), 163.

27 For an extensive development of the argument, see my *Convenient Myths*, chaps. 4–6.

28 Note Sura 30:41: "Corruption has flourished on land and sea as a result of people's actions."

29 Kaltner, *Qur'an*, 72.

30 It is interesting that, in spite of the strong Islamic emphasis on all of nature being, in some sense, "muslim," and therefore already submitting to Allah, there is a very long tradition in Islam of a commitment to human healing. To heal is apparently not to "change" nature but to pay attention to the "signs" that point to Allah, who has provided *in* nature a remedy for every disease. Ludwig, *Paths*, 488–89.

31 Consider alongside Stoicism, on this point, classical Daoism, where the whole point is to "accept nature" and get in harmony with the dao. The emphasis in doing this, however, lies on passivity, not on action. At most, then, we find here what Kohn (*Daoism*, 212) refers to as an attitude of "live and let live, but might just as easily be described as indifference. On the whole (disputed) topic, see further N. J. Girardot, James Miller, and Liu Xiaogan, *Daoism and Ecology: Ways within a Cosmic Landscape* (Cambridge, Mass.: Harvard University Press, 2001). "Live and let live" should not be understood, of course, as implying either that classical Daoism has any problem with using animals for "food, sacrifice, and service" or that it has provided any "specific directions for animal conservation." E. N. Anderson and Lisa Raphals, "Daoism and Animals," in *A Communion of Subjects: Animals in Religion, Science, and Ethics*, ed. Paul Waldau and Kimberley Patton (New York: Columbia University Press, 2006), 275–90 (286, 290).

32 Cicero, *The Nature of the Gods* 2.154, trans. Peter G. Walsh (New York: Clarendon, 1997), 103.

33 William O. Stephens, "Stoic Naturalism, Rationalism, and Ecology," *Environmental Ethics* 16 (1994): 275–86 (278). A similar anthropocentrism is found in the thinking of Confucius, perhaps best illustrated in the following anecdote from the *Analects*: "The stables caught fire. The Master, on returning from the court, asked, 'Was anyone hurt?' He did not ask about the horses" (10:17). And possibly further: "Tzu-Kung wanted to do away with the sacrificial sheep at the announcement of the new moon. The master said, 'Ssu, you are loath to part with the price of the sheep, but I am loath to see the disappearance of the rite'" (3:17).

34 Edward Westermarck, *The Origin and Development of the Moral Ideas*, 2nd ed., 2 vols. (London: Macmillan, 1924), 1:415.

35 Seneca, *De ira* 1.15. See further *Seneca: Moral Essays*, trans. John W. Basor (Cambridge, Mass.: Harvard University Press, 1923), 145, which translates the Latin in this way: "We drown even children who at birth are weakly and abnormal. Yet it is not anger, but reason that separates the harmful from the sound."

36 John Channing Briggs, "Bacon's Science and Religion," in *The Cambridge*

Companion to Bacon, ed. Markku Peltonen (Cambridge: Cambridge University Press, 1996), 172–99.

37 See further Iain Provan, "The Land Is Mine and You Are Only Tenants: Earth-Keeping and People-Keeping in the Old Testament," in *Many Heavens, One Earth: Readings on Religion and the Environment*, ed. Clifford C. Cain (Lanham, Md.: Lexington Books, 2012), 33–50.

CHAPTER 10

1 Mark Lilla, *The Stillborn God: Religion, Politics, and the Modern West* (New York: Knopf, 2007), 22.

2 Polybius, *Histories* 6.10.2–10, trans. W. R. Paton (Cambridge, Mass.: Harvard University Press, 1979), 3:291.

3 I am using new Jerusalem here as shorthand for the biblical vision of the eschatological polis—God's good world put back to rights—drawing on the imagery of passages like Revelation 21:1-4, where John sees "the Holy City, the new Jerusalem, coming down out of heaven from God" (21:2).

4 Wenham argues that fig leaves are "less than ideal for a covering," and with regard to the loincloths he suggests, "Perhaps again the skimpiness of their clothing is being emphasized" (*Genesis 1–15*, 76).

5 Kass, *Wisdom*, 147.

6 Moberly, *Theology*, 118.

7 Traditionally, the coat has been referred to as a coat of "many colors" (e.g., in the LXX [Greek] and Vulgate [Latin] translations of the Bible, and in the KJV), although some translators take it simply to be a coat with long sleeves (e.g., the RSV). The phrase is paralleled only in 2 Samuel 13:18-19, where it is used of a garment worn by the daughters of kings. This is probably the point. The robe indicates that Joseph has been elevated in status above his brothers.

8 Throughout this section (Genesis 37:25-36), the terms "Midianites" and "Ishmaelites" are used interchangeably (cf. 39:1). The latter term can be used in the general sense of Bedouin, rather than in reference to a particular people-group (Judges 8:24; cf. Genesis 16:12, where Ishmael is represented as a wild ass of a man, possibly indicating his itinerant lifestyle). The implication of the Hebrew of Genesis 37:28 is that the traders were recognized by the brothers in the first instance (and from a distance) only as "Ishmaelites" (itinerant traders in general)—and only subsequently (and close-up) as Midianites in particular.

9 Potiphar is explicitly *called* an "Egyptian" in Genesis 39:1 (Heb. *'ish mitsri*) because Pharaoh's high officials were not necessarily Egyptians; they could, for example, be Semites. The fact that Potiphar is an Egyptian is important to the story, because the plot partly turns on the fact that, in his new context, Joseph (a Semite) is an outsider in every sense. Potiphar's wife herself plays "the race card" to get herself out of trouble in 39:14, emphasizing that Joseph (her attacker) is a "Hebrew" (*'ish 'ibri*).

10 ESV; the NIV translates the Hebrew word *khesed* in this verse as "kindness," which is much too weak.

11 We must pass over for reasons of space the interesting story concerning *how* Joseph attains this position. Essentially, it is because he has been endowed with wisdom, such that he stands out even in a country renowned for its wisdom and its wisdom professionals (cf. Genesis 41:8, which mentions "all the magicians and wise men of Egypt"). The story is similar in this respect to the story told in the book of Daniel. Joseph's wisdom is already on display, not just in the story of Potiphar's wife but also in the story about Joseph's successful interpretation

of two fellow prisoners' dreams (Genesis 40). He communicates the meaning of these dreams using some rather grim humor. In the case of the first man, the Egyptian pharaoh is going to "lift up his head"—that is, restore his honor (v. 13). In the case of the second man, the king is also going to "lift up his head"—i.e., cut it off (v. 19). He is then going to impale him on a pole.

12   The NIV obscures the symbolism of this action (power transferring from one "hand" to the other) while accurately describing it in its translation: "Pharaoh took his signet ring from his finger and put it on Joseph's finger."

13   Joseph's treatment of his brothers when they come down to Egypt perhaps also raises questions about his character. Moberly, *Theology*, 237–41.

14   Jacob also remains an ambiguous character all the way through this story. He is still playing favorites, for example, in Genesis 42:38, where he is prepared to abandon Simeon rather than risk Benjamin.

15   Walter Brueggemann, *Genesis*, Interpretation (Atlanta: Westminster John Knox, 1982), 347.

16   Moberly, *Theology*, 120.

17   *Torah* covers more ground that the English term "law" and often has the broader sense of "direction, instruction."

18   They might have been captured in war or sold as slaves or have sold themselves into slavery because of poverty.

19   Duane L. Christensen writes, "This command runs contrary to all known ancient Near Eastern law codes, which forbade the harboring of runaway slaves." *Deuteronomy 21:10–34:12*, WBC 6B (Dallas, Tex.: Word Books, 2002), 549.

20   Debt slavery arising from a failure to pay debts was commonly found throughout the ancient Near East, and it is not just in Israel that we find it regulated to prevent it from becoming overly oppressive. The Code of Hammurabi of Babylon, for example, also instructs that a person enslaved because of his or her debts should be released after a set period (three years, in this case). In ancient Assyria, however, there was no set limitation: "In theory it was always possible for a debt slave to pay off his debts and regain his freedom. In practice, however, manumission was rare in Assyria . . . high interest rates . . . meant that it was not only easy to fall into debt slavery but that once in that situation it was very difficult to amass enough resources to buy one's way out of debt." A. Kirk Grayson, "History and Culture of Assyria," *ABD* 4:732–55 (751).

21   George Bernard Shaw, "The Future of Political Science in America: An Address to the Academy of Political Science at the Metropolitan Opera House, New York, on the 11th April 1933," *Political Quarterly* 4 (1933): 313–40 (316). See also G. K. Chesterton, *Autobiography* (London: Burns, Oates & Washbourne, 1937), who says of the English middle-class male of his childhood, "He was already an anarchist to those above him; but still an authoritarian to those below" (28).

22   Kass, *Wisdom*, 168.

23   Note Kass, *Wisdom*, who says of the law about murder in Genesis 9, "We have here impersonal retribution, precisely limited in extent, universal in scope, with no exceptions for the mighty, and based on a recognizable ontological standard ('image of God')" (191).

24   Kass, *Wisdom*, 173.

25   Judah's preeminence is then explained in verse 10 in terms of monarchy: "the scepter will not depart from Judah, nor the ruler's staff from between his feet, until he comes to whom it belongs and the obedience of the nations is his." As Wenham says, "This line is predicting the rise of the Davidic monarchy and the

establishment of the Israelite empire, if not the coming of a greater David" (*Genesis 16–50*, 478). On the "greater David," see our chap. 11.

26   Judah "sees . . . takes . . . goes into" this woman (Genesis 38:2); almost the exact same set of verbs is employed earlier in Genesis in the story of the rape of Dinah (Genesis 34:2)—a story with other significant similarities to this one.

27   The situation is similar with respect to Islam, which on the one hand did not set out in its first centuries to abolish the multifaceted legal inferiority of women and yet can also be said, in that context, to have greatly improved their position in various ways. Ruthven, *Islam*, 95–97.

28   John E. Hartley writes, "There is no indication, such as the need for making a confession, that either the act of conception or the process of birth was considered an act of sin. That the focus is not on some specific act of sin is evident in that a purification offering, not a reparation offering, is required and that the animal for this offering is the least expensive possible." *Leviticus*, WBC 4 (Dallas, Tex.: Word Books, 2002), 169.

29   Hartley touches on this reality in his comments on Leviticus 11:1–47: "in following these dietary laws, the Israelites obeyed God's instructions several times each day, developing deep in their consciousness an attitude of obedience to God" (*Leviticus*, 163). See further Jacob Milgrom, "Ethics and Ritual: The Foundations of the Biblical Dietary Laws," in *Religion and Law: Biblical-Judaic and Islamic Perspectives*, ed. Edwin B. Firmage et al. (Winona Lake, Ind.: Eisenbrauns, 1990), 159–98: "in the biblical view the Decalogue would fail were it not rooted in a regularly observed ritual, central to the home and table, and impinging on both senses and intellect, thus conditioning the reflexes into patterns of ethical behavior" (191). At the same time, I believe, the rules about not eating wild predatory animals (for example) may well have a moral aspect (see our chap. 9).

30   Lilla, *Stillborn God*, 298.

31   Shmuel N. Eisenstadt, "The Axial Age Breakthroughs: Their Characteristics and Origins," in *The Origin and Diversity of Axial Age Civilizations*, ed. Shmuel N. Eisenstadt (Albany: State University of New York Press, 1986), 1–28 (1).

32   Eisenstadt, "Breakthroughs," 3. See also idem, "The Axial Age: The Emergence of Transcendental Visions and the Rise of Clerics," *European Journal of Sociology* 23 (1982): 294–314; and idem, *Fundamentalism, Sectarianism, and Revolution: The Jacobin Dimension of Modernity* (Cambridge: Cambridge University Press, 1999). See further my *Convenient Myths*, chap. 2.

33   Eisenstadt, *Fundamentalism*, 15.

34   Eisenstadt, *Fundamentalism*, 14–38.

35   Eisenstadt, *Fundamentalism*, 16–17.

36   *Relative* passivity becomes *principled* passivity in the (still this-worldly) Daoist teaching of the third-century B.C. *Zhuangzi*, which abjures active political involvement on the part of the truth seeker and pictures the ideal person as "free from feelings and at one with Dao, completely spontaneous and at ease with all that happens, living with a sense of strong immediacy that precludes thinking, evaluating, and critical mentation." Kohn, *Daoism*, 45.

37   Ruthven, *Islam*, 4, 75.

38   Ruthven, *Islam*, 75, 86.

39   Ruthven, *Islam*, 54–56, 73–74.

40   Ruthven, *Islam*, 131.

41   Ruthven, *Islam*, 86.

42   Ruthven, *Islam*, 6.

43 Ruthven, *Islam*, 10–11.

44 Ruthven, *Islam*, 90.

45 Kaltner, *Qur'an*, 92–95.

46 See further Ruthven, *Islam*, 77–86. This is one of the reasons Shari'a courts have been so divisive and destructive in the Muslim countries where they have been introduced. What is blasphemy, for example? By whose definition are we to be guided? What is the role of the Qur'an and the hadith in determining this? Which collections of hadith may be added to the Qur'an in answering our question? It is not just the adherents of other religions who have suffered. Consider the case of Pakistan, where Shia Muslims have been actively persecuted by fellow Muslims ever since Shari'a courts were introduced—more so even than Christians. I am grateful to Don Curry for this observation.

47 Ludwig, *Paths*, 479.

48 Ruthven, *Islam*, 86.

49 Ruthven, *Islam*, 91.

50 Ruthven, *Islam*, 129–30. See further Kaltner, *Qur'an*, 155 63 for Muslim scholars writing on pluralism.

51 Ruthven, *Islam*, 74.

52 Here the biblical perspective differs from the perspective not only of utopian Islamists but also of utopian Christians—like the "Christian Reconstructionists" who make up one section of the Tea Party in U.S. politics. These Christians believe that the Bible should form the sole basis upon which U.S. society is organized and, specifically, that biblical law should form the sole basis for all U.S. law. For example, if taxes are not biblical, then there should be no taxation: Sarah Posner, "Huckabee Denies He's a Christian Reconstructionist," *American Prospect*, January 11, 2008, accessed June 17, 2013, http://prospect .org/article/huckabee-denies-hes-christian-recontructionist. If the Bible says that the penalty for adultery should be death, then so it should be in U.S. law: "Christian Reconstructionism," accessed June 17, 2013, http://www.conserva pedia.com/Christian_Reconstructionism#cite_note-1.

53 See further McConville, *Power*, 125–31, and especially his agreement with Dennis Olson that the book of Judges "shows the provisionality of all kinds of human rule"—that it considers any system of governance (quoting Olson now) as "necessary but provisional, helpful for a time, but eventually replaced by another." Dennis T. Olson, *The Book of Judges,* New Interpreter's Bible (Nashville: Abingdon, 1998), 727.

54 For the unusual adjective "middled," see chap. 1.

CHAPTER 11

1 Aeschylus, *Agamemnon*, line 1668. Aegisthus is taunting the chorus for believing (an "empty hope") that revenge will be taken for the death of Agamemnon.

2 Jensen, *Endgame*, 1:330.

3 See further our chap. 5.

4 Athanasius, "On the Incarnation of the Word," 4.6; 5.2, in *Nicene and Post Nicene Fathers: Second Series*, ed. Alexander Roberts et al., 14 vols. (Peabody, Mass.: Hendrickson, 1996), 4:38.

5 See further my comments on both of these thinkers in chap. 7.

6 I shall in a moment cite a couple of examples of this kind of reading offered by "ordinary" readers. For a scholarly perspective that appears to tend in this direction, see Barry G. Webb, *The Message of Isaiah: On Eagles' Wings* (Downers Grove, Ill.: InterVarsity, 1996). Commenting on Isaiah 11:6, Webb writes, "The

effect of his [the Messiah's/Root of Jesse's] rule will be universal peace (6–9), an ideal described here in symbolic language which recalls the paradise of Eden. It is a picture of the whole creation put back into joint" (75). Commenting on Isaiah 65:19, he writes, "The chapter ends with an unmistakable allusion to the final undoing of the work of the serpent who brought sin and death into the world in the first place (25). The new world will be history perfected and paradise regained, and it will be full of the modest and simple delights that God always intended us to have: joy (18), fullness of life (20), security (21–23a), rewarding work (22b), fellowship with God (23b–24), and peace (25)" (245).

7   Note, e.g., the following example from the Internet: "There were no weeds, thorns or thistles in the garden as it was a perfect garden. There was no heat, hot humid type weather or cold climate, it was just perfect, and it was a paradise. It was a place where there was no pain, no tears, no sorrows, no hardships, no trials and difficulties, my beloved this was heaven on earth." Nick Bibile, "A Taste of Heaven," accessed October 26, 2012, http://www.sounddoctrine.net/Nick/topical/A_Taste_of_Heaven.htm.

8   Note, e.g., this blog designed for children (which also picks up the "tears" theme): "In the Garden of Eden, there were no tears, no pain or no hunger. Adam worked in the garden, but he never got tired. All the animals were like pets." Jack Foster, "The Garden of Eden," *Mr. Bible Head*, accessed October 26, 2012, http://mrbiblehead.blogspot.com/2010_02_01_archive.html.

9   Theophilus of Antioch, *Theophilus to Autolycus* 2.17, in *The Ante-Nicene Fathers*, ed. Alexander Roberts and James Donaldson (Grand Rapids: Eerdmans, 1975), 2:101. I am again grateful to Sollereder, "Evolutionary Theodicy," for alerting me to this quotation (and to the Aquinas quotation ahead) in the course of her discussion of the origin of the concept of a "cosmic fall."

10   I leave aside here the question of whether there is even any good reason, from a biblical perspective, to interpret the goodness *of God* as involving a static perfection *in God*. It was the Eleatic philosophers of Greece in the fifth century B.C. who first "demonstrated that the divine being must be absolutely without any change." Reijer Hooykaas, *Religion and the Rise of Modern Science* (Vancouver, BC: Regent College, 2000), 2. In my opinion the biblical authors would have regarded as a form of idolatry all such attempts to prove by reason what God *must* be. They were much more interested in who God had *revealed* himself, in fact, to be (e.g., as a person, certainly, of stable and dependable character). They were not prone to speculations of a Greek kind about metaphysical realities beyond these revealed realities.

11   This is to assume, of course, that even *this* act constitutes an "ending," but might it perhaps be only the beginning of a new journey?

12   I leave aside for present purposes the obvious question as to whether we are even *supposed* to read the picture of pastoral tranquility in a passage like Isaiah 11 as anticipating a lack of predation in the eschatological future. It is at least possible that the passage is to be understood more metaphorically—an understanding already adopted by such ancient readers as Cyril of Alexandria. See Robert L. Wilken, trans. and ed., *Isaiah: Interpreted by Early Christian and Mediaeval Commentators* (Grand Rapids: Eerdmans, 2007), 151–52. Might it be that when the prophet Isaiah envisions the future peaceable society, he *pictures* human beings as animals, just as, e.g., Ezekiel 22:27 and Zephaniah 3:3 portray rapacious rulers as wolves?

13   Thomas Aquinas, *Summa Theologica* 1.96.1, trans. Fathers of the English Dominican Province, 2 vols. (New York: Benziger Bros., 1947), 1:486. For Augustine's

view, see *The Literal Meaning of Genesis* 1.3.16, *ACW* 41, trans. John Hammond Taylor, S.J. (New York: Newman, 1982), 92.

14 They did not, of course, think this. See, e.g., Isaiah 43:19; 48:6-7; 65:17.

15 Irenaeus, *Against Heresies* 5.21.1, in *Genesis 1–11*, ed. Andrew Louth, ACCS Old Testament 1 (Downers Grove, Ill.: InterVarsity, 2001), 90–91.

16 There is, therefore, something quite strange about the footnote to this verse in the NIV, which tells us that the first verb could also be translated simply as "strike." It could, and it *should*. We are not dealing here with a situation in which the translation might as readily go in one direction as the other.

17 The recent defense of a hope-filled reading of this text by Collins (*Genesis 1–4*, 155–59) appears to me to miss the main point here. He gets bogged down in a discussion about whether the "offspring" of the woman is one or many, but he fails to *argue* the more important point about the nature of the conflict. He simply assumes that we are dealing here with a text that tells us that "God will act for the benefit of mankind by defeating the serpent" (157; cf. 176)—even though he has just referred to "mutual bruising" (156). Wenham gets the actual sense of the line: "the human race, 'her offspring', and the serpent race, 'your offspring', will forever be at loggerheads" (*Genesis 1–15*, 79). Even Wenham, however, cannot let things rest there (80–81); he has to bring in the idea of ultimate human victory. Hope springs eternal, but sometimes from the wrong sources.

18 Genesis 15 is the first explicit reference to this "covenant," to which the promise of Genesis 12:1-3 is intrinsically connected.

19 Durham writes, "Israel as the 'special treasure' is Israel become uniquely Yahweh's prized possession by their commitment to him in covenant. Israel as a 'kingdom of priests' is Israel committed to the extension throughout the world of the ministry of Yahweh's Presence" (*Exodus*, 263).

20 See further McConville, *Power*, 50–73, particularly 69–71.

21 For further information, see Moshe Weinfeld, "Deuteronomy, Book of," *ABD* 2:168-83.

22 See Iain Provan, "The Messiah in the Book of Kings," in *The Lord's Anointed: Interpretation of Old Testament Messianic Texts*, ed. Philip E. Satterthwaite et al. (Carlisle, U.K.: Paternoster, 1995), 67–85.

23 On the nature of the monarchy in Israel and the hope grounded in it, see McConville, *Power*, 133–67.

24 E.g., Isaiah 2:1-4; Jeremiah 31:10-14; Ezekiel 37:24-28; Joel 3:17-21; Zephaniah 3:14-20; Zechariah 8:1-8, 20-23.

25 See also, e.g., Isaiah 43:5; Jeremiah 24:4-7; 50:20.

26 See Gerald L. Keown, Pamela J. Scalise, and Thomas G. Smothers, *Jeremiah 26–52*, WBC 27 (Dallas, Tex.: Word Books, 2002): "The heart and mind inscribed with the revelation of God cannot turn to sin again" (135). See further Leslie C. Allen, *Ezekiel 20–48*, WBC 29 (Dallas, Tex.: Word Books, 2002): "Their lives would be governed by a new impulse that was to be an expression of Yahweh's own spirit. He would re-make their human natures, so that they marched to the music of the covenant terms that expressed Yahweh's nature and will" (179).

27 See also Isaiah 2:2-4; and 66:18-23.

28 Emily Dickinson, *The Complete Poems of Emily Dickinson*, ed. Thomas H. Johnson (New York: Little, Brown, 1961), 116 (poem 254).

29 Ludwig, *Paths*, 340.

30 Kaltner, *Qur'an*, 215–43. Along with similarity there is also difference, as we have seen in other cases where we have compared Islamic and biblical faith. Perhaps most obviously, the Qur'an possesses a noticeably hierarchical view of the

afterlife, in which women and children continue to serve the needs and desires of the adult males. Note, e.g., 55:56, which promises that in paradise there will be "maidens . . . untouched beforehand by man or jinn." In 44:51-54, "maidens with large, dark eyes" are promised as wives to the "mindful of God," and in 52:24, "devoted youths like hidden pearls wait on them [the mindful]."

31 See further chap. 8 of my *Convenient Myths*.

32 It is, of course, especially obvious that if cycles of existence *do* endlessly repeat (and *have* endlessly repeated), a fundamental pessimism must naturally arise regarding the possibility of real transformation of the world, and hope must inevitably dissipate—if, indeed, it could ever emerge in the first place. See further Stanley L. Jaki, *Science and Creation: From Eternal Cycles to an Oscillating Universe* (Edinburgh: Scottish Academic Press, 1974), who touches on such matters while discussing why some worldviews precluded the rise of modern science. I am grateful to Paul Teel for drawing my attention to this book.

33 Ludwig, *Paths*, 194.

34 Ludwig, *Paths*, 194.

CHAPTER 12

1 The Gospel of Matthew is one of four New Testament books that record the life and teachings of Jesus of Nazareth, a first-century Palestinian Jew around whom all the literature of the New Testament coalesces and revolves.

2 This letter is one of many that have been preserved from the early Christian centuries (A.D.) in the New Testament.

3 Each answer will be "fuller," of course, only from a Christian point of view. Jewish literature does not develop biblical faith in the same manner as the New Testament, precisely because its authors do not share the same core convictions about Jesus. As to each answer being an "outline," it should go without saying that I do *mean* "outline"; space allows for nothing more. I shall try to suggest good books in the footnotes, however, for those who wish to take their explorations of the New Testament further. Here is my first suggestion: N. T. Wright, *Simply Jesus: A New Vision of Who He Was, What He Did, and Why He Matters* (New York: HarperOne, 2011).

4 Matthew 7:11; 5:45; James 1:5, 17.

5 See also 1 Thessalonians 5:24; 2 Thessalonians 3:3.

6 For a thorough discussion of the developments in the earliest Christian centuries that led to these ultimate outcomes, see Larry W. Hurtado, *Lord Jesus Christ: Devotion to Jesus in Earliest Christianity* (Grand Rapids: Eerdmans, 2003).

7 It is, however, difficult to blame outsiders to the Christian faith for misunderstandings about the doctrine of the Trinity when so many "insiders" themselves appear to have such a shaky hold on it and to require exhortations to return to it—such as those found in Mark Russell et al., eds., *Routes and Radishes: And Other Things to Talk about at the Evangelical Crossroads* (Grand Rapids: Zondervan, 2010), esp. chaps. 3 and 4.

8 See also Acts 14:15; 17:24; Romans 1:19-20; Hebrews 1:10; 11:3; Revelation 10:6.

9 The analysis here and ahead is indebted to Günther Bornkamm, "The Stilling of the Storm in Matthew," in *Tradition and Interpretation in Matthew*, ed. Günther Bornkamm, Gerhard Barth, and Heinz Joachim Held (Philadelphia: Westminster, 1963), 52–57.

10 E.g., Matthew 24:7; Revelation 6:12.

11 E.g., in Psalms 6:4; 7:1; 31:16; 69:1; 106:47.

12 The comment on a preceding use of the word in Matthew 7:21 by Donald A.

Hagner is also apt here: "Matthew's community can hardly have failed to think here of the primary Christian confession, that Jesus is Lord (cf. Rom 10:9; Phil 2:11; 1 Cor 12:3)." *Matthew 1–13*, WBC 33A (Dallas, Tex.: Word Books, 1993), 187.

13 On the significance of Jesus forgiving sins, see further ahead.

14 Donald A. Hagner, *Matthew 14–28*, WBC 33B (Dallas, Tex.: Word Books, 1995), 637.

15 As Robert G. Bratcher and Eugene A. Nida say, "Though the context may suggest mere 'knowledge about God,' it is more likely that the Greek term implies 'experience of' or 'coming into a relationship with,' as occurs in so many other contexts, especially in Paul's writings." *A Handbook on Paul's Letters to the Colossians and to Philemon* (New York: United Bible Societies, 1993), 84.

16 James D. G. Dunn, *The Epistles to the Colossians and to Philemon: A Commentary on the Greek Text* (Grand Rapids: Eerdmans, 1996), 223.

17 Bratcher and Nida, *Handbook*, 84.

18 Richard N. Longenecker, *New Testament Social Ethics for Today* (Grand Rapids: Eerdmans, 1984), 75.

19 E.g., Matthew 9:23-26; Mark 5:25-34; Luke 10:38-42; John 4:1-26; see also Matthew 28:9-10 for women as paradigmatic disciples. We gain some insight into just how radical the implications potentially were in women taking Jesus as their Lord (*kurios*) when we discover that *every* woman in ancient Athens already had a *kurios* (guardian), who was either her closest male birth relative or her husband. Although she could own her own clothing, jewelry, and personal slaves and she could purchase inexpensive items, she was otherwise unable to buy anything, own property, or enter into any contract. Her *kurios* controlled everything about her life. What happens to a person's sense of self, then, when she enters the community of brothers and sisters in which *Jesus* is *kurios*?

20 The NIV misleads us both with respect to Phoebe, who is described only as a "servant," and Junia, who appears as the (male) "Junias." On the second mistake, James D. G. Dunn notes that "the masculine form has been found nowhere else, and the name is more naturally taken as . . . Junia . . . as was taken for granted by the patristic commentators, and indeed up to the Middle Ages." *Romans 9–16*, WBC 38B (Dallas, Tex.: Word Books, 1988), 885–95 (894).

21 As Anthony C. Thiselton says, "Part of the observed *traditions* [NIV's "teachings" in 1 Corinthians 11:2] probably included the Christian practice of women leading a congregation in the *Godward* ministry of *prayer*, and leading in *preaching* a pastorally applied message or discourse *from God*." *The First Epistle to the Corinthians: A Commentary on the Greek Text* (Grand Rapids: Eerdmans, 2000), 828. On "prophesying," Thiselton says further that the term "allows for short utterances or, in accordance with Paul's own wishes, for longer stretches of speech to which the nearest modern parallel is probably that of an informed pastoral sermon which proclaims grace and judgment, or requires change of life, but which also remains open to question and correction by others" (1094). For a more general study of women in the New Testament, see Richard Bauckham, *Gospel Women: Studies of the Named Women in the Gospels* (Grand Rapids: Eerdmans, 2002).

22 Matthew 4:3; 13:39; 1 Thessalonians 3:5; Revelation 10:9.

23 Mark 3:27; Luke 22:32; Acts 26:18; Colossians 2:15; Revelation 12:7; 20:10.

24 That is to say, Satan is de facto the chosen god of those who reject the true God. Human beings have made the non-god a god in much the same way that Paul insists in Philippians 3:19 that it is true for some that "their god is their stomach."

25 See Timothy G. Gombis, *The Drama of Ephesians: Participating in the Triumph*

of God (Downers Grove, Ill.: IVP Academic, 2010): "Broken relationships give Satan and the powers of darkness and destruction an opening to infect and destroy our communities" (167).

26 See also Philippians 4:6; Colossians 4:2; 1 Thessalonians 5:17.

27 E.g., in Matthew 9:36; 14:14; 15:32; 20:34.

28 E.g., in Romans 12:8; Philippians 1:8; 2:1; Colossians 3:12.

29 Hebrews 13:12; 1 Peter 2:21; 4:1.

30 See also Hebrews 2:18; 4:15-16.

31 Following Jesus' lead, the early church *also* understood him as the suffering servant of the book of Isaiah. In 1 Peter 2:24, e.g., we read, "By his wounds you have been healed"—a direct quotation from Isaiah 53:5.

32 For a readable and extensive exploration of what this looks like, see Mike Mason, *Practicing the Presence of People: How We Learn to Love* (Colorado Springs: WaterBrook, 1999).

33 I. Howard Marshall, *The Gospel of Luke: A Commentary on the Greek Text*, NIGTC 3 (Exeter: Paternoster, 1978), 449.

34 Horace, *Epistles* 1.18:67-93, in *Satire, Epistles and Ars Poetica*, trans. H. Rushton Fairclough (Cambridge, Mass.: Harvard University Press, 1978), 375.

35 Longenecker, *Ethics*, 74.

36 Marshall, *Luke*, 697.

37 Marshall, *Luke*, 276.

38 Paul puts it in this way, in Romans 5:7-8: "Very rarely will anyone die for a righteous man, though for a good man someone might possibly dare to die. But God demonstrates his own love for us in this: While we were still sinners, Christ died for us."

39 See further on this theme Jonathan Lunde, *Following Jesus, the Servant King: A Biblical Theology of Covenantal Discipleship* (Grand Rapids: Zondervan, 2010).

40 William L. Lane, *Hebrews 1–8*, WBC 47A (Dallas, Tex.: Word Books, 1991), 48.

41 Hebrews 1:1-2, 10; 2:10. See further Loren Wilkinson, "Christ as Creator and Redeemer," in *The Environment and the Christian: What Can We Learn from the New Testament?*, ed. Calvin DeWitt (Grand Rapids: Baker, 1991), 25–44.

42 As James D. G. Dunn points out, the Greek word lying behind "frustration" in Roman 8:20 (*mataiotes*) has previously appeared in Romans 1:21 of the "futile" thinking of humanity in its rebellion against God. *Romans 1–8*, WBC 38A (Dallas, Tex.: Word Books, 1988), 470. There has been "frustration" in creation insofar as human beings "neither glorified him as God nor gave thanks to him, but their thinking became *futile* and their foolish hearts were darkened" (emphasis added). This is the New Testament counterpoint to what I have already said about the early chapters of Genesis: the "frustration" of creation is closely connected to the "frustration" of the divine-human relationship.

43 So, rightly, Collins, *Genesis*, 182–84.

44 Dunn, *Romans 1–8*, 471. Consistent with the idea that the interests of creation as a whole are bound up with those of the "sons of God," Revelation 12 describes the earth itself as acting in defense of God's people ("the woman" in this passage) when they are attacked by Satan (the "red dragon"). Having failed to devour the Christ child (12:4-6), the dragon "spewed water like a river" from his mouth, hoping to "overtake the woman and sweep her away with the torrent" (12:15). However, "the earth helped the woman by opening its mouth and swallowing the river that the dragon had spewed out of his mouth" (12:16).

45 See further Richard Bauckham, *Bible and Ecology: Rediscovering the Community of Creation* (London: Darton, Longman & Todd, 2010), chap. 5.

46 Revelation 11:18; 17:1–19:4. On Revelation 18, see Iain Provan, "Foul Spirits, Fornication and Finance: Revelation 18 from an Old Testament Perspective," *JSNT* 64 (1996): 81–100.

47 For further development of this theme, see, e.g., N. T. Wright, *Simply Christian: Why Christianity Makes Sense* (San Francisco: HarperSanFrancisco, 2006), esp. chaps. 11–16.

48 In fact, Paul commends that slaves be obedient to their masters and generally restricts his advice to slave owners to exhortations to treat their slaves well (Ephesians 6:5-9; Colossians 3:22–4:1; Titus 2:9-10). The same is true of Peter (1 Peter 2:18-25).

49 Compare the story in Acts 16:1-4, where Paul circumcises Timothy "because of the Jews who lived in that area, for they all knew that his father was a Greek," with what he has to say about Gentile Christians accepting circumcision in his letter to the Galatians.

50 See further William J. Webb, *Slaves, Women & Homosexuals: Exploring the Hermeneutics of Cultural Analysis* (Downers Grove, Ill.: IVP Academic, 2001).

51 See also Colossians 4:1.

52 Longenecker, *Ethics*, 75.

53 See further Richard Bauckham, *God and the Crisis of Freedom: Biblical and Contemporary Perspectives* (Louisville, Ky.: Westminster John Knox, 2002), 116–27.

54 I am thinking here especially of Paul's reading (apparently) of the opening chapters of Genesis in 1 Corinthians 11:2-9 and 1 Timothy 2:11-15. Readers who are persuaded by my own reading of Genesis 1–3 will immediately see the problems.

55 For the unusual adjective "middled," see chap. 1.

56 On the theme of New Testament hope, see further N. T. Wright, *Surprised by Hope: Rethinking Heaven, the Resurrection, and the Mission of the Church* (New York: HarperOne, 2008).

57 Augustine, "Answer to Adimantus, A Disciple of Mani," 3.4, in *The Works of St. Augustine: A Translation for the 21st Century*, ed. Boniface Ramsey, 26 vols. (Hyde Park, N.Y.: New City Press, 2006), 19.1.180.

CHAPTER 13

1 John Maynard Keynes, *The General Theory of Employment, Interest, and Money* (London: Macmillan, 1960), 383.

2 Chesterton, *Autobiography*, 223–24.

3 I have borrowed this useful term from Ched Myers, *Binding the Strong Man: A Political Reading of Mark's Story of Jesus* (Maryknoll, N.Y.: Orbis, 1988), 16, who himself borrowed it from Amos Wilder.

4 This attitude is extensively found among modern scientists, e.g., who often seem to believe that science "just tells the truth." For critical engagements with this idea, see Nancy Cartwright, *The Dappled World: A Study of the Boundaries of Science* (Cambridge: Cambridge University Press, 1999); and Connor Cunningham, *Darwin's Pious Idea: Why the Ultra-Darwinists and the Creationists Both Get It Wrong* (Grand Rapids: Eerdmans, 2010).

5 I cannot resist the comment here that this is precisely why it is such a disaster for the Christian church when "practical men" get themselves in charge of theological education and insist that what the church needs is ever greater numbers of men (and women) who are just like themselves. The consequence is typically a theological curriculum skewed toward "practice" rather than "theory" (a.k.a. "thinking"), which is guaranteed to produce leaders of the church who are

merely the blind leading the blind, albeit ever more efficiently. They know how to maintain an organization, but they have nothing meaningful to say.

6   Hitchens, *God*, 98.

7   C. S. Lewis, *The Great Divorce* (San Francisco: HarperSanFrancisco, 2001), 33–44. On this theme note further G. K. Chesterton's comments (*Autobiography*, 157) concerning the intelligentsia of "the artistic and vaguely anarchic clubs" of his younger life: "While it thought a great deal about thinking, it did not think. Everything seemed to come at second or third hand; from Nietzsche or Tolstoy or Ibsen or Shaw; and there was a pleasant atmosphere of discussing all these things, without any particular sense of responsibility for coming to any conclusion on them."

8   Ludwig, *Paths*, 479.

9   Blaise Pascal, *Pensées: Thoughts on Religion and Other Subjects*, trans. William Finlayson Trotter, ed. H. S. Thayer and Elizabeth B. Thayer (New York: Washington Square, 1965), 85. The original was published in 1671.

10 Harris, *End*, 225.

11 Richard Dawkins, *The Selfish Gene*, 2nd ed. (Oxford: Oxford University Press, 1989), 198.

12 Alister E. McGrath and Joanna Collicutt McGrath, *The Dawkins Delusion? Atheist Fundamentalism and the Denial of the Divine* (Downers Grove, Ill.: InterVarsity, 2007).

13 I note that the biblical tradition itself certainly does not set faith and reason against each other but demands of the believer the devotion of his or her whole self to God (including the mind), who himself can plead with human beings to "reason" with him (Isaiah 1:18). The Apostle Peter later urges his readers, "Always be prepared to give an answer to everyone who asks you to give the reason for the hope that you have" (1 Peter 3:15).

14 In the following two chapters, as in chap. 12, I shall inevitably only *touch* upon a whole range of different issues relevant to my inquiries. As there, however, I shall provide suggestions in the footnotes for further reading for those interested in exploring these matters more fully.

15 Most scientists appear still to believe in a "punctiliar big bang," although this has recently been questioned by some, including Stephen Hawking and Leonard Mlodinow, *The Grand Design* (New York: Bantam, 2010).

16 Here and at other points in chap. 13 I am drawing again on Provan and Wilkinson, "Stutterers"—an essay cited first in chap. 1. On the ultimate beginning of things as "shrouded in mystery" in both Genesis and modern cosmology, see Kass, *Wisdom*, 28.

17 Rowan Williams, transcript of "Soul of the Universe," BBC, 1991, quoted in Angela Tilby, *Soul: God, Self and the New Cosmology* (New York: Doubleday, 1992), 108.

18 See John Polkinghorne and Nicholas Beale, *Questions of Truth: Fifty-One Responses to Questions about God, Science, and Belief* (Louisville, Ky.: Westminster John Knox, 2009), 11–14.

19 Voltaire, *Les systemes et les cabales, avec des notes instructives* (London, 1772), 9.

20 See Edward Young, *Night Thoughts* (Edinburgh: James Nichol, 1853), who writes, "The course of Nature is the art of God" (293).

21 That is to say, these aliens are themselves aspects of the larger cosmos, but they are nonetheless responsible for some of its workings. Among others, Professor Edward Harrison of the University of Massachusetts has entertained such an idea. See John P. Wiley Jr., "Phenomena, Comment & Notes," *Smithsonian*,

accessed October 26, 2012, http://www.smithsonianmag.com/science-nature/phenom_dec95.html.

22 See further Alister E. McGrath, *A Fine-Tuned Universe: The Quest For God in Science and Theology* (Louisville, Ky.: Westminster John Knox, 2009).

23 G. K. Chesterton, *Orthodoxy* (San Francisco: Ignatius Press, 1995), 66.

24 William A. Dembski, *No Free Lunch: Why Specified Complexity Cannot Be Purchased without Intelligence* (Lanham, Md.: Rowman & Littlefield, 2002).

25 The quoted words are borrowed from Stephen Jay Gould, "Impeaching a Self-Appointed Judge," review of *Darwin on Trial*, by Phillip E. Johnson, *Scientific American* 267 (1992): 118–21 (119), *Stephen Jay Gould Archive*, accessed October 26, 2012, http://www.stephenjaygould.org/reviews/gould_darwin-on-trial.html. In context, Gould is referring to the beliefs of his scientific colleagues: "Either half my colleagues are enormously stupid, or else the science of Darwinism is fully compatible with conventional religious beliefs."

26 Kass, *Wisdom*, 47.

27 For a high-level discussion of a complicated issue, see Alexander Bird and Emma Tobin, "Natural Kinds," in *Stanford Encyclopedia of Philosophy*, ed. Edward N. Zalta, Winter 2012, accessed October 26, 2012, http://plato.stanford.edu/entries/natural-kinds/#NatKinBio.

28 Kass, *Wisdom*, 47–48.

29 It is not, in fact, perceived in this way by many notable scientists, including the renowned geneticist Francis S. Collins, *The Language of God: A Scientist Presents Evidence for Belief* (New York: Free Press, 2006). The "war" between science and faith is nonetheless still widely conducted in the trenches of popular culture, not least in the writings of the new atheists (e.g., Hitchens' *God*, chap. 6, where he assails "arguments from design"). The difficulty many people have in putting process and design together is well illustrated even in the form of a question in a recent Gallup poll, reported by Sam Harris in his *Letter to a Christian Nation* (New York: Knopf, 2006), x. The pollsters asked respondents whether they believed that "life on earth has evolved through a natural process, *without the interference of a deity*" (emphasis added). It is the word "interference" that reveals the problematic mindset. It implies that God is not normally to be found *in* scientifically describable natural processes but only in interventions *into* these processes from *outside*. See further (but briefly) McGrath and McGrath, *Delusion*, 29–31, and, more extensively on science and faith, their chap. 2.

30 See further Hooykaas, *Religion*, and (more challengingly) Michael B. Foster, "The Christian Doctrine of Creation and the Rise of Modern Natural Science," *Mind* 43 (1934): 446–68.

31 Tony Castle, ed., *The New Book of Christian Quotations* (New York: Crossroad, 1983), 239.

32 So it is (for example) that a colleague of mine who lived and worked in a majority Hindu area of Pakistan for a number of years can say this: "The average practitioner of Hinduism is constantly seeking the personal in God, and almost all the people that we knew focused on one of the incarnations. The area where we lived particularly worshiped Krishna, told stories about him, celebrated his birthday and the events of his life. From that perspective I met very few practitioners of 'classical' Hinduism" (Don Curry, personal communication with the author, October 15, 2012).

33 Chesterton, *Autobiography*, 336.

34 It is certainly to misread Genesis, e.g., to hold that Genesis 1 is a sequential, historical description of the "order of events" over a six-day period during which the

entire cosmos was created. Such a reading results in all kinds of absurdities long noted by biblical interpreters, including ancient ones like Origen (who wanted to know what "evening" and "morning" could possibly mean before there was a sun and a moon) and Augustine (who wanted to know why it would take the almighty God as long as six days to create everything). See, e.g., R. Walter L. Moberly, "How Should One Read the Early Chapters of Genesis?" in Barton and Wilkinson, *Reading Genesis after Darwin*, 5–21; among other good essays in the same volume are those by Francis Watson ("Genesis before Darwin: Why Scripture Needed Liberating from Science," 23–37); and Andrew Louth ("The Six Days of Creation According to the Greek Fathers," 39–55).

35 One of the consequences of misreading the Story along such lines, in fact, is the necessity of producing a new "science" ("creation science") that is entirely different from modern science and represents in most people's estimation an unhelpful misreading of the *world*. Museums designed to inculcate this "science" are now to be found all over the world. See further "Creation Museums," accessed October 26, 2012, http://nwcreation.net/museums.html.

36 Max Weber, "Science as a Vocation," in *Science as a Vocation*, trans. M. John, ed. Peter Lassman and Irving Velody (London: Unwin Hyman, 1989), 3–31 (17–18).

37 G. S. Kirk and J. E. Raven, *The Presocratic Philosophers: A Critical History with a Selection of Texts* (Cambridge: Cambridge University Press, 1957), 168.

38 Euripides, "Heracles," ll. 341–42, 347, in *Euripides*, trans. William Arrowsmith, 5 vols. (Chicago: University of Chicago Press, 1969), 2:43–115 (72).

39 Basil Mitchell, "War and Friendship," in *Philosophers Who Believe: The Spiritual Journeys of Eleven Leading Thinkers*, ed. Kelly James Clark (Downers Grove, Ill.: InterVarsity, 1997), 36.

40 Mitchell, "War and Friendship," 37.

41 Ludwig, *Paths*, 80–81, 86–87.

42 Ludwig, *Paths*, 136.

43 Ludwig, *Paths*, 220.

44 Ludwig, *Paths*, 220.

45 Chesterton, *Autobiography*, 150.

46 Leo Tolstoy, *Last Diaries*, trans. Lydia Weston-Kesich, ed. Leon Stilman (New York: G. P. Putnam's Sons, 1960), 65.

47 C. S. Lewis, *Mere Christianity*, rev. ed. (San Francisco: HarperSanFranscisco, 2001), 53. Hitchens, *God*, 118–20, attacks this argument and dismisses it in a couple of lines, without actually attempting any explanation of what is wrong with it.

48 Kass, *Wisdom*, 38.

49 Quoted in "Readings from *The Peasants' Revolt*," *BBC Radio*, accessed October 26, 2012, www.bbc.co.uk/radio4/history/voices/voices_reading_revolt.shtml.

50 Consider, e.g., how compelling the biblical vision of humanness was to women in the Roman Empire during the first few centuries of the Christian church. As Rodney Stark reminds us, "Amidst contemporary denunciations of Christianity as patriarchal and sexist, it is easily forgotten that the early church was so especially attractive to women that in 370 the emperor Valentinian issued a written order to Pope Damasus I requiring that Christian missionaries cease calling at the homes of pagan women." *The Rise of Christianity: How the Obscure, Marginal Jesus Movement Became the Dominant Religious Force in the Western World in a Few Centuries* (Princeton: Princeton University Press, 1996), 95–128 (95).

51 There is, in fact, a rare genetic disorder (anhidrosis, or CIPA) that results in an inability to feel pain. Those who think that pain is simply "evil" should consider

what the mother of one young girl who suffers from this disease has to say: "Some people would say [an inability to feel pain is] a good thing. But no, it's not. . . . Pain's there for a reason. It lets your body know something's wrong and it needs to be fixed. I'd give anything for her to feel pain." "Rare Disease Makes Girl Unable to Feel Pain," *MSNBC*, accessed October 26, 2012, http://www.msnbc.msn.com/ id/6379795#.T31BU_UQoTA. See further Philip Yancey and Paul Brand, *The Gift of Pain: Why We Hurt and What We Can Do about It* (Grand Rapids: Zondervan, 1997).

52 For a brief introduction, see Lee Pullen, "Plate Tectonics Could Be Essential for Life," *Astrobiology Magazine*, accessed October 26, 2012, http://www.astrobio .net/exclusive/3039/. For a relevant book, see Peter Ward and Donald Brownlee, *Rare Earth: Why Complex Life Is Uncommon in the Universe* (New York: Copernicus, 2004).

53 On what is good about storms and other "disasters," see further Holmes Rolston III, "Disvalues in Nature," *Monist* 75 (1992): 250–78 (264–66).

54 See further Anne Maczulak, *Allies and Enemies: How the World Depends on Bacteria* (Upper Saddle River, N.J.: FT Press, 2010). See further Loren E. Wilkinson, "A Christian Ecology of Death: Biblical Imagery and the Ecologic Crisis," *Christian Scholar's Review* 5 (1976): 319–38, who discusses how death is intrinsic to the good, created order.

55 Terence E. Fretheim, *Creation Untamed: The Bible, God, and Natural Disasters* (Grand Rapids: Baker Academic, 2010), 27. This is, I believe, the right kind of response to the questions raised by new atheists like Sam Harris (e.g., *Letter*, 50–57) with respect to "natural evil."

56 Such an answer was already offered as early as the second century A.D. by the Christian bishop Irenaeus of Lyons. God purposes, he suggested, to take human beings over time from the immature state in which they are born to a mature state in which they are truly "like God." He is in the business of "soul making." Suffering, much of which (Irenaeus agrees) is indeed intrinsic to the way in which the good world works, is also necessary in pursuit of that goal, both in the present world and in the next. It teaches us knowledge and compassion, and it builds our character as we make good choices in the face of it. To explore this question further in Irenaeus, see Robert M. Grant, *Irenaeus of Lyons* (London: Routledge, 1997). The relevant primary sources are *Against Heresies* and *Demonstration of the Apostolic Preaching*. It seems to me that, as one component of the "answer" to the question of evil and suffering, Irenaeus' thinking is helpful. God's good purposes include having moral creatures who freely choose to be like him. From this freedom arises moral evil, which hugely inflates the amount of suffering in the world. God then works with this evil also, striving to turn it always toward the good.

57 See further Christopher Southgate, *The Groaning of Creation: God, Evolution, and the Problem of Evil* (Louisville, Ky.: Westminster John Knox, 2008), passim; and John Polkinghorne, *Science and Religion in Quest of Truth* (New Haven: Yale University Press, 2011), chap. 4.

58 Alfred Lord Tennyson, *In Memoriam* (New York: Macmillan, 1912), 69.

59 See further Rolston, "Disvalues," 253–55; and Southgate, *Groaning*, passim.

60 Kass, *Wisdom*, 177 (emphasis original).

61 See further John Polkinghorne, *Exploring Reality: The Intertwining of Science and Religion* (New Haven: Yale University Press, 2007), 38–59. Having briefly reviewed "a number of characteristics that support a claim for unique human status" (41), Polkinghorne perceptively says this: "Even so brief a survey indicates

how strange it is that many biologists can claim not to be able to see anything really distinctive about *Homo sapiens*. They regard human behaviour as just another instance of animal behaviour, and humanity as a not particularly special twig on the burgeoning bush of evolutionary development. In fact, even the ability to articulate these assertions is sufficient to deny their premise" (45).

62 Kass, *Wisdom*, 119; see further 155–56.

63 This is true of the Assyrian king Ashurbanipal, e.g., who adorned his palace in Nineveh with wall reliefs that are now preserved in the British Museum in London.

64 For an accessible introduction to the thought of both men as it relates to politics, see Lilla, *Stillborn God*, 107–62.

65 See further Hans-Jürgen Goertz, *The Anabaptists* (London: Routledge, 1996).

66 David Andress, *The Terror: The Merciless War for Freedom in Revolutionary France* (New York: Farrar, Straus & Giroux, 2006); Ian Kershaw, *Hitler: A Biography* (New York: Norton, 2008); and Jung Chang and Jon Halliday, *Mao: The Unknown Story* (New York: Anchor, 2006).

67 Mohandas K. Gandhi, *Gandhi on Non-Violence: Selected Texts from Mohandas K. Gandhi's "Non-Violence in Peace and War"* (New York: New Directions, 1964), 70.

68 J. R. R. Tolkien, "Fairy Stories" (Andrew Lang Lecture, University of St. Andrews, St. Andrews, Scotland, March 8, 1939). This lecture (entitled "On Fairy Stories") may now be found in *The Monsters and the Critics, and Other Essays*, ed. Christopher Tolkien (London: HarperCollins, 2006), 109–61. I am once again grateful to my friend Loren Wilkinson for drawing my attention to this lecture.

69 Tolkien, "On Fairy Stories," 155–56.

70 Kass, *Wisdom*, 189, referring to Aeschylus, *Prometheus Bound*, 2:250–53.

71 François Duc de La Rochefoucauld, *Reflections; Or, Sentences and Moral Maxims*, trans. J. W. Willis Bund and J. Hain Friswell (London: Sampson Low, Son, & Marston, 1871), 21.

Chapter 14

1 Jaspers, *Origin*, 19–20.

2 Karl Jaspers, "The Axial Age of Human History: A Base for the Unity of Mankind," *Commentary* 6 (1948): 430–35 (435).

3 Marc H. Ellis, *Israel and Palestine—Out of the Ashes: The Search for Jewish Identity in the Twenty-First Century* (London: Pluto Press, 2002), 75.

4 Regina M. Schwartz, *The Curse of Cain: The Violent Legacy of Monotheism* (Chicago: University of Chicago Press, 1997).

5 E.g., Rodney Stark's *Rise of Christianity*; and idem, *For the Glory of God: How Monotheism Led to Reformations, Science, Witch-Hunts, and the End of Slavery* (Princeton: Princeton University Press, 2003); see also Jonathan Hill, *What Has Christianity Ever Done for Us?* (Downers Grove, Ill.: InterVarsity, 2005).

6 Rodney Stark, *God's Battalions: The Case for the Crusades* (New York: HarperOne, 2009).

7 John V. Tolan, *Saint Francis and the Sultan: The Curious History of a Christian-Muslim Encounter* (Oxford: Oxford University Press, 2009). I am grateful to my student Tina Boesch, who alerted me to this and other sources in the course of a very fine master's essay on Christian-Muslim encounters in medieval times.

8 Philip Jenkins, *The Lost History of Christianity: The Thousand-Year Golden Age of the Church in the Middle East, Africa, and Asia—and How It Died* (New York: HarperCollins, 2008), 1–95.

9   Jenkins, *History*, 16. See further William Montgomery Watt, *Muslim-Christian Encounters: Perceptions and Misperceptions* (London: Routledge, 1991).

10   Moberly, *Theology*, 100.

11   Laurence Weschler, "Books," *New Yorker*, November 24, 1997, 131–33 (132). Ronald Wright, in *A Short History of Progress* (New York: Carroll & Graf, 2005), draws attention to the blood already on the hands of Cro-Magnon man in early human times (chap. 1). On violence among "primitive" peoples, see my *Convenient Myths*, chap. 5; see also Steven LeBlanc, *Constant Battles: The Myth of the Peaceful, Noble Savage* (New York: St. Martin's, 2003), and Napoleon A. Chagnon, *Noble Savages: My Life Among Two Dangerous Tribes—the Yanomamö and the Anthropologists* (New York: Simon & Schuster, 2013). Among the Amazonian Yanomamö, Chagnon writes, "native warfare was not just occasional or sporadic but was a *chronic* threat, lurking and threatening to disrupt communities at any moment" (26).

12   Thomas W. Neumann, "The Role of Prehistoric Peoples in Shaping Ecosystems in the Eastern United States: Implications for Restoration Ecology and Wilderness Management," in Kay and Simmons, *Wilderness and Political Ecology: Aboriginal Influences and the Original State of Nature*, 141–78 (143).

13   Michael S. Alvard, "Testing the 'Ecologically Noble Savage' Hypothesis: Interspecific Prey Choice by Piro Hunters in Amazonian Peru," *Human Ecology* 21 (1993): 355–87 (384). For a more extensive discussion of the myth of the "ecologically noble savage," see my *Convenient Myths*, chap. 6.

14   G. W. F. Hegel, for example, understands the modern state as "the divine will as present spirit, unfolding as the actual shape and organization of a world." *Elements of the Philosophy of Right*, trans. H. B. Nisbet, ed. Allen W. Wood (Cambridge: Cambridge University Press, 1991), 292, quoted in Lilla, *Stillborn God*, 206. This divinization of the state (and indeed the self) played a significant role in creating the circumstances out of which emerged the horrendous bloodshed of the first part of the twentieth century, including the Nazi Final Solution.

15   See further McGrath and McGrath, *Delusion*, chap. 4 ("Is Religion Evil?").

16   Ludwig, *Paths*, 80.

17   Peter Padfield, *Himmler: Reichsführer-SS* (London: Cassell, 1990), 401–4 (402).

18   Lilla, *Stillborn God*, 131.

19   Kass, *Wisdom*, 177n8.

20   Such a view of the world is often referred to as "social Darwinism." It is usually connected with the writings of philosophers like Herbert Spencer and linked especially with Nazi Germany, where the notion of the "survival of the fittest" became a central component of Fascist ideology and policy. At the present moment in history we do not typically find it overtly expressed in such extreme ways, but it does come to expression in public discourse nonetheless, wherever people are found arguing that what Darwin discovered about evolutionary processes *ought* to lead us to live in this or that way, organize our society in this or that way, and so on. For one example from the business world, see Jerry W. Thomas, "Survival of the Fittest," *Decision Analyst*, accessed October 26, 2012, http://www.decisionanalyst.com/publ_art/survival.dai. More broadly, it is clear that much of the contemporary political discourse in the United States, concerning questions such as whether the state should fund social programs, is informed by this kind of thinking and draws inspiration from an important progenitor of contemporary social and political conservative thought, William Graham Sumner (1840–1910). Sumner certainly believed (among other things) that

state-sponsored social welfare worked against the universal "law" of the survival of the fittest.

21   For how the spread of the Christian story in the Roman Empire impacted females, in particular, see Stark, *Rise*, chap. 5; note further his more general comment: "Christianity brought a new conception of humanity to a world saturated with capricious cruelty and the vicarious love of death" (214).

22   The extent to which the "Western" view of human rights has *not* marked much of the rest of the world was illustrated (in tragic circumstances) by the 2009 assassination in Afghanistan of women's rights activist and provincial legislator Sitara Achakzai. Describing the situation in that country, Achakzai's fellow women's rights campaigner Fauzia Kofi is quoted as follows: "if you speak of human rights or women's rights in Afghanistan, you get accused of having converted to Christianity." Kamron Pasha, "Sitara Achakzai, Martyr for Muslim Women," *Huffington Post*, accessed January 17, 2013, http://www.huffingtonpost.com/kamran-pasha/sitara-achakzai-martyr-fo_b_186744.html. On the situation of women in nearby India, see the following newspaper articles: Helen Pidd, "Why Is India So Bad for Women?," *Guardian*, 2012, accessed January 3, 2013, http://www.guardian.co.uk/world/2012/jul/23/why-india-bad-for-women; and Sunny Hundal, "India's Bitter Culture of Rape and Violence," *Guardian*, 2013, accessed January 3, 2013, http://www.guardian.co.uk/commentisfree/2013/jan/03/india-rape-violence-culture.

23   In Canada, e.g., abortion is legally unrestricted through all nine months of pregnancy up until the point of birth, and the abortion rate runs at around 105,000 per year. See "Legal Abortion in Canada," accessed October 26, 2012, http://www.abortionincanada.ca/history/legal_abortion_canada.html.

24   The Netherlands is one of the countries that have gone furthest down this road, enacting law in 2002 that allowed both assisted suicide and euthanasia. See André Janssen, "The New Regulation of Voluntary Euthanasia and Medically Assisted Suicide in the Netherlands," *International Journal of Law, Policy and the Family* 16 (2002): 260–69. On the dangers of making assisted suicide and euthanasia legal (with some reference to the Netherlands situation), see Ezekiel Emanuel, "Whose Right to Die?," *Atlantic*, March 1997, accessed January 17, 2013, http://www.theatlantic.com/magazine/archive/1997/03/whose-right-to-die/304641/. Emanuel is a previous chief of the Department of Bioethics at the Clinical Center of the U.S. National Institutes of Health.

25   Ben Mattlin, "Suicide by Choice? Not So Fast," *Opinion Pages*, accessed November 8, 2012, http://www.nytimes.com/2012/11/01/opinion/suicide-by-choice-not-so-fast.html?smid=fb-share&_r=1&.

26   Note, e.g., the following striking example published in a respected academic journal: Alberto Giubilini and Francesca Minerva, "After-Birth Abortion: Why Should the Baby Live?," *Journal of Medical Ethics*, March 2012, accessed October 26, 2012, http://jme.bmj.com/content/early/2012/03/01/medethics-2011-100411.full. The authors argue that since neither babies in the womb nor newborns have the same moral status as actual persons, "after-birth abortion" (killing a newborn) should be permissible in all the cases where abortion is permissible, including cases where the newborn is not disabled.

27   E.g., does everyone have the same right as everyone else to proper, humane treatment under war conditions and to a speedy and fair trial? See further Joseph Margulies, *Guantánamo and the Abuse of Presidential Power* (New York: Simon and Schuster, 2006); and Mark P. Denbeaux and Jonathan Hafetz, eds., *The Guantánamo Lawyers: Inside a Prison, Outside the Law* (New York: New York University Press, 2009).

28   Chesterton, *Autobiography*, 176.

29   Felix Adler, *The Reconstruction of the Spiritual Ideal: Hibbert Lectures, Delivered in Manchester College, Oxford, May 1923* (New York: Appleton, 1924), 17–18.

30   Abraham J. Heschel, "What Ecumenism Is," in *Moral Grandeur and Spiritual Audacity: Essays*, ed. Susannah Heschel (New York: Farrar, Straus & Giroux, 1996), 286–89 (289).

31   Hans-Georg Moeller, *The Moral Fool: A Case for Amorality* (New York: Columbia University Press, 2009), 187.

32   Moeller, *Fool*, 2.

33   Kass, *Wisdom*, 44–45 (emphasis original).

34   Islam itself does recognize that "in the ordinary human state, people are weak and negligent, subservient to their surroundings and prisoners of their own needs and passions," that each human being is naturally "asleep to his or her true nature." Ludwig, *Paths*, 477. The question that arises, then, is how one is supposed to get to the *starting point* of desiring right knowledge? It is not clear that all human beings just naturally *desire* it, as any parent or educator will confirm. G. K. Chesterton recalls his own schooling as "the period during which I was being instructed by somebody I did not know, about something I did not want to know." *Autobiography*, 58. This is, I think, a problem for Islam.

35   Ludwig, *Paths*, 477.

36   Taylor, *Religion*, 75.

37   Taylor, *Religion*, 79. Here Taylor is summarizing the novelist Daniel Quinn in Quinn's work *Ishmael: A Novel* (New York: Bantam, 1992).

38   James Lovelock, *The Revenge of Gaia: Earth's Climate Crisis and the Fate of Humanity* (New York: Basic Books, 2006), 137, quoted in Taylor, *Religion*, 36. Lovelock is best known for his "Gaia theory" (the title alludes to this) about the biosphere as a self-regulating organism.

39   Taylor, *Religion*, 99. Taylor is describing here the position of Paul Watson, the cofounder of Greenpeace, in "Biocentric Religion, a Call For," in *Encyclopedia of Religion and Nature*, ed. Bron Taylor, 2 vols. (London: Continuum, 2005), 1:176–79.

40   Berry, *Dream*, 124. I quoted this line already in the second epigraph to chap. 1.

41   For a thorough exploration of the myth of the dark green golden age, see my *Convenient Myths*, chaps. 5–6.

42   C. S. Lewis captures this picture perfectly in *The Magician's Nephew* (New York: Macmillan, 1955), which imagines the first king and queen of Narnia as a London cabdriver and his wife, thrown unexpectedly into their new roles after living their ordinary lives well (149–58).

43   A good historical example would be Savitri Devi—a Nazi spy in India during the Second World War, a synthesizer of Hinduism and Nazism who proclaimed Hitler to be an avatar of the god Vishnu and after the war a (still-Nazi) writer who significantly influenced the later "green movement." See Nicholas Goodrick-Clarke, *Hitler's Priestess: Savitri Devi, the Hindu-Aryan Myth, and Neo-Nazism* (New York: New York University Press, 2000).

44   Hill, *Christianity*, passim.

45   For a brief description, see Frederick Clarkson, "Christian Reconstructionism: Theocratic Dominionism Gains Influence," *Public Eye Magazine*, accessed October 26, 2012, http://www.publiceye.org/magazine/v08n1/chrisrec.html.

46   Ruthven, *Islam*, 4.

47   On the "mystical and messianic impulses cultivated by the biblical tradition,"

which preceded and have also survived modern attempts to separate religion and politics into different realms, see Lilla, *Stillborn God*, 251–95 (254).

48 Lilla, *Stillborn God*, 260.

49 The phrase came into common parlance as a result of the 1984 book by Richard John Neuhaus, *The Naked Public Square: Religion and Democracy in America* (Grand Rapids: Eerdmans, 1984). Neuhaus used it to refer to the exclusion of popular values from the public forum, which he believed would result in the death of democracy.

50 Plato, *Theaetetus*, line 152, in *The Collected Dialogues of Plato Including the Letters*, ed. Edith Hamilton and Huntington Cairns (New York: Bollingen Foundation, 1961), 856.

51 Plato, *Republic* 1.336b–342c.

52 Niccolò Machiavelli, *The Prince and Other Writings*, trans. Wayne A. Rebhorn (New York: Barnes & Noble Classics, 2003), 66.

53 Leo Strauss, "Three Waves of Modernity," in *An Introduction to Political Philosophy: Ten Essays by Leo Strauss*, ed. Hilail Gildin (Detroit: Wayne State University Press, 1989), 81–98 (85).

54 Thomas Hobbes, *Leviathan*, ed. J. C. A. Gaskin (Oxford: Oxford University Press, 1998). For an accessible introduction to Hobbes' importance in the history of Western political thought, see Lilla, *Stillborn God*, 55–103.

55 Michael Stolleis, *The Law under the Swastika: Studies on Legal History in Nazi Germany*, trans. Thomas Dunlap (Chicago: University of Chicago Press, 1998).

56 See Littleton (*Shinto*, 58–63), who reminds us that in Shinto theology evil is that which disrupts the benign harmony "inherent in nature and human relationships" (58) and that "the Shinto ethic reached its apogee during the 'State Shinto' era (1872–1945), when obedience to the emperor became the noblest form of behavior—up to and including sacrificing one's life for his benefit" (59). See further Helen Hardacre, *Shinto and the State, 1868–1988* (Princeton: Princeton University Press, 1991).

57 The correlation of the two is found, e.g., in Long, *Jainism*, 115, 182–84. In relating part of his own story, Long recounts, "In the idea that all paths lead to the same goal, and that there are many names for the one ultimate reality, I felt that I had come upon the central truth of my existence: that exclusionary boundaries are false creations which keep people apart" (183). The Jain doctrine of *anekāntavāda* (nonabsolutism) is, then, for him, "one of the most important of Jain doctrines" (115).

58 I believe that we would discover this to be true even of Hans-Georg Moeller (*Fool*), if we were to get to know him better.

59 Along similar lines, see further the penetrating work of Canadian law professor Mary Anne Waldron, *Free to Believe: Rethinking Freedom of Conscience and Religion in Canada*, 3rd ed. (Toronto: University of Toronto Press, 2013).

60 It is illegal in the U.K., e.g., to refuse a couple in a homosexual civil partnership, on religious and moral grounds, a double room in one's home, if letting out rooms for bed and breakfast accommodation. The Christian Institute, "Homosexuals Try to Crush Christian B&B," accessed October 26, 2012, http://www.christian.org.uk/news/homosexuals-try-to-crush-christian-bb/. It is also illegal to wear a Christian cross in the workplace. St. George Church of Prescott, "Orthodox Woman Resigns after Being Banned from Wearing the Cross," accessed October 26, 2012, http://www.prescottorthodox.org/2012/03/orthodox-woman-resigns-after-being-banned-from-wearing-the-cross/.

61 The recent erosion of the right to privacy with respect to the U.S. government in relation to home, telephone, car, and Internet use is quite striking. Adam Cohen, "The Government Can Use GPS to Track Your Moves," *Time*, November 25, 2010, accessed October 26, 2012, http://www.time.com/time/ magazine/article/0,9171,2015765,00.html; Peter S. Vogel, "Invasion of Privacy? Federal Government Secretly Monitored Personal Webmail," *Internet, Information Technology, & e-Discovery Blog*, March 7, 2012, accessed October 26, 2012, http://www.vogelitlawblog.com/2012/03/articles/internet -privacy/invasion-of-privacy-federal-government-secretly-monitored-personal -webmail/; and "Edward Snowden and the NSA Files—Timeline," *Guardian*, 2013, accessed June 24, 2013, http://www.guardian.co.uk/world/2013/jun/23/ edward-snowden-nsa-files-timeline.

62 I have borrowed the excellent phrase "utopian spasms" from Kass (*Wisdom*), who uses it specifically of "political and cultural efforts to rationally solve the problem of man and woman . . . [which] will almost certainly be harmful, even dehumanizing, to man, to woman, and especially to children" (121). This is the essence of utopian politics: to seek to achieve a good society and good people (from the perspective of the powerful) through the imposition of simple political and legal "solutions" upon exceedingly complex (including moral) reality, without attention to the likely negative consequences even of "success," much less failure.

63 A number of the examples noted earlier make this clear.

64 The advance of the illiberal modern state is sure to be greatly *facilitated*, in fact, where there are large numbers of "postmodern" citizens inhabiting it. It is common to encounter among such citizens a rhetoric that is infatuated with "rights" yet is, at the same time, profoundly skeptical about larger stories (metanarratives), especially the biblical Story, which might ground those rights. This skepticism often extends to absolute claims concerning "right" and "wrong." Such people are not children merely of "postmodernity," however. G. K. Chesterton describes in his own day those who talk about things like "a right to life" at the same time as "saying that there is no such thing as right and wrong." He notes wryly, "It is a little difficult, in that case, to speculate on where their rights came from." *Autobiography*, 335.

65 On the "third way," see further Lilla, *Stillborn God*, 217–50, 301–2.

66 By way of example, note the following lines from Alexandre Dumas' novel, *The Count of Monte Cristo*, trans. Lowell Bair (Toronto: Bantam, 1985): "Until the day God deigns to reveal the future to man, the sum of all human wisdom will be contained in these two words: 'wait and hope'" (473).

67 See Albert Camus, *Camus at Combat: Writing 1944–1947*, ed. Jacqueline Lévi-Valensi (Princeton: Princeton University Press, 2006), 275–76.

68 Lilla, *Stillborn God*, 109.

69 Ouida [Marie Louise Ramé], *A Village Commune* (London: Chatto & Windus, 1882), 206.

70 Kass, *Wisdom*, 188–89 (emphasis original).

71 Kass, *Wisdom*, 8.

72 Strauss, "Three Waves," 97.

73 Jensen, *Endgame*, 1:332 (emphasis original).

POSTSCRIPT

1 Armstrong, *Transformation*, xi.
2 Suzuki, *Legacy*, 36.
3 Jaspers, "Age," 430.
4 Knudtson and Suzuki, *Wisdom*, 186.
5 Knudtson and Suzuki, *Wisdom*, 185.
6 See my *Convenient Myths*, chaps. 1–6.

Bibliography

Abdel Haleem, M. A. S. *The Qur'an.* Oxford World's Classics. Oxford: Oxford University Press, 2005.

"Adam." In *Dictionary of Biblical Imagery*, edited by Leland Ryken, James C. Wilhoit, and Tremper Longman III, 9–14. Downers Grove, Ill.: InterVarsity, 1998.

Adams, Douglas. *The Hitchhiker's Guide to the Galaxy.* London: Pan Books, 1979.

Adler, Felix. *The Reconstruction of the Spiritual Ideal: Hibbert Lectures, Delivered in Manchester College, Oxford, May 1923.* New York: Appleton, 1924.

Alighieri, Dante. *The Comedy of Dante Alighieri, the Florentine.* Cantica I, *Hell.* Translated by Dorothy L. Sayers. Harmondsworth, U.K.: Penguin, 1949.

Allen, Leslie C. *Ezekiel 20–48.* WBC 29. Dallas, Tex.: Word Books, 2002.

Allen, Woody. *Without Feathers.* New York: Random House, 1975.

Alter, Robert. *Genesis: Translation and Commentary.* New York: Norton, 1997.

Alvard, Michael S. "Testing the 'Ecologically Noble Savage' Hypothesis: Interspecific Prey Choice by Piro Hunters in Amazonian Peru." *Human Ecology* 21 (1993): 355–87.

Anderson, E. N., and Lisa Raphals. "Daoism and Animals." In *A Communion of Subjects: Animals in Religion, Science, and Ethics,* edited by Paul Waldau and Kimberley Patton, 275–90. New York: Columbia University Press, 2006.

Andress, David. *The Terror: The Merciless War for Freedom in Revolutionary France*. New York: Farrar, Straus & Giroux, 2006.

Angelou, Maya. *Wouldn't Take Nothing for My Journey Now*. New York: Bantam, 1994.

Annas, Julia. "Plato's *Republic* and Feminism." In Fine, *Plato*, 747–61.

Aquinas, Thomas. *Summa Theologica*. Translated by Fathers of the English Dominican Province, 2 vols. New York: Benziger Bros., 1947.

Arberry, Arthur J. *The Koran Interpreted*. Oxford: Oxford University Press, 1983.

Aristotle. *Politics*. Translated by Benjamin Jowett. New York: Random House, 1943.

―――. *Politics*. Translated by H. Rackam. Cambridge, Mass.: Harvard University Press, 1944.

Armitage, David. "John Locke, Carolina, and the *Two Treatises of Government*." *Political Theory* 32 (2004): 602–27.

Armstrong, Karen. *The Great Transformation: The Beginning of Our Religious Traditions*. New York: Knopf, 2006.

―――. *A Short History of Myth*. Toronto: Knopf, 2005.

Arnason, Johann P., S. N. Eisenstadt, and Björn Wittrock, eds. *Axial Civilizations and World History*. Jerusalem Studies in Religion and Culture 4. Leiden: Brill, 2005.

Athanasius. "On the Incarnation of the Word." In *Nicene and Post-Nicene Fathers: Second Series*, edited by Alexander Roberts et al., 14 vols. Peabody, Mass.: Hendrickson, 1996.

"Atheist Bus Campaign," accessed October 11, 2013, https://humanism.org.uk/about/atheist-bus-campaign/.

Augustine. "Answer to Adimantus, A Disciple of Mani." In *The Works of St. Augustine: A Translation for the 21st Century*, edited by Boniface Ramsey, 26 vols. Hyde Park, N.Y.: New City Press, 2006.

―――. *The Literal Meaning of Genesis*. ACW 41. Translated by John Hammond Taylor, S.J. New York: Newman, 1982.

―――. *The Trinity*. Translated by Arthur W. Haddan. Buffalo, N.Y.: Christian Literature, 1887.

Barnes, Jonathan. *Aristotle: A Very Short Introduction*. Oxford: Oxford University Press, 2000.

Barton, Stephen C., and David Wilkinson, eds. *Reading Genesis after Darwin*. Oxford: Oxford University Press, 2009.

Bauckham, Richard. *Bible and Ecology: Rediscovering the Community of Creation*. London: Darton, Longman & Todd, 2010.

————. *God and the Crisis of Freedom: Biblical and Contemporary Perspectives*. Louisville, Ky.: Westminster John Knox, 2002.

————. *Gospel Women: Studies of the Named Women in the Gospels*. Grand Rapids: Eerdmans, 2002.

BBC Radio, "Readings from *The Peasants' Revolt*," accessed October 26, 2012, www.bbc.co.uk/radio4/history/voices/voices_reading_revolt .shtml.

Beard, Mary, John North, and Simon Price, *Religions of Rome*. 2 vols. Cambridge: Cambridge University Press, 1998.

Berlinski, David. *The Devil's Delusion: Atheism and Its Scientific Pretensions*. New York: Crown Forum, 2008.

Berndt, Ronald M. *Australian Aboriginal Religion*. Leiden: Brill, 1974.

Berry, Thomas. *The Dream of the Earth*. San Francisco: Sierra Club, 1988.

Berthrong, John H., and Evelyn Nagai Berthrong. *Confucianism: A Short Introduction*. Oxford: Oneworld, 2000.

Bibby, Reginald W. *The Emerging Millennials: How Canada's Newest Generation Is Responding to Change and Choice*. Lethbridge, AB: Project Canada Books, 2009.

Bibile, Nick. "A Taste of Heaven," accessed October 26, 2012, http:// www.sounddoctrine.net/Nick/topical/A_Taste_of_Heaven.htm.

Bird, Alexander, and Emma Tobin. "Natural Kinds." In *Stanford Encyclopedia of Philosophy*, edited by Edward N. Zalta, Winter 2012, accessed October 26, 2012, http://plato.stanford.edu/entries/ natural-kinds/#NatKinBio.

Boardman, John, Jasper Griffin, and Oswyn Murray. *Greece and the Hellenistic World*. Vol. 1 of *The Oxford History of the Classical World*. Oxford: Oxford University Press, 1986.

Boethius. *The Consolation of Philosophy*. Translated by Richard Green. Indianapolis: Bobbs-Merrill, 1962.

Bornkamm, Günther. "The Stilling of the Storm in Matthew." In *Tradition and Interpretation in Matthew*, edited by Günther Bornkamm, Gerhard Barth, and Heinz Joachim Held, 52–57. Philadelphia: Westminster, 1963.

Bostock, David. "The Soul and Immortality in the *Phaedo*." In Fine, *Plato*, 886–906.

Bottéro, Jean. *Religion in Ancient Mesopotamia*. Translated by Teresa Lavender Fagan. Chicago: University of Chicago Press, 2001.

Bratcher, Robert G., and Eugene A. Nida. *A Handbook on Paul's Letters to the Colossians and to Philemon*. New York: United Bible Societies, 1993.

Briggs, John Channing. "Bacon's Science and Religion." In *The Cambridge Companion to Bacon*, edited by Markku Peltonen, 172–99. Cambridge: Cambridge University Press, 1996.

Brown, Robert McAfee, ed. *The Essential Reinhold Niebuhr: Selected Essays and Addresses*. New Haven: Yale University Press, 1987.

Brueggemann, Walter. *Genesis*. Interpretation. Atlanta: John Knox, 1982.

———. *Theology of the Old Testament: Testimony, Dispute, Advocacy.* Minneapolis: Fortress, 1997.

Calvert, Brian. "Slavery in Plato's *Republic.*" *Classical Quarterly* 37 (1987): 367–72.

Calvin, John. *Commentaries on the First Book of Moses Called Genesis.* 2 vols. Translated by John King. Edinburgh: Calvin Translation Society, 1847.

Campbell, Joseph. *The Power of Myth*. New York: Anchor Books, 1991.

Camus, Albert. *Camus at Combat: Writing 1944–1947*. Edited by Jacqueline Lévi-Valensi. Princeton: Princeton University Press, 2006.

———. *La peste*. Paris: Gallimard, 1947.

Cartwright, Nancy. *The Dappled World: A Study of the Boundaries of Science*. Cambridge: Cambridge University Press, 1999.

Cassuto, Umberto. *A Commentary on the Book of Genesis I, from Adam to Noah: Genesis 1–6:8*. Translated by Israel Abrahams. Jerusalem: Magnes, 1978.

Castle, Tony, ed. *The New Book of Christian Quotations*. New York: Crossroad, 1983.

Chagnon, Napoleon A. *Noble Savages: My Life among Two Dangerous Tribes—the Yanomamö and the Anthropologists*. New York: Simon & Schuster, 2013.

Chang, Jung, and Jon Halliday. *Mao: The Unknown Story*. New York: Anchor, 2006.

Chapple, Christopher K., ed. *Jainism and Ecology: Nonviolence in the Web of Life*. Cambridge, Mass.: Harvard University Press, 2002.

———. *Nonviolence to Animals, Earth, and Self in Asian Traditions*. Albany: State University of New York Press, 1993.

Chesterton, G. K. *Autobiography*. London: Burns, Oates & Washbourne, 1937.

———. *Orthodoxy*. San Francisco: Ignatius Press, 1995.

Choy, Wayson. *All That Matters*. Toronto: Doubleday Canada, 2004.

Christensen, Duane L. *Deuteronomy 21:10–34:12*. WBC 6B. Dallas, Tex.: Word Books, 2002.

Christian Institute. "Homosexuals Try to Crush Christian B&B," accessed October 26, 2012, http://www.christian.org.uk/news/homo sexuals-try-to-crush-christian-bb/.

"Christian Reconstructionism," accessed June 17, 2013, http://www .conservapedia.com/Christian_Reconstructionism#cite_note-1.

Christie, Agatha. *The Murder of Roger Ackroyd*. London: Collins, 1926.

Cicero. *The Nature of the Gods*. Translated by Peter G. Walsh. New York: Clarendon, 1997.

Clarkson, Frederick. "Christian Reconstructionism: Theocratic Dominionism Gains Influence." *Public Eye Magazine*, accessed October 26, 2012, http://www.publiceye.org/magazine/vo8n1/chrisrec.html.

Cohen, Adam. "The Government Can Use GPS to Track Your Moves." *Time*, November 25, 2010, accessed October 26, 2012, http://www .time.com/time/magazine/article/0,9171,2015765,00.html.

Collins, C. John. *Genesis 1–4: A Linguistic, Literary and Theological Commentary*. Phillipsburg, N.J.: P & R, 2006.

Collins, Francis S. *The Language of God: A Scientist Presents Evidence for Belief*. New York: Free Press, 2006.

"A Common Word between Us and You." *A Common Word*, accessed October 26, 2012, http://www.acommonword.com/the-acw-document.

Confucius. *The Analects*. Translated by D. C. Lau. New York: Penguin, 1979.

Council for a Parliament of the World's Religions. "Towards a Global Ethic: An Initial Declaration." *Urban Dharma*, accessed October 26, 2012, http://www.kusala.org/udharma/globalethic.html.

Craig, William Lane, ed. *God Is Great, God Is Good: Why Believing in God Is Reasonable and Responsible*. Downers Grove, Ill.: InterVarsity, 2009.

"Creation Museums," accessed October 26, 2012, http://nwcreation.net/ museums.html.

Cunningham, Connor. *Darwin's Pious Idea: Why the Ultra-Darwinists and the Creationists Both Get It Wrong*. Grand Rapids: Eerdmans, 2010.

David, Larry. "The Big Salad." *Seinfeld*, season 6, episode 2, directed by Andy Ackerman, aired September 29, 1994. Culver City, Calif.: Sony Pictures Home Entertainment, 2005. DVD.

Dawkins, Richard. *The God Delusion*. New York: Houghton Mifflin Harcourt, 2006.

———. *The Selfish Gene*. 2nd ed. Oxford: Oxford University Press, 1989.

de La Rochefoucauld, François Duc. *Reflections; Or, Sentences and Moral Maxims*. Translated by J. W. Willis Bund and J. Hain Friswell. London: Sampson Low, Son, & Marston, 1871.

Dembski, William A. *No Free Lunch: Why Specified Complexity Cannot Be Purchased without Intelligence*. Lanham, Md.: Rowman & Littlefield, 2002.

Denbeaux, Mark P., and Jonathan Hafetz, eds. *The Guantánamo Lawyers: Inside a Prison, Outside the Law*. New York: New York University Press, 2009.

Dennett, Daniel C. *Breaking the Spell: Religion as a Natural Phenomenon*. New York: Viking, 2006.

Dickinson, Emily. *The Complete Poems of Emily Dickinson*. Edited by Thomas H. Johnson. New York: Little, Brown, 1961.

Dumas, Alexandre. *The Count of Monte Cristo*. Translated by Lowell Bair. Toronto: Bantam, 1985.

Dunn, James D. G. *The Epistles to the Colossians and to Philemon: A Commentary on the Greek Text*. Grand Rapids: Eerdmans, 1996.

―――. *Romans 1–8*. WBC 38A. Dallas, Tex.: Word Books, 1988.

―――. *Romans 9–16*. WBC 38B. Dallas, Tex.: Word Books, 1988.

Durham, John I. *Exodus*. WBC 3. Dallas, Tex.: Word Books, 1987.

Eagleton, Terry. *Reason, Faith, and Revolution: Reflections on the God Debate*. New Haven: Yale University Press, 2009.

"Edward Snowden and the NSA Files—Timeline." *Guardian*, 2013, accessed June 24, 2013, http://www.guardian.co.uk/world/2013/jun/23/edward-snowden-nsa-files-timeline.

Eisenstadt, Shmuel N. "The Axial Age: The Emergence of Transcendental Visions and the Rise of Clerics." *European Journal of Sociology* 23 (1982): 294–314.

―――. "The Axial Age Breakthroughs: Their Characteristics and Origins." In *The Origin and Diversity of Axial Age Civilizations*, edited by Shmuel N. Eisenstadt, 1–28. Albany: State University of New York Press, 1986.

―――. *Fundamentalism, Sectarianism, and Revolution: The Jacobin Dimension of Modernity*. Cambridge: Cambridge University Press, 1999.

Ellis, Marc H. *Israel and Palestine—Out of the Ashes: The Search for Jewish Identity in the Twenty-First Century*. London: Pluto Press, 2002.

Emanuel, Ezekiel. "Whose Right to Die?" *Atlantic*, March 1997, accessed January 17, 2013, http://www.theatlantic.com/magazine/archive/1997/03/whose-right-to-die/304641/.

Engel, David M. "Women's Role in the Home and State: Stoic Theory Reconsidered." *Harvard Studies in Classical Philology* 101 (2003): 267–88.

"Enki and Ninhursag: A Paradise Myth." Translated by S. N. Kramer. In *Ancient Near Eastern Texts Relating to the Old Testament*, edited by J. B. Pritchard, 37–41. Princeton: Princeton University Press, 1969.

"Enuma Elish." Translated by Benjamin R. Foster. In Hallo and Younger, *Context of Scripture*, 1.111.390–402.

Euripides. *Euripides*. Translated by William Arrowsmith. 5 vols. Chicago: University of Chicago Press, 1969.

Fine, Gail, ed. *Plato*. Oxford: Oxford University Press, 2000.

Foster, Jack. "The Garden of Eden." *Mr. Bible Head*, accessed October 26, 2012, http://mrbiblehead.blogspot.com/2010_02_01_archive.html.

Foster, Michael B. "The Christian Doctrine of Creation and the Rise of Modern Natural Science." *Mind* 43 (1934): 446–68.

Freedman, David Noel, et al. *Anchor Bible Dictionary*. Toronto: Doubleday, 1992.

Fretheim, Terence E. *Creation Untamed: The Bible, God, and Natural Disasters*. Grand Rapids: Baker Academic, 2010.

Gal-Or, Benjamin. *Cosmology, Physics and Philosophy*. New York: Springer Verlag, 1981.

Gandhi, Mohandas K. *Gandhi on Non-Violence: Selected Texts from Mohandas K. Gandhi's "Non-Violence in Peace and War."* New York: New Directions, 1964.

Garrett, Duane A. *Proverbs, Ecclesiastes, Song of Songs*. NAC 14. Nashville: Broadman & Holman, 1993.

"Gilgamesh." Translated by Benjamin R. Foster. In Hallo and Younger, *Context of Scripture*, 1.132:458–60.

Girardot, N. J., James Miller, and Liu Xiaogan. *Daoism and Ecology: Ways within a Cosmic Landscape*. Cambridge, Mass.: Harvard University Press, 2001.

Giubilini, Alberto, and Francesca Minerva. "After-Birth Abortion: Why Should the Baby Live?" *Journal of Medical Ethics*, March 2012, accessed October 26, 2012, http://jme.bmj.com/content/early/2012/03/01/medethics-2011-100411.full.

Goertz, Hans-Jürgen. *The Anabaptists*. London: Routledge, 1996.

"Golden Rule." *Wikipedia*, accessed October 26, 2012, http://en.wikipedia.org/wiki/Golden_Rule.

Gombis, Timothy G. *The Drama of Ephesians: Participating in the Triumph of God*. Downers Grove, Ill.: IVP Academic, 2010.

Goodrick-Clarke, Nicholas. *Hitler's Priestess: Savitri Devi, the Hindu-Aryan Myth, and Neo-Nazism*. New York: New York University Press, 2000.

Gordis, Robert. "The Knowledge of Good and Evil in the Old Testament and the Qumran Scrolls." *JBL* 76 (1957): 123–38.

Goshen-Gottstein, Alon. "Abraham and 'Abrahamic Religions' in Contemporary Interreligious Discourse: Reflections of an Implicated Jewish Bystander." *Studies in Interreligious Dialogue* 12 (2002): 165–83.

Gould, Stephen Jay. "Impeaching a Self-Appointed Judge." Review of *Darwin on Trial*, by Phillip E. Johnson, *Scientific American* 267 (1992): 118–21 (119), accessed October 26, 2012, http://www.stephen jaygould.org/reviews/gould_darwin-on-trial.html.

Grant, Robert M. *Irenaeus of Lyons*. London: Routledge, 1997.

Grayson, A. Kirk. "History and Culture of Assyria." In Freedman et al., *Anchor Bible Dictionary*, 4:732–55.

Guthrie, W. K. C. *A History of Greek Philosophy*. Vol. 1, *The Earlier Presocratics and the Pythagoreans*. Cambridge: Cambridge University Press, 1962.

Hagner, Donald A. *Matthew 1–13*. WBC 33A. Dallas, Tex.: Word Books, 1993.

———. *Matthew 14–28*. WBC 33B. Dallas, Tex.: Word Books, 1995.

Hallo, William W., and K. Lawson Younger, eds. *Context of Scripture*. 3 vols. New York: Brill, 1996–2003.

Hamilton, Victor P. *Genesis 1–17*. NICOT. Grand Rapids: Eerdmans, 1990.

Handy, Lowell K. "Serpent (Religious Symbol)." In Freedman et al., *Anchor Bible Dictionary*, 5:1113–16.

Hanson, Paul D. *Isaiah 40–66*. Interpretation. Louisville, Ky.: Westminster John Knox, 1995.

Hardacre, Helen. *Shinto and the State, 1868–1988*. Princeton: Princeton University Press, 1991.

Hardy, Thomas. *Tess of the D'Urbervilles*. London: Octopus, 1986.

Harris, Sam. *The End of Faith: Religion, Terror, and the Future of Reason*. New York: Norton, 2004.

———. *Letter to a Christian Nation*. New York: Knopf, 2006.

Hartley, John E. *Leviticus*. WBC 4. Dallas, Tex.: Word Books, 2002.

Hawking, Stephen, and Leonard Mlodinow. *The Grand Design*. New York: Bantam, 2010.

Hegel, G. W. F. *Elements of the Philosophy of Right*. Translated by H. B. Nisbet. Edited by Allen W. Wood. Cambridge: Cambridge University Press, 1991.

Herodotus. *Histories*. Translated by A. D. Godley. Cambridge, Mass.: Harvard University Press, 1920.

Heschel, Abraham J. "What Ecumenism Is." In *Moral Grandeur and Spiritual Audacity: Essays*, edited by Susannah Heschel, 286–89. New York: Farrar, Straus & Giroux, 1996.

Hesiod. *Theogony*. Translated by Norman O. Brown. Indianapolis: Bobbs-Merrill, 1953.

Hick, John. *An Interpretation of Religion: Human Responses to the Transcendent*. 2nd ed. New Haven: Yale University Press, 2004.

Hill, Jonathan. *What Has Christianity Ever Done for Us?* Downers Grove, Ill.: InterVarsity, 2005.

Hitchens, Christopher. *God Is Not Great: How Religion Poisons Everything*. New York: Twelve Books, 2007.

Hobbes, Thomas. *Leviathan*. Edited by J. C. A. Gaskin. Oxford: Oxford University Press, 1998.

Hooykaas, Reijer. *Religion and the Rise of Modern Science*. Vancouver, BC: Regent College, 2000.

Horace. *Satire, Epistles and Ars Poetica*. Translated by H. Rushton Fairclough. Cambridge, Mass.: Harvard University Press, 1978.

Hundal, Sunny. "India's Bitter Culture of Rape and Violence." *Guardian*, 2013, accessed January 3, 2013, http://www.guardian.co.uk/commentisfree/2013/jan/03/india-rape-violence-culture.

Hurtado, Larry W. *Lord Jesus Christ: Devotion to Jesus in Earliest Christianity*. Grand Rapids: Eerdmans, 2003.

I Ching: Book of Changes. Translated by James Legge. New York: Bantam, 1969.

Inge, William R. *The Philosophy of Plotinus*. 2 vols. London: Longmans, Green, 1918.

Jaki, Stanley L. *Science and Creation: From Eternal Cycles to an Oscillating Universe*. Edinburgh: Scottish Academic Press, 1974.

Janssen, André. "The New Regulation of Voluntary Euthanasia and Medically Assisted Suicide in the Netherlands." *International Journal of Law, Policy and the Family* 16 (2002): 260–69.

Jaspers, Karl. "The Axial Age of Human History: A Base for the Unity of Mankind." *Commentary* 6 (1948): 430–35.

———. *The Origin and the Goal of History*. Translated by M. Bullock. New Haven: Yale University Press, 1953.

Jeffrey, David L. "The Self and the Book: Reference and Recognition in Medieval Thought." In *By Things Seen: Reference and Recognition in Medieval Thought*, edited by David L. Jeffrey, 1–17. Ottawa, Ont.: University of Ottawa Press, 1979.

Jenkins, Philip. *The Lost History of Christianity: The Thousand-Year Golden Age of the Church in the Middle East, Africa, and Asia—and How It Died.* New York: HarperCollins, 2008.

Jensen, Derrick. *Endgame.* Vol. 1, *The Problem of Civilization.* New York: Seven Stories, 2006.

Jha, Prabhat, Maya A. Kesler, Rajesh Kumar, Faujdar Ram, Usha Ram, Lukasz Aleksandrowicz, Diego G. Bassani, Shailaja Chandra, and Jayant K. Banthia. "Trends in Selective Abortions of Girls in India: Analysis of Nationally Representative Birth Histories from 1990 to 2005 and Census Data from 1991 to 2011." *Lancet* 377, no. 9781 (2011): 1921–1928, accessed December 29, 2012, http://www.thelancet.com/journals/lancet/article/PIIS0140-6736%2811%2960649-1/abstract.

Johansen, Thomas Kjeller. *Plato's Natural Philosophy: A Study of the Timaeus-Critias.* Cambridge: Cambridge University Press, 2004.

Johnson, Thomas H., ed. *The Complete Poems of Emily Dickinson.* New York: Little, Brown, 1961.

Kaltner, John. *Introducing the Qur'an for Today's Reader.* Minneapolis: Fortress, 2011.

Kass, Leon R. *The Beginning of Wisdom: Reading Genesis.* New York: Free Press, 2003.

Kay, Charles E., and Randy T. Simmons, eds. *Wilderness and Political Ecology: Aboriginal Influences and the Original State of Nature.* Salt Lake City: University of Utah Press, 2002.

Keown, Gerald L., Pamela J. Scalise, and Thomas G. Smothers. *Jeremiah 26–52.* WBC 27. Dallas, Tex.: Word Books, 2002.

Kershaw, Ian. *Hitler: A Biography.* New York: Norton, 2008.

Keynes, Geoffrey, and Brian Hill, eds. *Samuel Butler's Notebooks.* New York: E. P. Dutton, 1951.

Keynes, John Maynard. *The General Theory of Employment, Interest, and Money.* London: Macmillan, 1960.

Kirk, G. S., and J. E. Raven. *The Presocratic Philosophers: A Critical History with a Selection of Texts.* Cambridge: Cambridge University Press, 1957.

Kline, Meredith. "Divine Kingship and Genesis 6:1-4." *WTJ* 24 (1962): 187–204.

Knudtson, Peter, and David Suzuki, *Wisdom of the Elders.* Toronto, Ont.: Stoddart, 1992.

Kohn, Livia. *Introducing Daoism.* London: Routledge, 2009.

Kooliman, Dick. *Conversion and Social Equality in India.* New Delhi: South Asia, 1983.

Krech, Shepard, III. *The Ecological Indian: Myth and History*. New York: Norton, 1999.

Lambert, Wilfred G. "Destiny and Divine Intervention in Babylon and Israel." *OtSt* 17 (1972): 65–72.

Lane, William L. *Hebrews 1–8*. WBC 47A. Dallas, Tex.: Word Books, 1991.

LeBlanc, Steven. *Constant Battles: The Myth of the Peaceful, Noble Savage*. New York: St. Martin's, 2003.

"Legal Abortion in Canada," accessed October 26, 2012, http://www.abortionincanada.ca/history/legal_abortion_canada.html.

Lerner, Max, ed. *The Mind and Faith of Justice Holmes: His Speeches, Essays, Letters and Judicial Opinions*. Boston: Little, Brown, 1946.

Levy, David J. "The Religion of Light: On Mani and Manichaeism." In Arnason, Eisenstadt, and Wittrock, *Axial Civilizations and World History*, 319–36.

Lewis, C. S. *The Great Divorce*. San Francisco: HarperSanFrancisco, 2001.

———. *The Last Battle*. Harmondsworth: Puffin, 1964.

———. *The Lion, the Witch and the Wardrobe*. New York: HarperCollins, 2009.

———. *The Magician's Nephew*. New York: Macmillan, 1955.

———. *Mere Christianity*. Rev. ed. San Francisco: HarperSanFrancisco, 2001.

Lichfield, John. "Disbelief and Anger in the Cradle of Western Democracy." *Independent*, May 8, 2010, accessed June 20, 2013, http://www.independent.co.uk/news/world/europe/disbelief-and-anger-in-the-cradle-of-western-democracy-1968232.html.

Lilla, Mark. *The Stillborn God: Religion, Politics, and the Modern West*. New York: Knopf, 2007.

Littleton, C. Scott. *Shinto: Origins, Rituals, Festivals, Spirits, Sacred Places*. New York: Oxford University Press, 2002.

Lodahl, Michael. *Claiming Abraham: Reading the Bible and the Qur'an Side by Side*. Grand Rapids: Brazos, 2010.

Long, Jeffery D. *Jainism: An Introduction*. London: I.B. Taurus, 2009.

Longenecker, Richard N. *New Testament Social Ethics For Today*. Grand Rapids: Eerdmans, 1984.

Louth, Andrew, ed. *Genesis 1–11*. ACCS Old Testament 1. Downers Grove, Ill.: InterVarsity, 2001.

———. "The Six Days of Creation According to the Greek Fathers." In Barton and Wilkinson, *Reading Genesis after Darwin*, 39–55.

Lovelock, James. *The Revenge of Gaia: Earth's Climate Crisis and the Fate of Humanity*. New York: Basic Books, 2006.

Ludwig, Theodore M. *The Sacred Paths: Understanding the Religions of the World*. 4th ed. Upper Saddle River, N.J.: Pearson Prentice Hall, 2006.

Lunde, Jonathan. *Following Jesus, the Servant King: A Biblical Theology of Covenantal Discipleship*. Grand Rapids: Zondervan, 2010.

Machiavelli, Niccolò. *The Prince and Other Writings*. Translated by Wayne A. Rebhorn. New York: Barnes and Noble Classics, 2003.

MacIntyre, Alasdair. *After Virtue: A Study in Moral Theory*. Notre Dame: University of Notre Dame Press, 1981.

Maczulak, Anne. *Allies and Enemies: How the World Depends on Bacteria*. Upper Saddle River, N.J.: FT Press, 2010.

Margulies, Joseph. *Guantánamo and the Abuse of Presidential Power*. New York: Simon & Schuster, 2006.

Marshall, I. Howard. *The Gospel of Luke: A Commentary on the Greek Text*. NIGTC 3. Exeter: Paternoster, 1978.

Marsman, Hennie J. *Women in Ugarit and Israel: Their Social and Religious Position in the Context of the Ancient Near East*. Leiden: Brill, 2003.

Mason, Mike. *Practicing the Presence of People: How We Learn to Love*. Colorado Springs: WaterBrook, 1999.

Mather, Cotton. *Soldiers Counseled and Comforted: A Discourse Delivered unto Some Part of the Forces Engaged in the Just War of New England against the Northern and Eastern Indians, Sept. 1, 1689*. Boston: Samuel Green, 1689.

Mattlin, Ben. "Suicide by Choice? Not So Fast." Opinion Pages, *New York Times*, accessed November 8, 2012, http://www.nytimes.com/2012/11/01/opinion/suicide-by-choice-not-so-fast.html?smid=fb-share&_r=1&.

McCalla, Arthur. *The Creationist Debate: The Encounter between the Bible and the Historical Mind*. London: Continuum, 2006.

McConville, Gordon. *God and Earthly Power: An Old Testament Political Theology, Genesis-Kings*. LHBOTS 454. London: T&T Clark, 2006.

McGrath, Alister E. *A Fine-Tuned Universe: The Quest For God in Science and Theology* Louisville, Ky.: Westminster John Knox, 2009.

McGrath, Alister E., and Joanna Collicutt McGrath. *The Dawkins Delusion? Atheist Fundamentalism and the Denial of the Divine*. Downers Grove, Ill.: InterVarsity, 2007.

Mellinkoff, Ruth. *The Mark of Cain: An Art Quantum*. Berkeley: University of California Press, 1981.

Mencken, H. L. *Minority Report*. Baltimore: Johns Hopkins University Press, 2006.

Middleton, J. Richard. *The Liberating Image: The Imago Dei in Genesis 1*. Grand Rapids: Brazos, 2005.

Milgrom, Jacob. "Ethics and Ritual: The Foundations of the Biblical Dietary Laws." In *Religion and Law: Biblical-Judaic and Islamic Perspectives*, edited by Edwin B. Firmage et al., 159–98. Winona Lake, Ind.: Eisenbrauns, 1990.

Mitchell, Basil. "War and Friendship." In *Philosophers Who Believe: The Spiritual Journeys of Eleven Leading Thinkers*, edited by Kelly James Clark. Downers Grove, Ill.: InterVarsity, 1997.

Mitchell, Donald W. *Buddhism: Introducing the Buddhist Experience*. New York: Oxford University Press, 2002.

Moberly, R. Walter L. "How Should One Read the Early Chapters of Genesis?" In Barton and Wilkinson, *Reading Genesis after Darwin*, 5–21.

———. *The Theology of the Book of Genesis*. Cambridge: Cambridge University Press, 2009.

Moeller, Hans-Georg. *The Moral Fool: A Case for Amorality*. New York: Columbia University Press, 2009.

Muesse, Mark. *The Hindu Traditions: A Concise Introduction*. Minneapolis: Fortress, 2011.

Murray, Oswyn. "Life and Society in Ancient Greece." In Boardman, Griffin, and Murray, *Greece and the Hellenistic World*, 204–33.

Myers, Ched. *Binding the Strong Man: A Political Reading of Mark's Story of Jesus*. Maryknoll: Orbis, 1988.

Neuhaus, Richard John. *The Naked Public Square: Religion and Democracy in America*. Grand Rapids: Eerdmans, 1984.

Neumann, Thomas W. "The Role of Prehistoric Peoples in Shaping Ecosystems in the Eastern United States: Implications for Restoration Ecology and Wilderness Management." In Kay and Simmons, *Wilderness and Political Ecology*, 141–78.

O'Keefe, Tim. *Epicureanism*. Berkeley: University of California Press, 2010.

O'Neill, Eugene. *The Plays of Eugene O'Neill*. 3 vols. New York: Random House, 1954.

Olson, Dennis T. *The Book of Judges*. New Interpreter's Bible. Nashville: Abingdon, 1998.

Ophuls, William. *Plato's Revenge: Politics in the Age of Ecology*. Cambridge, Mass.: MIT, 2011.

Ouida [Marie Louise Ramé]. *A Village Commune*. London: Chatto & Windus, 1882.

Padfield, Peter. *Himmler: Reichsführer-SS*. London: Cassell, 1990.

Parker, Robert. "Greek Religion." In Boardman, Griffin, and Murray, *Greece and the Hellenistic World*, 254–74.

Pascal, Blaise. *Pensées: Thoughts on Religion and Other Subjects*. Translated by William Finlayson Trotter. Edited by H. S. Thayer and Elizabeth B. Thayer. New York: Washington Square, 1965.

Pasha, Kamron. "Sitara Achakzai, Martyr for Muslim Women." *Huffington Post*, accessed January 17, 2013, http://www.huffingtonpost .com/kamran-pasha/sitara-achakzai-martyr-fo_b_186744.html.

Peirce, Charles S. *Collected Papers*. Vol. 6, *Scientific Metaphysics*. Edited by Charles Hartshorne and Paul Weiss. Cambridge, Mass.: Harvard University Press, 1935.

Pidd, Helen. "Why Is India So Bad for Women?" *Guardian*, 2012, accessed January 3, 2013, http://www.guardian.co.uk/world/2012/ jul/23/why-india-bad-for-women.

Plato. *The Collected Dialogues of Plato Including the Letters*. Edited by Edith Hamilton and Huntington Cairns. New York: Bollingen Foundation, 1961.

———. *Laws*. Translated by Trevor J. Saunders. New York: Penguin, 1970.

———. *Phaedrus*. In *The Works of Plato*. Vol. 3, *Timaeus and Other Dialogues*. Translated by Benjamin Jowett. New York: Tutor, 1937.

———. *Timaeus and Other Dialogues*. Vol. 3 of *The Dialogues of Plato*. Translated by Benjamin Jowett. London: Sphere Books, 1970.

Polkinghorne, John. *Exploring Reality: The Intertwining of Science and Religion*. New Haven: Yale University Press, 2007.

———. *Science and Religion in Quest of Truth*. New Haven: Yale University Press, 2011.

Polkinghorne, John, and Nicholas Beale. *Questions of Truth: Fifty-One Responses to Questions about God, Science, and Belief.* Louisville, Ky.: Westminster John Knox, 2009.

Pollock, Sheldon. "Axialism and Empire." In Arnason, Eisenstadt, and Wittrock, *Axial Civilizations and World History*, 397–450.

Polybius. *Histories*. Translated by W. R. Paton. Cambridge, Mass.: Harvard University Press, 1979.

Posner, Sarah. "Huckabee Denies He's a Christian Reconstructionist." *American Prospect*, January 11, 2008, accessed June 17, 2013, http:// prospect.org/article/huckabee-denies-hes-christian-recontruc tionist.

Prasad, Ashok. "Harsh Reality of India's Unwanted Girls." *BBC*, October 22, 2007, accessed October 26, 2012, http://news.bbc.co.uk/2/hi/programmes/this_world/7050657.stm.

———. "India's Missing Girls." *BBC*, October 18, 2007, accessed October 26, 2012, http://news.bbc.co.uk/2/hi/programmes/this_world/7039681.stm.

Provan, Iain. *Convenient Myths: The Axial Age, Dark Green Religion, and the World That Never Was*. Waco, Tex.: Baylor University Press, 2013.

———. "Daniel." In the *Eerdmans Commentary on the Bible*, edited by John W. Rogerson and James D. G. Dunn, 665–75. Grand Rapids: Eerdmans, 2003.

———. *Ecclesiastes and Song of Songs*. NIV Application Commentary. Grand Rapids: Zondervan, 2001.

———. *1 & 2 Kings*. Understanding the Bible. Grand Rapids: Baker, 1995.

———. "Foul Spirits, Fornication and Finance: Revelation 18 from an Old Testament Perspective." *JSNT* 64 (1996): 81–100.

———. *Lamentations*. NCB. London: Marshall Pickering, 1991.

———. "The Land Is Mine and You Are Only Tenants: Earth-Keeping and People-Keeping in the Old Testament." In *Many Heavens, One Earth: Readings on Religion and the Environment*, edited by Clifford C. Cain, 33–50. Lanham, Md.: Lexington Books, 2012.

———. "The Messiah in the Book of Kings." In *The Lord's Anointed: Interpretation of Old Testament Messianic Texts*, edited by Philip E. Satterthwaite et al., 67–85. Carlisle: Paternoster, 1995.

———. "On 'Seeing' the Trees while Missing the Forest: The Wisdom of Characters and Readers in 2 Samuel and 1 Kings." In *In Search of True Wisdom: Essays in Old Testament Interpretation in Honour of Ronald E. Clements*, edited by Edward Ball, 153–73. JSOTSup 300. Sheffield, U.K.: Sheffield Academic, 2000.

———. "Pain in Childbirth? Further Thoughts on 'An Attractive Fragment' (1 Chronicles 4:9-10)." In *Let Us Go Up to Zion: Essays in Honour of H. G. M. Williamson on the Occasion of His Sixty-Fifth Birthday*, edited by Iain Provan and Mark Boda, 285–96. VTSup 153. Leiden: Brill, 2012.

———. "To Highlight All Our Idols: Worshipping God in Nietzsche's World." *Ex Auditu* 15 (2000): 19–38.

———. "2 Kings." In *1 & 2 Kings, 1 & 2 Chronicles, Ezra, Nehemiah, Esther*, Zondervan Illustrated Bible Backgrounds Commentary 3, edited by John Walton, 110–21. Grand Rapids: Zondervan, 2009.

Provan, Iain, and Loren Wilkinson. "'Unscripted, Anxious Stutterers': Why We Need Old Testament (Hi)story." *Sapientia Logos* 1 (2008): 12–36.

Provan, Iain, V. Philips Long, and Tremper Longman III. *A Biblical History of Israel*. Louisville, Ky.: Westminster John Knox, 2003.

Pseudo-Demosthenes. *Against Neaera by Apollodorus*. In *Legal Speeches of Democratic Athens: Sources for Athenian History*, edited by Andrew Wolpert and Konstantinos Kapparis, 187–226. Indianapolis: Hackett, 2011.

Pullen, Lee. "Plate Tectonics Could Be Essential for Life." *Astrobiology Magazine*, accessed October 26, 2012, http://www.astrobio.net/exclusive/3039/.

Quinn, Daniel. *Ishmael: A Novel*. New York: Bantam, 1992.

"Rare Disease Makes Girl Unable to Feel Pain." MSNBC, accessed October 26, 2012, http://www.msnbc.msn.com/id/6379795#.T31BU_UQoTA.

Ray, Benjamin C. *African Religions: Symbol, Ritual, and Community*. 2nd ed. Upper Saddle River, N.J.: Prentice Hall, 2000.

Rolston, Holmes, III. "Disvalues in Nature." *Monist* 75 (1992): 250–78.

Rose, Jenny. *Zoroastrianism: An Introduction*. London: I. B. Tauris, 2011.

Russell, Mark, et al., eds. *Routes and Radishes: And Other Things to Talk about at the Evangelical Crossroads*. Grand Rapids: Zondervan, 2010.

Ruthven, Malise. *Islam: A Very Short Introduction*. New York: Oxford University Press, 1997.

St. George Church of Prescott. "Orthodox Woman Resigns after Being Banned from Wearing the Cross." Accessed October 26, 2012, http://www.prescottorthodox.org/2012/03/orthodox-woman-resigns-after-being-banned-from-wearing-the-cross/.

Santas, Gerasimos. "The Form of the Good in Plato's *Republic*." In Fine, *Plato*, 249–76.

Sarna, Nahum M. *Genesis*. Philadelphia: Jewish Publication Society, 1989.

Schearing, Linda S. "Parturition (Childbirth), Pain, and Piety: Physicians and Genesis 3:16a." In *Mother Goose, Mother Jones and Mommie Dearest: Biblical Mothers and Their Children*, edited by Cheryl Kirk-Duggan and Tina Pippin, 85–96. SemeiaSt 61. Atlanta: Society of Biblical Literature, 2009.

Schüle, Andreas. *Die Urgeschchte (Genesis 1–11)*. Zürcher Bibelkommentare. Zurich: Theologischer Verlag, 2009.

Schwartz, Regina M. *The Curse of Cain: The Violent Legacy of Monotheism*. Chicago: University of Chicago Press, 1997.

Seneca: Moral Essays. Translated by John W. Basor. Cambridge, Mass.: Harvard University Press, 1923.

Shaw, George Bernard. "The Future of Political Science in America: An Address to the Academy of Political Science at the Metropolitan Opera House, New York, on the 11th April 1933." *Political Quarterly* 4 (1933): 313–40.

Skinner, John. *Genesis.* 2nd ed. ICC 1. Edinburgh: T&T Clark, 1930.

Snell, Daniel C. *Religions of the Ancient Near East.* Cambridge: Cambridge University Press, 2011.

Sollereder, Bethany N. "Evolutionary Theodicy: An Evangelical Perspective." Master's thesis, Regent College, 2007.

Southgate, Christopher. *The Groaning of Creation: God, Evolution, and the Problem of Evil.* Louisville, Ky.: Westminster John Knox, 2008.

Speiser, E. A. *Genesis.* AB 1. Garden City, N.Y.: Doubleday, 1964.

Stark, Rodney. *For the Glory of God: How Monotheism Led to Reformations, Science, Witch-Hunts, and the End of Slavery.* Princeton: Princeton University Press, 2003.

———. *God's Battalions: The Case for the Crusades.* New York: HarperOne, 2009.

———. *The Rise of Christianity: How the Obscure, Marginal Jesus Movement Became the Dominant Religious Force in the Western World in a Few Centuries.* Princeton: Princeton University Press, 1996.

Steinbeck, John. *East of Eden.* New York: Viking, 1952.

Stephens, Autumn. *Drama Queens: Wild Women of the Silver Screen.* Berkeley, Calif.: Conair, 1998.

Stephens, William O. "Stoic Naturalism, Rationalism, and Ecology." *Environmental Ethics* 16 (1994): 275–86.

Stolleis, Michael. *The Law under the Swastika: Studies on Legal History in Nazi Germany.* Translated by Thomas Dunlap. Chicago: University of Chicago Press, 1998.

Strauss, Leo. "Three Waves of Modernity." In *An Introduction to Political Philosophy: Ten Essays by Leo Strauss,* edited by Hilail Gildin, 81–98. Detroit: Wayne State University Press, 1989.

Suzuki, David. *The Legacy: An Elder's Vision for Our Sustainable Future.* Vancouver, BC: Greystone, 2010.

Taylor, Bron. *Dark Green Religion: Nature Spirituality and the Planetary Future.* Berkeley: University of California Press, 2010.

Tennyson, Alfred, Lord. *In Memoriam.* New York: Macmillan, 1912.

Theophilus of Antioch. "Theophilus to Autolycus." In *The Ante-Nicene Fathers,* edited by Alexander Roberts and James Donaldson, 2.17. Grand Rapids: Eerdmans, 1975.

Thiselton, Anthony C. *The First Epistle to the Corinthians: A Commentary on the Greek Text*. Grand Rapids: Eerdmans, 2000.

Thomas, Jerry W. "Survival of the Fittest." *Decision Analyst*, accessed October 26, 2012, http://www.decisionanalyst.com/publ_art/survival.dai.

Thoreau, Henry David. *The Journal of Henry David Thoreau*. Boston: Houghton Mifflin, 1906. Accessed October 11, 2013, http://www.walden.org/documents/file/Library/Thoreau/writings/Writings1906/20Journal14/Chapter%206.pdf.

Tilby, Angela. *Soul: God, Self and the New Cosmology*. New York: Doubleday, 1992.

Tolan, John V. *Saint Francis and the Sultan: The Curious History of a Christian-Muslim Encounter*. Oxford: Oxford University Press, 2009.

Tolkien, J. R. R. *The Lord of the Rings*. London: HarperCollins, 1991.

———. "On Fairy Stories." In *The Monsters and the Critics, and Other Essays*, edited by Christopher Tolkien, 109–61. London: HarperCollins, 2006.

Tolstoy, Leo. *Last Diaries*. Translated by Lydia Weston-Kesich. Edited by Leon Stilman. New York: G. P. Putnam's Sons, 1960.

Trible, Phyllis. *God and the Rhetoric of Sexuality*. Overtures to Biblical Theology 2. Philadelphia: Fortress, 1978.

Twain, Mark. *Mark Twain's Notebook*. Edited by Albert Bigelow Paine. New York: Harper & Brothers, 1935.

Van Buren, Maud. *Quotations for Special Occasions*. New York: H. W. Wilson, 1938.

Voegelin, Eric. *Plato*. Baton Rouge: Louisiana State University Press, 1957.

Vogel, Peter S. "Invasion of Privacy? Federal Government Secretly Monitored Personal Webmail." *Internet, Information Technology, & e-Discovery Blog*, March 7, 2012, accessed October 26, 2012, http://www.vogelitlawblog.com/2012/03/articles/internet-privacy/invasion-of-privacy-federal-government-secretly-monitored-personal-web mail/.

Voltaire. *Les systemes et les cabales, avec des notes instructives*. London, 1772.

Vonnegut, Kurt. *The Sirens of Titan: A Novel*. New York: Dial Press Trade, 2009.

Waldron, Mary Anne. *Free to Believe: Rethinking Freedom of Conscience and Religion in Canada*. 3rd ed. Toronto, Ont.: University of Toronto Press, 2013.

Walton, John. *Ancient Near Eastern Thought and the Old Testament: Introducing the Conceptual World of the Hebrew Bible*. Grand Rapids: Baker Academic, 2006.

Ward, Peter, and Donald Brownlee. *Rare Earth: Why Complex Life Is Uncommon in the Universe*. New York: Copernicus, 2004.

Watson, Francis. "Genesis before Darwin: Why Scripture Needed Liberating from Science." In Barton and Wilkinson, *Reading Genesis after Darwin*, 23–37.

Watson, Paul. "Biocentric Religion, a Call For." In *Encyclopedia of Religion and Nature*, edited by Bron Taylor, 2 vols., 1:176–79. London: Continuum, 2005.

Watt, William Montgomery. *Muslim-Christian Encounters: Perceptions and Misperceptions*. London: Routledge, 1991.

Webb, Barry G. *The Message of Isaiah: On Eagles' Wings*. Downers Grove, Ill.: InterVarsity, 1996.

Webb, William J. *Slaves, Women & Homosexuals: Exploring the Hermeneutics of Cultural Analysis*. Downers Grove, Ill.: IVP Academic, 2001.

Weber, Max. "Science as a Vocation." In *Science as a Vocation*, translated by M. John, edited by Peter Lassman and Irving Velody, 3–31. London: Unwin Hyman, 1989.

Weinfeld, Moshe. "Deuteronomy, Book of." In Freedman et al., *Anchor Bible Dictionary*, 2:168–83.

Wenham, Gordon J. *Genesis 1–15*. WBC 1. Waco: Word Books, 1987.

———. *Genesis 16–50*. WBC 2. Waco: Word Books, 1994.

Wentheim, Arthur Frank. *Radio Comedy*. New York: Oxford University Press, 1979.

Weschler, Laurence. "Books." *New Yorker*, November 24, 1997, 131–33.

Westermann, Claus. *Genesis 1–11*. BKAT 1. Neukirchen-Vluyn: Neukirchener Verlag, 1974.

Westermarck, Edward. *The Origin and Development of the Moral Ideas*. 2nd ed. 2 vols. London: Macmillan, 1924.

White, Lynn. "The Historical Roots of Our Ecologic Crisis." *Science* 155 (1967): 1203–7. Reproduced in *Western Man and Environmental Ethics*, edited by I. G. Barbour, 18–30. Reading, Mass.: Addison-Wesley, 1973.

"Why Was Eve Created Second? (Women in Church Leadership, Part 7)." *The Passionate Follower's Journal*, October 2, 2007, accessed October 26, 2012, http://thepfjournal.wordpress.com/2007/10/02/why-was-eve-created-second-women-in-church-leadership-part-7/.

Wiley, John P., Jr. "Phenomena, Comment & Notes." *Smithsonian*, accessed October 26, 2012, http://www.smithsonianmag.com/science-nature/phenom_dec95.html.

Wilken, Robert L., trans. and ed. *Isaiah: Interpreted by Early Christian and Mediaeval Commentators*. Grand Rapids: Eerdmans, 2007.

Wilkinson, Loren. "Christ as Creator and Redeemer." In *The Environment and the Christian: What Can We Learn from the New Testament?* edited by Calvin DeWitt, 25–44. Grand Rapids: Baker, 1991.

———. "A Christian Ecology of Death: Biblical Imagery and the Ecologic Crisis." *Christian Scholar's Review* 5 (1976): 319–38.

Wood, James L. "Is There an *Archê Kakou* in Plato?" *Review of Metaphysics* 250 (2009): 349–84.

Wright, Christopher J. H. *Deuteronomy*. NIBCOT 4. Peabody, Mass.: Hendrickson, 1996.

———. *The Mission of God: Unlocking the Bible's Grand Narrative*. Downers Grove, Ill.: InterVarsity, 2006.

Wright, N. T. *Simply Christian: Why Christianity Makes Sense*. San Francisco: HarperSanFrancisco, 2006.

———. *Simply Jesus: A New Vision of Who He Was, What He Did, and Why He Matters*. New York: HarperOne, 2011.

———. *Surprised by Hope: Rethinking Heaven, the Resurrection, and the Mission of the Church*. New York: HarperOne, 2008.

Wright, Ronald. *A Short History of Progress*. New York: Carroll & Graf, 2005.

Yancey, Philip, and Paul Brand. *The Gift of Pain: Why We Hurt and What We Can Do about It*. Grand Rapids: Zondervan, 1997.

Young, Edward. *Night Thoughts*. Edinburgh: James Nichol, 1853.

Younger, K. Lawson, Jr. *Ancient Conquest Accounts: A Study in Ancient Near Eastern and Biblical History Writing*. JSOTSup 98. Sheffield: JSOT Press, 1990.

Zerzan, John. *Twilight of the Machines*. Port Townsend, Wash.: Feral House, 2008.

Scripture Index

481

Index of Authors

SUBJECT INDEX